Jerash, Irbid & the Jordan Valley p80

⭐ **Amman** p46

Azraq & the Eastern Desert Highway p226

Dead Sea Highway p111

Madaba & the King's Highway p126

Petra p158

Aqaba, Wadi Rum & the Desert Highway p194

VITAL PRACTICAL INFORMATION TO HELP YOU HAVE A SMOOTH TRIP

THIS EDITION WRITTEN AND RESEARCHED BY

Jenny Walker

welcome to **Jordan**

Ancient Allure

Jordan has welcomed high volumes of visitors since camel caravans plied the legendary King's Highway transporting frankincense in exchange for spices. Nabataean tradesmen, Roman legionnaires, Muslim armies and zealous Crusaders have all passed through the land we now call Jordan, leaving spectacular monuments behind. In turn, these monuments have provoked a modern wave of visitors who, since the early 19th century, have been fascinated to discover this potent past or who have gone in search of the origins of their faith.

Jordan, then, is no stranger to the tourist and there are many ways to enjoy a visit – on a short package holiday, on a specialist archaeological tour, by hiring a Bedouin guide on arrival, or simply by hopping in a hire car and travelling where the fancy takes you. Minimal planning and only a modest budget is required to reach the main sites of interest, although booking a room in major destinations is recommended during the peak season in April.

One of the World's Wonders

Thanks to its small size and large diversity, Jordan repays even the shortest visit with sights and activities that are truly world-class. Petra, the ancient Nabataean city locked in the heart of Jordan's sandstone

At the crossroads of history for more than 2000 years, the kingdom of Jordan is a treasure trove of world-class heritage sites and spectacular desert scenery.

(left) Sunset at Petra (p160)
(below) Bedouin man with oud

escarpments, is the jewel in the crown of the country's many antiquities. The walk through the Siq to the Treasury (Petra's defining monument) is sublime in every sense and leaves an indelible impression on even the most jaded of visitors. It takes at least two days to make the most of a visit, particularly as the sites are far flung and require a fair amount of walking.

A Taste of the Middle East

Petra is a highly persuasive reason to visit Jordan but it is far from the only reason. Apart from the many other spectacular historical and biblical sites, the country offers striking desert landscapes, a salty sea at the lowest point on earth, magnificent springtime flowers scattered across the interior, and rural towns that keep continuity with the traditions of the past.

It takes tolerance to host endless volumes of incomers and Jordan has displayed that virtue in spades, absorbing in recent times hundreds of thousands of refugees from Palestine and Iraq, as well as accommodating ever-growing numbers of tourists who are often insensitive to conservative Jordanian values. While the country has challenges, particularly in terms of modernisation and growing urbanisation, it remains one of the best countries in which to gain an impression of the Middle East without the often attendant difficulties.

❯ Jordan

Umm Qais
Atmospheric ruins laced with wildflowers (p101)

Jerash
The region's finest Roman ruins (p83)

Wadi Jadid
Remote valley of ancient dolmens (p140)

Mt Nebo
View of Moses' Promised Land (p138)

Madaba
King's Highway town of mosaics (p128)

Mukawir
Spectacular site of Salome's dance (p141)

Dead Sea
The lowest point on earth (p113)

Mujib Biosphere Reserve
Waterfalls in adventure-lover's paradise (p123)

Dana Biosphere Reserve
Terraced oasis in desert hills (p151)

Petra
Jordan's 'must see' ancient city (p158)

Red Sea
World-class coral gardens (p26)

Azraq
Desert forts and pleasure domes (p231)

Karak
Crusader castle with a haunting history (p145)

Wadi Rum
Lawrence of Arabia's magical desert (p210)

MEDITERRANEAN SEA

34°E   35°E   LEBANON

33°N

Quneitra

Golan Heights

Sea of Galilee

Haifa   Fiq

Umm Qais   Der'a

Irbid   Suweida   Jebel Druze (1735m)

Netanya   Jordan River   Ramtha   Bosra   Salkhac

Ajloun   Mafraq   Umm al-Jimal

West Bank   Jerash   Zarqa River   Zarqa   Qasr al-Hallabat

32°N   Suweileh   Qasr al-Azraq   Az Wet Res

TEL AVIV   Salt   AMMAN   Qusayr Amra   Azraq

Ramallah   Wadi Jadid   Qasr Kharana

JERUSALEM   Mt Nebo (820m)

Suweimeh   Madaba   Dhab'a

Gaza   Dead Sea   Machaerus (Mukawir)

Mujib Biosphere Reserve   Ariha   Wadi Mujib

ISRAEL & THE PALESTINIAN TERRITORIES   Lisan Peninsula   Qatrana

Karak   Mu'tah

Safi   Wadi Hasa

The Negev   Fifa   Bayir

Dana Biosphere Reserve   Tafila   Qasr al-Bint

Qadsiyya   Jebel Atatia (1641m)   Jebel al-Adhriyat (986m)

Shobak

Wadi Musa   Udruh   Al-Jafr

Jebel Haroun   Petra   Ma'an   Qa'al Jafr

EGYPT   Ras an-Naqb

Jebel al-'t'nn (10.2m)

Quweira   Jebel 'Atrah (1382m)

Eilat   Ar-Rashidiyyah

Rum   Wadi Rum   Diseh

Aqaba   Jebel Rum (1754m)   Jebel al Khazali

Ad-Durra   Jebel Wmm Adani (1830m)   Al-Mudawwara

SINAI   Gulf of Aqaba (Red Sea)

Haql

Nuweiba

SYRIA

Az-Zulaf

Rutbah

Burqu Reserve Qasr Burqu

Tarbil

IRAQ

Ar-Ruwayshid

10

awi

Turayf

mari

Al-Haditha Ghatti

Al-Qurayat

Al Jalamid

Al Tsawiyah

SAUDI ARABIA

Subayhah

Sakakah

Al Jawf

ELEVATION

1000m
500m
0
-250m

N 0 — 50 km
0 — 30 miles

15
TOP
EXPERIENCES

Petra

1 Ever since the Swiss explorer Jean Louis Burckhardt rediscovered this spectacula site in 1812, the ancient Nabataean city of Petra (p158) has been drawing the crowds – and with good reason. This is without doubt Jordan's most treasured attraction and whe the sun sets over the honeycombed landsca of tombs, carved facades, pillars and golden sandstone cliffs, it's a hard-hearted visitor w is left unaffected by its magic. Allow a coupl of days to do the site justice and to visit the main monuments at optimum times of the d
Treasury, Petra

Ruins of Empire

2 For a country so small in size, Jordan punches well above its weight in world-class monuments, boasting some of the fine Roman ruins outside Rome. Most countries would be pleased to have attractions like the Citadel (p49) or the Roman Theatre (p52) in Amman, but these pale into insignificance compared with the superbly preserved ruins Jerash (p83). Visit during a chariot race whe commentary from a red-plumed centurion v help bring this ancient outpost of Rome aliv
Temple of Artemis, Jerash

HUW JONES / LONELY PLANET IMAGES ©

MARK DAFFEY/LONELY PLANET IMAGES ©

Lawrence's Desert

3 It wasn't just the sublime vista of Wadi Rum (p210), with its burnished sandstone cliffs and vivid-coloured dunes, that impressed Lawrence of Arabia as he paced on camel back through the land of the Bedouin. He was also impressed by the stoicism of the people who endured hardships associated with a life in the desert. Today, it's possible to get a glimpse of that traditional way of life, al-beit with a few more creature comforts, by staying in one of the Bedouin camps scattered across this desert wilderness. *Red sand dunes against Jebel Umm Ulaydiyya*

The Dead Sea Experience

4 Floating in the Dead Sea (p113) ⊙ is one of the world's great natural experiences. Floating is the right word for it: with an eye-stingingly high salt content it is virtually impossible to swim in the viscous waters of a sea that is 415m below 'sea level'. The experience is usu-ally accompanied by a mud bath, a bake in the sun and a health-giving spa treatment at one of the modern pleas-ure palaces lined up along the Dead Sea's shores.

Crusader Castles

5 As a frontier in the battle for the soul between Muslim and Christian forces, the land east of the Mediterranean is dotted with castles. In Jordan, there are well-preserved exam-ples at Ajloun (p92) and Shobak (p155), but Karak Castle (p145), commanding the semi-arid hills midway along the King's Highway, is the best. You don't need to be military-minded to be impressed by the ramparts of this enormous construc-tion, but imagination helps to hear the dying howls of those pitched from the parapet by the sadistic Renauld de Chatillon. *Karak Castle*

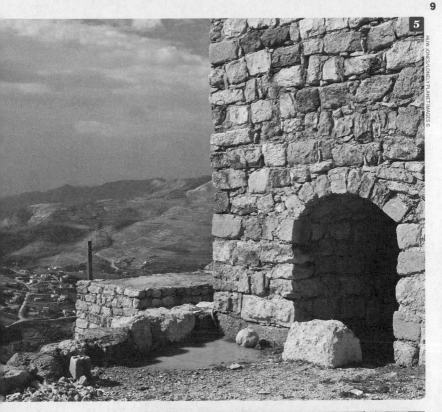

HUW JONES/LONELY PLANET IMAGES ©

Madaba's Handmade History

6 For centuries, Madaba (p128), at the head of the ancient King's Highway, has been a crossroad for caravans transporting goods, legions of armies pushing the borders of their empires, and pilgrims driven by faith in search of the Promised Land. To this day the town, with its churches, museums, markets and craft workshops, retains the marks of those cultural exchanges. Perhaps the best evidence of this rich past is Madaba's magnificent collection of mosaics, a heritage continued through the town's unique mosaic school (p131).

RICHARD I'ANSON/LONELY PLANET IMAGES ©

NPR/IMAGEBROKER ©

Diving with Damsels

7 It's no secret that the Red Sea is home to some of the most spectacular underwater seascapes in the world (p26). Jordan's Red Sea shoreline along the Gulf of Aqaba is admittedly short, but this comparatively unexploited stretch of water encompasses pristine reefs, crumbling wrecks and kaleidoscopic coral gardens. Snorkelling and diving among damsel fish, turtles and seahorses is an unforgettable experience easily arranged through dive centres in and around the lively seaside city of Aqaba (p196). *Cedar Pride* shipwreck

Getting in Touch with the Soul

8 For many people Jordan is more than just a traveller's destination: it is a place of pilgrimage. Sites that resonate with spiritual significance abound in a country delineated by the Jordan Valley, where John is believed to have baptised Jesus (at Bethany-Beyond-the-Jordan, p109), and Wadi Araba (p124) where, according to the Bible, the towns of Sodom and Gomorrah attracted the wrath of God. It is perhaps at Mt Nebo (p138), however, with its sublime view of the Promised Land, that one most senses this is 'hallowed, holy ground'. Bronze memorial, Mt Nebo

Walks on the Wild Side

9 In a region not commonly associated with hiking, Jordan has a surprising number of excellent walking paths. Trails thread through Ajloun Forest Reserve (p93) in the north of Jordan, adventurous routes lead above the waterfalls of Wadi Mujib (p123), and Bedouin guides help visitors negotiate the myriad livestock trails of Petra (p158) and Wadi Rum (p210). For some of the most inspiring walks on the wild side, a trip to Dana Biosphere Reserve (p151) is a must with its turquoise lizards, secretive ibex, terraced orchards and ecofriendly lodges. Trekking in Wadi Mujib

xploring the Desert
astles

10 The plains of eastern Jordan are home to the iconic 'desert castles', a collec-
n of early Umayyad pleasure palaces, bath-
uses and hunting lodges that are strikingly
congruous with their barren surroundings.
hile visiting Jordan's eastern frontier requires
me planning, this region is full of surprises,
cluding Qusayr Amra's saucy frescos (p236),
wrence's winter redoubt at Azraq (p233),
ast refuge of the Arabian oryx at Shaumari
ildlife Reserve (p235) and an unlikely lake in
e desert at Burqu (p243). Fresco, Qusayr Amra

Blooming Beautiful

11 Carpets of scarlet poppies strewn
across the desert, ribbons of oleander
in the wadis, the surprise flutter of velvet pet-
als on a black iris along the King's Highway;
Jordan is home to some of the region's most
magnificent floral displays. For a truly sublime
show, visit the Roman ruins of Umm Qais
(p101) in the far north of the country on a
sunny afternoon in April: armfuls of knee-high
daisies and thistles, yellow hollyhocks and
pink mallow compete for a sliver of warmth
between fallen masonry. Flowers at Umm Qais

IMAGE GROUP LTD/ALAMY ©

LYLE SCOTT NASH/GETTY IMAGES ©

The King's Highway

12 It may not be the path of literal kings, but the King's Highway (p126) follows some pretty big footsteps. These include those of the Nabataeans (their fabled city of Petra lies at the end of the King's Highway), the Romans (whose military outpost at Umm ar-Rasas is a Unesco World Heritage site) and the Crusaders (their Karak and Shobak castles are highlights in their own right). Smaller footsteps include those taken by Salome in her Dance of the Seven Veils at the desolate hilltop of Mukawir (p141). Ruins of Herod the Great's castle, Mukawir

Miraculous Mujib

13 Fresh water is in short supply in Jorda and it has already become an issue o intense political importance in dialogue with neighbouring states. Various projects, such as the 'Red to Dead' Sea Canal and a pipeline from Wadi Rum's aquifers to Amman, are being explored with ever-greater urgency. That's one reason why the miraculous spring of Mujib Biosphere Reserve (p123) are a high light. The other reason is that the water flows through a spectacular wadi into a series of heavenly pools – paradise for the adventure-seeking traveller. Wadi Mujib

12

The Hand of Hospitality

14 Despite its modest size, Jordan is home to diverse peoples who share a traditional sense of responsibility towards the visitor. It may sound unfashionably romantic to claim that Jordanians are more hospitable than most, but it doesn't take long to realise that it's an integral part of their culture. Whether you're invited for mint tea by Palestinians, bread and salt by Bedouins, or pomegranate salads by the Chechens of Azraq, your interactions with Jordanian people will be a highlight of your visit. Bedouin man

Wadi Jadid

15 There's nothing new about Wadi Jadid ('New Valley' in Arabic, p140). This undisturbed valley in the middle of nowhere typifies all that is constant in rural Jordanian life – sheep-grazing, shepherds trotting through thistles astride their pot-bellied donkeys, the smell of sage in the hot summer sun. In fact the valley would be entirely unremarkable were it not for the clusters of ancient Bronze Age dolmen that dot the terraced hillsides. Heaved into place between 5000 and 3000 BC, these impressive stone monuments are worth the effort it takes to locate them. Dolmen, Wadi Jadid

need to know

Currency
» Jordanian Dinar (JD)

Language
» Arabic (English is widely spoken)

When to Go?

Irbid
GO Mar–May

Azraq
GO Jun–Aug

Aqaba
GO Sep–Feb

Warm to hot summers, mild winters
Dry climate
Desert, dry climate

High Season
(Mar–May)

» The weather is perfect throughout Jordan with warm days and cool nights.

» Northern Jordan is blanketed in wildflowers in April.

» Book rooms in advance in main tourist areas and expect higher rates.

Shoulder Season
(Sep–Feb)

» The best time to visit the Red Sea; prices in and around Aqaba rise accordingly.

» Bitter nights in the desert and even rain or snow curtail many activities such as camping.

Low Season
(Jun–Aug)

» The desert in the middle of the summer is extreme. Temperatures throughout Jordan can be stifling.

» Prices are at their best but many places close in the low season.

Your Daily Budget

Budget less than
JD40

» Shared room in budget guesthouse: JD10–40

» Street fare and local markets: under JD5

» Public transport: JD5

» International Student Identity Card reduces cost of some tourist sites: JD5

Midrange
JD40– 120

» Double room in *mid-range hotel: JD40–90

» Eating in local restaurants: JD5–10

» Car hire: JD25

» Entry costs/unguided activities: JD10

Top end over
JD120

» Double room in five-star hotel: over JD90

» Buffet lunch/dinner: from JD10

» 4WD car hire: JD140

» Guided activities: JD50

Money

» ATMs are available throughout the country and credit cards are widely used.

Visas

» Visas, required by all visitors, are available on arrival at international airports and most of Jordan's land borders.

Mobile Phones

» Local SIM cards can be used for international calls and can be topped up with readily available prepaid cards.

Driving

» Drive on the right; the steering wheel is on the left side of the car. Seat-belt wearing is compulsory.

Websites

» **Jordan Jubilee** (www.jordanjubilee. com) Practical website about southern Jordan.

» **Jordan Tourism Board** (www.visitjordan. com) Excellent official website.

» **Lonely Planet** (www.lonelyplanet. com/jordan) Destination information, hotel bookings, traveller forum.

» **RSCN** (www.rscn. org.jo) Online booking of accommodation and eco-adventures in nature reserves.

» **Bible Places** (www. bibleplaces.com) Biblical sights in Jordan.

Exchange Rates

Australia	A$1	JD0.761
Canada	C$1	JD0.711
Egypt	E£1	JD0.118
Europe	€1	JD0.934
Israel & Palestinian Territories	1NIS	JD0.191
Japan	Y100	JD0.933
Syria	S£10	JD0.124
UK	£1	JD1.123
US	US$1	JD0.711

For current exchange rates see www.xe.com.

Important Numbers

Country code	☏962
International access code	☏00
Ambulance	☏911
Fire	☏911
Police	☏911

Arriving in Jordan

» **Queen Alia International Airport**
Bus – Airport Express Bus runs regularly between the airport and Amman (see p76)
Taxi – JD17, 30 to 40 minutes to central Amman
Car Hire – Available in arrivals hall

» **Ferry Terminal, Aqaba**
Taxi – JD8, 20 minutes to central Aqaba

» **Wadi Araba (Yitzhak Rabin) Border Crossing**
Taxi – JD8, 15 minutes to central Aqaba; JD50, two hours to Petra

Don't Leave Home Without

□ Your driver's licence

□ A Syrian visa if heading north (see p36)

□ A Jordanian visa if heading from Israel & the Palestinian Territories across King Hussein/Allenby Bridge (see p34)

□ Tampons (hard to find outside main tourist centres)

□ A sleeping sheet to waylay roaming scorpions if you're staying overnight in Wadi Rum

□ Mosquito repellent and a net if you want any chance of sleep while camping in wadis or sleeping outside (permitted on the roof of some guest houses)

□ A hat, sunscreen, sunglasses, lip balm, long sleeves and neck covering if you're planning a summer visit

□ Warm clothing for the cold desert nights between October and April

if you like...

Roman Ruins

Pillars, pediments and pavements from ancient Rome are liberally strewn across Jordan, making the country one of the best in the world to see evidence of this once-mighty empire.

Jerash Modern-day centurions clash swords daily in the hippodrome in the heart of the exquisite and well-preserved ruins of Jerash (p83)

Umm Qais With a view of the Golan Heights, these atmospheric ruins still command a strategic location; they are particularly picturesque surrounded by spring wildflowers (p101)

Pella One of the 10 cities of the ancient Decapolis (p104)

The Citadel Perched above the modern capital, these ruins afford a great view of downtown and its ancient amphitheatre (p49)

Colonnaded Street, Petra The presence of the Romans in the pink city of Petra is found in the detail – in an acanthus leaf carving, a tomb to a fallen hero or in the fallen pillars of the main thoroughfare (p171)

Views of the Promised Land

On the east bank of the river Jordan latter-day pilgrims can follow in the footsteps of former prophets. More than 100 sites in Jordan are mentioned in the Bible.

Bethany-Beyond-the-Jordan The most important biblical site in Jordan, this is where Elijah is said to have ascended into heaven and where Jesus was believed to have been baptised (p109)

Mt Nebo Casting his eyes across the Jordan Valley to Jericho beyond, Moses supposedly finally saw the Promised Land from here before dying (p138)

Madaba Famed for the mosaic map, the earliest map of the Holy Land, Madaba is a living testament to the Bible with its devout population of Christians (p128)

Herod's Castle, Mukawir Only a pillar remains atop the hill at Mukawir but this atmospheric site conjures the rhythm of Salome's dance in the wind (p141)

Lot's Cave She looked back, and for that Lot's wife was sait to have been cast into a pillar of salt near here (p125)

Crusader Castles

Most people love a good castle and Jordan has plenty. Once guarding ancient trade routes or repelling religious adversaries, their crumbling battlements are a highlight of Jordan.

Karak Castle The king of castles, the crusader stronghold of Karak is a highlight of Jordan (p144)

Shobak Castle Built by the Crusaders in the 12th century, this picture-perfect castle wins over even the most ruin-weary traveller (p155)

Qala'at ar-Rabad (Ajloun Castle) Part of Saladin's defensive chain of forts against the Crusaders (p92)

Azraq Castle On the edge of an important oasis, Azraq Castle was a chilly winter home for T E Lawrence and Sharif Hussein in 1917 (p233)

Eastern Desert Castles Collectively misnamed as castles, this collection of Umayyad bathhouses, hunting lodges and pleasure palaces is a monument to early Islamic architecture (p229)

TIM BARKER/LONELY PLANET IMAGES ©

» Entry hall in the Umayyad Palace (p51), the Citadel, Amman

Healthy Bathing

Jordan boasts dozens of thermal hot-water springs where the water ranges from 35°C to 45°C and contains potassium, magnesium and health-giving minerals. If you like a bath with bubbles, Jordan is the place to have one.

Hammamat Ma'in Steam vents pepper the sulphurous hillside at this famous and beautiful spring near Madaba; it's suitable for single women (p120)

Hammamat Burbita and Hammamat Afra West of the King's Highway near Tafila, these springs have a sequence of pools and basic facilities (p150)

Al-Pasha Turkish Bath Steam rooms, Jacuzzi and obligatory scrubbing are available at this Amman favourite (p60)

Petra Turkish Bath With a separate section for women, this is a great place to soothe aching muscles after a day of hiking in Petra (p179)

Dead Sea Spas The place to be for the ultimate in healthy bathing and luxurious pampering (p117)

Flora & Fauna

The desert may look deserted but it is home to some of the greatest survivors on earth – both animal and vegetable. If you want to see the desert come alive then time your visit for mid-April.

Wildflowers In profusion across Jordan in mid-April, the best floral displays are around the hills of the north (p101)

Strawberry Oaks Ajloun Forest Reserve protects this rare woodland (p93)

Bird-watching Azraq Wetland Reserve hosts migrants and residents in the heart of the desert (p234)

Black Iris Jordan's national flower blooms along the King's Highway in April (p126)

Ibex Perched on crags above the oleander-filled wadis of Dana Biosphere Reserve, this is one elusive goat! (p151)

Oryx The origin of the myth of the unicorn, this magnificent antelope can be seen at Shaumari Wildlife Reserve (p235)

Fish The Red Sea is renowned the world over for its diversity of life underwater (p26)

Crafts with a Conscience

The revival of cottage industries is helping to sustain traditional ways of life in Jordan. If you want to help the process, there are lots of places to buy a souvenir that leaves behind more than you take away.

Hand-loomed Rugs Goat-hair rugs are bringing life-changing opportunities to the women of Bani Hamida (p142)

Palestinian Embroidery The Haret Jdoudna Complex in Madaba provides an outlet for the once-dying art of cross-stitch (p137)

Mosaics Jordan has been associated with the art of mosaic for centuries and some superb pieces have been preserved for posterity; buy your own tree of life in Madaba, home of the mosaic map (p136)

Painted Ostrich Eggs Ostriches once roamed the land now called Jordan; the art of egg painting has been preserved in Azraq (p234)

Environmentally Friendly Products Wild Jordan in Amman sells a range of lovely eco-crafts from Jordan's nature reserves (p72)

» Bedouin guide with camels, Wadi Rum (p217)

Lawrence of Arabia

Jordan is 'El Lawrence' country, the land the eccentric, camel-riding, dagger-wielding Englishman made his own during the Arab Revolt of 1917–19.

Wadi Rum Lawrence's ghost haunts 'Rumm the Magnificent', floating past 'crags like gigantic buildings' now named 'Seven Pillars of Wisdom' in his honour (p210)

Wadi Umran The words 'to Aqaba' float in the wind for those who camel trek along this wadi – ask at Wadi Rum for a guide (p201)

Hejaz Railway The goods train rattles by on mended tracks once dynamited by Lawrence (p55)

Dana The 'chess-board houses of Dana village' give a vantage point into sunny Araba, 'fresh and green, thousands of feet below' (p151)

Azraq Castle Lawrence was proud to ride between Aqaba and 'Azraq the Remote' in three days; the journey now takes only one day (p233)

The West Lawrence left Azraq 'riding into a glowing west, while...schools of cranes flew into the sunset' – a good place to let Lawrence's memory rest (p234)

Bedouin Experiences

For centuries the Bedouin have inspired admiration for their ability to withstand the hardship of life in the desert. Nowadays they often make their living from sharing their traditional way of life with visitors – an experience not to be missed.

Camping under Goat Hair With a sky full of stars, mint tea and a good story, a Bedouin camp at Wadi Rum or Diseh offers a night to remember (p220)

Camel Trek The ships of the desert are more often driven than ridden by the Bedouin these days but treks are possible in Wadi Rum and Petra (p217)

Sampling Mensaf Camels' milk, dried dates and goats' cheese are the staples of Bedouin food; at the Al-Wadi Restaurant in Petra they prepare *mensaf*, the traditional Bedouin dish of lamb, rice and pine nuts (p187)

Walks on the Wild Side

Jordan's most exciting hikes are across sand dunes, through rare forests, and via the lush gorges, waterfalls and pools of seasonally dry riverbeds (wadis). Taking a guide with transport is advisable as hikes are only flood-proof from mid-March to mid-October. See Taylor & Howard's *Jordan: Walks* for full route descriptions.

Siq Trail A rewarding scramble (2km, three hours) through Wadi Mujib's narrow canyon in knee-high water (p123)

Wadi Dana Trail This classic Dana hike (16km, six hours) descends through a geography lesson of ecosystems and Bedouin grazing grounds (p151)

Prophet's Trail A beautiful hike (8km, four hours) through Ajloun's fig and pear orchards to the alleged birthplace of Prophet Elijah (p95)

Makharas Canyon Hike This plod through soft sands (8km, 2½ hours) opens up the best of Wadi Rum (p218)

Wadi Muthlim Enter Petra the Indiana Jones way (5km, 90 minutes) through this unnervingly narrow canyon (p174)

month by month

Top Events

1 **Jerash Festival**, July

2 **Hiking Season**, March–April

3 **Peak Wildflower Blooms**, April

4 **Dead Sea Ultra Marathon**, April

5 **Distant Heat**, August

January

If you thought the desert was hot by default, then think again. The desert is bitter cold in winter. But while most of Jordan shivers under chilly skies, those in the know head for Aqaba.

Red Sea Snorkelling & Diving

Aqaba, with its warm winter sunshine, hosts the annual holiday exodus of urbanites from the hills. The winter months, from December to March, are the perfect time for an underwater adventure, with clear blue skies and crystal-clear waters.

April

April is the most popular month to visit Jordan, and with good reason. The weather is balmy and clear and the semi-arid hills of Northern Jordan burst into magnificent, knee-high bloom.

Nature Walking

The spring, late March to mid-May, is the best time to visit Jordan's excellent nature reserves (p293). The elusive black iris (Jordan's national flower) blooms and nature lovers can hike through narrow wadis without fear of flash floods.

Jordan Rally

The annual Jordan Rally (www.jordanrally. com) is organised by the FIA World Rally Championship and attracts cheering crowds to the shores of the Dead Sea. The world's leading rally drivers participate in the 1008km route.

Dead Sea Ultra Marathon

Not just for a few crazed locals, the Dead Sea Ultra Marathon (www.deadsea marathon.com) attracts athletes and amateurs – all heading below zero. The 50km race begins in Amman at 900m above sea level and ends 400m below the international tideline.

May

Still peak tourist season, the country hots up in May and by the end of the month low-lying areas are toasting. It's also peak season for flowering oleander, making the wadis pretty in pink.

Independence Day

On 25 May, Jordanians celebrate their national day with bunting and flags and military parades in the capital. It's a good excuse for a chat, a water pipe and a mint tea with friends, and visitors are always made welcome.

Hiking & Camel Trekking

It may be hotting up in Petra and Wadi Rum but May is the perfect time to experience the desert. With hot days and warm nights, you quickly slip into the rhythm of Bedouin life, rising early and napping after lunch.

July

The midsummer months of June and July bring hazy skies and suffocating heat and few choose this time of year for a visit. Thankfully the tedious summer months are cheered up by open-air cultural events.

Jerash Festival

Hosted within world-class ruins, Jordan's

best-loved cultural event (p87) brings ancient Jerash to life with plays, poetry recitals, opera and concerts. Held annually since 1981, the festival (www.jerashfestival.jo) runs for 17 days from mid-July to mid-August.

☆ Traditional Concerts & Plays

In summer (July and August), traditional concerts and plays are held at the Odeon (p53) and Roman Theatre (p52) in Amman, as well as in the towns of Salt (p106) and Fuheis (p79).

August

Until 2015, the summer is associated with high points in the Islamic calendar. Each year Islamic holidays fall 11 days earlier than the previous year. The precise dates depend upon the sighting of the moon.

🍴 Ramadan

During the holy month of Ramadan, Muslims must refrain from eating, drinking and smoking between dawn and dusk. While there are some restrictions for visitors, Ramadan also brings special cuisine and sweetmeats unavailable at other times.

⭐ Eid al-Fitr

Marking the end of Ramadan, Eid al-Fitr is a time of festivity for Muslims. Disruptions to opening hours, and heavily booked transport and hotels are likely; on the upside, an invitation to join the party is an opportunity not to be missed.

☆ Distant Heat

August is hot, so if you can't beat the heat, you may as well join it by building up a sweat at Jordan's annual dance in the desert. This all-nighter (www.distantheat.com) takes place in Wadi Rum and features top international electronic-dance-music artists.

October

Residents of Jordan sigh with relief in late September and early October as temperatures cool and the parched earth returns to life with the first showers. Markets abound with figs, corn and fresh olive oil.

⭐ Eid al-Adha

Marking the end of Hajj, the annual pilgrimage to Mecca, this Islamic holiday falls in October until 2014. Shops close as owners join their families on these important days of celebration and feasting.

November

Blustering with wind and often heavy rains, November signals the season of flash floods as water chases through sun-dried wadis towards Wadi Araba. Not the best month for hiking, then, but good for sightseeing.

🏃 Jordan Running Adventure Race

Covered in a single stage between Petra and the Dead Sea via Wadi Rum, this 190km ultra trail is a new addition to Jordan's sporting calendar. A shorter route of 80km attracts less masochistic participants.

🏃 Floating in the Dead Sea

With fewer tourists than in spring, you may be bobbing alone in the Dead Sea (p113) in November. Early harvests of mangos and bananas from the Jordan Valley give extra enticement!

itineraries

Whether you have six days or 60, these itineraries provide a starting point for the trip of a lifetime. Want more inspiration? Head online to lonelyplanet. com/thorntree to chat with other travellers.

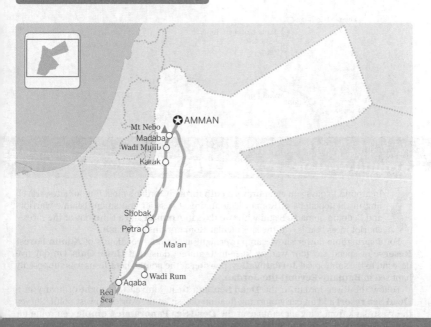

Mt Nebo
AMMAN
Madaba
Wadi Mujib
Karak

Shobak
Petra
Ma'an

Aqaba
Wadi Rum
Red Sea

Seven Days
Amman to Aqaba Return

> Thanks to its relatively compact size, Jordan rewards even the shortest of getaways, especially if you're prepared to hire a car. On day one take the pulse of the modern Middle East in the souqs and coffeehouses of **Amman**. On day two, piece together a biblical history in the mosaic town of **Madaba** and, like Moses, survey the Promised Land from neighbouring **Mt Nebo**.

Spend day three following the caravans of history along the ancient King's Highway, crossing mighty **Wadi Mujib**. Visit the Crusader castles in **Karak** and **Shobak** en route to **Petra** and listen for hooves clattering through cobbled corridors.

Make an early start on day four to experience the Siq at Petra at its best. Climb to a High Place and picnic under an oleander bush. On day five, slither through Wadi Muthlim and end your visit to the rose-red city at the iconic Monastery. From here, the seaside town of **Aqaba** is only two hours away. On day six, wash off the desert dust in the spectacular coral gardens of the **Red Sea**. On day seven, return to Amman (four hours via Ma'an and the Desert Highway); with an early start, you could have lunch on a **Wadi Rum** sand dune en route.

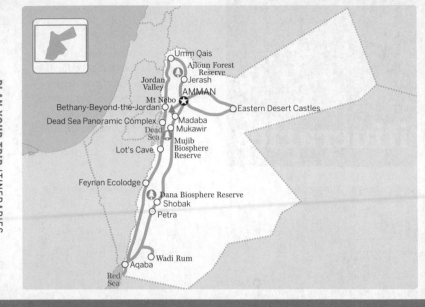

Two to Three Weeks
Around Jordan

> In around 18 days you can unravel a path through Jordan's most famous sites, travelling in the footsteps of Roman legionnaires, Crusader craftsmen, Islamic warriors and Bedouin nomads. Begin with two days in **Amman** and a third day at the races – chariot races that is – at the spectacular Roman ruins of **Jerash**.

For a springtime flower show, camp overnight at the oak woodlands of **Ajloun Forest Reserve** or spend day four wading knee-high among daisies at **Umm Qais**. On day five descend to the subtropical **Jordan Valley**, pausing at the point where Jesus was supposedly baptised in **Bethany-Beyond-the-Jordan**.

Follow the River Jordan to the **Dead Sea** and treat yourself to a night of luxury in a **Dead Sea resort** and an early morning float on day six at the world's lowest point. Survey the West Bank from a higher vantage at the **Dead Sea Panoramic Complex** en route for **Mujib Biosphere Reserve**. Splash, swim and struggle through 'Petra with water' on the unguided Siq Trail. Dry out along the Dead Sea Highway to **Lot's Cave** and swap stories about the adventure at candlelit **Feynan Ecolodge**.

Begin week two chilling in **Aqaba** for two days, sparing time for a dive or snorkel in the fabled **Red Sea**. With batteries recharged, tackle a hike in **Wadi Rum** on day 10 and stay overnight in a Bedouin camp. Spend the next three nights in Wadi Musa, joining Petra by Night for a magical introduction to the world-wonder of **Petra**. End your second week travelling back to Amman along the Desert Highway.

If you have a third week to hand, head north from Petra via the ancient **King's Highway** on day 15, sparing time to pause at the imposing castle of **Shobak**. Break the journey at **Dana Biosphere Reserve** and relax on day 16, taking village walks or a longer hike with a guide.

Spend day 17 making the most of the King's Highway to Madaba, pausing at Karak and Herod's Castle in **Mukawir** en route. Allow two days for some souvenir shopping in **Madaba**, the closest town to the international airport, or at craft shops in nearby **Mt Nebo**. If energy allows, end your visit with a day trip to **Azraq** and the **Eastern desert castles**.

» (above) Horse-drawn carriage, the
  Siq, Wadi Musa (p179)
» (left) Roman theatre (p52), Amman

Ten Days
Border to Border

Jordan is plumb in the middle of a richly historic region, making it an essential part of a Middle East adventure. This 10-day route by public transport assumes an entry point by ferry from Egypt or by taxi from Israel and the Palestinian Territories. If coming from the latter, check the visa and security situation for onward travel to Syria or Iraq (not recommended at the time of writing).

Spend the first two days acclimatising to a new country in **Aqaba**: Jordan has a distinct character, immediately felt in the souqs and open-air restaurants of this seaside town. Spare time for a swim – Jordan's access to the **Red Sea** may be diminutive but the coral gardens are pristine and relatively unvisited. On day three take the morning bus and go in search of 'El Lawrence' in the magnificent desert of **Wadi Rum**. Don a bandana and hop astride a camel and head into the red sand dunes for an overnight camp with the Bedouin.

On day four rise at dawn with the locals, ready to catch the minibus to **Petra**. With two days in the pink city you can hike to the High Places, learn to cook Jordanian food at Petra Kitchen and watch the sunset from the Monastery.

On day six head north to Amman on the frequent Desert Highway buses via Ma'an. Spend a night sampling city nightlife, including an evening's stroll downtown through Amman's Roman ruins. Hike from the Citadel on day seven and reward the effort with the capital's best-loved Arabic street food at Hashem Restaurant.

If you're heading for the Iraqi border on day eight, stop over for two nights at **Azraq**. Azraq Fort was Lawrence's winter hideout and the nearby Azraq Wetland Reserve is a reminder of the fragility of life in the black Badia (stone desert). After crossing such barren lands, the shrunken waters of the oasis seem miraculous. Getting to the border from here requires patience but is possible.

If heading for the Syrian or Israeli border, spend day eight roaming the Roman ruins of **Jerash** and stay overnight in **Ajloun**. With a crumbling castle, Qala'at ar-Rabad, and a nature reserve with easy hiking trails, Ajloun is a peaceful place to spend a last day in Jordan. Although the borders with Syria or Israel and the Palestinian Territories are nearby, allow time for a change of minibus in Jerash or Irbid.

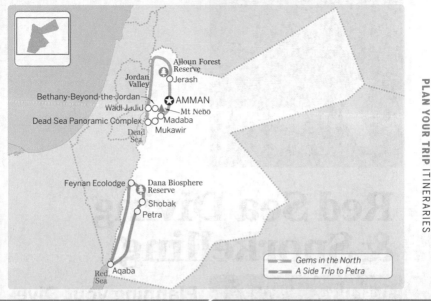

Gems in the North
A Side Trip to Petra

Four Days
Gems in the North

With a long weekend, most visitors head straight for Petra on an overnighter from Amman. For a more rewarding use of time, leave the pink city for a longer visit and focus instead on Jordan's gems in the north. This trip bypasses the capital.

Collect a car from the airport in Amman and head to the Roman ruins of **Jerash**. On day two, amble down to the **Jordan Valley** via **Ajloun** and the Islamic castle of Qala'at ar-Rabad. Pause at the point where John supposedly baptised Jesus at **Bethany-Beyond-the-Jordan** and book in for some extreme R&R at the lowest place on earth. If you can tear yourself away from the fluffy towels of the region's best **spas** (which come complete with a bob in the **Dead Sea** and a therapeutic mud pack), then drive via the **Dead Sea Panoramic Complex** on day three to steaming Hammamat Ma'in and take the scenic road to **Mukawir**, where Salome is said to have danced for John's head on a platter. Skirt the plateau ridge to the friendly mosaic town of **Madaba** and on day four visit **Mt Nebo**, or take an escort to the dolmens of **Wadi Jadid**. From Madaba, allow an hour to return the car to the airport.

Six Days
A Side Trip to Petra

Travellers frequently ask the question: 'Is it worth making the effort to get to Petra as a side trip from Israel or Egypt?' The answer is a resounding 'yes!' While you can just about do the round trip in three days, the experience will be much more rewarding in four or five days. Add one additional day and be prepared to use taxis to make this trip viable in the time available.

A trip to Petra from neighbouring countries invariably involves an overnight stop in **Aqaba**. With plenty of accommodation, a lively ambience and excellent seafood, this is no hardship. On day two, take the early bus to Wadi Musa, the town closest to the Nabataean treasures of **Petra**. Amble through the Siq at midday, missing the morning tour groups. Watch the sunset turn the Royal Tombs pink, and return to the lively traveller scene in the town's Cave Bar. On day three, hike through Wadi Muthlim and end the day at the Monastery.

Follow the ghosts of centurions and Crusaders along the King's Highway to **Shobak** on day four and stay overnight at the **Dana Biosphere Reserve**. Hike down to ecofriendly **Feynan Ecolodge** on day five, prearranging transport along the Dead Sea Highway back to Aqaba on day six.

Red Sea Diving & Snorkelling

Best Dive

The Cedar Pride The coral-encrusted hulk of this sunken ship is Jordan's most famous dive site.

Best Snorkel

Japanese Garden Shore access and a gradual slope to a colourful reef make this the best place to hoist a snorkel.

Best Underground Garden

Gorgonian I Renowned for 16m fan coral and house-sized cabbage coral.
Gorgonian II Spectacular trimming of fire, stony and raspberry corals.

Best Turtle Encounter

Power Station Turtles regularly frequent this dive site. Don't be unnerved by the hammerheads – shark attacks are extremely rare.

Best Watering Holes

Royal Diving Club This is *the* place to dry your flippers while you wet your whistle.
Bedouin Garden Village Swapping fishy stories under a Bedouin tent is an 'après dive' highlight.

Planning your Dive or Snorkel

A Low-Key Experience

The Red Sea has a legendary reputation among underwater enthusiasts. Conglomerations of coral rise from the seabed, shallow reefs team with brightly coloured fish, sheer drop-offs disappear into unplumbed depths and an eerie, ethereal blue pervades the cutglass water.

While it's no secret that the Red Sea is one of the world's finest marine destinations, it's less known that Jordan has 27km of precious access to this underwater wonderland alongside the Gulf of Aqaba. This is good news for those divers and snorkellers who seek pristine reefs. It's also good news for those who favour an altogether low-key experience; indeed, the whole diving scene here is delightfully relaxed and unpretentious.

Clear Visibility

Surrounded by desert on three sides, the Red Sea was formed 40 million years ago when the Arabian Peninsula split from Africa, and it is the only tropical sea that is almost entirely enclosed by land. No river flows into it and the influx of water from the Indian Ocean is slight, resulting in minimal tides and high salinity. It is also windy – on average the sea is flat for only 50 days a year. This unique combination of elements means that visibility underwater is almost unfailingly crystal-clear.

High Accessibility

Enjoying the wonders of the deep is easy to organise, with many of the dive sites readily accessible to snorkellers. Dive centres offer accommodation close to the shore (see p208) – handy for those who want to make diving and snorkelling the main focus of their visit to southern Jordan. Those who prefer the buzz and amenities of Jordan's seaside city can easily find transport to and from Aqaba, making the dive sites accessible as a day trip from town.

When, Where & How

When to Go

The water temperature is warm (an average 22.5°C in winter and 26°C in summer), making the in-water experience pleasant at any time of year.

Best Times

» **Late January–mid-May** This is the best time to dive weather-wise. Bear in mind that late winter attracts holiday-makers from Amman, pushing up the price of accommodation in Aqaba. Spring is peak tourist season for international visitors and the busiest time for dive centres.

» **October–November** The second most popular time to dive but prepare for the odd overcast or rainy day.

Avoid

» **Mid-May–September** The shore is usually miserably hot in the middle of the summer and the risk of burning is high both in and out of the water.

» **Late December–late January** Although usually mild in Aqaba, freezing cold weather and occasional thunderstorms can sweep in from the desert at any time during winter.

Where to Go

Jordan's short coastline along the Gulf of Aqaba stretches between Israel and the Palestinian Territories and Saudi Arabia. Diving and snorkelling is focused between the port

> ### RED SEA ROYALS
>
> Sultan Ibrahim, king fish and king soldier bream are not the only royals in the water. Diving in Jordan enjoys support from the very top, with King Abdullah II reported to be an avid diver. In fact his patronage was instrumental in the establishment of Jordan's premier artificial reef, the wreck of the *Cedar Pride*. Running aground after a fire in the engine room, this Spanish-built cargo ship was towed back out to sea in 1986 by the World Wildlife Fund (WWF) and sunk as an artificial reef. Today, the freighter lies on her port side at a depth of 25m, within easy reach from the shore and is now one of the premier dive sites in the Red Sea.

and the Saudi border. This stretch of coast is protected within the Red Sea Marine Peace Park, run in cooperation with Israel and the Palestinian Territories. Reefs here are in excellent condition, and the soft corals, especially those found on the *Cedar Pride,* are beautiful.

There are about 15 sites worth visiting. The majority can be enjoyed by snorkellers as well as divers as they are easily accessible from either a jetty or the beach. Although you can enter the water at any spot along the coast, snorkellers tend to gravitate towards the private beach at the Royal Diving Club.

Sites are not signposted, nor are they remotely obvious from the road. If you want to dive or snorkel independently you'll have to ask for directions, or take your chances and search for obvious offshore reefs.

How to Go
Dive Centres

Trips are easily organised through specialist operators in Aqaba or along the Red Sea coast and many hotels facilitate diving and snorkelling trips too. Dive centres with a long-standing reputation for excellence include those listed below.

Aqaba Adventure Divers (Map p198; ☏079-5843724; www.aqaba-diving.com) Operates dives in conjunction with Bedouin Garden Village.

Aqaba International Dive Centre (Map p198; ☏079-7774211; www.aqabadivingcenter. com) Popular, well-equipped and one of Aqaba's best.

Arab Divers (Map p198; ☏03-2031808; www. aqaba-divevillage.com) Highly recommended year after year by Lonely Planet readers.

Dive Aqaba (Map p198; ☏03-2108883; www. diveaqaba.com) A highly professional training centre known for its high-quality teaching staff.

Red Sea Diving Centre (Map p198; ☏03-2022323; www.aqabascubadiving.com) One of the most established dive centres in Aqaba.

Royal Diving Club (Map p198; ☏03-2017035; www.rdc.jo) Around 12km south of the city, this is one of Aqaba's most famous institutions.

Choosing a Dive Centre

» Choose a reputable dive centre that makes safety a priority.

» If you haven't dived for more than three months, take a refresher dive. The cost is usually applied towards later dives.

» Check hoses, mouthpieces and valves for cuts and leakage.

» Choose your wetsuit carefully: it's easy to get chilled in winter months.

» Check that there is oxygen on the dive boat in case of accidents.

Costs

The satisfying part of diving and snorkelling in Jordan is that it doesn't have to cost an arm and a leg. In fact, for under JD10 per day you can bask above fan corals, swim with sardines, tread water among angels and float among clowns. The following table, based on prices offered at the Royal Diving Club, gives a rough idea of what costs to expect. With competitive rates for courses, Jordan is a good place to learn to dive or to enhance your skills at all levels.

DIVING COSTS	
One-/two-tank shore dive	JD25/40
Full equipment rental for one/ two dives	JD12/15
PADI open-water course/crew pack/certification	JD230/50/25
Advanced open-water course/ crew pack/certification	JD180/40/25
Emergency first-response course/crew pack/certification	JD85/15/25
Rescue-dive course/crew pack/ certification	JD210/50/25
Divemaster training/ certification/application	JD550/250/70
SNORKELLING COSTS	
Full equipment rental	JD8 per day
Half-day from shore/whole day trip by boat	JD8/25

RESPONSIBLE DIVING & SNORKELLING

The Red Sea's natural wonders are just as magnificent as Jordan's historical and cultural splendours – and they need just as much protection. To help preserve the ecology and beauty of the reefs for posterity, please heed the following advice:

» Do not touch, remove or stand on coral and avoid dragging equipment across the reef.

» Minimise your disturbance of marine animals. In particular, do not ride on the backs of turtles or feed fish.

» Avoid large surges of water or kicking up sand with your fins; this may smother the delicate organisms of the reef.

» Do not throw rubbish into the sea or leave it on the beach. Plastics in particular are a serious threat to marine life. Turtles often mistake plastic for jellyfish, their favourite food.

» Ensure boats are anchored to buoys, not attached to precious coral, and are not grounded on coral.

» Practise and maintain proper buoyancy control. Major damage can be done by divers descending too fast and colliding with the reef.

» Resist taking marine souvenirs which depletes the beauty of a site and is illegal in Jordan.

The Underwater Experience

What to See Underwater

According to the **Royal Marine Conservation Society of Jordan** (☎06-5676173; www.jreds.org), the gulf has more than 110 species of hard coral and 120 species of soft coral forming spectacular reefs. These reefs are home to about 1000 species of fish, including colourful clownfish, parrotfish and angelfish, and a whole variety of life from dolphins to molluscs and sponges. Protected green turtles frequent the dive sites and harmless whale sharks pay a visit in summer.

Buy the plastic *Red Sea Fishwatchers Field Guide,* which can be taken underwater to identify species of fish and coral.

Further Information

Books

Lonely Planet's *Diving and Snorkelling Guide to the Red Sea* concentrates on sites along the Egyptian coast, but also has a detailed section about diving around the Gulf of Aqaba. The major bookshops in Aqaba have a good range of books about diving, including *Introduction to the Marine Life of Aqaba. The Red Sea: Underwater Paradise* by Angelo Mojetta is one of the better glossy coffee-table books, with beautiful photos of marine flora and fauna.

Internet Resources

Among the hundreds of internet references to help inform your underwater experience, the following are recommended.

Wind Finder (www.windfinder.com/forecast/aqaba) Check on current conditions day-by-day to ensure you pick the best day for your dive.

H2O Magazine (www.h2o-mag.com) The website of the quarterly publication of the Red Sea Association for Diving and Watersports, with articles and updates on diving in the region.

Reef Check (www.reefcheck.org) A membership organisation working to save coral reefs in the Red Sea and elsewhere in the world.

Health & Safety

Hazards of the Sea

It's worth familiarising yourself with the main marine hazards before snorkelling or

THE RED SEA – A SEVENTH WONDER

Ever wondered where the Mare Rostrum, or Red Sea, got its name? Some believe it was named after the red sandstone mountain ranges that surround the sea. Others insist it was named after the periodic blooms of algae that tinge the water reddish-brown. But whatever the etymology of the name, the Red Sea is now synonymous with underwater spectacles par excellence – and that's official! In 1989 a panel of scientists and conservationists selected the northern portion of this 1800km-long body of water as one of the Seven Underwater Wonders of the World.

diving – single-page colour guides to the Red Sea's common culprits can be bought in hotel bookshops around diving areas.

» **Stonefish** A poisonous fish with a nasty habit of lying half-submerged in the sand: wear something on your feet if you're wading out to a dive site. If stung by a stonefish, you should see a doctor immediately.

» **Lionfish** These have poisonous spikes like stonefish. Calamine lotion, antihistamines and analgesics may reduce the reaction and relieve pain. Some swear by the application of urine!

» **Jellyfish** Sometimes occurring in enormous groups, jellyfish can be something of a scourge of warm waters. Depending on the species, their sting can be very painful. The best remedy is to douse the rash with vinegar.

» **Sharks** In this part of the Gulf of Aqaba, you're most likely to encounter white- or black-tipped reef sharks. Tiger sharks, and the enormous, plankton-eating whale sharks, are generally found only in deeper waters. Attacks from these apex predators are extremely rare in this area but obvious common sense applies if you have a bad cut or bleeding wound.

» **Coral** The cuts from coral are notoriously slow to heal. Make sure you clean wounds thoroughly to avoid infection. Unlike the cold waters of northern seas, subtropical seawater is full of troublesome organisms that can cause serious infection.

» **Crown of Thorns Starfish** Known as COTS, these invasive starfish feed on and kill local coral.

NPR/IMAGEBROKER ©

» (above) Soft corals on the *Cedar Pride* shipwreck
» (left) Hawksbill sea turtle

Divers should notify their divemaster if they spot them.

» **Other Creatures to Avoid** Moray eels, sea urchins, fire coral, blowfish, triggerfish and turkeyfish are also better left alone.

Safety Advice

Any underwater adventure incurs some element of risk but with planning, knowledge and a bit of common sense, the risks can be minimised. Use the 'dive safe' checklist (p32) before you book your trip. If it's too late for that, the excellent **Princess Haya Hospital** (Map p198; ☏03-2014111; Ash-Shrif al-Hussein bin Ali St) in Aqaba is well-equipped for diving mishaps, including cuts, bites and stings. It also has a **decompression chamber** (☏03-2014117), where the staff is trained to deal with diving accidents. The reputable dive centres are equipped with emergency oxygen tanks, a first-aid kit and a mobile phone.

Jordan's Best Dives

The Power Station

» **Location:** Around 500m south of Aqaba

» **Rating:** Intermediate

» **Access:** Shore or boat

» From a shallow fringing reef of fire coral, a sloping plateau of coral and sand patches leads to a 200m sheer wall, dropping from 12m to a narrow shelf at 40m.

First Bay

» **Location:** Next to the Marine Science Station

» **Rating:** Novice

» **Access:** Shore or boat

» First Bay is a shallow reef plateau with lagoons and sandy channels leading to a fringing reef of fire coral. Just south is Cazar Reef, noted for black coral trees.

Cedar Pride

» **Location:** 5km north of the Royal Diving Club

» **Rating:** Intermediate

» **Access:** Shore or boat

» Intact and festooned with soft corals, the wreck of the *Cedar Pride* is a true highlight with magnificent sea fans, basket stars and rainbows of fish caught in the sunlight.

Diving & Snorkelling

Japanese Garden

» **Location:** 4km north of the Royal Diving Club

» **Rating:** Novice

» **Access:** Shore or boat

» Just south of the *Cedar Pride*, this reef sports large coral heads, including black coral. Lionfish, angelfish and schools of snapper and butterfly fish inhabit the magnificent colourful reef.

Gorgonian I and II

» **Location:** 3km north of the Royal Diving Club

» **Rating:** Novice

» **Access:** Shore or boat

» Gorgonian I and II take their names from large, solitary fan corals. Nearby wonders include giant cabbage corals and green turtles that feed on the sea grass.

DIVE SAFE CHECKLIST

Before You Go

□ **Are you insured?** If something happens to you, treatment in the decompression chamber can cost thousands. If you hadn't planned to dive before arriving in Jordan, many of the better dive centres can provide insurance.

□ **Have you informed your doctor?** Diving can affect your metabolism and if you're on medication, your dosage of prescription drugs might need to be changed.

□ **Have you been drinking?** Alcohol dehydrates, especially in Jordan's dry climate, and increases susceptibility to decompression sickness.

During the Dive

□ **Do you know your diving depth limit?** The Red Sea's clear waters and high visibility often lure divers into going too deep. The depth limit for casual divers is 30m – stick to it.

□ **Will you remember what your boat looked like?** Some dive sites get crowded and boats can look similar from underneath. It's not unknown for divers to be left behind because they didn't realise that their boat was leaving.

After Care

□ **Have you allowed 24 hours before flying?** Divers are in serious danger of decompression sickness if they attempt to fly too soon.

□ **Have you allowed 12 hours before leaving Aqaba?** As most routes out of town involve an uphill drive, the change in altitude may trigger decompression sickness. If you're heading for Petra or Wadi Rum, leave your journey until tomorrow.

Big Bay

» **Location:** 2km north of the Royal Diving Club

» **Rating:** Intermediate

» **Access:** Shore or boat

» There are four sites in Big Bay – **Blue Coral, Kalli's Place, Moon Valley** and **Paradise** – which feature lacy blue and black coral. The 'long swim' (1km) to the Royal Diving Club is popular.

The Aquarium & Coral Gardens

» **Location:** Offshore from the Royal Diving Club

» **Rating:** Intermediate

» **Access:** Shore or boat

» The Aquarium is home to a spectacular fringing reef with a giant wall of fire corals. Immediately south lies Coral Gardens, home to lots of reef fish, seahorses and moray eels.

Overland Travel

Don't Leave Home Without...

Visas If Syria or Saudi Arabia are part of your itinerary, you'll need a visa in advance before you leave home.

Easiest Overland Route

Syria–Jordan–Israel and the Palestinian Territories–Egypt This route in this direction avoids problems connected with having an Israeli stamp in your passport.

Check with the Consulate

Syria At the time of writing, the escalating violence in Syria has put the country off-limits to travellers.
Iraq The ongoing war continues to make casual travel in Iraq inadvisable.
Saudi Arabia The visa situation makes access highly challenging, but the rules change so it's worth checking the current status before you leave.

Top Spots in Easy Reach of Jordan

Egypt Mt Sinai, St Catherine's Mount
Israel & the Palestinian Territories Jerusalem, Bethlehem
Syria Damascus, Palmyra
Saudi Arabia Madein Saleh

Planning Your Overland Expedition

At the Heart of the Middle East

Ever since the King's Highway was established more than 2000 years ago, Jordan has enjoyed a strategic status at the very heart of the Middle East. With its stable political situation, world-class sites of cultural and natural interest and easy accessibility, Jordan is therefore an obvious choice on a twin- or multi-country trip to the region. This chapter helps you plan around some of the logistical challenges of overland travel via Jordan and ensures you don't arrive at a border without being able to proceed.

Overland Travel in a Nutshell

» **Entry Formalities** Entering Jordan at any border crossing or at the port in Aqaba is straightforward. For information regarding visas on arrival from Jordan's neighbours, see Visas (p36).

» **Transport** It's easy to reach Jordan by land from any of the neighbouring countries. Most travellers arrive in Jordan by bus or service taxi, although there is no problem in bringing your own car or motorcycle (see p323). Bringing a hire car is not possible.

WHAT DOES 'OVERLAND' MEAN?

Strictly speaking, 'overland' ought to mean just that – 'over land'. Throughout this chapter, however, the term is redefined to mean 'any form of travel that doesn't involve a flight'. It therefore covers crossing the Gulf of Aqaba by boat – and, for that matter, it also covers crossing the River Jordan at King Hussein Bridge.

» **Leaving Jordan by Land** This requires a little more planning on account of certain visa stipulations: if you're intending to visit Syria, in particular, read the information about obtaining visas for other Middle Eastern countries (p315).

Border Crossings
Planning Which Crossing to Use

It may help to sequence your planning of an overland trip in the following way:

» Begin by choosing your ideal route, ignoring any logistical challenges – you can consult Itineraries (p21) for some ideas.

» Familiarise yourself with the border crossings on the map in this chapter and read the descriptions.

» Consult the visa section of this chapter to see what restrictions are associated with each entry/exit point.

» Check whether transport is available (see p317).

» Amend your route accordingly.

Facilities at Jordan's Border Crossings

» **Syria** Post office and **tourist office** (⊘8am-5pm Sat-Thu, to 2pm Fri), places to eat and drink, and moneychangers (open most of the time)

» **Israel & the Palestinian Territories** Post office and a **tourist information counter** (⊘8am-2pm, closed Fri), places to eat and drink, duty-free shops and moneychangers. Borders are closed on the Jewish holiday of Yom Kippur and the Islamic New Year (see p313).

Getting to & from Jordan's Borders

Getting by public transport to and from Jordan's borders is easy (see p318).

Note that if you're planning to depart from Jordan to Israel and the Palestinian Territories on a Friday or Saturday, arrive at the border early as public transport on the Israeli side doesn't run during the Jewish Shabbat (between sunset Friday and sunset Saturday).

Jordan's Border Crossings
Wadi Araba Crossing

» **Israeli/Palestinian Name** Yitzhak Rabin

» **Opening Times** ⊘6.30am-10pm Sun-Thu, 8am-8pm Fri & Sat

» **Transport Details** See p319

» Linking Aqaba to Eilat, this is the most user-friendly of the Israel and the Palestinian Territories borders.

King Hussein Bridge Crossing (Jisr al-Malek Hussein)

» **Israeli/Palestinian Name:** Allenby Bridge

» **Opening Times** ⊘8am-8pm Sun-Thu (arrivals into Jordan), 8am-2pm Sun-Thu (departures from Jordan), 8am-1pm Fri & Sat

» **Transport Details** See p319

» Most direct route between Amman and Jerusalem but expect lengthy delays, especially between 11am and 3pm.

Sheikh Hussein Bridge Crossing (Jisr Sheikh Hussein)

» **Israeli/Palestinian Name** Jordan Bridge

» **Opening Times** ⊘24 hours

» **Transport Details** See p319

» Links northern Jordan with Beit She'an in Galilee, 6km away.

Border Crossings

Ramtha

» **Syrian Name** Der'a

» **Opening Times** ⊙24 hours

» **Transport Details** See p319

» The best crossing with your own car, it's also handy for travelling between local destinations in northern Jordan and southern Syria.

Jabir

» **Syrian Name** Nasib

» **Opening Times** ⊙24 hours

» **Transport Details** See p319

» Most transport between Amman and Damascus uses this crossing. It's also useful for eastern Jordan, via Zarqa or Mafraq.

Karama

» **Iraqi Name** Tarbil

» **Opening Times** ⊙24 hours

» **Transport Details** See p318

» The journey between Amman and Baghdad through the notorious 'Sunni triangle' remains a dangerous journey.

Al-Umari

» **Saudi Name** Al-Haditha

» **Opening Times** ⊙24 hours

» **Transport Details** See p319

» This is the border most public transport uses but be aware that it's difficult obtaining even a transit visa to Saudi.

Al-Mudawwara

» **Saudi Name** Halat Ammar

» **Opening Times** ⊙24 hours

» **Transport Details** See p319

» The least useful of the Saudi crossings, with large distances to the nearest town on either side of the border.

Ad-Dura

» **Saudi Name** Haql

» **Opening Times** ⊙24 hours

» **Transport Details** See p319

» If you are a resident of Saudi and drive your own car, this is a useful border crossing.

Visas

Visas for Jordan

All nationalities require a visa for Jordan but these are issued with a minimum of fuss at any of Jordan's land borders, with the exception of King Hussein Bridge. If you intend to enter Jordan using this crossing from Israel and the Palestinian Territories, then you need to obtain a single/multiple entry visa (cost JD20/60) from

---

BORDER BOTHERS

If you're thinking of a day trip to Jerusalem from Amman, think again! Many readers complain of difficulties using the King Hussein Bridge border crossing, particularly on the Israeli side, reporting intrusive security, luggage X-rays, chaotic queues and rude officials. You'll be grilled about why you want to visit Israel – a hard question to answer if you've spent half the day at the border.

---

one of Jordan's embassies or consulates abroad. This only applies, however, if you're entering Jordan through this crossing for the first time. If you are re-entering Jordan (after visiting Jerusalem as a side trip from Amman, for example) you do not need to reapply for a Jordanian visa at King Hussein Bridge, providing you return within the validity of your Jordanian visa or its extension. Remember to keep the stamped exit slip and present it on returning. Note that you also must return through the same border – this option does not apply at any of Jordan's other border crossings.

If you arrive in Jordan's southern city of Aqaba by sea or by land, you are entitled to a free visa. See p315 for details.

Visas for Other Middle Eastern Countries

Travelling between Jordan and neighbouring countries is possible by obtaining the relevant visas (see p315 for important details). Note that you must obtain a Syrian visa before you arrive in Jordan.

You will be refused entry to Syria, Iraq and Saudi Arabia if there is any indication in your passport of entry to Israel and the Palestinian Territories.

For addresses of embassies and consulates, see p307.

Transport To/From Jordan

Jordan is well connected with its neighbours. However, at the time of writing, travel to Iraq and Syria was not recommended. For a full account of how to reach the countries listed, read the details in the Transport chapter (p318).

Egypt

The journey to Egypt involves a short boat ride. At most times of the year this is a matter of turning up and buying your ticket. During hajj, however, when Aqaba is abuzz with thousands of Egyptian pilgrims returning home from Mecca, you may find the journey becomes an epic.

It's slightly quicker and cheaper to travel to Egypt overland via Israel and the Palestinian Territories – but read the boxed text

ISRAELI BORDER-STAMP STIGMA

Our mailbags are full of questions about the infamous 'Israeli stamp stigma'. Here are a few frequently asked questions.

I've never heard of this Israeli stamp business – what's it all about? Given the tensions between Arab countries and the Jewish state of Israel, any evidence of a visit to Israel in your passport (such as an entry or exit stamp from a border crossing) will bar you from entering a number of countries in the region, including Syria.

So what can I do if I plan to combine my visit to Jordan with a trip to Israel and Syria? When you enter or leave Israel, you can ask immigration officials to stamp a separate piece of paper instead of your passport.

So there's no problem then? That depends on where you go to next. If you have, say, an exit stamp from one border and an entry stamp dated a week later from a different border in Jordan, it will be obvious to the Syrian authorities, for example, that you must have been in Israel and the Palestinian Territories in the meantime. Indeed, travellers have been turned away from Syria's border with Jordan for having unexplained periods of time in their passport, such as six weeks in Jordan without any evidence of a Jordanian visa extension.

So how do I get round that problem? You can fly into and out of Ben-Gurion airport; enter and depart through King Hussein Bridge border crossing with a multiple entry visa and ask the Jordanian officials to stamp a piece of paper instead of your passport; or plan to visit Israel and the Palestinian Territories at the end of your trip.

Is an Israeli stamp a problem when trying to enter most Arab countries? No, it's not a problem when entering Jordan, Egypt, Turkey, Tunisia and Morocco. Officially, Bahrain, Qatar, the UAE and Oman will refuse you entry if you have evidence of a visit to Israel in your passport, but in reality they don't usually look for an offending stamp.

For which countries in the Middle East is it a problem? Syria, Lebanon, Iran, Saudi Arabia, Libya and Yemen. If you get an Israeli or Jordanian exit or entry stamp in your passport, there's little you can do. If you report that your passport is 'lost' to your embassy in any country in the Middle East, it may be met with cynicism and even rejection. The bottom line is that the restrictions that some Arab countries make are in place for a purpose and if you try to sidestep those rules, you can expect your intentions to be misinterpreted at some point.

(this page) regarding the Israeli border-stamp stigma before making a decision.

Iraq

Occasional service taxis run the gauntlet between Baghdad and Abdali bus station in Amman.

Israel & the Palestinian Territories

Buses link several cities in Jordan and Israel and the Palestinian Territories. Travelling by bus directly between Amman and Tel Aviv saves getting to/from the borders on your own, but it's more expensive than crossing independently, and you'll have to wait for all passengers to clear immigration.

If you're driving from Israel and the Palestinian Territories, you must use the border crossings at Sheikh Hussein Bridge or Wadi Araba.

Saudi Arabia

Getting a visa, even a transit visa, to Saudi Arabia is a very difficult feat – see p315 for details. If you are eligible for a visa, several bus companies run services to and from Jeddah and Riyadh from Amman's Abdali bus station.

Syria

Travel to Syria was not recommended at the time of writing due to escalating violence throughout the country. During more peaceful times, however, it is simple to travel between Jordan and Syria. You will find that it is quicker and cheaper to take a direct bus or service taxi between Amman and Damascus rather than negotiate local transport and border-crossing formalities on your own.

If you're heading to Syria from Jordan, make sure you get a Syrian visa before arriving in Jordan. To do this, you'll need to apply either in your home country or in İstanbul, Ankara or Cairo.

Elsewhere in the Middle East

For other destinations in the Middle East, travellers need time, patience and, most importantly, the necessary visas. Most trips involve long, hot journeys with frustrating delays so most people end up flying.

JETT has occasional bus through-services to Cairo (JD25), Baghdad (JD28,400) and Damascus (JD8) departing from the international bus office in Amman. Check with the JETT office ahead of departure as schedules and prices change frequently.

Travel with Children

Best Regions for Kids

Jerash
Kids studying the Romans will love Jerash where centurions bring history alive, and there are chariot races.

Dead Sea
You won't need to worry whether the kids can swim: the water is so salty, it's impossible to sink.

Karak
With tunnels and passageways, there's heaps to explore at Karak while the museum makes sense of Crusader history.

Petra
The horse rides and coloured caves are fun but a pre-visit viewing of *Indiana Jones & the Last Crusade* should nail it.

Aqaba
Teenagers can learn to dive while younger kids paddle in the calm, warm sea.

Wadi Rum
Camel rides, 4WD adventures and sandboarding make Wadi Rum a hit. Get the guide to spin the kids a Bedouin yarn.

Shaumari Wildlife Reserve
Youngsters will enjoy searching for oryx and ostriches on the night safari.

Jordan for Kids

Children are universally adored in Jordan so you'll find that taking the kids adds a welcome dimension to your trip. As instant ice breakers children will invite guaranteed contact with local people, especially as foreign families are still something of a novelty.

Expect a Warm Welcome

While few concessions are made for youngsters, except the occasional high chair in a restaurant and baby-changing facilities in modern city malls, you'll find people go out of their way to make your family feel welcome, especially on buses and in shops, hotels and restaurants.

The Jordanian Family Way

Child-oriented activities are still a novel concept in Jordan as normally kids are included in adult outings and entertainments. Jordanians enjoy socialising in groups so there's usually an extra pair of hands to mind the kids. As a result of this child-inclusive approach, most adult highlights are treated as children's highlights too.

Cultural Highlights a Hit with the Kids

Feedback from parents on Lonely Planet's Thorntree forum is very positive about the experience of taking children to Petra, Jerash, Karak and Wadi Rum, although it pays to get the family curious about the destination in advance. Jordan is a gold mine for school projects on the Romans, for example.

Children's Highlights
Dining Experiences

» **Jordanian Sweet Shops** A treat for all the family with honey-drenched pastries and giant, colourful platters of *kunafa* – shredded dough with cream cheese

» **Fruit Juice Stalls** A healthy way to beat the heat – watermelon and pomegranate juices are favourites

» **Brunch Wild** Brunch at Wild Jordan Café in Amman offers opportunities for eco-education

Rainy Day Activities

» **Haya Cultural Centre** Includes an interactive eco-museum

Amusement Parks

» **Amman Waves** A Western-style waterpark between the airport and Amman is a hit with all ages

» **Luna Park Rides** Offers rides and amusements for kids

Planning
When to Go

Spring is the best time for a family visit. The weather is great, attractions are open and the peak tourist season brings evening amusements.

The heat of summer (mid-May to mid-September) is difficult for children to tolerate, restricting your activities to early morning and late afternoon. Winter months (mid-November to mid-February) can be freezing cold and many activities are either restricted or it's too cold to be enjoyable. The risk of flash floods in wadis is an added anxiety.

Coping with High Temperatures

At any time of year, temperatures are high in parts of Jordan, particularly around noon. Trips to Petra and Wadi Rum involve long periods of sun exposure and it's not always easy to find shade. This doesn't mean that it's impossible to go; it's just advisable to plan your visit around early mornings and late afternoons. You can follow local custom and take a nap after lunch to avoid the worst of the sun.

Avoiding Sickness

To prevent stomach complaints, children should stick to bottled mineral water, which is readily available, and avoid peeled fresh fruit and washed salads.

Fresh and powdered milk is available but it is worth checking that fresh dairy products (such as milk, cream, yoghurt and cream cheese) are made with pasteurised milk. Unhappily for the kids, ice cream is usually best avoided in rural areas where the electricity supply is often unreliable, leading to frozen goods defrosting and refreezing.

General hygiene may not be the priority it is in many Western countries; carrying hand sanitisers is a good idea in case the local water supply is suspect.

Nursing Infants

Breast-feeding in public is culturally acceptable providing you are reasonably discreet about it. Carrying an extra garment, like a shawl or a cardigan, to tuck around you and the babe may help keep male curiosity at bay.

What to Pack

Disposable nappies are not readily available outside Amman and Aqaba. Come prepared with plastic bags to avoid contributing to Jordan's ubiquitous litter problem.

Mosquito nets and repellent are handy in the warmer months; malaria is not an issue in Jordan but itchy bites can easily become infected in the heat.

Car seats are not a big thing in Jordan so bring one with you. Pavements, or lack of, will be challenging for most prams but the locals seem to cope with them!

Jordanians are tolerant of Western norms but you will earn local respect if the kids dress appropriately. This is particularly the case with teenage girls: provocative clothing, however fashionable elsewhere, will bring unwanted attention and stares.

Safety Check

Travelling in Jordan is generally safe for the family with low incidences of crime. At the time of writing, the political situation after the spring disturbances of 2011 was calm but it's a good idea to check with your local Jordanian consulate before travelling.

Further Reading

See the boxed text (p64) for details of kids' highlights in Amman. Comprehensive advice about travelling with children can be found in Lonely Planet's *Travel with Children* by Cathy Lanigan.

regions at a glance

While there's much to see and do in Amman, it's important to get beyond the capital to have any sense of Jordan. With even the shortest of visits you can make a circuit around the semi-arid highlands of the north – a highlight in spring when wildflowers bloom among Jordan's main Roman and biblical sites and grace the hills above the Dead Sea.

Of course, with a tad more time, few can resist travelling south to Jordan's top spot, Petra. From here it's easy to explore the sands of Wadi Rum or go diving or snorkelling in the Red Sea.

Those seeking more adventure will head along the legendary King's Highway or strike out east to the home of the desert castles.

Amman

Roman Ruins ✓✓
Modern Middle East ✓✓
Shopping ✓✓

Roman Ruins
With mega-ruins to the north in Jerash, many overlook the antiquities of Amman and yet the Citadel and Roman Theatre downtown define the heart of the city, and are well worth exploring. Amman's museums give context to the experience of Jordan's major historical attractions.

Modern Middle East
Sophisticated malls, buzzing coffee shops and happening nightlife challenge the regional perception of Jordan as a sleepy backwater. Values are conservative and there is plenty of evidence of the traditional Middle East but if you want to feel the pulse of the country's youthful, well-educated and techno-savvy population the capital is the place to be.

Shopping
From gold bangles to Iraqi currency bearing Saddam Hussein's image, Amman's souqs and streets are full of intriguing souvenirs. To make your spending mean more, root out the neighbourhood cooperatives.

p46

Jerash, Irbid & the Jordan Valley

Roman Ruins ✓✓✓
Hiking ✓✓
Scenic Views ✓✓

Roman Ruins

Don't think twice about visiting Jerash: this remarkably well-preserved outpost of the Roman empire has been wowing the visitors for over two centuries and is one of the top three highlights of Jordan. Spare some time for the lesser antiquities at Umm Qais, especially in spring when the ruins are decorated with wildflowers. Archaeological buffs will love Pella.

Hiking

The socially and environmentally aware nature reserve at Ajloun is a byword for sustainable tourism. Hikes from here take you through the heartland of rural Jordan, passing traditional communities and providing an opportunity to see rare strawberry tree woodlands.

Scenic Views

Take any route from the juniper uplands of Jerash, Salt or Umm Qais to the fertile and subtropical Jordan Valley and a natural-history lesson awaits.

p80

Dead Sea Highway

Spas & Springs ✓✓✓
Hiking ✓✓
Dramatic Drives ✓✓✓

Spas & Springs

No one should come to Jordan and miss out on the extraordinary experience of a Dead Sea float. With luxury spas along the sea's southern shore this is the place to schedule some serious R&R. Nearby hot springs complete the opportunity for healthy treatments.

Hiking

With unexpected waterfalls, oleander-trimmed oases and glimpses of wildlife, Mujib Biosphere Reserve is a great place for an outdoor adventure. Expect to get wet in year-round pools. Further along Wadi Araba, the sea-level end of Dana Biosphere Reserve has good trails and the prospect of a great vegetarian feast at Feynan Ecolodge.

Dramatic Drives

Switchbacking from the vineyards of the King's Highway to the tomato fields and potash plants of the Dead Sea Highway, this region is peppered with exciting drives.

p111

Madaba & the King's Highway

Religious Relics ✓✓✓
Handicrafts ✓✓✓
Hiking ✓✓

Religious Relics

Moses, Elijah, Jesus Christ and John the Baptist are just some of the many biblical figures that have blessed Jordan's soil with a visit. Mt Nebo is a place of pilgrimage to this day. Crusader castles at Karak and Shobak and the Christian town of Madaba show how this inheritance has been embraced over the centuries.

Handicrafts

Some of the best handicrafts in Jordan are made by hand in cottage industries in and around Madaba. Traditional weaving near Mukawir and mosaic-making along the King's Highway are just two of many crafts helping sustain rural communities.

Hiking

The best and arguably the most beautiful hikes in Jordan are to be had in the upper wadis of Wadi Mujib and Dana Biosphere Reserve. However, it can snow in winter here.

p126

Petra

Ancient Ruins ✓✓✓
Hiking ✓✓✓
Stunning Scenery ✓✓✓

Ancient Ruins
There are not enough superlatives to describe the ancient city of Petra. Make sure you allow enough time to reach the Treasury in early morning, picnic at a High Place by noon, watch the sunset at the Monastery and walk the Siq by candlelight at night – at least two days in other words.

Hiking
Petra has some of the best and most accessible hikes in Jordan. Engaging a local Bedouin guide will help bring the recent history of Petra to life. Avoid the ovenbaking summer months when the heat is overbearing. It's not possible to hike after the winter rains.

Stunning Scenery
Outrageously colourful sandstone, wind-eroded escarpments and oleander-trimmed wadis make the rose-pink landscape of Petra a worthy consort of the ancient architecture. Don't forget your camera!

p158

Aqaba, Wadi Rum & the Desert Highway

Red Sea Diving ✓✓✓
Desert Camping ✓✓
Stunning Scenery ✓✓✓

Red Sea Diving
Whether you dive, snorkel or simply like to swim, Jordan's Gulf of Aqaba gives easy access to the magnificent underwater spectacle of the Red Sea. Early spring and late autumn offer the most comfortable temperatures. Check out p26 for information.

Desert Camping
You don't have to be a *Lawrence of Arabia* fan to enjoy hanging up your boots with the Bedouin after a day's camel trekking. The desert camps are comfortable but can be freezing in midwinter and stifling in midsummer.

Stunning Scenery
Even if you don't have time to stay overnight, it's worth driving as far as the Wadi Rum visitor centre. From here you can see the Seven Pillars of Wisdom and it'll be instantly clear why this is a highlight of Jordan.

p194

Azraq & the Eastern Desert Highway

Architecture ✓✓
Wildlife ✓✓✓
Remote Travel ✓✓

Architecture
With bathhouses, hunting lodges and caravan staging posts, the Eastern Desert is liberally strewn with Umayyad architecture collectively known as the 'Desert Castles'. It's not so much the buildings as the arid desert context that make these outposts of civilisation worth the effort to visit.

Wildlife
Oryx used to roam the deserts of Jordan before they were hunted nearly to extinction. You can see these magnificent antelope at the Shaumari Wildlife Reserve; your visit will help support their reintroduction. The nearby oasis at Azraq is a top spot for birdwatching.

Remote Travel
Few make it to the black wastelands of the Badia but if you're happy to spend some days in the suspended animation of the extreme desert then head for Burqu Reserve, which redefines the term 'remote'.

p226

> Every listing is recommended by our authors, and their favourite places are listed first.

> Look out for these icons:

 TOP CHOICE Our author's top recommendation

 A green or sustainable option

 FREE No payment required

See the Index for a full list of destinations covered in this book.

On the Road

Amman عمان

♪06 / POP 2.8 MILLION / ELEV 850M

Best Places to Eat

» Hashem Restaurant (p65)

» Afrah Restaurant &
Coffeeshop (p65)

» Wild Jordan Café (p66)

» Fakhr El-Din Restaurant
(p66)

» Romero Restaurant (p66)

Best Places to Stay

» Jordan InterContinental
Hotel (p61)

» Hisham Hotel (p61)

» Jordan Tower Hotel (p60)

» Caravan Hotel (p61)

» Palace Hotel (p61)

Why Go?

Jordan's capital city, Amman, is one of the easiest cities in the region to enjoy the Middle East experience. The city has two distinct parts: urbane Western Amman, with leafy residential districts, cafes, bars, modern malls and art galleries; and earthy Eastern Amman, where it's easier to sense the more traditional, conservative and Islamic pulse of the capital.

At the heart of the city is the chaotic, labyrinthine 'downtown', a must-see of a capital visit. At the bottom of the city's many hills, and overlooked by the magisterial Citadel, it features spectacular Roman ruins and the hubbub of Jordanian life – best understood by joining the locals in the nightly promenade between mosque, souq and coffeeshop.

When the intense conurbation of the city becomes claustrophobic, there are village escapes within the urban fringe – reminders that despite thousands of years of settlement, Jordan remains a largely rural experience.

When to Go

The capital's hilly location brings sharp winds during cold winters making March to May and October to November the best time for a visit.

If you can bear the claustrophobic heat of mid-summer which radiates off densely-packed buildings and lurks in breezeless alleyways, then July and August is recommended for the annual Jerash Festival. At this time the Roman Theatre comes alive and the capital penchant for an evening promenade comes into its own.

In September, the Hakaya storytelling festival brings a Bedouin experience to the heart of the city.

To North Bus Station
(Tabarbour - 2km)

0 — 2 km
0 — 1 miles

QATANEH

Al-Jame'ah Rd

Al-Riyadhah Rd

Ghaz Arabiyyat St

Wasfi al- Tal Rd

Maysaloon St

Nasser bin Jameel St

Yousef bin Tasheen St

Al-Malekah Alia St

Haroun al-Rasheed St

Abu Sufyan St

Nablus St

JEBEL AL-HUSSEIN

SHMEISANI

Abdul Hameed Sharaf St

Moh'del-Basheer St

Al-Istiqlal Rd

Khaled bin al-Walid Rd

Al-Imam Muslem St

King Abdullah Gardens

Bi'r al-Saba'St

Ein Jarout Rd

Ilya Abu Madhi St

Abu Hamed al-Ghazali St

ABDALI

Wadi Saqra Rd

Wadi Saqra Rd

Qurtubah St

King Abdullah Mosque

Sa'id Khair St

Citadel

Ibn Seena Rd

Zahran St

Darat al-Funun 5

JEBEL AL-QALA'A

Zahran St Al-Mutanabbi St

Al-Ameerah Basma bin al-Hussein Rd

Uqbah bin Nafi St

Bin Khaldour St

Al-Amir Mohammed St

Hashem Restaurant 8

Al-Ameerah Basma bin Talal Rd

Abdul Mun'em Riyadh St

Wild Jordan Café 6

Al-Qahira St

Al-Nee St

Downtown 4 2

Al-Ameer Ali bin al-Hussein Rd

ABDOUN

Wadi Abdoun Rd

Roman Theatre

Omar Matar St

Dimashq St

National Museum 3

Al-Quds Rd

ZAHRAN

To South Bus Station
(Wahadat - 2.5km)

Amman Highlights

1 Visit the ruins (and museum) of the ancient **Citadel** (p49)

2 Admire the engineering precision of the **Roman Theatre** (p52), Amman's most spectacular ancient monument

3 Be one of the first visitors to the **National Museum** (p53), set to open in 2012

4 Stroll **downtown** (p49) and rub shoulders with Amman's immigrant population

5 See an exhibition at **Darat al-Funun** (p54), and sip tea amid the Byzantine ruins

6 Have lunch at **Wild Jordan Café** (p66) and book your nature-reserve adventure with the RSCN at the same time

7 Have a glass of wine in the **bars and cafes** (p67) of Shmeisani and Abdoun

8 Queue at **Hashem Restaurant** (p65), downtown's legendary felafel eatery

9 Visit **Fuheis** (p79) for lunch in the excellent Zuwwadeh Restaurant and amble through **Wadi as-Seer** (p77)

History

Despite its ancient lineage, Amman as it appears today is largely a mid-20th century creation and visitors looking for the quintessential vestiges of a Byzantine Middle East will have to look quite hard. What they will see instead is a homogeneous, mostly low-rise, cream-coloured city of weathered concrete buildings, some sparklingly clad in white marble, others rather grey and in need of a facelift.

That's not to say that Amman is without history. In fact, impressive remnants of a Neolithic settlement from 8500 BC were found in the 1970s at Ain Ghazal in Eastern Amman. They illustrate a sophisticated culture that produced the world's earliest statues and carvings from limestone and plaster. Today, you can see some of these finds at the archaeological museum (p51).

Then there is Jebel al-Qala'a, the present site of the Citadel, and one of the oldest and most-continuously inhabited parts of the city, established around 1800 BC. Referred to subsequently in the Old Testament as Rabbath, the city was besieged by King David who burnt many inhabitants alive in a brick kiln. Rabbath continued nonetheless to flourish and supplied David with weapons for his ongoing wars.

Visitors bump into Amman's Egyptian heritage each time they see a company or restaurant called Philadelphia, after the Ptolemy ruler Philadelphus (283–246 BC). He rebuilt the city during his reign and it was named Philadelphia after him. It was one of the cities of the Roman Decapolis (see the boxed text, p82) before being assumed into the Roman Empire under Herod in around 30 BC. Philadelphia, meaning 'City of Brotherly Love', was redesigned in typically grand Roman style, with a theatre, forum and Temple to Hercules, the striking remains of which can be seen to this day.

The city's fortunes largely declined with the empire although it regained some of its former glory after the Muslim invasion in AD 636. From about the 10th century little more is heard of Amman until the 19th century when a colony of Circassians settled there in 1878.

You might not think it if you visit the sleepy tracks of Amman train station today, but the Hejaz Railway led to an early-20th-century boom in the city's fortunes when it became a stopover on the new 'pilgrimage route' between Damascus and Medina (Saudi Arabia). Emir Abdullah chose Amman as the headquarters of the new state of Trans-Jordan in 1921; it was officially declared the capital of the Hashemite kingdom two years later.

Over the intervening years, the city has weathered successive waves of immigration (from Palestine and in the last decade from Iraq), sprawling well beyond its original seven hills. As a result Amman has had to contend with severe water shortages, compounded by the lack of urban planning.

Despite the challenges, the citizens of Amman are ever-optimistic, many grateful for the opportunity of rebuilding their lives in a generous and stable environment. This is best evidenced by the almost continual expansion, embellishment and development projects that besiege the city, most of which take longer to complete than anticipated. No one complains, however, as the capital plays an ever-increasing role on the regional stage. Only minimally troubled by the Arab Spring of 2011, it remains a vibrant, open-minded city, famed in the region for its educational institutions and confident about the future.

Dangers & Annoyances

Despite some localised uprisings during the Arab Spring of 2011, Amman remains a safe city for visitors. It has had a few skirmishes in the past (see p300), which is why there are security guards and metal detectors in and around tourist sites and hotels. Many see this as a positive response on behalf of the government to protect foreigners in the capital.

In fact, crime of any sort in Amman is extremely rare, and Jordanians take pride in reminding foreigners that their country remains an oasis of peace in a notoriously belligerent region.

Nature Reserves

There are no nature reserves within the capital area, but it is worth mentioning that Amman is the best place to organise trips to any of Jordan's Royal Society for the Conservation of Nature (RSCN) reserves. Accommodation in most of these reserves has to be booked in advance and this is easily managed through the RSCN's **Wild Jordan Centre** (Map p50; ☎4616523; www.rscn.org.jo; Othman Bin Affan St) in downtown.

◉ Sights

A largely modern construction, Amman is home to few vistas that evoke images of grand empires. That said, scattered amid the concrete streetscapes are several spectacular remnants of Philadelphia, particularly the ruins on top of Jebel al-Qala'a, and the Roman Theatre downtown. The most interesting part of this open-hearted city, however, is the chance that it affords to meet its cosmopolitan inhabitants – in the souqs of downtown, for example, or in the coffeeshops and modern malls of its fashionable hilltop neighbourhoods of Jebel Amman and beyond.

DOWNTOWN

Citadel
RUIN

(Map p50; ☑4638795; Jebel al-Qala'a; admission JD2; ☺8am-4pm Sat-Thu Oct-Mar, to 7pm Sat-Thu Apr-Sep, 10am-4pm Fri year-round) The area known as the Citadel sits on the highest hill in Amman, Jebel al-Qala'a (about 850m above sea level), and is the site of ancient Rabbath-Ammon. Artefacts dating from the Bronze Age show that the hill was a fortress and/or agora (open space for commerce and politics) for thousands of years. The complex is surrounded by 1700m-long walls, which were rebuilt many times during the Bronze

and Iron Ages, as well as the Roman, Byzantine and Umayyad periods.

The Citadel ticket office is on the road leading up to the Citadel's entrance. Multilingual, fully licensed guides (up to JD15 per hour) usually congregate near the ticket office and can really enhance your visit.

The only access roads to the Citadel are from Al-Malek Ali bin al-Hussein St. It's better to hire a taxi for the trip up (around JD1 from downtown) but save some energy for the recommended walk down. Steps lead from east of the Citadel complex, past a viewing platform to Hashemi St, opposite the Roman Theatre. This makes a fine start to a walking tour of downtown.

Temple of Hercules

The most striking attraction of the Citadel are two giant standing pillars, remains of the Roman Temple of Hercules. Once connected to the Forum (downtown), the temple was built during the reign of Marcus Aurelius (AD 161–80). The only obvious remains are parts of the podium and the columns, which are visible from around town. There's also a rather touching remnant of a stone-carved

---

NAVIGATING AMMAN

Like Rome, Amman was originally founded on seven major hills, but today it spreads across more than 20. It's not really a city to explore on foot, apart from the downtown area – known by locals as *il-balad*. A straight, flat road is almost unheard of so the only way to make any sense of Amman in a short time is to pick out the major landmarks on the hills (jebels).

The main hill is Jebel Amman, home to several embassies, a few hotels and trendy restaurants. The traffic roundabouts in this central area (some now replaced with tunnels and major intersections) are numbered west of downtown from 1st Circle to 8th Circle. If you're travelling in a taxi, street names will mean little so ask for the nearest 'circle' and walk from there, or give the driver a nearby landmark (like an embassy or hotel).

Jebel al-Hussein, northwest of downtown, is notable for the Housing Bank Centre; its mossy, terraced facade sticks out a mile. This also marks the start of the upmarket Shmeisani area, which stretches out to the north as far as the leafy Sports City. It has plenty of restaurants, shops, top-end hotels and a few nightclubs. Another trendy and affluent area is Abdoun, a few hills south of Shmeisani and the location of supercool cafes and several embassies.

Closer to downtown is the grittier Abdali area, from where buses leave for Syria. A few budget hotels are in the area. It can be readily identified by the distinctive blue dome of the King Abdullah Mosque.

In the far west is swanky Sweifieh, a booming shopping area. Further out, the city's outlying towns, suburbs and refugee camps have now pretty much merged into one sprawling urban area.

The maps in this guidebook should be sufficient for most casual visitors. If you plan to stay for some time, or intend to visit places out of the centre, the *Maps of Jordan, Amman and Aqaba* published by Luma Khalaf is worth picking up. It shows just about every street in the city, and pinpoints embassies and other landmarks, though it doesn't cover the southern or eastern suburbs. It's available from most bookshops.

Downtown Amman

AMMAN

JEBEL
WEIBDEH

35

To Jebel Amman

38

Al-Malek Ali bin al-Hussein St

**Umayyad
Palace**
2

JEBEL AL-
QALA'A

JEBEL
AL-
QALA'A

Nadim al-Mallah St

Citadel
31

Nimer bin Adwan St

3

Omar al-Khayyam St

To Sydney Hostel (50m)

8

**Temple of
Hercules**

Parcel
Post Office

33

Central
Post Office

17

21

13

Sa'id Khair St

Shabsough St

Yaqout al-Hamawi St

32

20

16

22

12 27

24

Al-Amir Mohammed St

Mu'ath bin Jabal St

Othman bin Affan St

Al-Malek Faisal St

19

Cinema al-Hussein St

4

37

Hashemi St

36

Al-Madeenah
Police Station

Basman St

15

Al-Qabartay St

Ibn al-Atheer St

9

1

**Fruit &
Vegetable
Souq**

Italian St

Mohd al-Shabeeb St

Fawzi al-Malouf St

30

Abu Bakr as-Siddiq St (Rainbow St)

29

28

18

Hardware
Souq

Petra St

11

Al-Mahmoud Taha St

26

Omar bin al-Khattab St (Mango St)

**Fruit &
Vegetable
Market**

Quraysh St

Al-Malek Talal St

Quraysh St

Quraysh St

Italian St

34

Hashemi St

To National Museum (200m)

hand which shows something of the level of detail that would have adorned the temple in its glory days. Nearby is a **lookout** with sweeping views of the downtown area.

National Archaeological Museum

This modest museum, just northwest of the Temple of Hercules, has some rather astonishing items, including the famous Ain Ghazal figures. Dating from 6500 BC they are among the world's earliest known free-standing statues. Other items in the collection include 6000-year-old skulls from Jericho and Umayyad-period jewellery. It also boasts a copy of the Mesha Stele (see the boxed text, p145) – the famous tablet found near Wadi Mujib. Finds from the Citadel itself include the head from a statue of the Greek goddess Tyche and some Egyptian-style carvings. Most exhibits are well labelled in English. Note that there are rumours that this collection might one day be shifted to the new National Museum (see the boxed text, p53), though at the time of writing, only the Dead Sea Scrolls had been relocated.

Umayyad Palace

The Citadel's most impressive series of historic buildings is focused around the Umayyad Palace, behind the National Archaeological Museum. Believed to be the work of Umayyad Arabs and dating from about AD 720, the palace was an extensive complex of royal and residential buildings and was once home to the governor of Amman. Its lifespan was short – it was destroyed by an earthquake in AD 749 and was never fully rebuilt.

Coming from the south, the first major building belonging to the palace complex is the domed **audience hall**, designed to impress visitors to the royal palace. The most intact of the buildings on the site, the hall is shaped like a cross, mirroring the Byzantine church over which it was built. After much debate as to whether the central space had originally been covered or left open to the elements, consensus came down on the side of the ceiling dome, which was reconstructed by Spanish archaeologists.

A **courtyard** immediately north of the hall leads to a 10m-wide **colonnaded street**, lined with numerous arches and columns, and flanked by residential and administrative buildings. Further to the north is the former **governor's residence**, which includes the **throne room**.

Downtown Amman

◎ Top Sights
Roman Theatre	E4
Temple of Hercules	C3
Umayyad Palace	C2

◎ Sights
1	Al-Husseiny Mosque	C5
2	Byzantine Basilica	C2
3	Darat al-Funun	B3
4	Duke's Diwan	C4
5	Folklore Museum	E3
6	Forum	E3
7	Museum of Popular Traditions	F4
8	National Archaeological Museum	C2
9	Nymphaeum	D5
10	Odeon	F3

◎ Activities, Courses & Tours
11	Al-Pasha Turkish Bath	A6

◎ Sleeping
12	Cliff Hotel	B4
13	Farah Hotel	C3
14	Jordan Tower Hotel	E3
15	Palace Hotel	C4

◎ Eating
16	Afrah Restaurant & Coffeeshop	B3
17	Al-Quds Restaurant	B3
18	Cairo Restaurant	C5
19	Habibah	C4
	Habibah	(see 17)
20	Hashem Restaurant	B3
21	Jabri Restaurant	B3
22	Sara Seafood Restaurant	B4
	Wild Jordan Café	(see 36)

◎ Drinking
23	Al-Hail Restaurant & Café	F4
24	Al-Rashid Court Café	B4
25	Al-Sendabad Coffee Shop	E4
	Auberge Café	(see 12)
26	Books@café	A6
	Darat al-Funun Café	(see 3)
27	Jordan Bar	B4
	Orient Bar & Restaurant	(see 12)
	Peace Café	(see 20)
	Salamon Bar	(see 22)
28	Shaher's Penthouse Cafeteria	C5

◎ Shopping
29	Bawabet al-Sharq	A5
30	Jordan River Foundation	A5
	Wild Jordan	(see 36)

◎ Information
31	Citadel Ticket Office	D2
32	Communication International	B3
33	Customs Office	B3
34	Italian Hospital	C7
35	New Zealand Consulate	B1
36	Wild Jordan Centre	B4

◎ Transport
37	Bus 26 stop	C4
38	KLM	B2

East of the audience hall is the **Umayyad Cistern**, an enormous circular hole with steps leading down to the bottom, which once supplied water to the palace and surrounding areas. The small disc on the floor in the centre once supported a pillar that was used for measuring water levels.

Near the museum to the south is the small **Byzantine Basilica**, most of which has been destroyed by earthquakes. It dates from the 6th or 7th century AD, and contains a few dusty mosaics.

Roman Theatre   ROMAN AMPHITHEATRE
(Map p50; admission incl Folklore Museum & Museum of Popular Traditions JD1; ◎8am-4pm Sat-Thu & 9am-4pm Fri Oct-Mar, 8am-7pm Apr-Sep) This magnificently restored amphitheatre is the most obvious and impressive remnant of Roman Philadelphia, and is the highlight of Amman for most foreign visitors. The

theatre itself is cut into the northern side of a hill that once served as a necropolis and has a seating capacity of 6000. It was built on three tiers: the rulers, of course, sat closest to the action, the military secured the middle section, and the general public perched and squinted from the top rows.

The theatre was probably built in the 2nd century AD during the reign of Antoninus Pius (AD 138-61). Theatres often had religious significance, and the small shrine above the top row of seats once housed a statue of the goddess Athena (now in the National Archaeological Museum), who was prominent in the religious life of the city.

Full restoration of the theatre began in 1957. Unfortunately, non-original materials were used, which means that the present reconstruction is partly inaccurate. However, the final product is certainly impressive, especially considering that the theatre has again become a place of entertainment in recent years. Productions are sometimes put on here in July and August – check with the tourist office or ask at your hotel.

The best time for photographs is the morning, when the light is soft – although the views from the top tiers just before sunset are also superb. At night the theatre is floodlit, providing a spectacular backdrop to the bustle of downtown.

Folklore Museum   MUSEUM
(Map p50; 4651742; Roman Theatre complex; 8am-7pm Sat-Thu & 10am-4pm Fri May-Sep, 8am-5pm Sat-Thu & 10am-4pm Fri Oct-Apr) Immediately to the right as you enter the Roman Theatre, this small museum houses a modest collection of items illustrating traditional Jordanian life. They include a Bedouin goat-hair tent complete with tools; musical instruments such as the *rababa* (a one-stringed Bedouin instrument); looms; *mihbash* (coffee grinders); some weapons; and various costumes, including traditional Circassian dress. Don't miss the B&W photos of old Amman by the entrance. Captions are in English. It was closed for restoration at the time of writing but is expected to reopen with a similar focus.

Museum of Popular Traditions   MUSEUM
(Map p50; 4651670; Roman Theatre complex; 8am-7pm Sat-Thu & 10am-4pm Fri May-Sep, 8am-5pm Sat-Thu & 9am-4pm Fri Oct-Apr) This small museum, immediately to the left as you enter the Roman Theatre, has well-presented displays of traditional costumes, jewellery, face masks and mosaics from Jerash.

Forum   ROMAN PLAZA
(Map p50) The row of columns immediately in front (north) of the Roman Theatre is all that's left of the forum, once one of the largest public squares (about 100m by 50m) in Imperial Rome. Built in AD 190, the square was flanked on three sides by columns, and on the fourth side by the Seil Amman stream, though almost everything lies underneath the modern streets. The current plaza project, which is nearly complete, will help bring back something of the sense of grand public space, albeit with a modern aesthetic.

FREE **Odeon**   ROMAN AMPHITHEATRE
(Map p50; daylight) On the eastern side of the forum stands a 500-seat amphitheatre. Built in the 2nd century AD, it served mainly as a venue for musical performances. It

NATIONAL MUSEUM

Amman's congested downtown is midway through a major redevelopment project and already the outline of public gardens, panoramic vantage points and pedestrian trails linking the Citadel and the Roman Theatre are beginning to take shape. The highlight of this project is the new international-standard **National Museum** (Map p56; Omar Matar St), which is located next to the City Hall. While the museum is reportedly complete, and key items such as Jordan's share of the Dead Sea Scrolls, have been relocated, the museum was still closed at the time of writing. Rumour has it that the authorities are awaiting a suitable occasion to give fanfare to the museum's inauguration. Come what may, the first visitors are expected in 2012 (*in sha' Allah!*).

was probably enclosed with a wooden or temporary tent roof to shield the performers and audience from the elements. Like its bigger sibling, it is seasonally used for performances.

FREE **Nymphaeum**   FOUNTAIN
(Map p50; Quraysh St; daylight Sat-Thu) Built in AD 191, this elaborate public fountain was once a large, two-storey complex with water features, mosaics, stone carvings and possibly a 600-sq-metre swimming pool – all dedicated to the nymphs (mythical young girls who lived in and around the rivers). Up until 1947, the ancient stream and Roman bridge still stood where the road now runs. Excavations started in earnest in 1993, and restoration will continue for many years. Except for a few columns, an elegant archway and a few alcoves, there is little to see, though the workers toiling away may yet reveal hidden treasures in the years to come.

FREE **Al-Husseiny Mosque**   MOSQUE
(Map p50; Hashemi St) Built by King Abdullah I in 1924, and restored in 1987, this compact mosque is in the heart of downtown on the site of an earlier mosque built in AD 640. The mosque is more interesting as a hive of activity than for any architectural splendour and the precinct is a popular local meeting place. Non-Muslims are not normally admitted.

FREE Duke's Diwan   MUSEUM
(Map p50; Al-Malek Faisal St; ☉dawn-dusk) This historic townhouse, built in 1924, has served as a post office, the Ministry of Finance and a hotel. Today, it has been restored with period furnishings by a prominent Jordanian businessman, who is also the duke of the village of Mukhaybeh. There's not much to see, and the staircase has seen better days, but it gives an interesting glimpse of a bygone age.

FREE Darat al-Funun   GALLERY
(House of Arts; Map p50; ☎4643251; www.daratal funun.org; 13 Nadim al Mallah St; ☉10am-7pm Sat-Thu) On the hillside to the north of the downtown area, this cultural haven is dedicated to contemporary art. The main building features a small **art gallery** with works by Jordanian and other Arab artists, an art library, and workshops for Jordanian and visiting sculptors and painters. A schedule of upcoming exhibitions, lectures, films and public discussion forums is available on the website and in the *Jordan Times* newspaper.

Almost as significant as the centre's artistic endeavours are the architectural features of the site. At the base of the complex, near the entrance, are the excavated ruins of a 6th-century **Byzantine church**. Buildings further up the hill are mostly restored residences from the 1920s – it was in one of these that TE Lawrence wrote part of *Seven Pillars of Wisdom*. There is also a peaceful cafe (p69) and gardens with views over Amman.

Access is easiest on foot. From near the southern end of King Hussein St, head up the stairs under the 'Riviera Hotel' sign. At the top of the stairs, turn immediately right onto Nimer bin Adwan St and walk uphill for 50m where you need to take the left fork. The entrance gate (no English sign) is on the right after a few metres.

ⓘ WHEN CIRCLES ARE SQUARES

With its endless one-way streets, stairways, narrow lanes and jebels, Amman is confusing enough to get around anyway, but the ambiguous names for the streets and circles would challenge the navigational skills of even the most experienced explorer. We have used the more common names on maps and in the text, but if street signs, directions given by locals and queries from taxi drivers are still confusing, refer to the list below.

Don't forget that Al-Malek means King, so King Faisal St is sometimes labelled Al-Malek Faisal St. Similarly, Al-Malekah is Queen and Al-Emir (Al-Amir) is Prince. And don't be too surprised that some 'circles' are now called 'squares' *(maidan)*...

Circles

» 1st Circle – Maidan al-Malek Abdullah
» 2nd Circle – Maidan Wasfi al-Tal
» 3rd Circle – Maidan al-Malek Talal
» 4th Circle – Maidan al-Emir Gazi bin Mohammed
» 5th Circle – Maidan al-Emir Faisal bin Hussein
» 6th Circle – Maidan al-Emir Rashid bin al-Hassan
» 7th Circle – Maidan al-Emir Talal bin Mohammed
» Ministry of the Interior Circle – Maidan Jamal Abdul Nasser
» Sports City Circle – Maidan al-Medina al-Riyadiyah

Streets

» Rainbow St – Abu Bakr as-Siddiq St
» Zahran St – Al-Kulliyah al-Islamiyah St
» Mango St – Omar bin al-Khattab St
» Saqf Sayl St – Quraysh St
» Police St – Suleiman al-Nabulsi St

TUNNEL UNDER AMMAN

In ancient Roman Philadelphia, royalty considered it beneath them to mingle with the general public unless they had to. To ease their path between the major sites, an underground tunnel was built to connect the Citadel high on the hill with the Nymphaeum and the Theatre. While modern visitors to Amman might welcome having such access without having to negotiate the streets of downtown, the tunnel's precise location and state of repair is a closely guarded secret.

JEBEL AMMAN & AROUND

King Abdullah Mosque   MOSQUE
(Map p56; ☎5672155, ext 219; Suleiman al-Nabulsi St, Jebel Weibdeh; admission incl museum JD2; ◷8-11am & 12.30-2pm Sat-Thu) Completed in 1989 as a memorial by the late King Hussein to his grandfather, this blue-domed landmark can house up to 7000 worshippers, with a further 3000 in the courtyard. There is also a small women's section for 500 worshippers, and a much smaller royal enclosure.

The cavernous, octagonal prayer hall is capped by a magnificent blue dome 35m in diameter, decorated with Quranic inscriptions. The blue represents the sky while the golden lines depict rays of light illuminating the 99 names of Allah.

The **Islamic Museum** inside the mosque houses a small collection of photographs and personal effects of King Abdullah I. Shards of ancient pottery are also on display together with coins and stone engravings.

This is the only mosque in Amman that openly welcomes non-Muslim visitors. A Friday visit may be possible if you avoid prayer time but call ahead to be sure. Women are required to cover their hair – headscarves are available at the entrance to the mosque together with *abeyyas* (black, full-length outer clothing) to cover bare arms, legs or jeans. Shoes must be removed before entering the prayer hall.

Jordan National Gallery of Fine Arts
GALLERY
(Map p56; ☎4630128; www.nationalgallery.org; Hosni Fareez St, Jebel Weibdeh; admission JD5; ◷9am-5pm Wed-Mon) This small but impressive gallery is a wonderful place to gain an appreciation of contemporary Jordanian painting, sculpture and pottery. Renovated in 2005, the attractive space highlights contemporary art from around the Middle East and the greater Muslim world. Temporary exhibitions here are of high quality, and serve as a valuable introduction (or refresher) to the world of Islamic art. There's an on-site Art Cafe and an excellent gift shop.

The gallery is signposted from Suleiman al-Nabulsi St, opposite the King Abdullah Mosque.

OTHER SUBURBS

FREE **Military Museum**   MUSEUM
(Map p58; ☎5664240; ◷9am-4pm Sat-Thu) The simple and solemn Martyr's Memorial houses a small but interesting collection of documents, chronicling Jordan's recent military history, from the Arab Revolt in 1916 (in which 10,000 Arab fighters were killed) through to the Arab-Israeli Wars. The intention, however, is a focus on remembrance rather than historical verisimilitude.

The memorial is on the road to Zarqa, 1km east of the Sports City junction, in the grounds of the Sports City. Take any minibus or service taxi towards Zarqa, but check whether it goes past the Sports City *(al Medina al-Riyadiyah)*. A private taxi from downtown costs around JD6.

Hejaz Railway   TRAIN STATION
(Map p78; ☎06-4895413; King Abdullah I St; admission JD2; ◷dawn-dusk) Except for the occasional cargo train, only the breeze rolls through this historic old station at present. For years speculation has been that a functioning passenger service to Aqaba would return to the tracks of the Hejaz Railway, made famous in the West by the pursuits of TE Lawrence. For a while one or two intrepid and patient travellers sat out the long journey to Damascus but sadly, the Arab Spring in 2011 has now put paid to that journey too. It is still worth calling in on the station, though, to visit the small on-site museum, chat to the station master whose grandfather fought in the Arab Revolt, and to sit in the elaborately decked Royal Carriage. The station is 2.5km east of the Theatre, on the edge of the downtown area.

Abu Darwish Mosque   MOSQUE
On top of Jebel al-Ashrafiyeh, this mosque was built in 1961 with alternating layers of black and white stone. Non-Muslims are generally not permitted inside. Take service

AMMAN

Jebel Amman

0 _____ 1 km
0 _____ 0.5 miles

Mousabin Nusayr St

AL-RADHWAN

Adeeb Wahbeh St

Al-Ri'Asah St

Zahran St

Tripoli St

Ibrahim Ayoub St
Al-Salhouni St
31
37
28
4th Circle
Al-Malekah Noor St
Abou Madyen St
Uqbah bin Nafi St
Al-Ameerah Basma bin al-Hussein Rd

Al-Qahira St

Abdoun Circle
16
38
18
Al-Emir Hashem bin al-Hussein St
13 21
19
Al-Neel St
ABDOUN
Hims St
Dimashq St

To Blue Fig Café (500m)

29

Mahmoud al-Abedi
Fawzi al-Mulqi St
Abdul Mun'im al-Rifa'i St

Wadi Saqra Rd

Ahmad ibn Taymmiyah St

41
44

Al-Hussein bin Ali St

Ministry of Foreign Affairs

20
4
22
33
6
10
35
Zahran St
3rd Circle

30
Al-Mutanabbi St
Mithqal al-Fayez St

Bin Khaldoun St

26
5
Barada St

Amr bin al-'Ass St

34
27
Al-Rawabi St

Al-Ameerah Basma bin Talal Rd

King Abdullah Mosque

40
3
Suleiman al-Nabulsi St
Al-Ma'moun St

8
39
Umayyah bin Abd Shams St
Al-Malek al-Hussein St
Salah al-Deen al-Ayoubi St
43

Hosni Fareez St
Al-Karmali St
2
Ahmad ibn Hanbal St

1
Ibn Seena Rd

Mansour Kraishan St

Al-Amir Mohammed St

25
24
7
9
15
23
14
2nd Circle
Al-Kulliyah al-Islamiyah St
Al-Matbaeh St

Ma'n bin Za'edah St

Abdul Mun'em Riyadh St

Kamil al-Qassab St
Abdul Mun'em Riyadh St
Muhajireen Police Station

Muhajireen Bus Station
(Minibuses to Dead Sea & Wadi as-Seer)
N'oor al-Deen Zanki St

Kulliyat al-Sharee'ah St
Ahmad bin Adwan St
Nimer bin Dhikar bin al-Azwar St
Omar al-Khayyam St

Al-Baqoumiyah St

9 Sha'ban Rd
Al-Rjoum
42
32
17
11
12
1st Circle
36
Abu Bakr as-Siddiq St (Rainbow St)
Zayd bin Harethah St
Al-Buhturi St
Ali bin Abi Taleb Rd
Al-Muhajereen St

Omar Matar St

National Museum
AL-MATALLAH

Abdul Qader Koshak St

Jebel Amman

◎ Top Sights
King Abdullah Mosque E1
National Museum................................... G4

◎ Sights
1 Jordan National Gallery of Fine
   Arts F1

◎ Activities, Courses & Tours
Club Olympus................................(see 4)

◎ Sleeping
2 Canary Hotel... F1
3 Caravan Hotel... E1
4 Grand Hyatt Amman D2
5 Hisham Hotel.. D3
6 Hotel Le Royal D2
7 Jordan InterContinental Hotel E2
8 Toledo Hotel.. F1

◎ Eating
9 Abu Ahmad Orient Restaurant E2
10 Bonita Inn... E2
11 Fakhr El-Din Restaurant........................F3
12 Haboob Grand Stores F3
13 Noodasia... B4
14 Reem Cafeteria E3
15 Romero Restaurant...............................E3

◎ Drinking
16 Big Fellow Irish Pub A3
17 Grappa.. F3
Living Room................................... (see 15)
18 Tche Tche Café B3

◎ Entertainment
Cine Le Royal..................................(see 6)
19 Galleria B3

20 Grand Zara Cinema............................... D2
21 Harir Lounge B4
JJ's.. (see 4)
22 Kanabayé.. E2

◎ Shopping
23 Al-Alaydi Jordan Craft Centre E3
24 Al-Burgan E2
25 Artisana F2
Oriental Souvenirs Store............. (see 22)

◎ Information
26 Al-Khalidi Medical Centre......................C3
27 British Embassy......................................C4
28 Dutch Embassy...................................... B2
29 Egyptian Embassy................................. A1
30 French Embassy......................................C2
31 German Embassy................................... A2
32 Iraqi Embassy F3
33 Jacob's Pharmacy.................................. E2
34 Lebanese Embassy.................................C4
35 Ministry of Tourism &
   Antiquities D2
36 Saudi Arabian Consulate......................G3
37 Syrian Embassy..................................... A2
Tourist Police Centre................... (see 35)
38 Yemeni Embassy....................................A4

◎ Transport
39 Abdali Bus Station................................. F1
40 Airport Express Bus E1
41 Emirates D1
42 Firas Car Rental.....................................G3
43 Gulf Air F1
Royal Jordanian Airlines................ (see 7)
Trust International Transport
   (booking office) .... (see 39)
44 Turkish Airlines......................................D2

taxi 25 or 26 from Italian St in downtown to the mosque, or charter a taxi. It's a very long and steep climb southeast of downtown if you decide to walk.

Royal Automobile Museum   MUSEUM
(☏5411392; www.royalautomuseum.jo; King Hussein Park; admission JD3; ☺10am-7pm Wed-Mon, 11am-7pm Fri) Car enthusiasts will like this display of over 70 classic cars and motorbikes from the personal collection of King Hussein. It's in the northwestern suburbs, north of 8th Circle. The best way to reach the museum from downtown is to take a taxi.

🏃 Activities

The top-end hotels offer a day-rate to non-guests for use of their **swimming pools** and other facilities (from around JD25).

Sports City   SWIMMING
(Map p58; ☏5667181) This complex in northern Amman has an Olympic-size pool. Non-members are charged JD15 (including locker), depending on how early you arrive in the day (it gets cheaper as the day goes on). Note that women may feel uncomfortable swimming here. The Sports City complex also has tennis courts, which you can rent for JD4 per hour.

Shmeisani

Bisharat Golf Course   GOLF

(Map p78; ☏5520334) If you can't be away
without a game of golf, this nine-hole brown
course is located 14km south of downtown.
It is signposted from the Desert Hwy on the
way to Queen Alia airport.

Royal Racing Club   CAMEL RACES

(Map p78; ☏5850630) Horse and camel races
take place in spring and summer and horse-
riding lessons are available. The club is
located off the Desert Hwy on the way to
Queen Alia airport.

Power Hut   GYM

(Map p58; ☏5686349; 11 August St, Shmeisani;
☉5.30am-11pm Sun-Thu & Sat, 9am-6pm Fri) One
of the best gyms in town. A day/week pass
costs JD10/45 and gives access to a wide
range of machines, free weights, spin and
taebo classes, and a sauna and steam room.

Club Olympus   GYM

(Map p56; ☏4651234; Grand Hyatt Amman, Al-Hussein bin Ali St, 3rd Circle, Jebel Amman; ☉6am-10pm)
Charges JD25 for a day's use of the gym, indoor and outdoor pools, Jacuzzi and sauna.

Strikers   BOWLING

(Map p58; ☏5200200; Kempinski Amman, Abdul
Hamid Shouman St, Shmeisani) Tenpin bowling
is available here or at the **Jordan Bowling
Centre** (☏5512987; Makkah al-Mukarramah Rd)
at Mecca Mall in the northwestern suburbs.
The simplest way to reach both bowling centres is to take a taxi.

☞ Tours

The main backpacker hotels – the Cliff, Farah,
Jordan Tower and Palace – all offer a variety
of day trips from Amman. The most popular
are to the desert castles, Jerash, Ajlun and/or
Umm Qais. Prices vary depending on the size
of the party and the number of stops on the

Shmeisani

AMMAN SLEEPING

tour, but a day trip is usually in the region of JD15 to JD25 per person. These tours generally only run with a minimum of three but the hotels usually run a registration scheme among the guests so you don't have to find the other passengers yourself. Day trips are also available to Madaba, Mt Nebo and the Dead Sea. All four hotels can also arrange tours to more far-flung destinations such as Petra, Wadi Mujib Gorge, Karak, Shobak and the Dana Nature Reserve.

These tours provide an excellent way to visit key destinations if you are short on time as public transport is infrequent and inconvenient. They do not pretend, however, to provide a guided tour of the destination. Make sure you understand the nature of your tour before you commit to avoid disappointment.

🎊 Festivals & Events

Concerts, plays and performances are occasionally held at the Odeon and the Roman Theatre in July and August. The Ministry of Tourism office, near 3rd Circle, is the best source of information, but also check out the English-language newspapers.

See p87 for information about the Jerash Festival, Jordan's best-known cultural event (generally visited as a day trip from Amman).

The **Hakaya cultural project** (☑5687557; www.hakaya.org/en) connects organisations and individuals from around the Mediterranean who believe in the power of storytelling to effect positive cultural change. The project facilitates a programme of events throughout the year and there is hope of making 2011's successful September festival an annual event.

🛏 Sleeping

If you're just visiting the capital, then it's best to be based either in Jebel Amman, where there's a range of top-end and midrange accommodation close to downtown; or in downtown itself, where most of the budget options are located. The five-star hotels compete favourably with others in the region and represent reasonable value for money. The midrange options include wifi, air-conditioning and satellite TV and are usually tucked into quieter suburbs away from the noisy main streets. The budget hotels downtown vary considerably in cleanliness and facilities but all those recommended here sport clean linen, at least a fan, and friendly, experienced management. In addition, most can arrange onward connections. All the hotels listed here include breakfast in their room rates unless otherwise indicated.

BATHING WITH BRUISERS IN AMMAN'S HAMMANS

If you thought you felt sore after walking up and down Amman's multiple hills, then just wait until you see what they do with you at the local hammam (Turkish bath). The large, muscular attendants (male or female, depending on your sex) could easily retrain as Sumo wrestlers and you can rely on them to find parts of the body you didn't know you had. In fact, they'll remove parts of the body you didn't know you had, as the art of extreme exfoliation counts as one of their many talents.

A largely Ottoman creation, based no doubt on a Roman obsession with communal bathing, Turkish baths have existed as places of social gathering and ritual cleansing across the Middle East for centuries. Amman's bathhouses, despite being largely modern affairs, belong to this decidedly masochistic tradition. Think we're exaggerating? Then pay a visit to the **Al-Pasha Turkish Bath** (Map p50; ☑4633002; www.pashaturkishbath.com; Al-Mahmoud Taha St; ☺9am-2am, last booking midnight) and you can make up your own mind about this quintessential Middle Eastern experience.

The torture begins with a brief spell in the steam room: while you meekly sip ice-cold *karkade* (sweetened hibiscus tea), you'll be scalded with missile precision by occasional boiling-hot drops of condensed water from the ceiling. The next ordeal is a dip in the Jacuzzi, softening you up with dislocating jets of water for the scrubbing to come. Don't even think about backing out now as the bathhouse attendant will have spotted you, waiting to beckon you to an alcove in the wall.

Using what can only be described as a glorified Brillo pad, the attendant will quite literally scour the visible surface area of your body. For a few extra dinars, they will even set to work on your callused feet with a precision file! Don't expect phrases like 'no' and 'please don't' – uttered in either Arabic or English – to help you. More often they invite an almost sadistic acceleration of pummelling, pounding and slapping, accompanied by snorts of laughter. In fact, a sense of humour seems to be a prerequisite on both sides of the fluffy white towels handed out so thoughtfully in the antechamber of the baths: in emergencies (as when a nose hair is plucked without warning or two ears are lifted independently of the scalp) these towels can be used as a flag of surrender by battered bathers to signal that enough is enough.

After five to 10 minutes (which will feel like a lifetime) you'll be led to marble slabs for an olive-oil massage. If you opt for an additional full-body mud pack, then prepare to be pinched as the masseur checks you're still breathing under the caking armour. This is not the moment to try to strut off with attitude, nor to look back in anger, as there is enough olive-oil soap on the marble tiles to make sure you aren't the one having the last laugh.

If, by now, the prospect of being bullied in the bath is putting you off the idea altogether, don't let it. The bizarre part about the experience is that the moment you step out of the steaming pools of indistinct water and are laid to rest on the marble platform, or the moment you expose your newly scraped and kneaded flesh to the outside air, you'll feel so rejuvenated that you'll be booking your next appointment before you leave.

The full service costs around JD28. Generally speaking, women are welcome during the day, while evenings are men only. Book ahead as, believe it or not, this is a very popular pastime. Also, be sure to bring a modest swimming costume. Al-Pasha is easiest to find if you're coming along Abu Bakr as-Siddiq St (Rainbow St) from the 1st Circle; it's the fifth street on the right. Taxis know it as near Ahliya School for Girls.

DOWNTOWN

TOP CHOICE Jordan Tower Hotel HOTEL $
(Map p50; ☑4614161; www.jordantoweramman.com; 48 Hashemi St; male & female dm JD9, s/d/tr with bathroom JD20/32/38; ✳@🛜) A wonderful new addition to downtown accommodation, this warm and friendly hotel (probably the only no-smoking hotel in Amman) is run by a Jordanian man and his British wife. Rooms are bright and snug with flat-screen TVs though the bathrooms are small. The location is a winner: you couldn't be closer to the key sights without offering beds in the Forum! With a fantastic view of the Roman amphitheatre from the roof terrace (where smokers can take a puff with impunity), a cosy *majlis* designed as a place to relax on

cushions in front of the TV, and a big, bright and homely reception-cum-lounge area, this could be just the place to rest up for a few days before the exertions of a trip around Jordan. The helpful, English-speaking management can facilitate this with a number of popular day trips and transport options that start from around JD15. All tours include English-speaking drivers and there are daily departures to the most popular destinations.

Palace Hotel
HOTEL $
(Map p50; ☑4624326; www.palacehotel.com.jo; Al-Malek Faisal St; s/d/tr JD14/20/25, s/d/tr with bathroom JD25/30/40; ❈@❀) The Palace has offered good-value budget accommodation for many years and its location in the heart of King Faisal St can't be bettered. Some of the basic, airy rooms even have tiny balconies from which to enjoy the bustle of downtown's most characterful street below. An attractive lounge is a popular meeting place. Guests can add their name to the lists of day trips and onward transport options.

Farah Hotel
HOTEL $
(Map p50; ☑4651443; www.farahhotel.com.jo; Cinema al-Hussein St; 4- to 6-bed dm JD6, s/d/tr JD14/20/27, s/d/tr with bathroom JD22/30/39; @❀) A firm favourite with travellers, this is the only hotel downtown to have a shady garden. The presence of trees and the fact that it is off the main road give this well-managed establishment a homely, tranquil atmosphere unlike its neighbours off the high street. A roof terrace offers great views of downtown and the hotel owners have many years of experience in facilitating tours and onward transport. There are many security features in this hotel and women travelling alone are likely to feel comfortable here. Wi-fi (JD2) is free after a stay of three days.

Cliff Hotel
HOTEL $
(Map p50; ☑4624273; Al-Amir Mohammed St; s/d/tr/q JD8/10/12/15, breakfast JD1.500; ❀) This long-standing shoestring favourite has basic and quite dark rooms but there's a big bright lounge area that acts as a sociable meeting place. The shared showers have hot water. A popular choice among younger travellers, the Cliff also offers a mattress on the roof in summer.

Sydney Hostel
HOTEL $
(off Map p50; ☑4641122; sydney_hostel@yahoo. com; 9 Sha'ban St; dm JD7, s/d/tr JD15/25/33; ❈@❀) Not as conveniently located as other downtown options and lacking the social atmosphere of other travellers' haunts, this hotel nonetheless boasts big rooms – something of a novelty for the price. There's a huge communal area surrounding reception.

JEBEL AMMAN & AROUND

TOP CHOICE Jordan InterContinental Hotel
HOTEL $$$
(Map p56; ☑4641361; www.intercontinental.com; Al-Kulliyah al-Islamiyah St; r from JD140; ❈@❀☲) The grandaddy of luxury hotels in Amman, the much-loved InterCon has been hosting foreign dignitaries since the early days of Jordan's founding. Today it continues to attract an interesting mix of distinguished guests, including top brass on R&R from Iraq and visiting royalty from the Gulf. While it's certainly not the newest hotel, nor the most expensive on the block, there is an aged grace here not found at other top-end properties. A great favourite for local weddings, complete with traditional drumming, and with excellent Jordanian and Lebanese restaurants, and quality craft and antique shops, this is as good a place as any for an introduction to local city culture.

Caravan Hotel
HOTEL $
(Map p56; ☑5661195; caravan@go.com.jo; Al-Ma'moun St; s/d/tr/q JD22/28/33/38; @) Almost opposite the King Abdullah Mosque, the Caravan Hotel is something of a travellers' institution with a quiet side street location near downtown. The big clean rooms have a bright aspect and en-suite toilets and showers. If you detect a family-feel to this friendly hotel, that is because it's very much a family affair. The owner, Abu Charl, is the father of the owner of the ever-popular Mariam Hotel in Madaba. With 45 years experience helping travellers, the Caravan also offers a comprehensive transport service with English-speaking drivers. It costs JD3 for a taxi to the north bus station.

Hisham Hotel
HOTEL $$
(Map p56; ☑4644028; www.hishamhotel.com. jo; Mithqal al-Fayez St; s/d from JD65/76; ❈@❀) This delightful hotel in a leafy embassy district of Jebel Amman is an excellent choice if you're looking for a hotel removed from the hustle and bustle of the city while still within easy reach of downtown. The rooms are comfortable with flat-screen TVs and minibars, and are brought to life with small, personal touches. The family atmosphere, attractive decor and convivial Seven Barrels bar make this a frequent haunt of discerning travellers.

JEBEL AL-QALA'A

Al-Malek Ali bin al-Hussein St

Al-Qalat St

START ❶

❷

Salah bin Al-Akwa St

Hashemi St

Hashemite Square

Al-Malek al-Hussein St

Cinema al-Hussein St

Yaqout al-Hamawi St

Sa'id Khair St

Shabsough St

❻

❹

END ❷⓿ Al-Malek Faisal St

❶⓿ ❶⓿

❶❼

❶❻

❺

❸

❼

Hashemi St

❶❺

Basman St

Al-Qabartay St

Ibn al-Atheer St

❽

❶❹ ❶❸

❾

❶❷

❶⓿

❶❶ Petra St

Walking Tour
Amman

❯ The best way to experience the key sights of Amman, which are largely clustered downtown, is on foot. Stroll across the forum with promenading locals or immerse yourself in the narrow lanes of the souq, and you'll soon see that downtown remains the beating heart of the city. The walk is best suited to the morning (perfect for photographs) or early evening when the souqs are at their liveliest.

Begin at the hilltop ❶ **Citadel**. The pillars of the Temple of Hercules is the best place to gain a sense of Amman's ancient Philadelphian roots and to survey how the city has spread beyond the original seven hills.

Follow Al-Qalat St round the edge of the Citadel walls. A flight of steps (by a school with a flag) leads down to Salah bin Al-Akwa St; this is the shortcut locals take to reach downtown. A ❷ **viewpoint** to the right offers great views of the Roman amphitheatre. A further flight of stairs leads steeply downtown, past the Amman Panorama Art Gallery – a cooperative of four Jordanian artists.

Head gingerly across the busy main road at the bottom (Hashemi St), cross the newly reconstructed Hashemite Sq, and climb the hill to the left of the theatre. The coffeehouse here, ❸ **Hail Restaurant & Café**, is a popular spot for *nagileh*-smoking locals, especially at night. Take in the view of the Citadel and the hotchpotch of facades that line the main road, most of which date from the mid-19th to the mid-20th centuries. Follow the stairs in front of the coffeehouse and pass by the souvenir shops en route to the theatre complex.

The small building on your right is the Roman ❹ **Odeon**, a beautiful little amphitheatre still used for occasional performances. It is somewhat overshadowed, however, by the neighbouring ❺ **Theatre**, which seems to extend indefinitely up the hillside. Walk between the Theatre and the Roman columns, all that remains of the ❻ **forum**; the newly rebuilt plaza here provides space for the traditional evening stroll beloved by Ammanites. Pick up a map from the ❼ **tourist information office** before lunging into the heart of downtown. On the pavements around this area are Iraqi street vendors selling souvenir coins from the Saddam Hussein era; they're usually happy to invite conversation about their recent immigration to Jordan.

Cross the road onto Hashemi St, passing nut shops, perfumeries and a store selling mosque accessories such as brass crescents for minaret tops. Turn left at the traffic lights and you'll come to the **8** **Nymphaeum**. It takes imagination to resurrect this Roman fountain complex from the remaining ruins and even more imagination to picture the stream that ran nearby until recently and which now flows under the road.

Pluck up courage and dive into the **9** **fruit and vegetable souq** opposite. If you can find a space in which to stand unjostled by the throngs of shoppers, then close your eyes and just listen to the calls of the vendors. You don't have to speak Arabic to understand the bargains they are professing, interlaced with abuse for truculent customers. It's possible to travel the Middle East in this part of the souq as you pass sticky mounds of Saudi dates, Iranian pistachios and Syrian olives. Best of all are the bulging stalls of Jordanian cauliflowers, irregular-sized cabbages and organic carrots, reminders that not everywhere in the world is obsessed with regulation size and colour.

Turn left at the yellow shop, passing flatbread bakeries, and then right, through the **10** **hardware souq** of aluminium kettles and giant ladles. Turn right into Petra St (spelt 'Betra' – there's no distinction between 'p's and 'b's in Arabic) and take a sniff: the gorgeous aroma of spice-grinding and coffee-roasting is almost better than the flavour. On either side of the road are traditional **11** **Arabic medicine stalls**, recognisable by the dangling dried alligators, trays of starfish and drawers of herbs and henna. You can buy mascara from here – traditionally used by both men and women among the Bedouin and around babies' eyes to keep the evil eye at bay.

A right turn onto Quraysh St takes you past a tiny **12** **keffiyah shop** in a converted stairwell and brings you, four shops later, to **13** **Al-Husseiny Mosque**. At Friday lunchtime hundreds of men stream out of the mosque after the weekly sermon, pausing perhaps to buy prayer beads or a copy of the Quran from the surrounding mosque shops.

In the precinct in front of the mosque, craftsmen sit cross-legged behind their tools waiting for their next job.

Cross the street and enter the tiny **14** **Al-Afghani souvenir store**. Every conceivable space is occupied by chess sets, old postage stamps, plastic mosque clock-radios or some other items of treasure, largely of interest to the Jordanian visitor to the big city.

Turn left into Basman St, passing fine examples of Palestinian embroidered dresses, and turn right down a flight of stairs just before House 22. The **15** **women's souq** here challenges any preconceptions about prudish Arab women: the alleyways flutter with risqué Islamic lingerie, diaphanous above the doorways. It may be no accident that the **16** **gold souq**, where Arab men are expected to spend a portion of their salary, is immediately opposite, on the other side of King Faisal St (Al-Malek Faisal St). A bangle in 21-carat gold is one of the best souvenirs of a visit to an Arab souq and as you are only charged for the weight and not for the workmanship, it represents a good investment too. A cheaper purchase from the gold souq is a bag of peanuts from **17** **Abu Ahmed's peanut stall** – a family concern established decades ago.

Continue along King Faisal St, with its grand central aisle of Washington palms, and you'll come to the **18** **Duke's Diwan**; it's worth a quick trip upstairs to see yellowing newspaper cuttings from Amman's former glory days. The city is enjoying a renaissance at present and now old establishments like this are being highlighted with signs in English along the length of King Faisal St. Just past the ornate Arab Bank, for example, a sign indicates **19** **Habibah**, the perennially popular sweetmeat store with its brass platters of *kunafa* (shredded wheat and syrup dessert). A few paces further up King Faisal St and you'll reach legendary **20** **Hashem Restaurant**, a Turkish family-run establishment since 1956. The queue says it all: if a queue can be that long for a place that looks that bad, then you know it will be worth waiting for. And indeed it is. Don't bother to select: just wait patiently and the whole set (felafel, hummus, beans, bread, onions, leaves and tea) will come to you. There's no better way to end a trip downtown. But after the full works, you'll need to factor in time for another local custom – the afternoon nap.

Toledo Hotel
HOTEL $$

(Map p56; ☏4657777; www.toledo hotel.jo; Umayyah bin Abd Shams St; s/d/tr from JD70/80/90; ✳@🛜🏊) The Moorish-style Toledo offers a quality experience on the cusp of the top-end sector. Modern rooms with soft and subdued lighting boast business-friendly amenities, and the bathrooms are pleasingly spacious. The big draw of the hotel, however, is the ornate foyer with its Moroccan-style tiles and keyhole arches and free wi-fi access.

Hotel Le Royal
HOTEL $$$

(Map p56; ☏4603000; www.leroyalamman.com; Zahran St, 3rd Circle; r from JD140; ✳@🛜🏊) Amman doesn't get more ostentatious than this huge beacon on top of Jebel Amman, currently the tallest building in the capital. A favourite of visiting sheikhs and oil ministers, this is not the place for intimacy, but it is an address that will impress. Opulent rooms incorporate traditional Middle Eastern design elements, though the highlight of the property is its award-winning health-and-beauty spa, which is the biggest in Amman.

Grand Hyatt Amman
HOTEL $$$

(Map p56; ☏4651234; www.hyatt.com; Al-Hussein bin Ali St, 3rd Circle; r from JD130; ✳@🛜🏊) An enormous complex with hundreds of rooms, suites and apartments as well as restaurants, bars, clubs, swimming pools and even a shopping mall, the Grand Hyatt is truly a class act. The majority of the hotel is constructed from polished Jerusalem sandstone, an elegant touch that tones down the sheer extravagance of it all.

Canary Hotel
HOTEL $

(Map p56; ☏4638353; canary_h@hotmail.com; 17 Al-Karmali St; s/d JD24/32; @) In the leafy Jebel Weibdeh area, the cosy B&B-style Canary feels a million miles from the chaos of downtown. The rooms are more comfortable than luxurious, although everything is kept spick and span, including the bathrooms. There's a pleasant garden area in front of the hotel.

OTHER SUBURBS

AlQasr Metropole Hotel
HOTEL $$$

(Map p58; ☏5689671; www.alqasr-hojo.com; 3 Arroub St, Shmeisani; s/d JD100/110; ✳@🛜) Straddling the boundary between midrange and top-end in terms of facilities if not price, this hotel is the closest thing to a boutique establishment in Amman, with large contemporary paintings making a splash in the foyer. Located in fashionable Shmeisani, AlQasr has only 70 rooms, each artistically designed with wood floors, crown moulding and soft lighting. The hotel has an excellent range of restaurants and bars, including Vinaigrette (p67).

Kempinski Amman
HOTEL $$$

(Map p58; ☏5200200; www.kempinski.com; Abdul Hamid Shouman St, Shmeisani; r from JD210; ✳@🛜🏊) Amman's most chic and sophisticated accommodation option, this European-styled hotel is rightfully home in Shmeisani with immaculate rooms, designer furnishings

---

AMMAN FOR CHILDREN

While Amman is not exactly the most exciting city for kids, they will feel welcome, even in a restaurant late at night. See p39 to gain an idea of how to cater for children's needs in this family-friendly country.

Amman Waves
WATERPARK

(Map p78; ☏4121704; www.ammanwaves.com; Airport Rd; adult/child JD14/8; ◷10am-7pm) This Western-style waterpark is about 15km south of town on the highway to the airport. Note that adults should respect local sensibilities and wear appropriate swimwear (no Speedos or bikinis).

Haya Cultural Centre
CULTURAL CENTRE

(Map p58; ☏4637341; Ilya Abu Madhi St, Shmeisani; free; ◷9am-6pm Sat-Thu) Designed especially for children, this centre has a library, playground, an interactive eco-museum and an inflatable castle. It also organises regular activities and performances for kids.

Luna Park
AMUSEMENT PARK

(Map p58; ☏5698925; Khaled bin al-Walid Rd, Shmeisani; admission JD3; ◷10am-10pm) Has rides and amusements for the kids. Another branch is located at King Abdullah Gardens (Map p58).

and positively regal bathrooms. Offering a wide range of upmarket bars and restaurants, there's also an impressive list of entertainment, including a bowling alley, cinema and games centre for the kids.

Ocean Hotel   HOTEL $$$
(☑5517280; www.oceanhotel.com.jo; Shatt al-Arab St, Umm Utheima; s/d from JD77/100; ❄@🛜) Located in the western suburbs, far from the hustle and bustle of the downtown area, the Ocean Hotel is a good choice if you want peace and quiet and a flavour of everyday life in the capital – on the wealthy side of town. The best way to get here is by taxi. Rooms are warm and inviting as opposed to chic and luxurious but the opulent lobby with its oriental carpets lifts the hotel into the top-end category. Wi-fi is available for JD3 per hour or JD10 per day. The hotel encompasses the cavernous, almost legendary Diwan al-Sultan Ibrahim Restaurant, regarded as one of the best Lebanese dining venues in the capital.

Le Meridien   HOTEL $$$
(Map p58; ☑5696511; www.lemeridien.com; Al-Malekah Noor St, Shmeisani; r from JD120; ❄@☒) For those vital first impressions, the Le Meridien is grand and stylish. While it primarily targets business travellers, the hotel is considerably more affordable than the competition, yet still manages to win guests over with its flawless rooms and world-class service. Like other hotels in this up-market category, the Meridien has a private gym, swimming pools and health spa.

✖ Eating

Amman has a wide range of eating options, with budget places concentrated in downtown, while the more upmarket restaurants serving Arab and international cuisine are concentrated in Jebel Amman, Shmeisani and the western suburbs. If you fancy taking the local approach to choosing a dinner venue, then promenade Rainbow St in Jebel Amman, Culture St in Shmeisani or Waqalat St around the 7th Circle in Swafei, and just pop into whichever of the many restaurants appeals the most.

Note that many of the pubs and bars in Amman also serve food – for listings, check out p68. Although there are small grocery stores throughout the capital, the larger supermarkets are located in the more affluent and far-flung suburbs.

DOWNTOWN

TOP CHOICE **Hashem Restaurant**   FELAFEL $
(Map p50; Al-Amir Mohammed St; the works JD3; ☀24hr) You haven't tried falafel until you've eaten here. To fit in with the locals, pop in a handful of mint leaves first, park a wedge of raw onion between your teeth and don't touch the scalding copper vats of beans (harder than you'd imagine given the space available). This legendary eatery, run for half a century by a Turkish family, is so popular with locals and visitors alike that there's stiff competition for tables, many of which overflow into the alleyway. Aim for an early lunch or supper if you want to avoid the queues, although it has to be said that Hashem does a fantastic job of feeding the multitude in record time. Mid-afternoon, it makes a great place to sup a mint tea and watch downtown slide towards siesta.

Afrah Restaurant &
Coffeeshop   MIDDLE EASTERN $$
(Map p50; ☑4610046; Al-Malek Faisal St; mains from JD5; ☀9am-1am) This popular new restaurant in the heart of downtown is more about the ambience than the food. Squeezed into every nook and cranny of the renovated upper stories of this typical townhouse, the tables fill up quickly in the evening, particularly those with a balcony view of King Faisal St below. Old coffee pots, brass trays and other Oriental bric-a-brac are strewn in various alcoves, suspended from pillars and strung from the ceiling, recalling days of yore. Live Arab pop entertainment is offered nightly after around 9pm. Access is via a steep staircase up an alleyway, next to the Farah Hotel.

WILD JORDAN CAFÉ

Don't visit the RSCN booking office without sparing time for a bite at the wonderful, ecofriendly **Wild Jordan Café** (Map p50; 4633542; Othman Bin Affan St; mains JD7-12; 11am-midnight;). The emphasis is on locally sourced produce, healthy wraps, organic salads and locally plucked herbs. Smoothies are a welcome change from the ubiquitous coffee of cafes elsewhere. The glass walls and open-air terrace offer vistas of the Citadel and the downtown area – a great way to gain a perspective of Amman's main sights. While you're there, pop into the **Wild Jordan Nature shop** where you can buy olive-oil soaps and handcrafted silver earrings; profits are returned to the local communities that made them. Before you leave, pick up a downtown walking-trail brochure for some backstreet revelations.

Sara Seafood Restaurant SEAFOOD $
(Map p50; 4561115; Al-Malek al-Hussein St; fish dish from JD5; 10am-1am) A hit with locals, this new restaurant doesn't look much from the outside and looks positively uninviting from the street entrance (next to Cliff Hotel) but it turns out some of the best seafood in the neighbourhood. There's a tiny balcony overlooking busy King Hussein St or quieter tables inside. The restaurant offers an impressive choice of salads, whipped up at the micro-shop opposite the entrance downstairs – takeaways are possible.

Al-Quds Restaurant BEDOUIN $
(Jerusalem Restaurant; Map p50; 4630168; Al-Malek al-Hussein St; pastries from 800 fils, mains from JD6; 7am-10pm) The Jerusalem Restaurant specialises in sweets and pastries, but it has a large, good-value restaurant at the back that provides a great opportunity to try typical Jordanian dishes. The house speciality is *mensaf*, a Bedouin dish of lamb on a bed of rice, and *maqlooba* is frequently on the menu.

Cairo Restaurant MIDDLE EASTERN $
(Map p50; 4624527; Al-Malek Talal St; meals JD2-5; 6am-10pm) Recommended by travellers, this simple restaurant serves good local food at budget prices. Most of the locals opt for the mutton stew and boiled goat's head, but

you may prefer the *shish tawooq* with portions of grilled chicken large enough for two.

Habibah DESSERTS $
(Map p50; Al-Malek al-Hussein St; pastries from 500 fils) This legendary shop is a good bet for Middle Eastern sweets and pastries. Sweet tooths of all ages line up for honey-infused, pistachio-topped and filo-crusted variations on the region's most famous desserts. There is another branch on Al-Malek Faisal St.

Jabri Restaurant DESSERTS $
(Map p50; 4624108; Al-Malek al-Hussein St; pastries from 800 fils, mains JD4-6; 8am-8pm Sat-Thu) Like Habibah, Jabri is famed for its baklava and other local sweet delicacies.

JEBEL AMMAN & AROUND

Romero Restaurant ITALIAN $$$
(Map p56; 4644227; www.romero-jordan.com; Mohammed Hussein Haikal St; mains JD10-18) It may seem odd to recommend an Italian restaurant in Jordan but this exceptional place is no pizza parlour. A revered local favourite, it was established by Italian immigrants half a century ago in an elegant traditional townhouse and comes complete with period furniture, Venetian chandeliers and a roaring fire in winter. With intimate tables tucked in unexpected corners, attentive waiters who understand the concept of Mediterranean time, a fine wine list to savour, and succulent homemade pasta, this romantic venue is just the place to come for a celebration. But don't forget to book – even on a weekday in winter it's full of jovial groups of friends. The restaurant is virtually opposite the InterCon.

Fakhr El-Din Restaurant MIDDLE EASTERN $$$
(Map p56; 4652399; Taha Hussein St; mains JD8-15) Tastefully decorated and with crisp white linen cloths, this fine-dining restaurant is located in a 1950s house with a beautiful little garden. Over 10 years, a million guests have visited this establishment in search of what the proprietor terms 'genuine Arabic cuisine and hospitality'. A range of raw meat dishes, including lamb fillet, make an interesting addition to all the familiar Middle Eastern favourites. The restaurant is situated opposite Grappa if you fancy a nightcap after dinner.

Blue Fig Café FUSION $$
(off Map p56; 5928800; Al-Emir Hashem bin al-Hussein St; mains JD4-8; 8.30am-1am) If you're wondering where Amman's fashionable set go to escape their own cuisine, look no

further than this supercool, glass-and-steel restaurant near Abdoun Circle. Offering an extensive and imaginative mix of world fusion dishes (try a Kyoto green tea and mint flavoured crème brulée), the Blue Fig creates its ambience with seductive world music and the occasional Arabic poetry reading.

Abu Ahmad Orient
Restaurant   MIDDLE EASTERN **$$**
(Map p56; ☑3522520; 3rd Circle; mains JD5-11; ◷noon-midnight) This excellent midrange Lebanese place has a leafy outdoor terrace that bustles with life during the summer months. The standard fare comprises grilled meats, but the real highlights are the hot and cold mezze – try a *buraik* (meat or cheese pie) or the *yalenjeh* (stuffed vine leaves).

Bonita Inn   SPANISH **$$$**
(Map p56; ☑4615060; off Al-Kulliyah al-Islamiyah St; mains JD12-25; ◷noon-midnight) If you're looking for a change from Middle Eastern fare but still want to mix with a Jordanian clientele, this primarily Spanish restaurant is a great favourite with locals. The authentic paella Valenciana and gazpacho soup are recommended. The restaurant is located in a typical Jebel Amman townhouse (opposite the InterCon), lending a cosy charm to the venue. Don't eat too many tapas if you want to do justice to the paella!

Reem Cafeteria   SHWARMA **$**
(Map p56; ☑4645725; 2nd Circle; shwarma JD1.500) There are hundreds of shoebox-sized shwarma kiosks in Amman but few that have the customers queuing down the street at 3am. Even the royal family is rumoured to have dropped in here for a late-night kebab. And if it's good enough for them…

Haboob Grand Stores   SUPERMARKET **$**
(Map p56; ☑4622221; Al-Kulliyah al-Islamiyah St; ◷7am-midnight) Between 1st and 2nd Circles, this is a handy place to stock up with picnic material. It sometimes closes on Friday.

OTHER SUBURBS
Vinaigrette   FUSION **$$$**
(Map p58; ☑5695481; AlQasr Metropole Hotel, 3 Arroub St, Shmeisani; mains JD8-15) Located on the top floor of the AlQasr, and in keeping with the hotel's boutique theme, this restaurant offers trend-setting Middle East fusion food and gourmet sushi and salads – build your own salad and sushi combo, or let the house choose for you. Mellow jazz complements the superb views over the city.

La Terrasse   JORDANIAN **$$$**
(Map p58; ☑5601675; 11 August St, Shmeisani; mains JD10-25; ◷1pm-1am) This Shmeisani favourite offers some delicious local dishes and soups in a cosy, relaxed upper-storey dining area. The wine list is extensive, with labels representing Jordan and Tunisia (JD30 to JD40 a bottle). Most nights, after 10.30pm, the tiny stage is given over to live Arab singers and musicians, making it a popular venue for locals.

Diwan al-Sultan Ibrahim
Restaurant   MIDDLE EASTERN **$$**
(☑5517383; Ocean Hotel, Shatt al-Arab St, Umm Utheina; mains JD10-15; ◷noon-midnight) The Diwan comes highly recommended by locals and expats for its high-quality Lebanese food. The fresh fish is the speciality with options arrayed on ice. A whole Ibrahim fish (JD30) is fun for a party. The ambience in the cavernous dining area is good if there's a crowd but a bit impersonal if you arrive early.

Kan Zeman   JORDANIAN BUFFET **$$$**
(Map p78; ☑4128391; dinner buffet JD23; ◷7.30pm-midnight) Located in a historic inn with vaulted ceiling, this restaurant is brought to life each night when traditional live music fills the ancient halls. On-site workshops housed in old stable blocks sell glass, rugs and jewellery among other souvenirs. It's aimed primarily at tour groups, and at around 15km south of 8th Circle in the village of Al-Yadoudeh – 3km east of the Desert Hwy – it's only worth the effort if you happen to be in the area. A taxi fare from downtown costs around JD15 each way.

Safeway outlet   SUPERMARKET **$$**
(Map p58; ☑5685311; Nasser bin Jameel St, Shmeisani; ◷24hr) Located around 500m southwest of the Sports City junction.

C-Town Shopping Centre   SUPERMARKET **$$**
(☑5815558; Zahran St, Sweifieh; ◷7am-midnight) Branches close to 7th Circle and in **Shmeisani** (Map p58; Abdul Hameed Sharaf St; ◷7am-midnight).

Drinking

There is plenty of nightlife in Amman. The areas to head for are Jebel Amman, Shmeisani and the western suburbs, where numerous fashionable cafes and bars abound, as well as a few nightclubs and live houses that stay open until the early hours. For an authentic local experience, the bars downtown are an eye-opener but are recommended for men only. Otherwise nightlife here is limited to restaurants. Almost all bars serve food of some description.

Bars

Several bars in downtown, patronised almost exclusively by men, are tucked away in the alleys near Al-Husseiny Mosque.

MOSTLY MEN

Orient Bar & Restaurant   BAR

(Map p50; ☑4636069; off Al-Amir Mohammed St, downtown; beer from JD3; ☺11am-late) Also known as Al-Sharq, this spit-and-sawdust bar serves a range of beers, spirits and the local arak (if you dare) – if you've had a bit to drink, mind your head on the stairs on the way down.

Other local haunts include the **Salamon Bar** (Map p50; ☑5902940; off Al-Amir Mohammed St, downtown; ☺noon-midnight) and **Jordan Bar** (Map p50; ☑5796352; off Al-Amir Mohammed St, downtown; ☺10am-midnight). All of these places are tiny and full of smoke, but are at least the real deal.

WOMEN WELCOME

Living Room   COCKTAIL BAR

(Map p56; ☑4655988; Mohammed Hussein Haikal St, Jebel Amman; drinks JD3-5, mains JD6-10; ☺1pm-1am) Part lounge, part sushi bar and part study (think high-backed chairs, a fireplace and the daily newspaper), the Living Room is so understated that it's easily missed. It offers quality bar meals, fine music and delicious iced tea with lemon grass and mint. Non-teetotallers can enjoy the full complement of expertly crafted cocktails on offer which are served up deliciously strong.

Grappa   BAR

(Map p56; ☑4651458; Abdul Qader Koshak St, Jebel Amman; beer JD4-5; ☺6pm-1.30am) Stylish wooden benches and B&W photos on the wall give this rustic bar a hip feel but it's the huge windows with views and the summer terrace seating that really draw the crowds.

Big Fellow Irish Pub   PUB

(Map p56; ☑5934766; Abdoun Circle, Jebel Amman; drinks JD2-4; ☺noon-2am) It looks like an Irish pub, it even smells like an Irish pub, but with Arabic music sliding out of the stereo, it doesn't really sound like an Irish pub. If in doubt, tucking into a pint of bitter and a Guinness pie should help.

Rovers Return   PUB

(☑5814844; Ali Nasouh al-Taher St, Sweifieh; drinks JD3-5, meals JD5-8; ☺1pm-late) A godsend for homesick *Coronation St* fans, this popular, cosy English pub near the 7th Circle has wood panelling and a lively atmosphere. The comfort food includes authentic fish and chips, and roast beef with gravy. The entrance is round the back of the building and can be hard to find – look for the red 'Comfort Suites' sign.

Blue Fig Café   BAR

(off Map p56; ☑5928800; Al-Emir Hashem bin al-Hussein St; mains JD4-8; ☺8.30am-1am) Another convivial place to spend an evening, with a chic crowd, pleasant atmosphere and live music several times a week.

Cafes

Some of the cafes in downtown are perfect retreats to write up your journal, tweet a friend, smoke a scented nargileh, meet locals and play cards or backgammon – or to simply watch the world go by. The first group of cafes listed here are generally men only; women, while not unwelcome, may feel uncomfortable.

MOSTLY MEN

Auberge Café   COFFEEHOUSE

(Map p50; Al-Amir Mohammed St, downtown; ☺10am-midnight) One floor below the Cliff Hotel this gritty Jordanian spot is popular with local men. You'll have to make your way through the tobacco haze to reach the balcony, which overlooks the main street. You'll have to fight with the regulars to sit there, mind.

Peace Café   COFFEEHOUSE

(Map p50; ☑079 5297912; Al-Amir Mohammed St, downtown; ☺9am-midnight) Try to ignore the filthy staircase on your way up to this utterly basic smoking den. If you can land one of the two balcony tables overlooking the street, you'll have one of the prime vantage points in downtown. As with the Auberge Café, do it like the locals – puff at a nargileh (JD2.500) and just watch the world go by.

WOMEN WELCOME

Downtown, around Hashemite Sq and along Hashemi St, the dozen or more cafes attract locals and tourists alike, especially in summer. The place to be seen at night is anywhere around Abdoun Circle where there are plenty of cool cafes. Take local advice – fashions change frequently in this part of Amman.

Al-Rashid Court Café CAFE
(Map p50; ✆4652994; Al-Malek Faisal St, downtown; tea or coffee from JD3; ☺10am-midnight Sat-Thu, 1-11pm Fri) The 1st-floor balcony here is *the* place to pass an afternoon and survey the chaos of the downtown area below, though competition for seats is fierce. Also known as the Eco-Tourism Café, this is one of the best places for the uninitiated to try a nargileh (JD2). Although you won't see any local women here, it's well accustomed to foreign tourists. To find it, look for the flags of the world on the main facade; the entrance is down the side alley.

Books@café CAFE
(Map p50; ✆4650457; Omar bin al-Khattab; mains JD5-12; ☺10am-midnight) You may need to keep your sunglasses on when you enter this establishment – the retro floral walls and beaded curtains in psychedelic colours are a fun if dazzling throwback to the '70s. This is typical modern Jordanian coffeehouse chic and the tasty global food is far less interesting than the hip young Jordanians lounging on sofas in corners or with their noses in a new book. The on-site bookshop stocks Lonely Planet titles.

Darat al-Funun Café CAFE
(Map p50; Nimer bin Adwan St, downtown; snacks from JD1; ☺10am-7pm Sat-Thu) In the heart of a cultural centre, this is a peaceful place to escape from downtown, especially as it's surrounded by a garden and the ruins of a Byzantine church. Lawrence wrote part of *Seven Pillars of Wisdom* in the neighbouring house so who knows what creative spirits linger here. Closed during Ramadan.

Shaher's Penthouse Cafeteria CAFE
(Map p50; Sahat al-Malek Faysal al-Awal St, downtown; coffee JD3; ☺9.30am-11pm) This cosy cafe has a traditionally decorated indoor dining area as well as an outdoor terrace overlooking the street far below. Hussein, the resident musician, will happily play the oud (lute) or violin to provide a cultured counterpoint to the street noise below.

Al Hail Restaurant & Café CAFE
(Map p50; ✆78-6702270; Hashemite Sq, downtown; ☺9am-midnight) A glass of mint tea (JD3) here comes with perhaps the best view of the Citadel on offer downtown. It's an unpretentious place, despite the decorative well in the front garden, and it's popular with locals in the evening when the neighbouring theatre is illuminated.

Al-Sendabad Coffee Shop CAFE
(Map p50; ✆4632035; Hashemite Sq, downtown; ☺10am-midnight) About 150m west of the Roman Theatre, this place has good views over the city (though not of the theatre itself). You can sit on the roof in summer.

Tche Tche Café CAFE
(Map p56; ✆5932020; Abdoun Circle, Jebel Amman; snacks JD1-3; ☺10am-11pm) You'll have to arrive early to get a seat in this bright and buzzing cafe, one of a chain that stretches across the Middle East. Far from a traditional coffeehouse, it's a hit with Jordanian women who come to smoke nargileh and enjoy the Arabic pop.

Wild Jordan Café CAFE
(Map p50; ✆4633542; Othman Bin Affan St; ☺11am-midnight; mains JD7-12; ✆) Don't forget the Wild Jordan Café, which has the best organic teas, coffees and light bites in the capital.

☆ Entertainment

Cinemas

There are several modern cinema complexes that offer recent releases. Ticket prices vary. Programs for cinemas are advertised in the English-language newspapers (see p72). Note that the less-than-salubrious cinemas downtown usually feature Arabic, Indian and Thai films subtitled in Arabic and may not be of much interest to Western visitors. The cinemas listed below are modern complexes showing Western films.

Cinema City CINEMA
(✆5527948; Mecca Mall) Far from downtown, Cinema City is best reached by taxi.

Cine Le Royal CINEMA
(Map p56; ✆4603022; 3rd Circle, Jebel Amman) Part of Le Royal Hotel.

Galleria CINEMA
(Map p56; ✆5934793; Abdoun Circle, Jebel Amman)

Grand Zara Cinema CINEMA
(Map p56; ✆4613260; 3rd Circle, Jebel Amman) In the Zara Centre behind the Grand Hyatt, with several fast-food outlets.

Books@café (Map p50; ✆4650457; Omar bin al-Khattab, downtown) has film nights on Monday. The various cultural centres also show foreign films regularly (check in the English-language media).

LOCAL KNOWLEDGE

HIS EXCELLENCY NAYEF HMEIDI AL-FAYEZ: MINISTER OF TOURISM & ANTIQUITIES

His Excellency, the Minister of Tourism & Antiquities, is proud of his country and its heritage. Though quick to identify his own Bedouin and tribal ancestry, which he describes as lying at the root of Jordanian culture, he also emphasises Jordan's modern role on the international stage. In the following interview, HE Nayef Al-Fayez identifies the key elements that make Jordan a special and unique destination for the visitor, and describes the balance between heritage and progress that must be maintained to safeguard the country's future.

With so much heritage, how do you persuade tourists that Jordan is not all about ruins? Jordan is a very modern country, as you can see from Amman, but there is always a link between past and present. That link is the people. In fact, the people are the most wonderful part of our country. Jordanian hospitality is legendary and I read many stories on the internet about visitors who have rediscovered their confidence in people after their interactions with the local communities here. Tourism is a bridge between cultures and we welcome visitors as 'guests of God'.

With limited public transport to key destinations, and with high entry fees to national parks and Petra, is it fair to say that Jordan is actively targeting the wealthier tourist? Jordan is open for everyone. We are a small country and we depend a lot on tourism – it is a major pillar of our economy and given the treasures we have, it has the potential to be the number one pillar. We do have plans for scheduled tourist transportation, and we already operate JETT buses to the main destinations, but as with any government our main task is to move the population around at affordable prices. This is why we subsidise public transport. We are working with the private sector, however, to establish transport with guaranteed departures that will benefit all our visitors.

This year, 2011, has obviously been a tough one with problems in neighbouring countries impacting on tourism to Jordan. What measures have been taken to reassure tourists that Jordan is safe? The Middle East comprises 22 countries and each country is different. The Arab Spring was not about cross-border issues, nor about targeting foreigners. Jordan is what we call the 'Switzerland of the Middle East' because of its stability. Studies have been conducted that show that in the last six months it is safer than home for many visitors. As such, Jordan shouldn't be made guilty by geography!

To what extent do you have trouble convincing foreign tourists that Jordan is worth visiting as a destination in its own right as opposed to a stopover between Egypt and Syria? We have established the Jordanian Tourism Board to emphasise Jordan's value as a stand-alone destination. There is plenty of interest for a two-week visit because Jordan is so much more than just Petra. Wadi Rum is a Unesco heritage site, for example, and of course the Bible is your guidebook for the sites of the Holy Land in Jordan. The length of stay has increased and we're sure it will continue to do so as visitors learn about what we have to offer.

With water a major problem in the country, how can the demands of tourism be balanced against environmental concerns? Our responsibility is to preserve our heritage sites and natural resources for posterity and we have a Ministry of Environment that takes care of this. In fact, we consume the least water in the region and we have campaigns to educate children to be aware of environmental issues. The young are the future of our country and it is vital they are aware and proud of their inheritance.

How can visitors play their part in a sustainable future for tourism in Jordan? Integrating with local communities is key – if people feel the value of tourism, they will work hard to preserve and protect sites for the future. But it's more than that: visitors are touched by the experience of interacting with Jordanian people. That's what the future of tourism here is about – a sharing of cultures.

Exhibitions & Music

Various foreign cultural centres organise lectures, exhibitions and musical recitals. Darat al-Funun (p54) often features recitals of classical and traditional music. The Jordan National Gallery of Fine Arts (p55) sometimes has visiting exhibitions of contemporary art.

For the exquisite Arabic art of calligraphy, you can watch a master at work in Hassan Ali Hassan Kanaan's **workshop and gallery** (☑0777-888007 or 079-6796391909) downtown. Call ahead for an appointment to view.

Events are advertised in the local English-language newspapers.

Nightclubs

The clubs and lounges inside the top-end hotels offer an international atmosphere, more forgiving of Jordanians who want to let their hair down (both figuratively and literally). Cover charges vary depending on the night and the entertainment but JD15 per person is fairly standard. Locals dress to impress and expect visitors to make a bit of sartorial effort too!

Some of the more established nightspots include the following.

JJ's   NIGHTCLUB
(Map p56; ☑4651234; Grand Hyatt Amman, Al-Hussein bin Ali St, Jebel Amman; ⊙8.30pm-late Mon-Sat) The Grand Hyatt's disco is where Amman's glamorous set enjoy an evening out. The music varies greatly depending on the whims of the DJ, though it's always fresh and innovative.

Harir Lounge   NIGHTCLUB
(Map p56; ☑5925205; Abdoun Circle, Jebel Amman; ⊙1pm-1am, to 3am Sat & Sun) A flamboyant upper-floor lounge and restaurant, Harir is the place to wear your best threads, especially if you want to feel at home among local socialites.

Kanabayé   NIGHTCLUB
(Map p56; ☑4642830; 3rd Circle, Jebel Amman) A quiet place for a drink, the couches (*kanabayé* in Arabic) and seductive lighting give this lounge bar a sleek, sexy feel. In a bid to attract a savvy international clientele, Kanabayé mixes it up nightly with everything from Arabic pop to salsa ballads.

Sport

Football (soccer) is followed religiously by most locals. The capital's two main teams are Wahadat (generally supported by Palestinians) and Faisaly (supported by other Jordanians). The games are mostly played on Friday at the **Amman International Stadium** (Map p58), near Sports City in Shmeisani.

🔒 Shopping

Jordan has a rich craft tradition and there are several quality craft centres where you can buy handmade items and antiques on Rainbow St and near the InterContinental Hotel. Many of these outlets are run by women's cooperatives to benefit threatened communities and help preserve the environment. Lots of souvenir shops selling sand bottles, headdresses, miniature brass coffee pots and Bedouin jewellery, are dotted around the tourist sights of downtown. Don't assume on your travels in Jordan that if you see an item you like, then you will find something similar in Amman – a lot of the arts and crafts are quite localised. See p282 for an idea of Jordan's best buys, hints about where to buy ethically sourced goods that help contribute to the local community, and tips about bargaining, tax and buying antiques.

Mall mania is sweeping through areas of Amman. The biggest is **Mecca Mall** (☑5527948; Makkah al-Mukarramah Rd) in the northwestern suburbs, with a cinema, bowling alley, video arcade and dozens of restaurants. **Abdoun Mall** (☑5920246; Al Umawiyeen St, Zahran) is a smaller version of the same concept. There are several others, including a **City Mall** (☑5868500), on the outskirts of the city.

There are several bookshops selling English language publications and there's at least a kiosk for maps, guidebooks and newspapers in each top-end hotel. For a bigger selection of reading materials, head for **Books@café** (Map p50; ☑4650457; Omar bin al-Khattab, downtown).

Jordan River Foundation   HANDICRAFTS
(Map p50; ☑4613081; www.jordanriver.jo; Bani Hamida House, Fawzi al-Malouf St, Jebel Amman; ⊙8.30am-7pm Sat-Thu, 10am-5pm Fri) Supporting top-notch worthy causes through selling equally top-notch crafted items, this shop has become something of an institution in Amman. The showroom supports hand-loomed rugs from Bani Hamida and exquisite Palestinian-style embroidery. Cushions, camel bags, candles, embroidery, baskets (from Wadi Rayan in the Jordan Valley)

and Dead Sea products make it an excellent place to do some gift-buying as the items are less about souvenirs and more about stylish decor. Only the highest-quality pieces make it into the showroom.

Wild Jordan HANDICRAFTS
(Map p50; ☑4633718; Othman bin Affan St, downtown; ☺10am-10pm) The nature store at the Wild Jordan Centre sells beautiful products made in Jordan's nature reserves, including silver jewellery, organic herbs and jams from Dana, and candles made and decorated by Bedouin women as part of an income-generating project in Feynan. Decorated ostrich eggs are another speciality of this outlet. All profits are returned to the craftspeople and to the nature-reserve projects.

Bawabet al-Sharq HANDICRAFTS
(Map p50; ☑4637424; Abu Bakr as-Siddiq St, downtown; ☺9am-7pm) The 'Gate of the Orient' has locally made (some on site) home decor items tending towards the kitsch. Sales benefit several Jordanian women's groups.

Al-Alaydi Jordan Craft Centre HANDICRAFTS
(Map p56; ☑/fax 4644555; off Al-Kulliyah al-Islamiyah St, Jebel Amman; ☺9am-6pm Sat-Thu) Spread over several floors, this vast showroom includes jewellery, Hebron glassware, Palestinian embroidery, kilims, wood carvings, old kitchen implements and Bedouin tent accessories.

Al-Burgan HANDICRAFTS
(Map p56; ☑4652585; www.alburgan.com; 12 Tala't Harb St, Jebel Amman; ☺9.30am-6.30pm Sat-Thu) Al-Burgan has a smaller selection of items but the staff is knowledgeable and prices are reasonable. It's behind Jordan InterContinental Hotel.

Oriental Souvenirs Store SOUVENIRS
(Map p56; ☑4642820; 3rd Circle, Jebel Amman; ☺8am-7pm Sat-Thu) This friendly, family-run store is more rustic than the others listed here, but it's something of an Aladdin's Cave.

Artisana SOUVENIRS
(Map p56; ☑/fax 4647858; Mansour Kraishan St, Jebel Amman; ☺9.30am-6pm Sat-Thu) This excellent small showroom has a wide range that includes scarves, bottles of holy water from the Jordan River and reproductions of the famous 6000-year-old statues from Ain Ghazal.

Beit al-Bawadi CERAMICS
(☑5930070; www.beitalbawadi.com; Fawzi al-Qawoaji St, Jebel Amman; ☺9am-6pm Sat-Thu) This is the place for quality ceramics, created to support local artisans, whom you can see working in the basement. Designs are both traditional and modern (lampshades and dinner sets), some decorated with Arabic calligraphy, and pieces cost around JD50 to JD80.

Silsal Ceramics CERAMICS
(☑5931128; Innabeh St, North Abdoun; ☺9am-6pm Sat-Thu) Has a small showroom of superb modern pottery. If you're coming along Zahran St from 5th Circle, it's the third small street on the right.

ℹ Information

Emergency
The tourist police have an office at the Ministry of Tourism & Antiquities and there is a small tourist-police booth (Map p50) on Hashemi St near the Roman Theatre.
Ambulance (☑911)
Fire department (☑911)
Police (☑911)
Tourist Police (Map p56; ☑4603360, ext 254; Ministry of Tourism & Antiquities, ground fl, Al-Mutanabbi St, Jebel Amman; ☺8am-9pm)
Traffic police/accidents (☑911)

Internet Access
Amman has plenty of internet cafes, particularly in downtown. Most hotels now offer wi-fi connectivity and/or use of a PC with internet for minimal or no charge.
Books@café (Map p50; ☑4650457; Omar bin al-Khattab, downtown; per hr JD2; ☺10am-midnight) A professional set-up with fast connections.
Internet Yard (Map p50; ☑5509569; dweib@joinnet.com.jo; Al-Amir Mohammed St, downtown; per hr JD1; ☺9.30am-midnight)
Meeranet (Map p58; ☑5695956; Ilya Abu Madhi St, Shmeisani; per hr JD2; ☺24hr)
Welcome Internet (Map p50; ☑4620206; Al-Amir Mohammed St, downtown; per hr JD1; ☺10.30am-1am)

Media
Jordan Today is a free monthly booklet that includes a Yellow Pages listing of embassies, airlines, travel agencies and car-rental companies in both Amman and Aqaba, as well as restaurant listings and news of upcoming events.

The monthly *Where to Go* includes a useful collection of Amman restaurant menus. To track down a copy of either, ask at one of the tourist offices or at top-end hotels and restaurants.

The English-language *Jordan Times* and *Star* newspapers both print entertainment listings and useful phone numbers.

ℹ CROSSING THE STREET IN AMMAN

When you first arrive in Amman, one of your greatest challenges is likely to be making it safely to the other side of the street. This is especially true of the downtown area, although the faster-moving thoroughfares elsewhere also pose a serious hazard to your health. Contrary to what you may think, Amman's drivers have no desire to run you over; they just want to get to their destination as quickly as possible.

The installation of more traffic lights has made the situation a little easier, but you'll still have a better chance of survival if you follow a few simple 'rules'. In slow-moving traffic, the name of the game is brinkmanship – whoever yields last will win. A car missing you by inches may scare the hell out of you but is actually a normal and precisely calculated course of events.

Cross wide roads a lane at a time – if you wait for a big gap you'll be there all day. Some unscrupulous travellers have even been known to hail a taxi so that it will block traffic and give them a lane's head start. Make your decision and then don't hesitate – Amman's drivers will make their decisions based on a reasonable assumption of what you'll do next.

Above all, have patience; an extra minute's wait is infinitely preferable to a nasty accident. And if all else fails, put your pride behind you and ask some old lady to lead you by the hand – or at least follow in her slipstream.

Medical Services

Amman has more than 20 hospitals and some of the best medical facilities available in the Middle East. The English-language *Jordan Times* and *Star* list hospitals and doctors on night duty throughout the capital. They also publish a list of pharmacies open after-hours.

Al-Khalidi Medical Centre (Map p56; ☑4644281; www.kmc.jo; Bin Khaldoun St, Jebel Amman) Southwest of 3rd Circle.

Islamic Hospital (Map p58; ☑5101010; just off Al-Malek al-Hussein St, Jebel al-Hussein)

Italian Hospital (Map p50; ☑4777101; Italian St, downtown)

Jacob's Pharmacy (Map p56; ☑4644945; 3rd Circle, Jebel Amman; ☺9am-3am) One of the more conveniently located pharmacies.

Palestine Hospital (Map p58; ☑5607071; Al-Malekah Alia St, Shmeisani)

University Hospital (☑5353666; University of Jordan complex, northern Amman) Located about 10km northwest of downtown. Take any minibus or service taxi to Salt from Raghadan bus station or charter a taxi.

Money

Changing money in Amman is quick and easy, especially since there are dozens of banks downtown and in Jebel Amman, the two areas most visitors are likely to find themselves. The Arab Bank, Jordan Gulf Bank and the Housing Bank for Trade & Finance are among those with widespread ATMs for Visa and MasterCard, while Jordan National Bank and HSBC ATMs allow you to extract dinars from your Master-Card and are Cirrus-compatible. The Housing Bank has an ATM in the arrivals hall at Queen Alia International Airport after passing through customs. Although there's a bank before immigration it is not always open so make sure you have some local currency to buy your Jordanian visa.

Many moneychangers are located along Al-Malek Faisal St in downtown. For changing travellers cheques, try **Sahloul Exchange Co** (ground fl, Aicco Bldg, Al-Malek Faisal St, downtown; ☺9am-7pm Sat-Thu).

Post

There are lots of small post offices around town (ask your hotel for the nearest), including at the Jordan InterContinental Hotel between 2nd and 3rd Circles in Jebel Amman, and in the Housing Bank Centre in Shmeisani.

If you wish to send a large parcel home by post you must first weigh the item at the Parcel Post Office, in an alleyway behind the central post office in downtown (it looks more like a shop, so look out for the weighing machine on the counter). Then take it unwrapped to the nearby Customs Office, diagonally opposite (look for the sign with the word 'Customs' in English on the crest), where a customs declaration must be completed. Then take the parcel back to the Parcel Post Office for packing and paying.

Central Post Office (Map p50; Al-Amir Mohammed St, downtown; ☺7.30am-5pm Sat-Thu, 8am-1.30pm Fri)

Customs Office (Map p50; ☺8am-2pm Thu-Sat) Diagonally opposite the Parcel Post Office.

Parcel Post Office (Map p50; Omar al-Khayyam St, downtown; ☺8am-3pm Mon-Thu & Sun, to 2pm Sat)

Telephone

There is no central telephone office in Amman. To make a local call, use a telephone in your hotel (ask the price and minimum call length before dialling), or one of the numerous payphones (see p313 for more information). Telephone cards are available at shops close to telephone booths and grocery stores around town.

The private telephone agencies around downtown are the cheapest places for international and domestic calls.

Communication International (Map p50; Nimer Bin Adwan St, downtown) charges 200 fils per minute to North America and Europe through a mobile phone.

Tourist Information

Ministry of Tourism & Antiquities (Map p56; ☎4603360, ext 254; fax 4646264; ground fl, Al-Mutanabbi St, Jebel Amman; ☺8am-9pm) The most useful place for information is this office, southwest of the 3rd Circle, which is also the centre for the tourist police. The staff is friendly, and speaks good English.

Wild Jordan Centre (Map p50; ☎4616523; www.rscn.org.jo; Othman Bin Affan St, downtown) Provides information and bookings for activities and accommodation in any of Jordan's nature reserves, including Dana and Wadi Mujib. The centre is run by the Royal Society for the Conservation of Nature (RSCN; see p297). There's also a small crafts shop and organic cafe here.

Visa Extensions

You must extend your visa if you wish to stay in Jordan longer. This is a relatively simple process but takes some paperwork – see p315 for details.

Al-Madeenah Police Station (Map p50; ☎4657788; 1st fl, Al-Malek Faisal St, downtown) Opposite the Arab Bank. Start the process of lodging your paperwork here.

Muhajireen Police Station (Markaz Amn Muhajireen; Map p56; Al-Ameerah Basma bin Talal Rd, downtown) West of the downtown area. Police stations are usually open for extensions from 10am to 3pm Saturday to Thursday, although it's best to go in the morning. Complete the process at this station.

ⓘ Getting There & Away

For information about international services to/from Amman, see p317.

Air

Amman is the main arrival and departure point for international flights, although some touch down in Aqaba as well.

The head office for **Royal Jordanian Airlines** (Map p58; ☎5100000; www.rj.com; Al-Malekah

Noor St, Shmeisani) is inconveniently located in the Housing Bank Centre (9th floor). There are more convenient offices in the **Jordan Inter-Continental** (Map p56; ☎4644267) and along Al-Malek al-Hussein St.

The Royal Jordanian subsidiary, **Royal Wings** (☎4895103; www.royalwings.com.jo), has an office at Marka Airport, but it's easier to book and confirm tickets at a Royal Jordanian office in town.

See p317 for contact details of airlines that fly to Amman.

Bus, Minibus & Service Taxis

There are two main bus and minibus stations in Amman, the north station (serving northern destinations and sometimes referred to as Tabarbour) and the south bus station (serving southern destinations and sometimes referred to as Wahadat).

In addition, there are smaller bus stations serving specific destinations such as the Dead Sea, as well as private coaches from the JETT and Trust offices.

Service taxis are generally faster, but they don't always follow fixed schedules. They depart from the same stations as the minibuses.

All departures are more frequent in the morning and most dry up completely after sunset.

MAIN PUBLIC BUS STATIONS

North Bus Station (Tabarbour) Located in the northern suburbs, this station offers services to the north. A taxi to this station from downtown costs from JD3. Fairly regular minibuses and service taxis leave between 7am and 6.30pm for the following destinations: Ajloun (900 fils, every 30 minutes, two hours), Jerash (800 fils, hourly, 1¼ hours) and Madaba (750 fils, every 10 minutes from 6am to 8pm, 45 minutes). Services are also available for Deir Alla (for Pella, one hour), Fuheis (45 minutes), Irbid (two hours), Ramtha (two hours), Salt (45 minutes) and Zarqa (for Azraq, 30 minutes); all these services cost under JD1.

There's also a daily airport bus (JD3, every 30 minutes from 6.15am to midnight, 45 minutes).

South Bus Station (Wahadat) Almost all buses and service taxis heading south leave from this station in the southern suburbs by Middle East Circle (Duwaar Sharq al-Awsat). A taxi to this station from downtown costs from JD2.500.

For Petra, minibuses and service taxis (JD5, four hours) depart for Wadi Musa when full from the far corner of the lot between around 7am and 4pm. Buses to Aqaba (JD5.500, five hours) leave every two hours or so until 9pm. There are regular buses to Karak (JD1.650, two hours) until 5pm, Shobak (JD4, 2½ hours) and Ma'an

(JD2.750, three hours). Most services stop running around 4pm.

For Dana there are three buses a day from 11am for Qadsiyya (JD3, three hours); otherwise take a bus to Tafila (JD2.550, 2½ hours) and change.

There are semiregular service taxis to Karak (JD3, 2½ hours), Ma'an (JD6, three hours) and also infrequently to Aqaba (JD10, five hours).

OTHER PUBLIC BUS STATIONS

The **Abdali Bus Station** (Map p56; Al-Malek al-Hussein St, Jebel Amman) is a 20-minute walk (2km uphill) from downtown; service taxi 6 or 7 from Cinema al-Hussein St goes right by. This is the station to use for air-conditioned buses and service taxis for international destinations, especially Syria (see p318). The bus station is transformed into a giant flea market on Fridays and there are plans to redevelop the entire site as part of an ambitious urban regeneration project.

The **Muhajireen Bus Station** (Map p56) is opposite the Muhajireen police station. Minibuses to Wadi as-Seer leave frequently from here during daylight hours (300 fils, 30 minutes). There are also services to Madaba and Mt Nebo (500 fils, 45 minutes) between 6am and 5pm.

Minibuses for the Dead Sea leave from here. There are no direct services: the route involves a minibus to Shuneh al-Janubiyyeh (South Shuna, JD1, 45 minutes) and then a wait for another minibus to Suweimah. At Suweimah, you'll have to hire a taxi or hitch for the last stretch. It has to be said that few will want to attempt this route, which is unreliable and can leave you stranded in the Jordan Valley. More recommendable is to take a taxi or a tour straight to the Dead Sea from one of the downtown hotels in Amman (or the Black Iris Hotel or Mariam Hotel in Madaba).

The **Raghadan Bus Station** (off Map p50) in downtown Amman is a few minutes' walk east of the Roman Theatre. It is mainly used for service taxis to surrounding suburbs although there is talk of widening the network with minibuses to nearby towns.

PRIVATE COACH STATIONS

The domestic **JETT office** (Map p58; 5664146; www.jett.com.jo; Al-Malek al-Hussein St, Shmeisani) is about 500m northwest of the Abdali bus station. Passengers board the bus outside the office. There are six buses daily to Aqaba (JD7.500, five hours, 7am, 9am, 11am, 2pm, 4pm and 6pm), and one bus to King Hussein Bridge (JD7.250, one hour, 7am), for entry into Israel and the Palestinian Territories. There are daily services to Irbid (JD1.900, every 30 minutes from 6am to 7.30pm, two hours).

A daily JETT bus connects Amman with Petra, largely designed for those wanting to visit on a day trip. The service leaves at 6.30am (single/return JD8/16, three hours) and drops passengers off at Petra Visitor Centre in Wadi Musa at 9.30am. The return bus leaves at 4pm so bear in mind this option leaves very little time for visiting the sites of Petra.

A weekly Jett bus departs for Amman Beach at the Dead Sea (single JD8) on Fridays at 8am and returns at 4pm. If there are insufficient passengers, however, the service is cancelled.

Trust International Transport (5813427) has daily buses to Aqaba (JD7, four daily, four hours) between 7.30am and 7pm. All buses leave from the office inconveniently located at 7th Circle, near the Safeway shopping centre. A taxi to/from downtown costs JD2.500 to JD3. Trust also has a **booking office** (Map p56; 4644627) at Abdali bus station. Other services, such as to Irbid and to Damascus in Syria, are sometimes on offer. Check with the office for current timings.

Hijazi Travel & Tours (02-724 0721) runs daily buses to Irbid (JD1.900, every 15 to 20 minutes from 6am to 7pm, 1½ hours). The buses leave from the North Bus Station.

Car

The transport chapter covers general information on driving in Jordan. Listed here are reliable local and international car-rental agencies. There are many more to choose from in King Abdullah Gardens (Map p58), where there is a collection of around 50 car-rental companies.

Avis (Map p58; 5699420, 24hr line 777-397405; www.avis.com.jo; King Abdullah Gardens, Shmeisani) Branches at the airport, Hotel Le Royal and Hotel InterContinental.

Budget (Map p58; 5698131; www.budget jordan.com; 125 Abdul Hameed Sharaf St, Shmeisani)

Europcar (Map p58; 5655581; www.europ car.jo; Isam Al-Ajlouni St, Shmeisani) Branches at Radisson SAS and King Abdullah Gardens.

Firas Car Rental (Map p56; 4612927; 1st Circle, Jebel Amman) The agent for Alamo Car Rental.

Hertz (Map p58; 5920926, 24hr line at airport 4711771; www.hertz.com; King Abdullah Gardens, Shmeisani) Offices at the airport, Grand Hyatt and Sheraton.

National Car Rental (Map p58; /fax 5601350, 24hr line 5591731; www.1stjordan. net/national/) Also has offices at Amman Marriott and Sheraton hotels.

Reliable Rent-a-Car (5929676; www.reliable.com.jo; 19 Fawzi al-Qawoaji St, Abdoun)

ⓘ Getting Around

To/From the Airports

Queen Alia International Airport is 35km south of the city. The **Airport Express Bus** (Map p56; ☑0880 022006, 4451531) runs between the airport and the North Bus Station (Tabarbour), passing through the 4th, 5th, 6th and 7th Circles en route. This service runs hourly between 7am and 11pm, and at 1am and 3am, from the airport daily. From Amman, it runs from at 6am to 10pm hourly and at 2am and 4am. Sariyah buses (JD3, 45 minutes) run every 30 minutes between 6.15am and midnight. From the airport, buses depart from outside the arrivals hall of Terminal 2. Buy your ticket from the booth at the door.

There are branches of **Avis** (☑5699420) and **Hertz** (☑4711771) and other car-rental companies. Those that don't have an office at the airport will meet you at the airport or otherwise will arrange for you to pick up a car from there.

The quickest and easiest way to reach the airport is by private taxi (JD20 to JD25 from downtown).

To get to Marka Airport, take a service taxi for 200 fils from Raghadan station.

Bus

Buses 26, 27, 28, 41 and 43 can be useful for getting to downtown – if you have the patience to wait and enough Arabic to communicate with the driver. Tickets cost around 70 fils.

For 7th Circle, take bus 41 or anything headed to Wadi as-Seer.

Taxi

PRIVATE TAXI

Private taxis are painted yellow. They are abundant, can be flagged from the side of the road and fares are cheap. A taxi from downtown to Shmeisani, for example, costs JD2.500 and it's JD3 to Tabarbour. For longer journeys around town, then you're best off agreeing a price per hour (JD10 was the current going rate at the time of writing).

SERVICE TAXI

These white cabs are shared taxis that stick to specific routes and are not permitted to leave the city limits. Fares cost from 350 fils per seat, and you usually pay the full amount regardless of where you get off. After 8pm, the price for all service taxis goes up by 25%.

There can be long queues at rush hour (8am to 9am and 5pm to 6pm). The cars queue up and usually start at the bottom of a hill – you get into the last car and unusually the whole line rolls back a car space and so on.

ⓘ TAKING A TAXI IN AMMAN

Only the brave or the foolhardy would sit behind the wheel in Amman, where driving is complicated by extremely complex roads twisting around the contours of the city's many hills, and is further made miserable by dense, unpredictable traffic. Buses are slow and unreliable and you need to be in the right place at the right time to rely on a service taxi. Without doubt, therefore, the best way of getting around is to do what the locals do and hop in a cab.

Most drivers of private taxis use the meter as a matter of course, but some may refuse to do so – or may simply refuse the ride. This is not necessarily indicative of an intention to overcharge: meter charges are set by the government and often don't reflect the realities of petrol price rises and the unprofitable business of waiting in long traffic queues, especially in congested downtown traffic.

If you're in town for a couple of days, it's well worth identifying a taxi driver who speaks English and who is used to working with tourists. These gear-stick warriors of the city have Knowledge to rival a London cabby, knowing every shortcut and unusual attraction in town and ensuring you don't get stuck for hours in a queue. They'll drop you off and pick you up at the time of your choice and if they're on another fare when you call, they'll often send a reliable friend. Many of these drivers are willing and able to take visitors on longer trips around Amman, to Jerash, the Dead Sea or the desert castles.

Ask at your hotel for a recommended driver or contact **Mosa Kanan** (☑079-9966621), a veteran English-speaking driver of Palestinian origin. With over 30 years of experience and an expert knowledge of tourist travel patterns, this taxi driver is highly recommended by many travellers. Another safe pair of hands is **Shawki Dahier** (☑079-5818993; shawki -drive@yahoo.com) who speaks excellent English and has similar experience in taking visitors on extended out-of-city tours. Both drivers cover destinations throughout Jordan.

SERVICE TAXI ROUTES

All departure points are listed on Map p50.

Service taxi 1 From Basman St for 4th Circle.

Service taxi 2 From Basman St for 1st and 2nd Circles.

Service taxi 3 From Basman St for 3rd and 4th Circles.

Service taxi 4 From the side street near the central post office for Jebel Weibdeh.

Service taxi 6 From Cinema al-Hussein St for the Ministry of the Interior Circle, past Abdali station and JETT international and domestic offices.

Service taxi 7 From Cinema al-Hussein St, up Al-Malek al-Hussein St, past Abdali station and King Abdullah Mosque, and along Suleiman al-Nabulsi St for Shmeisani.

Service taxis 25 & 26 From Italian St, downtown, to the top of Jebel al-Ashrafiyeh and near Abu Darwish Mosque.

Service taxi 27 From Italian St to Middle East Circle for Wahadat station.

Service taxi 35 From opposite the Amman Palace Hotel, passing close to the Muhajireen Police Station.

Service taxi 38 From downtown to Makkah al-Mukarramah Rd.

AROUND AMMAN

With the exception of downtown, uncovering remnants of the ancients is no easy task in Amman as the capital is largely a 20th century creation. However, you don't have to look far beyond the city limits for historical reminders of the country's illustrious past. Indeed, the outskirts of the capital are home to Roman ruins, biblical landmarks, Byzantine churches and Ottoman structures, all of which are set against beautiful landscapes that are a world apart from the streets of Amman. All of the destinations listed in this section can be reached on a half-day trip from Amman.

Wadi as-Seer & Iraq al-Amir   وادي السير & عراق الأمير

West of the capital lies the fertile Wadi as-Seer, standing in marked contrast to the treeless plateau surrounding Amman. The stream-fed valley is lined with cypress trees, and dotted with fragrant orchards and olive groves. In the springtime, particularly April and May, as-Seer plays host to spectacular wildflower blooms that include the Jordanian national flower, the black iris.

The village itself, which is largely Circassian in origin, is now virtually part of sprawling western Amman. However, there still remains a sense of distinct community, especially in the Ottoman stone buildings

and mosque that lie at the centre of the village. The main attractions of the area, however, lie further down the wadi.

About 4km past Wadi as-Seer, on the road to the village of Iraq al-Amir, you can spot part of an ancient **Roman aqueduct** (Map p78). Shortly past the aqueduct, look up to the hillside on the left to a facade cut into the rock. Known as **Ad-Deir** (monastery; Map p78), it most likely served as an elaborate medieval dovecote.

If you continue for a further 6km, you'll come to the caves of **Iraq al-Amir** (Caves of the Prince). The caves are arranged in two tiers – the upper tier forms a long gallery (partially damaged during a mild earthquake in 1999) along the cliff face. The 11 caves were once used as cavalry stables, though locals have taken to using them to house their goats and store fodder. Steps lead up to the caves from the paved road – keep an eye out for the ancient Hebrew inscription near the entrance.

Opposite the caves is the village of Iraq al-Amir, home to the **Iraq al-Amir Handicraft Village** (Map p78; ☻8am-4pm, closed Fri), selling handmade pottery, fabrics, carpets and paper products. The project was founded by the Noor al-Hussein Foundation, and employs many women from the surrounding area. Profits are returned to the community.

About 700m further down the road, just visible from the caves, is the small but impressive **Qasr al-Abad** (Palace of the Slave; admission free; ☻daylight hours). Despite

Around Amman

Around Amman

appearances and indeed its name, it was most likely built as a fortified villa rather than a military fort. Its precise age isn't known, though it's thought that it was built by Hyrcanus of the powerful Jewish Tobiad family sometime between 187 and 175 BC. Although never completed, much of the palace has been reconstructed, and it remains an impressive site.

The palace was built from some of the biggest blocks of any ancient structure in the Middle East – the largest is 7m by 3m. The blocks were only 20cm or so thick, making the whole edifice quite flimsy, and susceptible to the earthquake that flattened it in AD 362. Today, the setting and the animal carvings on the exterior walls are the highlights. Look for the carved panther fountain on the ground floor, the eroded eagles on the corners and the lioness with cubs on the upper storey of the back side.

The gatekeeper will open the interior, as well as a small museum (which includes drawings of what the complex once looked like) for a tip of JD1. If he's not around, ask for the *miftah* (key) at the small shop near the gate.

ⓘ Getting There & Away

Minibuses leave regularly from the **Muhajireen bus station** (Map p56; Al-Ameerah Basma bin Talal St, Amman) for Wadi as-Seer village (300 fils, 30 minutes) and less frequently from the Raghadan bus station (off Map p50) in downtown. From Wadi as-Seer, take another minibus – or walk about 10km, mostly downhill – to the caves. Look for the signpost to the Iraq al-Amir Handicraft Village, which is virtually opposite the stairs to the caves. Alternatively take bus 26 from Shabsough St in downtown to its terminus and then change to a bus for Wadi as-Seer or take a taxi. From the caves, it's an easy stroll down to the *qasr* (but a little steep back up).

If you're driving, head west from 8th Circle and follow the main road, which twists through Wadi as-Seer village.

Cave of Seven Sleepers (Ahl al-Kahf) أهل الكهف

The legend of the 'seven sleepers' has several parallels throughout literature. It involves seven Christian boys who were persecuted by the Roman Emperor Trajan, then escaped to a cave and slept there for 309 years. This is one of several locations (the most famous being Ephesus in Turkey) that claim to be that cave. Inside the **main cave** (Map p78; admission free; ⊙8am-6pm) – also known as Ahl al-Kahf (Cave of the People) – are eight smaller tombs that are sealed, though one has a hole in it through which you can see a creepy collection of human bones. Above and below the cave are the remains of two mosques. About 500m west of the cave is a large Byzantine cemetery, the tombs of which are sadly full of rubbish.

The cave is to the right of a large new mosque complex in the village of Rajib, off the road from Amman to Sabah. Buses from Amman to Sabah pass 500m from the mosque; catch them at Wahadat bus station (less than 500 fils, 15 minutes). Alternatively, take a minibus from Quraysh St in downtown, ask for 'al-Kahf' and the driver will show you where to get off to change for a Sabah bus. The easiest way there is by chartered taxi (around JD8 each way).

Fuheis فحيص

🎵06 / POP >5000 / ELEV 1050M

Just 15km northwest of Amman, this pleasant village is famous for fruit growing and, somewhat incongruously, cement production. First built in about 2000 BC, Fuheis is now a largely Christian village, with several Orthodox and Catholic churches. The main reason for a visit, however, is to have lunch or dinner in the town's celebrated restaurant.

The Jordanian cuisine at the **Zuwwadeh Restaurant** (🎵4721528; mains JD6-14; ⊙10am-midnight) is delicious, especially the *fatteh* (fried bread) with hummus, meat or chicken and pine nuts – the 'wedding *fatteh*' is complemented by tomato and cardamom. You can choose between shady outdoor tables or an intimate indoor dining area, and most nights there are live oud performances upstairs (after 7pm). Highly popular with locals and discerning expats from Amman, the ambience is lively and warm, helped much by the jovial, attentive staff.

ⓘ Getting There & Away

Fuheis is easy to reach by minibus from Abdali bus station (Map p56) in Amman (500 fils, 40 minutes). The town is also connected to Wadi as-Seer, making it possible to visit both destinations as a day trip from Amman. If you're dining at the restaurant, it's best to pre-arrange a chartered taxi back to Amman for around JD10.

The minibus stop in the older Al-Rawaq neighbourhood (also known as *il-balad*) is at a roundabout, close to the Zuwwadeh Restaurant and marked by a statue of St George (known locally as Giorgis) slaying a dragon.

Jerash, Irbid & the Jordan Valley

جرش & إربد & الشمال

Best Places to Stay

Best Places to Eat

Why Go?

You might expect that the far north of Jordan, with its exceptional Roman ruins, biblical associations, lively cities and complex terrain, would feature as a standard part of any visitor's trip to the country. This, however, is not the case and the region receives relatively few visitors compared with Petra and the south. For those in the know, this is excellent news as it means that it is quite possible to enjoy epic sites like Jerash without the epic crowds normally associated with a world-class destination.

Although many of the sites can be covered in a day trip from Amman, this ancient and populous region, dotted with olive groves and pine forests and liberally strewn with the ruins of Rome's great Decapolis cities, repays a longer visit. The availability of public transport and friendly accommodation facilitate this and if the springtime flowers happen to be blooming, it will prove to be a hard region to leave.

When to Go

The natural time to visit the northern part of Jordan is in spring (March to mid-May) when the black iris, the country's national flower, puts in a shy appearance along roadsides and a profusion of knee-high wildflowers spill across the semiarid hillsides.

For culture vultures, the hot summer months of July and August bring music and poetry to the Roman ruins in the Jerash Festival of Culture & the Arts.

From early November to January, while the region's hill towns shiver through winter, sub-tropical fruits ripen in the Jordan Valley.

History

When travelling around the far north of Jordan, you may notice the name 'Gilead' crop up from time to time. This was the region's name in biblical times, defined by the sculpting waters of the Yarmouk River to the north and the once-mighty River Jordan to the west. The hills of Gilead have been occupied since antiquity, and were once home to the Roman Decapolis. Largely established during the Hellenistic period, these 10 city-states flourished along the boundaries of the Greek and Semitic lands. The Romans transformed these cities into powerful trading centres – the torchbearers of Roman culture at the furthest reaches of the empire.

If you're wondering where these cities are today, chances are you are walking on them! Northern Jordan is the most densely populated area in the country, and is home to the major urban centre of Irbid as well as dozens of small towns and villages which have largely engulfed many of the ancient sites. With a bit of amateur investigation it's easy to make out the ancient tells (mounds) and archaeological remains of the Decapolis, scattered among Gilead's rolling hills. If you haven't the time or inclination for such sleuthing, just head for Umm Qais (Gadara), Pella and most especially Jerash, where there are enough clues among the standing columns, amphitheatres and mosaic floors to conjure the full pomp and splendour of the Roman past.

Nature Reserves

There are two reserves in the north of Jordan, both encompassing rare woodland. **Ajloun Forest Reserve** (p93) is the more developed of the two, with excellent hiking trails and accommodation options. **Dibeen Forest Reserve** (p91) is a popular spot for weekend picnics.

Dangers & Annoyances

This region is bordered by Israel and the Palestinian Territories to the west and by Syria to the north. Given the sensitivity of relations between these countries, a bit of discretion is advised when travelling near the Yarmouk or Jordan Valleys. There are many checkpoints, particularly around the convergence of those two valleys near Umm Qais so, it is imperative to carry your passport and, if driving, your licence and car-rental details. Don't hike too close to either border. Avoid taking photographs near the border area – this includes photographing the River Jordan near checkpoints.

Northern Highlights

1 Wander the colonnaded streets of **Jerash** (p83), a spectacularly well-preserved Roman provincial city

2 Hike along the trails of **Ajloun Forest Reserve** (p93) in the shade of trees

3 Visit the fairy-tale castle of **Qala'at ar-Rabad** (p92), one of Jordan's most impressive Islamic structures

4 Survey views of three countries from the basalt ruins of **Umm Qais** (p101)

5 Conjure all eras of Jordanian history at the complex archaeological site of **Pella** (p104)

6 Peruse the exhibits at the **Museum of Archaeology & Anthropology** (p96), within the vibrant campus of Yarmouk University in Irbid

7 Travel the subtropical **Jordan Valley** (p100), sampling seasonal fruits

8 Scoop water from the River Jordan at **Bethany** (p109), where Jesus was reputedly baptised

9 Amble by traditional houses in the souq town of **Salt** (p106) and discover how the town came by its name

ℹ Getting There & Away

Amman is the gateway to the north so most public transport from other regions transits through the capital, though there are connections from Madaba and Aqaba directly to Irbid. There are four international borders in the north with public transport to Israel and the Palestinian Territories and Syria. See the Overland Travel chapter for a full account of all border crossings. By car, you can enter the region either via Jerash from Amman or along the Jordan Valley from the Dead Sea.

ℹ Getting Around

Compared with other parts of Jordan, the north is well-served by public transport. Minibuses link most towns and villages and run at irregular intervals along the Jordan Valley. A bit of patience is required waiting for buses to fill up and forget trying to establish the 'correct fare'; that said, no journey in the north is likely to cost more than JD1. Driving in this region requires a few navigational skills as promising rural roads often lead to dead ends due to steep-sided wadis.

JERASH & AROUND

Often referred to as the 'Pompeii of Asia', the ruins at Jerash (known in Roman times as Gerasa) are one of Jordan's major attractions, and one of the Middle East's best examples of a Roman provincial city. Remarkably well preserved through the centuries by the dry desert air, Jerash comprises a collection of triumphal arches, two amphitheatres, a hippodrome where live chariot races are conducted each day, temples and a spectacular colonnaded forum. Whether you're an aspiring archaeologist, an admirer of the ancients, or simply a visitor looking for a morning's diversion, the ruins at Jerash cannot fail to impress.

Although the ruins are the undoubted key attraction in the area, there is more to Jerash (which also comprises a thriving modern town) and the surrounding area than just the ruins. Nearby Ajloun, for instance, has a grand castle and offers hiking trails, picnic opportunities and lots of places to buy fresh

THE DECAPOLIS

The Roman commercial cities within modern Jordan, Syria and Israel and the Palestinian Territories became known collectively as the Decapolis in the 1st century AD. Despite the etymology of the word, it seems that the Decapolis consisted of more than 10 cities, and possibly as many as 18 (Decaoctodecapolis?!). The league of cities served to unite Roman possessions and to enhance commerce in the region. In Jordan the main Decapolis cities were Philadelphia (Amman), Gadara (Umm Qais), Gerasa (Jerash), Pella (Taqabat Fil), and possibly Abila (Qweilbeh) and Capitolias (Beit Ras, near Irbid).

Rome helped facilitate the growth of the Decapolis by granting the cities a measure of political autonomy, within the protective sphere of Rome. Each city operated more like a city-state, maintaining jurisdiction over the surrounding countryside and even minting its own coins. Indeed, coins from Decapolis cities often used words such as 'autonomous', 'free' and 'sovereign' to emphasise their self-governing status.

The cities may have enjoyed semi-autonomy but they were still recognisably Roman, rebuilt with gridded streets and well-funded public monuments. A network of Roman roads facilitated the transport of goods from one city to the next, and the wheel ruts of carriages and chariots can still be seen in the paving stones at Umm Qais and Jerash. The so-called 'imperial cult', which revolved around mandatory worship of the Roman emperor, helped unify the cities in the Decapolis while simultaneously ensuring that its residents didn't forget the generosity of their Roman benefactors.

Wandering the streets of the ruined cities today, it's easy to imagine life 2000 years ago: the centre bustling with shops and merchants, and lined with cooling water fountains and dramatic painted facades. The empty niches would have been filled with painted statues; buildings clad in marble and decorated with carved peacocks and shell motifs; and churches topped with Tuscan-style terracotta-tiled roofs.

The term 'Decapolis' fell out of use when Emperor Trajan annexed Arabia in the 2nd century AD although the sister cities continued to maintain connections with one another for another 400 years. Their eventual demise was heralded by the conquest of the Levant in 641 by the Umayyads. Political, religious and commercial interests shifted to Damascus, marginalising the cities of the Decapolis to such an extent that they never recovered.

fruit from the surrounding hillside orchards. As such, although Jerash is usually visited as a day trip from Amman, there's more than enough of interest in the area to warrant at least one overnight stop.

Jerash
جرش

🚗 U2 / POP 123,190 / ELEV 618M

Arriving in the modern town of Jerash today, with its provincial streets and small market gardens, there's little to suggest its illustrious past. But the moment you cross from the new town into the ancient city boundaries, marked by the imposing Hadrian's Arch, it becomes immediately apparent that this was once no ordinary backwater but a city of great wealth and importance. And how did Jerash, which was never on a major trade route, come to be so important? The answer lies in the soil. Whatever route you take to reach the town of Jerash, and at whatever time of year, you will pass the ubiquitous fruit stalls that characterise the area. Figs, apples, plums, berries, and most especially olives all grow prodigiously in the surrounding hillsides and the surplus of crops helps the local farming communities to prosper just as in ancient times.

Jerash is cleaved in two by a deep and cultivated wadi. Today, as in Roman times, the bulk of the town's inhabitants live on the eastern side of the wadi. The walled city on the west side of the wadi, graced with grand public monuments, baths and fountains, was reserved for administrative, commercial, civic and religious activities. The two were once linked by causeways and processional paths and magnificent gates marked the entrance. Access to the remains of this walled city today is through the most southerly gate, known as Hadrian's Gate or the Arch of Triumph.

While there are certainly other surviving Roman cities that boast similar architectural treasures, the ancient ruins at Jerash are famous for their remarkable state of preservation. Enough structures remain intact for archaeologists and historians, and even the casual visitor, to piece together ancient life under the rule of an emperor.

History

Although inhabited from Neolithic times, and settled as a town during the reign of Alexander the Great (333 BC), Jerash was largely a Roman creation and well-preserved remains of all the classic Roman structures – forum, cardo maximus, hippodrome, nymphaeum – are easily distinguishable among the ruins. If you need a refresher course on key technical terms before you reach the site, see the boxed text (p338) and you'll soon remember your pediments from your porticos.

Following General Pompey's conquest of the region in 64 BC, Gerasa became part of the Roman province of Syria, and then a city of the Decapolis. Over the next two centuries, trade with the Nabataeans (of Petra fame) flourished, and the city grew extremely wealthy, thanks to local agriculture and iron-ore mining. In the 1st century AD the city was remodelled on the grid system with a colonnaded main north-south street (cardo maximus – one of the great highlights of the site today) intersected by two side streets running east-west.

The city was further enhanced in AD 106, under Emperor Trajan, and the triumphal arch at the far southern end of the city (through which the site is accessed today) was constructed in AD 129 to mark the important occasion of Emperor Hadrian's visit. Jerash's fortunes peaked around the beginning of the 3rd century, when it was bestowed with the rank of Colony and boasted a population of 15,000 to 20,000 inhabitants.

The city declined with a devastating earthquake in 747 and its population shrank to about one-quarter of its former size. Thereafter, apart from a brief occupation by a Crusader garrison in the 12th century, the city was completely deserted until the arrival of the Circassians from Russia in 1878. The site's archaeological importance was quickly realised, heralding over a century of excavation and restoration and the revival of a new town on the eastern flank of the ruins.

⊙ Sights

The ruins at Jerash cover a huge area and can seem daunting at first, especially as there is virtually no signage. To help the ruins come alive, engage one of the knowledgeable guides (JD20) at the ticket checkpoint to help you navigate the main complex. Alternatively, visit the main structures in the sequence in which they're presented below. The whole route, walking at a leisurely pace and allowing time for sitting on a fallen column and enjoying the spectacular views, takes a minimum of three to four hours; two opportunities are suggested following, however, to cut the visit short.

0   200 m
0   0.1 miles

To Irbid (42km)

8

Synagogue
Church

Church of
Bishop
Isaiah   9   10

Church
of Bishop
Genesius

**Temple of
Artemis**   16

Church of St John
the Baptist   3   12

Church of
St George   Courtyard
of the Fountain   11   Propylaeum Church

2

Church of
St Theodore

Umayyad
Houses

Church of St
Peter & St Paul   South Decumanus

14

Mortuary
Church   4

Market

1

**Forum
(Oval Plaza)**   7

**South
Theatre**   15

13

Upper
Temple
of Zeus   20

18   22

6

Hippodrome

21   5

17

19

To Buses to Amman (100m);
Amman (52km)

(Colonnaded Street)

Cardo Maximus

Al-Qayrawan St

Al-Malek Abdullah St

Bab Amman St

Jerash

The entrance to the site is south of the ancient city, close to Hadrian's Arch. The **ticket office** (☎6351272; admission JD8; ⊗8am-4.30pm Oct-Apr, to 7pm May-Sep) is in a modern souq with souvenir and antique shops, a post office and a semi-traditional coffeehouse. Keep your ticket as you will have to show it at the South Gate.

Hadrian's Arch　　MONUMENTAL GATEWAY
There's no better way of gaining a sense of the pomp and splendour of Rome than walking through the triumphal, 13m-tall Hadrian's Arch at the entrance to Jerash. Don't be tempted to bypass the gate by nipping up the neighbouring slope or you will miss the intentional framing of the city from the top of the arch steps. From here you can see a honey-coloured assortment of columns and walls, some delicately carved with acanthus leaves, some solid and practical, extending all the way to a pale view of hills in the distance – just as the Roman architects intended.

Built to honour the visiting Emperor Hadrian, the gateway was originally twice this height and encompassed three enormous wooden doors.

Hippodrome　　STADIUM
Stepping through the arch, you can begin to hear the pounding of horse's hooves and the creak of wooden wheels. Chances are you are not imagining the chariot races that

once took place in the hippodrome on your left, but hearing the sound of the twice daily re-enactment (see the boxed text, p86). The show, a joint Swedish-Jordanian venture, has become one of the highlights of a modern visit to the ancient city and is simply too good to miss. It begins with the parading of 40 Roman legionnaires (Jordanian special forces) who complete a range of military drills, from the tortoise manoeuvre to the use of a catapult, and is followed by gladiators fighting it out with tridents, nets and *gladius* (swords) and four chariots racing seven laps around the hippodrome's central wooden *spina*.

Even if you miss the show, it's still worth sitting on the bleachers above the hippodrome and imagining the roar of the crowd. Built sometime between the 1st and 3rd centuries AD, this ancient sports field (244m by 50m) was once surrounded by seating for up to 15,000 spectators, 30 times the current seating capacity, and hosted mainly athletics competitions and chariot races. Recent excavations have unearthed remains of stables and pottery workshops, plus indications that it was used for polo by invading Sassanians from Persia during the early 7th century.

South Gate　　MONUMENTAL GATEWAY
From the hippodrome, stroll the 200m to the South Gate, which was most likely constructed in AD 130, and originally served as

DON'T MISS

SALUTE THE TROOPS AT JERASH'S CHARIOT RACE

Have you ever considered how and why Rome managed to conquer the lands of the Middle East so easily? Pay a visit to the spectacular ruins at Jerash, and you may just find the answer.

The answer doesn't lie in the ruins of empire scattered around the site but in the novel re-enactment, held twice daily at the hippodrome. Bringing entertainment back to the playing field for the first time in 1500 years, the **Roman Army & Chariot Experience** (www.jerashchariots.com; admission JD12; ⊙shows 11am & 2pm Sat-Wed, 11am Fri) is faithful to history, right down to the Latin commands.

Visitors will have a chuckle at the lively repartee of the master of ceremonies, one Adam Al-Samadi, otherwise known as Gaius Victor. Dressed as a Roman legionnaire with a feather pluming from his helmet, he stands erect like a true centurion. 'Salute the troops,' he demands in a cockney English accent as he hitches his tunic and raises a spear to the amassed veterans of the Jordan army – in their new uniform of the Sixth Roman Legion.

'These men,' Gaius says imperiously to the huddled audience on the bleachers, 'they didn't want to die in some godforsaken battlefield. They wanted to go home to their wives and mistresses in civilised Rome and draw their pensions.' That's why, he argues, the Roman soldiers were the best in the world: 'Get in, get out, stop messing about – eight minutes of fighting, then fresh men for the next eight minutes of fighting.'

A trundle of soldiers shuffles into formation and slams down gleaming shields; they advance across the arena like a gleaming, metal-plated, human tank, impervious to the lances of the leather-clad natives – if rather more vulnerable to the giggles from spectators. 'So Gaius Victor,' I ask after the show. 'What is it that makes such an erudite fellow like you do a job like this?' 'Call it bread and circuses,' he says. 'That's what kept people happy under the Romans and I guess that's what keeps us happy today.'

That sounds like a logical enough answer, but then his eyes mist over and he adds: 'You know, there's the moment in the performance when you say "Salute the troops" and watch them salute you back. To this day, it gives me a thrill that I can't explain.' Forget the disciplined armies; forget the orderly organisation of labour and provisions – local people fell under the magic of Rome. As a spare soldier blasts the horn from atop Jerash's triumphal arch, his scarlet cloak furling behind him and the flag of Jordan blowing in the wind, it's easy to see how.

Jenny Walker

one of four entrances along the city walls. Along the way you can see how the Roman city, then as now, spilt over both sides of Wadi Jerash, with most of the residential area lying to the east of the wadi.

The visitor's centre (see p91) is on the right before you reach the gate and this is the place to hire a guide, or have a drink in the site's only restaurant before entering the city proper. One square kilometre of the city is encased by the 3m-thick, 3.5km-long boundary walls.

Don't forget to look up as you pass under the South Gate: like Hadrian's Arch, the columns bear elaborately carved acanthus-leaf decorations and would once have supported three wooden doors. Framed by the archway is the first hint of the splendours ahead – the columns of the forum start appearing in ever greater profusion as you walk towards them.

Vaulted Gallery
MUSEUM

As tempting as it is to make a beeline for the forum, veer instead into the vaulted passageway, under the courtyard of the Temple of Zeus. When your eyes become accustomed to the gloom, you'll see a superb display of columns, pediments and masonry carved with grapes, pomegranates and acanthus leaves. This is a good place to swat up on the three main column styles; Doric, Ionic and Corinthian. But it is the gallery that is worth seeing: the legacy of Rome has endured because of the 'built to last' quality of each structure. Take a look at the model of the Temple of Zeus here as it will help to recreate the ruins in your mind later.

Forum
ROMAN PLAZA

The stairs outside the gallery lead to one of the highlights of Jerash. Whatever the light, whatever the weather, the forum, with its organ-pipe columns arranged around an unusual oval-shaped plaza, is always breathtaking. This immense space (90m long and 80m at its widest point) in the heart of the city, linking the main thoroughfare (the cardo maximus) with the Temple of Zeus, served as a marketplace and the main locus of the city's social and political life. Today it still draws the crowds, with Jordanian families picnicking and site guards napping among the columns.

And what superb columns they are! Constructed in the middle of the 1st century AD, the forum is surrounded by 56 unfluted Ionic columns, each constructed from four solid cuts of stone that appear double in number because of their shadow. The plaza itself is just as spectacular, paved with extremely high-quality limestone slabs. The slabs, which increase in size as they radiate from the middle, create a sense of vortex that draws your eye to the centre point. To appreciate this effect fully, you need an aerial view which can be gained from climbing the steps to the Temple of Zeus.

Temple of Zeus
TEMPLE

Built in AD 162 over the remains of an earlier Roman temple, the Temple of Zeus was once approached by a magnificent monumental stairway, leading from the *temenos* (sacred courtyard). Today lizards sun themselves in the cracks of pavement, oblivious of the holy sacrifices that used to take place here. The temple, on the summit of the hill, towers above the city. Enough of this once-beautiful building remains, despite erosion and earthquakes, to understand its former importance.

A path leads from the *temenos* to the temple, via a welcome stand of trees. You can pause here for a panorama of the forum and a small hill of pines (home to the site museum). As you walk from the trees to the temple, notice the intricate friezes of floral and figurative motifs unearthed by French excavations. The delicacy of the design contrasts strikingly with the massive size of the building blocks that comprise the inner sanctum of the temple.

South Theatre
ROMAN AMPHITHEATRE

It is a short walk from the temple to the neighbouring South Theatre. Entering through a wooden door between the arches, there's little to suggest the treasure encased by the plain exterior. But then suddenly you emerge in the upper seating of the theatre and you can't help but be impressed. Built between AD 81 and 96 and once housing 5000 spectators amid two storeys of seating (only one tier of which remains), the theatre is almost perfect.

Sit in Row 30 of the 32 rows of seats (if you can read the Greek numbers) and you'll see how the elaborately decorated stage is just a foreground for the backdrop of ancient and modern Jerash. At sunset, the lighting melts the stage surface. Cue music? That's provided by the visitors who whisper experimental choruses and the members of the Jordanian Scottish bagpipe band who, with less subtlety, blast sporadic tunes to the four winds to illustrate the excellent acoustics.

The theatre comes into its own during the **Jerash Festival of Culture & Arts** (see the boxed text, p90) when it proves as worthy a venue today as it was to the ancients two thousand years ago.

South Decumanus
STREET

If the heat is proving a challenge, or you're experiencing ruin fatigue, descend from the theatre to the forum and exit the way you entered. It's about a 10-minute walk back to Hadrian's Gate. If you have energy to spare, keep to the high ground and follow the path from the theatre towards the Temple of Artemis. On the way, you'll notice a double colonnade to your right formed by the South Decumanus, or main east-west access. At the end of this line of sight is a modern mosque, a fitting reminder of how Jordan has embraced many different religions over the years and continues to tolerate different forms of worship to this day.

Tolerance was not always a given, as you'll see if you take the left fork up to what might be termed 'Church Hill', where a number of churches lie in ruins.

Church of St Cosmos & St Damianus
CHURCH

When Christianity became the official state religion under Emperor Constantine in AD 324, all Roman monuments that were tainted by so-called pagan practices were quickly abandoned. These structures were subsequently pilfered for building materials as Roman cities competed with one another to build glorious churches and cathedrals in the name of 'the Lord'. As testament to the

Byzantine presence in Jerash, a total of 15 churches have been uncovered among the ruins, with many more thought to be in the vicinity.

The Church of St Cosmos & St Damianus (look for a complex with four bulbous columns and a thick outer wall) is one of the best-preserved of these churches. Consecrated in 533 in memory of twin brothers – both doctors, who devoted themselves to the care of the poor and the needy, and who were martyred during the reign of Diocletian – the church boasts the best-preserved mosaics at Jerash. Stand above the retaining wall and you can clearly make out zoomorphic figures, geometric designs and medical symbols. Some of the mosaics from this church are now housed in the Museum of Popular Traditions (p53) in Amman.

Continue up hill and just before you reach the great temple in front of you, sit on the stone sarcophagus nearby and survey the view: this is one of the best vantage points in Jerash, showing the extent of the ruins from North Gate to Hadrian's Gate.

Temple of Artemis TEMPLE

If you're lucky enough to visit Jerash on a partially cloudy day, you're in for a treat as the sandstone pillars of the magnificent Temple of Artemis light up like bars of liquid gold each time the sun comes out of the clouds. It's a magical sight, and magic, or the sense of the world beyond, was exactly what the architects of this gem of a building would have been trying to capture in temple design.

Dedicated to Artemis, the goddess of hunting and fertility, and the daughter of Zeus, the temple (deservedly one of the most photographed buildings of the ancient city) was built between AD 150 and 170, and flanked by 12 elaborately carved Corinthian columns, 11 of which are still standing. The construction of the temple is particularly impressive given that large vaults, housing temple treasure, had to be built to the north and south to make the courtyard level. The whole of the building was once clad in shimmering marble and prized statues of Artemis would have adorned the niches.

Alas, the edict of Theodorius in AD 386, permitting the dismantling of pagan temples, led to the demise of this once-grand edifice as the temple was picked apart for materials to construct new churches. The Byzantines further disgraced the site by converting it into a mere artisan workshop for kitchenware and crockery. In the 12th century the structure was temporarily brought back to life as an Arab fortification, only to be destroyed by the invading Crusaders.

If the wanton destruction gets the better of you, this is another good place to cut and run. You can descend through the **propylaeum**, built in 150 AD as the monumental gateway to the Temple of Artemis, and originally flanked by shops. From here, it is a 20-minute walk along the cardo maximus to Hadrian's Gate. Alternatively, if you want to get a sense of the complete extent of Jerash, head towards the North Gate and be rewarded by one or two extra surprises.

North Theatre ROMAN AMPHITHEATRE

Just downhill from the Temple of Artemis, partially hidden by the hill, is the beautiful little North Theatre. Built in about AD 165 and enlarged in 235, it was most likely used for government meetings rather than artistic performances. Originally it had 14 rows of seats with two vaulted passageways leading to the front of theatre, as well as five internal arched corridors leading to the upper rows.

Like many of the grand monuments at Jerash, the North Theatre was destroyed by earthquakes and then partially dismantled for later Byzantine and Umayyad building projects. However, in recent years it has been magnificently restored and still maintains a capacity of about 2000 people. Take a seat in the lower rows, and you'll be in good company: many of the seats are inscribed with the names of the delegates who voted in the city council. The theatre may not have been used for performances but there's still plenty of rhythm in the design details, with round niches and inverted scallop shells, and exuberant carvings of musicians and dancers at the base of the stairs. Exit stage left and head for the North Gate.

North Gate MONUMENTAL GATEWAY

Built in about AD 115, the North Gate forms an impressive full stop at the northern limit of the ruins. Commissioned by Claudius Severus, who was responsible for building the road to Pella, it still makes a fine, if somewhat neglected, frame for the cardo maximus which stretches in all its glory along the entire length of the ancient walled city.

If you've reached the North Gate, you deserve a pat on the back because very few visitors bother to walk this far. The good news is it's all downhill from here on the 35-minute nonstop walk back to Hadrian's Gate; if you want to savour the many monuments on the way, however, it will take at least an hour.

Cardo Maximus   STREET
Jerash's superb colonnaded cardo maximus is straight in the way that only a Roman road can be straight, ignoring all of the natural bends and contours of the landscape that may have suggested a more serpentine approach. This is one of Jerash's great highlights and the opportunity to walk along its entire 800m length from North Gate to forum well rewards the effort.

Built in the 1st century AD and complete with manholes to underground drainage, the street was redesigned and rebuilt several times and bears the hallmarks of the city's principal street, with the ruts worn by thousands of chariots scored into the original flagstones. The 500 columns that once lined the street were deliberately built at an uneven height to complement the facades of the buildings that once stood behind them. Although most of the columns you see today were reassembled in the 1960s, they give an excellent impression of this spectacular thoroughfare.

There are many buildings of interest on either side of the cardo maximus, in various states of restoration and ruin. From north to south, the highlights include the **northern tetrapylon** (archway with four entrances), built over the intersection with the **north decumanus** (one of two main streets running east to west); rebuilt in 2000, it was probably designed as a gateway to the North Theatre.

Western (and Eastern) Baths   BATHHOUSE
Beside the intersection, on the eastern side of the cardo maximus, lie the earthquake-stricken remains of the **Western Baths** – once an impressive complex of hot- *(calidarium)*, warm- *(tepidarium)* and cold-water *(frigidarium)* baths. In Roman times, public bathing fulfilled the role of a social club (much as Jordan's modern bathhouses do today), and attracted a wide variety of people who gathered to exchange news and gossip as well as to enjoy music, lectures and performances. Dating from the 2nd century AD, the Western Baths represent one of the earliest examples of a dome atop a square room.

The **Eastern Baths** lie outside the gated city on the other side of the wadi in the modern town of Jerash. They are lit up at night and are interestingly juxtaposed with a modern mosque.

Nymphaeum   FOUNTAIN
After the stairway leading to the Temple of Artemis, on the western side of the cardo maximus is the elegant nymphaeum, the main ornamental fountain of the city that was dedicated to the water nymphs. Built in about AD 191, the two-storey construction was elaborately decorated, faced with marble slabs on the lower level, plastered on the upper level and topped with a half dome. Water would cascade over the facade into a large pool at the front, with the overflow pouring out through seven carved lions' heads into drains in the street below.

Although it's been quite some time since water poured forth from the nymphaeum, the well-preserved structure remains one of the highlights of Jerash. Several finely sculpted Corinthian columns still frame the fountain, and there is a lovely pink-granite basin at its base, which was probably added by the Byzantines. At one point the entire structure was capped by a semi-dome in the shape of a shell, and you can still make out the elaborate capitals lining the base of the ceiling.

Cathedral   CHURCH
Next to the nymphaeum, an elaborate staircase rises from the cardo maximus to the city's only cathedral. Little more than a modest Byzantine church, it was constructed in the second half of the 4th century on the site of earlier temples. At the height of its glory, the cathedral consisted of a soaring basilica supported by three naves, and boasted a magnificent portal that was finely decorated with elaborate marble carvings.

Southern Tetrapylon   MONUMENT
Marking the intersection with the **south decumanus**, this four-pillared structure is in good repair. Nearby on the western side of the cardo maximus is the **agora** or **macellum**, where people gathered for public meetings around the central fountain.

Museum   MUSEUM
(☏6312267; admission free; ⊙8.30am-6pm Oct-Apr, to 5pm May-Sep) Before you finish exploring the ancient city, visit the small museum just above the forum. It houses a small but worthwhile selection of artefacts from the site, such as mosaics, glass, gold jewellery and coins found in a tomb near Hadrian's Arch. Almost as good as the exhibits is the view the hill affords of Jerash, ancient and modern, spread either side of the town's defining wadi.

WORTH A TRIP

JERASH FESTIVAL OF CULTURE & ARTS

If you happen to be in Jordan in the middle of summer, it's worth catching a show in one of the Roman amphitheatres. Since 1981 the ancient city of Jerash has hosted the annual **Jerash Festival of Culture & Arts** (www.jerashfestival.jo), under the sponsorship of Queen Noor. Events are held in the South Theatre, North Theatre and Oval Plaza in Jerash, as well as the Royal Cultural Centre in Amman, and other places like Umm Qais and Mt Nebo. Special programs for children are also held at the Haya Cultural Centre in Amman.

The festival is held over 17 days from mid-July to mid-August, and features an eclectic array of performances including plays, poetry readings, opera and musical concerts from around the world. Events are listed in English in the official souvenir news sheet, the *Jerash Daily*, printed every day of the festival, and the English-language newspapers published in Amman.

Tickets cost around JD10 for events in Jerash, and around JD30 for more formal events in Amman and elsewhere. Since the events change from year to year, it is best to check online regarding the locations of ticketing venues. There is also a **festival office** next to the visitor centre near the South Gate, though it's only open during the festival. Several bus companies, including JETT, offer special transport to Jerash, which is useful considering public transport usually finishes early in the evening.

🛏 Sleeping

Many people visit Jerash as a day trip from Amman, which is possible on a tour but quite difficult using public transport unless you make a very early start. An overnight stop is more rewarding: the modern town of Jerash, which encompasses the ruins of the Eastern Baths, comes to life after sunset and is a pleasant place to explore in the early evening. With only one hotel in the middle of the town, and only one other place to stay nearby, it is important to book ahead. If you have a car, Ajloun has more accommodation and is only about a 20-minute drive away.

Olive Branch Resort   HOTEL $$
(☎6340555; www.olivebranch.com.jo; s/d/tr incl breakfast from JD35/50/60, camping own tent/hired tent JD11/14; ☀) Around 7km from Jerash on the road to Ajloun, this hilltop countryside hotel is located in a picturesque and tranquil spot amid olive groves and pine trees. The spacious rooms have some oddities, such as a bathtub in the bedroom, but the private balconies with rural views compensate. Country fare, including kebab suppers and *labneh* breakfasts, are served in the poolside garden or in the modest restaurant with panoramic views. Unstructured camping is possible in the grounds. A taxi from Jerash costs JD3. By car, drive from Jerash towards Ajloun for 5km; turn right and continue steeply uphill for 1km. Turn right again at the bend in the road – it is signposted but it's hard to read the signs at night.

Hadrian Gate Hotel   HOTEL $$
(☎077-7793907;   s/d/tr/penthouse   from JD25/40/50/70; ☀) Run by the always friendly and accommodating Ismail Khasim and his son Walid, Jerash's only hotel boasts a spectacular location overlooking the ruins and walking distance to Hadrian's Gate. Breakfast is served on the rooftop terraces with a panoramic view of the Temple of Artemis to the west and Jerash's market gardens to the east. A range of private rooms with shared bathrooms (priced individually) are humble but spotless; more commodious is the en-suite penthouse with aircon. What the hotel lacks in amenities it makes up for in good old-fashioned hospitality and both father and son go out of their way to make their guests comfortable and welcome.

🍴 Eating

Modern Jerash is a bustling town with several outdoor markets, as well as the obligatory smattering of kebab and felafel shops. It is also home to one of Jordan's best-loved restaurants, the Lebanese House. There's a string of no-fuss restaurants on the main street opposite the visitor's centre. Around the entrance to the ruins there are some eating options, but there is only one place to buy refreshments inside the ruins proper.

TOP CHOICE Lebanese House   LEBANESE $$
(☎6351301; mains JD4-9; ⊗noon-11pm; ☝) Nicknamed 'Umm Khalil', this rambling restaurant, which has served more than five

million customers since 1977, is a national treasure. If it's good enough for King Hussein, Kofi Annan and Richard Gere, it's certainly good enough for us! Try the fresh almonds while you wait for sizzling mezze and fresh-baked bread. If you can't decide what to sample, try the regular meal (JD15) or the house special (JD22) for a selection of the best dishes. The quality is consistently high, in line with the house motto: 'A good reputation is more valuable than money'. The indoor and outdoor seating gets busy with local families after 9pm. It's a five- to 10-minute walk from Jerash's centre.

Jerash Rest House   BUFFET $

(☑ 6351437; buffet JD5; ☺ noon-5pm) The only restaurant inside the ruins, this is a welcome stop for weary visitors. Located near the South Gate it attracts large volumes of tourists but service is quick and efficient, if not always entirely friendly. The lunch buffet is more conducive to an afternoon nap than a jaunt round the ruins but it's tasty nonetheless.

Jordan House Restaurant   BUFFET $$

(☑ 07778675; buffet JD6; ☺ 8am-9pm) Serving a comprehensive buffet between 11am and 5pm, this friendly establishment at the entrance to the ruins is a good place for a Turkish coffee before tackling the ruins, and a fresh lemon and mint drink over lunch on your return.

ℹ Information

Books & Maps

Published by the Jordan Tourism Board, the free *Jerash* brochure includes a map, some photos and a recommended walking route. It can be found at the visitor centre in Jerash or the Jordan Ministry of Tourism & Antiquities (p72).

Anyone with a particular interest in the history of Jerash should pick up one of the three decent pocket-sized guides: *Jerash: The Roman City; Jerash: A Unique Example of a Roman City;* or the most comprehensive and readable *Jerash*. All three are available at bookshops in Amman. *Jerash* by Iain Browning gives a more detailed historical account.

Tourist Information

Next to the South Gate, the **visitor centre** has informative descriptions and reconstructions of many buildings in Jerash as well as a good relief map of the ancient city. Toilets are available at the entrance (in the middle of the souvenir souq), at Jerash Rest House and at the visitor centre.

Allow at least three hours to see everything in Jerash, and make sure you take plenty of water, especially in summer. It's best to avoid walking around the site in the middle of the day between April and September as there is little shade from the sun. It's possible to leave limited luggage at the Jerash Rest House, for no charge, while you visit the site. Guides (JD20) are available at the ticket checkpoint in front of the South Gate – they can do wonders in bringing the ruins to life.

ℹ Getting There & Away

Jerash is located approximately 50km north of Amman, and the roads are well signed from the capital, especially from 8th Circle. If you're driving, be advised that this route can get extremely congested during the morning and afternoon rush hours.

From the North Bus Station (Tabarbour) in Amman, public buses and minibuses (800 fils, 1¼ hours) leave regularly for Jerash, though they can take up to an hour to fill up. Leave early for a quick getaway, especially if you are planning a day trip.

Jerash's bus and service-taxi station is a 15-minute walk southwest of the ruins, at the second set of traffic lights, behind the big white building. You can pick up a minibus to the station from outside the visitor centre for a few fils. From here, there are also plenty of minibuses travelling regularly to Irbid (JD1, 45 minutes) and Ajloun (600 fils, 30 minutes) until around 4pm. You can normally flag down the bus to Amman from the main junction in front of the site to save the trek to the bus station.

Transport drops off significantly after 5pm. Service taxis sometimes leave up to around 8pm (later during Jerash Festival) from the bus station, but it's not guaranteed.

A private taxi between Amman and Jerash should cost around JD18 to JD25 each way, with a bit of determined bargaining. From Jerash, a taxi to Irbid costs around JD14 to JD20.

Dibeen Forest Reserve

متنزة دبين الوطني

Established in 2004, this small area (around 8 sq km) of Aleppo pine and oak forest is a **nature reserve** (☑ 02-6370017; ☺ year-round). Managed by the Royal Society for the Conservation of Nature (RSCN), Dibeen is representative of the wild forests that once covered much of the country's northern frontiers but which now account for only 1% of Jordan's land area. Despite its small size, Dibeen is recognised as a national biodiversity hotspot, and protects 17 endangered animals (including the Persian squirrel) and several rare orchids.

As Dibeen is still very much a work in progress, facilities are currently limited compared with other RSCN reserves. There are some short marked (but unmapped) **hiking trails** through the park. In March and April carpets of red crown anemones fill the meadows beneath the pine-forested and sometimes snow capped hills. Most trails are either small vehicle tracks or stony paths, some of which continue beyond the park's boundaries. The area is very popular with local picnickers on Fridays, and litter is a problem.

Impinging on the park, construction is underway for a seven-star hotel, financed by an Emirati national, expected to be completed by 2015. There is currently no other place to stay.

The park is only usefully accessed by car. Follow the signs from Jerash and expect to get lost! Keep heading for the obvious hillside woodland as you pass through nearby hamlets and you will eventually stumble on the entrance.

Ajloun عجلون

📞 02 / POP 94,458 / ELEV 744M

It may look a bit rough around the edges, but Ajloun (or Ajlun) is founded on an ancient market town and boasts a 600-year-old mosque. Most visitors, however, don't come to experience this chaotic little hub and its limited attractions. They come for the impressive castle that perches on top of a nearby hill, where it has commanded the high ground for nearly 1000 years.

With the biblical site of Mar Elias and one of Jordan's best nature reserves in the vicinity, Ajloun makes a good base for a couple of days of exploration. It is also reasonably close to Jerash (30 minutes by minibus, 20 minutes by car), offering alternative accommodation and making a rewarding weekend circuit from Amman.

◉ Sights

Qala'at ar-Rabad (Ajloun Castle) CASTLE
(admission JD1; ⊙8am-4pm Oct-Apr, to 7pm May-Sep) This historic castle was built atop Mt 'Auf (1250m) between 1184 and 1188 by one of Saladin's generals (and also nephew), 'Izz ad-Din Usama bin Munqidh. It was enlarged in 1214 with the addition of a new gate in the southeastern corner, and once boasted seven towers as well as a surrounding 15m-deep dry moat.

The castle commands views of the Jordan Valley and three wadis leading into it – the Kufranjah, Rajeb and Al-Yabes – making it an important strategic link in the defensive chain against the Crusaders, and a counterpoint to the Crusader Belvoir Fort on the Sea of Galilee (Lake Tiberias) in present-day Israel and the Palestinian Territories. With its hilltop position, Qala'at ar-Rabad was one in a chain of beacons and pigeon posts that enabled messages to be transmitted from Damascus to Cairo in a single day. The rearing of pigeons in the area is still a popular pastime.

After the Crusader threat subsided, the castle was largely destroyed by Mongol invaders in 1260, only to be almost immediately rebuilt by the Mamluks. In the 17th century an Ottoman garrison was stationed here, after which it was used by local villagers. The castle was 'rediscovered' by the well-travelled JL Burckhardt, who also just happened to stumble across Petra. Earthquakes in 1837 and 1927 badly damaged the castle, though slow and steady restoration is continuing.

Note that there is a useful explanation in English just inside the main gate, although nothing else is signposted. However, not much explanation is needed to bring the castle to life, especially given that the views from these lofty heights are nothing short of spectacular.

The castle is a tough (3km) uphill walk from the town centre, but minibuses very occasionally go to the top (about 100 fils). Alternatively, take a taxi from Ajloun (JD1 to JD2 each way). A return trip by taxi from Ajloun (JD7 to JD10), with about 30 minutes to look around, is money well spent. The **visitors centre** and ticket office is about 500m downhill from the castle entrance; there is a small model of the castle on display here and, perhaps more usefully, clean toilets.

FREE Mar Elias ARCHAEOLOGICAL SITE
(⊙8am-7pm Apr-Oct, to 4pm Nov-Mar) This little-visited **archaeological site**, believed to be the birthplace of the prophet Elijah, gives you just the excuse you need to explore the countryside around Ajloun. To be honest, it's not a spectacular site by any stretch of the imagination, though it is certainly worth checking out solely for its religious and historical significance.

Elijah (also known as Elias) is mentioned in both the Quran and the Old Testament, and is thought to have been born around 910 BC in the village of Lesteb, next to Mar Elias. The prophet died not far away in Wadi al-Kharrar (see p109), before supposedly ascending to heaven on a flaming chariot. During Byzantine times, a pilgrimage site grew up around Mar Elias under the guidance of the nearby Bishopric of Pella. In 1999 excavations unearthed a church complex dating back to the early 7th century.

From the car park, stairs lead up above the ruins of the earliest church, the apse of which has a tree growing directly above it. The foundations of the main cross-shaped church are easy to make out and are decorated with wonderfully fresh floor mosaics. Look for the tomb chambers to the back right of the church, and an earlier chapel with plain white tiles to the south. Water cisterns and bits of masonry dot the rest of the site.

There's no public transport to the site. From Ajloun take a right by the Qalet al-Jabal Hotel, climb the hill for 1km and take a left at the junction, heading downhill after this for 2.7km. At the junction/army post take a right for another 1.8km until you see a signpost pointing left (the right branch leads to Ishfateena and the Ajloun Forest Reserve). After 1km take the paved track on the left for 400m up to the site (a total of 8.3km from Ajloun).

If you're heading on to Ajloun Forest Reserve, take a left when you get back to the junction, 1.4km from the site, and head towards Ishfateena. After 1.6km you'll reach the main road; take a right here and after 5km the reserve is signposted to the left, 300m before the main Irbid–Ajloun highway.

Mar Elias can also be reached by foot along the spectacular Prophet's Trail, which connects the site to the Ajloun Forest Reserve.

Sleeping & Eating

There are two hotels on the road up to the castle, either of which are a good option if you want to enjoy the sunset from the castle ramparts.

Qalet al-Jabal Hotel   HOTEL $
(6420202; www.jabal-hotel.com; s/d/tr from JD28/38/48) About 1km downhill from Ajloun Castle, this busy little hotel boasts a gorgeous garden of flowering jasmine, grapevines and roses. The proprietors even make their own wine. The decor is a tad tired and the furnishings on the minimal side but there are expansive views from many of the rooms. Ask for a room with a balcony to enjoy the sunset. The highlight of the hotel is the outdoor terrace (open to non-residents) where slow-cooked meals are served.

Ajloun Hotel   HOTEL $
(6420524; s/d incl breakfast from JD25/35) Located just 500m down the road from the castle, this is a handy option for an early morning visit to the castle. There's a comfortable lounge area in the foyer but most of the rooms are very basic. Choose a top-floor room for grand views of the countryside.

There are a few places for a snack and a drink inside Ajloun Castle. For something more substantial, both **Abu-Alezz Restaurant** (meals JD2-3) and **Al-Raseed** (meals JD2-3) near the main roundabout in Ajloun offer standard Jordanian fare, including chicken, hummus and shwarma. Alternatively, pick up some supplies in the many Ajloun grocery stores, supplement your rations with freshly picked fruit from the many roadside fruit stands, and head into the surrounding hills for a picnic.

ℹ Information

Just south of the main roundabout in Ajloun, the Housing Bank changes money and has an ATM. The **tourist office** (/fax 6420115) was not functioning at the time of writing.

ℹ Getting There & Away

Ajloun is approximately 75km northwest of Amman and 30km northwest of Jerash. The castle can be clearly seen from most places in the area. If you're driving or walking, take the signposted road (Al-Qala'a St) heading west at the main roundabout in the centre of Ajloun.

From the centre of town, minibuses travel regularly to Jerash (600 fils, 30 minutes along a scenic road) and Irbid (JD1, 45 minutes). From Amman (900 fils, two hours), minibuses leave half-hourly from the North Bus Station.

Ajloun Forest Reserve
محمية عجلون الطبيعية

Located in the Ajloun Highlands, this small (just 13 sq km) but vitally important **nature reserve** (02-6475673; ☼year-round) was established by the RSCN in 1988 to protect oak, carob, pistachio and strawberry tree forests. The reserve also acts as a wildlife sanctuary for the endangered roe deer (which is being brought back from the brink of extinction through captive breeding programs) as well as wild boar, stone martens, polecats, jackals and even hyena and grey wolves.

The RSCN has worked hard to develop tourist infrastructure within the reserve and woodland cabins are perfect for a romantic retreat. Of course, the real appeal of the reserve is its good network of **hiking trails**, with a variety of paths suited to hikers of all fitness levels. The landscape of rolling hills and mixed forest is lovely, especially if you've been spending a few too many hours in Jordan's barren deserts or congested capital. Even if you don't complete any of the hiking trails listed here, it's worth entering the woodland at the start of the Roe Deer Trail just to enjoy the strawberry trees, so named because of their vivid, strawberry-red peeling bark.

◉ Sights

The RSCN supports a number of local community projects in and near the reserve to help develop new sources of income for the local population. These small-scale, high-value projects include three workshops that produce olive-oil soap, screen-printed items and traditional Jordanian cuisine, all of which can be purchased on site or in the reserve's Nature Shop. The three houses are free to visit and are within a 10-minute drive of the reserve (follow the signposts from the main road near the reserve) or, more rewardingly, can be reached via a hiking trail. Pick up a map from the visitors centre before you set out.

🖉 The Soap House   CRAFT WORKSHOP
(Orjan Village; ⊙9am-4pm) Ever wondered what pomegranate soap smells like? Local women demonstrate the art of making all kinds of health-promoting soaps using natural local ingredients and comprising 90% pure olive oil. Pomegranate is one of a dozen exotic fragrances.

🖉 House of Calligraphy   CRAFT WORKSHOP
(⊙9am-4pm) You don't have to be a linguistic scholar to enjoy the dynamic rhythms of Arabic script. Reinforcing Islamic heritage, the women in this workshop aim to educate visitors about Arab culture and there is even an opportunity to try your hand at calligraphy using a reed to write your name in Arabic.

🖉 The Biscuit House   CRAFT WORKSHOP
(Orjan Village; ⊙9am-4pm) Delicious Jordanian delicacies are prepared for sale in RSCN Nature Shops here in this cottage-industry kitchen. With an on-site cafe selling locally produced herbal teas, olive-oil crisps and molasses and tahini sandwich cookies, it's tempting to stay until morning – quite possible at the Biscuit House Bed & Breakfast.

🏃 Activities

Hiking

It's important to arrange return transport at the reserve visitor centre before you leave on any of the following hikes except the Roe Deer and the Rockrose Trails. Most hikes require a guide (see Information, p96).

Roe Deer Trail   HIKING
(⊙year-round) If you're just stopping by for the day, the 2km-long Roe Deer Trail takes about an hour and can be self-guided. It starts from the accommodation area, looping over a nearby hill – past a 1600-year-old stone wine press and lots of spring wildflowers (April) – and returning via a roe deer enclosure.

Soap House Trail   HIKING
(⊙year-round) This guided, three-hour, 7km trail combines a visit to the reserve's oldest strawberry tree with a panoramic vista at Eagle's Viewpoint. Descending from the 1100m lookout, the trail leads through evergreen woodland to the soap house where enterprising women make natural olive-oil soap.

Houses Trail   HIKING
(⊙year-round) This guided, three-hour, 7km trail links the three RSCN handicraft workshops – the Soap House, the House of Caligraphy and the Biscuit House. Pause at the Biscuit House for coffee and home-baked delights. Allow extra time for visiting each workshop.

Orjan Village Trail   HIKING
(⊙1 Apr-31 Oct) A guide is needed for this rural, six-hour, 12km trail that weaves alongside a brook, following poplar trees and fruit orchards. The olive trees at the end of the hike date back to Roman times.

Rockrose Trail   HIKING
(⊙1 Apr-31 Oct) This scenic, four-hour, 8km trail involves some steep scrambling and requires a guide. The route passes through heavily wooded valleys, rocky ridges and

LOVING THE LAND

It's easy to spot a guide at one of the six flagship nature reserves run by the Royal Society for the Conservation of Nature (RSCN) – they exude such a passion for their place of work. This is hardly surprising when you consider that, as part of the RSCN's far-sighted policy to involve local people, the rangers are almost all born and raised nearby.

Take Majid, a ranger at Ajloun. He loves the evergreen oak forests because he played in them when he was young; he remembers village grandfathers harvesting the strong strawberry-tree timber to build houses and local grandmothers using the fruit to settle stomach ailments. There were also hunts for roe deer and wild boar – the same species Majid is now helping to reintroduce and protect today.

Hunting may be banned within the parks, but local communities are still given a vested interest in the land they call their own. At Ajloun, six of the surrounding villages are involved in the maintenance of the reserve: 'Our families want to protect their sons' employment,' says Majid, 'so they are keen to support the reserve and make it work for the benefit of the whole community.'

Naturally, not everyone is equally committed and the reserve faces problems such as illegal cutting of firewood for valuable oils and the odd attempt at poaching. The clever part of the RSCN philosophy, however, is that villagers are not banned from exploiting their birthright resources without being offered an alternative income. At Ajloun, for example, a guided trail offers visitors a chance to meet with the area's soap makers: these enterprising women make their ecofriendly products from natural resources in low-impact cottage industries and sell them at fair prices in the Ajloun Reserve shop.

At each of the reserves, the challenges may be slightly different (extraction of water in Mujib and Azraq, overgrazing in Dana), but the story of culturally sensitive and sustainable development is the same. To quote Chris Johnson, director of Wild Jordan (the marketing arm of the RSCN), it is this 'amazing relationship between landscape and people' that is securing Jordan's ancient wild lands for future generations – indeed, saving them for the sons of Majid.

olive groves and offers sweeping views of the Palestinian West Bank.

Prophet's Trail
HIKING

(⊙year-round) Terminating at the archaeological site of Mar Elias, where the prophet Elijah was reportedly born, this five-hour, 8.5km guided route winds through fig and pear orchards. At Wadi Shiteau the trail plunges into a dense forest of oak and strawberry trees.

Ajloun Castle Trail
HIKING

With prior arrangement it's possible to continue hiking from Mar Elias for another 9.5km through Wadi Al-Jubb to Ajloun Castle – a tough extra four hours over rough and steep terrain. The trail is 'donkey-assisted', which helps considerably on the difficult final ascent towards the castle.

Sleeping & Eating

TOP CHOICE Biscuit House Bed & Breakfast
B&B $$

(☑6475673; s/d incl breakfast JD49/70) It's an experience just getting to this rural homestead in the village of Orjan, where a stream, olive groves and ancient poplars make a welcome contrast to the dry and dusty hills of Ajloun. Just about negotiable by car along a very steep but graded road, this wonderful B&B is situated in a lush wadi with its own orchards. All the furniture in the two bedrooms and shared bathroom and sitting room are made from recycled wood. The highlight of the stay, however, is breakfast, rustled up by the ladies of the cooperative who run a commercial kitchen on site producing goods for the RSCN's Wild Jordan Nature Shops. The thyme, olives, cheese and jam are all locally sourced. The Biscuit House is 1.5km from the Soap House on the main road in Orjan.

Ajloun Reserve Tented Bungalow
LUXURY TENT, BUNGALOW $$

(☑6475673; s/d/tr/q incl breakfast JD60/70/80/90) The reserve encompasses luxury tents perched on a treehouse-style wooden platform, and light and breezy canvas bungalows (open from 1 April to 31 October). Both are a short walk from an ablution block containing environmentally sound composting toilets and solar-heated showers. Bring plenty of mosquito repellent during the summer months.

Ajloun Reserve Cabin CABIN $$$
(☑6475673; s/d/tr/q incl breakfast from JD91/103/113/124) Also within the reserve are rustic cabins equipped with private facilities and terraces overlooking a patch of forest. These make for a delightful retreat if you're looking for a place to relax in rural surroundings.

Meals (lunch and dinner) are available in the tented **rooftop restaurant** (meals JD13) by the visitors centre if you give some notice, though you can always cook for yourself on the public barbecue grills. From the rooftop, there are wonderful views of snowcapped Jebel ash-Sheikh (Mt Hermon; 2814m) on the Syria–Lebanon border; snow is common in the reserve between December and February.

ⓘ Information

At the entrance to the reserve is a modest **visitor centre** (☺dawn-dusk) with a helpful reception where you'll find information and maps on the reserve and its flora and fauna. There is also a Nature Shop selling locally produced handicrafts.

You should book accommodation and meals in advance with the RSCN through its Wild Jordan Centre in Amman (see p74). If you're planning to take a guided hike, it's also a good idea to book. Guided hikes require a minimum of four people and start from around JD10 per person, depending on the choice of trail.

ⓘ Getting There & Away

You can reach the reserve by hiring a taxi from Ajloun (9km) for around JD5 to JD7; ask the visitor centre to book one for your departure. If you're driving, take the road from Ajloun towards Irbid and take a left turn by a petrol station 4.8km from Ajloun towards the village of Ishfateena. About 300m from the junction take a right and follow the signs 3.8km to the reserve, which is next to the village of Umm al-Yanabi.

IRBID & AROUND

Jordan's far-flung northern hills see few travellers aside from overlanders heading to Damascus in Syria. This is a shame as the region's rolling hills and verdant valleys are home to characterful rural villages, country lanes overrun by goats, and ubiquitous olive groves among whose ancient trunks lie the scattered remains of forgotten eras.

And then, of course, there is Irbid. This thriving university town is generally overlooked by visitors, despite some national treasures; in this densely populated part of the country, Irbid is a key place in which to feel the pulse of modern Jordan.

All minibuses, in whatever village you find them, appear to make a beeline for Irbid, from where connections can be made to almost anywhere in the country. With a car, it's possible to visit the remote battleground of Yarmouk or the ruins of the Decapolis city of Umm Qais as a day trip from Irbid.

Irbid اربد

☑02 / POP 751.634 / ELEV 582M

Jordan's second-largest city is something of a glorified university town. Home to Yarmouk University, which is regarded as one of the most elite centres of learning in the Middle East, Irbid is in many ways more lively and progressive than staid Amman. The campus, which is located just south of the city centre, is home to shady pedestrian streets lined with outdoor restaurants and cafes.

Historians and archaeologists have identified Irbid as the Decapolis city of Arbela. The area, in all likelihood, predates the Romans with significant grave sites suggesting settlement since the Bronze Age. Aside from the tell lying at the centre of town, however, there is little evidence today of such antiquity.

◉ Sights

Yarmouk University UNIVERSITY
(☑7211111; www.yu.edu.jo) There are two **museums** in the grounds of Jordan's largest university. Established in 1977, the campus now boasts over 22,000 students from across the Middle East. Visitors are welcome to wander around the grounds, where it is easy to strike up a conversation with students.

FREE **Museum of Archaeology & Anthropology** MUSEUM
(☑7211111; ☺10am-1.45pm & 3-4.30pm Sun-Thu) This highly recommended museum features exhibits from all eras of Jordanian history arranged in chronological order. The collection opens with 9000-year-old Neolithic statuettes found near present-day Amman,

covers the Bronze and Iron Ages, continues through the Mamluk and Ottoman occupations, and closes with more modern displays on rural Bedouin life. One of the highlights of the museum is a reconstruction of a traditional Arab pharmacy and smithy. Worth a visit is the adjacent Numismatic Hall which has some fascinating displays on the history of money over the last 2600 years. All displays are labelled in English.

FREE Jordan Natural History Museum   MUSEUM
(☎ 7211111; ⊙8am-5pm Sun-Thu) Encompassing a range of stuffed animals, birds and insects, as well as rocks from the region, this may not be to everybody's taste but it is at least a good place to identify some of Jordan's most elusive species. The museum is in the huge green hangar No 23.

FREE Dar As Saraya Museum   MUSEUM
(☎245613; Al Baladia St; ⊙8am-6pm) Located in a stunning old villa of basaltic rock, just behind the town hall, this new museum is a real gem. Built in 1886 by the Ottomans, the building is typical of the caravanserai established along the Syrian pilgrimage route with rooms arranged a paved internal courtyard. It was used as a prison until 1994 and now houses a delightful collection of local artefacts illustrating Irbid's long history. Don't miss the olive press in the courtyard, nor the impressive basalt doors with 'iron' bolts carved in stone.

FREE Beit Arar   MUSEUM
(off Al-Hashemi St; ⊙9am-5pm Sun-Thu) Set up to host cultural events, Beit Arar is located in a superb old Damascene-style house. The rooms are set around a courtyard paved with volcanic black stones and there are manuscripts and photo displays of Arar, one of Jordan's finest poets.

🛏 Sleeping

It has to be said that the standard of hotels in Irbid is not great. The redeeming feature, especially among the budget options, is the great friendliness of the welcome.

Al-Joude Hotel   HOTEL $
(☎7275515; off University St; s/d/tr incl buffet breakfast from JD30/35/60; ❋@☀) Located near the campus of Yarmouk University, Irbid's only midrange hotel has seen better

days – which to be fair is reflected in the budget price. Rooms are clean and spacious but sparse, noisy (especially those by the antiquated lift) and tired. The good part is that you don't have to go looking for nightlife – of an evening, half of Irbid pours into the hotel's popular News Cafe, or the Al-Joude Garden Restaurant.

Omayah Hotel   HOTEL $
(☎7245955; omayahhotel@yahoo.com; King Hussein St; s/d JD20/30; ❋) Good value for money, this recently renovated budget hotel boasts satellite TV, as well as large picture windows overlooking the heart of the city. The friendly proprietor is kind and helpful and solo women will feel comfortable here. Rooms towards the back of the property are a bit quieter – a good choice for light sleepers who don't want to be woken by the sounds of honking car horns.

Al-Ameen al-Kabeer Hotel   HOTEL $
(☎7242384; Al-Jaish St; dm/s/d from JD8/12/15) The friendly management gives personal and attentive service at this city-centre hotel. Of course, this is very much a budget option with basic concrete rooms and shared bathrooms, though the property is well tended and there's a reliable supply of hot water. Affected by the lack of tourist trade at the time of writing, this family-run enterprise may well not weather the latest economic storm. Call ahead to be sure.

🍴 Eating

It's hard to imagine how the restaurants along the length of University St all make a living. Every other establishment along the 'Champs Elysees of Irbid' (so-called by the proprietor of Al-Ameen Al-Kabeer Hotel) is dedicated to some kind of eatery or other. And then you remember that there are 22,000 hungry students living just over the road. The fare is pretty standard but the attraction is not the food but the evening vibe: after 9pm the streets swell with gregarious crowds looking for a good night out and seeming to find it on the promenade between roundabouts.

Self-caterers and would-be picnickers should head to the **Alia Supermarket** (King Hussein St) near the Omayed Hotel, which has a good selection of local produce, including the region's justifiably famous olives. The nearby street market sells all manner of fresh fruits from northern orchards.

Irbid

Al-Joude Garden Restaurant JORDANIAN **$$**

(off University St; mixed grill meals JD6-10) Students, visiting parents and local families crowd into the courtyard outside Al-Joude Hotel to sip fresh fruit juices and smoke a strawberry nargileh (water pipe). The waiters are kept in a constant state of rush between tables in this teeming venue as they are summoned for hot embers and top-ups of Turkish coffee. Eating is an entirely secondary pastime. If you decide to eat, then expect the food – which is tasty enough – to arrive just as your patience runs out. Chilly even in the summer once the moon comes up, the management thoughtfully provides Arab overcoats – strictly, mind, for the ladies as the lads are expected to tough it out. Dessert is best had in one of the many juice and cake shops in the neighbouring streets.

Clock Tower Restaurant JORDANIAN **$**

(Al Jaish St; meals JD3-5; ◷8.30am-9.30pm) The name of this popular local is written in Arabic but as it's right next to the clock tower and has a huge spit of shwarma roasting in the window, it's hard to miss. There's a family seating area upstairs for a bit of peace and quiet away from the street and the Jordanian staple dishes are cheap, cheerful and delicious. This is one budget restaurant where you won't have to worry about stomach ache in the heart of downtown.

❶ Information

Irbid has plenty of banks for changing money and most have ATMs. The police station is above the market area, and offers great views of the city. There are literally dozens of internet cafes along the southern end of University St (Shafeeq Rshaidat St) near Yarmouk University; most are open year-round.

Post office (King Hussein St; ◷7.30am-5pm Sat-Thu, to 1.30pm Fri)

Royal Jordanian Airlines (☎7243202; cnr King Hussein & Al-Jaish Sts)

❶ Getting There & Away

Approximately 85km north of Amman, Irbid is home to three main minibus/taxi stations.

From the North bus station, there are minibuses to Umm Qais (45 minutes), Mukheiba (for Al-Himma; one hour) and Quwayliba (for the ruins of Abila; 25 minutes) for between 400 fils and JD1.

From the large South bus station (New Amman bus station), air-conditioned Hijazi buses (JD1.90, 90 minutes) leave every 15 to 20 minutes between 6am and 7pm for Amman's North Bus Station. There are also less comfortable buses and minibuses from Amman's North Bus Station (less than JD1, about two hours) and plenty of service taxis (JD1). Minibuses also leave the South Bus Station for Ajloun (45 minutes), Jerash (45 minutes) and the Syrian border for around 800 fils.

Irbid

From the West bus station (Mujamma al-Gharb al-Jadid), about 1.5km west of the centre, minibuses go to Al-Mashari'a (45 minutes) for the ruins at Pella, Sheikh Hussein Bridge (for Israel and the Palestinian Territories; 45 minutes) and Shuneh ash-Shamaliyyeh (North Shuna; one hour) for between 800 fils and JD1.20. For transport to Syria contact **Trust International Transport** (⌨7251878; Al-Jaish St) near Yarmouk University.

❶ Getting Around

Getting between Irbid's various bus stations is easy, with service taxis (200 fils) and minibuses (100 fils) shuttling between them and the centre. Service taxis and minibuses to the South bus station can be picked up on Radna al-Hindawi St, while for the North station head to Prince Nayef St. For the West station take a bus from Palestine St, just west of the roundabout.

The standard taxi fare from the centre (al-Bilad) to the university (al-Jammiya) is 500 fils; few taxis use meters in Irbid. A minibus from University St to the university gate costs 200 fils. Otherwise it's a 25-minute walk.

If you have a car, be aware that the one-way roads and lack of parking can make driving a stressful experience.

Abila (Quwayliba) أبيلا (قويلبا)

Lying just 10km north of Irbid, between the twin hills of Tell Abila and Tell Umm-al-Amad, are the ancient remains of the Decapolis city of **Abila** (admission free; ⊙daylight hr). At first glance you'd be forgiven for thinking that this site could only be enjoyed by the committed ruin hunter or the aspiring archaeologist. Indeed, little remains of this once-great city, especially since the earthquake of AD 747 did a pretty thorough job of turning Abila into a rock-strewn field.

To date, much of Abila remains largely unexcavated and the site certainly isn't set up for visitors. Of course, you don't need a guide to find the Roman-Byzantine **theatre** or the scattered remains of **columns** from the markets, temples and baths lying around the site.

However, if you're looking for a real Indiana Jones experience and have a torch, explore the eerie **tomb caves** that arc carved into the hillsides surrounding the site. At one point the caves were full of corpses, but tomb raiders stripped them clean over the millennia. However, the spectacular **frescoes** adorning the walls and ceilings are marvellously intact, and made all the more dramatic by their remoteness.

The Abila site is close to the village of Quwayliba, about 10km north of Irbid. Buses leave from the North bus station in Irbid (less than JD1, 25 minutes) for Quwayliba; ask the driver to drop you off at the ruins.

Yarmouk Battleground

If you have a car and are intrigued to know why all roads out of Irbid seem to lead to Yarmouk battleground, then follow the signs northeast towards the village of Saham Al Kfarat. The site is of great significance to Muslim Arabs as this was where, on the 12th of August in AD 636, an army of 40,000 Arabs confronted 125,000 Byzantine fighters and emerged victorious. A lot of blood was spilled that day with 4000 Muslims and 80,000 of their adversaries killed, and the battleground remains something of a pilgrimage site to this day.

The signposted road from Irbid leads not to the battleground itself but to a spectacular viewpoint, high above the Yarmouk River which marks the border with Syria. The battle took place in the valley below but from this vantage point it's easy to see how the disciplined, motivated, mobile and homogenous Arabs, united by faith and good leadership, were able to overcome the mercenary Byzantine groups. The latter, who had no belief in the fight, lacked strategy and were ill-disciplined, were particularly disadvantaged by their heavy armour – as can easily be imagined on a hot August day overlooking the steep, sun-parched hillsides opposite the viewpoint.

The viewpoint, which has an interpretive plaque and a monument but no facilities, is not accessible by public transport. By car, it is a 30-minute drive from Irbid; don't give up on the signs – they're just widely spaced.

A short cut to Umm Qais is signposted halfway between the viewpoint and Irbid.

THE JORDAN VALLEY

When Moses reputedly surveyed the Promised Land from Mt Nebo, surely it wasn't the semi-arid hills surrounding the Dead Sea that gave hope for the future, but the great green ribbon of fertility extending from the sea's northern shore towards the distant mountains. The River Jordan has supported human settlement since antiquity, sustained by the rich soil that to this day makes farming an obvious pursuit.

Visitors will be struck by the contrast between the olive-growing hillsides and the subtropical Jordan Valley; they will also probably be struck by the heavily policed border with Israel and the Palestinian

THE JORDAN VALLEY

Forming a part of the Great Rift in Africa, the fertile valley of the Jordan River was of considerable significance in biblical times, and is now regarded as the food bowl of Jordan.

The hot dry summers and short mild winters make for ideal growing conditions, and (subject to water restrictions) two or three crops are grown every year. The main crops are tomatoes, cucumbers, melons and citrus fruits, many of which are cultivated under plastic.

The Jordan River rises from several sources, mainly the Anti-Lebanon Range in Syria, and flows down into the Sea of Galilee (Lake Tiberias), 212m below sea level, before draining into the Dead Sea. The actual length of the river is 360km, but as the crow flies the distance between its source and the Dead Sea is only 200km.

It was in the Jordan Valley, some 10,000 years ago, that people first started to plant crops and abandon their nomadic lifestyle for permanent settlements. Villages were built and primitive irrigation schemes were undertaken; by 3000 BC produce from the valley was being exported to neighbouring regions, much as it is today.

The Jordan River is highly revered by Christians, mainly because Jesus was said to have been baptised in its waters by John the Baptist at the site of Bethany-Beyond-the-Jordan. Centuries earlier, Joshua also supposedly led the Israelite armies across the Jordan near Tell Nimrin (Beth Nimrah in the Bible) after the death of Moses, marking the symbolic transition from the wilderness to the land of milk and honey:

And while all Israel were passing over on dry ground, the priests who bore the ark of the covenant of the Lord stood on dry ground in the midst of the Jordan, until all the nation finished passing over the Jordan.
Joshua 3: 17

Since 1948 the Jordan River has marked the boundary between Jordan and Israel and the Palestinian Territories, from the Sea of Galilee to the Yarbis River. From there to the Dead Sea marked the 1967 ceasefire line between the two countries – it now marks the continuation of the official frontier with the Palestinian Territories.

During the 1967 war with Israel, Jordan lost the West Bank, and the population on the Jordanian east bank of the valley dwindled from 60,000 before the war to 5000 by 1971. During the 1970s, new roads and fully serviced villages were built and the population has now soared to over 100,000.

Territories which runs along the length of the River Jordan. The valley has been the site of fight and flight for centuries and is still a sensitive area as disputes about territory give way to concerns over water (see p294).

Despite the frisson of political friction, there is absolutely no danger in visiting the area and indeed there are many worthwhile sights, from the Roman ruins of Umm Qais in the north, to the assumed baptism site of Jesus at Bethany-Beyond-the-Jordan. The valley itself, with commercial farms of bananas, papaya, potatoes, tomatoes and aubergines rubbing alongside market gardens of locally sold produce, is worth a trip in its own right, especially when the valley's many flame trees are in full, glorious flower. At sunset, the encasing hills turn an extraordinary colour of pink and egrets flap across the reed beds, oblivious of the border. Incidentally, the only place where you can actually see the River Jordan is at Bethany, as the demands of irrigation have reduced this once-mighty river to a mere brook, hidden between the fields.

There is plenty of public transport plying the valley from village to village. With a car, however, it is considerably easier to make the side trips from the valley floor (which is at an altitude well below sea level) to places of interest above sea level, such as the ruins at Pella or the bustling town of Salt. It takes about an hour and a half to drive the full length of the valley, with accommodation possible in Umm Qais at the northern end, Pella in the middle or the Dead Sea in the south. A sample of the valley can also be included in a roundtrip from Amman and Jerash. Don't forget your passport to show in the numerous police checkpoints.

Al-Himma (Mukheiba)
الحمى (مخيبا)
📞 02 / POP >5000 / ELEV -130M

If you have just paid a visit to the Yarmouk Battleground viewpoint (see p99) you may be interested to descend to the hot springs of Al-Himma in the village of Mukheiba. At the confluence of the Yarkmouk and the Jordan Rivers, you can gain a good idea of the battle site from the ground, although access to the site proper is currently restricted. The hills (almost an escarpment) up which the conflicting armies had to run look considerably steeper from here and make the Muslim victory all the more impressive.

In Roman and Byzantine times, al-Himma was the site of Gadara's bath complex, famous throughout the empire for its lavish design and architecture. Most of the ruins today lie across the border in the Israeli-occupied Golan Heights and the modern incarnation of the baths has not endured the downturn in tourism of the past decade.

Mukheiba marks the northern most reach of Jordan's portion of the Jordan Valley, 10km north of Umm Qais. This edgy border town can be reached via a scenic road (with checkpoints) giving views of the Golan Heights in Syria and Lake Tiberias (Sea of Galilee) in Israel and the Palestinian Territories. Public transport is not reliable here and the village is not a good place to be marooned.

Umm Qais (Gadara) أم قيس
📞 02 / POP >5000 / ELEV 310M

And when he came to the other side, to the country of the Gadarenes, two demon-possessed men met him, coming out of the tombs, so fierce that no one could pass that way. And behold, they cried out, 'What have you to do with us, O Son of God? Have you come here to torment us before the time?' Now a herd of many swine was feeding at some distance from them. And the demons begged him, 'If you cast us out, send us away into the herd of swine'. And he said to them, 'Go'. So they came out and went into the swine; and behold, the whole herd rushed down the steep bank into the sea, and perished in the waters.
Matthew 8:28-32

In the northwest corner of Jordan, in the hills above the Jordan Valley, are the ruins of the Decapolis city of Gadara (now called Umm Qais). Although the site is far less complete than Jerash, it is nonetheless striking due to the juxtaposition of Roman ruins with an abandoned Ottoman-era village. Umm Qais is especially visit-worthy in spring when an explosion of wildflowers adorns the fallen masonry.

Umm Qais has another claim to fame as the site where, according to the Bible, Jesus performed one of his greatest miracles: casting demons from two men into a herd of pigs. Since the first millennium, Gadara has resultantly been a Christian place of

Umm Qais (Gadara)

Temple of Zeus

Decumanus Maximus

7

To Baths (400m); Roman Mausoleum (400m); City Gate (800m)

9 ⊙1 ⊙2

⊗11

5 ⊙

⊙6

Museum (Beit Russan)

Ottoman-era Village ⊙3 (Acropolis)

West Theatre

⊙8

Tomb of Chaireas

Tomb of Germani

4⊙

Tomb of Modestus

Ticket Office

10⊗

To Umm Qais Hotel (400m)

0 ——— 200 m
0 ——— 0.1 miles

Umm Qais (Gadara)

pilgrimage, though an alternative Israeli site on the eastern shore of Lake Galilee also claims to mark the spot.

The site boasts spectacular views of three countries (Jordan, Syria, and Israel and the Palestinian Territories), encompassing the Golan Heights, Mt Hermon and the Sea of Galilee (Lake Tiberias). Over the past decade or more, Umm Qais has become a rallying point

for homesick Palestinians (many of whom are now Jordanian nationals – see p277), yearning for a glimpse of their former homeland. The Resthouse, a popular restaurant located amid the ruins, is a particular favourite with families congregating to swap stories of the Holy Land.

History

The ancient town of Gadara was ruled by a series of powerful nations, including the Ptolemies, the Seleucids, the Jews and, from 63 BC, the Romans who transformed the town into one of the great cities of the Decapolis (see p82).

Herod the Great was given Gadara following a naval victory and he ruled over it until his death in 4 BC – much to the disgruntlement of locals who tried everything to put him out of favour with Rome. On his death the city reverted to semi-autonomy as part of the Roman province of Syria and it flourished under various guises until the 7th century when, in common with other cities of the Decapolis, it lost its trading connections and became little more than a backwater.

The town was partially rebuilt during the Ottoman Empire and many structures from this period, built in the typical black basaltic rock of the region, remain well preserved alongside the earlier Roman ruins.

In 1806 Gadara was 'discovered' by Western explorers but excavation did not commence in earnest until the early 1980s. Thanks to German funding, considerable restoration of the Roman ruins has taken place but much remains still to be excavated.

◉ Sights

West Theatre
AMPHITHEATRE

Entering the site from the south, the first structure of interest is the well-restored and brooding West Theatre. Constructed from black basalt, it once seated about 3000 people. This is one of two such theatres – the **North Theatre** is overgrown and missing the original black basalt rocks which were recycled by villagers in other constructions.

Basilica Terrace
RUIN

A bit of imagination is needed to reconstruct the next structure – a **colonnaded courtyard**, the western section of which housed a row of **shops** (the shells of which remain). More interesting are the remains of the 6th-century **church**, with an unusual octagonal interior sanctum, marked today by the remaining basalt columns. The church was destroyed by earthquakes in the 8th century.

Decumanus Maximus
STREET

The main road passing through the site, and still paved to this day, once linked Gadara with other nearby ancient cities such as Abila and Pella. In its heyday, the road extended as far as the Mediterranean coast.

Baths
BATHHOUSE

West along the decumanus maximus are the overgrown public baths. Built in the 4th century, this would once have been an impressive complex of fountains (like the nearby **nymphaeum**), statues and baths, though little remains today after various earthquakes.

Roman Mausoleum
TOMB

The decumanus maximus continues west for 1km or so, leading to some ruins of limited interest, including **baths**, **mausoleums** and **gates**. Japanese and Iraqi archaeologists are currently excavating here. Most interesting is the basilica built above one of the Roman mausoleums. You can peer down into the subterranean tomb through a hole in the basilica floor. The sarcophagus of Helladis that once lay here can be seen in the Museum of Anthropology and Archaeology (p96) in Irbid.

FREE Museum
MUSEUM

(☎7500072; ⊗8am-6pm Sat-Thu, to 4pm Fri) Housed in Beit Russan, a former residence of an Ottoman governor, this modest museum is set around an elegant and tranquil courtyard of fig trees. The main mosaic on display (dating from the 4th century and found in one of the tombs) illustrates the names of early Christian notables. Another highlight is the headless white marble statue of the Hellenic goddess Tyche, which was found sitting in the front row of the West Theatre.

Ottoman Village
RUIN

Surrounding the museum are the comprehensive ruins of an Ottoman village dating from the 18th and 19th centuries. Two houses, **Beit Malkawi** (now used as an office for archaeological groups) and the nearby **Beit Heshboni**, are still intact. A **mosque** and the remains of a **girls' school** are also worth a cursory visit if you choose to amble around the derelict lanes.

⊨ Sleeping & Eating

Not many people spend the night in Umm Qais, especially since the ruins can easily be accessed on a day trip from Jerash or Irbid. Staying here does give the option, though, of making a full day's excursion along the Jordan Valley the following day.

Umm Qais Hotel
HOTEL $

(☎7500080; www.umqaishotel.com; s/d/tr incl breakfast from JD15/30/40) With modest rooms above a bakery (guess where bread for breakfast comes from), and a stone's throw from the ruins, this family-run hotel makes up for the lack of attractions with hearty hospitality. A rooftop cafe is due to reopen if tourism picks up. Alternatively, home-cooked Jordanian food is available on request from the landlady. Half-day trips into the local countryside can be organised from here for JD3 (for a minimum of four people).

TOP CHOICE Umm Qais Resthouse
JORDANIAN $$

(☎7500555; meals JD5-10; ⊗10am-7pm, to 10pm Jun-Sep; ☑) Without doubt, one of the best parts of the Umm Qais site is pausing to have a mint and lemon, or a tabouli salad at the Umm Qais Resthouse, perched atop a small hill in the heart of the ruins. With stunning views over Galilee, the Golan and the snow-capped peaks of Lebanon, it's the perfect venue for lunch or an early dinner.

Located inside a converted Ottoman house, the restaurant is part of a famed consortium of top-notch restaurants in Jordan and offers an impressive seasonal menu highlighting fresh produce, local wines and locally raised meats. The open-air terrace is surrounded by flowers in spring that look good enough to sprinkle on the salad.

Shine Cottage Grilling CAFE $
(☻9am-9pm) A small open-air cafe, that has great views from the terrace and is the only other opportunity for casual refreshments near the ruins. It is opposite the parking lot.

❶ Information

The easiest way to enter ancient **Gadara** (admission JD3; ☻24hr) is from the western end of the car park. There are minimal signs in the site so it's worth collecting the brochure about Umm Qais from the ticket office. *Umm Qais: Gadara of the Decapolis* (JD3), published by Al-Kutba, is ideal for anyone who wants further information. Guides (JD10) are available from the ticket office.

There are toilets at the Umm Qais Resthouse. The tourist police are along the lane between the museum and the Resthouse.

❶ Getting There & Away

Umm Qais village, and the ruins 200m to the west, are about 25km northwest of Irbid, and about 110km north of Amman. Minibuses leave Irbid's North bus station (800 fils, 45 minutes) on a regular basis. There's no direct transport from Amman.

With a car you can descend to the Jordan Valley road via the village of Adasiyyeh. The occasional minibus runs down this road to Shuneh ash-Shamaliyyeh but if you are relying on public transport to get to Pella from here, it's easier to backtrack via Irbid.

Pella (Taqabat Fahl) بيلا

In the midst of the Jordan Valley are the ruins of the ancient city of Pella (Taqabat Fahl), one of the 10 cities of the fabled Roman Decapolis. Although not as spectacular as Jerash, Pella is far more important to archaeologists as it reveals evidence of 6000 years of continuous settlement. In fact, it's regarded as the most historically significant site in all Jordan. Centred on a large tell, and surrounded by fertile valleys that together comprise a rich watershed, Pella has fostered human civilisation from the Stone Age to medieval Islamic times.

Many of the ruins are spread out and in need of excavation, so some walking and a bit of imagination are required to get the most from the site. Unlike Jerash, which overwhelms visitors with its monumental grandeur, Pella is harder to visualise but the superb setting just above the Jordan Valley rewards even the most cursory of visits.

History
Pella was inhabited a million years ago by hunters and gathers who followed herds of game animals through the Stone Age forests

---

FORBIDDEN FRUIT IN THE JORDAN VALLEY

This is border country, historically disputed land, where the names alone (Golan Heights, West Bank) cast a long shadow over the fields of onions and tomatoes. Mr Abu Eiad, in this year of drought, casts an eye up to the cloudless sky and pronounces with profound stoicism, 'It's God's will'. He is happy, he says. With two wives, four sons and two daughters, why shouldn't he be? It also transpires that he has something else to smile about. Hidden between the limes and lemons of his family plot, water gushes into a beautiful vale of emerald green. It's a far cry from the plastic-sheeted fields of corporate neighbours, some dry-baked like old leather, others artificially green under their polythene coating.

The spring is diverted by stones into the orchard one day and the potato fields the next, the excess siphoned off to help neighbours. Abu Eiad's wife wants help for new technologies to develop their enterprise. Casting a look at the Garden of Eden in front of us, with its plump, organic fruit and glossy aubergines, it's hard to imagine that anything could improve on their winning formula.

'Take a picture!' Abu Eiad insists, as he stands in waving distance of the Jordan River – and the armed border guard who thankfully is looking the other way. But it isn't the border that's the focus of the shot: the focus is on two farmers, either side of the thin ribbon of reeds, plucking weeds from their onion beds, just as other *fellaheen* (subsistence farmers) have been doing in the Jordan Valley for centuries.

and savannahs. By 5000 BC permanent Neolithic farming villages sprung up around the tell and attracted the attention of the Egyptians, who referred to the site in written texts in the 2nd millennium BC.

Pella thrived due to its strategic position on the trade routes running between Arabia, Syria, Egypt and the Mediterranean. Luxury items, including ivory sculpture and gold jewellery have been excavated from the site, suggesting that Pella was a prosperous settlement throughout the Bronze and Iron Ages.

Under the Greeks, the settlement earned the name 'Pella' after the birthplace of Alexander the Great. The Jews largely destroyed Pella in 83 BC as the inhabitants were not inclined to adopt Jewish customs. Twenty years later, the legions of Roman Emperor Pompey swept into the Levant and rebuilt it, along with neighbouring cities in the Decapolis. Life under the Romans was embraced in Pella and the city enjoyed an era of political autonomy and economic stability; it even had the power to mint its own coins.

It was to Pella that Christians fled persecution from the Roman army in Jerusalem in AD 66. Although they later returned to Jerusalem, they left a strong mark on Pella, helping to ease the city's adoption of Christianity a few centuries later.

Pella reached its peak during the Byzantine era, and by the year 451 the city was influential enough to warrant its own bishop. The population at this time may have been as high as 25,000, and there is evidence that Pella was part of an expansive trade route that encompassed most of Asia Minor as well as North Africa.

The city was virtually destroyed by the earthquake that shook the whole region in 747. The last occupiers of Pella were the Mamluks of the 13th and 14th centuries. While Pella enjoyed a brief renaissance, the defeat of the Mamluks by the Ottomans caused the residents of Pella to flee, ending more than 6000 years of continuous settlement. Today the ruins of Pella lie a few kilometres away from the modern Arab village of Taqabat Fahl.

◉ Sights

At the base of the main mound (on your right as you pass through the main entrance) are the limited remains of a **Roman gate** to the city. Atop the hill are the ruins of an **Umayyad settlement**, which consisted

Pella (Taqabat Fahl)

Pella (Taqabat Fahl)

◉ Sights
1 Abbasid Settlement	B1
2 Byzantine Fort	B2
3 Canaanite Temple	A2
4 Civic Complex Church (Middle Church)	B2
5 East Church	B2
6 Mamluk Mosque	A2
7 Nymphaeum (Baths)	B2
8 Odeon (Theatre)	B2
9 Roman Gate	B1
Roman Temple	(see 2)
10 Umayyad Settlement	B2

⊗ Eating
11 Pella Rest House	B1

of shops, residences and storehouses. The small, square **Mamluk mosque** to the west dates from the 14th century. Carved into the south side of the hill is the recently excavated **Canaanite temple**, which was constructed in around 1270 BC, and dedicated to the Canaanite god Baal.

The main structure, and indeed one of the better preserved of the ruins at Pella, is the Byzantine **civic complex church** (or **middle church**), which was built atop an earlier Roman civic complex in the 5th century AD, and modified several times in the subsequent two centuries. Adjacent is the **odeon** (a small theatre used for musical performances). It once held 400 spectators, but you will need considerable imagination to picture this now. East of the civic complex church are the low-lying remains of a Roman **nymphaeum**.

Up the hill to the southeast is the 5th-century **east church**, which has a lovely setting perched high above the lower city. From there a trail leads down into Wadi Malawi and then climbs **Tell al-Husn** (note the remains of tombs cut into the hillside), atop which are the stones of a **Byzantine fort** and **Roman temple**. There are good views of the Jordan Valley from here.

Outside the main site, there are the ruins of a small **Abbasid settlement** about 200m north of the main entrance. There are also a few limited **Palaeolithic ruins** (4km), **Roman baths** and a **rock bridge** (3km) reached via the road past the turn-off to the Pella Rest House.

Enquire at the rest house about how to get to the rubble of a **Hellenistic temple** high on Jebel Sartaba to the southeast. From there, Jerusalem is visible on a clear day. The return hike takes a good couple of hours.

🛏 Sleeping & Eating

Pella Countryside Hotel B&B $
(☎079-5574145, 077-6184337; dheebjawahreh575@hotmail.com; s/d incl breakfast from JD30/40) This charmer of a B&B has lovely rural views from a shared guest lounge. The seven comfortable rooms, with private bathrooms, have plenty of country-style flourishes. It's a good place to relax for a couple of nights and the owners can arrange picnics in the surrounding hills. From February to May, black irises, the national flower of Jordan, bloom in the garden. The hotel is signposted off the road to the ruins.

TOP CHOICE **Pella Rest House** JORDANIAN $$
(☎079-5574145; meals JD8-10; ☺8.30am-7pm) This famous restaurant is renowned for its exceptional views over Pella and the Jordan Valley – Israel and the Palestinian Territories is visible to the right of the communications towers, the West Bank is to the left, and the Jenin Heights and Nablus are in the middle. Of course, you shouldn't let the views distract you too much from the enticing menu, which highlights regional cuisine including fresh St Peter's fish from the Jordan River.

ℹ Information

The **site** (☺8am-6pm) can be entered free at several points, including via the Pella Rest House on the hill.

Anyone with a specific interest should buy *Pella* (JD3), published by Al-Kutba and available in major bookshops around Jordan.

ℹ Getting There & Away

From Irbid's West bus station, minibuses go to Al-Mashari'a (800 fils, 45 minutes), though be sure to get off before Al-Mashari'a at the junction. Pella is a steep 2km walk uphill from the signposted turn-off but occasional minibuses ascend to the rest house if they see visitors heading for the ruins. Minibuses and service taxis travel regularly from Amman's North Bus Station to Deir Alla (800 fils, one hour) close to the Pella junction.

With your own car, the ruins are an easy day trip from Irbid, Jerash or Amman. Exploring the scenic back roads to Ajloun (25km) takes a bit of a nose for navigation but is worthwhile for the insights into rural life among the olive groves that it affords.

Salt السلط

☑ 05 / POP 70,000 / ELEV 814M

Progressing along the Jordan Valley in either direction, it is worth taking a 30-minute detour into the hills to visit the characterful old town of Salt. Part of the fun of the visit is climbing to a viewpoint and marker, 10 minutes from the valley floor, which indicates sea level (see p114 for an account of the route). If you were just about anywhere else on the planet, you'd be surfacing for air at this point.

The town itself is set in a steep-sided, narrow valley. During Ottoman rule, Salt was the region's administrative centre, but was passed over as the new capital of Trans-Jordan in favour of Amman. Consequently, Salt never experienced the intense wave of modernisation that swept across the capital, and as a result has retained much of its historic charm. Today, much of Salt's downtown is a living museum of Ottoman-period architecture.

Salt is visited by few foreign tourists, and remains one of the undiscovered highlights of the Jordan Valley area. A multimillion-dollar aid package awarded to the city in 2004 by Japan has been used to preserve many of the city's old buildings and to create facilities for tourists. While infrastructure is still largely lacking, it's heartening to see that the residents of Salt have embraced their city's architectural heritage in a country where concrete urbanisation is the norm.

History

While you'd be forgiven for thinking that the town was named after the table condiment, Salt was either named after the Greek word *saltus* meaning 'forests' (although these are long gone), or from *sultana* for the grapes that were once abundant in the region.

Construction began on Salt's characteristic limestone buildings in the late 19th century thanks to the arrival of merchants from Nablus. Over several decades, Salt began to thrive as trade networks sprang up between the city and neighbouring Palestine.

Following the establishment of Trans-Jordan, the new emir chose Amman as his capital due to its proximity to the railway. Almost overnight, Salt went into decline. War with Israel separated Salt from the port of Haifa in 1948, and later from its trading partner of Nablus in 1967, ending Salt's significance as anything more than a rural town above the Jordan Valley.

◉ Sights & Activities

There are some fine examples of **Ottoman architecture** (see the boxed text, p108) in town dating from the late 19th and early-20th century. Few of these gracious limestone buildings are open to the public, but some of the elegant facades are worth viewing. Stairways lead up to fine views from atop Jebel al-Qala'a.

Salt Archaeological Museum   MUSEUM

(☑3555651; admission JD1; ☺8am-6pm May-Oct, to 4pm Nov-Apr) This delightful little museum is located in a well-restored Ottoman-era building and covers the local history of the Jordan Valley area with excellent information boards in English. The downstairs rooms focus on glass and pottery (some dating back 5000 years), spanning the Roman, Byzantine and Islamic eras, mostly from around Salt but also from Deir Alla and Tell Nimrin (from where Joshua is thought to have led the Israelites across the River Jordan into the Promised Land). Upstairs are some examples of local traditional dress, displays on traditional farming activities and mosaic fragments from churches around Salt.

Salt Handicraft Training
Centre   CRAFT WORKSHOP

(☑3550279; Nageb al-Daboor district; ☺8am-3pm Sun-Thu) Visitors can watch weaving, pottery, mosaics and other handicrafts being made at this women's cooperative, 3km out of town. The centre specialises in both train-

ing and production and has a showroom for displaying the finished products. A taxi here costs JD1 to JD2 from the centre; ask for the Balkhar Islamic School (Bejanib Maddaris al-Balkhar al-Islamiy). The turn-off is at a set of traffic lights by a bridge, 2km from Salt along the road to Amman.

Wadi ash-Shu'aib   HIKING

If you have a car it's worth exploring Wadi ash-Shu'aib, a refreshing valley named after the prophet Jethro ('Shu'aib' in Arabic).

DISCOVERING SALT ON FOOT

Salt is one town that really rewards a bit of on-foot exploration as much of the old quarter can only be accessed by stairways and the best of the souq area is clustered into pedestrian-only alleyways. The following 3km route, which takes about 90 minutes to complete, leads you on a circular tour of Salt's backstreets, taking in its bazaars and old Ottoman architecture.

From Salt bus station walk up Dayr St, past the impressive doorway of **Beit Mismar** and the lovely balcony columns of **Beit Muasher**, both grand old Ottoman residences. Continue along Dayr St as it passes the curved walls of Salt's Orthodox church to the recently restored **Beit Abu Jaber**, which houses a small local-history museum. Head across the plaza and take the stairs up to the right of the mosque, curving round to the entry of the former **English Hospital** (look for the letters 'EH' on the green gate). From here you can wind your way uphill for fine views over the town and descend along a neighbouring staircase.

Alternatively, return to the plaza and head down **Hammam St**, Salt's most atmospheric backstreet, past the ornate **Ottoman mosque** to the junction with Maydan St. Across the street is the colonnaded entry of **Muhammed al-Bashir's House** (built between 1890 and 1910), now a traditional coffeehouse (with a tree in front). Next door is Beit al-Sulibi (built between 1920 and 1930).

Break for lunch at the **Al-Salam Restaurant** and end your tour at the **archaeological museum**.

There are some hiking opportunities here and interesting caves. It's 2.5km southeast of Salt.

✖ Eating

There is nowhere to stay in Salt but there are several unpretentious places to eat. The northern end of Maydan St is lined with traditional cafes, full of men drinking tea and smoking nargileh. Basic restaurants along the same street and by the bus station serve kebabs, though the best place in town for Arabic food is the **Al-Salam Restaurant** (☑3552115; Maydan St; meals JD3-5; ◷7am-10.30pm Sat-Thu), which serves up rotisserie chicken and good shish kebab meals.

ⓘ Information

The friendly **tourist office** (☑3555652; Dayr St; ◷8am-3pm Sun-Thu) is upstairs in the impressive old residence of Beit Mismar, but catching it open as per the advertised hours is something of an art.

ⓘ Getting There & Away

The bus station is on the main road south of the town centre. There are minibuses to Salt (800 fils, 45 minutes) from Amman's North Bus Station, via the University of Jordan, and occasional service taxis from Raghadan. From Salt, minibuses head fairly regularly down to the Jordan Valley to Shuneh al-Janubiyyeh (South Shuna; 800 fils, 45 minutes). Minibuses also go to Wadi as-Seer (600 fils, 30 minutes) and Fuheis (600 fils, 30 minutes), with which Salt can be combined as a day trip from Amman. Taxis can be chartered to Amman for around JD10 to JD15.

The drive to Salt from the Jordan Valley, along either the road south of Deir Alla or from South Shuna, is spectacular. The 30-minute route winds through Bedouin encampments to the coniferous and windswept hillsides of the Zay National Park (little more than a municipal picnic spot) and affords many panoramic views of the Jordan Valley.

Shuneh al-Janubiyyeh (South Shuna) الشونة الجنوبية

☑05 / POP 6000 / ELEV -240M

Serving as a junction for public transport along the Jordan Valley and King Hussein Bridge, as well as for the Dead Sea, this town is well connected by minibus with Amman's Muhajireen bus station (800 fils, 45 minutes), as well as Madaba (600 fils, 45 minutes) and Salt (500 fils, 45 minutes). There are also frequent minibuses to Suweimeh, 3km from the Dead Sea resorts.

A few simple restaurants and grocery stores are scattered around town. Consider chartering a taxi (if you can find one) for a few hours from Shuneh al-Janubiyyeh to places like Bethany-Beyond-the-Jordan (JD15) and Amman Beach (JD15).

Bethany-Beyond-the-Jordan (Al-Maghtas) المغطس

> Then Jesus came from the Galilee to the Jordan to be baptised by John.
>
> *Matthew 3:13*

> This took place in Bethany beyond the Jordan, where John was baptising.
>
> *John 1:28*

Whatever one's religious persuasions, it's hard not to be moved by this minimal pile of ruins with its preposterously long name, lying at the end of the Jordan Valley near the Dead Sea. This is the site, archaeologists assure us, where John the Baptist preached, where Jesus was baptised, where the first five apostles met and where, thereby, the foundations of the early Christian faith were laid. They chose an auspicious spot, as many also believe that this was the place from where prophet Elijah (who was born in Mar Elias in north Jordan) ascended to heaven in a whirlwind:

> And as they still went on and talked, behold, a chariot of fire and horses of fire separated the two of them. And Eli'jah went up by a whirlwind into heaven.
>
> *2 Kings 2:11*

Although John was later beheaded by Herod at Machaerus (see p141) and Jesus was crucified in Jerusalem, the meeting between the two men at this spot in the fertile Jordan Valley was one of hope and new beginnings. It is little surprise, then, that it became a focus for early pilgrimage, and remains so to this day.

History
The name Bethany comes from the Aramaic Beit Anniya (House of the Crossing). As you stand by the almost-stagnant river at this point, Israel and the Palestinian Territories is almost within arms' reach. Pilgrim churches, guesthouses and a 6th-century pilgrim road developed around the crossing as pilgrims broke their journey between Jerusalem and Mt Nebo. Today, there's little visible evidence of the early passage of pilgrims but the sense of crossing is still disturbingly apparent: as one traveller, Nathalie Ollier, remarked, 'It's hard for Christian visitors on either side of the water to pray when watched over by Jewish and Muslim armed guards intent on making sure you don't cross the border'.

The sense of fight and flight at this point is captured in the famous mosaic map of Madaba where a gazelle turns towards a lion (identifiable only by its tail) in hot pursuit. They're running through the Jordan Valley towards the Dead Sea, just above the place where John baptised Jesus, and are symbolic, perhaps, of the human flight that has marked this poignant patch of land for centuries.

The site has only relatively recently been identified. Some ancient ruins were discovered in 1899 but it wasn't until the clearing of landmines (following the 1994 peace treaty with Israel and the Palestinian Territories) that the remains of churches, caves, extensive wells and several baptism pools were unearthed. After much debate, scholars identified the site of John the Baptist's mission and Jesus' baptism from descriptions in the Bible and from 3rd- to 10th-century pilgrim accounts. Pope John Paul II sanctified the claim with an open-air mass at the site in the spring of 2000.

◉ Sights

Tell Elias   RUIN
The shuttle bus makes a brief stop at Tell Elias, where Elijah is said to have ascended to heaven. This is a significant spot for pilgrims of the three religions 'of the book', although there is little to see here. The rebuilt arch marks the 5th- to 6th-century pilgrim chapel, where the late Pope John Paul II authenticated the site in March 2000. The nearby 3rd-century rectangular prayer hall is one of the earliest Christian places of worship ever discovered, dating from a period when Christianity was still illegal. The bus continues to a modern baptism pool with filtered water from the Jordan River (the river is badly polluted).

Spring of John the Baptist   SPRING
The tour continues on foot (hot in summer so take a hat and water) to one of several places where John is believed to have carried out baptisms. Most baptisms were conducted in the spring-fed waters of Wadi al-Kharrar, rather than in the Jordan River. The path leads through thickets of tamarisk and *argul* (wild cherry) and the yellow rose of Jericho in spring.

Site of Jesus' Baptism   RUIN

The main archaeological site comprises the remains of three churches, one on top of the other. Steps lead down to the original water level and a building nearby marks the likely **site of Jesus' baptism**. Byzantine churches were built to mark the site during the 5th and 6th centuries, and rebuilt on the same site after they were destroyed by flooding. All that remains today are traces of original mosaic.

Jordan River   RIVER

The walking trail passes a golden-roofed Greek Orthodox church and leads, under the watchful eye of border guards, to the river – little more than a stagnant ditch. It's not very inviting but you can be baptised in the Jordan if accompanied by a priest. Across the river (and the border) is a rival Israeli baptism complex. This is the only place where civilians can currently touch the Jordan River as the remainder runs through a military no-man's-land.

Other Sights

Tours often return via the **House of Mary the Egyptian**, a 'reformed sinner' who lived and died in the two-room house in the 4th century. The trail continues left, up some wooden stairs to a two-room **hermit cave** burrowed into the soft rock.

The hill behind holds the presumed cave of John the Baptist, a 5th-century monastery (built around the site) and the **Rhotorios Monastery**, which has a mosaic floor with Greek inscriptions. In the 3rd to 4th century, the plaster-lined pools were used by pilgrims for bathing. In the early years of Christianity, John was a more celebrated figure than Jesus and this was the more important of the two pilgrimage sites.

✖ Eating

Bethany Touristic Restaurant   FISH **$$$**
(☑079 6076060; fish JD12; ☺10am-midnight) Attached to a thriving fish farm, this restaurant specialises in excellent tilapia (*talloubi* in Arabic), locally known as Baptism fish. The fish is fried, or baked with sweet peppers and fresh coriander. It's a popular spot at weekends, particularly at dusk when the sun sets over distant Jerusalem. Look for signs along the road halfway between the baptism site and the main Amman–Dead Sea road. This was the only place to eat near Bethany at the time of writing.

❶ Information

Entry to the **site** (adult/child under 10 JD12/free; ☺8am-4pm Nov-Mar, to 6pm Apr-Oct) includes a one-hour guided tour and shuttle-bus service which departs every 30 minutes to the main complex, close to the sensitive border with Israel and the Palestinian Territories. Collect a brochure and map at the main gate, where there are toilets and a few desultory souvenir shops, hit hard by the recent downturn in tourism. The flies here are of plague proportions in spring so bringing repellent is a good idea.

❶ Getting There & Away

The site is near South Shuna, at the southern end of the Jordan Valley. Coming from Amman, follow signs to the 'Baptism Site' along the main road to the Dead Sea. Tours from the budget hotels in Amman and Madaba often include this site in a Dead Sea day trip from around JD50 for a maximum of four people. Getting there by public transport is more difficult. Take any minibus to Suweimah and ask to be dropped at the Al-Maghtas junction. The Dead Sea is to the left of the junction, the baptism site to the right. There's no public transport for the 5km trip to the visitor centre. Take plenty of water if you intend to walk or hitch.

Dead Sea Highway
الطريق البحر الميت

Best Places to Stay & Eat

» Mövenpick Resort & Spa (p118)

» Dead Sea Marriott (p119)

» Mujib Biosphere Reserve (p123)

» Panorama Restaurant (p120)

» Feynan Ecolodge (p122)

Best Spa Experiences

» Zara Spa (p118)

» Anantara Spa (p118)

» Dead Sea Marriott Spa (p118)

» Evason Ma'In Hot Springs Six Senses Spa (p122)

Why Go?

There are not many places on earth where you can walk below sea level, but along the shores of the Dead Sea you are in one of them! In fact, this is the lowest point on earth. If this isn't inducement enough for a visit, try the swimming. Bobbing in the intensely salty water is one of the most extraordinary aquatic experiences to be had. Add the luxury soaking, massaging and therapeutic treatment that is part and parcel of a night or two in a spa resort and you'll soon see why the Dead Sea area is a highlight of a visit to Jordan.

The attractions of the Dead Sea are no secret but there's more to the region than just the northern strip of five-star hotels. Wadi Mujib encompasses a beautiful little nature reserve that offers outdoor adventure, and the entire Wadi Araba is especially magnificent at sunset.

When to Go

Blisteringly hot and humid between May and October, and chilly between December and January, the best time to enjoy the Dead Sea pleasure domes is around February and November – perfect for sunny swims and balmy dinning al fresco. Catering to the peak tourist season at this time, resorts offer live entertainment.

Those looking for adventure should aim for spring: the Dead Sea Ultra Marathon brings physical activity to a seashore more famous for sunning than running and hikes along water-bound Wadi Mujib are free from the danger of flash flooding.

Western Highlights

1 Descend to the depths for a bob in the **Dead Sea** (p113), at the lowest point on earth, before scaling the heights with a cocktail at a lavish spa resort

2 Relax mind and body at a famous **Dead Sea spa** (p117), applying mud used for cosmetic purposes since the time of Herod

3 Place the Dead Sea in historical and geographical context at the informative **Dead Sea Panoramic Complex** (p120)

4 Wallow in hot springs at **Hammamat Ma'in** (p120), one of the region's thermal oases

5 Drive from high-ground to low-ground towards the **Dead Sea Highway** (p114) for the best views in Jordan

6 Splash through the canyon pools of **Mujib Biosphere Reserve** (p123), keeping an eye open for ibex

7 Taste a freshly plucked tomato before exploring the rainbow hills of **Wadi Araba** (p125)

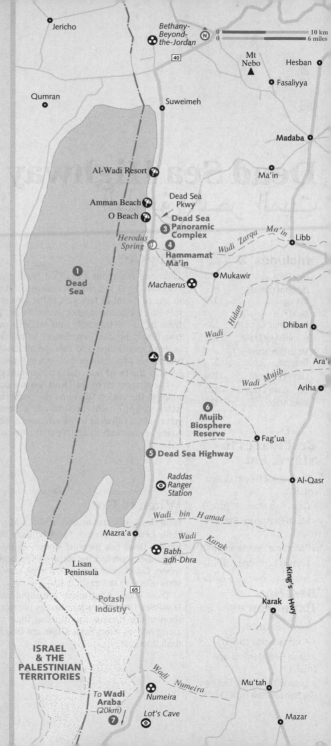

History

It's easy to sense the antiquity of a region that has supported human endeavour for thousands of years. All along the highway, fresh water springs bring a hopeful abundance of life (as at Wadi Mujib) in vivid contrast to the surrounding barren escarpment. In season, the parched soil is threaded with crates of blood red tomatoes and glossy-coated eggplants (aubergines), proving the unexpected fecundity of a region that looks to all intents and purposes like a desert.

Belying its name, even the Dead Sea has contributed to the pattern of human civilisation. Known to the ancients as the Sea of Asphalt, it produced bitumen harvested by the Nabataeans and sold to neighbours for embalming processes in a nascent oil industry.

Travel along the Dead Sea Highway today, with its proximity to the Israel and Palestinian Territories, and you quickly feel how oil, albeit of a different kind, defines the territory still. Police checks, border posts, cautious eyes across the Rift Valley – this is disputed soil, a land cleaved in two, geologically, historically and politically. You may try to float in peace in a Dead Sea spa but you can't help but be aware that the calm has been bought at a high price. For more about the history of the Dead Sea area, see p252.

Nature Reserves

One of the most delightful wilderness areas in Jordan, Mujib Biosphere Reserve (p123) lies just around the corner from the Dead Sea resorts. Unfortunately this is partially why there are concerns for the long-term viability of the reserve as the water that flows through the wadi is siphoned off to supply the demands of tourism. Whatever the future of the reserve, for now the area offers waterfalls, canyon adventures and a chance to catch sight of the elusive ibex.

The Dead Sea Highway also gives secondary access to the spectacular Dana Biosphere Reserve (p151) and to Dana's Feynan Ecolodge (p122) – the only accommodation in Wadi Araba. The main entrance to Dana Biosphere Reserve, however, is via the village of Dana off the King's Highway. See p151 for full coverage of the reserve.

Dangers & Annoyances

Due to the proximity of the Israel and Palestinian Territories border, there are numerous police checkpoints in the area. Keep your passport, driver's licence, rental contract and *ruksa* (car registration card) handy on any of the roads near or along the Dead Sea Highway.

There are few petrol stations in the vicinity, and little accommodation (except at the Dead Sea resorts and within the national parks of Wadi Mujib and Wadi Dana). It's therefore important you honour the desert code and fill up each time you see a petrol station or you stand a very real chance of getting stranded.

There is very little shade at the Dead Sea or indeed anywhere along the Dead Sea Highway so it is important to bring a hat and plenty of water, particularly in the summer when temperatures can soar to an intolerable 50°C.

On Friday and public holidays the hotels and public areas are crowded; some will see this as a good thing, others might find the typically Jordanian noise levels an annoyance!

❶ Getting There & Away

The Dead Sea Highway is most easily reached by road from Amman but other access points include Madaba, Karak and Wadi Mousa, all of which make suitable bases for exploring the region. Although the Dead Sea Highway (Hwy 65) ends in Aqaba, there's not much to see or explore along the southern reaches of the highway and no public transport. It's just about possible to get to the Dead Sea resorts with a frustrating and unreliable combination of minibuses and taxis, but tours offer the most realistic way of reaching the area.

❶ Getting Around

Pretty much the only way to explore the Dead Sea Highway (Hwy 65) is with a car. The Dead Sea Highway runs along the edge of the Dead Sea, between the honey-coloured Moab Mountains and the distant cliffs of Judaea on the West Bank, and offers an interesting alternative to the Desert Highway between Amman and Aqaba.

If you're not in a hurry, there are some **spectacular roads** (p114) that link the Dead Sea Highway with the King's Highway. With the intimate insight these roads afford into Bedouin communities and striking desert landscape, they are almost destinations in their own right.

Dead Sea البحر الميت

☑ 05 / POP >5000 / ELEV -400M

It would be a travesty to come to Jordan and miss the Dead Sea. At 400m below sea level, this extraordinary body of intense blue water, polished smooth like oiled skin on a

DRIVING BELOW ZERO

The switchback roads that link the high ground with the low ground (often below sea level) are a highlight of Jordan, especially if you are driving and can stop to admire the panoramic views. The roads twist through terraced fields of onions, hug contours of sheep-cropped hills, edge past nomadic communities of Bedouin with their black tents and attendant goats, before spiralling into a painted desert, vermilion with iron ore, olive green with copper oxides and laced with hanging gardens. Here is a summary of the best of these drives. You won't find the roads indicated on all maps but they are all well paved, suitable for a 2WD car (beware sharp bends) and usually marked 'Dead Sea' or 'Wadi Araba' on signs. Remember to carry your passport with you as there are numerous checkpoints along the roads to the Jordan Valley and Dead Sea Highway.

Salt to Dead Sea

1½ hours, 23km descent and 60km along the Jordan Valley

A varied drive along a busy road of Aleppo pines, red-barked strawberry trees and gardens of early-summer hollyhocks, giving way to tamarisks and acacias. Let your brakes cool at the sea-level marker and enjoy the view of the fertile Jordan Valley, lit up with flowering flame trees in May.

Follow signs for Zay National Park and Dayr 'Alla on Hwy 30 from Salt. Watch out for truck drivers on their mobile phones on the hairpin bends! Add a 14km detour (well signposted) to Mountain Breeze Country Club for a tea break. Notice the humidity and heat as you approach the Dead Sea.

Mt Nebo to Dead Sea Resorts

30 minutes, 21km

An easy drive, passing wildflowers and clumps of prickly pear, and driving through Bedouin grazing grounds before descending to a colourful, semi-arid desert with spectacular Dead Sea views.

The start of the descent is to the left of the Mt Nebo entrance gate. After 14.5km, turn left for the Dead Sea resorts or right for Bethany.

Madaba to Dead Sea Panoramic Complex

50 minutes (half-day with stops), 30km plus 5km return trip to Hammamat Ma'in

The best of the Dead Sea drives, through avenues of windswept junipers and firs, vines and olive groves, and alongside a wadi decorated with flowering oleander. Don't miss the steep descent of the sulphurous hillside to Hammamat Ma'in (p120). Recover at the aptly named

windless day in winter or ruffled into salty whitecaps during the summer winds, lies at the lowest point on earth. The extreme salinity of the water has nothing to do with the Dead Sea being below sea level; rather it comes about because of the high evaporation rate. This salinity makes for an almost intolerable environment for all but the most microscopic of life forms. Indeed, the only things you're likely to see in the Dead Sea are a few buoyant tourists.

Dead Sea salts and minerals have long been exploited for their skin-friendly properties – although they don't always feel that friendly. While swimming in the sea, you'll discover cuts you never knew you had (don't shave before visiting), and if any water gets in your eyes, be prepared for a few minutes of agony. In fact, 'swimming' is probably a misnomer – bobbing is nearer the mark as the buoyancy experienced in the Dead Sea makes it difficult to move through the water.

The best way to visit the Dead Sea is to stay at one of the luxury resorts at the northeastern end of the sea. Here you can enjoy a spa treatment, watch the sunset across the water and toast the rising night lights of Jerusalem, perched 1200m above the West Bank.

Alternatively, the Dead Sea can be reached as a day trip from Amman or Madaba.

Panorama Restaurant (p120). Follow signs for Hammamat Ma'in from King's Highway, 1km south of Madaba. The road, sometimes referred to as the 'Dead Sea Parkway', is incorrectly shown on most maps. Use low gear if you're making a detour to Hammamat Ma'in. Continue to the Dead Sea resorts (7km), Bethany (25km) or Amman (60km).

Karak to Safi
30 minutes, 40km

This is an easy drive along steep-sided wadi, with expansive views of potash production. Take a side trip to Lot's Cave (p125).

Time this drive for midafternoon, when the sunset turns the sandstone to molten gold. Follow signs from the King's Highway in Karak to Mazra'a or 'Dead Sea' along Hwy 50. Turn left at the Dead Sea Highway for Safi.

Tafila to Fife
40 minutes, 26km

Descend from cypress woodland, through weather-beaten rock formations and palm oases to tomato fields at Fifa.

Give extra time to this trip – it's a veritable geography lesson in habitats at different altitudes. Take Hwy 60 from the centre of Tafila, following signs for Wadi Araba; take care on the sharp bends.

Little Petra to Wadi Araba
One hour 15 minutes (half-day with stops), 45km plus 2km return to Little Petra and 20km return to Feynan Ecolodge

This fantastic drive begins with Nabataean sites such as the Elephant Rock and a side trip to the Siq at Little Petra (p191). Look out for rock-cut wine presses and dams through Siq Umm Al-Alda, decorated with ancient carob trees. Pass through the psychedelically green landscape surrounding a reclaimed-water project and visit a pre-pottery Neolithic tell (look for a wire fence on the left of the road) at Shkarat Msaiad. The mountain road thereafter twists through magnificent rainbow rocks before gliding into Wadi Araba, dotted with Bedouin camps, acacia trees and sand dunes.

Head through Umm Sayhoun to Little Petra. Turn right to Hesha and Bayder and immediately left, following signs to Wadi Araba. The road, which doesn't appear on most maps and isn't numbered, is damaged but not impassable at the bottom. At the junction in Wadi Araba, turn right to Qurayqira to stay at Feynan Ecolodge (p122) or left to reach the Dead Sea Highway. From the highway junction, it is 130km to Aqaba.

DEAD SEA HIGHWAY DEAD SEA

History

The Dead Sea has been called many names in its time, including the logical 'Salt Sea' and the less flattering 'Stinking Sea' (slap a little Dead Sea mud on your face and you'll soon see why). A Greek traveller, Pausanias, first gave it the current name, noticing that the extreme brackishness of the water made it unsupportive of life. The high salinity is due to the fact that the sea has no outlet and the high summer temperatures evaporate the fresh water more quickly than it is replenished. Each year, due to intensive irrigation in the Jordan Valley, the sea shrinks. This, together with the potash industry on the southern shore, has caused many environmentalists to lament the imminent death of this extraordinary stretch of water.

🏃 Activities

People come to the Dead Sea to engage with the sea and its mineral properties, either by taking a dip or by wallowing in a spa. About the only other activity on offer is a chance to ride on a camel or a horse. The Bedouin bring their magnificently liveried animals to the corniche between the resorts and pace them up and down the pavement between ad hoc tea stalls. A five-minute ride or photo opportunity costs around JD2.

DON'T MISS

BRAVING LUXURY IN A DEAD SEA SPA

You can't come to the Dead Sea and not try a spa. Even if you're a die-hard, old-school traveller who feels that sleeping on a bed with a soft mattress is a sign of weakness, there's a certain gratification in succumbing to the spa experience. You'll be in good company: Herod the Great and Cleopatra, neither noted as wimpish types, both dipped a toe in spa waters. So ditch the hiking boots for a day, step into a fluffy bathrobe and brave the clinically white, marble entrance hall of a Dead Sea pleasure dome.

The **spa experience** (from around JD30) usually begins with a mint tea and a spa bag to stow your worldly goods – this isn't going to be a chlorinated swim in the municipal pool back home. You'll then be shown to the mirrored changing rooms, with Dead Sea soaps and shampoos and more towels than you'll have body to towel down. This marks the point of no return: the silent-padding assistants waft you from here along marble corridors to the opulent bathhouses.

All the spas offer a range of cradling Dead Sea waters with different levels of salinity. There's usually a foot spa and a float in a Damascene-tiled Jacuzzi. Outside pools assault visitors with a variety of bullying jet sprays. Best of all are the little pots that bubble when you sit in them and ought to be X-rated.

Luxury of this kind is an extreme sport and by the time you reach the spa's private infinity pool, you'll be so seduced by the ambience you won't have the energy to try the saunas, steam rooms or tropical sprays, let alone the gym. Lie instead under an oleander by the pool, sip a chilled carrot juice and wonder why you resisted the spa experience for so long.

Swimming

Although technically you can take a dip anywhere along the Dead Sea coast, unless you are staying at one of the resorts it can be surprisingly difficult to reach the sea. This is especially the case as each year the sea retreats further from the shore, making it less and less accessible. Secondly, after a dip in the Dead Sea you'll find yourself coated in uncomfortable encrustations of salt that are best washed off as soon as possible. Thirdly, there's the utter lack of privacy to consider: the road follows the shoreline closely, and so do the border police! For these three reasons, it's better to reserve your swim for the comfort of the Dead Sea resorts or day beaches where freshwater showers are available and where access to the sea is generally cleared of sharp and lethally slippery rocks. The following day beaches are listed north to south.

Al-Wadi Resort   SWIMMING

(adult/child JD25/18; ⊙9am-6pm Sat-Thu, to 7pm Fri) This privately run resort has a variety of water games, including a wave machine and slides, in pleasantly landscaped surroundings. There are two restaurants (open 10am to 5pm), one selling snacks and the other offering an Arabic menu. Children are measured on entry: those under 95cm are admitted free! The resort is about 500m north of the Convention Centre at the head of the resort strip.

Amman Beach   SWIMMING

(☑3560800; adult/child JD15/10; ⊙9am-8pm) This public facility goes under the full title of **Amman Beach Tourism Resort, Restaurant & Pools**. The beach, 2km south of the main resort strip, is run by Amman municipality to give affordable access to the Dead Sea. The grounds are attractively landscaped and the beach is clean, with sun umbrellas, freshwater showers and a vibrant local flavour, making it a great place to strike up conversation with a Jordanian family.

There are also a number of swimming pools, a **restaurant** (JD12 buffet; ⊙11am-5pm), some drinks stalls, basketball courts and an amusement park next door. It gets very busy at weekends (especially Friday afternoon and Saturday morning).

Locals will generally swim fully clothed, though foreigners shouldn't feel uncomfortable in a modest swimming costume. Women on their own may attract less unwanted attention in shorts and a T-shirt.

Amman Beach is the finishing line for the annual Dead Sea Ultra Marathon in April. See p19 for details.

O Beach   SWIMMING

(☑3492000; www.obeach.net; adult/child JD20/17; ⊙9am-6pm) This excellent luxury private beach, stepped down the hillside in a series of landscaped terraces and infinity pools, is a great way to enjoy the Dead Sea in comfort without having to pay for a night in the neighbouring hotels. Various packages are available with discounts on weekdays (adult/child JD15/12). If you're looking for an extra-restful experience, VVIP areas are provided for an extra JD30 (couples only) with king size beds. Towels are free. A range of spa treatments and massages is also available. There are several restaurants and bars and a buffet at the weekend.

In addition to the previously discussed day beaches, some of the resorts offer day rates outside holiday periods. The Mövenpick charges JD40 for access to the pools, beach and buffet (couples and families only) and an extra JD50 for access to the spa. The Marriott charges JD60 (JD35 entrance only; JD25 for food). The Dead Sea Spa Hotel charges JD30 with a snack and a drink thrown in.

The Holiday Inn charges JD25 on weekdays and JD45 at weekends and holidays.

Mud Bathing
Most beaches have mud pots by the sea's edge where you can self-administer a full-body mud-pack. Leave it in place to bake under the sun for five to 10 minutes and then wash it off in the sea. It tightens the skin and leaves it feeling smooth, tingling and refreshed.

Spa Treatments
Many people go to the Dead Sea area for the therapeutic treatments on offer in the Dead Sea spas. The low levels of UV rays and high oxygen levels are good for the health, and the Dead Sea mud contains high concentrations of minerals. These include calcium and magnesium, helpful remedies against allergies and bronchial infections; pungent

DEAD SEA HIGHWAY DEAD SEA

THE DEAD SEA IS DYING *DR ALON TAL*

The Dead Sea is the lowest place on earth, and probably one of the hottest. The resulting evaporation produces an astonishing salinity of 31%, about nine times higher than the oceans, making a dip in the Dead Sea a very salty experience. The high mineral concentrations mean incredible buoyancy and great photo opportunities – get a snapshot of your travel companions happily sitting upright on the water reading newspapers. The water's oily minerals also contain salubrious properties. German health insurance covers periodic visits to the Dead Sea for psoriasis patients to visit and luxuriate in the healing waters.

Sadly, no natural resource in the Middle East shows more signs of relentless population growth and economic development than the Dead Sea. Technically, the sea is a 'terminal lake' into which the Jordan River, along with other more arid watersheds, deposit their flow. Despite the folk song's characterisation of the River Jordan as 'deep and wide', in fact it has never been much of a gusher. When Israeli and Jordanian farmers began to divert its water to produce a new agricultural economy in the 1950s, the flow was reduced to a putrid trickle and the Dead Sea began to dry up.

In 1900, the river discharged 1.2 trillion litres a year into the Dead Sea, but water levels in the river today are hardly 10% of the natural flow. The Jordanian and Israeli potash industries in the southern, largely industrial Dead Sea region exacerbate the water loss by accelerating evaporation in their production processes. The impact is manifested in sink holes, created when underground salt gets washed away by the infiltrating subsurface freshwater flow. Particularly ubiquitous on the western (Israeli side) of the sea, the ground literally opens up – with people, farming equipment and even trucks falling in. Perhaps the most acute environmental consequence though is the 27m drop in the sea's water level, and the long and discouraging walks now required to reach the edge of the retreating beach.

Several solutions have been considered to bring back water to the Dead Sea. A 'Med-Dead' canal utilising the height drop from the Mediterranean Sea was discarded because of the prohibitively expensive price tag. But a similar pipeline from the Red Sea is seriously being considered. Dubbed the 'Peace Conduit', the project would pipe water from the Gulf of Aqaba to the Dead Sea's southern shore, producing hydroelectricity as well as a desalination plant that would provide water to Amman. Environmentalists question the anticipated unnatural water chemistry reaction and the seismic instability of the area. The World Bank, however, recently decided that the US$5 billion project was sufficiently serious to justify a $15 million feasibility study.

Dr Alon Tal is a professor in the Desert Ecology Department at Israel's Ben-Gurion University.

bromine that promotes relaxation; iodine which alleviates certain glandular ailments; and bitumen that has skin-rejuvenating properties. Many of these Dead Sea properties are made into easy-to-use preparations such as soaps, shampoos and lotions, and sold at the Dead Sea spas and in tourist shops throughout Jordan.

Of course, you don't need to be under-the-weather to enjoy the benefits of a spa treatment. If you feel like a scrub or a massage, or just a bit of pampering, it's easy to book in for an hour or two.

Anantara Spa
SPA

(☑3568888; www.spa.anantara.com/deadsea; Kempinski Ishtar Hotel; ☺10am-10pm) The highlight of this highly luxurious spa is the Royal Hammam Ritual (JD130, 90 minutes), touted as 'pure bliss for mind and body'. It includes massage, body scrub and body wrap applied with traditional Jordanian-style vigour.

Zara Spa
SPA

(☑3491310; www.zaraspa.com; Mövenpick Resort & Spa; ☺8.30am-8.30pm) One of the largest spas in the Middle East, Zara Spa offers a range of facilities and treatments in a beautiful environment and costs JD20 for hotel guests and JD50 for nonguests. These rates include access to a gym, private beach, pool, sauna, steam room, foot-massage pool, infinity pool and aqua-pressure pool. Extra services include a mud wrap (JD60, one hour), dry flotation, hot-stone therapy, shiatsu and other massages (from JD60 for 50 minutes). A day package costs JD190 for 3½ hours of treatments; a three-day package is JD365.

Dead Sea Marriott Spa
SPA

(☑3560400; Dead Sea Marriott; ☺8.30am-8.30pm) This spa is JD19 for guests and JD30 for nonguests. It costs an extra JD40 for access to the beach, pools and gym. The spa includes a heated pool, Dead Sea saltwater pool, Jacuzzi, steam room and sauna. Treatments include massage (JD74, 55 minutes), body wraps, salt scrubs, phytomer facials, mud facials, dry flotation and hydro baths. An Arabic loufa experience (JD94, 75 minutes) has to be tried to be believed!

Dead Sea Spa
SPA

(☑3561000; www.deadseaspahotel.com; Dead Sea Spa Hotel; ☺8am-6pm) This spa focuses primarily on medical treatments, with an in-house dermatologist and physiotherapist. Entry to the beach, pools and spa costs JD30 at weekends (JD25 on weekdays) and includes a

fitness room, solarium and Dead Sea saltwater pool. A full-body Swedish massage (JD25) and mud application (JD30) are also available.

🛏 Sleeping & Eating

Along the Dead Sea Highway, about 5km south of Suweimeh, there are a number of first-class resorts. They don't look much from the highway but, once inside, they tumble into landscaped gardens, terraced sun spots, cascading pools and pristine Dead Sea beaches. They all have excellent restaurants and offer vantage points for watching the sun set over the hills of Judaea. Reservations are necessary at weekends (Friday and Saturday). At other times, discounts are often offered for walk-in customers. Unfortunately, there are no budget or midrange hotels in the vicinity. Madaba is the nearest town for cheaper accommodation, but as public transport to or from Madaba is so impractical you'll spend more time on the road than you will in the sea – unless you take a tour.

In addition to the long-established hotels following, a new Hilton and a Crowne Plaza are due to open by this book's publication.

🏆 Mövenpick Resort & Spa
RESORT $$$

(☑3561111; www.moevenpick-hotels.com; r from JD215; ❈@⧉) This wonderful haven of dates and hibiscus boasts a river that ambles through the village-style complex of rustic two-storey apartments. Wooden screens and balconies allow guests to enjoy the view (of sea or gardens) in private, while secluded seating areas around a superb infinity pool add to the ambience of discreet, gentle pleasure. The Zara Spa is justifiably renowned as one of the best in the Middle East. Culinary high points include Al-Saraya buffet, a Thursday night barbecue and prodigious Friday brunch. If five-star luxury is your thing, you won't want to stay anywhere else.

Kempinski Hotel Ishtar
RESORT $$$

(☑3568888; www.kempinski.com; s/d from JD200/220; ❈@⧉) Dominating the shore, this grand resort is not shy in its bid to be the best. Floor-to-ceiling windows stretch the length of the Dead Sea vista, a Sumerian-style lobby overlooks a spectacular, circular infinity pool, and a series of water features tumbles down to the Dead Sea, making this a palace among hotels. Each of the modern rooms has a semi-shaded balcony and semi-sunken bath. Champagne is served with breakfast and the restaurant cuisine, including Thai and Mediterranean, is excellent. Visit at night time when a walk through the floodlit grounds is like participating in a piece of conceptual art.

Dead Sea Marriott RESORT $$$
(☑3560400; www.marriott.com; s/d from JD175/190; ✳@☲♪) Polished marble floors, brass fixtures and fittings, and spacious rooms contribute to the general opulence of this much-loved resort. Eating spots include seaview cafes and a brasserie-style French restaurant. Two cinemas, high-speed internet access, a jungle playground, mini waterfall and family pool ensure the kids are kept happy while parents luxuriate in the spa.

Holiday Inn Resort Dead Sea RESORT $$$
(☑3495555; www.ichotelsgroup.com; s/d from JD100/120; ✳@☲♪) One of the newest hotels in the area, this excellent resort will appeal to families with its easier access to the Dead Sea. It is located at the far northern end of the hotel strip, well away from the current construction boom.

Dead Sea Spa Hotel RESORT $$
(☑3561000; www.deadseaspahotel.com; r from JD120; ✳☲) Not as refined as its neighbours, this hotel is pleasant nonetheless. There's a medical/dermatological spa, private beach access, a big pool and separate kids' pool with slides. Choose from rooms in the main block or bungalows.

There is one restaurant complex at the northern end of the hotel with some uninspiring chain outlets but the complex does at least have a view of the sea from the upper storey and this is the only place to eat near the Dead Sea beaches without being in a resort or a day beach. You can't miss the place: it's right beside the police checkpoint. There are no shops or general amenities in the area so if you intend to picnic, bring everything with you!

❶ Getting There & Away
Bus & Minibus
JETT buses offer a Friday-only service from Amman (JD8 return) at 8am, returning at 4pm if there are sufficient passengers. The bus leaves from the JETT office near Abdali bus station. Check with the JETT office in Amman (p75) for the latest timetable.

Minibuses from Muhajireen bus station only run as far as Suweimeh. For details of getting to/from the Dead Sea from Amman, see p75. See p138 for details on reaching the Dead Sea from Madaba.

Car
From Amman, it takes about an hour to reach the Dead Sea resorts, along Hwy 40 and Hwy 65. Alternatively, you can drive from Madaba via Mt Nebo (see the boxed text, p114). If you choose this route, your first view of the Dead Sea will be a spectacular blue lozenge beyond the iron-coloured hills.

Hitching
If you miss the last bus back to Amman from Amman Beach, you can try hitching. Friday and Sunday are the best days, but don't rely on this in summer or winter when infrequent traffic and extreme temperatures make this hazardous. Women should not attempt to hitch from here.

Taxi
A return taxi from Amman costs about JD50 including three hours waiting time (minimum required to make the trip worthwhile) or JD15 for a one-way journey. From Shuneh al-Janubiyyeh, taxis cost from JD30, including side trips to Bethany-Beyond-the-Jordan and the Dead Sea Panoramic Complex. If you take a taxi from Shuneh to the Dead Sea in only one direction (JD10 depending on your negotiation skills), bear in mind that it's very hard to find an onward taxi from the beach area.

Some budget hotels in Amman and Madaba organise day trips (see p58 and p138) via Mt Nebo, the Dead Sea Panoramic Complex and Hammamat Ma'in.

Herodus (Zara) Spring
نبع هيرودس
These hot springs, around 5km south of Amman Beach, have been famous for centuries, and are even marked on the Madaba mosaic map. Indeed, nearby is the site of ancient **Callirhoë**, a favourite spa of the ancients. Herod came here in 4 BC to find treatment for, according to Josephus, 'an unbearable itching all over his body' – quite possibly psoriasis. Little remains to be seen at the archaeological site (discovered in 1807) other than remnants of Roman bathhouses and the ancient harbour from which Herod's boats sailed. But with a bit of imagination, it's easy enough to conjure poor Herod's itching form being led to the therapeutic hillside.

Despite the popularity of the spot with locals, especially on Friday, it's hard to recommend swimming here either in the hot-spring pools (which are unclean), or at the beach, which affords no privacy from the road.

FAST FACTS

» The Dead Sea is part of the Great Rift Valley; it is the lowest spot on earth at 408m below sea level and more than 390m deep

» It is not actually a sea but a lake filled with incoming water with no outlet

» It is the second-saltiest body of water on earth (after Lake Aral in Djibouti) with a salt content of 31%

» Egyptians used Dead Sea mud (bitumen) in their mummification process; the last lump of floating bitumen surfaced in 1936

» The majority of Dead Sea minerals (including calcium and magnesium) occur naturally in our bodies and have health-giving properties

» The Dead Sea is 3 million years old but has shrunk by 30% in recent years (half a metre per year) due to evaporation and the demands of the potash industry, one of Jordan's most valuable commodities

The site is adjacent to the police station. Follow the sign for Mukawir and Dhiban uphill for 300m and the Callirhöe ruins are on the left. There is no public transport.

Dead Sea Panoramic Complex البحر الميت بانوراما

Walk among the cacti to this **lookout** (admission per person JD2; ⊙8am-10pm), high above the Dead Sea, watch the raptors wheel in the wadis below and you will have to pinch yourself to think that you are standing at sea level. This wonderful museum and restaurant complex offers some breathtaking views, especially on a crisp day in winter when the Judaea Mountains across the water seem as if they are an arm's stretch away.

For an excellent introduction to the geology, history and environment of the Dead Sea, spare an hour for the **Dead Sea Museum** (⊙9am-4pm) and lay hands on a set of touchable stones. Drive the roads in the area (see p114) and you'll notice the rich pattern, texture and hue of the exposed rocks alongside the road. This is particularly the case

on the Dead Sea Parkway, which extends above the Dead Sea Panoramic Complex to Hammamat Ma'in and Madaba, or below to the Dead Sea Highway. Along the cut of the steepest section of road, rich layers of sedimentary rock create natural murals that add to the beauty of the journey. In the museum, you can identify and touch specimens of this geological treasure.

A short hiking trail called the **Zara Cliff Walk** (1.4km; easy) follows the edge of the wadi and highlights local flora and fauna. You will hear the Tristram's Grackles before you see these birds as they screech across the wadi. Hyrax can also be spotted here.

To recharge, try at least one mezze in the **Panorama Restaurant** (☑3245500; mains JD10-18; ⊙noon-10pm; ☑), which more than lives up to its name. The excellent cuisine makes it a popular venue for weekend lunch and dinner. Try the ground-walnut (JD3) or *shanklish* (local cheese, rolled in thyme and mixed with tomatoes, onion and parsley; JD2), and follow it up with marinated, locally reared lamb chops (JD12) or *sawda dajaj* (chicken livers with grenadine syrup and lemon), which are a meal in themselves (JD4).

The complex is clearly signposted off the Dead Sea Highway, about 10km south of the Dead Sea resorts. The Dead Sea Panoramic Complex makes a worthwhile stop on a day circuit from Madaba, Mt Nebo, Bethany, the Dead Sea and Hammamat Ma'in, either by hired car or taxi (JD50 through Charl at the Mariam Hotel – see p133). There is no public transport.

Hammamat Ma'in
حمامات ماعين (زرقاء ماعين)
☑05 / ELEV -90M

Drive anywhere in the hills above the Dead Sea and you'll notice occasional livid green belts of vegetation, a trickle of water as it catches the sunlight, or a curtain of ferns across a disintegrating landscape of sulphurous rock. On closer inspection, you may catch a puff of steam and the hiss of underground water. These hills are alive with the sound of thermal springs – about 60 of them suppurate below the surface, breaking ground with various degrees of violence.

The most famous spring is **Hammamat Ma'in** (admission per person JD15; ⊙9am-9pm), a spectacular resort in Wadi Zarqa Ma'in.

The water, ranging from 45°C to a blistering 60°C, tumbles off the hillside in a series of waterfalls and less assuming trickles, and is collected in a variety of pools for public bathing. It contains potassium, magnesium and calcium.

The entrance fee permits use of the Roman baths at the base of the waterfall closest to the entrance and a swimming pool. Visitors are requested not to bring their own picnic, but this is rarely enforced. The valley is hugely popular on Friday during spring and autumn.

🏃 Activities
Thermal Bathing
Two main baths are open to the public. The **Roman baths** have clean, indoor, hot baths (separate for men and women). There is also a small **family pool** beside a waterfall (turn left after the entrance), restricted to women, families and couples.

The large, clean, cold-water **swimming pool** closes around 4pm. A steaming waterfall downstream makes a striking backdrop for tea on the terrace of the hotel.

WORTH A TRIP

A WALK ON THE WET SIDE

If you're in the Wadi Mujib vicinity and fancy a walk on the wild side, then try the 2km **Siq Trail**, the shortest hike in the reserve. Late spring and summer are the perfect times for hiking, at least for the reserve's so-called 'wet trails'. And by wet, they really mean wet, as you have to wade through the wadi's permanent standing pools of water. After rains, water height can reach well over 1m and may make the wadi inaccessible.

Leave your valuables behind (you can leave a locked backpack at reception), wrap your camera in a watertight bag, wear hiking sandals rather than leather hiking boots and brave the surprisingly noisy rush of water.

The Bad Bits
» Even on a summer morning it gets surprisingly cold wading between the canyon walls
» Ignore the macho types telling you it's just a 'gentle splash': depending on water levels, it's more like an assault course
» There are three or four points where you need a steadying hand to help cross fast-moving water (ask for a guide if you're on your own)
» Several giant, slippery boulders or obstructions at best require inelegant scrambling, shunting and stretching, and at worst invite a dislocated hip or shoulder
» On the descent, the leap of faith into a deep pool of water takes quite a bit of courage

The Good Bits
» 'Petra with water' is how the reserve ranger described the Siq Trail, and the comparison is a fair one
» Beautiful pockets of lime-green reeds harbour toads and the occasional snake
» The wadi is decorated with outrageously banded rock, scooped out and smoothed by the water
» Being pushed by the water from one rock pool to the next has its moments
» The adrenalin rush as the water thunders past a precarious foothold is exhilarating
» Relief on surfacing easily from the bubbling cauldrons of water is almost worth the fear on leaping in
» You'll be happy the pictures came out even though the camera didn't make it

So is it worthwhile? Without doubt! If you're fit but not a great water-goer you'll be surprised by how benignly exciting it is to be alone in a raging torrent, bounced down small waterfalls and flipped into gorgeous pools of sunlight in what must be one of the region's most accessible little adventures.

Spa Treatments

The exquisite little **Six Senses Spa** (☎3245500; www.sixsenses.com; ☺9am-8pm) offers a range of different treatments and experiences. There are two thermal pools naturally hovering at 42°C and a natural sauna cave (65°C to 70°C) buried discreetly in the heart of the wadi. It's a beautiful place to relax with grouse scuttling over the rocks and eagles wheeling above. In addition, there is a dry sauna and treatment rooms, each with a private garden. Use of the facilities costs JD38 including towels and green tea. A range of treatments include a one-hour Swedish massage (JD83) and a 90-minute holistic massage (JD115). If you book in at the spa, the JD15 entry fee to Hammamat Ma'in is waived.

Hiking

It's possible to **hike** the 8km from the springs through Wadi Zarqa Ma'in to Herodus Spring on the Dead Sea Highway. The seven-hour, moderate to hard trail involves negotiating deep pools, reed beds and slippery surfaces and is closed after rains. The hike requires a guide (JD130 per person for a minimum of two people), which can be organised through the resort reception if you book one day ahead. The fee includes the price of transport to collect you from the end of the trail.

Another small trail leads from the security guard hut, above the main waterfall. It is an easy hike, taking around 1½ hours. There is no need for a guide but you are requested to let the resort reception know that you are attempting it. If you prefer a guide to manage the small steep section it costs JD35 per person for a minimum of two people. For JD65 the price includes breakfast, which is winched across the wadi in a basket to a shaded picnic spot in full view of the main waterfall.

🛏 Sleeping & Eating

TOP CHOICE **Evason Ma'In Hot Springs**

Six Senses Spa   RESORT $$$

(☎3245500; www.sixsenses.com/evason-ma-in; s/d JD150/170; ❄@☎⚡) The new management of this excellent resort has magically transformed this hotel into an elegant, luxurious complex, shaded with mature trees and made characterful with extravagant Arabesque features. There are lots of retreats, either in alcoves of feathery cushions inside or in hidden landscaped arbours in the gardens. Many of the rooms – with

---

ⓘ OASES OF THE DEAD SEA HIGHWAY

There are virtually no eating or sleeping stops along the southern part of the Dead Sea Highway – bar one, the exceptional Feynan Ecolodge.

Owned by Dana Nature Reserve and privately managed (see p151), **Feynan Ecolodge** (☎2270497; www.feynan.com; Wadi Feynan; s/d incl breakfast & park entry fee JD85/95; ☺1 Sep-30 Jun; ❄⚡) is the only sleeping option south of Wadi Mujib. More usually found at the end of a long, hard day's hike through the Dana Nature Reserve, this lodge is more grail than guesthouse. The 26 adobe rooms are quirky in design, with patchwork mirrors and 'balconies' that are integral to the room rather than appended to the outside. At night the lodge is lit solely by locally made candles (4000 are used a month!), adding to the reverential atmosphere somewhere between medieval monastery and desert fortress.

It gets very hot here in summer (air-conditioning is available in extreme temperatures only) and you should bring a torch and mosquito repellent. The hot water (available between 11am and 7pm) is solar-heated. Dinner comprises a delicious vegetarian feast of potato, rice, eggplant (aubergine), tomato and bean dishes, garnished with local herbs and served with wafer-thin Arabic bread. Staff is recruited from local Bedouin tribes; food and supplies are purchased locally and a share of profits from tourism is invested in the care of Dana Reserve.

Set in magnificent multihued desert, Feynan Ecolodge is 22km off the Dead Sea Highway, via the Bedouin village of Greigra. Park at the office on the edge of the reserve and you'll be transported the rest of the distance by 4WD.

For a pit stop an hour's drive north of Aqaba, **Beir Mathkour** has a restaurant, craft shop and petrol station within a garden of palms.

sumptuous bathrooms – share a view of the piping, sulphurous hillsides. Windows onto the waterfalls from the superb restaurant bring the hot springs to your table. Fine dining includes home-grown herbs and vegetables from the hotel's organic cabbage patch in the wadi. The hotel organises daily excursions to Holiday Inn for those wanting to spend the day at the Dead Sea but chances are you'll find it hard to leave the sanctuary of the resort's own intimate spa.

Minimal snacks and soft drinks are for sale in the shop near the entrance of Hammamat Ma'in.

❶ Getting There & Away

The resort is 18.5km from the Dead Sea resorts and 27km from Madaba, and well signposted in either direction. If you're driving, the 2.5km descent into Hammamat Ma'in is scenic (with bands of green, yellow and red streaking the hillside) but very steep, so use low gear.

From Madaba a taxi costs around JD15 one way, or JD25 for a return journey including around an hour's wait. Alternatively, take a tour from the Black Iris in Madaba for JD28 with a three-hour waiting time. There is no public transport.

Mujib Biosphere Reserve
محمية الموجب

Straddling the Dead Sea Highway, this wonderful reserve, which ranges from 900m above sea level to 400m below, was originally established by the Royal Society for the Conservation of Nature (RSCN) for the captive breeding of the Nubian ibex. It now supports a surprising variety of over 400 species of plants (including rare orchids), 186 species of birds and 250 animal species, including Syrian wolves, striped hyenas, caracals and Blandford's fox. It's also an important staging post for migratory birds travelling between Africa and Europe.

The reserve faces several challenges. Water in the permanently flowing wadis of the reserve has significantly reduced as water is siphoned off for use in Amman and the Dead Sea resorts. With illegal hunting, overgrazing of livestock and the demands of mining companies for licences to start mineral extraction, the future of the park is looking precarious. Against all the odds, the RSCN is doing a first-class job in managing the 215 sq km reserve and it can only be hoped

that increased tourism to the reserve – with its crystal-clear pools of water, hanging gardens and desert escarpments – will increase the pressure on the government to guarantee its long-term protection.

Hiking

Siq Trail   HIKING
(per person JD15.500) The easiest hike on offer, this exciting 2km wade and scramble into the gorge ends at a dramatic waterfall (see p121).

Malaqi Trail   HIKING
(per person JD64) This wet trail is the reserve's most popular hike. It's a half-day trip involving a hot and unremitting climb into the wadi, a visit to the natural swimming pools of Wadi Hidan and descent (often swimming) through the siq (gorge). The finale involves rappelling down the 18m waterfall (not suitable for non-swimmers or those with a fear of heights). If you have limited time, tackle the wet **Canyon Trail** (per person JD42) instead. The trails start 3km south of the visitor centre.

Ibex Trail   HIKING
(per person JD25) This dry winter trail is a half-day guided hike that leads up to a Nubian ibex enclosure at the Raddas ranger station, along a ridge with views of the Dead Sea, and an optional excursion to the ruined Qasr Riyash.

Mujib Trail   HIKING
(from JD48) Starting from the ranger station at Fag'ua, near the King's Highway, this dry trail descends through a number of wadis to the Raddas ranger station or Wadi Mujib gorge.

🛏 Sleeping & Eating

The reserve operates 15 **chalets** (☎07-97203888; s/d/tr incl breakfast JD60/71/81; ❉) on the windy shores of the Dead Sea. You need to book in advance, either by calling the chalet manager direct, or when booking your hike through the RSCN. The chalets have twin beds, a fridge and a shaded patio overlooking the Dead Sea in a plot that is still under development. The communal shower block has hot and cold water, and there are freshwater showers by the beach. The small restaurant serves an early breakfast (open 7am to 8.30am) for hikers. For JD13, guests can also order a lunch or dinner of chicken, salad and mezze.

IN SEARCH OF SODOM

Say the words 'Sodom and Gomorrah' and dens of iniquity spring to mind. The Book of Genesis (Gen 19:24–25), responsible for the wicked reputation of these two terrible towns, describes the last straw – namely, when local Sodomites demanded to have sex with the angels sent by God to visit Lot. In response 'the Lord rained upon Sodom and upon Gomorrah brimstone and fire...and he overthrew those cities, and all the plain, and all the inhabitants of the cities, and that which grew upon the ground...'

Fanciful legends of a fevered biblical imagination? Not necessarily. The edge of Wadi Araba is located on a major fault line, and it's possible that the towns were swallowed up by collapsing soil. Another possibility is that an earthquake released large amounts of underground flammable gas and bitumen (the infamous 'slime pits' referred to in the Old Testament), which were ignited by fire or a lightning strike.

Whatever the cause of their demise, archaeologists have long speculated about the location of the world's most sinful cities. Many archaeologists favour the southern shore of the Dead Sea. But there's also the Bronze Age site of Babh adh-Dhra, on the edge of Wadi Karak. This town (population roughly 1000) was destroyed in 2300 BC, but intriguingly it holds the remains of 20,000 tombs, containing an estimated half a million bodies – as such it's odds-on favourite for Sodom. Both Babh adh-Dhra and the nearby site of Numeira, believed to be Gomorrah, are covered in a 30cm-deep layer of ash, suggesting the cities ended in a great blaze.

Natural disaster or the wrath of God? Some believe it amounts to the same thing.

ℹ️ Information

The **visitor centre** (☑07-97203888) is along the Dead Sea Highway, about 20km south of the Dead Sea resorts, beside a suspension bridge across Wadi Mujib. Guides are compulsory for all but the Siq Trail and should be booked in advance through the RSCN's **Wild Jordan Centre** (☑4616523; www.rscn.org.jo; Othman Bin Affan St, downtown, Amman). Only 25 people per day are allowed on each trail and there's a minimum group size of three on some trails. Apart from the Ibex Trail, children under 18 years are not allowed. Life jackets are provided.

There are three wet trails (open between 1 April and 31 October) and two dry (1 November to 31 March). The best time to visit is April and May, although February and March, and October and November, are the high seasons. The region is extremely hot and dry for most of the year, so guided treks usually begin early in the morning. For the wet trails, you may be wading up to your chest in water (or swimming) so bring a swimming costume, towel, walking shoes that can get wet, and a waterproof bag for your valuables and camera. A spare set of clothes is also recommended.

ℹ️ Getting There & Away

There's no public transport to the reserve: hire a car or take a taxi from Amman (125km), the Dead Sea resorts, Madaba or Karak.

Lisan Peninsula
ليسان شبه جزيرة

From Wadi Mujib, the Dead Sea Highway continues along the remaining length of the sea until it veers inland at the Lisan Peninsula. This area, together with the shallow waters of the Southern Ghor (Depression), is now dominated by the potash plant. Huge quantities of potassium chloride (Jordan's most valuable commodity), calcium and bromide are reclaimed from the Dead Sea through solar evaporation, leaving piles of discarded rock salt along the shoreline. The area was once settled during the early-Byzantine period and a number of minor ruins are scattered across the landscape.

The fields to the south of the Lisan Peninsula are highly fertile and produce tomatoes in biblical quantities, as well as eggplants (aubergines), cucumbers and potatoes, groves of bananas and date palms. It's a colourful region to visit during the winter harvest (January) when trucks, laden with produce, lumber up the mountain roads, leaving a trail of off-loaded vegetables strewn behind them.

Lot's Cave   كهف لوط

> Now Lot went up out of Zo'ar, and dwelt in the hills with his two daughters, for he was afraid to dwell in Zo'ar; so he dwelt in a cave with his two daughters.
>
> *(Genesis 19:30)*

Lot, the nephew of Abraham, features repeatedly in the colourful annals of the Dead Sea's southern shores. **Lot's Cave** (admission free; ☉daylight hours), just past the Lisan Peninsula, is where he and his daughters apparently lived after fleeing the destruction of Sodom and Gomorrah. Lot's wife famously turned into a pillar of salt after looking back at the smouldering city.

In an eyebrow-raising incident of incest that's remarkable even for the Bible, Lot's two daughters spiked their father's drink, had sex with him and then nine months later gave birth to his grandsons/sons Moab and Ben-Ammi, the forefathers of the Moabite and Ammonite peoples.

The cave, a 10-minute climb up a steep flight of steps, is surrounded by the ruins of a small Byzantine church (5th to 8th centuries), a reservoir and some mosaics, which were excavated by the British Museum. Remains from the cave date to the early Bronze Age (3300–2000 BC) and an inscription in the cave mentions Lot by name.

The **Lowest Point on Earth Museum**, at the base of the hill, was closed at the time of research.

The cave is 2km northeast of Safi and well signposted from the Dead Sea Highway. Look for the circular museum building on the hillside. Regular minibuses run between Karak and Safi (800 fils, one hour). If you're relying on public transport, be prepared for a 2km walk from the highway.

Wadi Araba   وادي عربة

Beyond the town of Safi, the Dead Sea Highway enters the arid landscape of Wadi Araba, and the desert quickly reasserts its dominance. The odd sand dune encroaches upon the road, the escarpment recedes to the distance and the sky assumes the epic quality of uninterrupted space. As such, there is not much to see along the final run into Aqaba – although the sensation of driving uphill to the Red Sea is an odd one. You can make the journey more interesting by diverting to the King's Highway, along the remarkable roads to Karak, Tafila or Little Petra (see p114 for details of these routes).

Madaba & the King's Highway
مأدبا & الطريق الملوكي

Best Places to Stay

» Black Iris Hotel (p133)
» Mariam Hotel (p133)
» Karak Rest House (p147)
» Dana Guest House (p153)

Best Places to Eat

» Haret Jdoudna Complex & Cafe (p136)
» Adonis Restaurant (p136)
» Ayola Coffeeshop & Bar (p136)
» Asa Moses Restaurant (p139)

Why Go?

Occupying the central highlands and interrupted by the mighty Wadi Mujib, Madaba and the points of interest that punctuate the King's Highway lie at the heart of ancient Jordan. From prehistoric dolmens in rolling pastureland, panoramic sites of biblical importance and exquisite Roman mosaics lying along old trade routes, to well-preserved Crusader castles, there is something fascinating to see along the entire length of this central region.

That doesn't mean to say that the region is only of interest to history buffs or religious pilgrims. As home to some of the most diverse communities, including Jordan's Christian minority, and encompassing dramatic and highly varied landscapes, this is quintessential Jordan. With good accommodation, typical Jordanian dining and opportunities for outdoor adventure, it's easy to engage with both town and country in a region that is still surprisingly off the beaten track for most visitors.

When to Go

Enjoyable year-round, the higher altitude towns along the King's Highway often experience snow in winter providing a spectacular backdrop to crusader castles. The cold air brings cut-glass clarity to the region's sweeping panoramas by day, and chilly nights inspire huddles around wood fires in true Arab tradition.

For hiking, the season extends from March (when trailside flowers are at their best) until 30th October. At this time, while Jordan's lowlands shrivel in the heat, this region's uplands offer relative cool, grapes and figs in abundance, raptor migration and grand sunsets.

Central Highlights

1 Piece together early Christian history in the mosaics of **Madaba** (p129) and visit a modern workshop to see how they were made

2 Take shade under an ancient stone dolmen in **Wadi Jadid** (p140)

3 Survey the Promised Land – that took almost 2000 years to deliver and cost the region dearly – from Moses' memorial at **Mt Nebo** (p138)

4 Dance with Salome's ghost at **Mukawir** (p141), before unveiling the spot where a reluctant Herod supposedly beheaded John the Baptist

5 Watch the ladies at **Bani Hamida** (p142) weave their past into the shape of a new future

6 Savour an eagle-eye view of **Wadi Mujib** (p143) from the viewpoint

7 Listen to the thunder of ghostly hooves at **Karak Castle** (p145) and **Shobak Castle** (p155), Jordan's most impressive Crusader castles

8 Find peace (and ibex if you're lucky) at **Dana Biosphere Reserve** (p151), on a hike from the temperate high ground to the desert landscape of Wadi Araba

History

The landscape either side of the great yawning gap of Wadi Mujib is identical. There are neat olive groves, avenues of poplars, prickly pear fences, gently undulating hills, sheep driven along a network of paths, villages of flat-roofed houses – and occasional piles of fallen masonry from antiquity. North and south of the divide, the rural communities seem to form part of a seamless continuum along the surface of the upper plateau and, unless you have driven along the King's Highway, you might never guess at the great hiatus that divides the region in two.

There is surely no better metaphor for the continuity of human life along this ancient trade route. For the past 3000 years, the King's Highway has been traversed by the Israelites en route to the Promised Land; by Nabataeans to and from their sacred city at Petra; by Christian faithful on pilgrimage to Moses' memorial at Mt Nebo; by Crusaders to their castle fortifications; and by Muslim pilgrims heading to and from Mecca. Travel the road today, with all its difficulties, and you follow in the path of history.

See p259 for a fuller history of this ancient thoroughfare.

Nature Reserves

The Royal Society for the Conservation of Nature (RSCN) runs two nature reserves straddling the central plateau, wedged between the King's Highway and the Dead Sea Highway. **Mujib Biosphere Reserve** (p123) is more usually accessed from the Dead Sea and is covered in that chapter. **Dana Biosphere Reserve** (p151) is accessed via the small upland village of Dana, just off the King's Highway. Protecting a rich diversity of flora and fauna, Dana Biosphere Reserve offers the visitor a chance to camp and hike in the reserve's stunning landscape.

Dangers & Annoyances

Hiking in any of the wadis that crisscross the region from November to February should be approached with caution, if not avoided, because of the danger of flash floods. After rains, walls of water roll out of the canyons without warning, even on a cloudless day, uprooting trees and strewing boulders in their wake. Take advice before setting out, or tell your hotel manager where you are heading.

It can get seriously cold in winter with snow and hailstones. Many visitors get caught out without adequate clothing as the daytime temperatures may still be beguilingly warm.

Because of the gap in public transport where the King's Highway crosses Wadi Mujib, it's easy to get stranded either side of the wadi. Plan an early start to be sure of reaching the nearest town in daylight.

ⓘ Getting There & Away

Of Jordan's three highways running north to south, the King's Highway is by far the most interesting, with a host of historical attractions lying on the road or nearby. The highway, which is little more than a rural road for most of its length, connects Madaba to Petra via Crusader castles, Roman forts, biblical sites, a windswept Nabataean temple and some epic landscapes – including the majestic Wadi Mujib.

The King's Highway is connected with the Dead Sea Highway via spectacular hairpin roads (see p114) that are a highlight in their own right. Most public transport, however, connects with the King's Highway via the Desert Highway. Madaba is directly accessible from the main international airport (without the need to enter Amman).

ⓘ Getting Around

It's not possible to travel the length of the King's Highway by public transport. This is because Wadi Mujib gets in the way. Minibuses serve the communities on either side of the wadi, but through traffic uses the Desert Hwy. Chartering a taxi for the day, however, is feasible.

The most convenient way to explore the King's Highway is to hire a car. You can drive the whole route from Madaba to Petra in a day. Allowing time to stop at all the places of interest and with a return along the Dead Sea Highway takes four to five days.

Hotels in Madaba and downtown Amman run minibus tours that stop in Wadi Mujib and Karak (and sometimes Dana and Shobak) en route to Petra.

If all else fails, hitching is possible but be prepared for long waits on deserted stretches – not advisable in the extreme temperatures of summer or winter.

Madaba

مأدبا

🚗 05 / POP 152,900 / ELEV 800M

The amiable market town of Madaba is best known for a collection of Byzantine-era mosaics. The most famous of these is the mosaic map on the floor of St George's Church, but there are many others carpeting different parts of the town, many of which are even more complete and vibrant in colour.

Wonderful though they are, the mosaics are not the only reason to pay Madaba a visit. A traveller in the early 20th century described being shot at by the people of Madaba just so they could bring him back to town as 'their guest and to eat their food'. No-one is likely to shoot at you today but the town remains one of the most traveller-friendly in Jordan.

Madaba has an interesting cultural mix. One third of the population is Christian (the other two thirds are Muslim), making it one of the largest Christian communities in Jordan. The town's long tradition of religious tolerance is joyfully – and loudly – expressed on Friday. This is one day when you shouldn't expect a lie-in. The imam summoning the faithful before dawn leavens the sky. Then the carillon bells bid the Orthodox Christians to rise, and finally Mammon gets a look in with the honks and groans of traffic. The rest of the day is punctuated with yelps to buy apricots, and friendly greetings from children.

Madaba is easily and best explored on foot. With its lively shops dangling with strings of shoes, skinned goats tended by men in white Wellington boots, sewing machines rattling off repairs by the roadside, piles of fat cabbages, and giant aluminium pots and pans, Madaba is a typical King's Highway town. Unlike most other towns along the highway, however, it has a good choice of hotels and restaurants.

Less than an hour by public transport from Amman, Madaba makes an alternative base for exploring King's Highway and Dead Sea highlights. You can even come by taxi from Queen Alia International Airport, bypassing Amman altogether.

History

The region around Madaba has been inhabited for around 4500 years and was one of the towns divided among the 12 tribes of Israel at the time of the Exodus. The region passed from Ammonites to Israelites, Nabataeans and eventually, by AD 106, to Romans, under which Madaba became a prosperous provincial town with colonnaded streets and impressive public buildings. The prosperity continued during the Christian Byzantine period, with the construction of churches and the lavish mosaics that decorated them.

The town was abandoned for about 1100 years after a devastating earthquake in AD 747. In the late 19th century, 2000 Christians from Karak migrated to Madaba after a bloody dispute with Karak's Muslims. The new arrivals found the town's signature mosaics when they started digging foundations for houses. News that a mosaic map of the Holy Land had been found in St George's Church in Madaba reached Europe in 1897, leading to a flurry of excavation that continues to this day. Various NGOs have assisted in restoration and rejuvenation projects in Madaba; at the time of writing, US Aid was taking an active initiative in this field. To find out more, see www.jordan.usaid.gov.

◉ Sights

Madaba is sprinkled over the top of a tell. The most interesting part of town is the old quarter on top of the hill, rather than the new developments along the King's Highway. Follow signs for the 'Visitors Centre', or any of the hotels, to reach the centre of town.

Most tourists file dutifully in and out of St George's Church and pay scant attention to the rest of Madaba. This is good news for the discerning visitor who can pore over the town's other stunning mosaics, untroubled by the crowds. A combined ticket to the Archaeological Park, Madaba Museum and Church of the Apostles costs JD2 (for one or all sites). Children under 12 are free. There's no student discount. With the exception of St George's Church, all the sites below are listed in a logical order from the visitors centre and follow the same sequence as the walking tour.

St George's Church & Mosaic Map   CHURCH

(Talal St; admission JD1; ⊙8am-5pm Sat-Thu Nov-Mar, 8am-6pm Sat-Thu Apr-Oct, 9.30am-5pm Fri year-round) It's easy to understand why this rather modest 19th-century **Greek Orthodox church** has such a magnetic attraction. Imagine the excitement in 1884 when Christian builders came across the remnants of an old Byzantine church on the site of their new construction. Among the rubble, having survived wilful destruction, fire and neglect, the mosaic they discovered wasn't just another mosaic, it was one with extraordinary significance: to this day, it represents the oldest map of Palestine in existence and provides many historical insights into the region.

Crafted in AD 560, the map has 157 captions (in Greek) depicting all the major biblical sites of the Middle East from Egypt to Palestine. It was originally around 15m to 25m long and 6m wide, and once contained more than two million pieces. Although

Madaba

To Mt Nebo (9km)

Al-Mouhafada Circle

Aisha Umm al-Mu'meneen St

Palestine St

Al-Yarmouk St

Al-Quds St

King Hussein St

King Abdullah St

Ash-Shuhada St

Al-Jame St

Prince Hassan St

St George's Church & Mosaic Map

To Queen Alia International Airport (28km); Amman (33km)

Abu Bakr as- Seddiq St

Madaba Archaeological Park I & Virgin Mary Church

Souq (Market)

Local Bus Station

Shrine of the Beheading of St John the Baptist

To Dana Restaurant (150m); Tche Tche Cafe (100m); Church of the Apostles (300m); Hammamet Ma'in (27km)

Al-Nuzha St

To Mukawir (35km)

King's Hwy

---

much of the mosaic has been lost, enough remains to sense the majesty of the whole.

On Friday and Sunday morning the church opens at 7am for Mass (visitors welcome); viewing the map at these times is not permitted. A small shop by the exit sells copies of the map and reproduction Orthodox icons.

Before viewing the map, take a look at the full-size replica in the ticket office and spot the details that you want to see in the church. The ticket office was being converted into an interpretative centre at the time of writing and prices may increase to JD2

on reopening. The centre will offer visitors the chance to listen to a CD explaining the mosaic map in several languages.

Visitors Centre   OTTOMAN HOUSE
(☎3253563; Abu Bakr as-Seddiq St; ⏰8am-5.30pm Oct-Apr, to 7pm May-Sep) This helpful interpretative centre is worth a visit in its own right as it is housed in a beautifully restored traditional house from the late 19th century, belonging to the al-Batjali family. Note the open central courtyard – unusual in Jordan where the predominantly Muslim culture normally dictates a closed courtyard

Madaba

for family privacy. Two of the rooms house interesting information panels in English on the history of Madaba and there's a 10-minute film setting the town in its historical context.

The visitors centre makes a good starting point for visiting the highlights of Madaba.

FREE **Madaba Institute for Mosaic Art & Restoration (MIMAR)** MOSAIC WORKSHOP
(☑3240723; Abu Bakr as-Seddiq St; ⊗8am-3pm Sun-Thu) Originally set up as a school in 1992 by the Jordanian Government, this institute trains Jordanian artists in the production and restoration of mosaics, spreads awareness of mosaics in Jordan and actively preserves mosaics throughout the country. The restoration work of the school's artisans is evident in the Archaeological Park, the Church of the Apostles and at Khirbet Mukhayyat.

Visit the administration office first to arrange a visit of the workshop and for an appreciation of the painstaking nature of mosaic making and restoration.

Madaba Archaeological Park I & Virgin Mary Church MUSEUM
(☑3246681; Abu Bakr as-Seddiq St; combined ticket JD2; ⊗8am-4pm Oct-Apr, to 5pm May-Sep) Some careful restoration and excavation in the early 1990s led to the creation of this open-air museum which houses a collection of ruins and mosaics from the Madaba area.

As you enter, you'll see a 1st-century BC mosaic from Machaerus, which is said to be the oldest mosaic found in Jordan. Follow the walkway to the right, above the Roman street. This street once ran east to west between the Roman city gates and was lined with columns. Continue past the faded but elegant mosaics of the **Church of the Prophet Elias** (built AD 607), pausing to enjoy the details (such as the fine green bird) and then descend to the crypt (AD 595).

The large, roofed structure in front of you contains the most impressive mosaics on the site, including those of **Hippolytus Hall**, an early-6th-century Byzantine villa. Spot the four seasons in each corner and notice the beautiful depictions of flowers and birds. The middle section shows characters from

NAVIGATING THE MADABA MAP

It takes some orientation to be able to 'read' the Mabada Map spread across the floor of St George's Church. Chances are you will intuitively look at the mosaic expecting north to be in front of you, towards the altar. In fact, the map, and indeed the church itself, is oriented towards the east. Imagine, therefore, as you approach the map, that you are in the hills west of Jerusalem, looking over the crenulated tops of the great city residences towards the Dead Sea and follow the guide below for the highlights.

North (top left)

In the most touching part of the mosaic, fish in the River Jordan scamper back upstream from the lethal waters of the Dead Sea, swimming under the cable-drawn ferries of the river crossing (marked today by King Hussein Bridge). A bodiless lion pursues a gazelle just above Bethany, the supposed site of Jesus' baptism (marked as 'Sapsafas' on the map).

East (straight ahead)

The most exquisitely detailed part of the map is that depicting Jerusalem, complete with city walls, gates and the central road (cardo). Becalmed on the waters of the Dead Sea, their oars at the ready, lie two boats going nowhere. Perhaps they were trying to ferry Herod to the spa at Callirhöe (Zara), marked by three springs and two palm trees. Lot's Cave, where the old man was seduced by his two daughters, lies just above the oasis of Safi (Balak or Zoara). The walled town of Karak appears in the uppermost portion of the map, at the end of vertical Wadi Al-Hasa.

South (far right)

Mt Sinai is recognisable by the multicoloured mountains from which Moses descended with the Ten Commandments. Look for fish in the mosaic fingers of the Nile Delta; they swim towards the Mediterranean, only a snippet of which remains. Almost fragmented from the rest of the Holy Land by damage, but resolutely connected to Egypt and the Mediterranean Sea, is Gaza. This accident of history gives the map a kind of presentiment that matches its historical vision.

the classic Greek Oedipal tragedy of Phaedra and Hippolytus. The upper image shows Adonis and a topless Aphrodite spanking naughty, winged Eros, while the Three Graces (daughters of Zeus, representing joy, charm and beauty) float nearby.

The **Church of the Virgin Mary**, included in the site, was built in the 6th century and was unearthed beneath the floor of someone's house in 1887. The central mosaic, thought to date from AD 767, is a masterpiece of geometric design.

FREE **Archaeological Park II**
(Burnt Palace)   MOSAIC
(Hussein bin Ali St; ⊙8am-3pm Sun-Thu Oct-Apr, to 5.30pm Sun-Thu May-Sep) Walkways lead around the ruins of this late-6th-century luxury private mansion, destroyed by fire and earthquake around AD 749. From this vantage point, there's a good view of assorted mosaics, the best of which are the hunting sequences in the east wing, and the lion attacking a bull in the west wing.

On the site (which takes more imagination than most) is the continuation of the ancient **Roman road** that runs through what is now the Archaeological Park, as well as the 6th-century **Martyrs Church**, which was destroyed in the 8th century. If the on-site guard is willing, ask to see the buried mosaics of the church: protected from the light by sand until restoration takes place, the few tesserae (squares) of buried mosaic that he'll expose for you are astonishing in the vibrancy of their colour.

Dar Al-Saraya   MUSEUM
(Talal St) The administrative centre of the Ottomans, this grand old building was subsequently used as the headquarters of the British administration in 1922. While not yet open to visitors, this newly restored structure near Madaba's hilltop is planned as the new home of the Madaba Museum. In the meantime, the adjacent plaza makes a good place to catch the breeze.

FREE **Shrine of the Beheading of John the Baptist (Latin Church)** MUSEUM
(☎3244065; Talal St; ⊙9am-5pm) This operational early 20th-century Roman Catholic Church has recently been transformed into an intriguing destination for visitors and pilgrims by the restoration of the ancient sites upon which the church sits. The **church facade** was built with ancient stones, and Roman columns with Corinthian capitals dot the courtyard. In the 19th-century chapel, which now acts as a visitors centre and gift shop, there is a fascinating **exhibition of photographs** dating from 1902-11, but the real gem of the complex is the **Acropolis Museum**, housed in the ancient, vaulted underbelly of the church. Here, an ancient well dating to the Moabite era, 3000 years ago, is still operational.

Spare some time and energy to scale the **belfry**. The last section involves steep metal ladders with handrails and a bit of dexterity manoeuvring around the bells and bell ropes, but it's worth the effort for the best panorama in Madaba.

There are spotlessly clean toilets in the visitors centre.

Madaba Museum MUSEUM
(☎3244189; Haya Bint Al-Hussin St; combined ticket JD2; ⊙8am-5pm, to 7pm May-Sep) Housed in several old Madaba residences, some highlights of this museum include a 6th-century mosaic depicting a naked satyr, a saucy (and partially damaged) mosaic of Ariadne dancing with cymbals on her hands and feet, and a mosaic in the courtyard depicting two rams tied to a tree – a popular image recalling Abraham's sacrifice.

Spare a few minutes in the **Folklore Museum**, housed at the Madaba Museum and included in the admission price. It features jewellery, traditional costumes and a copy of the Mesha Stele.

There have long been plans to move the museum to Dar Al-Saraya, but nothing has come of this yet. It may explain, however, why the museum is rather under par. The open courtyard with grape vines and palms makes a pleasant place to sit.

Church of the Apostles CHURCH
(King's Highway; combined ticket JD2; ⊙9am-4pm Oct-Apr, 8am-5pm May-Sep) This insignificant-looking church contains a remarkable mosaic dedicated to the Twelve Apostles. The embroidery-like mosaic was created in AD 568 and is one of the few instances where the name of the craftsman (Salomios) is included. The central portion shows Thalassa, a female personification of the sea, surrounded by fish and slippery marine creatures. Native animals, birds, flowers and fruits, and cherubic faces decorate the corners.

🛏 Sleeping

Madaba has a good range of hotels, mostly run by Christian families, and all within easy walking distance of the town's main sights. Prices include breakfast and private bathroom unless otherwise noted. Although the hotels below are listed in order of recommendation, it's hard to select a clear favourite as all offer very good value for money.

TOP CHOICE **Black Iris Hotel** GUESTHOUSE $
(☎3241959; www.blackirishotel.com; near Al-Mouhafada Circle; s/d/tr JD22/30/40; ⊛) For a 'home away from home' feeling, it's hard to beat this family-run hotel. The carpeted rooms, with thick blankets and fresh towels, are cosy and there's a spacious sitting area where guests can drink coffee and read up on the town without being harassed. Its 'very special breakfast' is part of a long tradition at the guesthouse and includes date cake and homemade fig jam. The owner (trained hotelier and former chef in Switzerland) makes home-cooked Jordanian dishes on request in the evening, garnished with home-grown herbs from his garden. The warm and knowledgeable assistance in organising onward travel gives the Black Iris continuing popularity with readers. Arrive in spring and you may spot the national flower of Jordan – the namesake of this hotel. Women travelling alone will feel comfortable here. The hotel is easy to spot from Al-Mouhafada Circle.

Mariam Hotel HOTEL $$
(☎3251529; www.mariamhotel.com; Aisha Umm al-Mumeneen St; s/d/tr/q JD30/40/48/60; ⊛@☎⊠) The Mariam has built a prodigious reputation over the years. The hotel offers good facilities including a bar, restaurant by the pool and internet access in a cheerful communal lobby area. A restaurant and bar on the 5th floor offers views across the town. Reservations are recommended. The hotel can organise a taxi to/from the airport (around JD12) and transport to Petra among other tours. Ask Charl, the owner, about a trip to see the local dolmens (p140) – a subject he is knowledgeable and passionate about.

START VISITORS CENTRE
FINISH VISITORS CENTRE
DISTANCE 3KM
DURATION 3 HOURS

Walking Tour
Madaba

❯ From the ① **visitors centre** leave via Abu Bakr as-Seddiq St, pausing at the bend to admire the town view. Call into ② **Archaeological Park I**, catching topless Aphrodite spanking Eros. Turn right and immediate left along colourful, pedestrianised 'Prince Hassan St', with its flapping kilims. Duck into ③ **Archaeological Park II** for a preview of yet-to-be-restored mosaics. The antique shop opposite is an Aladdin's cave of copper coffee pots.

At the T-junction with Talal St, turn right for ④ **St George's Church**, famed for its mosaic map, and visit cosy Ayola Coffeeshop opposite. Backtrack along Talal St, passing clothing shops with their ancient mannequins. The renowned restaurant ⑤ **Haret Jdoudna** is tucked into a traditional Madaba residence on the right; the craft shop here supports good causes. Continue uphill along Talal St towards ⑥ **Dar Al-Saraya**, preparing to become Madaba's main museum. The road curves uphill to ⑦ **The Shrine of the Beheading of John the Baptist**, a Catholic church constructed with Roman fragments. Compare the modern town vista (from the belfry) with the black-and-white photographs exhibited in the gallery.

From the church, turn left along Ishac Al-Shuweihat St, passing ⑧ **Adonis Restaurant**, atmospherically housed in a grand old residence. Turn right on Princess Haiya St to ⑨ **Madaba Museum** – a shady spot to absorb Madaba's layered history.

Backtrack to Sulaiman Al-Alamat St and pass an unexcavated cathedral and fine houses. Turn right at the T-junction and head downhill, turning left onto Rocks Al-Ozizi St. Call into the tiny ⑩ **Church of the Apostles** to see imagined marine creatures in mosaic.

Walk north along the King's Highway past hardware stores abuzz with Bedouin shoppers in traditional headdresses. Turn uphill along Prince Faisal bin Al-Hussain St, noting the mosque's minaret rising majestically above Madaba's skyline. At the crossroads, adorned with gold shops, tailors and haberdashers, turn right onto Firas Al Ajlouni St.

KEEPING IT IN THE FAMILY

You may be wondering why it is that the newest hotel in Madaba has located itself right next to two of its competitors, the Mariam and Salome. The answer lies in a photograph of grandmother Mariam in the dining room of the Rumman Hotel. This formidable lady bequeathed the land to her four sons. The younger generation of cousins, all belonging to the long-established Twarl family of Madaba, have inherited the passion for the hotel trade and have transformed the visitor experience.

Salome Hotel
HOTEL $

(☎3248606; www.salomehotel.com; Aisha al-Mumeneen St; s/d/tr JD24/30/35; ❄@☎) With the family-run appeal of a small residential hotel, the Salome is a good choice for a quiet stay. It may lack the buzz of fellow travellers plotting their onward routes, but it nonetheless has a welcoming reception-cum-lounge, a licensed restaurant and an ever-charming owner. The small rooms all have TV and spotless bathrooms. The hotel is located next to the Mariam Hotel, an easy five-minute walk from the town centre.

Mosaic City Hotel
HOTEL $$

(☎3251313; www.mosaiccityhotel.com; Yarmouk St; s/d JD32/44, extra bed JD15; ❄) This attractive, family-run 21-room hotel has bright and spacious rooms with matching curtains and bedspreads. Some have balconies overlooking lively Yarmouk St but all rooms are double-glazed, keeping the street noise to a minimum. The 1st-floor reception of this recommended hotel is accessed from the neighbouring street.

Queen Ayola Hotel
HOTEL $

(☎3244087; www.queenayolahotel.com; Talal St; s/d/tr JD20/25/30, s/d with shared bathroom JD10/18; ☎) A cosmopolitan Russian-speaking owner (an engineer by trade) has transformed this former dive into one of the most happening places in town. With a bar offering happy hour and serving excellent food, the hotel looks set to become a favourite with travellers. The rooms are attractively decorated and two have balconies onto the street – fun for people-watching in the heart of town.

St George's Church Pilgrim House
GUESTHOUSE $

(☎/fax 3253701; pilgrimshousemadaba@gmail.com; Talal St; s/d/tr JD25/35/45; ☎) For a characterful place to stay, consider this pilgrim house, attached to St George's Church. Although it receives mainly Christian pilgrims, travellers can expect a warm welcome too. Rooms are ascetically simple. If you encounter the patron of the house, the urbane and charming Father Innocent (self-confessedly 'Innocent by name, guilty by every other means'), then your stay will find an extra blessing! Profits from the guesthouse are invested in the neighbouring church school. See the Directory for a voluntary work opportunity here (p316).

Rumman Hotel
HOTEL $

(☎3252555; www.info@rummanhotel.com; Aisha Umm al-Mumeneen St; s/d/tr JD24/30/38; ❄@☎) A new establishment with a friendly owner, spacious rooms and the only bathtubs in town, Rumman looks set to live up to the Twarl family reputation.

Moab Land Hotel
GUESTHOUSE $

(☎/fax 3251318; moabland_hotel@orange.jo; Talal St; s/d/tr JD30/35/40) With grand views of St George's Church and beyond, this family-run hotel couldn't be more central. The prize draw, apart from the welcome, is the glorious rooftop terrace where breakfast is served in summer. The reception is on the upper floor.

Madaba Inn Hotel
HOTEL $$

(☎3259003; www.madaba-inn.com; Talal St; s/d/tr JD45/70/80; ❄@☎) Though needing refurbishment, this 33-room hotel is in a good central position and has car parking. Wi-fi is restricted to the lobby.

Phoenix Palace Hotel
HOTEL $

(☎3253550; www.palacehotel.com.jo; Hamra Al-Assad St; s/d/tr JD25/35/45) With an attractive foyer, quiet location, big rooms and large garden under an aged grapevine, this hotel should be a winner. The hotel management, however, is lacking in experience and this shows in the reception and services on offer.

Madaba Hotel
GUESTHOUSE $

(☎/fax 3240643; Al-Jame St; s/d/tr from JD18/25/35, with shared bathroom JD15/20/30) This central, eight-room family-run guesthouse has had a recent makeover but is still on the spartan side with dorm-style beds. There's a ground-floor lounge and kitchen that guests can use.

✕ Eating & Drinking

Madaba is a good place to sample traditional Jordanian food. Most of Madaba's restaurants serve beer, some interesting local wines and the local firewater, arak.

TOP CHOICE Haret Jdoudna Complex
JORDANIAN **$$**

(☎3248650; Talal St; mains JD8-15; ⊘noon-midnight;☑) Popular with locals and discerning diners from Amman, and set in one of Madaba's restored old houses, this restaurant is a Madaba favourite. Sit indoors by a roaring fire in winter or in the shaded courtyard in summer and sample the traditional Jordanian dishes such as *mutaffi bethanjan* (fried eggplant with sesame), *fatteh* (fried bread with garlic-laced yoghurt and hummus, sometimes with chicken) and *sawani* (meat or vegetables cooked on trays in a wood-burning oven). Buy a souvenir of a good night out from the handicraft shop within the complex and you'll have the added satisfaction of contributing to a good cause.

Adonis Restaurant & Cafe
JORDANIAN **$$**

(☎3251771; jehadalamat@yahoo.com; Ishac Al Shuweihat St; mixed grill JD6; ⊘11am-2am) Housed in a beautifully restored typical Madaba residence, and run by one of the town's returning sons, this excellent restaurant has quickly become established as the place to be at weekends. Serving typical Jordanian fare in a space that expands almost magically into unseen corners, the restaurant has the added charm of live music on Thursday and Friday nights.

Ayola Coffeeshop & Bar
CAFE **$**

(☎3251843; ayola@hotmail.com; Talal St; snacks around JD2; ⊘8am-11pm; ☑☑) If you want a toasted sandwich (JD2), Turkish coffee (JD1), glass of arak with locals, or simply a comfortable perch on which to while away some time with fellow travellers, then this is the place to come. Fries, a soft drink and a salad costs JD3.500. There's free internet access if you have a laptop.

Bowabit Restaurant
CAFE **$$**

(☎3240335; www.bowabitmadaba.com; Talal St; mains JD7.500; ⊘10am-midnight) With two tables overhanging the road opposite St George's Church, photographs of old Madaba on the wall and excellent Italian-style coffee (cappuccino JD3), this is a number-one place to relax after strolling round town. Alternatively, make a night of it over a dish of Madaba chicken (JD7) and a beer (JD3.500).

Dardasheh Restaurant & Bar
CAFE **$**

(☎776530034; Al-Hassan bin Ali St; snacks JD2.500; ☎) The blue and red velveteen cushions and foreign money pinned to the wall give this unassuming little cafe a cosy and cosmopolitan atmosphere. Wi-fi is available and is helping to make this central venue a popular meeting point for travellers.

Tche Tche Café
CAFE **$**

(☎3244416; Rocks Al-Ozizi St; mains JD6; ⊘10am-midnight) A fashionable chain restaurant with branches throughout the Middle East, this cafe is set in a bright hall with a rare outdoor seating area. The menu offers a 'mind map' (after Buzan) of tasty options.

Dana Restaurant
BUFFET **$$**

(☎3245749; Rocks Al-Ozizi St; lunch buffet JD10; ⊘noon-3pm) Popular with tour groups, this restaurant serves a good quality buffet in a pleasant dining hall. It makes a useful stop if you've worked up an appetite on the walking tour.

Stop & Go
CAFE **$**

(☎776530034; Al-Hassan bin Ali St; snacks 500 fils) The doughnuts may not always be today's, but the frank and thoroughly likeable owner is the first to tell you as much. A cup of coffee in the upper gallery of this tiny cafe is like tea in a carpet shop: an essential experience of being in town.

Quick Eats

There are a number of snack shops along Yamouk St and the King's Highway, selling felafel, shwarma and roasted chicken. For freshly baked Arabic bread, head for the ovens opposite the Church of the Apostles. There are several grocery stores in the centre of town. Fresh fruit and veg for a picnic can be bought along King Abdullah St.

Don't miss out on the Arabic sweet shops, such as **Al-Baraka Sweets** (cnr Sameh al Farah & King Abdullah Sts) where you'll find round trays of honey-drizzled pastries, some filled with local cheese, others with nuts and sugar.

There's little going on in Madaba after dark, except drinks in the bar at Queen Ayola, Ayola Coffeeshop or poolside at the Mariam Hotel.

🔒 Shopping

You can visit private mosaic workshops (with no obligation to buy) around town and purchase your own copy of the Madaba map or a more modest Tree of Life (from

JD15, depending on size). Another large handicraft centre specialising in mosaics is the **Jordan Jewel** (☎3241364), located 1km before Mt Nebo on the road from Madaba. The owner of this large emporium employs a large number of physically challenged locals to help offer marginalised people a way back into society.

Madaba is also famous for its colourful hand-loomed kilims (see p282), which flap and dance outside shops throughout town (especially between the Burnt Palace and St George's Church). Buying one of these rugs is more than just a purchase, it's a great way to get under the skin of the town: chats and tea with the rug-sellers are de rigueur.

Spare some time to amble along Al-Yarmouk St: here you will find water pipes, women's headscarves and shops selling Jordanian sweets. The street comes alive at night and it's a good place to mingle with local shoppers to gain a flavour of the town.

There are several warehouse-like emporiums selling handicrafts but they are mainly intended for tour groups and lack the personal touch of shops in town. If you are into one-stop shopping, however, you can find these outlets along the road to Mt Nebo.

Haret Jdoudna Complex   HANDICRAFTS
(☎3248650; Talal St; ☉10.30am-11pm) Selling an extensive range of crafts, including mosaics, ceramics, textiles and clothing, this shop, attached to the restaurant of the same name, stocks particularly exquisite embroidery. Many of the items for sale are sponsored by the Arab Cultural Society, which supports Jordanian war widows. Indeed, most items come from local non-profit organisations, including the Jordan River Foundation which supports marginalised communities.

Hanania Silver Shop & Rafidi for Silver   JEWELLERY
(Al-Hassan bin Ali St) There are a number of quality jewellery shops in town including these locally renowned master silversmiths along Prince Hassan St. There is little on display in the windows but every piece is hand-crafted to the highest standards.

Holy Treasures Centre   SOUVENIRS
(☎3248481; Talal St) Opposite St George's Church, this shop has an extensive range of Dead Sea products. It also sells consecrated holy water from the River Jordan.

Spice   FOOD
(Sameh al Farah St) For an unusual present, take back a selection of spices or freshly ground coffee beans from this aromatic grocers, opposite the Housing Bank.

Madaba Studio & Lab   ELECTRONICS
(☎3245932; Talal St; ☉8am-8.30pm) Has memory cards and batteries. It's near the Moab Land Hotel.

ℹ Information

Collect a brochure called *Madaba and Mount Nebo*, summarising Madaba's attractions, from the visitor centre. Other good Jordan Tourist Board brochures include *Madaba Mosaic Map* and *Mount Nebo*.

The American Center of Oriental Research publishes the definitive *Madaba: Cultural Heritage* (around JD20). More portable is the *Mosaic Map of Madaba* by Herbert Donner (JD10), with a fold-out reproduction of the map and detailed text. Also recommended is the pocket-sized *Madaba, Mt Nebo* published by Al-Kutba (JD3).

The bookshop opposite the Burnt Palace sells a range of international newspapers.

Arab Bank (Sameh al Farah St) Accepts Visa and MasterCard, and has an ATM.

Bank of Jordan (Sameh al Farah St & King Abdullah Sts) Changes cash and travellers cheques.

Housing Bank (Sameh al Farah St) Accepts Visa; has an ATM.

Jordan National Bank (cnr King Abdullah & Talal Sts) Changes cash and travellers cheques.

Ministry of Tourism & Antiquities (☎/fax 3252687; www.tourism.jo) Has an office above the Burnt Palace for specialised information about Madaba's preservation efforts.

Post office (Sameh al Farah St; ☉8am-5pm) Long-distance telephone calls can be made from here.

Tour.Dot Internet (Talal St; per hr 500 fils; ☉9am-2am)

Tourist Police Office (☎191; Talal St; ☉24hr) Just north of St George's Church and in the visitors centre.

Visitors Centre (☎3253563; Abu Bakr as-Seddiq St; ☉8am-5.30pm Oct-Apr, to 6pm May-Sep) This helpful information office has a range of brochures and some informative displays. Ask to see the 10-minute film that sets Madaba in the context of the surrounding highlights. There are toilets and a handy car park.

ℹ Getting There & Away

The bus station is about 15 minutes' walk east of the town centre on the King's Highway. Most attractions around Madaba (with the exception of Mt Nebo and Mukawir) are time-consuming if not impossible to reach by public transport. It's easy, however, to charter a taxi in Madaba or take one of the well-thought-out tours from the Black Iris Hotel or the Mariam Hotel, both of which have a wealth of experience in organising trips for independent travellers.

To/From the Airport

If you want to bypass the bustle of Amman, it's possible to reach Madaba from Queen Alia International Airport by private taxi (day JD19) in under half an hour (15 minutes when the new highway opens). Most hotels in Madaba can arrange a taxi (JD15) to or from the airport if you contact them in advance.

To/From Amman

From the Muhajireen, South (Wahadat) and North (Tababoor) Bus Stations in Amman, there are regular buses and minibuses (between 500 fils and 750 fils, one hour) throughout the day for Madaba. Minibuses return to Amman until around 8pm (earlier on Friday). Taxis cost JD12 during the day, JD15 at night.

To/From the Dead Sea

It's really not feasible to rely on public transport to reach the Dead Sea as the route involves two minibus rides, which are unreliable at best, and a taxi ride from Suweimah that can cost almost as much as a taxi from Madaba. If you're determined, check with your hotel for the latest information on these ad hoc services. To visit the Dead Sea by taxi with enough time for a swim, you need to factor in three hours' waiting time. The Black Iris offers this trip for JD28.

One popular trip from Madaba to the Dead Sea is via Mt Nebo and Bethany, returning via the Dead Sea Panoramic Complex and Hammamat Ma'in (around JD50).

With your own transport, you can drive to the Dead Sea via Mt Nebo and return along the Dead Sea Panoramic Complex road. Branch off to Hammamat Ma'in and the new Mukawir road for a spectacular detour. Alternatively, you can make

---

MA'AN NOT AMMAN!

If you're brave enough to try travelling by public transport in the region, be careful how you pronounce the transport hub of Ma'an. If you don't get your gutturals worked out, you may just find yourself heading back to the capital – no laughing matter if you've just spent a day of your trip trying to edge along the King's Highway.

---

a longer but equally stunning drive via Karak (see p114).

South Along the King's Highway

There is no public transport linking Madaba with Karak along the King's Highway as scaling the banks of Wadi Mujib on a regular basis costs more in vehicle maintenance than it earns in fares. If you wish to go this way you must take a minibus to Dhiban (450 fils, 45 minutes) and then charter a taxi to cross Wadi Mujib to Ariha (if you can find one) and wait for an onward minibus to Karak. From Karak, minibuses run to Tafila, where you can find transport for Qadsiyya (access to Dana). Public transport south of Qadsiyya is infrequent, so you may need to take a minibus to Ma'an and then another to Wadi Musa (Petra).

A much easier option is to take the daily service organised by the Mariam Hotel. Leaving at 10am, it goes to Petra (arriving around 6pm), with stops at Wadi Mujib for photos, and an hour in Karak. You can get off at Dana, but you may have to pay the full fare. The service requires a minimum of three people (the hotel will link you with other passengers staying at the hotel) and a maximum of four, and costs JD54 per taxi. The Black Iris Hotel offers a similar service for JD18 per person for a minimum of three people. Other hotels offer similar deals though with less frequency. A normal taxi fare for this service is around JD90 per car.

To/From Mukawir

From the local bus station in Madaba, minibuses go to Mukawir (for Machaerus castle; JD1, one hour) several times a day (not Fridays). The last minibus leaves at around 5pm. The service isn't wholly reliable – it will only run if there are enough passengers. A taxi costs JD20 with one hour of waiting time.

See p140 for details of getting to and from Mt Nebo.

ⓘ Getting Around

The walk from the bus station to the centre of town is quite a hike with bags but taxis (costing around JD1) are plentiful. If you are driving, note that it is not possible to park outside some of the cheaper hotels as they are on busy, narrow streets.

Mt Nebo   جبل نيبو

Go up unto...Mount Nebo in Moab, across from Jericho, and view Canaan, the land I am giving the Israelites as their own possession. There on the mountain that you have climbed you will die.

Deuteronomy 32:49-50

Mt Nebo (admission JD1; ☺8am-4pm Oct-Apr, to 6pm May-Sep) is where Moses is said to have seen the Promised Land, a land he was himself forbidden to enter. He died (allegedly aged 120) and was later buried in the area, although the exact location of the burial site is the subject of conjecture. The site flickered briefly into the international spotlight with the visit of Pope John Paul II in 2000.

The Mt Nebo region features several rocky outcrops, including Siyagha (the local name of the site, meaning 'monastery'). This is where you will find the Moses Memorial Church. It's a pleasant side trip from Madaba, just 9km away, and the mosaics are magnificent (unfortunately, they're closed for renovation until 2014). Aside from its religious significance, Mt Nebo commands sweeping views of the ancient lands of Gilead, Judah, Jericho and the Negev – the Promised Land.

History

A Roman nun, Etheria, stumbled across the original three-apsed church on this site during a pilgrimage in AD 393. A nave was added in the 5th century, the first baptistery chapel (with the mosaic) in 530, and the main basilica in 597, together with a large monastery.

By this time Nebo had grown into an important pilgrimage site, even earning a signpost off the main Roman road through the region (a Roman mile marker lies in the museum). Pilgrims would travel to Jerusalem, Jericho, Bethany, Ayoun Musa and Mt Nebo, before descending to Hammamat Ma'in for post-pilgrimage bathing.

The church was abandoned by the 16th century and only relocated in the 20th century, using 4th- and 5th-century pilgrim travelogues. The Franciscans bought the site in 1932 and have excavated most of the ruins of the church and the monastery, as well as reconstructing much of the basilica.

⊙ Sights

The museum has some interesting milestones, information on mosaics and a 3-D map of the area.

The basilica, built around 4th-century foundations in AD 597, is currently under reconstruction, but it houses important mosaics (from around AD 530). The masterpiece is a hunting and herding scene interspersed with an assortment of African fauna, including a zebu (humped ox), lions,

---

ⓘ MOSES MEMORIAL CHURCH RESTORATION

At the time of writing, the roof of Moses Memorial Church was being refitted in a project estimated to take at least three years. The church is being expanded at the same time so the famed mosaics are off limits until 2014. Although the church is closed, the view of Moses' Promised Land (Jerusalem is just 46km away) from the viewing platform still makes Mt Nebo a worthwhile trip en route between Madaba and the Dead Sea.

---

tigers, bears, boars, zebras, an ostrich on a leash and a camel-shaped giraffe.

In the courtyard, an Italian-designed bronze memorial symbolises the suffering and death of Jesus on the cross and the serpent that 'Moses lifted up' in the desert.

Some of the complex is part of a functioning monastery and is therefore off limits to visitors.

To enjoy the views away from the crowds, pack a picnic and hike along the road downhill from the site (towards the Dead Sea) for 100m and take the track to the left to the nearby hilltop.

✖ Eating

Asa Moses Restaurant   BUFFET $$
(☏3250226; buffet JD9; ☺12.30-4pm; ✎) If you happen to be around Mt Nebo at lunchtime, call into this recommended trestletabled place, also called Siyagha Restaurant. Every day it produces an excellent buffet, which includes Jordan's famous maqlubbeh (upside-down dish) and a variety of vegetarian options in this restaurant. The stone pillars and reed ceiling add to the 'been here forever' ambience and you can take a glass of after-lunch wine and stretch out on the majlis cushions. The restaurant is opposite the turning for Ayoun Musa, 1km back along the road towards Madaba.

Nebo Restaurant & Terrace   BUFFET $$
(☏3242442; buffet JD10; ☺11.30am-6pm Sat-Thu, till late Fri) For a spectacular view, try the neighbouring Nebo, a stylish new venture with panoramic windows and a roof terrace. It has its own ovens for fresh Arabic bread.

ℹ Information

The entrance to Mt Nebo is signposted on the Madaba–Dead Sea road, next to a visitor centre (built several years ago but still not open). Tickets are currently bought from the guard at the gate. Smoking is not allowed in the complex. Toilets can be found next to the museum.

The authoritative *Town of Nebo* by Fr Sylvestre J Salter and Fr Bellarmino Bagatti details this and other Christian sites in Jordan. More portable is *Mount Nebo* by Michelle Piccirillo. Both are usually available for sale inside the church. The Jordan Tourism Board publishes an excellent pamphlet entitled *Mount Nebo,* which summarises the site's significance. The encyclopaedic *Mosaics of Madaba* is on display inside the church.

ℹ Getting There & Away

From Madaba, shared taxis to Mt Nebo cost around JD1.500; a private taxi from Madaba costs JD4 (or JD8 return, with one hour waiting time).

From Mt Nebo the road continues for 17km into the Jordan Valley to meet the main Amman–Dead Sea Highway, offering excellent views of the Dead Sea. The drive takes you from the tree line of olives and root vegetables, past a rocky landscape of prickly pears to the ochre-coloured hills of the Dead Sea depression. The yellow turns to red as the road twists past iron-rich escarpments and finally descends to the highly cultivated Jordan Valley, dotted with greenhouse plastic. There is no reliable public transport along this route.

Around Mt Nebo

KHIRBET MUKHAYYAT   خربة مخيط

The village of Khirbet Mukhayyat marks the original site of ancient Nebo village, as mentioned on the 9th-century BC Mesha Stele (see p145) and in the Bible. Near the village, the **Church of SS Lot & Procopius**, originally built in AD 557, houses a remarkable **mosaic** with scenes of daily life such as agriculture, fishing and winemaking (the cutting and carrying of grapes). Sadly, the mosaics have been damaged by rainwater in recent years and the church remains closed for restoration.

The turn-off to Khirbet Mukhayyat is signposted 'Al-Makhyt', about 6km from Madaba and 3km before reaching the church complex at Mt Nebo. A good road leads 2.5km along the edge of the village to a car park surrounded by juniper trees. There is no public transport.

AYOUN ('AIN) MUSA   عين موسى

Ayoun Musa (Spring of Moses) is one of two places where the prophet is believed to have obtained water by striking a rock (see also p186). Six giant eucalyptus trees mark the spot and there's an occasional waterfall over the lip of the rocks if it's been raining. The littered site is disfigured by discarded concrete buildings and there's little to see except the low-lying **ruins** of a couple of churches nearby.

To reach the site, turn right at the sign about 1km before the church at Mt Nebo. A 2.4km switchback road to Ayoun Musa is steep (but sealed) and it offers a close-up view of Bedouin encampments, hunkered down against the elements. Arums grow in abundance among the rocky patches of tilled ground, and small, fertile wadis bristle with citrus and olive trees.

There is no public transport to the site. Walking down from the main road is easy; coming back is a killer.

HESBAN   حسبان

Amateur archaeologists will like **Tell Hesban** (admission free; ☉daylight hr), 9km north of Madaba. Over the centuries this strategic hill has been a Bronze Age settlement, an Amorite capital (900–500 BC), a Hellenistic fortress (198–63 BC), a Roman settlement called Esbus (63 BC–AD 350), a Byzantine ecclesiastical centre (AD 350–650), an Umayyad market town (650–750), a regional capital of the Abbasids (750–1260) and Mamluks (1260–1500) and, finally, an Ottoman village. All these layers of history are on view, albeit faintly.

The site is well signed, indicating the remains of a Byzantine church (the mosaics are displayed in Madaba), Roman temple and Hellenistic fort. There are lots of caves and cisterns both here and in neighbouring Wadi Majar. The largest Bronze Age cave can be explored with a torch. Read up on the site beforehand at www.hesban.org.

Minibuses run frequently from Madaba (300 fils, 20 minutes) to Hesban, or take a taxi for JD5. Coming from Madaba, the tell is on the left side of the road; if you are driving, turn left at the first set of traffic lights after the pedestrian bridge in the modern town of Hesban and follow your nose up the hill.

Wadi Jadid   جديد وادي

More terraced fields than wadi, Wadi Jadid is locally renowned for its remarkable collection of early Bronze Age burial chambers and stone memorials. Known as **dolmens**, these stone structures date back to around 5000 to 3000 BC and consist of two upright stones capped by a bridging stone. The term 'dolmen' means stone table and it remains a mystery as to how the huge bridging stones were winched into position: little wonder that social anthropologists regard them as proof of early social cohesion. There are about 40 dolmens scattered across the un-marked site, with at least 12 in good condition. There are thousands more scattered across Jordan, especially around ar-Rawdah.

From the road, it takes about 30 minutes to walk to the nearest dolmen, and an hour to reach more distant groups. The site is near the village of Al-Fiha, 10km southwest of Madaba, but you need to be 'in the know' to find it. The best way to visit is by checking on directions with the Mariam Hotel in Madaba. The hotel owner, Charl, is a geologist and is passionate about dolmens and it was he who rediscovered this remarkable site for tourists.

With your own vehicle, you can continue downhill to the Dead Sea (30 minutes) after Wadi Jadid. The road is narrow and potholed towards the end but it threads through beautiful and varied terrain, with Bedouin camps, green valleys of grapevines, olive groves and citrus orchards. As it descends to the desert floor, the road passes a spring with a small waterfall – almost miraculous in the arid landscape.

Mukawir (Machaerus)

مكاور(مكاريوس)

☑ 05 / POP >5000 / ELEV 700M

Just beyond the village of Mukawir (pronounced mu-*kar*-wir) is the spectacular 700m-high hilltop perch of Machaerus, the **castle of Herod the Great** (admission JD1.500; ☺daylight hr), and the place where Salome is said to have danced for the head of John the Baptist.

The pudding basin of a hill was first fortified in about 100 BC, and expanded by Herod the Great in 30 BC. The ruins themselves are of minor interest, but the setting, with the wind blowing through the columns like one of Salome's seven veils, is both haunting and breathtakingly beautiful. Most days you'll be alone with the ghosts.

Machaerus is known locally as Qala'at al-Meshneq (Castle of the Gallows), a fitting name given that it is renowned as the place where John the Baptist was beheaded by Herod Antipas, the successor of Herod the Great. According to the Bible, John the Baptist had denounced Herod Antipas' marriage to his brother's wife, Herodias, as Jewish law forbade a man marrying his brother's wife while he lived. Bewitched by his stepdaughter Salome's skill as a dancer, the king promised to grant her anything she wished. To take revenge on the Baptist, Herodias told her daughter to ask for his head on a platter:

> And she went out, and said to her mother, "What shall I ask?" And she said, "The head of John the Baptiser."
>
> *Mark 6:24*

So, at the request of Salome, John was killed at Herod's castle, Machaerus. Provocative Salome has inspired painters and writers ever since.

There was nowhere to stay in Mukawir at the time of writing but the Mukawir Visitor Centre (in the village, about 2km from the castle) is likely to open in 2012. Accommodation will be offered on site in old renovated buildings next to the ruins of Bishop Malechios Church. A restaurant is planned here too. In the meantime, water, tea and coffee (and tickets to the castle) are sold from a Bedouin tent at the entrance to the castle.

◎ Sights & Activities

From the car park, a stone staircase leads down to the main path, which climbs the hill in a clockwise direction. Near the base of the climb, a small track leads around the main hill to the right, past a number of **caves**. Legend has it that it was in one of these that the gruesome execution took place. Flocks of choughs wheel through the air in suitably ominous fashion.

The main path climbs eventually to the **castle**. At the top, the modest ruins are unlabelled. The reconstructed columns southwest of the deep cistern mark the site of Herod Antipas' **palace triclinium**; this is the site where Salome danced. You can also make out the low-lying remains of the eastern **baths** and defensive **walls**.

The Romans built a **siege ramp** on the western side of the hill when taking the fort from Jewish rebels in AD 72 and the remains are still visible.

The castle is about 2km past Mukawir village and easy to spot. If you don't feel in the mood for a climb, it's worth coming this way

WEAVING A FUTURE: THE WOMEN OF BANI HAMIDA

The Bani Hamida rug-making initiative was established in 1985, with help from Save the Children, to bring paid work to the newly settled Bedouin women of Mukawir district. The project began with only 12 women, all experienced hand-loom weavers. Ten years later, the cooperative involved 1500 women from the surrounding hillsides washing, carding, spinning and dyeing sheep's wool, and weaving the rugs. All these activities took place around the usual business of looking after husband, family and home. Now supported by the Jordan River Valley Foundation, the project employs 24 full-time staff, responsible for the coordination of the project, marketing in an international arena and promoting the vision of the enterprise.

There have been challenges (such as competition, cheap imports and failing tourism) but the project continues to be a success, empowering women in proportion to their involvement. Earning even a little extra money has brought independence and social manoeuvrability, allowing women to change their lives and most significantly, those of their children. When asked what the project meant for her family, one weaver at the showroom in Mukawir explained that she could afford to buy new pans from Madaba while another had funded a university education for her son.

These changes have been achieved by harnessing, rather than rejecting, the traditional skills that have been handed from mother to daughter since the days of Abraham, and which have helped define the Bedouin identity. As such, buying a Bani Hamida rug is more than just making a purchase; it is affirming an ancient but evolving way of life.

just to see the hilltop fortress framed by sea and sky beyond.

This is a great area for **hiking**, with plenty of shepherds' trails snaking around hilly contours. One particularly worthwhile track leads steeply down the west side of the castle hill from the top and along a ridge line towards the Dead Sea. The views are magnificent, particularly at sunset.

It's also possible to follow the shepherds' trails (or the 4WD road) to the hot springs at Hammamat Ma'in. You must exercise extreme caution if taking any of these trails as the terrain falls steeply away and many paths are only for the sure-footed. Women are advised not to hike alone.

You can arrange with a private tour operator to hike from Mukawir to Zara/Herodus Hot Springs, a hard three- to four-hour trek. See p310 for a list of recommended hiking agencies.

🛍 Shopping

In Mukawir village, by the side of the road leading to the castle, is a weaving centre and gallery. This women's cooperative is run by the Bani Hamida Centre and the gorgeous, colourful kilims and cushions are on sale in the attached **gallery** (✆3210155; www.jordanriver.jo; ◷8am-3pm Sun-Thu). An elaborate 100x50cm kilim costs around JD75 and prices are fixed. The women who run the centre speak little English, but welcome you

to the workshop. There's also a display video explaining the work of the cooperative. For an excellent anthropological perspective on the Bani Hamida story, it's worth picking up a copy of *A Bedouin Perspective* (JD5) by Sue Jones, who worked with the Jebel Bani Hamida women in the early 1990s. This booklet is on sale in the showroom.

❶ Getting There & Away

Frequent minibuses (600 fils, one hour) leave from outside the local bus station in Madaba for the village of Mukawir, via Libb (the last is around 5pm). From there, it's a pleasant downhill stroll to the foot of the castle, or ask the minibus driver to take you the extra distance for a few fils more. There is no return traffic between the castle car park and the village, although one delighted traveller reported that the bus driver kindly waited for her while she spent 30 minutes looking round the ruins.

By car, the road from the King's Highway snakes along a ridge with spectacular views. An impressive new road links the site with Hammamat Ma'in and the Dead Sea.

Umm ar-Rasas   أم الرصاص

Umm ar-Rasas is one of those delightful surprises that crops up along the King's Highway – although it doesn't look very promising from the outside! Despite being designated a Unesco World Heritage site in

2004, it's not as well promoted as other sites along the highway. A grand new visitor centre opened at the end of 2008 but is already badly in need of maintenance and sheds little light on the site. Visitors are accompanied to the ruins by tourist police; although kind and friendly, they are not able to give much in the way of interpretation.

The ruined **Church of St Stephen** (admission free; ☉8am-4pm), protected by an ugly hangar but with an ingenious interior hanging stairway, is one of four churches in the original village. Inside, the magnificent **mosaics** date back to about AD 785. If you have mosaic fatigue after Madaba and Mt Nebo, try to muster up one last flurry of enthusiasm for this well-preserved masterpiece. There are depictions of hunting, fishing and agriculture; scenes of daily life (such as boys enjoying a boat ride, a man astride an ostrich); and the names of those who helped pay for the mosaic. A panel consisting of 10 cities in the region includes Umm ar-Rasas, Philadelphia (Amman), Madaba, Esbounta (Hesban), Belemounta (Ma'in), Areopolis (Ar-Rabba) and Charac Moaba (Karak). A northern panel depicts Jerusalem, Nablus, Casearea, Gaza and others.

Beyond are the expansive ruins of **Kastron Mefaa** (mentioned in the Bible as the Roman military outpost of Mephaath), with another four churches (including the **Church of Lions** with impressive namesake mosaics) and city walls. Arches rise up randomly from the rubble like sea monsters and you can spot cisterns and door lintels everywhere, although a lack of signposts makes it hard to grasp the structure of the town.

About 1.5km north of the ruins is an enigmatic 15m-tall **stone tower**, the purpose of which baffles archaeologists as there are no stairs inside but several windows at the top. It was most likely a retreat for stylites, early Christian hermits who lived in seclusion on the top of pillars. Crosses decorate the side of the tower and several ruined monastery buildings lie nearby.

As part of the development of facilities at Umm ar-Rasas, a new museum is planned for the archaeological site of **Lehun**. Lehun was a garrison town built in AD 300 to house the 4th Roman Legion, forming part of a line of Roman forts called the Limes Arabicus, which defended the most remote borders of Rome. The site is 7km east of Dhiban and is worth a visit not so much for the random excavations as for the panoramic view across Wadi Mujib.

ⓘ Getting There & Away

As with all points along the King's Highway, the easiest way to get to either Umm ar-Rasas or Lehun is to drive or charter a private taxi from Madaba, 32km to the north. The turning is clearly signposted off either the King's Highway or the Desert Highway (Umm ar-Rasas lies halfway between the two).

A few minibuses go directly to Umm ar-Rasas via Nitil from the local bus station in Madaba. Alternatively, catch anything going to Dhiban, and try arranging a taxi (if you can find one) from there. It costs around JD10/18 one way/return, including waiting time. Failing that you could try hitching, although the road to Umm ar-Rasas is not a busy one.

Wadi Mujib   وادي الموجيب

Stretching across Jordan from the Desert Highway to the Dead Sea (covering a distance of over 70km) is the vast Wadi Mujib, proudly known as the 'Grand Canyon of Jordan'. Aside from being spectacular, it is also significant as the historic boundary between the ancient Amorites (to the north) and the Moabites (to the south). Moses is also believed to have walked through Wadi Mujib, when it was known as the Arnon Valley. The King's Highway crosses the upper reaches of the wadi while the lower reaches fall within the Mujib Biosphere Reserve (see p123) – normally accessed from the Dead Sea Highway.

The canyon measures 1km deep and 4km wide, but it takes the King's Highway 18km of road to switchback down one wall of the wadi, across the dam at the bottom and up the other side. From the picturesque olive groves of the upper plateau, either side of the wadi, there is no hint of the sublime upheaval that renders the land in two.

Travelling south, **Dhiban** is the last town you'll pass through before the descent into Wadi Mujib. Once the powerful capital of an empire carved out by King Mesha in the 9th century BC, Dhiban is where the Mesha Stele was discovered. There is nothing left of the ancient city and it's hard to imagine this unexceptional little town had such an illustrious past.

Even if you are not intending to make the crossing, it's worth travelling to the canyon rim. Past Dhiban, the road descends after 3km to an awesome **lookout** over Wadi Mujib. Some enterprising traders have set up a tea stall here and an assortment of fossils and minerals from the canyon walls are for

---

ℹ️ SLEEPING & EATING IN WADI MUJIB

There's nowhere between Madaba and Karak to stay or eat, except one outpost, high on the southern wall of Wadi Mujib. The strategically placed **Trajan Rest House & Restaurant** (📞079 5903302; trajan_resthouse@yahoo.com; bed in shared room JD5, with breakfast JD10) is perched like an eyrie on the canyon rim, and is mainly visited for its restaurant – a cavernous grotto of Bedouin artefacts, with hand-loomed rugs and cushions, and benches at the long trestle tables. Every day the hospitable owner, Mr Awad, and his family prepare an **open buffet** (JD10; ⏱11.30am-4.30pm). Mostly intended for tour groups, the generous buffet includes local dishes of spicy meatballs and herb chicken. The 'emergency' accommodation here is intended solely for those who get stuck and is basic to say the least, with curtains for doors. The views from the canyon rim on a morning walk are spectacular. For those hitching along the highway, you may find your best bet for a ride across Wadi Mujib is from this establishment.

---

sale. This is the easiest point on the road to stop and absorb the view, take a photograph and turn around if you're heading back to Madaba (there are no turning points after that until you reach the dam at the bottom).

Ariha is the nearest village to the canyon rim on the southern side of Wadi Mujib, although the village is about 2.5km off the main King's Highway.

ℹ️ Getting There & Away

Dhiban is where almost all transport south of Madaba stops. The only way to cross the mighty Wadi Mujib from Dhiban to Ariha is to charter a taxi for JD12 (bargain hard) each way. Finding a taxi in Ariha is even harder. Hitching is possible, but expect long waits.

Ar-Rabba عرّابه

The holy and historic city of Ar-Rabba came under the rule of King Mesha (9th century BC), then Alexander the Great (mid-4th century BC) and later the Nabataeans (from the 2nd century BC to the 2nd century AD). The Greeks named it Areopolis after Ares, the god of war, and the Romans based their Arab governorate here.

At the northern end of town are the minimal **ruins** (admission free; ⏱daylight hr) of a Roman temple from the end of the 3rd century AD (two niches contained statues of the Roman emperors Diocletian and Maximilian), and other Roman and Byzantine buildings. None of the ruins are signposted.

The site is accessible by minibus from Karak, 16km to the south, but is best visited on a 15-minute stop en route between Madaba and Karak.

Karak الكرك

🎵03 / POP 28,000 / ELEV 1000M

The ancient Crusader stronghold of Karak (or Kerak) lies within the walls of the old city and is one of the highlights of Jordan. The fortified castle that dominates the town was a place of legend in the battles between the Crusaders (Franks) and the Islamic armies of Saladin (Salah ad-Din). Now among one of the most famous Crusader castles, the castle at Karak was just one in a long line built by the Crusaders, stretching from Aqaba in the south to Turkey in the north.

Often ignored by travellers speeding south towards Petra, Karak deserves a detour.

History

Karak lies on the ancient caravan routes between Egypt and Syria, and was used by the Greeks and Romans. The city is mentioned several times in the Bible as Kir, Kir Moab and Kir Heres, capital of the Moabites, and later emerges as a Roman provincial town, Charac Moaba. The city also features in the famous mosaic map in St George's Church in Madaba.

The arrival of the Crusaders gave the city renewed prominence, especially after Crusader king Baldwin I of Jerusalem built the castle in AD 1142. Standing midway between Shobak and Jerusalem, Karak's commanding position and strategic value are obvious: it soon became the capital of the Crusader district of Oultrejourdain and, with the taxes levied on passing caravans and food grown in the district, helped Jerusalem to prosper.

Saladin's Muslim armies took the castle in 1183 after an epic siege. The Mamluk sultan Beybars took the fort in 1263 and strengthened the fortress, deepening the moat and adding the lower courtyard, but three towers collapsed in an earthquake in AD 1293.

Little more is known of the castle until Jean Louis Burckhardt (the Swiss explorer who rediscovered Petra) passed through Karak in 1812, describing the castle as 'shattered but imposing'.

In the 1880s, religious fighting compelled the Christians of Karak to flee north to resettle in Madaba and Ma'in; peace was only restored after thousands of Turkish troops were stationed in Karak.

◉ Sights

Karak's friendly, busy and chaotic town centre radiates around the statue of Saladin. The plaza near the entrance to the castle has been redeveloped, and it's in the surrounding streets that you'll find most of the tourist hotels and restaurants. Qala'a St is also known by the English name, Castle St.

Look for signs in the suburbs to two panorama points just southeast and northwest of town, providing grand views of the castle.

Karak Castle CASTLE
(☑2351216; admission JD1; ☺8am-4pm Oct-Mar, to 7pm Apr-Sep) The entrance to Karak Castle is at the southern end of Al Qala'a St, and throughout the castle, informative display boards give detailed descriptions of the history and function of each structure. Bring a torch (flashlight) to explore the darker regions, and watch your head on low doorways. Reconstruction and excavation work within the castle is ongoing.

The main entrance, **Ottoman's Gate**, is reached via a bridge over the dry moat. The **Crusader's Gate** (old entrance) is not open to the public.

From Ottoman's Gate, pass the ticket office and take the path to the left. Resist the temptation to head into the vaulted corridor straight ahead and instead turn left and enter the **Crusader Gallery** (stables). Near the far end of the gallery, steps lead down to the Crusader's Gate. Those entering the castle did so via a narrow winding passage (separated from the Crusader Gallery by a wall). This restrictive access is typical of Crusader castles, ensuring the entrance could be easily defended. On the north wall is a (now headless) **carved figure** that local legend claims to be Saladin, but which actually dates from the 2nd century AD and is believed by scholars to be a Nabataean funerary carving.

A small staircase leads up to the site of the ruined **northeast tower** while a long passageway leads southwest to the **soldiers barracks**. Note the small holes for light, walls

---

THE MESHA STELE

If you're travelling along the King's Highway, you'll keep coming across references to the Mesha Stele, but chances are you'll find little opportunity to discover what it is. Here's a quick ready reference to this significant artefact.

» **What is a stele?** It's an ancient upright stone, usually decorated in some way.

» **And the Mesha Stele?** It was a chest-high, black basalt tablet of stone carved with inscriptions.

» **Who discovered it?** It was found by a missionary at Dhiban in 1868.

» **Why was it so famous?** It provided historical detail of the battles between the Moabites and the kings of Israel and was also the earliest example of Hebrew script to be unearthed at that time.

» **Why was it made?** It was commissioned by King Mesha of Moab to advertise his successes against Israel.

» **What happened to it?** After surviving intact from about 850 BC to AD 1868, it quickly came to a rather unfortunate end. After finding the stele, the missionary reported it to Charles Clermont-Ganneau at the French consulate in Jerusalem, who made a mould of the tablet and returned to Jerusalem to raise the money to buy it. While he was away, local families, arguing over who was to benefit from the sale, lit a fire under the stone and poured water over it, causing it to shatter. Although most pieces were recovered, inevitably some were lost.

» **Where is it now?** The remnants were collected and shipped off to France, and the reconstructed stone is now on display in the Louvre in Paris. Copies can be seen in the museums at Amman, Madaba and Karak.

of limestone and straw, and a few Byzantine **rock inscriptions** on the walls. Across the corridor is the **kitchen**, which contains large, round stones used for grinding olives, and huge storage areas for oil and wheat. In a dark tunnel (only visible with a torch) are some **Greek inscriptions** of unknown meaning. A door from the kitchen leads to a giant **oven**.

Continuing southwest along the main passage, leave the cool, covered area and emerge into the light. Peer over the parapet at the **glacis**, the dizzyingly steep rocky slope that prevented invaders from climbing up to the castle and prisoners from climbing

down. This is where Renauld de Chatillon delighted in expelling his enemies.

Turn right into the overgrown **upper court**, which has a large **cistern** and the largely unexcavated domestic **residences** of the castle. At the northern end of the castle is the **terrace**, directly above the Crusader Gallery, with fine views. Above the far (southern) end of the castle rises **Umm al-Thallaja** (Mother of Snows), the hill which posed the greatest threat to the castle's defences during times of siege. To the west is the village of **Al-Shabiya**, which was once called Al-Ifranj because many

Karak

Crusaders (Franks) settled here after the fall of the castle.

Returning to where you emerged from the long corridor, head southwest. On the left is a **tower** and what is believed to have been a **Mamluk mosque**. On the right is the castle's main **Crusader church** with a **sacristy** down the stairs to the right (north). Note how in this lowered room there are arrow slits in the walls, suggesting that this originally formed part of the castle's outer wall.

Continue to the southern end of the castle towards the impressive, reconstructed **Mamluk keep**. Because it faces Umm al-Thallaja, it was here that the defences were strongest, with 6.5m-thick walls, arrow slits on all four levels and a crenellated section at the top. The keep was built from 1260 by the Mamluk sultan Beybars.

From the keep, find the stairs leading down to the **Mamluk palace**, built for Sultan al-Nasir Muhammad in 1311. The open-air **reception hall** is a variation of the classic Islamic design of four *iwans* (chambers) off the main hall; on two sides are barrel-vaulted rooms. The **mosque** here, with a clearly visible mihrab (niche) facing Mecca, was probably reserved for palace notables.

Pause near the top of the stairs for good **views** of Wadi Karak and the alleged site of the condemned cities of Sodom and Gomorrah (see p124). Return to the main Crusader church and you will find two corridors. The left (east) corridor leads past seven **prison cells** and the **prison administration office**. The right (west) corridor leads from the foot of the stairs through the **Rosettes Gallery**, named after the carved rosette at the bottom of the staircase.

If you're game, take the third passage to the left of the steps, which leads northwest through the bowels of the castle, roughly underneath the church. The corridor turns right (north) and emerges into the better-lit areas of the delightful underground **marketplace** with various **shops** and **cellars**.

At the northern end of the market, the path leads back to the entrance (also the exit) or you can detour down the hill to the **Mamluk ruins** and the excellent **Islamic Museum** (☺8am–1 hr before castle closing time).

🛏 Sleeping

TOP
CHOICE **Karak Rest House**   HOTEL $$
(☎2351148; moaweyaf@gmail.com; Al-Qala'a St; s/d incl breakfast JD28/47) You won't find a more convenient bed for the night than in this characterful hotel, right next door to the castle. With fantastic sweeping views of Wadi Karak from many of the rooms, elaborate Middle Eastern–style fixtures and fittings, and an elegant if somewhat faded lobby, this hotel is a great place to enjoy a

DON'T MISS

CARNAGE AT KARAK

For some reason, travellers often make the extra effort to travel the King's Highway and yet don't bother to pause at Karak. This is a great pity because it is home to one of the country's great highlights – the imposing crusader castle of Karak.

Built in 1142, the castle has a rather dark history. Indeed, some claim that if they stand above the parapet at Karak, with the wind in a particular direction, they can hear a wailful moaning on the wind. Rumour has it that these are the ghosts of the victims of one Renauld de Chatillon, a French crusader who inherited the castle by marriage soon after it was built.

De Chatillon, who arrived from France in 1148, was effective in seizing control of the trade routes to Egypt and Mecca, thereby disrupting the supply lines of the Islamic armies. De Chatillon's bigger claim to fame (or notoriety), however, was his sadistic gusto in interning the weakened soldiers in the dungeons of Karak castle. Here he delighted in torturing the hapless prisoners. After baiting them with descriptions of their forthcoming fate, he would then have them hurled off the castle walls into the rocky wadi, 450m below. That was the relatively good bit. The bad bit was that he went to the trouble of having a wooden box fastened over their heads first so they wouldn't lose consciousness before hitting the ground.

Hated by Saladin for his treachery, De Chatillon was later executed by the redoubtable Islamic warrior – the only Crusader leader to meet such a fate. Today, his brooding castle still dominates the King's Highway, providing a fascinating insight into the struggle for the Holy Land between Christians and Muslims that echoes down the centuries.

cup of Egyptian tea under the pergola and watch the goings-on of the busy street. The hotel continues to receive letters from satisfied guests.

Al-Mujeb Hotel
HOTEL $$

(☑2386090; almujeb_hotel@yahoo.com; King's Highway; s/d/tr incl breakfast JD30/45/55; ✳) This sprawling, three-storey hotel has recently had a makeover with all rooms refurbished. An assortment of interesting guests give the place character, especially when huddled round the gas heater in the foyer on a cold winter's evening. The hotel is around 5km from Karak, by the junction on the road to Ar-Rabba. If you are driving, consider parking here and taking a taxi (JD4 to JD5 one way) into town.

Qairwan Hotel
BOUTIQUE HOTEL $

(☑2396122; fax 2396022; King's Highway; s/d/tr JD23/30/38, 5-bed Jacuzzi suite with kitchen JD44; ✳🛜) Also spelt 'Cairwan', this eccentric, family-run hotel, with its tiled pitched roof and homely etceteras, is Karak's answer to a boutique hotel. Each of the nine rooms is unique, with quirky decoration. Quite unexpectedly, stairs lead down to a cavernous disco. The hotel is 500m from the bus station, outside the main town of Karak. Breakfast (JD4) is not included. Wi-fi costs JD3.

Towers Castle Hotel
HOTEL $

(☑/fax 2354293; Al-Qala'a St; s/d/tr incl breakfast JD15/25/35) Near to the castle, this friendly budget hotel is a good meeting place for younger travellers. Don't be put off by the dingy reception area: the rooms, with their floral motifs, are clean and many open onto balconies with views across Wadi Karak. You can find help with onward travel from here.

✖ Eating

Most restaurants are near the castle on Al-Mujamma St or near the statue of Saladin. Shwarma stands are clustered around Al-Jami St.

TOP
CHOICE ### Kir Heres Restaurant
JORDANIAN $$

(☑2355595; Al-Qala'a St; mains JD5-7; ⊗9am-10pm; ☑) A cut above the rest, this award-winning restaurant is a surprise find in Karak. The chef (and owner), Saddam, is from Karak and he has a passion for food, reflected in the inventive menu. There are ostrich steaks (JD10) and chicken dishes prepared with local herbs (JD7). Vegetarians can choose from dishes including fried haloumi (salty cheese; JD3.500) and mushrooms with garlic and thyme (JD3.100). The owner laments that people take fright at the smart tablecloths, serviettes and tasteful interior of draped kilims and imagine the prices will be prohibitive. The secret is out, however, among the discerning palates of Karak, and a reservation is necessary at weekends. This is also the only restaurant in town selling alcohol. Try the locally produced sweet white wine (JD4.250 per glass) in the upper gallery at lunchtime and you can forget about visiting the castle afterwards!

King's Restaurant   JORDANIAN $
(☎2354293; Al-Mujamma St; mezze JD2.500, mains JD5; ☺8am-10pm) Opposite an open area called Castle Plaza, this boulevard restaurant with tables on the pavement attracts travellers at all times of the day and night. It offers grills, pizzas and sandwiches, and local, home-cooked Jordanian dishes like *maqlubbeh*. The freshly squeezed orange juice is welcome after hot climbs up and down Al-Qala'a St.

King's Castle Restaurant   BUFFET $
(☎2396070; lunch buffet JD10, ☺noon-4pm) The daily buffet here is popular with tour groups. With pleasant outdoor seating, castle views and over 20 salads to choose from, it's easy to understand why. The eastern building is worth a visit for its impressive relief display of the castle.

Shehab Restaurant   JORDANIAN $$
(☎9513803; Al-Qala'a St; mains JD6; @) This restaurant offers free internet and a free drink if ordering a meal.

Al-Fid'a Restaurant   JORDANIAN $
(☎079 5037622; Al-Mujamma St; mains JD5; ☺8am-10pm) Another popular place selling standard local fare of chicken, dips and salads.

Al-Motaz Sweets   SWEETS $
(☎2353388; An-Nuzha St; ☺8am-10pm) This Arabic pastry shop is a must for those with a sweet tooth.

Al-Shubba   SUPERMARKET
(Al-Mujamma St) Try Al-Shubba if you need to stock up on supplies for the next leg of the King's Highway.

🛍 Shopping

While there is a small selection of souvenirs around the castle area, for an idea of how the people of Karak like to spend their money, take a walk down Al-Malak Hussein St – the road that leads from Castle Plaza to the Saladin statue. Here you will find tailors

stitching fake fur to collars; leather jackets and red woollen sweaters dangling in the wind; vendors with rakishly tied headscarves and broken-backed shoes (the local answer to slip-ons); bushy green bundles of coriander hanging from butchers' shops; fennel, turnips and shaggy-mopped carrots begging to be bought for a picnic; and locally gathered herbs in textile bags flagging the outside of spice and coffee bean shops. There is even a small gold souq – selling mostly silver.

ℹ Information

There are at least four banks that change money on An-Nuzha St, one block south of the Saladin roundabout, and most have an ATM for Visa and MasterCard.

Italian Hospital (Al-Maydan St)
Post office (Al-Khadr St) In the lower (northern) part of town.
Tourist police (☎191; Al Qala'a St)
Visitor centre (☎2354263; Al Qala'a St; ☺8am-4pm Sat-Thu)

ℹ Getting There & Away

Karak is difficult but not impossible to reach by public transport, accessed from the Desert Highway. The main bus station is outside the town, at the bottom of the hill by the junction of the King's Highway. If you are driving, there is a highly scenic road (Route 50) that leads from Karak down to the Dead Sea (see p114).

Bus & Minibus
From the main bus station, several daily buses go direct to Amman's South Bus Station (JD1.650, around two hours) via the Desert Highway. Minibuses also run about every hour along the King's Highway from Karak to Tafila (950 fils, one hour), the best place for connections to Qadsiyya (for Dana Biosphere Reserve) and Shobak. To Wadi Musa (for Petra), take a minibus to Ma'an (JD2.200, two hours) which leaves around 1pm daily, and change there. Alternatively, leapfrog on minibuses to Tafila, Shobak and Wadi Musa.

Buses to Aqaba (JD2.700, three hours) travel in the mornings via the Dead Sea Highway about four times a day. In the afternoon it's better to take the Amman bus to Qatrana on the Desert Highway and change to a southbound bus to Aqaba.

There are smaller minibus stands around town for services to Safi (800 fils) and Mazra'a (600 fils) on the Dead Sea Highway, south along the King's Highway to Mu'tah (400 fils) and Mazar (400 fils), and north to Al-Qasr, Ar-Rabba and Ariha.

Taxi

From Amman it's possible to charter a taxi to Karak via the Desert Highway for about JD45 one way. From Amman via the King's Highway, with a stop at Madaba and Wadi Mujib, it costs at least JD75.

From Karak, taxi fares cost around JD45 to Amman or Madaba, JD40 to Dana and JD60 to Petra.

ℹ Getting Around

The old city of Karak is easy to get around on foot but has a maddening system of narrow one-way streets. If you're driving, consider parking outside town and taking a taxi.

Khirbet Tannour خربة التنور

Travelling south from Karak, the King's Highway gradually descends from a brooding piece of black volcanic hillside into the impressive but arid Wadi Hasa (the biblical Zered Valley). Attempts at tomato growing are in evidence but it's hard to encourage the rocky topsoil into production, and the discarded and wind-strewn strips of plastic are a sorry blight on an otherwise wild landscape.

The highway skirts a reservoir, above which looms a small, conical hill. A track leads off to the right of the highway from where a steep 15-minute hike leads to the top of the hill. At the top are the neglected ruins of the 2000-year-old Nabataean temple of **Khirbet Tannour** (admission free; ☉daylight hr). A famous statue of Nike was found here, a copy of which is housed in Amman's National Archaeological Museum; the original is in Cincinnati. A statue of the goddess Atargatis (currently in Amman's National Archaeological Museum) was also unearthed from this auspicious little hilltop.

In truth there's not much to see here except for column bases and the outlines of a temple courtyard with adjoining rooms. Despite this, most people will relish the windswept site and epic location. In fact the term 'most people' is misleading: there is the strong suggestion among the scampering lizards and the desert larks that no one ever comes up here – except a conscientious guidebook writer or two. Even the dogs herding sheep along the fertile wadi to the south keep their distance, running in contours around the lower hills.

Access is only viable with private transport. The turn-off is 36km south of Karak

town, at the crest of the hill – a dam is clearly visible at the bottom of the hill. It is marked as 'AT TA NO I QUI ES SI', which isn't a Latin inscription, but a weather-beaten version of 'At-Tannour Antiquities Site'. The 1.5km access road is potholed but you can park off the track quite easily. Walk up to the communication tower and the path up the hill becomes obvious.

Hammamat Burbita & Hammamat Afra
حمامات بربيتا & حمامات عفرا

Hammamat Burbita (or Burbayta) and Hammamat Afra are two thermal hot springs near Wadi Hasa. Facilities at **Hammamat Afra** (JD7 per person) include private pools for men and women, changing rooms and picnic areas. It's very popular with locals at weekends and there's little chance of escaping the party as wardens prohibit you exploring the wadi upstream. Women on their own are likely to feel conspicuous.

The two springs are signposted about 23km north of Tafila; from the turn-off it's about 13km to Burbita; a green oasis at the base of a wadi with a small, uninviting rock pool marks the spot. The road continues for 5km to an entry gate where you pay the entrance fee and show your passport before continuing the extra 1km to the more picturesque Hammamat Afra. You can't see the springs from the road.

There is no public transport to either spot but it is adequately signposted if you are driving. A chartered taxi from Tafila to Afra costs around JD25 return, including waiting time.

Tafila الطفيله

☎03 / POP 85.600 / ELEV 1050M

Wrapped around a steep-sided wadi, Tafila (also spelled Tafileh) is a busy market centre and transport junction. There is nothing to see, except the decrepit exterior of a ruined **Crusader castle** (closed to visitors). It was in Tafila that one of the Prophet Mohammed's emissaries was beheaded, leading to the military conquest by the Islamic armies from AD 632.

The only reason to come here is to change minibuses. They leave almost hourly from Karak (JD1, one hour), crossing the inspiring desert scenery of Wadi Hasa. There are also direct minibuses to/from Wahadat station in Amman (JD2.500, 2½ hours) via the

Desert Highway; Aqaba (JD1.800, 2½ hours) via the Dead Sea Highway; Ma'an (JD1.300, one hour) via the Desert Highway; and Shobak (JD1.200, one hour) and Qadsiyya (for Dana Biosphere Reserve, JD1, 30 minutes) along the King's Highway.

Dana Biosphere Reserve
محمية دانا الطبيعية

🗓 03 / ELEV 1250M

The **Dana Biosphere Reserve** (adult/student JD8.120/4.060, free for guests staying in RSCN accommodation) is one of Jordan's hidden gems. The focal point of the reserve is the charming 15th-century stone village of **Dana**, which dangles beneath the King's Highway on a precipice, commanding exceptional views of the valley below.

The reserve is the largest in Jordan and includes a variety of terrain, from sandstone cliffs over 1700m high near Dana to a low point of 50m below sea level in Wadi Araba. Sheltered within the red-rock escarpments are protected valleys that are home to a surprisingly diverse ecosystem. About 600 species of plants (ranging from citrus trees and juniper, to desert acacias and date palms) thrive in the reserve, together with 180 species of birds. Over 45 species of mammals (25 of which are endangered) also inhabit the reserve, including caracal, ibex, mountain gazelle, sand cat, red fox and wolf. The recent installation of night traps is giving reserve wardens a better understanding of the movement of these rarely spotted animals.

In short, the reserve is a wonderful place to spend a few days hiking or simply reading and relaxing en route from Madaba or the Dead Sea to Petra, Wadi Rum and Aqaba.

The best time to visit Dana is in the spring, when the hillsides bloom with flowers, or during the autumn, when the auburn foliage thins out, making it easier to spot wildlife. The winter can be bitterly cold and some of the trails are closed, while the summer is simply too hot for comfort in the lower part of the reserve.

History
Dana village itself dates from the Ottoman period but was abandoned less than a generation ago as locals moved to nearby Qadsiyya in search of jobs. Farmed by only a handful of remaining residents, the neighbouring terraces, which once grew pistachio, almond, walnut, pomegranate, lemon and apple crops, are slowly slipping back to nature. Ongoing attempts by various parties to entice the villagers back into the reserve are hampered by the fact that housing with utilities, schooling and basic infrastructure is to be had in nearby towns that are far more accessible. That said, there are signs of green shoots in the village, thanks to the persistent efforts of the RSCN and the tourism it promotes. Several old houses are being renovated and shopkeepers, barbers and bakers are being invited to return.

About 50 Bedouin families drift in and beyond the lower reaches of the reserve. They are only permitted to herd their livestock in the Dana Valley at certain times of the year to allow the vegetation to recover.

The RSCN assumed control of the reserve in 1993 in an attempt to promote ecotourism, protect wildlife and improve the lives of local villagers in an integrated project. The reserve directly or indirectly employs locals from nearby villages, and income from tourism is helping to sustain a number of families beyond the reserve and provide environmental education in local schools. Villagers also make quality local crafts (organic herbs, fruit rolls, jams, olive-oil soaps, candles and silver jewellery) that are sold by the RSCN throughout Jordan. The leather goods and candles produced by local Bedouin women at Feynan Ecolodge, in particular, give local women a degree of economic independence and an incentive to move away from goat rearing, which is detrimental to the fragile environment.

Dana is unique because it has four ecosystems ranging from altitudes of 1700m to minus 50m, all of which occur within a very compact distance. For this reason Dana has now achieved official 'biodiversity reserve' status.

🏃 Activities
Hiking
The reserve begs to be explored on foot. It's only by getting out in the thick of it that you feel the special beauty of the terrain and invite the chance encounter with Dana's diverse wildlife.

The visitor centre can give information on a range of **hikes**, most of which are guided. The trails from Al-Barra require a short drive to get to the trailhead (RSCN charges JD11.600 for a shuttle). The major trails include the following:

EASY TRAILS

Rummana Campground Trail   HIKING

(1-2hr, self-guided; ☺15 Mar-31 Oct) This spectacular walk traces the fluted edge of Wadi Dana's canyons, circling through the trees and rock formations around the campground, and giving plenty of opportunities for a quiet sit among untroubled wildlife. Look out for griffon vultures wheeling above the stone turrets of Wadi Dana, brilliant turquoise agamas (a type of lizard) basking on rocks, jewel beetles and, if you get really lucky, an early-morning ibex in the creases and folds of neighbouring canyons.

Wadi Dana Trail   HIKING

(16km, 6hr, self-guided; ☺year-round) Although this is the most popular trail, you are still likely to have this long hike through majestic Wadi Dana to yourself. The trail is easy to follow, partially along a disused road, and latterly via Bedouin grazing paths. Although no scrambling is involved, be aware that the trail involves a relentless one-hour descent at the beginning of the hike that gives toes, calves and knees a good bruising. It's not feasible to complete the walk in both directions in a day unless you are super fit or plainly masochistic. Either stay the night at Feynan Ecolodge, at the bottom of the walk, or arrange with the RSCN office for a car (JD46) to bring you back to Dana either via Tafila (2½ hours) or Shobak (2¾ hours). See the boxed text (p156) for more detail.

MODERATE TRAILS

Rummana Mountain Trail   HIKING

(2.5km, 1-2hr, self-guided; ☺15 Mar-31 Oct) From Rummana Campground to the nearby Rummana (Pomegranate) Peak, this trail gives great views over Wadi Araba. One Rummana receptionist, Mahmoun, described the trail as a good metaphor for life: lots of ups and downs but greatly rewarding when you reach your goal.

Nawatef Trail   HIKING

(2.5km, 2½hr, guide required; ☺year-round) This great short walk, from Al-Barra to the luscious springs and Nabataean ruins of Nawatef, involves a steep uphill walk back to Dana.

White Dome Trail   HIKING

(8km, 3hr, guide required; ☺15 Mar-31 Oct) Taking you past dramatic wadi escarpments surrounding Rummana Campground, through the beautiful terraced gardens of Dana village, this trail leads through waist-high vegetation to Dana Guesthouse.

HARD TRAILS

Fida Canyon Trail   HIKING

(2.5km, 2hr, guide required; ☺year-round) This short but strenuous hike leads from Al-Barra to Shaq al-Reesh and is not for the faint-hearted.

Hammam Al-Dathnah Trail   HIKING

(17km, 9hr, guide required; ☺year-round) A spectacular but highly taxing trail, it leads from Al-Nawatef, crossing Hamra Valley and Palm Tree Valley to Feynan Ecolodge.

WORTH A TRIP

ANCIENT DANA

There's something rather magical about coming across a pile of smelted fragments and realising that this is evidence of industry, not from any industrial revolution, but from the activities of communities 6000 years ago.

There are almost 100 archaeological sites in Dana reserve, most still being excavated by British teams. The ruins of **Khirbet Feynan**, at the mouth of Wadi Feynan and Wadi Ghuweir, are particularly interesting: the 6000-year-old copper mines here were once the largest metal-smelting operations in the Near East and are mentioned in the Bible. The Romans later worked the mines using Christian slaves.

You can explore the slag heaps of the main mines of Umm al-Amad, together with the ruins of three churches and a Roman tower, on a fascinating 13km hike in the hills from Feynan Ecolodge or on the shorter **Feynan Ecolodge Copper Mine Tour** (1-2hr, guide required; ☺closed Jul & Aug) which includes Iron Age sites. The tour is very hot for much of the year so carrying water and wearing a hat is essential.

The hills of Dana still contain copper, but despite lobbying from mining companies, the Jordanian government has agreed not to allow mining in the reserve. A growing cement factory which quarries along the rim of the reserve is the nearest incursion permitted in this wildlife haven.

Al-Ghuweir Trail HIKING

(16km, 6-7hr, guide required; ☺year-round) This demanding hike leads along river beds and through a siq and a valley of palm trees to arrive at Feynan Ecolodge. It is to be avoided if rain is expected or has recently fallen because of flash floods. Transport to the start of this trail costs JD25.

In addition to the above, there's a two-day hike to Feynan Ecolodge, via Wadi Ghuweir, overnighting at the lodge and returning via Wadi Dana. Hotels in Dana can help organise longer treks to Shobak (two days) via Wadi Feynan, Wadi Ghuweir and the village of Mansourah, and even on to Petra (four days).

Al-Nawatef Camp organises several excellent guided hikes in Wadi Ghuweir and Wadi Hamra. Ask about Ali's Walk, a three-day hike to Petra (JD180 to JD200 per person for a minimum group of six), including guide, camping facilities, all meals and transportation of luggage.

Cycling

A **mountain-bike trail** (guide possible) offers cyclists opportunities to explore the park on saddleback: a four-hour ride costs JD18 (JD 29 with a guide); a full day's ride costs JD29 (JD47 with a guide). The trail starts at Feynan Ecolodge and uses gravel tracks past the archaeological site of Khirbet Feynan, ending at the villages of Rashaydeh and Greigra. There are opportunities to stop en route to hike or have tea with the Bedouin. The lodge has 10 bikes available. Contact the tourism manager at **Feynan Ecolodge** (☎079 9599507; rkhawaldeh@rscn. org.jo) for details . The trail is closed in July and August.

🍴 Sleeping & Eating

The RSCN operates three excellent places to stay, each of which should be booked in advance through the **Wild Jordan Centre** (☎4616523; www.rscn.org.jo; Othman Bin Affan St, downtown) in Amman. In addition, there are three privately run budget hotels in Dana village. Each arranges transfers and hiking but make sure you pay your reserve fees as it is illegal to walk in the reserve without a ticket, and besides money from tourism is the main hope for the long-term survival of this reserve. Camping in the reserve, except at the Rummana Campground, is not permitted.

TOP
CHOICE **Dana Guest House** ECOLODGE $$

(☎2270497; dhana@rscn.org.jo; s/d/tr/q with shared bathroom incl breakfast JD55/70/85/100, d with private bathroom JD80) With panoramic views across the reserve and a roaring fire in winter, enthusiastic park rangers and a collection of like-minded fellow travellers, this is one ecolodge that lives up to its reputation. Run by the RSCN, the lodge is cut into the hillside with the balcony and dining room on the ground floor and minimalist, stone-walled rooms on the floor below. All but the two single rooms have a balcony on which you can shiver in the dawn before sneaking back to bed before breakfast. The heating and hot water is provided by solar panels. Breakfast, a selection of fresh salads, local cheese, *labneh* and *halva,* and dinner (JD11) is shared around long trestle tables.

🏕 **Rummana Campground** CAMPGROUND $$

(s/d/tr/q tent incl breakfast & park entry fee JD44/54/64/74; ☺15 Mar-31 Oct) Location, location, location is what this wonderful RSCN campsite is all about. The price may seem steep given the minimal facilities but when you wake up to the sound of Dana's copious wildlife singing in your ear, it's easy to see why you have to book in advance during high season. With some fantastic hiking trails just beyond the tent pegs, you can step out of your dreams and into the cloudscape as the mist rises from the valley floor. Tents come with mattresses, copious bedding and kerosene lamps, and there's a cold-water shower block with locally made olive-oil soap. Dinner (JD11) and breakfast (included in the camp fee) are whisked up by a jolly cook intent on beefing you up for another day's exertions; meals are surprisingly lavish affairs of freshly prepared Jordanian specialities. You can drive here (see p155) or hike in three hours from Dana village (p152). You can use the barbecue grills if you bring your own food and fuel. There's a 20% discount for students.

🏕 **Feynan Ecolodge** ECOLODGE $$

(☎2270497; www.feynan.com; Wadi Feynan; s/d incl breakfast & park entry fee JD85/95; ☺1 Sep-30 Jun; ❄🔧) This one-of-a-kind ecolodge, owned by the RSCN and privately managed, is only accessible on foot from Dana or by 4WD from the Dead Sea Highway. See the box (p122) for a full review.

MADABA & THE KING'S HIGHWAY DANA BIOSPHERE RESERVE

LOCAL KNOWLEDGE

MALIK AL-NANAH: ECO GUIDE AT DANA

Graduated in biology from Ma'an University, Malik Al-Nanah knows and loves the reserve's residents – like the rockmartin whose nest is attached to the Feynan Ecolodge, a fitting metaphor for the relationship nurtured between people and nature here.

What's your favourite time of year here? All year! In summer, there's the bird migration, skies are cloudy and the sunsets are fantastic. You may see up to 40 griffin vultures and even short-eared owls.

And your most exciting wildlife encounter? I've seen wolf, wild cat and horned viper – all rare animals. But the best was probably seeing, at 5am one morning, a family of ibex.

What role does the community play? The whole philosophy of the RSCN is to protect nature by supporting local people – through employment, use of supplies and children's workshops.

Any famous visitors? Yes, the royal family have stayed here – in room 9 – and the king sends guests here too.

Why should people visit? Clean air, waking up early, seeing animals and hearing birdsong – in short, you can learn the meaning of nature here.

What if they can't make it to Dana? Go to the RSCN's Wild Jordan Centre in Amman – we've taken nature to the city there and it's inspiring!

Dana Tower Hotel GUESTHOUSE $
(☏079 5688853; dana_tower2@hotmail.com; s/d/tr with shared bathroom JD5/10/12, summer rooftop camping JD2) This quirky assembly of rooms, sitting areas and tiny, leafy courtyards has its own appeal, with a *majlis* draped in memorabilia, including plastic roses, sheesha bottles and backgammon sets. With names like 'Flying Carpet' and 'Sunset Royal', the small, unheated rooms, some of which are decorated with travellers' graffiti, are a winner with younger backpackers. There's free tea, a washing machine, shared hot showers and rooftop seating. Lunch and dinner of 22 dishes including chicken, salad and dips (JD5) can be provided on request. The guesthouse offers free transfer to and from the main road and good-value onward transport.

Al-Nawatef Camp CAMPGROUND $
(☏2270413, 079 6392079; nawatefcamp@hotmail. com; half board JD15) If the accommodation at Dana is full, consider staying at this privately owned camp. Perched on the edge of a neighbouring wadi, it has a fabulous location and is run by an enterprising local who knows the area 'because', he says, 'it runs in my blood'. The camp comprises a basic shared shower block, goat-hair chalets with beds and blankets (but no linen) and balconies with exceptional views. In spring, the camp is surrounded by black iris. Tea and coffee is available all day, delicious dinners are rustled up from the ground oven and a free transport service is offered to Dana village. You can set your own tent up in the grounds for JD5 and order dinner (JD5) or breakfast (JD2) to suit. The camp is signposted 2km off the King's Highway, 5km south of the Dana turning in Qadsiyya. The owner can collect you from the main road. He also organises onward travel via local buses and will drop you at the relevant junction.

Dana Hotel HOTEL $
(☏2270537, 079 5597307; www.danavillage.piczo. com; s/d JD12/20) This 17-room, no-frills hotel in Dana village is run by the Sons of Dana, a cooperative that provides social programs to around 150 local residents. It's the oldest hotel in Dana and rooms are stark and plain with metal bedposts. That said, this is a friendly establishment and it feels good to be giving patronage to a worthy self-help project. Meals, in a commodious dining room with en-suite *majlis* on the 1st floor, cost JD5.

Dana Moon Hotel GUESTHOUSE $
(☏079 7533581; dana.moonhotel@hotmail.com; half-board JD15 per person) Simple rooms with shared bathrooms characterise this guesthouse. A *majlis* under the pine trees is an attractive feature. This latest addition to accommodation in Dana needs more time to become better-established. A restaurant is planned for 2012.

❶ Information

The **visitor centre** (☎2270497; www.rscn.org.
jo; ☺8am-3pm) in the guesthouse complex in
Dana village includes an **RSCN shop**, nature exhibits, craft workshops (closed by 3.30pm) and
a food-drying centre for making organic food.
This is also the place to obtain further information about the reserve and its hiking trails, and
to arrange a guide. Rangers at the centre are
knowledgeable, enthusiastic and friendly, and
you sense a genuine commitment to the cause.

Spare 10 minutes for the wonderful little **museum** (visitor centre) that illustrates the various
wildlife at 1500m on the King's Highway, at
1100m at Dana Village and 50m below sea level
in Wadi Araba. It also explains the peculiar challenges to the ecosystem in a reserve that experiences 350mm of rain per year in winter on the
mountaintops, and soaring desert temperatures
and 10mm of rain per year at sea level.

Guides are available (and compulsory on some
hiking and cycling trails) to give visitors a deeper
understanding of the reserve. They cost (for a
minimum of four people) JD10 per person for up
to two hours; JD13 for three to four hours, JD16
for five to six hours. It costs JD16 per person
for a guide for a full day (for a minimum of 10
people).

See the Directory (p316) for a voluntary work
opportunity.

❶ Getting There & Away

The easiest way to get to Dana by public transport is from Tafila. Minibuses run every hour or
so between Tafila and Qadsiyya (JD1, 30 minutes). The turn-off to Dana village is 1km north of
Qadsiyya; from here it's a steep 2.8km downhill
walk to Dana village (there's no bus). Alternatively, you can take a private car with one of the
locals in Qadsiyya for JD4. Heading out of Dana,
ask around at the hotels for a ride as you won't
want to walk back up that hill. There are three
daily buses to Amman (JD3, three hours); the
first bus leaves Qadsiyya between 6am and 7am.

A taxi to Dana from Karak costs around JD25
to JD30 one way. The Dana Tower Hotel will pick
up travellers for free from Qadsiyya if you ring
in advance and stay at this hotel. A taxi to Petra
costs JD36 or JD12 in a shared taxi from the
hotel. The Dana Tower Hotel also organises a bus
from Amman's South Bus Station for JD5 if you
book with the hotel in advance.

If you're driving from Tafila or Karak, the
first signpost you'll see off to the right goes to
the Rummana Campground. A few kilometres
beyond this turning, pull over by the side of
the highway at a gap in the pines. If you don't
have time to visit Dana, you can at least enjoy
the spectacular view from the viewpoint here.
It's especially inspiring at sunset. The turn-off

to Dana Biosphere Reserve is signposted, just
before the village of Qadsiyya. Beware, it is a
steep descent: use low gear instead of relying on
your brakes.

To get to Rummana Campground from Dana
village, head 4.5km north of Qadsiyya along the
King's Highway and turn left at the signpost. The
campground is 6km along a road partially shared
by cement-factory traffic. RSCN can arrange
transport from Dana village for JD10.500 (for
one to four people).

Shobak Castle   شوبك

☑03

Perched in a wild, remote landscape,
Shobak Castle (admission free; ☺daylight
hr) wins over even the most castle-weary,
despite being less complete than its sister
fortification at Karak. Formerly called Mons
Realis (Mont Real, or Montreal – the Royal
Mountain), it was built by the Crusader king
Baldwin I in AD 1115. It withstood numerous
attacks from the armies of Saladin before
succumbing in 1189 (a year after Karak), after an 18-month siege. It was later occupied
in the 14th century by the Mamluks, who
built over many of the Crusader buildings.

Built on a small knoll at the edge of a plateau, the castle is especially imposing when
seen from a distance. Restoration work is
ongoing and hopefully this will include
some explanatory signs. In the meantime,
the caretaker shows visitors around for
about JD1 to JD2. Bring a torch for exploring the castle's many dark corners.

As you climb up from the entrance,
there are some **wells** on the left. Soon after
passing these, you'll see the reconstructed
church, one of two in the castle, down to
the left. It has an elegant apse supported by
two smaller alcoves. The room leading off to
the west was the **baptistery**; on the north
wall there are traces of water channels leading from above.

Returning to the main path, turn left. After passing under the arches, a door leads
into the extensive **market**. Turn left and
descend 375 steps into an amazing **secret
passageway** that leads to a subterranean
spring, finally surfacing via a ladder outside
the castle, beside the road to Shobak town.
Tread carefully, use a torch and don't even
think about coming down here if you're
claustrophobic. Alternatively, continue past
the tunnel for 50m and you'll pass a large
two-storey building with archways, built by

the Crusaders but adapted by the Mamluks as a **school**.

At the northern end of the castle is the semicircular **keep** with four arrow slits. Outside, dark steps lead down to the **prison**. Head to the northeast corner of the castle to see **Quranic inscriptions**, possibly dating from the time of Saladin, carved in Kufic script around the outside of the keep. Following south along the eastern perimeter, you'll pass the entrance to the **court of Baldwin I**, which has been partly reconstructed. The court was later used as a **Mamluk school**.

Continuing south, you'll pass some **baths** on the right. Off to the left is a reconstructed **Mamluk watchtower**. Just past the tower is the second **church**. On a room to the left as you enter, you can see above a door in the east wall a weathered carving of a **Crusader cross**. In the church proper, the arches have been reconstructed.

Beneath the church are **catacombs**, which contain Islamic tablets, Christian carvings, large spherical rocks used in catapults, and what is said to be Saladin's very simple throne. From the catacombs, the path leads back to the gate.

A new **visitor centre** (⊘9am-5pm Nov-Mar, to 7pm Apr-Oct) has limited facilities (and no telephone). The caretaker can rustle up a Turkish coffee in the attractive courtyard with great views of the castle.

ℹ️ A WALK IN THE PARK

One of the most popular trails at Dana is the 16km, 'easy hike' Wadi Dana Trail, from Dana to Feynan Ecolodge. As it's downhill all the way, it ought to be a mere walk in the park, but don't be deceived – it's not as easy as it looks! Start the walk after lunch: that way, you'll reach the hotter part of the walk in the cooler part of the day. Take more water than you think you'll need and wear a hat. Don't forget in your planning that it takes three hours, partly by 4WD, to return to Dana by road.

The Bad Bits:

» Interminable initial descent on a potholed vehicle track, wishing you'd worn thicker socks

» Blazing heat with little shade (there's only one tree in the first hour)

» Not having time to stop to chat with the Bedouin (some JD1 notes for tea would've been handy)

» The end of the wadi is nowhere near where you think it is

» Being overtaken by an encouraging old couple on a donkey saying 'Funduq (hotel) – only five minutes', when you're still an hour's walk from Feynan

» The prospect of no beer and no meat at the inn – Feynan Ecolodge is vegetarian-only

The Good Bits:

» A lizard sunning itself in the ash of an old fireplace

» A crest of goats marshalled into camera by an entrepreneurial herdsman

» Carnival-pink oleander flowers, waving like bunting along the entire lower wadi

» Secret gardens of reeds and oleander and huge, spreading trees

» A barefoot race by local lads conducted for the sheer fun of running

» A Sinai agama (lizard), whose brilliant turquoise livery demanded a second look

» The same encouraging couple returning on the donkey saying 'Funduq – only five minutes'

» The sampling of delicious cool water and superb vegetarian food at Feynan Ecolodge

So is it worthwhile? Without doubt! Chances are that even in peak season you'll have the reserve to yourself. Anyone who has hiked main trails in other popularly visited destinations will know what a treat that is.

🛏 Sleeping & Eating

There is limited accommodation in Shobak (properly known as Musallath) village; all options have fine views of the castle.

TOP CHOICE **Montréal Hotel**   HOTEL $
(☏077 6951714; www.jhrc.jo; r JD20, ste JD38; ☜)
This new hotel, with a spectacular view of the castle, has some lovely features including a stylish lounge around a central gas fire. The rooms are simple but comfortable. The hotel takes a sustainable approach and has solar panels for hot-water heating and electricity. Breakfast costs JD5 and dinner is available.

Jaya Tourist Camp   CAMPGROUND $
(☏079 5958958; http://jayatouristcamp.yolasite.com; JD20) With 15 tents in a tranquil spot on high ground opposite Shobak Castle, this friendly campsite has a clean shower block and Bedouin goat-hair tents for relaxing. The camp runs a number of hikes, including from Shobak to Feynan Ecolodge or to Little Petra (JD30 per day for a guide) and can organise transport of luggage (JD70 per day). If you want to gain a better insight into the nomadic way of life, consider visiting a local Bedouin family (JD5; JD30 to stay overnight). To reach the camp, follow the signs from the King's Highway. The road passes Montréal Hotel and ends after 1km at the camp.

Showbak Camp & Caves
Zaman Motel   GUESTHOUSE $
(☏077 7996834; showbakcavehotel@yahoo.com; incl breakfast JD12 per person) For an interesting experience, consider staying at the refurbished caves at the foot of the castle. The caves have been in the owner's family for generations and he remembers his grandparents living here. The interior of each shallow cave has been rendered and electric lights help to make sense of the uneven interior space. Vague privacy is offered by flimsy curtains but proper doors are planned. Shared bathrooms have hot water and dinner is available for JD13. Warm in winter and cool in summer, the caves are an intriguing way to get a feel for an ancient way of life.

There are a few grocery stores and cheap restaurants in Shobak village.

❶ Getting There & Away

Occasional buses link Shobak village with Amman's south station (JD4, 2½ hours), Aqaba and Karak. Some minibuses travelling between Wadi Musa and Ma'an also pass through Shobak. There are less reliable minibuses between Shobak and Tafila (JD1.200, one hour). For the 3km from Shobak village to the castle, you can charter a taxi (around JD6 return including waiting time) or walk.

If driving, there are two well-signposted roads from the King's Highway to the castle and there are signs from Shobak village.

Petra بترا

Best Places to Eat & Drink

» Cave Bar (p188)

» Sahtain (p187)

» Petra Kitchen (p183)

» Red Cave Restaurant (p187)

» Basin Restaurant (p184)

Best Places to Stay

» Mövenpick Hotel (p183)

» Amra Palace Hotel (p185)

» Taybet Zaman Hotel & Resort (p186)

» Petra Palace Hotel (p184)

» Petra Moon Hotel (p183)

Why Go?

It's dawn. The path winds down towards the Siq, the dramatic rift in the land that leads towards the hidden city of Petra. The only sounds are the ringing of hooves on cobblestones as horse carts pass into the narrow gorge. The corridor of stone narrows and the cliffs cast long shadows across the sacred way. At length, the path slithers into sunlight and there, bathed in morning glory, stands the Treasury, a beacon of hope to the ancients and a promise of 'wonderful things' for the modern visitor.

If this sublime experience isn't sufficient inducement to visit Petra, then the magnificent spectacle of the 'pink city' tombs at sunset surely will be. Ultimately, however, these dramatic gestures of immortality may prove less memorable than a quiet amble through forgotten tombs, glimpses of outrageously coloured sandstone or a satisfying hike to the top of a High Place.

When to Go

March to May is peak tourist season in Petra and for good reason. Hiking is at its safest, the wadis are seamed with prolific pink-flowering oleander and climbs to the 'high places' are accompanied by spears of flowering aloe.

Mid-October to the end of November, Petra's second high season, offers a last chance to visit in good weather before rains put some routes off-limits.

Bitterly cold by night and bright blue skies by day, Petra is almost empty in winter allowing for a more intimate engagement with the 'Pink City'.

History

Neolithic villages dating from around 7000 BC can be traced to the surrounding wadis and hillsides of Petra. Remains of the most famous of these, excavated in the 1950s, can be seen at Al-Beidha (p192), just north of Petra. Built at the same time as Jericho on the West Bank, Al-Beidha is one of the earliest known farming communities in the Middle East.

The Nabataeans, a nomadic tribe from western Arabia, settled in the area around the 6th century BC. They were organised traders (see p255) and over the next 500 years they used their wealth to build the city of Petra.

In its heyday, under King Aretas IV (8 BC–AD 40), the city was home to around 30,000 people, including scribes (the Nabataeans created their own cursive script; the forerunner of Arabic) and expert hydraulic engineers who built dams, cisterns and water channels to protect the site and its magnificent buildings.

By AD 106, as trade routes shifted from Petra to Palmyra and new sea trade routes via the Red Sea to Rome bypassed Petra altogether, the Romans assumed control of the weakened Nabataean empire. Far from abandoning the city of Petra, however, the invaders recast the ancient city with familiar Roman features, including a colonnaded street and baths. The city was honoured by a visit from Emperor Hadrian in AD 131, and in the 3rd century Petra once again became a capital city – this time of the newly created province of Palaestrina Tertia.

PETRA

Petra Highlights

1 Tread the path of history by winding through the **Siq** (p164), the sheer-sided chasm leading to an ancient world

2 Catch the early-morning sun slanting off the pillars of the **Treasury** (p166), the sublime spectacle at the end of the Siq

3 Climb the processional way to the **High Place of Sacrifice** (p167), pause

for tea with the Bedouin and return to the valley floor through a garden of wildflowers

4 Search the **Royal Tombs** (p169) for spirits, lurking in the rainbow-coloured hollows

5 Make the pilgrimage to the **Monastery** (p173) and watch the weather-burnished stones catch alight at sunset

6 Let your soul glide through the Siq's shadows, guided by music and candlelight on tour with **Petra by Night** (p182)

7 Prepare your own traditional Jordanian supper at **Petra Kitchen** (p183)

8 Visit **Little Petra** (p191) and enjoy Nabataean tombs and temples in a miniature siq without the company of tour groups

Earthquakes in 363 and 551 ruined much of the city and Petra became a forgotten outpost, a 'lost city' known only to local Bedouin who preferred to keep its whereabouts secret. In 1812, however, a young Swiss explorer, Jean Louis Burckhardt, ended Petra's splendid isolation, riding into the abandoned ancient city disguised as a Muslim holy man.

Throughout the 19th century, Petra became the focus of the Western European obsession with the Arabic Orient and the site was pored over by numerous archaeologists, travellers, poets and artists (including the famed British painter David Roberts in 1839). The first English archaeological team arrived in 1929 and excavations have continued unabated to the present day. In 1992 the mosaics of the Petra Church were unveiled and in 2003 a tomb complex was found underneath the Treasury. Part of the continuing allure of the 'rose red city' is that despite many years of scrutiny, Petra still has many secrets yet to be discovered.

Nature Reserves

Petra is a protected area although it comes under a different administration from Jordan's other nature reserves. Given the number of visitors it hosts each year, the area has its own challenges (see the boxed text, p169), particularly erosion and damage to antiquities. For the longevity of this extraordinary site, it's important to pay it the same respect as any other reserve and avoid littering, wandering off paths, picking flowers or uprooting plants, marking the monuments or disappearing behind a rock instead of using the toilet facilities.

Dangers & Annoyances

Some travellers have complained of overcharging and hard-sell techniques (not to mention persistent local children!). This is rarely aggressive, and waxes and wanes with the fortunes of local traders. If you visit in winter, people are too busy keeping warm to worry about sales. In the competitive high season, however, traders and animal handlers make up for lost time. Invariably, after establishing contact with a smile, greeting or snippet of conversation, you'll find almost all will reciprocate in kind.

When hiking from November to March and in September and October, pay careful attention to the weather as the narrow wadis are susceptible to flash flooding.

ℹ️ Getting There & Away

Petra is a three-hour drive from Amman, two hours from Aqaba and 1½ hours from Wadi Rum. See p190 for transport details. If driving to or from the Dead Sea, consider travelling along the spectacular and seldom-used road that links Little Petra with Wadi Araba. See the boxed text (p114) for details.

ℹ️ Getting Around

There are usually plenty of private (yellow) unmetered taxis travelling up and down the main road of Wadi Musa towards the entrance for Petra, especially in the early morning and late afternoon. The taxi fare around central Wadi Musa is JD2 to JD3; it costs a little more if you go as far as 'Ain Musa. See p179 for transport within the Ancient City.

The Ancient City

The ancient city of Petra is strewn over a vast area of mountains and wadis, but there's just the one main access point. Be careful not to underestimate the amount of time it takes to walk between sights, nor the uphill return journey when you're tired. See the boxed text (p175) for details of walking times.

Petra is open every day unless it rains heavily – rare but disappointing occasions if you only allow one day for your visit in winter. Sturdy footwear, a hat, sunscreen and water are essential at any time of year and a warm coat is needed in winter. Take spare batteries and memory cards with you as supplies are limited beyond the Siq.

Start your visit to Petra at the visitor centre plaza in Wadi Musa, across from the Mövenpick Hotel. This is where you can buy tickets, get leaflets and a map, and use the toilets (although there are now several sets of loos inside the ancient city).

At the time of writing the visitor centre was being rebuilt to house a greater range of facilities, and tickets were available from a portable building opposite. The construction is expected to take at least two years.

⊙ Sights

There are over 800 registered sites in Petra, including some 500 tombs, but the best things to see are easy to find and easy to reach. From the gate, a path winds 800m downhill through an area called **Bab as-Siq** (Gateway to the Siq; Map p164), punctuated with the first signs of the old city.

See the boxed text (p338) for a handy explanation of archaeological terminology used in this chapter. The following sights are, for the most part, in the order you are likely to encounter them if you follow the most direct path through the city. There are signs in English throughout Petra, helping to identify the main monuments.

A word of caution: the ancient city is strewn with 'high places', once used for sacrifice or other ritual. These locations, all of which afford magnificent views and are a highlight of a visit, usually involve a steep hike up steps to a hilltop where there is no railing or other safety features. Some readers have expressed dismay at this.

Djinn Blocks MONUMENT

Just past the entrance, look out for three enormous, squat monuments, known as Djinn Blocks (Map p164) or God Blocks. Standing guard beside the path, they take their name from the Arabic word for spirit, the source of the English word 'genie'. Other than the fact that they were built by the Nabataeans in the 1st century AD, little is known about their why or wherefore – they could have been tombs,

or funerary dedications, or even related to the worship of water and fertility. Whatever their intended function, they are the lodestar for the modern visitor – a tantalising taste of the monuments to come, or announcing journey's end on your weary return.

Obelisk Tomb & Bab as-Siq Triclinium MONUMENT

Further along the path to the left is a tomb (Map p164) with four pyramidal obelisks, built as funerary symbols by the Nabataeans in the 1st century BC. The four obelisks, together with the eroded human figure in the centre, probably represent the five people buried in the tomb. The monument comes into its own at sunset when the obelisks are thrown into relief.

The obelisk tomb at first appears to be multistorey. In fact it was built on top of a much earlier structure, with a Doric columned facade. This building is known as a triclinium, or dining room, and is one of several in Petra. This is where annual feasts were held to commemorate the dead, although it's hard to imagine the conviviality of a banquet in the silent hollow that remains.

PETRA THE ANCIENT CITY

FINDING YOUR OWN PACE IN PETRA

Instead of trying to tick off all the top spots (the quickest way to 'monument fatigue'), make Petra your own by sparing time to amble among unnamed tombs, have a picnic in the shade of a flowering oleander or sip tea at a stall on the valley floor and watch everyone else toiling to 'see it all'.

The following suggestions combine some of the obvious highlights with some off-the-beaten-track exploration. See the boxed text (p175) for tips about distances and best times to visit.

» **Half Day** (five hours) Amble through the Siq, absorbing its special atmosphere and savouring the moment of revelation at the Treasury. Resist the temptation to head for the Theatre; instead, climb the steps to the High Place of Sacrifice. Pause for tea by the Obelisk and take the path into Wadi Farasa, enjoying wildflowers and the Garden Tomb en route. The path reaches the Colonnaded Street via a paintbox of rock formations. If there's time remaining, visit the Royal Tombs then return to the valley floor for a chat with Bedouin stallholders and a hunt for the perfect sand bottle.

» **One Day** (eight hours) Spend the morning completing the half-day itinerary, but pack a picnic. After visiting the Royal Tombs, walk along to Qasr al-Bint and hike along the broad wadi that leads to Jebel Haroun as far as Snake Monument – an ideal perch for a snack and a snooze. Return to Qasr al-Bint and slip into the nearby Nabataean Museum to find out more about the snake you shared lunch with. Save some energy for the climb to the Monastery, a fitting finale for any visit to Petra.

» **Two Days** Spend a second day scrambling through exciting Wadi Muthlim and restore your energies over a barbecue in the Basin Restaurant. Walk off lunch exploring the hidden beauty of Wadi Siyagh with its pools of water before strolling back along the Street of Facades. Sit near the Theatre to watch the sun go down on the Royal Tombs opposite – the best spectacle in Petra.

Petra

WALKING TOUR

Splendid though it is, the Treasury is not the full stop of a visit to Petra that many people may imagine. In some ways, it's just the semicolon – a place to pause after the exertions of the Siq, before exploring the other remarkable sights and wonders just around the corner.

Even if you're on a tight schedule or worried the bus won't wait, try to find another two hours in your itinerary to complete this walking tour. Our illustration shows the key highlights of the route, as you wind through Wadi Musa from the **Siq 1**, pause at the **Treasury 2** and pass the tombs of the broader **Outer Siq 3**. With energy and a stout pair of shoes, climb to the **High Place of Sacrifice 4** for a magnificent eagle's-eye view of Petra. Return to the **Street of Facades 5** and the **Theatre 6**. Climb the steps opposite to the **Urn Tomb 7** and neighbouring **Silk Tomb 8**: these Royal Tombs are particularly magnificent in the golden light of sunset.

Is the thought of all that walking putting you off? Don't let it! There are donkeys to help you with the steep ascents and Bedouin stalls for a reviving herb tea. If you run out of steam, camels are on standby for a ride back to the Treasury.

Treasury
As you watch the sun cut across the facade, notice how it lights up the ladders on either side of Petra's most iconic building. These stone indents were most probably used for scaffolding.

Jebel Madba

Jebel al-Khubtha

To Entrance to Petra

Siq
This narrow cleft in the land forms the sublime approach to the ancient city of Petra. Most people walk through the corridor of stone but horse-carts are available for those who need them.

Down Differently

A superb walk leads from the High Place of Sacrifice, past the Garden Tomb to Petra City Centre.

TOP TIPS

» **Morning Glory** From around 7am in summer and 8am in winter, watch the early morning sun slide down the Treasury facade.

» **Pink City** Stand opposite the Royal Tombs at sunset (around 4pm in winter and 5pm in summer) to learn how Petra earned its nickname.

» **Floral Tribute** Petra's oleanders flower in May.

High Place of Sacrifice

Imagine the ancients treading the stone steps and it'll take your mind off the steep ascent. The hilltop platform was used for incense-burning and libation-pouring in honour of forgotten gods.

Outer Siq

Take time to inspect the tombs just past the Treasury. Some appear to have a basement but, in fact, they show how the floor of the wadi has risen over the centuries.

Street of Facades

Cast an eye at the upper storeys of some of these tombs and you'll see a small aperture. Burying the dead in attics was meant to deter robbers – the plan didn't work.

airs to High Place

5

6

Souvenir shops, teashops & toilets

Wadi Musa

Wadi Musa

To Petra City Centre

Jebel Umm al'Amr (1066m)

7

Royal Tombs

8

Royal Tombs

Head for Heights

For a regal view of Petra, head for the heights above the Royal Tombs, via the staircase.

Urn Tomb

Earning its name from the urn-shaped finial crowning the pediment, this grand edifice with supporting arched vaults was perhaps built for the man represented by the toga-wearing bust in the central aperture.

Silk Tomb

Perhaps Nabataean builders were attracted to Wadi Musa because of the colourful beauty of the raw materials. Nowhere is this more apparent than in the weather-eroded, striated sandstone of the Silk Tomb.

Theatre

Most stone amphitheatres are freestanding, but this one is carved almost entirely from the solid rock. Above the back row are the remains of earlier tombs, their facades sacrificed in the name of entertainment.

Petra

See Petra City Centre Map (p168)

Further down the track, a signposted detour to the right leads to several stepped tombs carved into the tops of domed hills. It's a secret little place, missed by almost everyone in their rush to get to the Siq.

The Siq
CANYON

The 1.2km siq (Map p164), or canyon, with its narrow, vertical walls, is undeniably one of the major highlights of Petra. The walk through this magical corridor, as it snakes its way towards the hidden city, is one full of anticipation for the wonders ahead and many people charge through it, impatient to get to Petra. That's a pity because the Siq is worth

enjoying for its own sake and the longer you take to travel through it, the more you can savour the final moment of arrival.

The Siq starts at an obvious bridge, beside a modern dam. The dam was built in 1963, on top of a Nabataean dam dated AD 50, to stop floodwater from Wadi Musa flowing through the Siq. To the right, Wadi Muthlim heads invitingly through a Nabataean tunnel – the start (or finish) of an exciting hike (see p174).

The entrance to the Siq was once marked by a Nabataean monumental arch. It survived until the end of the 19th century, and

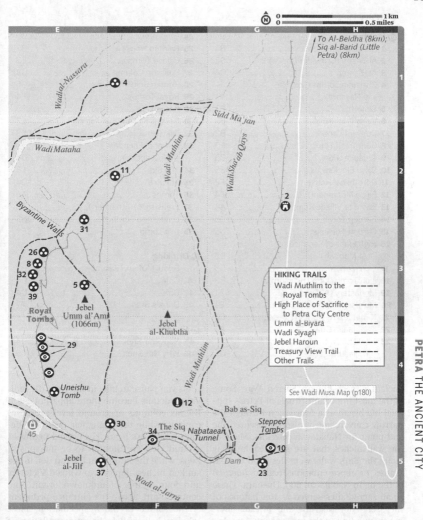

To Al-Beidha (8km);
Siq al-Barid (Little
Petra) (8km)

HIKING TRAILS

Wadi Muthlim to the
  Royal Tombs
High Place of Sacrifice
  to Petra City Centre
Umm al-Biyara
Wadi Siyagh
Jebel Haroun
Treasury View Trail
Other Trails

See Wadi Musa Map (p180)

PETRA THE ANCIENT CITY

some remains can be seen at twin niches on either side of the entrance.

Technically, the Siq, with its 200m high walls, is not a canyon (a gorge carved out by water), but a single block that has been rent apart by tectonic forces. At various points you can see where the grain of the rock on one side matches the other – it's easiest to spot when the Siq narrows to 2m wide.

The original channels cut into the walls to bring water into Petra are visible, and in some places the 2000-year-old terracotta pipes are still in place. A section of Roman paving was revealed after excavations in 1997 removed 2m of soil accumulation.

At one point the Siq opens out to reveal a square tomb next to a lone fig tree. A little further on, look for a weathered carving of a camel and caravan man on the left wall. The water channel passes behind the carving. Hereafter, the walls almost appear to meet overhead, shutting out the sound and light and helping to build the anticipation of a first glimpse of the Treasury. It's a sublime introduction to the ancient city.

Some historians speculate that the primary function of the Siq was akin to the

Petra

PETRA

ancient Graeco-Roman Sacred Way. Some of the most important rituals of Petra's spiritual life began as a procession through the narrow canyon, and it also represented the end point for Nabataean pilgrims. Many of the wall niches that are still visible today along the Siq's walls were designed to hold figures or representations (called *baetyls*) of the main Nabataean god, Dushara. These small sacred sites served as touchstones of the sacred for pilgrims and priests, offering them a link to the more ornate temples, tombs and sanctuaries in the city's heart, reminding them that they were leaving the outside world, and on the threshold of what was for many a holy city.

Treasury (Al-Khazneh)   TOMB

Tucked into a confined space, the Treasury (known locally as Al-Khazneh; Map p164) is protected from the ravages of the elements, and it is here that most visitors fall in love with Petra. The Hellenistic facade is an astonishing piece of craftsmanship of a scale and grandeur guaranteed to take your breath away.

As you pause to take in the view, the individual details become more apparent. Atop the six columns at ground level are floral capitals, while the triangular pediment depicts a gorgon's head. The carved figures at ground level are thought to be the sons of Zeus, while the figures on the top tier, in the sunken niches, depict two winged Victories and four figures of unknown origin. The central figure above the entrance pediment is the source of much speculation; most scholars believe it to be an assimilation of the Egyptian goddess Isis and the Nabataean goddess Al-'Uzza, while others suggest Tyche, the Roman goddess of fortune. Two eroded eagles stand sentry at the very top. Regularly spaced niches on either side of the facade are suggestive of scaffolding.

Although carved out of iron-laden sandstone to serve as a tomb for the Nabataean King Aretas III (c 100 BC–AD 200), the Treasury derives its name from the story that an Egyptian pharaoh hid his treasure here (in the urn in the middle of the second level) while pursuing the Israelites. Some locals clearly believed the tale because the

3.5m-high urn is pockmarked by rifle shots, the results of vain attempts to break open the secret.

As with all the rock-hewn monuments in Petra, it's the facade that captivates; the interior is just an unadorned square hall with a smaller room at the back. The Treasury, which is 43m high and about 30m wide, is at its most photogenic in full sunlight between about 9am and 11am.

From the Treasury, the Siq veers to the right; diagonally opposite is a **Sacred Hall**, which may have had ritual connections with the Treasury.

One of the great experiences of Petra is watching the beaming smiles on the faces of those emerging from the Siq. This can be easily enjoyed from the steps of the Treasury (though the smiles quickly change to grimaces if you're sitting in someone's picture) or better still from up high.

Street of Facades   ANCIENT THOROUGHFARE

From the Treasury, the passage broadens into what is commonly referred to as the Outer Siq. Riddling the walls of the Outer Siq are over 40 tombs and houses built by the Nabataeans in a 'crow step' style reminiscent of Assyrian architecture. Colloquially known as the Street of Facades (Map p164), they are pleasingly accessible. That said, most people ignore them, lured on by the majestic Theatre a few paces further on.

For those who prefer to savour the moment, there are a couple of tombs worth exploring. The first tomb (number 67) is unusual in that it has a funeral chamber in the upper storey. The low entryway highlights how the valley floor has risen over the centuries thanks to the debris washed down during flash floods. Nearby, tomb 70 is unusual in that it is freestanding, with a

ziggurat-style top that makes it look like a miniature fort.

If you can stay your curiosity even longer, take the steps up to the High Place of Sacrifice from here (while you have the energy) and leave the Theatre either for the way down or the way back from Petra city centre.

High Place of Sacrifice
(Al-Madbah)   VIEWPOINT

The most accessible of the many mountain-top sites (called 'High Places') at Petra is the High Place of Sacrifice (Map p164), referred to locally as Al-Madbah (the Altar). The Nabataeans levelled the top of Jebel Madbah to make a platform, digging large depressions with drains to channel the blood of sacrificial animals. At first there doesn't seem much to see except some weathered steps, but this is in fact one of the best-preserved sacred sacrificial sites from ancient times.

Look first for two **obelisks** that mark the entrance to the site. Over 6m high, these are remarkable structures because they are carved out of the rock face, not built upon it: looking at the negative space surrounding them, you can understand the truly epic scale of excavation involved. Dedicated to the Nabataean gods Dushara and Al-'Uzza, their iron-rich stone glows in the sun and they act like totems of this once-hallowed ground.

The altar area includes a large rectangular triclinium, where celebrants at the sacrifice shared a communal supper. In the middle of the High Place, there's a large stone block preceded by three steps. This is a *motab*, or repository, where the god statues involved in the procession would have been kept. Next to it is the circular altar, reached by another three steps; stone water-basins nearby were used for cleansing and purifying.

PETRA THE ANCIENT CITY

NAVIGATING PETRA

The town of Wadi Musa is the transport and accommodation hub for Petra, as well as for other attractions in the vicinity, such as Little Petra. The town is split roughly into three parts. The upper part comprises a few top-end hotels lining the main road, each of which has spectacular views of the weathered sandstone landscape. The town centre is where most of the cheaper hotels, the bus station and shops are located. The lower part of town, a 10-minute walk from the town centre, is where you'll find most of the top-end and mid-range hotels, together with souvenir shops, tourist restaurants and the famed Cave Bar.

Beyond this is the Petra Visitor Centre and entrance to Petra. The Ancient City is reached via the Siq, or gorge, which begins after a 15-minute walk (or horse ride) from the entrance. See the boxed text (p175) for details of walking times. There is another entrance near the village of Umm Sayhoun but tickets can only be bought from the main visitor centre.

Petra City Centre

Petra City Centre

The faint bleat of sheep or the clunk of a goat bell evokes the ancient scene – except that no ordinary person would have been permitted to enter this holy of holies at that time. Cast an eye across the superb panorama in front of you – far above the mortal goings-on of both ancient and modern city – and it's easy to see how this site must have seemed closer to the sky than the earth.

To reach the High Place of Sacrifice, look for a flight of steps signposted just before the Theatre, after the Why Not shop. The steps are well maintained, if unremitting, and it takes about 45 minutes up through the crevices and folds of the mountain to reach the obelisks. From here you fork right to reach the altar area. The route is steep but not unduly exposed, so is manageable (unless you suffer from severe vertigo) even without a head for heights. You can ascend by donkey (about JD10 one way), but you'll sacrifice both the sense of achievement on reaching the summit and the good humour of your poor old transport. From the altar area, descend the shelves of rock to a broad rim: about 50m down are regal views of the Royal Tombs.

It's worth sitting here for a while. From this lofty vantage point you can watch the everyday dramas of camel handlers arguing with their mounts, young children moving goats from one patch of sparse vegetation to the next and Bedouin stallholders regaling the unsuspecting traveller. They each move beyond the languishing tombs of ordinary folk, far too mindful of the needs of the living to worry much about the forgotten hopes of the ancient dead.

Return to the obelisks and continue to the city centre via a group of interesting tombs in beautiful Wadi Farasa. See p175 for details of this highly recommended hike.

Theatre   ROMAN AMPHITHEATRE
Originally built by the Nabataeans (not the Romans) more than 2000 years ago, the weathered Theatre (Map p164) was cut out of rock, slicing through many caves and tombs in the process. The seating area had an original capacity of about 3000 in 45 rows of seats, with three horizontal sections separated by two corridors. The orchestra section was carved from the rock, but the backdrop to the *frons scaenae* (stage, which is no longer intact) was constructed, as opposed to carved, in three storeys with frescoed niches and columns overlaid by marble. The performers entered through one of three entrances, the outlines of which are still partially visible.

The Theatre was renovated and enlarged to hold about 8500 (around 30% of the population of Petra) by the Romans soon after they arrived in AD 106. To make room for the upper seating tiers, they sliced through more tombs. Under the stage floor were storerooms and a slot through which a curtain could be lowered at the start of a performance. From near the slot, an almost-complete statue of Hercules was recovered.

The Theatre was badly damaged by an earthquake in AD 363, and parts of it were then removed to help build other structures in Petra. With a backdrop worthy of a David Roberts canvas, the Theatre (sometimes closed) now offers a vantage point from which to watch a modern tragi-comedy of the ill-costumed, cursing their high-heeled footwear; the ill-cast, yawning at tedious tour guides; and the ill-tempered – mainly in the form of irritable camels and their peevish owners.

Royal Tombs   TOMBS
Downhill from the Theatre, the wadi widens out to create a larger thoroughfare. To the right, the great massif of Jebel al-Khubtha looms over the valley. Within its west-facing cliffs are burrowed some of the most impressive burial places in Petra, known collectively as the 'Royal Tombs' (Map p164). They look particularly stunning in the late afternoon, bathed in golden light.

The Royal Tombs are reached via a set of steps that ascends from the valley floor, near

LOVING PETRA TO DEATH

It seems ironic that after 1000 years of obscurity, if not neglect, Petra owes its current fragility to a renaissance of interest. In a 'good' year half a million people visit, putting a huge strain on the management of one of the world's best-loved antiquities. The combination of thousands of footprints a day, increased humidity levels from the breath of tourists in the most popular tombs and erosion caused by adventurous travellers clambering over monuments and steep hillsides combine to threaten Petra's longevity.

Acutely aware of the problems, a number of local, national and international bodies have been cooperating for more than a decade to protect and enhance the 853 sq km site. For the most part Petra is now spotlessly clean, thanks to constant maintenance, more toilet facilities and a shift in attitude from visitors, who largely carry their rubbish back out with them.

Other improvements include the use of an invisible mortar to conserve fragile masonry and replace unsightly cement used in previous restoration attempts; major shoring up of the Siq; and ongoing conservation of tomb facades. Rampant development in Wadi Musa has also been checked, an infrastructure of drainage and sewerage systems installed and a moratorium enforced on the building of unsightly hotels that impinge on the sense of seclusion in Petra. Better signage and trail markers are yet to appear.

These conservation measures, however, will only save Petra for future generations with the cooperation of visitors. Each tourist can play their part by sticking to trails, not clambering over the monuments, resisting the temptation to touch crumbling masonry, removing their litter and using designated toilet facilities. These things sound obvious, but judging by a piece of graffiti that reads 'Daniel 2008' on top of one of the High Places, responsible tourism may still be a long time coming.

THE TOMBS OF PETRA

There are more tombs dotted around Petra than any other type of structure and for years visitors assumed that the city was a vast necropolis. One plausible reason why so few dwellings have been discovered is that many of the Nabataeans lived in tents, much like some Bedouin do today.

Petra's earliest rock tombs date from the 3rd century BC. The size and design of the tombs depended on the social status and financial resources of the deceased, ranging from simple cave-like tombs to the ornate facades of the Royal Tombs, the high point of Nabataean funerary architecture.

More sculptors than architects, the Nabataeans quickly realised that it was easier to carve tombs out of the soft sandstone rock than to build free-standing structures that were vulnerable to earthquakes. The larger tombs were carved out of the rock from the top down, using scaffolding support, and the facades were then plastered and painted (almost none of this decoration remains).

The dead were buried in *loculi* (small, separate cavities) carved from the plain walls inside the tomb, while the exterior decoration was made to represent the soul (and sometimes likeness) of the deceased. All but the most simple tombs contained banqueting halls where funerals and annual commemorative feasts were held. Some rooms were frescoed and you can still see traces of coloured decoration in Wadi Siyagh's Painted House and in Siq al-Barid (Little Petra).

The Nabataeans were a nomadic desert people without an architectural heritage of their own, but as traders they were cosmopolitan enough to borrow elements of art and architecture from neighbours. Thus you'll see Egyptian, Assyrian, Mesopotamian, Hellenistic and Roman styles throughout Petra, as well as unique local architectural inventions such as the Nabataean horned column. If you combine this eclecticism with the organic nature of Petra's cave-like tombs, the stunning natural colour of the rock and natural grandeur of the landscape, it's easy to see how Petra has captured the imagination of generations of travellers.

the Theatre. A fantastic hike from the Royal Tombs leads up to the numerous places of worship on the flattened High Place of Jebel Khubtha, together with a spectacular view of the Treasury. The steps are easily visible between the Palace and Sextius Florentinus tombs. The Royal Tombs also can be reached via the adventurous hike through Wadi Muthlim – see p174.

Urn Tomb

The most distinctive of the Royal Tombs is the Urn Tomb, recognisable by the enormous urn on top of the pediment. It was probably built in about AD 70 for King Malichos II (AD 40–70) or Aretas IV (8 BC–AD 40). Part of what makes it such a grand structure is the flanking Doric portico cut into the rock face on the left of the tomb, and the huge open terrace in front of it – a feature that encouraged its use, according to a Greek inscription inside the tomb, as a cathedral in AD 447. The double layer of vaults was added at a later date by the Byzantines. Look towards the top of the building and you'll see three inaccessible openings carved between the pillars. These are tombs, the central one of which still has the closing stone intact, depicting the king dressed in a toga. The naturally patterned interior of the Urn Tomb measures a vast 18m by 20m.

Silk Tomb and Corinthian Tomb

Spare some time to admire the neighbouring Silk Tomb, noteworthy for the stunning swirls of pink, white and yellow veined rock in its facade. The badly damaged Corinthian Tomb, immediately adjacent, is something of a hybrid, with elements of both Hellenistic and Nabataean influences. The portico on the lower level of the tomb is distinctively local in origin, while the upper decorative features are more Hellenistic in style. The tomb gets its name from the Corinthian capitals adorned with floral motifs.

Palace Tomb

Nearby is the delightful three-storey imitation of a Roman or Hellenistic palace, known as the Palace Tomb. Its rock-hewn facade, the largest in Petra, is thought to owe more to ornamental exuberance than to any religious significance. The two central doorways are topped by triangular pediments, while the two on either side have arched pediments. The doors lead into typically simple funerary chambers. The 18 columns on the upper level are the most distinctive and visually arresting elements of the tomb. Notice the top-left corner: pragmatically, it is built (rather than cut out) of stone because the rock face didn't extend far enough to complete the facade.

Sextius Florentinus Tomb

Continue a few hundred metres around the hill to reach the seldom-visited Sextius Florentinus Tomb, built from AD 126 to 130 for a Roman governor of Arabia, whose exploits are glorified in an inscription above the entrance. Have a cup of tea with the Bedouin grandmother who has set up shop here and admire the dazzling veining of the tomb in peace. The gorgon's head in the centre of the facade above the columns is eroded, but it's still possible to distinguish the vine tendrils emanating from the head. The horned capitals are a uniquely Nabataean creation. Unlike many other tombs, the interior is worth a look for the clearly discernible *loculi* (graves); there are five carved into the back wall and three on the right as you enter.

Colonnaded Street   ANCIENT THOROUGHFARE

Returning to the main thoroughfare downhill from the Theatre, the Colonnaded Street (Map p168) marks Petra's city centre. The street was built in about AD 106 (contemporaneous with the Colonnaded Street in Jerash), over an existing Nabataean thoroughfare. It follows the standard Roman pattern of an east–west *decumanus* (main street), but without the normal *cardo maximus* (north–south axis). Columns of marble-clad sandstone originally lined the 6m-wide carriageway, and covered porticoes gave access to shops.

At the start of the Colonnaded Street is the **Nymphaeum**, a public fountain built in the 2nd century AD and fed by water channelled from the Siq. Little can be seen today, although it's recognisable by the huge 450-year-old **pistachio tree**, giving welcome shade in summer.

Also along the Colonnaded Street are the limited remains of the market area and the unrecognisable ruins of the **Royal Palace**.

The street ends at the **Temenos Gateway**. Built in the 2nd century AD, the gateway originally had huge wooden doors and side towers. It marked the entrance to the *temenos* (sacred courtyard) of the Qasr al-Bint, separating the commercial area of the city from the sacred area of the temple. Look closely for the few remaining floral friezes and a figure with an arrow, which suggest that this was once a very grand structure. Opposite are the minimal ruins of the **Nabataean baths**.

Great Temple   TEMPLE

Excavations of the Great Temple (Map p168) have been under way since 1993 and have yielded impressive results. It was built as a major Nabataean temple in the 1st century BC and, despite being badly damaged by an earthquake not long after, was in use (albeit in different forms) until the late Byzantine period. The first set of stairs was fronted by a monumental *propylaeum* (gateway) while the courtyard at the top of the first stairs marked the lower *temenos*, flanked by a triple colonnade. The upper level housed the temple's sacred enclosure, with four huge columns (made from stone discs and clad in marble) at the entrance. A *theatron* (miniature theatre) stands in the centre. The temple was once 18m high, and the enclosure was 40m by 28m. The interior was originally covered with striking red-and-white stuccowork.

Qasr al-Bint   TEMPLE

One of the few free-standing structures in Petra, Qasr al-Bint (Map p168) was built in around 30 BC by the Nabataeans, adapted to the cult of Roman emperors and destroyed in about the 3rd century AD. Despite the name given to it by the local Bedouin – Qasr al-Bint al-Pharaun (Castle of the Pharaoh's Daughter) – it was built as a dedication to Nabataean gods and was one of the most important temples in the ancient city. In its original form, it stood 23m high and had marble staircases, imposing columns topped with floral capitals, a raised platform for worship, and ornate plaster and stone reliefs and friezes – small traces of which are still evident.

The central 'holy of holies', known as an *adyton*, would have housed an image of the deities. The sacrificial altar in front, once overlaid with marble, indicates that it was probably the main place of worship in the Nabataean city and its location at street level suggests that the whole precinct (and not just the temple interior) was considered sacred.

PETRA THE ANCIENT CITY

Temple of the Winged Lions   TEMPLE

The recently excavated Temple of the Winged Lions (Map p168), built in about AD 27, is named after the carved lions that once topped the capitals of each of the columns. The temple was probably dedicated to the fertility goddess, Atargatis, the partner of the male god Dushara.

This was a very important temple, centred around a raised altar, and with a colonnaded entry of arches and porticoes that extended across the wadi. Fragments of decorative stone and painted plaster found on the site, and now on display in the Nabataean Museum, suggest that both the temple and entry were handsomely decorated.

Petra Church   CHURCH

An awning covers the remains of Petra Church (also known as the Byzantine Church;

Map p168). The structure was originally built by the Nabataeans, and then redesigned and expanded by the Byzantines around AD 530. It eventually burned down, and was then destroyed by repeated earthquakes. It has recently been restored by the American Center of Oriental Research in Amman.

Inside the church are some exquisite Byzantine floor **mosaics**, some of the best in the region. The mosaics originally continued up the walls. A helpful map and explanations in English are located inside the church.

Al-Habis   VIEWPOINT

Beyond Qasr al-Bint is the small hill of Al-Habis (the Prison; Map p164). From the Nabataean Tent Restaurant, steps lead up the hill to the small **Al-Habis Museum** (☉8am-4pm), the smaller of Petra's two museums. The classical statues, tiny figurines and

---

'IBRAHIM' BURCKHARDT – EXPLORER EXTRAORDINAIRE

There can't be many explorers in history who can match the remarkable exploits of Jean Louis Burckhardt. Born in 1784 in Lausanne, Switzerland, he studied Arabic and attended lectures on science and medicine at Cambridge University in the UK before moving to Aleppo in 1809. Here he converted to Islam and took the name Sheikh Ibrahim bin Abdullah. Over the next two years he became a master of disguise, adopting local customs and putting his alias to the test among local Bedouin.

In 1812, travelling between Damascus and Cairo, he heard locals tell of fantastic ruins hidden in the mountains of Wadi Musa. Determined to see for himself, he had to think of a ploy to allay the suspicions of his guide and porters:

I, therefore, pretended to have made a vow to have slaughtered a goat in honour of Haroun (Aaron), whose tomb I knew was situated at the extremity of the valley, and by this stratagem I thought that I should have the means of seeing the valley on the way to the tomb.

Jean Louis Burckhardt, Travels in Syria and the Holy Land

The plan worked and soon he was riding down the Siq, trying hard to hide his astonishment. His guide wasn't fooled for long, and imagined that the pale Syrian had come hunting for treasure, declaring: 'I see now clearly that you are an infidel, who have [sic] some particular business amongst the ruins.' To avoid occasioning more suspicion, Burckhardt had to confine his curiosity to the briefest examination of the ancient monuments – enough, however, to conclude that this was Petra, a place which he understood 'no European traveller has ever visited'. Despite being a man not given to literary flourishes, his journals reveal something of the excitement of his discovery:

The situation and beauty of [the Treasury] are calculated to make an extraordinary impression upon the traveller, after having traversed...such a gloomy and almost subterranean passage [the Siq]...it is one of the most elegant remains of antiquity existing.

For many an explorer, this expedition would have been a lifetime's achievement – but not for Burckhardt. He went on to find the source of the Niger, stumbled on the magnificent Ramses II temple at Abu Simbel in Egypt, and still under disguise explored Mecca and Medina. In 1815 he contracted dysentery in Cairo which returned with fatal consequences in 1817. He was buried as a Muslim in the Islamic Cemetery in Cairo. He was only 33 years old.

painted stuccowork on display lend a human dimension to the huge scale of the site.

If you continue up the steps, beyond the museum, a little-used path leads around the back of Al-Habis, with striking views of fertile Wadi Siyagh and the junction with Wadi Numeir. The path soon skirts the tea shop and comfortable **cave home** of Bdoul Mofleh, one of the last residents of Petra. Asked why he didn't leave when the rest of his family were relocated to Umm Sayhoun, he replied, 'Why would I? This is my home; I've always lived here.' With a view to die for, and a garden of flowering jasmine, it's easy to see why this hardy resident chose to stay. Notice the red-capped aloe, standing to attention in early summer, billeted across the cliffs opposite.

The path continues around the hill, past the **Convent Group** of tombs to a flight of steps. These lead in turn (via a wooden plank bridge) to the top of Al-Habis, another of Petra's many High Places. At the summit (allow 10 to 15 minutes to reach the top) are the limited ruins of a small **Crusader fort**, built in AD 1116 by Baldwin I. The ruins are not impressive, but the views across the city certainly are.

From here you can either hike, via **Pharaun Column** (a good landmark), to Snake Monument in Wadi Thughra or along Wadi Farasa to the High Place of Sacrifice.

Alternatively, complete the circuit of Al-Habis by descending the hill behind Qasr al-Bint. On your way down, look out for the **Unfinished Tomb**. It offers a rare glimpse of the way the Nabataeans constructed their rock tombs, starting at the top on a platform of scaffolding and working their way down. Nearby is the enigmatic **Columbarium**, whose multiple niches remain a mystery; some suppose they housed votive images or urns, others say this was a dovecote for pigeons.

Nabataean Museum   MUSEUM
(Map p168; ⊗9am-5pm, to 4pm Oct-Mar) This small museum has an interesting display of artefacts from the region, including mosaics. Explanations are in English. The museum, together with a shop selling detailed maps and fixed-price, handmade jewellery sponsored by the Queen Noor Foundation, shares the same building as the Basin Restaurant.

Monastery (Al-Deir)   TOMB
Beyond the museum, hidden high up in the hills, is one of the legendary monuments of

ⓘ BACKDOOR TO PETRA

In the 1980s many of the Bdoul Bedouin, who had lived in Petra for generations, were resettled in villages such as neighbouring Umm Sayhoun. At the end of this village, there is an access road into the old city of Petra. It would be a pity to enter Petra this way on your first day (as the Siq is Petra's most spectacular highlight), but if you want a shortcut to the Monastery thereafter, take a taxi to the gate at the top of this road and walk down. Note that you can't buy tickets here and you can't enter without one so don't forget to bring your ticket with you.

Petra. The spectacular Monastery (known locally as Al-Deir; Map p164) is similar in design to the Treasury but far bigger (50m wide and 45m high). Built in the 3rd century BC as a Nabataean tomb, perhaps for King Obodas I (r 96–86 BC), the Monastery derives its name from the crosses carved on the inside walls, suggesting that the building was used as a church in Byzantine times. The courtyard in front of the Monastery was once surrounded by columns and was probably used for sacred ceremonies.

Opposite the Monastery there's a strategically placed drinks stall in a cave with a row of seats outside where you can sit and contemplate the majestic Hellenistic facade. It's particularly spectacular from mid- to late afternoon when the setting sun draws out the colour of the sandstone. Behind the drinks stand, tomb 468 is worth exploring for another fine facade, some defaced carvings and excellent views.

Beyond the drinks stand a trail leads up to two lookouts, with stunning views west over Wadi Araba towards Israel and the Palestinian Territories and south to the peak of Jebel Haroun, topped by a small white shrine.

The easy-to-follow **trail** to the Monastery starts from the Nabataean Museum and takes about 40 minutes (if in doubt, look for weary hikers coming down). Alternatively, donkeys (with a guide) can be hired for about JD7–12 one way, depending on your power of negotiation; you're better off walking coming down as the donkeys travel fast and the way is steep and slippery, making for an uncomfortable and at times dangerous journey for both you and your mount.

The trip is best started in mid-afternoon when there is welcome shade and the Monastery is at its most photogenic. The remarkable ancient rock-cut path of more than 800 steps follows the old processional route and is a spectacle of weird and wonderfully tortured stone. There are several side paths to explore, including a detour to the **Lion Tomb** (Lion Triclinium), set in a gully. The two weather-beaten lions that lend the tomb its name face each other at the base of the monument.

An exciting 6km **hike** leads from the Monastery to Siq al-Barid (Little Petra; it takes about 2½ hours and involves some easy scrambling). Ask at Petra Visitor Centre or at local travel agencies for a guide as the route is difficult to find.

🏃 Activities

Hiking

Anyone wanting to see some stunning landscapes, explore unexcavated tombs and meet the Bedouin should pack an extra bottle of water and go hiking.

None of the following hikes is all that strenuous and none involves camping overnight (which is not permitted within Petra). Only the hikes along Wadi Muthlim and to Sabra or Little Petra require a guide. Hikers should pick up the contoured *Map of Petra* (see p189). Note that the approximate hiking times are just that, and do not include time for pottering.

Experienced multilingual guides can be hired from Petra Visitor Centre from JD50 (for one to nine people) for a simple route to the Museum, or from local travel agencies. Unofficial Bedouin 'guides' may charge considerably less than the official rates: occasionally they are very good but there's no guarantee. Women on their own should be cautious of hiking with unregistered guides, particularly as most of the hikes involve spending time in isolated parts of Petra.

Please stick to trails and remove your litter to avoid degradation of the site.

WADI MUTHLIM TO THE ROYAL TOMBS

This adventurous 1½-hour canyon hike (Map p164) is an exciting alternative route into Petra if you've already taken the main Siq path, or a rewarding way out of the site if you still have energy. The hike is not difficult or strenuous, but there are several boulder blockages and in winter you may need to wade through pools of water. Flash floods are a serious issue in the area and, due to a recent fatality at the time of writing, a guide is now mandatory.

The trail starts from the dam, just before the entrance to the Siq. Before entering the ancient, 88m-long **Nabataean tunnel**, it's possible to make a short detour (veer right and double-back over the top of the tunnel) to the **Eagle Monument**, with its eponymous carvings.

Back on the hike, walk through the tunnel and you'll emerge into the sunlight of Wadi Muthlim with its thick ribbon of oleander. The wadi gradually narrows into a metre-wide siq and in three places you'll have to lower yourself down 2m-high boulder blockages. The first is easy enough to negotiate; the other two take a bit more strategy – not impossible if you have someone to lean on, but tricky if you attempt it on your own. If you're not comfortable on the second boulder, turn back or you could get stuck between boulder blockage two and three!

After 25 minutes from the start of the hike, look for the remains of a Nabataean dam above the trail. Five minutes later, you'll meet a T-intersection where the trail joins Wadi Mataha. Follow the painted arrow to the left. This is the most exciting part of the hike as the canyon narrows to little more than a crack in the rock. You can see here how treacherous this hike would be in a flash flood as there is little space between you and the parallel walls. At certain times of the year you may have to splash through residual pools of water here until at length you pass into the perfect picnic point. Surrounded by Nabataean niches, and shaded on two sides almost all day, this little square of ancient Petra has a presence far bigger than its dimensions.

From here, follow the cliff face to the left, past a series of little-visited tombs, including **Dorotheos' House** and the **Sextius Florentinus Tomb**, until you reach the Royal Tombs. Alternatively, you can turn northeast on a small track that begins from the wadi almost opposite the Tomb of Sextius Florentinus, and explore the interesting so-called 'Christian Tombs' of Moghar al-Nassara where excavations are ongoing.

Note that if you are doing this hike in the opposite direction, you can find the entry to the canyon after Dorotheos' House by following the curved wall around to the right – niches mark the entry to the canyon.

Some parts of the canyon may be impassable if it's been raining. Flash floods occur

ⓘ WALKING TIMES TO KEY SIGHTS IN PETRA

To make the most of Petra you need to walk. The good news is that you don't have to be a serious hiker with a week to spare to have a 'Burckhardt moment' in the ancient city – you just need to know where to go and when. Times in the following table indicate one-way walks (unless stated otherwise) at a leisurely pace. At a faster pace without stopping, you can hike from Petra Visitor Centre to the Treasury in 20 minutes and the museum in 40 minutes along the main thoroughfare. Don't forget to double the time for the uphill return journey, particularly if you're tired after a day's sightseeing. A variety of animal transport is usually on hand to get you back to base if you're seriously flagging: for example, you can take a donkey from the Monastery to the Museum, a camel to the Treasury, a horse carriage to the Siq entrance and a horse to the visitor centre. See Map p164.

DIRECT ROUTE	TIME	DIFFICULTY	ALTERNATIVES & INTERESTING DETOURS
Visitor Centre to Siq Entrance	15 minutes	Easy	**Horse ride** Ponies are for hire to help you reach the dam near the Siq entrance – useful on the uphill return journey.
Siq Entrance to Treasury	20 minutes	Easy	**Hike** Clamber above the Royal Tombs to a Treasury viewpoint and look down on everyone else looking up (one hour; strenuous).
Treasury to Royal Tombs	20 minutes	Easy	**Hike** Climb the steps between the Royal Tombs and Sextius Florentinus tomb for a regal-eyed view of Petra. Continue to the cistern and descend to the Urn Tomb (one to 1½ hours; strenuous). **Hike** As an alternative to the Siq, squeeze through sinuous Wadi Muthlim to reach the Royal Tombs (1½ hours; moderate, guide required).
Treasury to Obelisk at High Place of Sacrifice	45 minutes	Moderate	**Walk** Go beyond the High Place altar onto the solitary edge of the escarpment for a wide-angle view of Petra (15 minutes from Obelisk; easy).
Obelisk to Museum (via main thoroughfare)	45 minutes	Easy	**Hike** Instead of returning down the steps you ascended, hike via enchanting Wadi Farasa, passing rainbow-coloured rocks, Lion Monument and Garden Tomb (one hour from Obelisk; moderate).
Treasury to Museum	30 minutes	Easy	**Walk** Trace the path around the base of the Royal Tombs to Dorotheos' House, explore the rarely visited Christian Tombs and follow Wadi Mataha to the Museum (one hour; easy)
Museum to Monastery	40 minutes	Moderate	**Walk** Get a head-start to the Monastery via Umm Sayhoun access road, pausing at Turkmaniya Tomb, famous for its long Nabataean inscription (20 minutes to museum; easy). **Hike** For a rare glimpse of how tombs like the Monastery were cut, walk around Al-Habis to see the Unfinished Tomb (40 minutes return to museum; moderate).

PETRA THE ANCIENT CITY

along Wadi Muthlim because the dam at the start of Petra's main Siq deliberately diverts water along this wadi. As such, it's imperative that you don't start this trek if it's been raining, is raining or is likely to rain soon. Your guide should have the latest information on the condition of the route.

HIGH PLACE OF SACRIFICE TO PETRA CITY CENTRE

This one-hour hike (Map p164) starts from the High Place of Sacrifice and is a must. Refer to p167 for information about getting to the High Place via the steps near the Theatre. It's also possible to do this hike in reverse, making for a grand afternoon exit from the site.

ℹ TOP TIPS FOR MAKING THE MOST OF PETRA

Petra at Dawn The Treasury is sunlit in the morning; you may have seen photos but the real thing is indescribably magical.
Tip: Go before the 8am tours arrive.

Photogenic Petra Mid-afternoon and most of Petra's weary guests have returned to base. Those who linger catch the Royal Tombs turn pink at sunset.
Tip: The sun sets around 6pm in summer and 5pm in winter.

Petra on High The Siq, Street of Facades and museum all lie brooding in the wadi bottom. Climb a few steps, hike to a high place, sit on a camel and you'll find a whole new dimension to Petra.
Tip: The Theatre seats give grandstand views.

Hidden Petra Petra doesn't give up its secrets easily and most visitors leave without discovering the exquisite Monastery, at the top of 800 hand-hewn steps.
Tip: Best seen in the full sun of afternoon, beautiful views of Wadi Araba are just a 15-minute stroll from the Monastery to the lookouts.

Green Petra Explore a parallel world along the hidden wadis of Petra; lizards, snakes and scorpions are common but shy residents beside the rocky pools.
Tip: Magnificent pink oleander blossoms stripe the wadis in profusion in May.

Living Petra Petra may be a pile of ruins to some, but for others it's home; take Raami's Tours to see how the Bdoul Bedouin interact with their famous monuments.
Tip: Say yes to tea with the Bedouin and participate in Petra's age-old ritual.

Petra by Night (p182) Catch the spirit of Petra by candlelight.
Tip: Warm coat needed in winter.

PETRA

From the top of the path, near the obelisks, a trail with steps heads down towards Wadi Farasa (Butterfly Valley). The start of the trail is not obvious, so look for the helpful piles of stones indicating the trail, or ask for directions at the drinks stand.

The hike is immediately rewarding with magnificent veined rock formations and wild gardens of flowers. After about 10 minutes of descent, you'll come to the 5m-long **Lion Monument**, where water was channelled to pour out of the lion's mouth from the rock face above – an example of Nabataean engineering at its most sophisticated. A stone altar diagonally opposite suggests the fountain had some religious function. The steps wind further down the side of the cliff to the **Garden Tomb** (more likely to have been a temple) and the remains of a giant water cistern.

A little further down, on the left, is the elegant **Roman Soldier's Tomb**, named after the statue over the door. Almost opposite is the **Garden Triclinium**, a hall used for annual feasts to honour the dead placed in the Soldier's Tomb. The hall is unique in Petra because it has carved decoration on the interior walls. The tomb and triclinium were once linked by a colonnaded courtyard.

Hereafter, the trail branches to the right, above the dry wadi floor. A teashop here sells handmade strings of cloves, a good sniff of which is surprisingly reviving. The path forks at the ridge ahead. The right fork leads past some outrageously colourful but dilapidated tombs and descends eventually to the Colonnaded Street. The left fork passes **Az-Zantur**, a 1st century AD palace that's still under excavation. Nearby is a collection of ruined **Nabataean and Roman houses**, one of the few traces of habitations so far discovered in Petra. The trail continues west along the ridge to the **Pharaun Column**, the lone surviving column of another Nabataean temple. From here you can turn left to Snake Monument for a longer hike or go straight on for Qasr al-Bint and Al-Habis. If you're disoriented, look for Petra Church, north of the Colonnaded Street: its pale green awning makes a good landmark.

ABOVE THE TREASURY

There are two vantage points (Map p164) that have for many years been used to admire the Treasury. The first is a steep 20-minute hike and scramble with a trailhead to the left of the Treasury. This trail is now closed to visitors as the handkerchief-sized lookout above the vertical cliff is extremely dangerous.

For a similarly dramatic and unusual view of the Treasury, however, make the following 1½-hour return hike from the Palace Tomb, with the option of returning via the Urn Tomb. Start this hike in the early morning to catch the Treasury in sunlight. A recently renovated set of processional steps leads steeply uphill from about 150m northeast of the Palace Tomb (they are signposted). The stiff climb takes about 20 minutes and flattens out at a hilltop Nabataean cistern. Along the way there are wonderful views of the Roman Theatre.

Continue south from the cistern (currently occupied by a helpful Bedouin teashop owner) along a less obvious dirt path. Descend through the dry wadi for about 15 minutes and then pass into a small ravine; suddenly you will reach a dramatic lookout about 200m above the Treasury, with fantastic views of the mighty edifice. Watch your step and look out for landmarks on the way down as it is hard to find the path back to the top of the steps.

Back at the cistern, a tiny cleft in the rock reveals worn steps leading down a gully and along the rock face to a point next to the Urn Tomb. The trail isn't all that clear (and is rather dirty at the outset), but it is navigable with a bit of common sense. The author, lacking in this quality, ended up on a Nabataean drain dangling over a vertical drop. Of course, you can always return the way you came.

UMM AL-BIYARA

He the Judaean king, Amaziah was the one who defeated ten thousand Edomites in the Valley of the Salt and captured Sela in battle...

2 Kings 14:7

Umm al-Biyara (Map p164) is the flat-topped mountain (1178m) in the southwest of Petra. Legend maintains that it was once the Edomite capital of Sela, from where the Judaean king Amaziah (r 796–81 BC) threw 10,000 prisoners to their deaths over the precipice. There are ruins of a 7th-century BC Edomite village at the top as well as several cisterns. There are also many unexcavated tombs along the base of the eastern cliffs.

The return trip from Qasr al-Bint to Umm al-Biyara (the Mother of Cisterns) takes about three hours and offers stunning mountaintop views over Petra (you can even spot the Monastery). It's a fairly strenuous hike up hundreds of steps, but the trail is easy to follow. Start the hike in the mid-afternoon when most of the path is in shade but don't leave it too late as you don't want to be coming down in poor light.

From behind Qasr al-Bint, head to the Pharaun Column and descend to the road that leads along Wadi Thughra towards Snake Monument. The path up the rock face starts from the left of the largest of the rock-cut tombs on the southeast face of the mountain.

PETRA THE ANCIENT CITY

WORTH A TRIP

A DOZEN UNUSUAL WAYS TO ENJOY PETRA

» Enter Petra via the narrow Wadi Muthlim (p174) instead of the Siq.

» Gain an eagle-eye view of the Treasury from the path above the Royal Tombs (p169).

» Gallop across a plateau on horseback, high above the Treasury (p166).

» Descend from the High Place of Sacrifice via the garden valley of Wadi Farasa (p175).

» Take tea with one of the few remaining residents of Petra behind Al-Habis (p172).

» Unfurl a portable feast in a triclinium, a banqueting hall for honouring the dead.

» Hike with a guide to Little Petra (p191) from the Monastery.

» Find your own secret garden beyond the Siq at Little Petra (p191).

» Saddle up a donkey for the two-day hike to Sabra via Wadi Tibn (p178).

» Leave Petra with the Bdoul Bedouin via the road to Umm Sayhoun.

» Walk between Umm Sayhoun (p184) and Wadi Musa for a sublime view of Petra at sunset.

» Stop at the viewpoint on the scenic road to Tayyibeh for the ultimate Petra panorama (p185).

WADI SIYAGH

For a leg-stretcher that doesn't require a vertical take-off, try the trail (Map p164) that follows the dry riverbed of Wadi Siyagh beneath Al-Habis hill. Once a residential suburb of Petra, the wadi and the nearby slopes have unexcavated tombs and residences to explore and offer some peaceful picnic spots once you pass the noisy restaurant generator.

Enter Wadi Siyagh opposite the Basin Restaurant (Map p168). You'll soon see steps on the right leading to the **Painted House**, one of the very few tombs in Petra that still has traces of Nabataean frescoes. Further down, at a bend in the valley, is a **Nabataean quarry**.

The main attraction further along the valley is the dense oasis of green bushes, water pools and even waterfalls (in winter). In spring, the flowers are beautiful and in May and June it's worth making the hike just to enjoy the oleander and seams of aloe.

The trail along Wadi Siyagh is easy to follow, but becomes a bit rough in parts as it ascends the wadi walls. Don't attempt the hike if rain is imminent because flash floods are possible.

JEBEL HAROUN

Aaron will be gathered to his people: he will die there. Moses did as the Lord commanded: they went up to Mount Hor in the sight of the whole community.

Numbers 20:26-27

Jebel Haroun (1350m) is thought to be biblical Mt Hor, where Moses' brother Aaron (Haroun to Muslims) is believed to be buried. The small white shrine on top of Jebel Haroun (off Map p164) was built in the 14th century, apparently over Aaron's tomb, and some people consider this a place of pilgrimage. For most, however, the big drawcard of Jebel Haroun is the superb panoramic view from the top.

The return trip from Qasr al-Bint takes around six hours. Some people hire a guide with a donkey or even a camel for the trip, but if you're reasonably fit and not fazed by working out your own route from the network of goat tracks that head in the general direction, then this really isn't necessary.

The trail to Jebel Haroun starts at Pharaun Column, and follows the dirt road past Bedouin settlements to **Snake Monument**, a curled stone that resembles a snake on a rock pedestal. Continue to the southwest towards the obvious white shrine

(which looks deceptively close); the trail is not as steep as it looks. At the bottom of the mountain, find the caretaker if you want to enter the shrine.

SABRA

The trip from Qasr al-Bint to the remote Nabataean suburbs of Sabra (off Map p164) takes a minimum of five hours return. This was where trade caravans once unloaded their precious cargoes at the fringes of the main city and the remains here include some ruined walls, temples, bridges and a small Roman theatre. A guide is needed even to find the trail from Snake Monument. A return trip on donkey costs from around JD80, depending on your powers of negotiation.

An exciting option offered by some travel agencies is the adventurous two-day hike from Tayyibeh, through the Siq-like Wadi Tibn, to Sabra, camping overnight and continuing on to Petra the next day.

Horse-Riding

For those who know how to ride, it costs from around JD30 for a two- to three-hour horse ride around the surrounding hills. A particularly exciting ride leads across a plateau at the top of the Treasury – definitely not one for the faint-hearted as the horses pull up from a gallop to a stop at the vertiginous cliff edge. Book a ride through one of the tourist agencies in town or, for more of an adventure, ask the animal handlers near the entrance to Petra to take you to their favourite haunt.

ⓘ Information

The **ticket office** (Map p180; ☎/fax 2156044; ⏰6am-4pm, to 6pm in summer) is in the visitor centre at Wadi Musa. Although tickets are not sold after 4pm, you can remain in Petra until sunset (5pm in winter).

Entry fees are JD50/55/60 for one-/two-/three-day passes (payable only in Jordanian currency). Multiday tickets are non-transferable. Children under 15 are admitted free. If you're contemplating trying to enter Petra without paying, please don't. The preservation of Petra depends on the income from tourists and this is where responsible tourism begins. Note that if you are visiting Petra as a day trip from Israel and the Palestinian Territories the entry fee is JD90.

You can hire an **official guide** (JD50 for one to nine people) from the visitor centre to explain the sights between the entrance and the museum; these guides have a lot of knowledge and experience, and can bring a different dimension to your visit. Guided tours are available in English, Spanish, French and Arabic.

Toilets

There are 'super-deluxe' toilets at the visitor centre (Map p180), before the Theatre (Map p164) and near the Basin Restaurant (Map p168). Tea houses provide clean portaloos throughout the site – most people give a tip of JD1 to the caretakers who maintain them. Please avoid going to the toilet elsewhere as it spoils the site for others.

Tourist Information

Information is available at the **Petra Visitor Centre** (Map p180; 2156044; 6am-9pm), or at the portacabin during refurbishment, just before the entrance. It houses the ticket office (which closes at 4pm in winter, 6pm in summer) and a helpful information counter and is surrounded by souvenir shops.

Websites

American Museum of Natural History (www.amnh.org/exhibitions/petra) See an online Petra exhibition.

Brown University (www.brown.edu /departments/joukowsky_institute/Petra/) Take an online tour of the excavations of the Great Temple.

Complete Petra (www.isidore-of-seville.com/petra) A great collection of current and archived links on Petra.

Go 2 Petra (www.go2petra.com) For background and general travel info on Petra.

Nabataea Net (http://nabataea.net) Everything you could want to know about the Nabataean empire.

ⓘ Getting Around

If you buy your ticket at the Petra Visitor Centre, a return horse ride for the 800m stretch between the main entrance and the start of the Siq is included in your ticket (arrange a return time with the handler). A tip of JD3 or JD4 is appreciated. If you walk down you can usually find a ride back to the entrance for around JD5. Horses and carriages with drivers travel between the main entrance and the Treasury (2km) for JD25, and to the museum for JD50 per carriage (which seats two people).

Unofficial donkey rides (with handlers) are available all around Petra for negotiable prices. Donkeys can reach the High Place of Sacrifice (from JD10 one way) and the top of the Monastery (between JD7 and JD12 one way). They can also be rented for longer trips to the Snake Monument (from JD35), Jebel Haroun (JD60) and Sabra (JD80). Leading donkeys is a genuine occupation for local Bedouin, who prize their animals as an important part of their livelihood; that said, some of the younger animal handlers can be seen using a stick or whip with unnecessary aggression – perhaps in a misguided bid to look manly. If you have hired animal transport, don't feel shy to intervene if you feel the treatment is inappropriate. There is an animal clinic near Petra Visitor Centre called the Brooke Hospital for Animals.

Magnificently bedecked camels are available for rides between Qasr al-Bint and the Treasury (about JD15) and they will pause for a photograph near the Theatre. You may be able to hitch a ride on something four-legged back along the Siq for a few dinars at the end of the day.

Wadi Musa وادي موسى

03 / POP 20,000 / ELEV 1150M

The village that has sprung up around Petra is called Wadi Musa (Valley of Moses). It's an easy-going assemblage of hotels, restaurants and shops stretching about 5km from 'Ain Musa (Moses' Spring) to the main entrance of Petra at the bottom of the wadi.

Wadi Musa's fortunes depend almost entirely on tourism. Dozens of new hotels were hastily erected in the late 1990s (after the peace treaty with Israel), often with no aesthetic or social sensitivity. Many locals bought into the new opportunities that mass tourism offered only to be stung in the tourism slump after 9/11 and again in 2011 after the Arab Spring. A moratorium on hotel building is in place until 2012 in an effort to curb rampant expansion and to shift the focus to improving services rather than simply 'packing them in'.

Prices in Wadi Musa are inevitably higher than in other tourist destinations in Jordan, reflecting its status as guardian to one of the 'New Seven Wonders of the World', identified by an international public poll in 2008.

🏃 Activities

Hammams

A Turkish bath is the perfect way to ease aching muscles after a hard day's walking in Petra. See the boxed text (p60) for an idea of what to expect. The service typically includes steam bath, massage, hot stones, scrubbing and 'body conditioning'. The baths are popular with tourists and locals alike, and now several hotels, including the Amra Palace Hotel and the Petra Palace Hotel, offer excellent hammam facilities too. Book in advance; women can request a female attendant.

Petra Turkish Bath　　　　　BATHHOUSE

(2157085; JD24; 3-10pm) In the passage under the Silk Road Hotel, near the entrance

PETRA

Wadi Musa

To Al-Anbat Hotel I (1km);
Ain Musa (2km);
Post Office (2km)

To Tayyibeh (10km)

Police
Roundabout

Shaheed
Roundabout

Tourist Rd

To Al-Wu'ira (1.5km);
Sayhoun (3km);
Al-Beidha (8km)

Hertz
Rent-a-Car

Jett Bus
Stop

Brooke
Hospital
for Animals

Entrance
To Petra

To Petra (2.5km)

400 m
0.2 miles

Wadi Musa

of Petra, this hammam has a completely separate bath area for women, with female attendants.

Salome Turkish Bath   BATHHOUSE
(☎2157342; JD24; ⊙4pm-10pm) Entered via a grotto displaying old farming implements, this bathhouse has an atmospheric sitting area for relaxing with a herb tea after bathing. It's located near Al-Anbat Hotel III.

Sella Turkish Bath   BATHHOUSE
(☎2157170; www.sellahotel.com; JD20; ⊙5.30-10pm) The Sella bathhouse has a comprehensive list of services including sauna and separate baths for men and women. Dead Sea products are on sale here.

☞ Tours

A couple of the budget (and a few midrange and top-end) hotels can also arrange simple day trips around Petra and further afield.

There are many excellent local guides working independently in the Petra area. These include **Mahmoud Twaissi** (☎077-254658; mat65petra@yahoo.com), who has a well-earned reputation not just as a guide but also as a fixer for large-scale projects throughout the country. Equally well regarded is **Mohammed Al-Hasanat** (☎2156567; explorerone69@yahoo.com), who has been a licensed national guide since 1979. He has a passion for hiking and has had plenty of practice: 'I took my first steps [hiking] aged six,' he says, 'and I've been walking ever since.' Both these guides are reliable, knowledgeable both of the historical and cultural contexts of the areas they cover, and experienced in catering to the needs of individual or groups with special interests. They can organise camping tours over several days including camel and horse safaris.

Petra by Night
TOUR

(adult/child under 10 JD12/free) If you were wondering what Petra would be like under the stars, then you are not alone. The extremely popular Petra by Night Tour was introduced in response to numerous requests from visitors wanting to see Petra by moonlight. The magical tour of the old city starts from Petra Visitor Centre at 8.30pm on Monday, Wednesday and Thursday nights (it doesn't run when it's raining), and lasts two hours. It takes you along the Siq (lined with 1500 candles), in as much silence as is possible given the crowds, as far as the Treasury. Here traditional Bedouin music is played and mint tea served. The performance of Bedouin storytelling depends on the mood of the raconteur. Tickets are available from travel agencies in town, or from Petra Visitor Centre before 5pm.

Petra Moon Tourism Services
TOUR

(☑2156665; www.petramoon.com) Petra Moon is the most professional agency in Wadi Musa for arranging trips inside Petra and around Jordan (including Wadi Rum and Aqaba). The office is on the main road to Petra. It can arrange horses to Jebel Haroun, fully supported treks to Dana (four to five days), hikes from Tayyibeh to Petra and camel treks to Wadi Rum.

Raami Tours
TOUR

(☑ 2154010; www.raamitours.com) This tour company, based on the main road in the Bedouin village of Umm Sayhoun, organises traditional meals for visitors who want to try real homecooking. They also design tailor-made tours to fit all schedules, special interests and budgets (email at least three days ahead of arrival). The owner is the son of Marguerite van Geldermalsen, author of *Married to a Bedouin* – an expatriate who married into the Bdoul and who brought young Raami up in a Petra cave for the first few years of his life. Guided tours into Petra, therefore, don't come any more authentic than this!

Jordan Travel & Tourism
TOUR

(www.jordantours-travel.com) In addition to local tours, Jordan Travel organises tours to six countries (including visas) and daily trips to Israel and the Palestinian Territories and Syria (suspended at the time of writing). Near the Sella Hotel.

Jordan Experience
TOUR

(☑2155005; www.jordan-experience.com) On the main road to Petra.

La Beduina
TOUR

(☑2157099; www.labeduinatours.com) Near the Red Cave Restaurant.

Petra Night Tours
TOUR

(☑2154010; www.pntours.com) On the main road to Petra.

Zaman Tours & Travel
TOUR

(☑2157723; www.zamantours.com) In the same building as the Silk Road Hotel.

DON'T MISS

PETRA BY NIGHT

Like a grumbling camel caravan of snorting, coughing, laughing and farting miscreants, 200 people and one jubilantly crying baby make their way down the Siq 'in silence'. Asked to walk in single file behind the leader, breakaway contingents surge ahead to make sure they enjoy the experience 'on their own'. And eventually, sitting in 'reverential awe' outside the Treasury, the collected company show its appreciation of Arabic classical music by lighting cigarettes from the paper bag lanterns, chatting energetically, flashing their cameras and audibly farting some more.

Welcome to public entertainment in the Middle East! If you really want the Siq to yourself, come in the winter, go at 2pm or take a virtual tour on the internet.

But despite the promotional literature to the contrary, silence and solitude is not what the **Petra by Night Tour** (adult/child under 10 JD12/free; ◷8.30pm Mon, Wed & Thu) is all about. What this exceptional and highly memorable tour does give you is the fantastic opportunity to experience one of the most sublime spectacles on earth in the fever of other people's excitement. Huddles of whispering devotees stare up at the candlelit god blocks, elderly participants are helped over polished lozenges of paving stones, the sound of a flute wafts along the neck-hairs of fellow celebrants – this is surely much nearer to the original experience of the ancient city of Petra than walking through the icy stone corridor alone.

PETRA

🎓 Courses

Petra Kitchen   COOKING COURSE

(☎2155700; www.petrakitchen.com; cookery course per person JD35; 🍴) If you've always wanted to know how to whip up wonderful hummus or bake the perfect baklava, Petra Kitchen is for you. Located 100m up the main road from the Mövenpick Hotel, Petra Kitchen offers nightly cookery courses for those wanting to learn from locals how to cook Jordanian mezze, soup and main courses in a relaxed family-style atmosphere. A local Jordanian chef is on hand to make sure you don't make a camel's ear of the authentic Jordanian dishes. Dishes (including delicious vegetarian fare) change daily. The experience starts at 6.30pm (7.30pm in summer) and the price includes the printed recipes, food and soft drinks. Better still, buy a bottle of St George wine to share with your fellow apprentice chefs. Reservations are recommended. See the boxed text (p288) for an idea of what to expect.

🛏 Sleeping

In 1908 Macmillan's guide, *Palestine and Syria*, had the following advice:

> At Petra, there is no sleeping accommodation to be found, and travellers therefore have to bring with them camp equipment, unless they prefer to put up with the inconvenience of sleeping in the Bedwin huts at Elji, half an hour distant from Petra, or spend the night in some of the numerous temples. Such a course cannot be recommended to European travellers, especially if ladies are in the party.

Even as recently as 1991, there were only four official hotels in Wadi Musa. Visitors now have a choice of over 70 hotels (none of which are inside the site itself) and camping is no longer permitted.

The high season is generally from April to mid-May and October to November (check the heating works!). Outside these times, prices can drop quickly from the official rates, especially if you're staying more than a couple of nights. Most hotels have a variety of rooms in a variety of sizes; some with a balcony, some with no natural light, so ask to see some options. The prices quoted in this chapter are for high-season accommodation in an average room (neither the hotel's best nor worst), with bathroom

> **NAVIGATING WADI MUSA**
>
> The commercial centre of Wadi Musa is Shaheed roundabout, around 3km from the entrance to Petra. There is a second collection of midrange and top-end hotels, restaurants and souvenir shops 2km downhill, close to the Petra entrance. There are also a number of four- and five-star hotels on the 'rim' of Wadi Musa, on the road towards Wadi Rum, all of which have wonderful views – not of Petra but of the unique surrounding landscape.

(unless otherwise noted) and with breakfast – the norm in Wadi Musa, unlike in the rest of Jordan. Note that the views advertised by some hotels are of Wadi Musa valley, not of Petra itself.

Women travelling alone need to be more on their guard in budget hotels in Wadi Musa than in other towns (make sure doors lock properly and there are no peep holes).

If you get off the minibus at the Shaheed roundabout in Wadi Musa with a backpack, then you will be besieged by persuasive touts. Decide on your choice of hotel in advance if you want to be left alone.

LOWER WADI MUSA

The following hotels are located at the bottom end of town, within walking distance to the entrance to Petra.

Mövenpick Hotel   HOTEL **$$$**

(☎2157111; www.moevenpick-hotels.com; s/d JD155/170; ✳@🛜🏊🍴) This beautifully crafted Arabian-style hotel, 100m from the entrance to Petra, is worth a visit simply to admire the inlaid furniture, marble fountains, wooden screens and brass salvers. Petals are floated daily in the jardinière, a roaring fire welcomes winter residents to the Burckhardt Library (a lounge on the upper floor) and there's a pleasant ambience on the roof garden in summer. As the hotel is in the bottom of the valley, there are no views but the large and super-luxurious rooms all have huge windows regardless. The buffet breakfast and dinner are exceptional.

Petra Moon Hotel   HOTEL **$$**

(☎2156220; www.petramoonhotel.com; s/d/tr JD60/70/90; ✳@🛜🏊) Behind the Mövenpick Hotel, this friendly establishment is run by two brothers, who have poured

PICNIC AT PETRA

There are lots of ways to enjoy alfresco dining in Petra, from a simple take-your-own picnic to fine dining (well nearly) at the two Petra Valley restaurants.

For breakfast, spread your cloth in the little opening at the end of Wadi Muthlim; it's overlooked by god niches and as this is, after all, a necropolis, you may host unexpected guests of the ethereal kind. Entertain the wind for lunch on top of Umm al-Biyara and have high tea (or at least tea-on-high) with the Bedouin stallholder above the Royal Tombs. For dinner with a difference, choose a Nabataean dining room (the Garden Triclinium is a good bet) or share a candlelight supper. For the latter, join the Petra by Night Tour (p182) and spread your tablecloth in the middle of the Siq while the crowds race to the Treasury.

If a picnic takes too much forethought, snacks (including biscuits, fruit, ice cream) are sold at kiosks with outside tables and chairs throughout the site, or try the following:

Basin Restaurant (Map p168; lunch buffet JD17, fresh orange juice JD4; ⊙11am-4pm; ☑) Run by the Crowne Plaza Resort, the Basin serves a healthy selection of salads, fresh felafel and barbecued spicy sausage, followed by fruit and *umm ali* (bread-pudding-like dessert). Groups sit by the ravine under canvas; independent travellers are given tables under the trees. Flies can be a problem at certain times of the year.

Nabataean Tent Restaurant (Map p164; lunch buffet JD10, drinks JD2; ⊙11am-3pm) This eatery is similar to the Basin, with a slightly less appetising spread but a lovely spot under blue-flowering jacaranda trees (they flower in May).

Bdoul Mofleh Tea Shop (Map p164; ☑077-6094797; lunchbox JD3, tea by donation) A delightful ad hoc venture outside the owner's cave home.

In the neighbouring village of Umm Sayhoun, north of the city centre, you can try the original flavours of Petra in a Bedouin family home, prepared by the mother of the house (see p182). Not content just to watch? Then cook the food yourself at Petra Kitchen (p183) in Wadi Musa.

Throughout Petra, including at the High Place of Sacrifice and the Monastery, stalls sell bottled water, soft drinks and snacks. Best of all they sell sweet black tea laced with herbs; sharing a quite conversation with the aged or infant vendor is a guaranteed highlight of the ancient city.

major investment into this once modest hotel, transforming it into a luxurious complex of modern rooms, sumptuous bathrooms, and a rooftop swimming pool and barbecue area with splendid sunset views. The now-elegant pillared foyer remains a great meeting point for visitors to Petra, and readers' letters indicate that this is fast becoming the hotel of choice.

Petra Palace Hotel   HOTEL $$$
(☑2156723; www.petrapalace.com.jo; s/d/tr JD90/ 120/165; ✱@☎☲) Located on the main street, 500m from the entrance to Petra, this attractive and well-established hotel – with its palm-tree entrance, big bright foyer and helpful management – is an excellent choice. A whole suite of new rooms opens on to the outdoor swimming pool. The lively bar and restaurant are also drawcards. Up to 30% discounts are available in the low season.

This establishment also runs the Rock Camp near Little Petra.

Crowne Plaza Resort Hotel   HOTEL $$$
(☑2156266; www.crowneplaza.com; s/d/tr JD140/ 170/210; ✱@☎☲☲) A great location (close to the entrance to Petra and overlooking sandstone bluffs) makes this a popular top-end choice, although the rooms are not as luxurious as one might expect for the price. The heated swimming pool is useful outside of high summer and a lovely terrace offers summer barbecues. The hotel also has a Jacuzzi, sauna, tennis courts, coffee makers in rooms and self-service laundry facilities.

Petra Guest House   HOTEL $$$
(☑2156266; www.crowneplaza.com; s/d/tr JD97/ 105/130; ℗✱@☲) You can't get closer to the entrance to Petra without sleeping in a cave –

and indeed the hotel's bar (the famous Cave Bar) is located in one. Although not the same quality as its sister, the Crown Plaza, the guesthouse does offer use of the latter's facilities. Choose from motel-like chalets or sunny (if cramped) rooms in the main building.

La Maison HOTEL $$
(☏2156401; www.lamaisonhotel.com.jo; s/d/tr JD70/80/90, ❄) The brass jardinières decorating the foyer set the tone for this good-value hotel, just uphill from the entrance to Petra. With quality furniture, generous fluffy duvets, and a stylish recent makeover in black and white, La Maison gives some of the bigger hotels a run for their money. Ask about the brighter end rooms, which offer 120-degree views. The roof terrace is a great place to catch the sunset in summer.

Silk Road Hotel HOTEL $$
(☏2157222; www.petrasilkroad.com; s/d/tr JD60/70/90; P❄) Hand-painted panels of Bedouin camps stretch across the foyer and restaurant walls of this old favourite, 300m from the entrance to Petra. The common areas have been spruced up in lavender hues that may not be to everyone's taste but the rooms all sport decent furniture and big bathtubs. Some rooms are very dark so ask for one with a view. The buffet in the outside restaurant (JD10) is popular with tour groups.

WADI MUSA TOWN CENTRE
The following hotels are most convenient for the bus station and shops. It's just about possible to walk downhill to Petra from here but if you want to save your energy for Petra itself, then enquire about free transport to and from the gate (usually offered by hotels once a day in each direction).

TOP CHOICE **Amra Palace Hotel** HOTEL $$
(☏2157070; www.amrapalace.com; s/d/tr JD44/72/84; ❄@🛜🏊) This lovely hotel lives up to its name with magnificent lobby, marble pillars, giant brass coffeepots and Damascene-style furniture. The brothers who have run this establishment for many years take a personal interest in the details and they have a fine sense of interior design. Each room has spotless linen that's changed every day (there's a laundry on site), wooden headboards, upholstered furniture and satellite TV. Most rooms have views across the valley. Services include heated pool, Jacuzzi, summer terrace and excellent Turkish bath (JD13 per person). There's also a fun cave-style internet cafe with unlimited internet access and wi-fi availability for JD3 per hour. With pretty gardens of roses and jasmine, this is undoubtedly one of the best hotels in Wadi Musa.

Cleopetra Hotel HOTEL $
(☏2157090; www.cleopetrahotel.com; s/d/tr JD20/30/40; 🛜) This has to be one of the friendliest budget hotels in town. The whole hotel has recently undergone a complete refurbishment and now all rooms are bright and fresh and have private bathrooms with hot water. There's a communal sitting area in the lobby which is ideal for meeting fellow travellers and, if the mood takes you, you can still sleep on the roof for JD6 (JD7 with breakfast). Wi-fi is available for JD2. Two further improvements on the cards are air conditioning and double-glazing to reduce the street noise. The hotel can organise overnight 4WD trips to Wadi Rum (JD40 per person for a minimum of three) that travellers have recommended.

Al-Anbat Hotel III HOTEL $$
(☏2157200; www.alanbat.com; s/d/tr JD25/40/50; 🛜) The cavernous lobby and big, comfortable rooms of this new addition to the Al-Anbat estate (the family now own three hotels in the area) will start to find its feet once a few more guests have discovered it. There's an excellent view across Wadi Musa and surrounding hills from many of the rooms and from the roof terrace. The same friendly family run the budget option next door and there's an excellent Turkish bath opposite.

El-Rashid Hotel HOTEL $
(☏2156800; wailln@hotmail.com; s/d/tr from JD20/35/45) This well-run, friendly hotel has an attractive, marble-floored lobby and elegant furniture. The rooms are not quite so appealing, but the satellite TV will take your mind off the lime-green walls.

Rose City Hotel HOTEL $
(☏/fax 2156440; s/d/tr JD15/20/25) The delightful staff members make this tired hotel worth considering. A long overdue makeover is apparently on the cards but, in the current slump in tourism, it's unlikely to happen soon. Rooms vary considerably, but all have private bathrooms and are at least quiet.

UPPER WADI MUSA
The following luxury hotels are located at the top end of town, on the scenic road between the town centre and Tayyibeh,

a 10- to 15-minute drive from the Petra visitor centre. Perched at around 1400m above sea level, they offer fine views over the Rift Valley and most have beautiful terraces for a sunset drink. Unfortunately, lovely though the hotels are, they have somewhat blighted the once-secluded view from inside Petra.

Taybet Zaman Hotel & Resort
HOTEL $$$

(☎2150111; www.jordantourismresorts.com; s/d from US$93/104; ✱@✉⚡) With the rose-tinted sandstone typical of Petra's famous landscape spread beneath the lintels of this unusual hotel, you won't mind being a half-hour drive from the entrance to the site. Indeed, the sequestered nature of the accommodation, in renovated local village houses, is part of its unique appeal. With luxurious rooms, handicraft shops, swimming pool and Turkish bath set in tranquil gardens of fruiting figs and flowering plumbago, it is something of a rural idyll. The hotel is perched above expansive views of the Rift Valley in Tayyibeh village; a taxi from Petra (10km) costs about JD15 one way. Ask to pause at the spectacular viewpoint, just below the junction for the hospital. The hotel also has the highly recommended terrace restaurant, Sahtain. If you want to be closer to Petra, ask about their sister hotel in Wadi Musa, Beit Zaman.

Rocky Mountain Hotel
HOTEL $

(☎2155100; rockymountainhotel@yahoo.com; s/d/tr/q JD25/36/45/56, buffet lunch/dinner JD8/8; ✱@🛜) This delightful hotel near the junction with the main road downtown has caught just the right vibe to make it a successful travellers' lodge. The hotel is 'big on cleanliness' and there's a cosy communal area with free tea and coffee. If you're honeymooning in the area, ask for a double bed, as opposed to a twin, as extra care has been lavished on these double rooms (JD38). Seven of the rooms have a shared terrace from which to enjoy the magical views. A shuttle service to the Petra entrance at 7am and 8am, returning at 4pm and 5pm, is free.

Al-Anbat Hotel I
HOTEL $

(☎2156265; www.alanbat.com; s/d/tr JD20/35/45, buffet lunch/dinner JD8/8; ✱@🛜✉) Located some way out of town, on the road between 'Ain Musa and Wadi Musa, this three-storey resort offers midrange quality for budget

THE SPRING OF MOSES

Then Moses raised his arm and struck the rock twice with his staff. Water gushed out, and the community and their livestock drank.

Numbers 20:11

'Ain Musa (Spring of Moses) is one of two possible locations in Jordan for the site where Moses supposedly struck the rock with his staff and water gushed forth to the thirsty Israelites (the other possible site is near Mt Nebo). The simple site is marked by a modern three-domed building occasionally visited by local pilgrims. The site is located near the Golden Tulip Hotel, alongside the King's Highway at the main junction into Wadi Musa from the north.

prices. The large rooms (many with gorgeous sunset views) have satellite TV and come with a balcony. All rooms have been redecorated and those in the new extension are particularly attractive. Other facilities include a Turkish bath (JD15 for guests) and small pool but the best feature of the hotel is the new restaurant, perched like a nest on top of the new block and with extensive views of the Petra landscape from all windows. Free transport to/from Petra is available. Campers (JD7 per person) can use a designated area with showers and a kitchen, and you can park a campervan.

Petra Panorama Hotel
HOTEL $$$

(☎2157393; www.petrapanorama.com; r/half board JD90/100; ✱@🛜✉⚡) Popular with European tour groups, this hotel was designed for the package tourist with its cavernous corridors, little finesse and a *Marie Celeste* atmosphere during the day. That said, the rooms, which cascade in tiers down the mountain, are bright and spacious and they all come with unmatchable views. Most open on to terraces where you can enjoy your own private sunset and, for this, the hotel is a recommended choice.

Nabataean Castle Hotel
HOTEL $$$

(☎2157201; www.movenpick-hotels.com; s/d incl half board JD135/160; ✱@🛜✉⚡) Mövenpick runs this often fully booked hotel. It is an opulent choice although it plays second fiddle to its sister hotel near the entrance to

Petra. Most rooms have views over the valley, but the windows are surprisingly small. There's a free daily shuttle bus to and from Petra.

Sella Hotel
HOTEL **$$**

(☎2157170; www.sellahotel.com; s/d/tr JD40/66/85; ✳@🛜) This hotel is out of the town centre but compensates with views across Wadi Musa. Some rooms are either noisy or cramped – ask to see a few options. Free tea and coffee are available. The hotel runs the spotless Turkish baths opposite.

Petra Marriott
HOTEL **$$$**

(☎2156407; www.marriott.com; s/d JD125/140; ✳@🛜✖🍴) One of the most elegant hotels in the area, though remote in every sense from the experience of Petra, services include an outdoor pool, several restaurants, a Turkish bath and even a cinema for free use by guests.

✖ Eating

See the boxed text (p184) for details of where to eat inside the ancient city, together with information about authentic local dining experiences in Umm Sayhoun and Wadi Musa. The main road through Wadi Musa is dotted with grocery stores where you can buy the necessaries for a picnic in Petra; there's also a supermarket next to Al-Anbat Hotel I, slightly out of town on the road to 'Ain Musa. Some hotels can arrange snack-boxes with a boiled egg, bread and tomato. A felafel sandwich travels well and makes a filling lunch. Buy your dessert course at **Sanabel Bakery** (⊘5am-midnight), which sells a delicious range of Arab sweets around the corner from Rum Internet.

After a hot day's hiking in Petra, it's hard to resist a Swiss ice cream (JD2.500) from the foyer coffeehouse of the Mövenpick Hotel.

If you're climbing the hill between the Petra Visitor Centre and Shaheed roundabout, you might like to stop at the **Land of Peace Shop** (☎079-5738934; ⊘8am-midnight), a halfway house with a small craft shop, cafe with seating on the pavement, and four clean loos!

The cheapest places to eat are around Shaheed roundabout and Sanabel bakery. Most are similar in menu and price. More midrange options with a wider selection of dishes are near the entrance to Petra. Fine dining is confined to the five-star hotels.

Al-Saraya Restaurant
INTERNATIONAL **$$$**

(☎2157111; ⊘lunch/dinner JD18/JD22; ✳🍴) Serving a top-notch international buffet in an elegant banquet hall, this fine-dining restaurant offers a quality of dishes that matches the general opulence of the Mövenpick Hotel in which it is located. Leave time for a nightcap in the magnificent, wood-panelled bar afterwards which often sports a roaring fire in the hearth.

Sahtain
JORDANIAN, INTERNATIONAL **$$$**

(☎2150111; buffet JD20; ✳🍴) This delightful terrace restaurant at the Taybet Zaman is as much an experience as a seriously tasty supper. With cavernous, vaulted interior, the restaurant specialises in traditional Arabic and international home-cooked specialities. Simpler fare for lunch includes the chef's salad (JD4). The dinner buffet allows the chance to try a variety of local favourites, including more than 20 different salads.

Red Cave Restaurant
JORDANIAN **$$**

(☎2157799; starters JD1, mains from JD5; ⊘9am-10pm) Cavernous and friendly, this restaurant specialises in local Bedouin specialities including *mensaf* (lamb on a bed of rice topped with a lamb's head) and *maqlubbeh* (steamed rice with meat, grilled tomato and pine nuts). It's a popular travellers' meeting point and a cosy place to come on a chilly evening or to catch the breeze on a hot summer's day.

Oriental Restaurant
JORDANIAN **$$**

(☎2157087; mains JD6; ⊘11am-9.30pm) Together with the neighbouring **Sandstone Restaurant** (☎079-5542277; entrees/mains JD2/8), this main street favourite offers simple fare of tasty mixed grills, salad and mezze with pleasant outdoor seating. These are good places for a beer and a good-natured chuckle at the menu.

Mystic Pizza
PIZZA **$**

(☎2155757; small/medium/large pizza from JD4/8/10; ⊘8.30am-11pm; 🍴) A welcoming establishment serving fresh, tasty pizza. It also has vegetarian options, including lentil soup (JD3).

Al-Wadi Restaurant
JORDANIAN **$**

(☎2157151; salads JD1, mains JD4-5; ⊘7am-late) Right on Shaheed roundabout, this lively spot offers pasta, as well as a range of vegetarian dishes and local Bedouin specialities such as *gallayah* (meat, rice and onions in a spicy tomato sauce) and *mensaf*, most of which come with salad and rice.

PETRA WADI MUSA

Al-Arabi Restaurant MIDDLE EASTERN $
(☏2157661; mains from JD4; ⊙6am-midnight) Located off the Shaheed roundabout, it offers hummus, felafel and shwarma.

Cleopatra Restaurant & Coffee Shop BUFFET $
(☏079-5318775; buffet JD6; ⊙6am-11pm) This canteen offers a reasonable open buffet, with a range of Bedouin specialties.

🍷 Drinking & Entertainment

There's not a lot to do in the evening, other than take a bath in the hammam and plan your next day in Petra. Some hotels organise DVDs or other entertainment, but only when there are enough takers.

TOP CHOICE **Cave Bar** BAR
(☏2156266; beer/cocktails JD6.500/4.500; ⊙4pm-11pm; ❄) You can't come to Petra and miss the oldest bar in the world. Occupying a 2000-year-old Nabataean rock tomb, this blue-lit Petra hot spot has been known to stay open until 4am on busy summer nights. Sit among the spirits, alcoholic or otherwise, and you'll soon get a flavour of Petra you hadn't bargained on (including the 26% tax and service charge!). The menu includes delicious comfort food such as potato wedges and fish and chips that you may feel you've earned after a day's exercise in Petra. Don't be put off by the loud music at the entrance: the noise stops there. The restaurant and bar is next to the entrance to Petra Guest House, behind Petra Visitor Centre.

Al-Maqa'ad Bar BAR
(☏2157111; beer from JD2.500; ⊙4-11pm) The Mövenpick Hotel bar has a superb Moroccan-style interior with carved wooden grills and a chandelier: it's worth having a cocktail just to enjoy the ambience. The ice-cream specials are unforgettable and worth the 26% tax and service charge.

Wranglers Pub BAR
(☏2156723; beer JD3-5; ⊙2pm-midnight) The Petra Palace Hotel runs this sociable bar, decorated with assorted local memorabilia.

🛍 Shopping

There are many souvenir shops near the entrance to Petra and ad hoc stalls run by local Bedouin inside Petra. Throughout Wadi Musa you'll see craftsmen patiently pouring coloured sand into glass bottles; they will write your name if you give them time.

Top-end hotels sell good-quality handicrafts. Ask for Umm Raami's concession inside Petra where you can buy contemporary silver jewellery inspired by ancient Nabataean designs and crafted by local women originally trained through a Noor al-Hussein Foundation project.

Made in Jordan CRAFT
(☏2155700; www.madeinjordan.com) This excellent shop sells quality crafts from various local enterprises. Products include olive oil, soap, paper, ceramics, table runners, nature products from Wild Jordan in Amman, jewellery from Wadi Musa, embroidery from Safi, camel hair shawls, and bags from Aqaba as well as Jordan River Foundation goods. The fixed prices reflect the quality and uniqueness of each piece; credit cards are accepted.

Indiana Jones Gifts Shop GIFTS
(☏2155069; ⊙8am-10pm) Good place to buy a video of the main sites in Petra.

Rum Studio & Labs PHOTOGRAPHY
(☏2157467; ⊙8.30am-10pm) A range of digital accessories is available here; the shop is located in front of the Silk Road Hotel on the main road.

The **Wadi Musa Ladies Society** (⊙6am-9pm) and the **Society for the Development and Rehabilitation of Rural Women** (⊙6am-9pm) both have shops at the visitor centre selling a range of souvenirs, books and crafts.

Books on Petra can be found in the shops behind the visitor centre and along the main road through Wadi Musa. See p189 for information about maps and books.

ℹ Information

Emergency
Main police station (☏2156551, emergency 191) In Wadi Musa, adjacent to the police roundabout.
Tourist police station (☏2156441, emergency 196; ⊙8am-midnight) Opposite Petra Visitor Centre. A few tourist police can be found lounging around in the shade inside Petra.

Internet Access
There are lots of internet cafes around the town centre, including **Rum Internet** (per hr JD1; ⊙10am-midnight), located downhill from Shaheed roundabout. **Seven Wonders Restaurant** (per hr JD3.500; ⊙9am-11pm), near the entrance to Petra, a few doors up from the

PETRA

BOOKS & MAPS

A Good Read

There is some interesting literature about Petra, together with beautiful souvenir books, available at shops and stalls around Wadi Musa and Petra.

One of the best guidebooks, *Petra: A Traveller's Guide* by Rosalyn Maqsood, covers the history and culture of the site and describes several hikes. The pocket-sized *Petra: The Rose-Red City*, by Christian Auge and Jean-Marie Dentzer, is excellent on Petra's historical context. Jane Taylor's *Petra* is another good paperback introduction to the site. Taylor also wrote the authoritative *Petra & the Lost Kingdoms of the Nabataeans*. There's a chapter on hiking in Petra in Tony Howard and Di Taylor's *Jordan – Walks, Treks, Climbs & Canyons*.

For an engaging account of the Bdoul Bedouin who once lived in the caves surrounding the Petra valley and who now live on the rim of the ancient city, *Married to a Bedouin* is a recommended read. The author, Marguerite van Geldermalsen, raised three children among the Bdoul and ran the local clinic. Since the book's publication in 2006, Marguerite has become a local celebrity in Jordan, has received the Queen of England and Queen Noor in her cave, and her son now runs tours for those wanting to gain an understanding of Bedouin life in the area (see Tours, p181).

Finding Your Way

Very little in Petra is signposted or captioned, so a map and guidebook are essential. For most visitors the maps in this book should suffice.

If you plan to hike long distances in Petra without a guide, the best map is the Royal Jordanian Geographic Centre's contoured 1:5000 *Map of Petra* (2005; JD5). It's usually available at bookshops in Wadi Musa and at the stand outside the Nabataean Museum.

The *Petra* brochure, published by the Ministry of Tourism & Antiquities, has an easy-to-read map with useful photos that help identify certain monuments. Pick one up before coming to Petra as the visitor centre often runs out.

PETRA WADI MUSA

Mövenpick Hotel, also serves a luxury hot chocolate (JD2.500).

Laundry

Most hotels will do laundry for around JD2 per piece, through the drycleaners at Amra Palace Hotel.

Medical Services

The Queen Rania Hospital offers high-standard health care, and is open for emergencies without referral. It's located 5km from the police roundabout on the road to Tayyibeh.

The Wadi Musa Pharmacy, located near the Shaheed roundabout, has a wide range of medications and toiletries.

Money

Many hotels will change money, albeit at a poor rate. It's generally better to change travellers cheques before arriving in Petra.

The Housing Bank and Jordan Islamic Bank up from the Shaheed roundabout are good for money exchange; both have ATMs. The Arab Bank is downhill from the roundabout. Closer to the Petra entrance, the Cairo-Amman Bank

in the Mövenpick Hotel and the Arab Jordan Investment Bank both change cash and (usually) travellers cheques with a minimum of fuss. The banks are open from about 8am to 2pm Sunday to Thursday and (sometimes) 9am to 11am on Friday. A couple of moneychangers near the Silk Road Hotel keep longer hours.

Post

Main post office (⊙8am-5pm Sat-Thu) Located inside a mini-plaza on the Shaheed roundabout.

Post office (⊙8am-5pm Sat-Thu) Small office by the Mussa Spring Hotel in 'Ain Musa.

Visitor centre post office (⊙7.30am-5pm) The attraction of using the small post office behind Petra Visitor Centre is that mail is postmarked 'Petra Touristic Post Office', rather than Wadi Musa.

Telephone

International telephone calls can be made from private agencies along the main streets of Wadi Musa. The cheapest and easiest way to make a call is to buy a prepaid phonecard.

ⓘ PETRA: PUBLIC TRANSPORT AT A GLANCE

TO/FROM	DURATION	FREQUENCY	NOTES
Amman (210km) via Desert Highway	4 hours	1 bus daily/11 minibuses daily	**JETT Bus** Leaves 6.30am from the JETT bus office near Abdali Bus Station. Returns 4pm from Petra Visitor Centre. **Minibus** Leaves between 7am and 4pm to/from the south bus station (Wahadat) in Amman and Wadi Musa bus station. Leaves only when full.
Wadi Rum (90km)	2 hours	1 daily	**Minibus** Leaves 6.30am from Wadi Musa bus station. Leaves 8.30am from Petra Visitor Centre. May only leave if full: ask hotel/camp owner to contact bus driver in advance.
To/from Aqaba (120km)	2½ hours	4 daily	**Minibus** Leaves between 6.30am & 8.30am, with one midafternoon to/from Wadi Musa bus station and Aqaba minibus station. Leaves only when full.

Tourist information

The best source of information is the main **Petra Visitor Centre** (Map p180; ☏2156044; ☉6am-9pm) near the entrance to Petra. The easiest way to find information about minibuses and other transport is to ask at your hotel or one of the restaurants around the Shaheed roundabout. You can also log on to **Jordan Jubilee** (www.jordanjubilee.com); the author of the site, Ruth, is a long-term resident of Wadi Musa and local oracle.

ⓘ Getting There & Away

Public transport to and from Wadi Musa is less frequent than you'd expect, given that it's the number-one tourist attraction in Jordan. For a guide to transport between Petra and Jerusalem, see the boxed text (p322).

Bus & Minibus

A daily JETT bus connects Amman with Petra, largely designed for those wanting to visit on a day trip. The service leaves at 6.30am from the JETT office, near Abdali Bus Station (single/return JD8/16, four hours) and drops off passengers at Petra Visitor Centre in Wadi Musa. The return bus leaves at 4pm (sometimes earlier in the summer).

Minibuses leave from the bus station in central Wadi Musa. Most minibuses won't leave unless they're at least half full, so be prepared for a wait. If there are insufficient passengers, they may not leave at all, or you may be approached to pay for the empty seats. This is not a scam: it's just an attempt by the driver to cover the cost of the journey. You should establish the fare you are being charged before departing. There are far fewer services on Fridays.

Regular minibuses travel every day between Amman's south bus station (Wahadat) and Wadi Musa (JD5, four hours) via the Desert Highway. These buses leave Amman and Wadi Musa when full every hour or so between 7am and 4pm. Timings change frequently so ask at your hotel for the latest information.

Minibuses leave Wadi Musa for Ma'an (JD1.500, 45 minutes) fairly frequently throughout the day (more often in the morning), stopping briefly at the university, about 10km from Ma'an. From Ma'an there are connections to Amman, Aqaba and (indirectly) Wadi Rum. Minibuses also leave Wadi Musa for Aqaba (JD5, 2½ hours) at about 6am, 8.30am and 3pm – ask around the day before to confirm or check through your hotel.

For Wadi Rum (JD5, two hours) there is a daily minibus around 6am. It's a good idea to reserve a seat the day before – your hotel should be able to ring the driver. If you miss this bus, or the service isn't operating, take the minibus to Aqaba, get off at the Ar-Rashidiyyah junction and catch another minibus or hitch the remainder of the journey to Rum. You may well be charged extra for 'luggage' (around JD3), especially if it takes up a seat that could be used for a paying customer. Buy water for your journey in advance and make provisions for a Wadi Rum tour either from your hotel, a travel agent or on arrival in Rum to avoid falling victim to opportunistic touts at the station. Cleopetra Hotel, among other hotels, organises overnight tours to Wadi Rum.

To Karak, a minibus sometimes leaves at around 7am (JD3), but demand is low so it doesn't leave every day. Alternatively, travel via Ma'an.

Car

Hertz Rent-a-Car (☏2156981; ⊙8am-6pm)
rents out cars from JD30 per day. A 4WD costs
around JD160 per day.

Petra and Wadi Musa are well signposted along
the main highways. The road from Petra to Little
Petra extends to the Wadi Musa to Shobak road
offering a scenic alternative route out of town.
A spectacular road winds into Wadi Araba for
direct access to the Dead Sea Highway (see the
boxed text, p114). The road to Tayyibeh is also
particularly scenic.

Taxi

Private (yellow) taxis are easy to find in Wadi
Musa. A few 4WD taxis are available for much
the same cost, but they are not of much benefit
as you will still have to join a 4WD tour from the
Wadi Rum Visitor Centre if you want to explore
the protected area. One-way taxi fares cost
JD40 to Wadi Rum (one hour) or Aqaba (1½
hours); JD7 to Shobak (JD12 return including a
one-hour wait); and JD50 to Karak (1½ hours). If
you want to travel to Madaba or Amman via the
King's Highway, with stops at Shobak, Dana and
Karak, the fare is around JD90.

Siq al-Barid (Little Petra)

سيق البيضاء (البتراء الصغيرة)

Siq al-Barid (Cold Canyon) is colloquially
known as **Little Petra** and is well worth a
visit. It was thought to have served as an
agricultural centre, trading suburb and
resupply post for camel caravans visiting
Petra. The surrounding area is picturesque
and fun to explore, especially as it is home to
some of the oldest settlements in the world,
including Al-Beidha.

◉ Sights

FREE **Little Petra Siq**   RUINS
(⊙daylight hr) From the car park, an obvi-
ous path leads to the 400m-long siq, which
opens out into larger areas. The first open
area has a **temple**, which archaeologists
know little about. Four **triclinia** – one on
the left and three on the right – are in the
second open area, and were probably used
as dining rooms to feed hungry merchants
and travellers. About 50m further along the
siq is the **Painted House**, another small
dining room, which is reached by some exterior steps. The faded but still vivid frescoes
of vines, flowers and birds on the underside
of the interior arch are a rare example of
Nabataean painting, though the walls have
been blackened by Bedouin campfires. Cut
into the rock opposite the room is a large
cistern; there are also worn water channels
at various points along the siq.

At the end of Siq al-Barid are some steps.
You can climb to the top for great views and
plenty of picnicking opportunities. With
extra time and interest you can explore the

DAVID ROBERTS (1796–1864)

Stand in certain parts of Petra and Little Petra and it's almost impossible not to imagine
striped-robed Arabs from the 19th century lounging languidly in the foreground. Sit in the
cafes and hotel lobbies of Wadi Musa and you'll see the same characters and landscapes
writ large across otherwise-vacant walls. And who do we have to thank for this 'picturesque' peopling of ancient Petra? The culprit is one David Roberts, artist, Scot and much-
beloved topographer of the late Romantic era.

Given the continuing popularity of his images with tourists, it's safe to say that Roberts had the common touch. This may have had something to do with his seven-year
apprenticeship as a housepainter, or perhaps his stint as a scenery painter at the Theatre
Royal in Edinburgh. Whatever the reason, his compositions are full of human interest – an
unloaded caravan, friends waving across a wadi, a quarrel between traders cast against a
backdrop of exaggerated landscape.

Roberts visited the region in 1839 dressed as an Arab, in the tradition of Burckhardt
just two decades earlier, and travelled with a caravan of 20 camels and local bodyguards.
Petra was the high point of his journey, despite having to cut short his visit due to trouble
with local tribes. On his return to Britain, his watercolours, magnificently interpreted in
lithograph by the Belgian engraver Louis Haghe, were exhibited in 1840 and won instant
critical acclaim.

Roberts' images have now passed into the visual vocabulary of one of the world's most
treasured sites. For a shoemaker's son with no formal art training who began life painting
houses, that's a formidable legacy.

BEDOUIN HUMOUR

While you're in Petra, look out for the funny side of your visit. Locals are famous for their mischievous sense of humour, offering camels as 'air-conditioned taxis' and donkeys as 'Mercedes Benz'. Handicrafts are often prefaced with the words 'buy one for the wife and one for the girlfriend'. Beware, however, that 'Happy hour prices' charged for souvenirs in the evening may well mean they cost double!

Nabataean quarries and cisterns of Umm Qusa, located just before the entrance to Siq al-Barid.

FREE **Al-Beidha** RUINS
(⊙daylight hr) The Neolithic ruins of **Al-Beidha** date back some 9000 years and, along with Jericho, constitute one of the oldest archaeological sites in the Middle East. The remains of around 65 round (and later rectangular) structures are especially significant because they pinpoint the physical transition from hunter-gatherer to settled herder-agriculturalist communities. The settlement was abandoned around 6000 BC, which is why it's still intact (later civilisations didn't build upon it). For the casual visitor, the ruins require imagination. Follow the marked trails so the site is fragile.

To reach the site, follow the trail starting to the left of the entrance to Little Petra for about 15 minutes.

FREE **Al-Wu'ira** CASTLE
(Map p164; ⊙daylight hr) Built by the Crusaders in AD 1116, **Al-Wu'ira** was overrun by Muslim forces 73 years later. A fantastic bridge (previously a drawbridge) leads over the gorge to a gatehouse and the limited ruins.

Look for the unsigned turn-off, about 1.5km north of the Mövenpick Hotel, and on the left side of the road leading to Siq al-Barid (Little Petra).

🏃 Activities

If you come prepared, it's possible to **hike** from Siq al-Barid to Petra's Monastery (Al-Deir), or to Petra centre via Wadi Mu'aisireh al-Gharbiya. You'll need a guide for the four-hour trek (JD35 – ask at the car park by the entry to Siq al-Barid or at one of the camps

below) as route-finding is tricky. You must also have a valid ticket to Petra (you can't get one at Siq al-Barid).

🛏 Sleeping & Eating

There are several camps in the area which make a rural retreat from the slightly claustrophobic atmosphere of Wadi Musa.

The Rock CAMP $$
(☎079-777589; www.therockpetra.com; s/d half board in Bedouin tent JD45/JD66) This luxury new camp in Ba'ja has a gorgeous location in a wide valley with typical wind-blown rocks for a backdrop and an unusually green vista (thanks to the neighbouring farming project) stretched across the plain below. There is a choice between luxury, white army-style tents or more traditional hand-woven goat-hair tents and a variety of cosy perches for traditional suppers. If you sup a glass of wine from the outdoor bar (JD5) you'll be partaking in an ancient tradition as you'll see from the Nabataean wine press within the camp grounds. Remains of a dam and water channels are also visible. A two-hour walk and scramble in the adjacent Siq Ba'ja brings you to the ruins of a well-preserved 9000-year-old Neolithic village. To reach the camp, follow the Rock Camp signs from Little Petra towards Wadi Araba. The last 200m is just about accessible by 2WD vehicle car if you drive slowly over the bumpy track slowly.

Ammarin Bedouin Camp CAMP $
(☎079-5667771; www.bedouincamp.net; half board per person in tent JD50) A 10-minute walk from Little Petra and signposted off the approach road, this camp is in Siq al-Amti, hidden in a spectacular amphitheatre of sand and hills. Accommodation is a mattress and blankets in a sectioned Bedouin tent with concrete floors, but the shower and toilet block is clean. A wonderful little ethnographic museum on site spotlights the local Ammarin tribe – read the story of Torfa Bint Saleh Al-Ammarin for an idea of the everyday hardships of a life on the fringe. The camp offers guided hikes in the surrounding hills. Reservations are essential.

Seven Wonders Bedouin Camp CAMP $
(☎079-7958641; www.sevenwondersbedouincamp. com; half board per person in tent JD30, B&B JD20; ☑) Tucked discreetly into a hillside, this relaxed camp looks particularly magical at night when the open fires are burning and the rocks behind the camp are illuminated.

Accommodation is in simple but cosy cabins with electric light, carpets and mosquito nets. Hot water and towels are available. Tasty traditional fare is served from a *zerb* oven and *mendi* pits and wholesome vegetarian soups are made on the premises by an experienced chef. Follow the signs along a track off the road to Little Petra.

Little Petra Bedouin Camp   CAMP $$
(☏079-5300135 or 077-6331431; www.littlepetra bedouincamp.com; per person JD25, half board per person JD40, minimum 2 people) Hidden in the mountains on the road between Umm Sayhoun and Little Petra this secluded complex brings a touch of urban chic to the rural retreat. It offers camping in style with army tents that sport proper beds with mattresses, and full-length wood-rimmed mirrors. Dinner is prepared in a cave and served with finesse in a variety of dining areas, including romantic caverns. The camp is signposted just off the main road to Little Petra.

❶ Getting There & Away

Some hotels in Wadi Musa organise tours to Little Petra. If not, a private taxi costs about JD20 one way or JD30 return, including an hour's wait.

If you're driving, take the road north of the Mövenpick Hotel and follow the signs to 'Beda' or 'Al-Beidha'. Turn left at the junction from where it's just under 1km to the car park.

Alternatively, it's a pleasant 8km walk following the road. The route passes the village of Umm Sayhoun, the 'Elephant Rock' formation and then 'Ain Dibdibah, which once supplied Petra with much of its water. You can shortcut across fields to the left about 1km before the junction to Al-Beidha.

Hitching is possible, especially on Friday when local families head out for a picnic.

Aqaba, Wadi Rum & the Desert Highway
العقبة وادي رم & الطريق الصحراء

Best Places to Stay

» InterContinental Hotel (p202)

» Coral Bay Resort (p208)

» Bait Ali Lodge (p221)

» Rum Stars Camp (p221)

Best Places to Eat

» Blue Bay (p204)

» Ali Baba Restaurant (p203)

» Royal Yacht Club Restaurant (p203)

» Captain's Camp (p224)

Why Go?

Southern Jordan is the home of the Bedouin whose legendary courage and bravado were made famous by TE Lawrence in *Seven Pillars of Wisdom*. They inhabit the unforgiving Southern Desert, a quintessential landscape of sand dunes, oases and weathered escarpments, beautiful at sunset and awe-inspiringly extreme in midsummer. A trip to Wadi Rum makes all but the most unromantic at heart long to leave the modern world behind and attempt the life of a nomad. And that's possible – at least for a day or two amid the camps of Rum and Diseh, on camel back, by 4WD or floating above in a hot-air balloon.

Nearby Aqaba, together with neighbouring diving centres, give access to another of Jordan's natural splendours: the coral gardens of the Red Sea. Even if wet suits aren't your thing, Aqaba is a relaxed and pleasant destination in which to wash off the desert dust and enjoy a fish supper among Jordan's own holidaymakers.

When to Go

Aqaba enjoys year-round warmth, even in winter, and a crystal clear sea. This brings holiday-makers from the chilly uplands to the shore in large numbers – especially during national holidays and religious festivals.

The desert springs to life after rain making February to May and October to November the perfect time for desert adventure in Wadi Rum. With temperate days and balmy nights camping is blissful.

Despite high temperatures, the all-night music festival, 'Distant Heat', attracts party-goers to Wadi Rum in mid-August.

Beware! Mid-winter brings bitter night-time temperatures to the desert.

History & Culture

There is a magnificent road (A35) that leads from Wadi Musa, with westerly glimpses across expansive Wadi Araba, to the escarpment of Jebel Batra. Here the road joins the Desert Highway and hand in hand they sweep onto the majestic floor of what is commonly called the Southern Desert. For centuries this has been the home of the Bedouin whose tribes rallied together in the most convincing expression of the pan-Arab ideal during the 20th-century Arabic Revolt. The cry of 'to Aqaba' still rings between the towering walls of Wadi Rum, carried in the whistle of the freight train as it winds along the now-placid tracks of the Hejaz Railway.

As romantic as the nomadic life may seem, many of the Bedouin tribes have turned in the past two or three decades to a settled life. The desert, much of which is characterised not by the picturesque features of Wadi Rum but by inhospitable plains, doesn't take prisoners. Life to this day is hard here, even for the Bedouin and, in the words of Lawrence, 'a death in life' for strangers. Take the journey along the Desert Highway, along the edge of the mighty Badia, and you'll quickly learn a new respect for this extreme environment – and for the people and wildlife who have adapted to its privations.

Nature Reserves

There are two reserves in the south of Jordan. On land, **Wadi Rum Protected Area** (p210), run by the Aqaba authorities, offers desert adventure such as camping, camel treks, hiking, ballooning and off-road driving, amid beautiful sand dune and sandstone landscapes.

Off-shore, the **Red Sea Aqaba Marine Park** was established in 1997 to protect the complex marine environment of the Red Sea south of Aqaba and is best accessed through one of the diving clubs in the area. The park stretches from the Marine Science Station to the Royal Diving Club, and extends about 350m offshore. Enforced by rangers, there's a ban on fishing and boating is limited within the park. Jetties enable divers and snorkellers to jump into the water rather than wade out over coral from the beach.

Dangers & Annoyances

Like the plains of the Eastern Desert, the sand dunes of the Southern Desert are an unforgiving environment that must be treated with respect. It's easy to dehydrate, even in winter, and without a guide getting lost

Southern Highlights

1 Don mask and flippers and hover with the pipe fish over spectacular coral gardens in the **Red Sea** (p26)

2 Taste fresh tuna steaks in one of the excellent fish restaurants of **Aqaba** (p203), and ruin your love for the tinned version

3 Relax at one of Jordan's southerly **coastal resorts** (p208) and enjoy the three 'S's (sun, sea and sand)

4 Live a 'Lawrence moment' by riding through **Wadi Rum** (p210) on a camel, visiting the places made famous in *Seven Pillars of Wisdom*

5 Enjoy the banter between Bedouin drivers on a **4WD excursion** (p217) through Wadi Rum

6 Book a private tent and personally delivered dinner on your own sand dune in **Diseh** (p223) for the ultimate candlelit supper

7 Camp with the Bedouin in a goat-hair tent in **Wadi Rum** (p220) and experience the night sky in all its glory and disoriented is a serious hazard. Perhaps a less anticipated danger is the bitter cold of night-time temperatures in winter, when hypothermia can set in on an open-vehicle trip without you noticing.

The Red Sea is home to a number of hazards. See p29 for a description of the main dangers.

For divers, it's important to remember that most roads out of Aqaba lead uphill. This means that 'the bends' are a serious concern if you fail to acclimatise in Aqaba before heading on to Wadi Rum or Petra.

ℹ Getting There & Away

Aqaba is well served by public transport from Amman and even has an international airport. Aqaba is also a gateway into Jordan from Egypt (usually by boat) and Israel and the Palestinian Territories (through the blissfully straight-forward Wadi Araba border crossing – see p34). Wadi Rum is not as easy to get to without your own transport or without taking a tour from Aqaba or Petra. With a car it's possible to link this region with the Eastern Desert via Hwy 5.

ℹ Getting Around

It's possible to make a roundtrip of this most southerly part of Jordan by public transport from Aqaba in three to four days. Hiring a car from Aqaba makes accessing the South Coast and Wadi Rum much easier. You don't need a 4WD for Wadi Rum as you can drive to the Visitors Centre on tarmac. From there, unless you are an expert sand driver, it's advisable to take an excursion with a Bedouin driver.

AQABA & AROUND

Aqaba is the most important city in southern Jordan and, with feverish development underway, is being groomed as the country's second city, if not in size at least in terms of status, revenue and tourism potential. Perched on the edge of the Gulf of Aqaba, ringed by high desert mountains and enjoying a pleasant climate for most of the year, Aqaba has what it takes to make a major resort – a fact not lost on hotel chains: the glamorous $2.5 billion Saraya Project, which includes lagoons, marina, golf course and a British university, is well on the way to completion and the Tala Bay hotel and residential development is helping Aqaba and its surrounding coastline in the bid to become Jordan's answer to Eilat.

Aqaba   العقبة

♪ 03 / POP 133,200 / ELEV 50M

Surprisingly, given the radical makeover of its immediate vicinity, Aqaba retains the relaxed small-town atmosphere of a popular local holiday destination. For the visitor, although there's not much to 'do' as such, the town offers a sociable stopover en route to the diving and snorkelling clubs to the south, and the big destinations of Wadi Rum and Petra to the northeast. It's also an obvious place to break a journey to/from Israel and the Palestinian Territories or Egypt. There's plenty of good-value accommodation in the town centre and some excellent restaurants. The port mars the view a little and the beaches close to town are fairly unappealing (except at the top-end hotels), but overall Aqaba has an 'on holiday' atmosphere that's infectious.

While Amman shivers in winter with temperatures around 5°C and the occasional snowfall, the daytime temperature in Aqaba rarely goes below 20°C and is often quite a few degrees warmer. In summer the weather is hot, with daytime temperatures over 35°C, but the sea breezes make it bearable. It also helps to follow the traditional siesta: everything shuts down around 2pm and reopens after the afternoon nap, from around 6pm.

History

And king Solomon made a navy of ships in Ezion-Geber, which is beside Eloth (Eilat), on the shore of the Red Sea, in the land of Edom

1 Kings 9:26

In the 10th century, a Muslim traveller described Aqaba as 'a great city' and a meeting place of pilgrims en route to and from Mecca. Indeed, from as early as the 10th to 5th centuries BC, it was at the heart of ancient trade routes transporting copper ore, smelted from mines in Wadi Araba, and transported by King Solomon's fleets to far-flung destinations. Ceramics from China and coins from Ethiopia highlight the cosmopolitan nature of the port throughout its early history. Thereafter the Egyptians, Nabataeans and Romans all found their uses for 'Ayla', as it came to be known, and the discovery of a late-3rd-century purpose-built church – one of the oldest in the world – is suggestive of a prosperous community, embracing of change.

In AD 1068 the town's fortunes changed when a huge earthquake split the old city of Ayla in two. The shifting of trade routes to Baghdad in the middle of the 16th century led to the final eclipse of the port which dwindled to an insignificant fishing village for the next 500 years.

Aqaba returned to the spotlight during the Arab Revolt in the early 20th century when Ottoman forces were ousted after a raid by the Arabs (and TE Lawrence) in 1917. Thereafter the British used the town as a supply centre from Egypt to support the assault on Damascus.

After WWI, the border between Trans-Jordan and Saudi Arabia had not been defined, so Britain arbitrarily drew a line a few kilometres south of Aqaba. The Saudis disputed the claim but took no action. As the port of Aqaba grew, the limited coastline proved insufficient, so in 1965 King Hussein traded 6000 sq km of Jordanian desert for another 12km of coastline with Saudi Arabia. Today, with the value of tourism to the gross national product, that has proved to be a very foresighted deal.

⊙ Sights

To be fair, there isn't too much to see as most people come to Aqaba to relax by the beach, or go snorkelling or diving (see p26). The one or two sights listed are best enjoyed as part of a stroll around town (see the boxed text, p197). Alternatively, take a **horse and cart** (JD15 for 30 minutes) from outside Al-Cazar Hotel.

King Hussein St (written in full as King Al-Hussein bin Talal St, or referred to simply

DISCOVERING AQABA ON FOOT

The compact centre of Aqaba lends itself to a late afternoon amble. The following 3km circular route takes about two hours. It begins outside Al-Cazar Hotel on the Corniche where you can hire a horse carriage if you prefer.

Gain a sense of Aqaba's antiquity in the **ruins of Ayla**: there has been a port at the mouth of the gulf for many centuries. Continue along the Corniche to the **marina** to understand Aqaba's strategic location, with the mountains of Israel and Egypt just across the water and Saudi Arabia, 14km to the south.

Continue along the Corniche and take the path through the carefully tended allotments of spinach and radish to the **beach**. On the weekend, the beach comes alive with picnicking locals; on a weekday off season, you'll have the sand to yourself. Continue south to the large plaza at the base of the giant flag. Spare 30 minutes for a ride in a **glass-bottom boat** and a tantalising glimpse of the fabled Red Sea with its window-pane clarity.

From the flag, cut inland to the **Aqaba Fort** and catch the cry of 'To Aqaba' as you stroll through the giant wooden gates. This is where the Arab Revolt memorably ousted the Turks, with TE Lawrence in tow. For a memento of standing in the big man's shoes (or at least in his celebrity sandals), buy something from the **Noor al-Hussein Foundation** opposite, where profits are returned to the community.

Leave history behind and turn left onto the busiest section of the Corniche, dodging the invitations to snack with the locals from the town's popular shwarma vendors. Turn right up Ar-Razi St and first left, doglegging through the colourful **fruit & vegetable souq** selling monumental mounds of eggplants. Turn left on Zahran St – or be led by your nose as you're bound to smell the shops selling nuts, coffee and spices before you see them. Jewellery, bead, antique and **souvenir shops** punctuate the parade along the rest of its length. To feast the belly instead of the eyes, duck left through one of the alleyways into Raghadan St. The magnificently renovated **mosque** opposite was a recent project of the current king. Turn right along Raghadan St and buy desserts for later from the famous pastry shops at the bend in the road, then settle yourself into a street-side table at **Ali Baba Restaurant** for a tasty first course.

Cross the busy Amman Hwy and stroll along An-Nahda St, the teeming centre of modern Aqaba. Choose a **fish restaurant** for tonight's supper or stop off for an Arabic coffee and sheesha along As-Sa'dah St, stepping aside for the entrepreneurial young lads exercising their camels on the pavement. Turn left onto Ar-Rashid St by the ruins of the **ancient church**; a few paces will bring you to the Mövenpick Resort Hotel by the ruins of Ayla – a grand place for an end of tour ice cream.

Aqaba

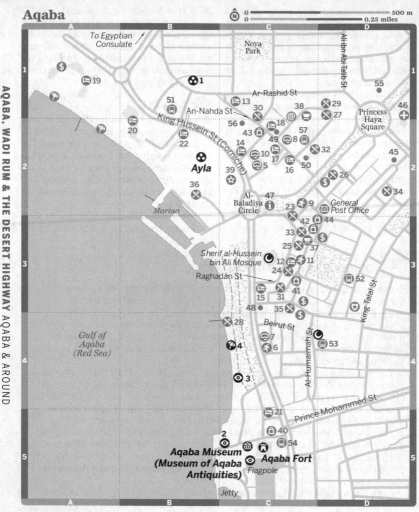

Gulf of Aqaba (Red Sea)

Noya Park

Marina

Ar-Rashid St

An-Nahda St

King Hussein St (Corniche)

Ayla

Al-Baladiya Circle

Sherif al-Hussein bin Ali Mosque

Raghadan St

Beirut St

Ali Ibn Abi Talib St

Princess Haya Square

General Post Office

King Talal St

Al-Humaimah St

Prince Mohammed St

Aqaba Museum (Museum of Aqaba Antiquities)

Aqaba Fort

Flagpole

Jetty

---

as the Corniche) is the main axis of Aqaba. It follows the languid Gulf from the border with Israel and the Palestinian Territories to the border with Saudi Arabia. In the centre of town, a walking path parallels King Hussein St along the beach, ending at a huge flag – the location of Aqaba Fort and the tourist office. The disappointingly obtrusive port is a few kilometres south of the centre of Aqaba.

FREE **Ayla**
RUIN
(Corniche; ☺24hr) Located along the Corniche, and incongruously squeezed between

the marina and the Mövenpick Resort, Ayla is the site of the ancient port of Aqaba. The ruins are limited, but noticeboards in English pinpoint items of interest. At the back of the parking space behind the JETT bus office is another small section of the old city, including the city wall and the ruins of an ancient church.

Aqaba Fort
FORT
(off King Hussein St; admission JD1, includes Aqaba Museum; ☺8am-4pm Sat-Thu, 10am-4pm Fri) This squat fortification, at the other end of the Corniche near to the giant flag,

Aqaba

measures around 50m by 50m, and is unusual in having sides of slightly uneven length. The castle was built between 1510 and 1517, as attested by the Arabic inscriptions inside the monumental gateway, and was used as a khan (travellers' inn) for pilgrims on their way to Mecca. The Ottomans occupied the castle until WWI when, in 1917, the fortress was substantially destroyed by shelling from the British Royal Navy. The Hashemite coat of arms above the main entrance commemorates the Arab Revolt that swept through Aqaba, ousting the Turks.

Aqaba Museum
MUSEUM

(Museum of Aqaba Antiquities; West of King Hussein St; admission JD1; ⊙8am-4pm Sat-Thu, 10am-4pm Fri) The museum, part of the Aqaba Fort complex, was previously the home of the great-great-grandfather of the present king, Abdullah II. The collection of artefacts includes coins, ceramics and 8th-century Islamic stone tablets. Anyone who has travelled the King's Highway may be interested to see an inscribed milestone from the Trajan Rd (the Roman incarnation of this famous thoroughfare). There's a small tourist information centre housed at the museum.

🏃 Activities

Beaches

Look at pictures of Aqaba in a brochure, and you may imagine that the town has already achieved resort status. While there are some good facilities in the top-end hotels, and plenty more in the pipeline, the public beaches at present are more about fully dressed bathing on board your own inflatable lilo than jet-skiing in designer swimwear across palm-fringed bays.

The main free **public beach** is the stretch of sand lined with cafes between the marina and Aqaba Fort. Forget the swimming and join the Jordanians at leisure instead. There are macho youths strutting along the beach in pointed, shiny leather shoes; babies being carried carefully in sports bags and wicker holdalls; footballers of all ages, congregating under the giant Arab revolutionary flag at the end of the beach; men in corduroy coats, sitting cross-legged on the seawall; pink-jacketed children racing between poles of candyfloss; young women seated demurely on a variety of four-legged transport; and listless vendors half bothering to wave snacks or Chinese trinkets at whoever

passes by. Inevitably, given the garrulous and hospitable nature of Jordanian people, you won't be left alone for long.

If you are determined to bare some skin and take a dip in the Gulf, head to a private beach attached to one of the five-star hotels.

Mövenpick Resort Hotel
SWIMMING

(⌨/fax 2034020; www.movenpick-aqaba.com; King Hussein St; day use JD40; ⊙8am until sunset) Day use of a clean beach, three pools, health club, sauna and Jacuzzi; includes a JD10 drink voucher.

InterContinental Hotel
SWIMMING

(⌨2092222; www.intercontinental.com; King Hussein St; day use JD50; ⊙8am until sunset) Day use of beautiful gardens, pools and beach; includes a JD25 food and drink voucher.

Water Sports

The top-end hotels are well equipped for various water sports (prices start from JD10 per hour). Water-skiing, jet-skiing, windsurfing and kayaking are some of the water sports on offer between March and October. All hotels can organise snorkelling and diving, although these activities are best carried out from the diving clubs south of town (see p27).

Cruises

Each of the big hotels has a cruise boat for swimming and lunch by day, or sundowners and belly dancing by night. In addition, several boats moor by the harbour office in the marina waiting for sufficient customers to leave.

Sindbad
CRUISE

(⌨2050077; www.sinbadjo.com; Marina) This local company operates a number of popular cruises around the Gulf of Aqaba. Prices range from JD15 per person for a two-hour sunset cruise, to JD29 for a half-day trip with snorkelling (equipment included) and barbecue. The cruises operate on a daily basis and depart from the end of the pier. Most hotels can book you on these trips, or simply turn up 30 minutes before departure (1pm for barbecue trip; 6pm for a sunset cruise) and buy a ticket from the Sindbad staff.

Saif Marine Transport
CRUISE

(3hr cruise JD12 per person, with dinner JD25) Runs a three-hour coffeeshop cruise each evening, or take the barbecue dinner cruise. There is no need to call or book – just turn up at sunset.

Glass-Bottom Boats

If you don't have time to go diving or snorkelling, the next best thing is a glass-bottom boat. The ride is fun, but the amount of fish and coral on view is usually disappointing unless you get away from central Aqaba. This entails hiring a boat for at least two to three hours.

Boats, which operate between 6am and sunset, congregate along the central public beach or at a jetty in front of Aqaba Fort. The rate for a boat (holding about 10 people) is JD15 per 20 minutes, JD25 for 40 minutes and JD35 for an hour. A three-hour trip costs JD100 and a half-day trip is around JD150. During any of the trips, you can swim, snorkel or fish (bring your own equipment) and it makes a great excursion if you can get a group together.

Hammam

Aqaba Turkish Baths   BATHHOUSE
(☎2031605; King Hussein St; ☉10am-10pm) Offers the full works – massage, steam bath and scrubbing – for a very reasonable JD12. Women are theoretically welcome to attend, but as 'special arrangements' need to be made (single men are evacuated for the session and a female attendant found), entry isn't guaranteed. Book a couple of hours ahead on a quiet day and you could be in luck. Couples can make similar arrangements.

Bab Al-Hara   BATHHOUSE
(☎07 99663800; Near Petra Moon Hotel; ☉10am-10pm) Offers similar services to the Aqaba Turkish Baths for the same price. Arrangements can be made for women.

☞ Tours

There are a number of good travel agents in town offering diving and snorkelling trips (see p27), tours in Jordan (including to Wadi Rum, see p220), and longer trips to neighbouring Egypt, and Israel and the Palestinian Territories. Some agencies also organise day trips to Petra (JD40 per person for a minimum of three; JD80 for one); these trips are worth considering if you only have one day to spend at Petra and don't want to spend half of it waiting for public transport. Bear in mind that the price doesn't include entrance fees and you'll find the amount of time you get to spend at the site is disappointingly brief. Some of the more experienced agencies include:

ON A RARE RAINY DAY IN AQABA...

Try visiting the **Jordan Experience Show** (☎2022200; Aqaba Gateway; admission JD7; ☉shows noon, 1pm, 3pm, 4pm & 5pm) This 35-minute multimedia experience features the highlights of Jordan, beginning with a Disney-style walk through the Siq and followed by a simulated flying-carpet tour of Jordan, complete with movable seats. At least four people are needed for the shows to run, so this attraction is only sporadically open. Unless you speak Arabic, ask your hotel to call ahead to ascertain current timings.

International Traders   TOUR
(☎2013757; www.traders.com.jo; Al-Hammamat al-Tunisieh St) The price reflects the reliable and quality service.

Nyazi Tours   TOUR
(☎2022801; www.nyazitours.com; King Hussein St) Recommended adventure tour company run by Nyazi Shaba'an, former Director of Antiquities & Tourism in Petra. Camping, hiking, jeep tours and camel trips along Wadi Umran.

Wadi Rum Desert Services   TOUR
(☎2063882; www.wadirumdesertservice.tripod.com; ☉8.30am-11pm) Located next to Al-Shami Restaurant, off Zahran St.

🛌 Sleeping

Aqaba is a popular place for Jordanian and Saudi tourists in winter (October to March), with the season (and hotel rates) peaking in April, May, October and November. Holidaymakers also flock to Aqaba from northern Jordan during long weekends and public holidays, especially around Eid al-Adha (immediately after the hajj). At these times, prices may increase by as much as 30% and you must book in advance.

Campers, overlanders and dive enthusiasts should consider staying at one of the camps along the beach south of Aqaba (see p220). The long-established camps have the budget sector well weighed off here.

Unless otherwise stated, all hotels listed here include satellite TV, air-conditioning and private bathroom with hot water. Most cheaper hotels don't include breakfast but can usually rustle up something uninspiring for around JD2 to JD5; better still, go for beans and *labneh* in the nearest cafe. On the whole, midrange accommodation in Aqaba offers better value for money. As for top-end accommodation, don't dismiss the big hotels as characterless chains: in Aqaba, as at the Dead Sea, each of these luxury complexes involves stunning design and sympathetic landscaping.

TOP CHOICE InterContinental Hotel   RESORT $$$

(☎2092222; www.intercontinental.com; King Hussein St; r from US$120; ✲@✈🏊) An imposing full stop at the end of the bay, the InterCon boasts less of an infinity pool than an 'infinity sea': on a calm day, the Gulf of Aqaba stretches in one seamless ripple all the way to Egypt. With exceptional landscape gardening, pools, a lazy river and a terracotta army of fully grown palm trees, the InterCon has stolen the top spot in Aqaba's luxury accommodation, providing the kind of practical service that has made this chain a favourite throughout the Middle East. With six restaurants and a shopping arcade among its many amenities, you won't want to move on in a hurry.

Aqaba Gulf Hotel   HOTEL $$$

(☎2016636; www.aqabagulf.com; King Hussein St; r JD130; ✲@🌐🏊) This excellent hotel (the only one in Aqaba with a tennis court) is just across the road from the Aqaba Gateway complex. It was the first hotel to be built in Aqaba and it has quite an honour roll of guests. The stained-wood, split-level dining room looks thoroughly dated, like the rest of the common-use areas, but this is not a criticism. The large, extremely comfortable rooms (ask for a double-window corner room for great sunsets), copious breakfasts and excellent staff make this an old favourite.

Mövenpick Resort Hotel   RESORT $$$

(☎2034020; www.movenpick-aqaba.com; King Hussein St; r from US$125; ✲@🏊🍽) This stylish hotel, spreadeagled across the main road, has a palatial interior decorated with mosaics and Moroccan lamps. The huge pool and beach complex has three pools, a gym (open 6am to 10pm), lovely gardens and the Red Sea Grill. Other restaurants include the Palm Court, and Italian and Lebanese restaurants, both with outdoor terraces.

Kempinski Hotel   RESORT $$$

(☎2090888; www.kempinski.com; King Hussein St; r from US$130; ✲@🏊🍽) Lavish, multilayered swimming pools, six restaurants and bars (including the renowned Fish Inn and Black Pearl) and a spa make this super-luxury hotel worth top dollar. Despite being more angular and austere than its neighbours, the service is flawless. A comprehensive tour service covers camping and balloon trips at Wadi Rum and overnight trips to Petra.

Captain's Hotel   BOUTIQUE HOTEL $$

(☎2060710; www.captains-jo.com; An-Nahda St; s/d JD75/85; ✲@✈🏊) Aqaba's version of a boutique hotel, the Captain's began life as a fish restaurant (still functioning on the ground floor and with an excellent reputation) and evolved, one storey at a time, into this stylish new accommodation. With a bronze horse in the foyer and copper-tiled flooring, compact rooms (with flat-screen TV), Arabian-style furniture and wonderful bathrooms with massage showers, this is an upmarket choice for a midrange price. Other facilities include an attractive pool, sauna and Jacuzzi.

Golden Tulip   HOTEL $$

(☎2051234; www.goldentulipaqaba.com; As-Sadah St; s/d JD65/80, low season weekdays JD35/50; ✲✈🏊) This thoroughly recommended hotel in the centre of town is comfortable and modern. It has a fashionable foyer (complete with vocal African Grey parrot) and tasteful karaoke bar where the teetotal bartender mixes a superb cocktail. The rooms are cosy and bright but beware knees and elbows in the surprisingly mean-sized bathrooms. The reception desk is manned by uniformly charming staff.

Al-Cazar Hotel   HOTEL $$

(☎2014131; www.alcazarhotel.orange.jo; An-Nahda St; s/d/tr from JD35/40/50; ✲🏊) If you're looking to stay somewhere with a bit of character, this faded old grand dame of Aqaba – with two dozen overgrown Washington palms in the front garden, an enormous empty lobby and a bar with outrageous filigree plaster – is the place to come. The spacious rooms have bathrooms with multiple mirrors and marble surfaces that must have looked grand in their day. A shuttle bus from the hotel to Club Murjan, a beachfront sports centre south of Aqaba, runs twice a day at 9am and 1.30pm for JD9 per person.

Moon Beach Hotel   HOTEL $

(☎2013316; ashrafsaad77@yahoo.com; King Hussein St; s/d/tr with sea view JD18/30/35; ✲) Near the fort, this is undoubtedly the best of the budget options. The foyer is a welcoming mixture of heavy wooden furniture, matching drapes and some interesting photographs of old Aqaba. Most rooms have sea views, though the dark red furnishings, faded carpet, chocolate paint and odd plastic-panelled corridors won't be to everyone's liking. The delightful family-run management easily makes up for the dodgy decor.

Al-Amer Hotel
HOTEL $

(☑/fax 2014821; Raghadan St; s/d/tr JD20/25/30; ❄) Don't get too excited at the powder blue reception with its gorgeous chandeliers: the French Rococo stops here! That said, the bright, clean rooms – especially those at the front – make this a quality budget option, though the rooms need a repaint. If you get peckish in the night, the Syrian Palace Restaurant is right next door.

Al-Shula Hotel
HOTEL $

(☑2015153; alshulahotel@yahoo.com; Raghadan St; s/d/tr JD22/27/34; ❄) With its black-and-white marble reception desk and painted mirrors, the Al-Shula has been thoughtfully redecorated. Most rooms have views to the sea across the new mosque complex – good for a 4.30am wake-up call!

Aquavista Hotel
HOTEL $$

(☑2051620; humanehabco@gmail.com; An-Nahda St; incl breakfast r JD50; ❄) The rooms in this functional, nondescript hotel are clean and comfortable – if you can look beyond the lime green walls and yellow ceilings.

Aqaba Star
HOTEL $

(☑2016480; fax 2018147; King Hussein St; s/d JD30/35; ❄) This modern, Arabian-style two-storey hotel with its pillars and blue linoleum tiles caters mainly for Arabic clientele but the rooms are reasonable, if under-decorated. Ask for a room with sea views and a balcony.

Al-Kholi Hotel
HOTEL $

(☑/fax 2030152; Zahran St; s/d JD15/20, d with balcony JD25; ❄) This very basic hotel is at least central. The low ceilings are a serious inconvenience to tall people but if you ignore the damp patches on the walls and the smell of food pervading the rooms, this is a clean enough option if you get stuck for somewhere cheap.

✖ Eating

Aqaba has a large range of places to eat to suit all budgets. The seafood is particularly delicious: try Aqaba's signature dish of *sayadieh* (fish layered onto rice with a tomato,

onion and pepper sauce). For shwarma (meat sliced off a spit and stuffed in a pocket of pita-type bread with chopped tomatoes and garnish), grills and snacks, the dusty array of stalls and restaurants along King Hussein St spill onto the pavement and are popular with locals. For a wider choice of budget meals, have a prowl along Raghadan St – the eateries range from little more than a collection of open-air tables serving tea, hummus, *fuul* (fava-bean paste) and felafel, to the larger restaurants listed here.

There are plenty of modern and sophisticated restaurants in the newer part of town, especially along either side of As-Sadah St, and in the Aqaba Gateway complex. The ones included in the recommendations below all serve excellent seafood, together with international meat and vegetarian dishes. Note that many restaurants do not have a license to sell alcohol.

TOP CHOICE Ali Baba Restaurant
JORDANIAN $$

(☑2013901; Raghadan St; mains JD5-12 ☺8am-midnight; ❄🌿) With its wooden awning, leafy cannas and potted palm trees, this favourite still draws the crowds. It has a large outdoor seating area wrapped around the corner facade and offers a large menu of mezze, grilled meats and fish, including *sayadieh* (JD8.500). It's a sociable place for breakfast or a fresh juice between meals, but it really comes into its own in the evening when it is more than just a restaurant – it is the amiable heart of old town Aqaba.

Captain's Restaurant
SEAFOOD $$$

(☑2016905; An-Nahda St; mains JD8-15; ☺8am-midnight; ❄) Serving consistently good quality seafood, including *sayadieh* and seafood salad, this is a perennially popular choice for locals with something to celebrate. The stylish and amiable restaurant was so successful, they built a whole boutique hotel on the same site for those too full to make it home!

Royal Yacht Club Restaurant
ITALIAN $$$

(☑2022404; www.romero-jordan.com; Royal Yacht Club; mains JD8-15; ☺noon-4.30pm & 6-11pm; ❄🌿) With views of the marina, this elegant, wood-panelled restaurant is the place to savour a romantic sunset and mingle with Aqaba's nouveau riche. The mostly Italian menu includes Mediterranean favourites like crab, avocado, shrimp and artichoke salad, mussels Provençale, and homemade vegetarian pasta. Reservations are recommended.

TOP CHOICE Blue Bay

SEAFOOD $$

(☑2070755; As-Sadah St; mains JD7; ⊘10am-1am; ❄☑) The seafood menu here is a cut above the rest with large portions of beautifully prepared catch-of-the-day, presented with finesse. The sleek glass tables and open-plan upper seating area attract Jordan's in-crowd and groups of 'in-the-know' expats. Imaginative salads make this a good choice for vegetarians.

Al-Mabrouk Beach Touristic Restaurant

SEAFOOD $$

(Raghadan St; mains JD10; ⊘9am-11.30pm; ❄) This attractive restaurant is a friendly and popular place for a large fish supper, with glass-top tables decorated with shells outside, or air-conditioned dining indoors. A local favourite is a pot of Al-Mabrouk fish, mussels, calamari and tomatoes (JD13).

Floka Restaurant

SEAFOOD $$$

(☑2030860; An-Nahda St; mains JD8-15; ⊘12.30-11.30pm; ❄) Choose from the catch of the day (which normally includes sea bream, silver snapper, grouper and goatfish) and select how you would like it cooked. Service can be a little slow but it's a friendly, unpretentious establishment. There's indoor and outdoor seating.

Formosa Restaurant

CHINESE $$

(☑2060098; Aqaba Gateway complex; mains JD5-10; ⊘noon-midnight; ❄☑) For an excellent Chinese perspective on seafood (and with plenty of meat and vegetable options on the menu too), you couldn't better this cosy, intimate restaurant.

Syrian Palace Restaurant

SYRIAN $

(☑/fax 2014788; Raghadan St; mains JD3-10; ⊘10am-midnight) As the name implies, this is a good option for Syrian and Jordanian food, including fish dishes. It's next to the Al-Amer Hotel.

Al-Tarboosh Restaurant

PASTRY $

(☑2018518; Raghadan St; pastries around 200 fils; ⊘7.30am-midnight) This is one of two neighbouring pastry shops that offer a great range of meat, cheese and vegetable *sambousas*. Order a bag for takeaway or sit and eat them straight from the oven at the tables outside.

Eibal Coffee

NUTS

(☑2035555; As-Sadah St; 1kg nuts from JD8.500; ⊘10am-midnight) For upmarket nuts scooped from wooden drawers, this is the place to come. Try the smoked nuts: the mixed pistachio, cashew and almonds are irresistibly moreish. Ask for a kilo of nuts to be bagged in 250g bags to avoid them going soft in the humidity.

Quick Eats

There are popular **beachfront cafes** between Aqaba Fort and the marina. The front-row seats are so close to the water that you can wet your toes while you whet your appetite. No alcohol is served at these public places.

The **juice stands** (750 fils-JD1.500) on Ar-Razi St are popular meeting places for travellers.

On a hot day, stop by **Hani Ali** (Raghadan St), a paradise of traditional sweets and delicious ice cream, or **Gelato Uno** (off An-Nahda St) behind the Hertz car-rental office. For something even more sublime, check out the **ice-cream parlour** and **cake shop** at the Mövenpick Resort Hotel and order a 'special' (you don't have to enter the hotel – there's access from King Hussein St).

Self-catering

The best supermarket is **Humam Supermarket** (☑2015721; Al-Petra St; ⊘8.30am-2.30pm & 4-11pm). **Safeway** (⊘8am-midnight) is quite a hike, 750m north of Princess Haya Hospital. There are a couple of modern American-style malls in and around town.

The **fruit and vegetable souq**, hidden at the southern end of Raghadan St, is the best place to buy healthy, locally grown items for a picnic. There are lots of **bakeries** around, including one on Al-Hammamat al-Tunisieh St.

🍷 Drinking

Many of the midrange and all the top-end hotels have bars, and most offer some kind of happy hour from 6pm to 7.30pm. Around the As-Sadah St loop, there are a number of open-air coffeehouses with armchairs on the pavement, selling sheesha, coffee and soft drinks.

Al-Fardos Coffee Shop

COFFEEHOUSE

(coffee 500 fils) Just off Zahran St, this is a traditional coffeehouse where local men sip *qahwa*, play backgammon and stare open-mouthed at Arabic music videos. It has a pleasant outdoor setting, and foreign women are welcome.

Friends

BAR

(☑2013466; upper storey, Aqaba Gateway; beer JD2.500-3; ⊘3.30pm-3am) This relaxed and friendly place, with sensible prices, is on a terrace that captures the sea breezes. Try the Dizzy Buddah (JD7); have two, and you may as well sleep over.

Rovers Return PUB
(☎2032030; Aqaba Gateway; large beer JD5; ☺12.30pm-12.30am) An aerial version of the Amman expat favourite (it's located in a mock lighthouse), this pub attracts a young crowd. If you're British and feeling homesick, stay for fish and chips or roast beef (JD9) and watch three-screen football. The only downside is that the compact space can get oppressively smoky.

Royal Yacht Club Bar BAR
(☎2022404; ☺5-11pm; beer JD3.500-4.500) Above the Romero Restaurant in the marina, this is an elegant rendezvous with a harbourside view of the sunset.

Wisalak Cafe CAFE
(☎2022600; sheesha JD3; milkshakes from JD3; ☺3pm-midnight; ✳) If you want to get off the road for a bit of peace and quiet, try this cosy cafe, which has an upstairs seating area.

☆ Entertainment

There's not too much in the way of entertainment in Aqaba, but **Aqaba Gateway** (☎2012200; Al-Baladiah Circle) has a popular collection of restaurants, fast-food outlets, shops and two bars.

🔒 Shopping

Aqaba is a fun place to shop, especially at night when Jordanian holidaymakers treat the shops as an excuse to cruise around in large groups, enjoying the company of strangers. Head for the souq in the older part of town, where shops are bulging at the seams with loofahs, colourful Arab headscarves, Dead Sea products, denim and cotton clothing, and of course nuts and spices.

Aqaba is also a good place to buy jewellery, with a few gold and silver shops in the souq and several shops selling beautiful beads (see boxed text, below).

Sam's Jewellers JEWELLERY
(☎2012100; btwn King Hussein St & An-Nahda St; ☺9.30am-11pm) With designs 'inspired by my

AQABA, WADI RUM & THE DESERT HIGHWAY AQABA

BUYING BEADS IN AQABA

Walk around Aqaba's souq in the middle of town, and your eye will soon be drawn to chaotic windows festooned with brightly coloured beads. There are strings of blue lapis lazuli; creamy tiger's eye; spangled goldstone; and smooth round beads of pink coral, draped next to their plastic imitations. Beads of amber, agate, turquoise, malachite, jet, amethyst and jade are stored in jars like a mixture of all-sorts in a corner sweetshop. Most of these magnificent beads of natural stone are imported from neighbouring countries but they are usually crafted locally into necklaces, earrings and bracelets, often by the shop owners themselves. If a piece is not 'Made in Jordan', the vendor is usually quick to tell you so.

You can ask the bead-shop owner to make a piece from your own design. Think 'Bedouin', and add a few silver beads among the stones, or think 'ethnic' and rope the stones onto leather or camel-hair cord. The price of beads depends on the quality of the stones used and the intricacy of the work, but a simple strand starts at around JD5, while a multiple strand of good stones can cost JD100 or more. Men not fond of wearing jewellery needn't feel left out: *misbah* (prayer beads – usually in sets of 33, 66 or 99 in honour of the 99 names and attributes of Allah) make a handy introduction into Arab society across the Middle East. Or you could buy an ever-popular agate ring. Note that the stones are almost invariably clasped in silver as it is considered *haram* (forbidden) for Muslim men to wear gold.

Jewellery may seem like mere decoration, but beware that this may not be the way the locals see it. Choose a necklace with a central medallion inscribed with Allah's name, for example, and you may be exhorted to remove the necklace before using the bathroom; if you admire someone else's jewellery, they may feel obliged to give it to you; ubiquitous eye-ball beads are accorded almost mystic powers in fending off the 'evil eye'. If the bead vendor is particularly pleased with the way a piece hangs about your neck, he or she may well say 'ma sha'Allah' to protect you from the envy of onlookers. In fact, enter a bead shop in Jordan and you quickly realise that jewellery is less about decorating the body than making a statement of the soul.

mother and my aunts', the jeweller takes personal pride in his very unusual necklaces of silver, coral, amber and semiprecious stones, which combine traditional motifs with modern settings.

Noor Al-Hussein
Foundation Shop HANDICRAFTS

(☑2012601; ☺8am-6pm, to 7pm May-Sep) For a fine selection of handicrafts, it's worth calling in on the Noor Al-Hussein Foundation shop, located in the Aqaba Fort complex, opposite the museum. Profits help support marginalised communities throughout Jordan. Items include silver jewellery from Wadi Musa, petroglyph designs from Wadi Rum, kilims, clothes, embroidery, basketware and ceramics. Credit cards are accepted.

Photo Hagop PHOTOGRAPHY

(☑2012025; Zahran St; ☺8.30am-11pm) Branches around town offer digital accessories.

Redwan Bookshop BOOKS

(☑2013704; redwanbook@hotmail.com; Zahran St; ☺7.30am-12.30pm & 4-9pm) One of the best bookshops in Jordan with an extensive selection of newspapers, hard-to-find Jordanian titles, Lonely Planet guidebooks, and English, German and French novels.

Yamani Library BOOKS

(☑/fax 2012221; Zahran St; ☺9am-2.30pm & 6-10pm) A few doors to the north, Yamani has a better range of English novels.

❶ Information

Dangers & Annoyances

Women travellers have reported varying degrees of harassment from local lads on the public beaches. Foreign women may feel less conspicuous wearing loose shirts and baggy shorts over a swimsuit or, better still, using the facilities of one of the hotels.

Emergency

Police station (☑2012411, 191; Ar-Reem St) Opposite the bus station.
Princess Haya Hospital (☑2014111; Ash-Shrif al-Hussein bin Ali St) Well-equipped and modern. It's just north of Princess Haya Square roundabout.

Internet Access

Aqaba has a good sprinkling of internet cafes, particularly along As-Sadah St, most of which charge around JD1 to JD2 per hour.
10zll Internet Cafe (☑2022009; As-Sadah St; per hr JD1, ☺24hr) Next to Days Inn, this large establishment has coffee & soft drinks.

Money

There are dozens of banks and ATMs around the city. Many are located along the southern side of Al-Hammamat al-Tunisieh St.

Numerous moneychangers are congregated around the corner of Zahran and Ar-Razi Sts. They keep longer hours than the banks, and most change travellers cheques without commission, though check the rate first.

Post

DHL (☑2012039, 2011385; Al-Petra St)
General post office (☺7.30am-7pm Sat-Thu, to 1.30pm Fri) Opposite Zahran St in the centre of town.

Telephone

There are a number of telephone booths outside the general post office, and several stalls nearby sell telephone cards. Other private telephone agencies are located on the main streets, and some moneychangers also offer telephone services. Note that international calls from Aqaba are up to five times cheaper than in Wadi Rum.

Tourist Information

The **tourist office** (☑/fax 2013363; Baladiya Circle; ☺8am-2.30pm Sun-Thu) is located in a kiosk in the middle of a new park between carriageways. The tourist office just east of the roundabout has lots of leaflets and precious little else despite friendly staff. There's another branch inside Aqaba Museum.

Visa Extensions

Aqaba Special Economic Zone Authority (ASEZA; ☑2091000; www.aqabazone.com; Ash-Sherif al-Hussein bin Ali St-Amman Hwy) Opposite Safeway. You need to register here if you were given a free visa on arrival in Aqaba and plan to stay in Jordan for more than 14 days. The website has some useful information about Aqaba.

Police station (☑2012411; Ar-Reem St; ☺7am-9pm Sat-Thu) Opposite the bus station. This is the place to come for an extension of your visa for up to three months. These extensions are usually available on the spot and are free. It's best to go earlier in the day (8am to 3pm). Aqaba is the only reliable place to get your visa extended outside Amman.

❶ Getting There & Away

Air

Aqaba has Jordan's only commercial **airport** (☑2012111) outside Amman, although it only awakes from slumber when a flight is about to leave or arrive. There are daily flights to Amman and intermittent charter flights. The airport is 10km north of town.

Royal Jordanian (☎2016555; www.rj.com; Ash-Sherif al-Hussein bin Ali St; ⏰9am-5pm Sun-Thu) Operates flights to Amman's Queen Alia International Airport on Friday and Saturday. Their office at the airport is the place to buy, confirm or change Royal Jordanian or Royal Wings air tickets. Tickets to Amman cost JD37 one way.

Royal Wings (www.royalwings.com.jo) A subsidiary of Royal Jordanian flies between Aqaba and Amman twice daily.

Boat

There are two daily boat services to Nuweiba in Egypt. For information about these services, see p320.

Buy your ticket at the ferry terminal when departing, except during hajj (see p313) when you may need to book in advance.

Bus

There are buses to Amman and Irbid from Aqaba. It's worth paying for the comfort, speed and air-conditioning of a JETT or Trust private bus. Book tickets for these at least a day in advance. Buses for both companies leave from outside their offices.

JETT bus office (☎2015222; King Hussein St), next to the Mövenpick Resort Hotel, has buses six times daily to Amman (JD7.500, four hours), between 7am and 6pm. The office is a 10-minute walk from the centre.

Trust International Transport (☎2032200; just off An-Nahda St) has four daily buses to Amman (JD7, four hours) at 7.30am, 11.30am, 2.30pm and 8.30pm. There are also buses to Irbid (JD9, 5½ hours) at 8.30am and 3.30pm.

Ordinary public buses travel between the main bus/minibus station in Aqaba and Amman's south (Wahadat) station (JD5.500, five hours) about every hour between 7am and 3pm, sometimes later.

Car

Aqaba has branches of all the major car-hire agencies. Most charge a 'drop fee' (JD35) if you wish to leave the car in Amman or at Queen Alia International Airport. Hiring in Aqaba makes some sense as public transport in the south of the country is less frequent and requires more connections than in the north. Aqaba is also far easier to drive around than Amman. The cost of car hire is between JD25 to JD35 per day plus Collision Damage Waiver (average JD8 per day). Enquire about seasonal discounts.

Al-Cazar Car Rental (☎2014131; An-Nahda St)

Avis (☎2022883; www.avis.com.jo; King Hussein St) Located inside the Housing Bank Centre.

Europcar (☎2019988; www.europcar.com.jo; An-Nahda St)

Hertz (☎2016206; www.hertz.com.jo; An-Nahda St)

Thrifty (☎2030313; An-Nahda St) Opposite the Al-Cazar Hotel.

Minibus

To Wadi Musa (for Petra) minibuses (JD5, 2½ hours) leave when full between 7am and 2pm; the exact departure times depend on the number of passengers and you may have a long wait as very few locals use this service. Drivers often offer passengers the option, however, to leave with a minimum of four to five people providing each passenger pays extra.

Two minibuses go to Wadi Rum (JD1.500, one hour) at around 6.30am and, more reliably, 11am. At other times, catch a minibus towards Ma'an, get off at the turn-off to Wadi Rum at Ar-Rashidiyya and then hitch a ride to Rum village (30km) from there.

Minibuses to Amman's south bus station (JD5, five hours) leave when full – approximately every two hours throughout the day.

All of the above minibuses leave from the main Aqaba bus/minibus station on Ar-Reem St. Minibuses to Karak (JD2.500, three hours), via Safi and the Dead Sea Highway, are the exception, leaving from the small station next to the mosque on Al-Humaimah St.

Taxi & Service Taxi

From the main bus/minibus station, service taxis head to Amman (JD9, five hours), but far less regularly than buses and minibuses. To Karak (JD6, three hours) they leave from the small station on Al-Humaimah St. Service taxis start lining up at either station at 6am and many have left by 8am, so get there early. Chartering a taxi costs around JD50 one way to Petra and JD30 to Wadi Rum (JD45 with two hours of waiting time).

Chartering a taxi between Aqaba and the Israel and the Palestinian Territories border costs around JD5. For details on crossing the southern border to/from Israel and the Palestinian Territories, see p320.

ⓘ Getting Around

To/From the Airport

Aqaba's **King Hussein Airport** (☎2012111) is located 10km north of town, close to the border with Israel and the Palestinian Territories. There's no bus to the airport, so take service taxi 8 (around JD2, 15 minutes) from the main bus/minibus station, or take a taxi for around JD8 to JD10.

To/From the Ferry Terminal & Southern Coast

Minibuses (JD1) leave from near the entrance to Aqaba Fort on King Hussein St for the Saudi border via the southern beaches, camps, dive

WORTH A TRIP

ON A WINTER'S DAY SOUTH OF AQABA YOU CAN...

» Snorkel or dive in safe hands at the **Royal Diving Club** (see p28). The club offers a day rate of JD15 to use the beach, pool and other facilities – free if you're coming to dive.

» Learn about what's under the sea without getting your feet wet at the **Aquarium** (☑2015145; admission JD3; ☉8am-5pm). Part of the Marine Science Station complex (7.5km south of Aqaba), the aging and dated tanks nonetheless provide a colourful glimpse of coral, moray eels, turtles and stonefish.

» Laze under a sunshade on the free public beach at the **Marine Park Visitors Centre** (☑2035801). As the headquarters of the Aqaba Marine Park (12km south of Aqaba) it has a jetty, museum, cafe, gift shop and park office. It gets busy on Friday and overrun on public holidays.

» Mull over fishermen's tales and a mint-and-lime juice at **Club Murjan** (☑2012794). This diving centre (13.5km south of Aqaba) offers a good beach, swimming pool, showers, bar and restaurant.

» Explore a Crusader castle on **Pharaoh's Island**. Hotels can book day trips to the island (off Egypt's coast) for around JD40 per person, which includes the entrance fee to the island, Egyptian visa, lunch and transport.

sites and Royal Diving Centre, passing the ferry terminal for boats to Egypt. Minibuses returning to Aqaba can be full of construction workers heading off shift from 2pm to 3pm. A taxi from central Aqaba to the ferry terminal costs around JD8 (JD12 to the southern beaches).

Taxi

Hundreds of private (blue-green) taxis cruise the streets beeping at any tourist (Jordanian or foreign) silly enough to walk around in the heat rather than take an air-conditioned taxi. Taxis are unmetered so prices are entirely negotiable, and the drivers in Aqaba enjoy the sport. Most rides cost between JD1 and JD2. A horse-drawn 'taxi' costs around JD25 for a 30-minute ride.

South Coast

There is only 27km of Jordanian coastline between Israel and the Palestinian Territories and Saudi Arabia. Much of the northern section of shoreline is paved over by the town and container ports of Aqaba. The shore south of the port is protected within the Red Sea Marine Peace Park, and is run in cooperation with Israel and the Palestinian Territories; it is managed locally by the Aqaba Marine Park. Resorts and dive centres are scattered along this precious seaside and the reefs here are in good condition.

While it's probably fair to say that the barren, treeless South Coast is not the prettiest place on earth, it's sufficiently pleasant to relax and enjoy the sunshine or, better still, take a dip or a dive in the clear, warm waters. The Red Sea in this northern end of the Gulf of Aqaba is highly saline; this, together with winds from the north and minimal tides, means the water stays crystal clear, while the average water temperature is 22.5°C in winter and 26°C in summer.

🛏 Sleeping & Eating

There are three main types of accommodation along the South Coast: the hotel attached to the Royal Diving Club at the far southern end of the beach; the budget and traveller-friendly camps clustered around the Bedouin Garden Village, and the luxury hotels of the Tala Bay complex. All include breakfast and have on-site bars and restaurants. They usually provide a free daily shuttle service into Aqaba for residents.

TOP CHOICE **Coral Bay Resort** RESORT $$
(☑2017035; s/d on weekdays JD65/75; weekends JD75/85; ❄@🛜🏊) Part of the Royal Diving Club, this excellent midrange option is a quintessential divers' paradise. If you're planning on undertaking a dive course, or arranging a lengthy dive package, you couldn't ask for a better base. Simple, elegant rooms have bright motifs and there's a sociable bar. The hotel and dive complex is committed to the sustainable development of tourism in and around the dive sites.

Bedouin Garden Village BACKPACKER HOTEL **$**
(☑079 5602521; camping per person JD6, caravan JD10, s/d/t/q JD26/36/46/56; meals JD5-7; ✹🛜🖢) Sun worshippers and dive bums alike will love this funky little spot, which aims to bring a bit of Dahab-style Bedouin flair to Jordan. There's a clutch of cosy rooms and camping pitches but the highlight is swapping stories with fellow travellers beneath the Bedouin tent. Internet use is JD2 per hour. Snorkelling gear costs JD6 for all day use. It's only a 50m walk from a dive site, and neighbouring dive centres can assist with water-bound activities.

Marina Plaza Hotel BOUTIQUE HOTEL **$$$**
(☑2092900; www.marinaplazahotel.com; r from JD100; ✹@🛜🖢) This boutique hotel was the first property to open at Tala Bay, a large project that includes several hotels, such as the Radison and Crowne Plaza, residences, marina, golf course and water-sports club. The developers have worked hard to minimise their impact on the environment, as demanded by the Red Sea Aqaba Marine Park, and the complex is well-landscaped. As is often the case with these complexes, however, it is detached from any sense of being in Jordan, except on public holidays when Jordanians flood in!

❶ Getting There & Around

It is helpful to have a car if you want to head into town from the coast. However, you can always call a cab, and hotels will pick you up in Aqaba with advanced reservations. If you're staying in Aqaba and planning on going diving, most operators will arrange transport to the dive sites.

Minibuses (JD2) leave from near the entrance to Aqaba Fort on King Hussein St for the Saudi border via the southern beaches, camps, dive sites and Royal Diving Club, passing the ferry terminal for boats to Egypt. Minibuses returning to Aqaba can be full of construction workers heading off shift from 2pm to 3pm. A private taxi from central Aqaba to the ferry terminal costs JD8.

WADI RUM & AROUND

Western visitors have been fascinated by the magnificent landscape of Wadi Rum ever since TE Lawrence wrote so evocatively about its sculpted rocks, dunes and Bedouin encampments in *Seven Pillars of Wisdom* in the early 20th century:

The crags were capped in nests of domes, less hotly red than the body of the hill; rather grey and shallow. They gave the finishing semblance of Byzantine architecture to this irresistible place: this processional way greater than imagination...Our little caravan grew self-conscious, and fell dead quiet, afraid and ashamed to flaunt its smallness in the presence of the stupendous hills.

The name Wadi Rum lends itself not just to the broad valley of Lawrence's description, but to a whole series of hills and dunes stretching north to south for over 100km. The central valley, 900m above sea level, fans into an arena dominated by Jebel Rum (1754m), once considered the highest peak in Jordan – an accolade that belongs to Jebel Umm Adaami (1832m) on the Saudi border.

The area has been protected since 1988 and is controlled by Aqaba Special Economic Zone Authority (ASEZA), which has a mandate to promote tourism for the benefit of local communities while protecting the fragile desert environment. With over 100,000 visitors per year using 600 4WDs, this is no mean feat.

Of course, the stewardship of the desert is shared with the local Bedouin who have been roaming the area for centuries. Many of the 5000 Bedouin remaining in the area have now opted for a settled life in the villages of Rum, Diseh and Shakriyyeh but, certainly as far as they are concerned, that does not make them any less Bedouin.

Although not part of the Wadi Rum protected area, the desert spills in equal magnificence into neighbouring areas including Diseh. Indeed, the sandstone monuments and intervening sand dunes are a feature of Jordan's Southern Desert that stretches right to the Saudi border to the south while running out into the plains of the Badia in the northeast.

The most comfortable months for a visit are early spring (March and April) and late autumn (October and November). Winter (December to February) is bitterly cold, summer (May to September) miserably hot: with temperatures of 40°C, this is when you really come to know the meaning of desert! Night-time temperatures can fall to 0°C throughout the year, so come prepared if you're camping or watching the sunset.

Wadi Rum

وادي رم

♪ 03 / ELEV 950M

Wadi Rum is everything you'd expect of a quintessential desert: it is extreme in summer heat and winter cold; it is violent and moody as the sun slices through chiselled siqs (canyons) at dawn or melts the division between rock and sand at dusk; it is exacting on the Bedouin who live in it and vengeful on those who ignore its dangers. For most visitors, on half- or full-day trips from Aqaba or Petra, Wadi Rum offers one of the easiest and safest glimpses of the desert afforded in the region. For the lucky few who can afford a day or two in their itinerary to sleep over at one of the desert camps, it can be an unforgettable way of stripping the soul back to basics.

History

With its many wells and springs, Wadi Rum has been inhabited since prehistoric times. Petroglyphs and burial mounds appear throughout the area, indicating its importance as a hunting and meeting point in ancient times. It was referred to by the Greeks and Romans, who noted its vineyards (now gone), and olive and pine trees (some of which remain on the mountaintops). Some Islamic scholars claim that this is the location of Ad (an ancient Arab tribe), described in the Quran.

About 30,000 inscriptions decorate Wadi Rum's sandstone cliffs. They were made firstly by tribes from Southern Arabia and later by the Nabataeans who settled in Wadi Rum around the 4th century BC. The two tribes lived peacefully side by side, honouring the same deities of Lat and Dushara.

The region owes its fame, however, to the indefatigable TE Lawrence, who stayed here in 1917 during the Arab Revolt – a campaign led by King Hussein bin Ali against the Ottoman Turks in a bid to establish an independent Arab nation. The king's camel- and horse-mounted troops passed through Wadi Rum on their way to conquer Aqaba and some units (including that of Lawrence) returned to use the area as a temporary base before moving north towards Damascus.

The discovery of a Nabataean temple (behind the Rest House) in 1933 briefly returned the spotlight to the desert. A French team of archaeologists completed the excavations in 1997.

ⓘ WADI RUM ITINERARY BUILDER

Even with only have a few hours to spend, you can enjoy some of what Wadi Rum has to offer. Below is a suggestion of what you can do in a given time under your own steam. For 4WD and camel excursions lasting from one hour to one day, see the boxed text on p217 & p219. Obviously, the longer you stay, the more your eyes (and heart) open to the desert.

WITH THIS TIME...	YOU CAN GO THIS FAR...	AND DO THIS MUCH...
En route to elsewhere	Visitor Centre (p222)	Have a panoramic view of Wadi Rum (lit up magnificently at sunset).
One hour	Visitor Centre (p213)	Enjoy a leisurely lunch overlooking Wadi Rum, then visit the museum.
Two hours	Rum Village (p215)	Walk through Wadi Rum on the tarmac road (7km) as far as Rum Village, snack at the Rest House and hitch a lift back.
Three hours	Lawrence's Spring (p215)	Hitch a ride to Rum Village and hike through the sand to Nabataean Temple & Lawrence's Spring.
Half day	Al-Hasany Dunes (p216)	Time your hike from Rum Village to the sands to coincide with sunset.
Overnight	Desert Camp (p220)	Book your accommodation at a Wadi Rum camp through the visitor centre (4WD transport included) or pay extra to ride there by camel.
Two days	Wadi Rum & Diseh Area (p223)	Choose a Wadi Rum camp near Barrah Canyon, then hike through the canyon (5km) to a Diseh camp for the following night

LAWRENCE OF ARABIA

You can't visit Wadi Rum and fail to bump into Lawrence. The legacy of the esoteric Englishman is everywhere – there's even a mountain named *Seven Pillars of Wisdom*, after his famous account of the Arab Revolt. Lawrence's ubiquitous local evocation is something of a cynical one, mind, designed to cash in on the chiefly foreign fascination with this legendary figure.

Lawrence the Legend

It was largely thanks to the promotion of *Seven Pillars of Wisdom* by an American journalist in 1926 that the Lawrence legend was born. In this adventurous account of derring-do, much of which takes place in the desert in and around Wadi Rum, Lawrence casts himself in the role of trusted adviser, brave soldier and ultimately a messiah figure of the Arab cause. However, that was not necessarily how he was regarded from an Arab perspective. Indeed for some he was 'Lawrence Who?' – one among 100,000 Arabs, 10% of whom died in their epic struggle to build a nation.

The Man Behind the Myth

So what are the facts? Born in 1888 into a wealthy English family, Thomas Edward Lawrence ('TE' to his friends) nurtured an early passion for the Middle East. He studied archaeology at Oxford and became bewitched by the region in 1909 while researching his thesis on Crusader castles. With the outbreak of WWI, Lawrence became a natural choice for the intelligence service in Cairo, where he became attached to the Hejaz Expeditionary Force. Lawrence felt a natural sympathy towards the fomenting Arab Revolt, the objective of which was to oust the Turks and create an Arab state. Learning to ride camels with the best of them, and wearing Arab clothing like so many other English adventurers before him, Lawrence accompanied the armies of the great Arab warrior (and later statesman) Emir Faisal in 1917 (p261) and learned a respect for his comrades that lasted a lifetime. Lawrence died in a motorcycle accident in 1935 – a lone and isolated figure, by all accounts, who never fully found in peacetime the sense of purpose and passion he experienced with his Arab comrades in the desert.

Lawrence's Legacy

Some say that Lawrence was embarrassed by the hero status conferred upon him by an adoring English public (in 1927 he changed his name to Shaw and chose to enrol as a private in the RAF); others say he did nothing to put his contribution into a more historically accurate perspective. But Lawrence's legacy is best judged not so much in terms of his disputed military accomplishments, eccentric and brave though they may be, but in the way he immortalised (at least for Western readers) some of the great characters of modern Arab history. It is not just the hallowed names of Auda and Faisal that ring out of these desert at Wadi Rum; to his credit, Lawrence also describes with great tenderness the ordinary foot soldiers of the Arab cause who gave their lives for a brave new world. In the process, Lawrence immortalised forever the magnificence of the Bedouin landscape from which these soldiers hailed, inspiring generations of visitors to see for themselves the wonder of Rum.

Flora & Fauna

Despite its barren appearance, Wadi Rum is home to a complex ecosystem. Small medicinal plants dot the desert and are used to this day by the Bedouin, and during the infrequent rains parts of the desert bloom with over 200 species of flowers and wild grasses. Around the perennial springs, hanging gardens of fig, fern, mint and wild watermelon topple over the rocks, creating shaded lairs for small mammals, birds and reptiles.

For most of the year, the extreme heat and lack of ground water mean that animals only venture out at night. If you sit tight, you may well see a hedgehog, hare or hyrax (a small furry animal implausibly related to the elephant). If you're extremely lucky, you could catch a glimpse of a jackal, wolf, caracal or giant-horned ibex. Sadly, you are not likely to see the highly endangered Arabian oryx, a small group of which were released into Wadi Rum in 2002 (see p236) but which

Wadi Rum

Wadi Rum

didn't like the new accommodation and set out for the rocky plains of neighbouring Saudi Arabia. A new program of reintroduction in a less sandy neighbourhood of Rum, supported by the United Arab Emirates, is so far meeting with better success.

This is big-bird country and there is usually a raptor or two (including sooty falcons, kestrels and eagle owls) circling on the thermals above the desert floor, on the lookout for the desert's plentiful geckos, agamas and lizards. If you see a scorpion, snake or camel spider, count yourself lucky, as they are all shy residents of Rum.

◎ Sights

For the distance between each of the following sights and the visitor centre, together with the time it takes to get there by 4WD or camel, see p217 and p219. These sights are listed in the sequence most visitors encounter them.

FREE Visitor Centre Museum MUSEUM
(◎8am-6pm) While you are buying your ticket to enter Wadi Rum, spare half an hour to visit the delightful and informative museum (next to the restaurant) which helps to give a human context to the desert. The displays also explain environmental issues through information panels in English and natural history exhibits. Ask to see the 10-minute film on some of the highlights of Wadi Rum, shown in the purpose-built cinema.

Seven Pillars of Wisdom ROCK FORMATION
Named in honour of Lawrence's book, this large rock formation, with seven fluted turrets, is easy to see from the road. If you fancy a closer look, a rewarding hike circumnavigates the mountain via **Makharas Canyon** (see p218).

Jebel Umm Ishrin MOUNTAIN
The Seven Pillars rock is connected to the deeply crevassed 'Mother of Twenty', a 20-domed mountain forming the east flank of Wadi Rum. The mountain acquired its name, according to local legend, after a woman killed 19 suitors; she was outwitted by the 20th, so she married him. The whole range turns a magnificent white-capped auburn during sunset.

Jebel Rum MOUNTAIN
The western flank of Wadi Rum is formed by Jebel Rum (1754m) which towers over Wadi Rum village. It is a popular destination for scramblers and climbers who tackle parts of the ancient Thamudic Way to the summit (guide required – ask at the visitor centre).

NAVIGATING WADI RUM

For more information on getting to/from Wadi Rum, see p223.

Highway to Visitor Centre

Wadi Rum is accessed from a tarmac road off the main Desert Highway, an hour's drive from Aqaba. The road is flanked at first by fields of watermelons, but shortly after crossing the Hejaz railway line the splendid scenery begins, becoming more and more spectacular as you reach the mouth of Wadi Rum. The road passes a police post and the junction for the small village of Diseh and continues towards the **visitor centre** (/fax 2090600; www.wadirum.jo; ⏰7am-7pm). This is where all visitors to Wadi Rum must report before venturing further into the valley.

Even if you don't have time to spend a whole day at Wadi Rum, it is worth coming as far as the visitor centre. From this attractive complex you can see Lawrence's **Seven Pillars of Wisdom** (a striking rock formation at the head of the valley), visit the museum, watch a short film about the desert, have lunch and get an idea of what Rum is all about. This is also where you pay the admission fee if you want to proceed further into the valley.

Visitor Centre to Rum Village

Beyond the visitor centre, the road is initially lined by a battered set of 4WDs, accompanied by their Bedouin drivers awaiting the next fare in strict rotation. The tarmac road continues for 7km to the village of Rum. The village, wedged between the towering dome-capped pillars of Wadi Rum, has a few concrete houses, a school, some shops and the Beau Geste-style fort, headquarters of the much-photographed Desert Patrol.

Again, if you don't have much time or can't afford one of the 4WD tours, consider at least reaching the village (you can drive in your own car, hitch or walk). In the village, there's a pleasant rest house with an outside terrace and camping facilities.

Rum Village to Desert Interior

To penetrate the desert beyond the village of Rum, you must either have organised a 4WD trip from the visitor centre, booked a camel or be prepared for an exhausting hike through soft sand. With your own 4WD you can make your own way in, provided you know how to drive off-road.

Beyond the village of Rum, the tarmac runs out and numerous tracks take over, slithering through the soft sand of Wadi Rum to an open area of converging valleys. From here, tracks lead to various points of interest such as rock bridges, desert mushrooms and yardangs. Most 4WD and camel tours make a circular route through the intersecting wadis of the area before returning to the visitor centre.

Outside this heavily visited area is a portion of desert known as the **Wilderness Area**. It is forbidden to take a 4WD into this protected zone but you can hike there with a guide.

For overnight stays, there are several Bedouin campsites with rudimentary facilities within Wadi Rum and the neighbouring Diseh area, on the rim of the reserve.

Books & Maps

If you are planning any hikes and scrambles, bring a detailed guidebook and map; if you plan to do some serious hiking and rock climbing, it's vital to organise a guide in advance.

British climber Tony Howard has spent a lot of time exploring Wadi Rum, and has co-written with Di Taylor the excellent and detailed *Treks & Climbs in Wadi Rum, Jordan* and a pocket-sized version called *Walks & Scrambles in Wadi Rum*. Treks and climbs around Wadi Rum are also mentioned in Howard and Taylor's *Walking in Jordan*. Buy these books before arriving in Wadi Rum.

The free Wadi Rum brochure has a map showing the major sites and is available from the visitor centre. The 1997 *Map of Rum* is contoured and detailed for a small section of northern Wadi Rum (ie around Rum village). The most detailed and informative map is *Wadi Rum Tourist Plan*, published by International Traditional Services Corp, but it's not widely available.

Similar pathways, once used for hunting ibex and collecting medicinal plants, link one massif to another throughout the area giving limitless scope for hiking, scrambling and climbing (see p216).

Rum Village & Village Plaza VILLAGE

Rum village, in the middle of Wadi Rum, houses a small community of Bedouin who have chosen to settle, rather than continue a more traditional nomadic life. The village has a rest house, restaurants and a couple of grocery shops. It also has the last piece of tarmac before the desert proper.

In the former police station, a local handicrafts centre is intermittently open and is expected eventually to house a small museum. The small, squat Rum Fort has been recently renovated.

Nabataean Temple TEMPLE

On a small hill in Rum village, about 400m behind the Rest House (follow the telephone poles), are the limited ruins of a 2000-year-old temple, dedicated to the deity Lat. Inside the Rest House an information board describes the temple and its excavation. The ruins are important because they are evidence of a permanent Nabataean settlement, built on the earlier foundations of a temple built by the Arab tribe of Ad. The baths in a villa behind the temple are the earliest so far discovered in Jordan. Near the temple are some **inscriptions** by hunters and nomads dating back to the 2nd century BC.

Lawrence's Spring (Ain Ash-Shallalah) SPRING

A short walk from the Nabataean temple, you'll see a white water tank at the opening of Wadi Shallalah. After the tank, a path climbs the hill to a spring named in honour of Lawrence's evocative description of it in the *Seven Pillars of Wisdom:*

> In front of us a path, pale with use,
> zigzagged up the cliff-plinth ... From
> between [the] trees, in hidden crannies
> of the rock, issued strange cries; the
> echoes, turned into music, of the voices
> of the Arabs watering camels at the
> springs which there flowed out three
> hundred feet above ground.

Together with other springs in the area, this natural water spout that tumbles into a leafy 'paradise just five feet square' allowed

SUNSET & SUNRISE VANTAGE POINTS

Dusk and dawn are the most magical (and cooler) times to be in the desert. The best vantage points differ according to the time of year but you can't go far wrong if you park yourself at **Umm Sabatah**. Jeep drivers can take you there and either wait or pick you up later (they are reliable about such things); or arrange a sunset tour which can include a traditional Bedouin dinner for a negotiable price. Ask at the visitor centre for details.

Rum to become an important waterhole for caravans travelling between Syria and Arabia. Look out for a small shrine dedicated to Lat, an aqueduct used to channel the water from the spring, and inscriptions on the rock face. Notice too the aroma of mint in the air: it grows wild among the ferns and trees of this shady place. To walk to the spring and back (2.5km) from the Rest House takes about 1½ hours.

Ain Abu Aineh SPRING

Often mistaken for Lawrence's Spring, the 'Father of Aineh Spring' is piped down the mountain into a large tank for Bedouin sheep, goats and camels. Look out for a large boulder near the tank: it is covered with Thamudic inscriptions, proving the spring has been used for a similar purpose for millennia. To reach Ain Abu Aineh, head south from the Rest House and follow the eastern side of Jebel Rum for 3km (a 1½-hour walk in soft sand). The site in itself is not particularly special but the views across to Jebel Khazali are wonderful, especially at sunset when the whole amphitheatre of stone and sand turns orange.

Lawrence's House (Al-Qsair) RUIN

There is little left of this building, erected on the Nabataean ruins of a water cistern. Nonetheless, legend has it that Lawrence stayed here during the Arab Revolt and that makes it a must on the regular 4WD circuits of the area. Near the building is a Nabataean inscription that mentions the area's ancient name of Iram. The remote location and supreme view of the **red sand dunes** are the main attraction.

Al-Hasany Dunes
SAND DUNES

While there are dunes in several places around Wadi Rum, the most striking are the red sands that bank up against Jebel Umm Ulaydiyya. If you are on a 4WD tour, drivers will stop near a pristine slope for you to plod your way to the crest of the dune. To reach the dunes on foot from the visitor centre takes about three hours, partly through soft sand.

Alameleh inscriptions
PETROGLYPHS

Thamudic and Nabataean inscriptions, depicting camel caravans, hunting warriors and various animals, are common throughout the Wadi Rum area. The Alameleh inscriptions, near to the Seven Pillars of Wisdom and on the edge of the Diseh district, are some of the most comprehensive and best preserved.

Anfaishiyya inscriptions
PETROGLYPHS

Another wonderful set, the Anfaishiyya inscriptions are scratched into the smooth surface of a huge, vertical rock face.

Rock Bridges

There are many chiselled rock formations in the area, where the wind has whittled away the softer parts of the sandstone, leaving the tortured forms of harder rock behind. The most striking of these formations are the rock bridges that arch from one rock mass to another. You can see several of these bridges around the area but there are three famous ones.

The largest of the three is the **Burdah Rock Bridge**, precariously perched about 80m above surrounding rock. There's a precipitous hike to the summit.

The smaller **Umm Fruth Rock Bridge** is tucked away in a remote corner of the desert and can easily be climbed without gear or a guide. It can be a busy spot at lunchtime but the best time to see it is in the late afternoon when full sunlight hits the rear side of the arch.

Little Rock Bridge (Rakhabat al-Wadak) is easier to climb and more accessible than Burdah Rock Bridge, but is not as impressive. The views, however, across a broad expanse of desert valley, are superb.

Siqs & Canyons

An easy siq to explore is the narrow fissure that cuts into **Jebel Khazali**. You can explore on foot for about 150m, far enough to appreciate the shade and the cool and to see inscriptions made by the ancients who used the siq for the same purpose. Look out for drawings of ostriches, pairs of feet and a woman giving birth. You need ropes and a guide to penetrate further and 4WD transport to reach the siq.

A popular destination by 4WD is **Siq Umm Tawaqi**, a beautiful area with mature trees sprouting apparently from the rock face. Locals have carved the humorous likeness of TE Lawrence (complete with Arab headdress), and two other prominent figures of the Arab Revolt, into a stone plinth in the middle of the siq.

Numerous other canyons riddle the area, including the 5km-long **Barrah Canyon**; they all offer opportunities for hiking, camel trekking, climbing or simply napping in the shade and absorbing the special atmosphere of Wadi Rum's hidden heartland.

🏃 Activities

Although you could have a pleasant day out in the Wadi Rum area by calling in at the visitor centre and ambling along to the village of Rum, you will have a more interesting experience if you penetrate deeper into the desert. This requires leaving the tarmac behind and going 'off-road'. You can do this most effectively by hiring a 4WD vehicle with driver; by hiring a camel or a horse with a mounted escort; or by hiking, scrambling or climbing with or without a guide. For a list of guides, see p224.

4WD Excursions

The easiest way to see the largest number of sights in the least amount of time is to arrange a 4WD trip. This is easily done through the excursion office at the visitor centre on arrival.

Rates for 4WD excursions are fixed and listed on a board outside the excursion office at the visitor centre. The prices are per vehicle, not per person, so it can help with costs if you put together a group in Wadi Musa or Aqaba (not easy to do on arrival at Wadi Rum). Most 4WDs seat six people; some have bench seats in the back offering better views than the closed-in cabs but they are fearfully cold or boiling hot in extreme seasons.

If you take the vehicle for a day, don't forget to pack food and water for you and your driver. You can buy the basics of a rudimentary picnic in Rum village on your way into the desert.

It's unlikely that anything will go wrong with your trip as the drivers are highly experienced in the desert terrain. Some of the vehicles, however, have seen better days so if you are involved in a breakdown try to avoid heated confrontation: the Bedouin take their responsibility towards the visitor very seriously and they will quickly arrange for a replacement – if everyone remains amicable!

You may be approached by the odd freelance guide in Rum village. Prices may be cheaper but there are no guarantees regarding the safety or quality of the trip and, more importantly, it cheats the lads waiting patiently in line for a fare. In addition, 60% of the profit from excursions goes back to the cooperative: someone who jumps the queue robs the community of that revenue. Rangers tour the Wadi Rum area, checking people have tickets. Entering without one is not only unethical, it is also illegal.

You can easily add on an overnight stay at a Bedouin camp (ask at the visitor centre when booking your vehicle). Your driver will simply drop you off in the afternoon and pick you up the next morning.

Camel Trekking

If you have the time, travelling around Wadi Rum by camel is highly recommended. Apart from being ecologically sound, it will enable you to experience Wadi Rum as the Bedouin have for centuries, and to appreciate the silent gravitas of the desert. That said, a ride of more than about four hours will leave you sore in places you never knew existed.

ℹ️ 4WD EXCURSIONS AROUND WADI RUM

When booking a 4WD excursion at Wadi Rum visitor centre you can either hire a driver for a whole day (make sure you agree on the destinations before leaving), or you can select a destination from two prescribed routes. 'Operator 1' routes cover the central areas of Wadi Rum; 'Operator 2' routes cover outlying (but just as beautiful) areas. Distances are measured from the visitor centre. Maximum times are given below: you could rush round the main sights of Wadi Rum in a few hours but the trip will be much more rewarding if you get out of the vehicle and explore each of the sights on foot, or simply sit and enjoy the peace and quiet. Drivers are assigned in strict rotation so you may get a driver who speaks English and is knowledgeable about the desert or you may not. If you want a guide to accompany you, ask at the visitor centre or book one in advance.

SITE	KM	TIME	PRICE PER VEHICLE
OPERATOR 1 ROUTES			
Lawrence's Spring	14km	1 hour	JD25
Khazali Canyon	30km	2 hours	JD35
Sunset sites of Rum	35km	2½ hours	JD44
Little Rock Bridge	35km	3 hours	JD44
Red Dunes	40km	3½ hours	JD51
Lawrence's House	45km	3½ hours	JD59
Umm Fruth Rock Bridge	50km	4 hours	JD67
Burdah Rock Bridge	60km	5 hours	JD75
Burdah Canyon	65km	8 hours	JD80
OPERATOR 2 ROUTES			
Alameleh inscriptions	15km	1 hour	JD25
Siq Umm Tawagi	18km	2 hours	JD35
Sunset sites of Diseh	20km	2½ hours	JD44
Barrah Canyon	49km	3 hours	JD51
Burdah Rock Bridge	50km	4 hours	JD67
Full-day tour	60km	8 hours	JD80

Rates for camel-trekking excursions are fixed and listed on a board outside the excursion office in the visitor centre. The prices are per person. You'll enjoy your ride much more if you ride yourself rather than being led. This will cost a bit more as you need to pay for your guide's camel but it's well worth the extra cost.

You can easily add on an overnight stay at a Bedouin camp (ask at the visitor centre when booking your camel). If you want to return by 4WD then you have to pay the price of returning the camel to where you collected it from. If you have a lot of gear, it's better to hire an additional camel (at the same rate) to bear the load. It is also possible to arrange longer camel excursions from Wadi Rum to Aqaba (three to six nights depending on the route); or towards Wadi Musa (for Petra; about five nights).

The camel is no longer a common form of transport for Bedouin; most now prefer the ubiquitous pick-up truck – in fact, it's not unusual to see a Bedouin transporting a prized camel in the back of a Toyota. These grumpy but loyal animals, however, are still very much part of the Bedouin culture and camel races are held weekly in winter, generally on a Friday, at the camel track near Diseh. Ask at the visitor centre for details.

Horse Trekking

An alternative and memorable mode of four-legged transport through Wadi Rum and surrounding areas is by horse. A hack costs around JD25 per hour. These trips are for people who have riding experience – novices should not underestimate the challenge of riding high-spirited Arab horses in open country. The highly recommended and long-established **Rum Horses** (☎2033508, 079-5802108; www.wadirumhorses.com) is the most professional trekking, camel- and horse-trekking agency. The owner, Atallah Swillheen, trained and qualified in horse management and endurance racing in Europe. One of his horses, Sasha, is a five-time winner of the FEI endurance race in Jordan. Day trips from Rum Horses cost JD90 (JD140 including overnight camping). The stables are located on the approach road to Wadi Rum visitor centre, about 10km from the Desert Highway. Look for a signboard beside the road.

Hiking

For those who prefer 'Shank's pony' to the real thing, there are many wonderful places to explore on foot and you can walk unguided to several of the main sights.

There is only space in this chapter to highlight a couple of routes but if you're serious about hiking (or scrambling and climbing), invest in one of the excellent books by Tony Howard and Di Taylor (see p214).

Avoid the extreme heat of summer (May to September). Remember that it's very easy to get disoriented amid the dozens of craggy peaks; temperatures (cold as well as hot) can be extreme; natural water supplies are not common and sometimes undrinkable; passing traffic is rare; and maps are often inaccurate. Walking in sand is particularly exhausting.

MAKHARAS CANYON HIKE

One excellent do-it-yourself option is to hike southeast across the plain from the visitor centre towards the Seven Pillars of Wisdom and then head up Makharas Canyon (take the left-hand wadi when it branches). The wadi narrows after about an hour from the visitor centre and then emerges onto a patch of gorgeous red sand with fabulous views of Jebel Barrah and Umm Nfoos to the east. From here cut north over the sand dunes and plod your way around the northern tip of Jebel Umm Ishrin until you get back to the Seven Pillars of Wisdom. This hike takes about 2½ hours.

JEBEL RUM ROUND TRIP

Another possible DIY hike is the circumambulation of the southern half of Jebel Rum via Wadi Leyyah, starting from Rum village and passing Lawrence's Spring and Ain

GOING IT ALONE

Although there is nothing to stop you driving your own 4WD in the desert or striking off on your own two feet, you should not attempt this unless you are experienced in the terrain. Soft sand is difficult to drive in and exhausting to walk through. If you get stuck or run out of steam, it may be a long time before anyone finds you – a serious danger if you are short of water in midsummer or ill-clothed in winter. Furthermore, it can be highly disorienting trying to navigate through the labyrinthine passages. Make sure you have a compass, map and water before attempting even a simple route on your own.

ⓘ CAMEL TREKS AROUND WADI RUM

Camel routes are sorted into two circuits for 'operational' purposes. Camel excursions normally begin from Rum village and distances are measured from the Rest House. Prices rise with the price of fodder and the routes on offer change from time to time.

SITE	KM	TIME	PRICE (MAX)
FROM RUM VILLAGE			
Nabataean Temple	1km	30 minutes	JD4
Lawrence's Spring	6km	2 hours	JD10
Khazali Canyon	14km	4 hours	JD20
Sunset sites	22km	4 hours	JD25
Red Dunes	25km	5 hours	JD20
Burdah Rock Bridge	40km	overnight	JD60
Full-day tour	unlimited	8 hours	JD30
Luggage camel		8 hours	JD30
FROM ALAMELEH			
Short Trip	2km	1 hour	JD10
Sunset sites	8km	2 hours	JD15
Siq Lawrence	9km	3 hours	JD20
Full-day tour	unlimited	overnight	JD60
Luggage Camel		8 hours	JD30

Abu Aineh. The route takes eight hours and offers some stunning 'big country' scenery.

JEBEL UMM ADAAMI ASCENT

A recommended 4WD-hiking trip is to Jebel Umm Adaami (1832m), Jordan's highest peak, on the rarely visited southern border with Saudi Arabia. The hour-long uphill hike is marked by cairns and offers fabulous views of Wadi Rum to the north and Saudi Arabia to the south. Find a driver who knows the 45-minute 4WD route south to Wadi Saabet, where the hike starts. On the way back, stop off at the rock carvings of nearby Siq al-Barid, a lovely spot for a picnic.

Scrambling

Scrambling lies somewhere between hiking and climbing. No technical skills are required but you may have to pull yourself up short rock faces on the following trips.

BURDAH ROCK BRIDGE

If you take a 4WD excursion to Burdah Rock Bridge, it's well worth making the hour-long scramble up to the bridge itself. There's nothing technical involved but you'll need a guide to find the route and a head for heights on one spot just before the bridge.

There are fabulous views from the top. To continue beyond the bridge you'll need ropes and some climbing skills (one climber fell to his death here in 1999).

RAKHABAT CANYON

With a local guide or a copy of Tony Howard's *Walking in Jordan* you can navigate the labyrinthine siqs of Rakhabat Canyon for an exciting half-day trip through the heart of Jebel Umm al-Ishrin. The western mouth of the canyon is just by Rum village. At the far (eastern) end of the canyon you can hike across the valley to the Anfaishiyya inscriptions, 600m south of the Bedouin camp, and then return on foot to Rum via the southern point of Jebel Umm al-Ishrin, with a possible detour to Ain Abu Aineh en route. Alternatively, with a guide and some experience of abseiling you can head back west through the mountain ridge along the Kharazeh Canyon for a great loop route.

Rock Climbing

Wadi Rum offers some challenging rock climbing (up to Grade 8). Although the Bedouin have been climbing in the area for centuries, climbing as a modern sport is still relatively undeveloped. That said, there are now several accredited climbing guides, most of whom have been trained in the UK. To arrange a climbing trip, contact the visitor centre a few days in advance; they will put you in touch with a guide with whom you can negotiate the price and organise camping gear, equipment and transport. Costs start at around JD200 for one to two days' climbing.

Guides often suggest Jebel Rum for less experienced climbers: minimal gear is needed and it's close to the Rest House. Another popular climbing location is Jebel Barrah. For information on routes see Tony Howard and Di Taylor's books and check out www.wadirum.net.

Other Activities

For a magnificent eagle-eye view of Wadi Rum, take to the air by balloon (JD130 per person for a minimum of two people). Trips take a minimum of two hours and are dependent on the weather. Alternatively, try a 20-minute 'flip' by microlight or ultralight. **Bait Ali Lodge** (✆079-5548133; www.baitali.com) acts as the local facilitator for the **Royal Aero Sports Club of Jordan** (✆20 58052; www.royalaerosports.com), providing the easiest way of making a booking for these sports. Bait Ali also rents out sand yachts, mountain bikes and quad bikes, along with maps of possible routes in the dry mud flats north of the camp.

The annual **Jebel Ishrin Marathon** takes place each September and the **Wadi Rum Endurance Race** (www.fei.org), a 120km-in-a-day FEI event, may interest horse enthusiasts.

☞ Tours

If you have limited time, you may find it easier to arrange a tour to Wadi Rum from Aqaba. Prices start from around JD70 per person per day (including transport, food and entrance fee) and can include an overnight stay in the desert (JD15 for facilities and breakfast). **Wadi Rum Safari** (✆20 63882; www.wadirumsafari.com) has one of the better reputations for these tours.

Some tours overnight at Diseh and do not even enter the main protected area of Wadi Rum. Diseh has some good camps in beautiful scenery but it is not part of the reserve area so you should be clear about what the tour entails to avoid disappointment.

🛏 Sleeping

There is no hotel in Wadi Rum, nor in the neighbouring village of Diseh, so if you want to spend time in the area, be prepared to camp. Camping can range from a goat-hair blanket under the stars at an isolated Bedouin camp or a mattress under partitioned canvas in a 'party tent' at Diseh, to a comfortable cabin at Bait Ali, just outside Wadi Rum. You can even pitch your own tent in designated areas (enquire about locations at the visitor centre). Mattress, blankets and food are provided by the camps but bring your own linen.

Rum Village

Rest House CAMPGROUND $
(✆2018867; mattress & blankets in 2-person tent per person JD3) The frayed tents at the back of the Rest House offer the most accessible accommodation, but they're only recommended if you arrive in Wadi Rum too late to head into the desert. You can pitch your own tent for JD2, which includes use of toilets and shower block.

In the Desert

The sky's the limit for those who stay in one of the Bedouin camps in Wadi Rum and this is definitely the best way to experience the desert. Unfurl your mat under the stars and let singing youths, together with the snorts of grumbling camels and the whistle of mint tea over the fire, lull you to sleep.

The Bedouin camps all conform to certain standards and are checked regularly. There are two types of camps – permanent (which usually have toilet-shower blocks and operate year-round) and temporary (used only occasionally by Bedouin groups or tourists). The camps are only permitted in certain areas and these fall either within Wadi Rum or within neighbouring Diseh. The Wadi Rum camps are best booked through the visitor centre, either in advance (especially if you want to stay at a particular camp), or on arrival. For camps in the Diseh area, see p223.

The price of accommodation at these camps, including food, tents and blankets, is generally around JD30 per person per night. Camps advertising half-board generally provide a simple barbecue supper with salads and Arabic bread, coffee or tea and a piece of fruit, and a breakfast of jam, cheese, bread and coffee. For groups staying in a temporary camp, there is an additional charge for the transportation of camping items to the campsite each day. If you have your own sleeping bag, tent and food, all you should have to pay is the cost of your four-wheeled or four-legged transport.

As there are many camps, all offering similar services in similarly beautiful parts of the desert, it is hard to recommend one over another. The ones listed below give you an idea of what is available and come recommended, but that is not to say others are not equally good.

Tour operators run their own camps scattered around the desert – see p224.

Mohammed Mutlak Camp CAMP $

(077-7424837; www.wadirum.org; half board in tent JD30 per person) In a beautiful spot overlooking Jebel Qattar, this camp is run by brothers who speak English well. Dinner may, if you're lucky, include delicious lamb cooked in a *zerb* (Bedouin oven buried in the sand). Transport by 4WD to the camp is free if you don't visit anywhere en route. You can come by camel (from JD25, 2¼ hours). Hiking opportunities include a 45-minute hike to see the merging of red and white sand dunes. There is no electricity, but light is provided by gas lamp.

Rum Stars Camp BEDOUIN CAMP $

(079-5127025; www.rumstars.com; half board in tent JD25 per person) One of the camps situated deepest in the desert, it takes about 20 minutes by 4WD to reach. In a magnificent spot, tucked into the side of a mountain and overlooking quintessential Wadi Rum landscape, the camp is simple but well-run by Bedouin brothers. The owner, who speaks excellent English and is passionate about his Bedouin heritage, will collect you from Rum Village. Half day jeep tours cost JD50 for a maximum of four people (full day with lunchbox JD70). Local guided hiking costs JD50 for a five-hour trip.

Around Wadi Rum

TOP CHOICE Bait Ali Lodge ECO-CAMP $$

(079-5548133; www.baitali.com; half board in tent JD35 per person, in small/medium/large cabin 45/48/53;) If you want to stay in the area but are not wild about roughing it, then Bait Ali offers a compromise. Tucked behind a hill, with a sublime view of the wilderness, this upmarket eco-friendly camp is clearly signposted just off the road, 15km from the Desert Highway and 9km from the Wadi Rum visitor centre. The accommodation (either in army tents or cabins, some with en suite showers and toilets) is basic but includes linen and there is a separate shower block with hot water for men and women. The facilities include an excellent restaurant with an extensive nightly barbecue. Wrapped up in blanket coats, reclining on sheepskin, peering through the roaring fire at cloaked Arab men – this is the way to eat roasted meats, in the company of great storytellers. There is even an attractively designed swimming pool. You can pitch your own tent (JD10) or park a campervan (JD10) and use the shower block. The owners are delightful and can advise on bike rides, hikes, ballooning and other activities in the local area. The hike around Lion Mountain (12km, three hours) is particularly recommended.

✗ Eating

Apart from the good Rum Gate Restaurant at the visitor centre, there are limited eating options in Wadi Rum. The small grocery stores along the main road through Rum village have basic supplies and mineral water. The area around Diseh has some of the cleanest aquifer water in Jordan. While out in the desert you may be lucky enough to try a *zerb* – a Bedouin barbecue, cooked in an oven buried in the sand.

Rest House BUFFET $$

(/fax 2018867; breakfast JD3, lunch JD10, dinner buffet JD10; 7am-8.30pm) Dining here is open-air and buffet-style. Sipping a large Amstel beer (JD4) while watching the sun's rays light up Jebel Umm al-Ishrin is the perfect way to finish the day.

Ali's Place CAFE $

(snacks JD4; 6am-1am) Along the main road in Rum village, next to Alfi's climbing shop (a grocery store), this local place serves tea and snacks, and is where the younger Bedouin guides go to unwind.

Rum Gate Restaurant BUFFET $$

(2015995; Wadi Rum visitor centre; buffet lunch JD10; 8am-5pm;) A fine selection of dishes is offered in the buffet between noon and 4pm (popular with tour groups); outside this time, the restaurant is a buzzing meeting place for guides, weary hikers and independent travellers who congregate over a non-alcoholic beer (JD2) and a chicken sandwich (JD5).

🔒 Shopping

Rum Arts HANDICRAFTS

(2032918; Wadi Rum visitor centre; 8am-5pm) This is a good place to look for quality silver items, embroidered bags and glass designs. Most items are made by local women to whom most of the profits are returned. It's possible to visit the workshop in Rum village (closed Friday and Saturday) – ask for directions at the Rest House. Almost adjacent, the **Bedouin Gallery** sells a fine selection of textiles and Bedouin goat-hair rugs.

ℹ️ Information

Admission to **Wadi Rum Protected Area** (per person JD5; children under 12 free) is strictly controlled and all vehicles, camels and guides must be arranged either through or with the approval of the visitor centre (no prior reservations necessary). You can also book a camp here or a guide for hiking, scrambling or climbing (best to book in advance, especially if you want a particular guide).

Essential items to bring include a hat, preferably with a brim or a flap to keep the sun off your neck, sunscreen, sturdy footwear and water.

A heavy coat, scarf, hat and gloves are needed in winter. If you are camping (including at the Rest House), bring a torch, a book to read and a padlock (many tents are lockable).

The Bedouin are a conservative people, so dress appropriately. Loose shorts and tops for men and women are acceptable around the Rest House, but baggy trousers/skirts and modest shirts/blouses will save you sunburn and earn you respect from the Bedouin, especially out in the desert.

Police station (☏2017050) Located in the old police fort 400m south of the Rest House. They will not receive complaints (go to the tourist police), but they will come looking for you if you get lost.

Tourist police (☏2018215) At the visitor centre.

Visitor Centre (☏/fax 2090600; www.wadi rum.jo; ⊙7am-7pm) Situated at the entry to the protected area, about 30km east of the Desert

---

LOCAL KNOWLEDGE

AHMED OGLA AL ZALABEYH: STEWARD OF THE DESERT

Until he was seven years old, Ahmed lived the life of the nomad in Jordan's southern desert. His parents were keen for him to be integrated into the modern world so Ahmed and his siblings donned shoes for the first time and went to school. Over, a decade later, after attaining a degree in English literature in Amman, Ahmed is back in Wadi Rum. Describing his four years in the big city as the worst of his life, he is relieved to come home to the desert and this is where he intends to stay. Newly married and now part of the tourist industry, Ahmed is both passionate and articulate about his Bedouin roots and he looks forward to bringing up his own family with a firm idea of what it means to be Bedouin.

What are the best places to visit in Jordan to have a Bedouin experience? There are many who claim to be Bedouin but who use the label for commercial ends. If you want to meet the real Bedouin, you must come to the desert – like here in Rum, or in Wadi Araba or in small pockets of the Eastern Desert. In these places you will encounter families who know what it means to live in the traditional nomadic way, moving with the seasons.

Where do the Bedouin go to escape the tourists? Ah, that's easier than you may think! We throw everything into the back of our pickup truck and follow the camels into the desert, beyond the camps and the car tracks. That's our spiritual home and we return to it often.

How do the Bedouin find sustenance in the desert? Livestock are the key to survival. The Bedouin trade among themselves, exchanging camels and sheep for products such as goat-hair tents, rugs, milk and cheese or items of hardware from the market.

What does it mean to be Bedouin in the modern world? Life in the desert is about the basic origins of humanity. For us this includes the concept of hospitality which runs very deep in our culture. Increasingly, though, thanks to the need for education and access to better transport, it also means settlement – usually near to the desert's edge.

How will you ensure your children love the desert the way you do? I will take them, like my father took me, to all the places where our story can be told. Knowing that our grandfathers sat by this rock or under that tree helps us connect to the land and ensures our history is passed along.

What advice have you for the tourist wanting to meet the Bedouin? Don't be suspicious of our motives – just come and talk, or share tea with us. Yes we want to make a living but we want our culture to be understood more.

Highway and 7km north of Rum village. This is where you buy your entry ticket to the reserve, book a 4WD or camel excursion, organise accommodation at a camp and book a guide.

ℹ Getting There & Away

Car

The most convenient way to get to Wadi Rum as an independent traveller is by car. You can hire a car in Aqaba and, if you intend to continue to Petra, you are well advised to keep it for the round-trip. This will save considerable time and frustration trying to fathom the limited public transport.

If you are accustomed to desert navigation and off-road driving in sandy conditions, you could hire a 4WD in Aqaba and drive into the desert yourself, providing you state your intention at the visitor centre at Wadi Rum and pay the JD2 (per person) entrance fee. Do not attempt this if you have no prior knowledge of desert driving.

Hitching

Because of the limited public transport to and from Rum village (which has only a small population), many travellers follow local custom and hitch (JD2) from the junction with the Desert Highway at Ar-Rashidiyya, 5km south of Quweira. All transport heading along the highway will stop at this junction – with the exception of JETT buses. You can normally hitch a lift in a pick-up between the visitor centre and Rum village for around JD5.

Minibus

At the time of research, there was at least one minibus a day to Aqaba (JD2, one hour) at around 7am. A second one may run at 8.30am, but check with your camp operator first. To Wadi Musa (JD5, 1½ hours) there is a fairly reliable daily minibus at 8.30am. Check current departure times at the visitor centre or Rest House when you arrive in Wadi Rum.

For Ma'an, Karak or Amman, the minibuses to either Aqaba or Wadi Musa can drop you off at the Ar-Rashidiyya crossroads with the Desert Highway (JD1.500, 20 minutes), where it is easy to hail onward transport.

Taxi

Occasionally taxis hang around the visitor centre (and very occasionally the Rest House) waiting for a fare back to wherever they came from – normally Aqaba, Wadi Musa or Ma'an. It costs about JD25 to JD30 to Aqaba, and JD45 to Wadi Musa (Petra). A taxi jeep from Rum village to the Ar-Rashidiyya crossroads with the Desert Highway costs around JD10.

Diseh   الديسي

Diseh is northwest of Rum village, about 12km as the vulture flies but 22km by road. The scenery is almost as spectacular as at Wadi Rum, and there are plenty of places to hike outside the official Wadi Rum protected area. There are seven camps in the desert near Diseh offering basic facilities. If you stay at one of these, you can organise transport to Wadi Rum visitor centre and book your desert excursion from there.

The paved road to Diseh from the turn-off to Rum offers some interesting places to explore. For a negotiable price, locals will drive you out into the desert area north of the railway line, which is dotted with Nabataean and Roman dams, artificial rock bridges, rock carvings and inscriptions. The landscape around **Jebel Amud** is the most interesting. A longer trip could take in the 2m-high rock carvings at **Abu Hawl** (Father of Terror), 7km north of the Bait Ali camp, and on to a rock bridge at Jebel Kharazeh. A three-hour 4WD trip costs around JD45.

🛏 Sleeping

A number of camps outside Diseh have been recommended by readers. The camps are roughly wrapped around a large hill with the first few camps adjacent to each other and accessible by 2WD (unless there's been heavy rain). They all offer traditional sitting areas with cushions and beds either in cramped individual tents or larger, partitioned Bedouin tents. The camps listed below have clean shower-toilet blocks. If you are looking for a quieter, more tranquil experience, the camps located in more isolated parts of the desert and requiring 4WD for access are a better bet – make sure you check on the location before you book to avoid disappointment.

Rahayeb Camp   BEDOUIN CAMP $$
(☑079-6909030; www.rahayebcamp.com; half-/full-board per person JD32/38) This beautiful new camp wedged into a secluded bend of the rocks, well away from the other Diseh camps, represents camping in style. Two professional chefs rustle up delicious traditional fare in the *zerb* oven while guests lounge under the stars around a central fireplace. For those who prefer the idea of camping more than the reality, there are five VIP tents (from JD45) with their own toilets and showers, solar-heated water and

AGENCIES & GUIDES

Jeep drivers and camel escorts do a good job of looking after visitors, but if you want more detailed or specialised information about Wadi Rum, or help in organising a particular activity, you'll need to hire a guide. Staff at the visitor centre can help you locate a guide, or you can contact one of the recommended guides listed here. Make contact at least 48 hours in advance and carry a copy of your email correspondence in case the staff at the visitor centre asks for it. For longer excursions, some planning is required on the part of the guide (eg buying provisions, arranging camels). April, September and October are the busiest seasons.

Al-Hillawi Desert Services (☑/fax 2018867, 079-5940117) Agency with several desert camps, run by the management of the Rest House.

Attayak Ali (☑079-5899723; www.bedouinroads.com) Climbing and adventure guide.

Attayak Aouda (☑079-5834736; www.rumguides.com) Climbing guide.

Eid Mohamed Al-Sowelleh (☑079-5624671) General guide.

Sabagh Eid (☑/fax 2016238; 03-7891243) Climbing guide.

electric lighting. Alternatively, there are super-secluded camping pitches near a miniature siq above the camp with nothing to disturb the peace but your own heartbeat.

Zawaideh Desert Camp   BEDOUIN CAMP $
(☑079-5840664; zawaideh_camp@yahoo.com; half-board per person JD20) Close to the road and accessible by car, this simple but atmospheric camp is in the undercliff of the escarpment, on the edge of a wide plain. It has a reputation for providing a sociable experience around the lively campfire and is popular with Jordanians from the city looking to reconnect with the desert.

Captain's Camp   BEDOUIN CAMP $$
(☑2016905, 079-5510432; captains@jo.com.jo; half-board per person JD35) A well-run mid-range camp with hot showers, lots of snug seating areas and good buffets, this camp is popular with tour groups, especially as it's easily accessible from the road. The camp also offers a romantic tent for two (JD90 per person) in the middle of the desert, with a candlelit supper delivered to the tent flaps.

Palm Camp   BEDOUIN CAMP $
(☑077-7244605; www.jordandesertpalmcamp.com; half-board per person JD17) A sociable place with a central campfire and lounging area, but with cramped accommodation. Ask at Zawaideh Desert Camp for transport across the sands.

❶ Getting There & Away

You're unlikely to find a minibus or service taxi headed all the way to Diseh, so follow the instructions for getting to Wadi Rum as far as the turn-off to Diseh (the police checkpoint 16km after leaving the Desert Highway). From there you can ring ahead to one of the camps where someone is usually happy to come and collect you. If you get stuck, you can hitch the 8km but be prepared for a wait; it's customary to give a few fils to the driver – JD1 should do it.

Minibuses often run from Diseh to the Desert Highway (JD1.700). A single bus runs to Aqaba daily at around 7am. Check at your camp for the latest information.

THE DESERT HIGHWAY

The Desert Highway, which follows the legendary tracks of the Hejaz Railway and a new water pipeline, connects Aqaba in the south of Jordan with Damascus in Syria. The section between Amman and Aqaba is a road of very limited interest, poorly maintained and usually bearing heavy traffic. As such, it hardly ranks as one of Jordan's highlights. It is, however, the shortest route between Amman and southern Jordan and it's likely that you'll end up using the highway in one direction or another. This is the only road in Jordan that actually looks like a highway, with dual carriageway for most of its length and lighting at main intersections.

There are very few places to sleep or eat along the Desert Highway and if you make it to Ma'an, you may as well continue on to Wadi Musa, Wadi Rum or Aqaba.

Ma'an

معان

📱03 / POP 116,000 / ELEV 1100M

Ma'an has been a transport junction and trading centre for many centuries, and is now one of the larger towns and administrative centres in southern Jordan. There's little of specific interest here, but the centre of town is pleasant enough and some travellers may have to stay overnight while waiting for transport to Wadi Rum, Wadi Musa (for Petra) or Aqaba. The town is particularly busy during hajj as it lies on the main pilgrimage route from Jordan and Syria to Mecca in Saudi Arabia. The main north-south thoroughfare is King Hussein St, centred somewhere around the mosque and the communication tower. Here you'll find restaurants and several banks with ATMs. To get here from the bus station head two blocks west then one block north (a five-minute walk) to the southern end of King Hussein St, where it meets Palestine St. The Hotel Kreashan is a further five minutes' walk north of here.

🛏 Sleeping & Eating

Grill and chicken restaurants abound along King Hussein St, including **Alroz Al Bokhary** (King Hussein St; mains JD3-5). There's a tempting sweet shop diagonally opposite the corner of King Hussein and Palestine Sts, and fruit shops nearby.

Hotel Kreashan   HOTEL $
(Krishan Hotel; 📱07-7719308; Al-Bayyarah St; r from JD10) If you get stuck and really can't muster onward transport then this basic hotel at least has large and sunny rooms and clean, shared bathrooms. It's not recommended for solo women who may feel uncomfortable with a proprietor who sports long johns instead of trousers. The hotel is a block east of the mosque off the northern end of King Hussein St.

ℹ Information

Horizon Internet Centre (📱2131700; King Hussein St; per hr JD1; ⏰9am-10pm) Opposite the Housing Bank; has fast connections.

ℹ Getting There & Away

If you can't get a direct bus to where you want to go in Jordan, there's a good chance that you can find a connection in Ma'an.

The station for buses, minibuses and service taxis is a five-minute walk southeast of the centre. Departures from Ma'an start to peter out around 2pm and stop completely around 5pm.

There are regular minibuses (JD2.750, three hours) and less frequent service taxis (JD6, three hours) to/from Amman's south bus station (Wahadat). To Aqaba, minibuses (JD2.200, 80 minutes) and service taxis (JD2.500) are also frequent. For Wadi Rum, take an Aqaba-bound minibus to the junction at Ar-Rashidiyya (JD1.700) then take a minibus or hitch from here. For Petra, minibuses to Wadi Musa (JD1.200, 45 minutes) leave fairly frequently when full and stop briefly at the university en route. To Karak, there are occasional service taxis (JD2, two hours) and three minibuses a day, via Tafila (JD1.300).

A chartered taxi to Petra/Wadi Musa costs around JD15, and JD30 to Karak or Aqaba.

Qatrana

القطرانه

📱03 / POP 5000 / ELEV 740M

One of the few towns along the Desert Highway is Qatrana, a couple of kilometres north of the turn-off to Karak, and a former stop on the pilgrim road between Damascus and Mecca. The only reason to stop here (if you have your own transport) is to have a quick look at **Qatrana Castle** (admission free), built in 1531 by the Ottomans. It has been nicely restored, but there are no explanation boards.

Azraq & the Eastern Desert Highway

الأزرق & شرق الطريق الصحراء

Why Go?

Imagine a space so desolate that not even a boulder or a bush troubles the 360-degree horizon. Now add a carpet of ancient black volcanic rock, unnavigable even by camels. And finally, factor in a ravaging heat so overpowering in the summer that the ground pulses before your eyes and mirages appear in the distance. Welcome to the Eastern Desert!

So why, you might well ask, would anyone bother to come here. Well the Eastern Desert may look like uncharted territory but it has been inhabited by Bedouin, crossed by caravans and visited by migrating birds since recorded history. Today you can see evidence of this traffic in a string of intriguing ruined forts, hunting lodges and caravanserai, collectively known as the 'desert castles'. At the miraculous oases of Azraq and Burqu, birds still break their journey across the otherwise featureless desert.

Best Places to Stay & Eat

» Azraq Lodge (p232)

» Al-Azraq Resthouse (p232)

» Azraq Palace Restaurant (p233)

Best Castles to Visit

» Qasr al-Azraq (p233)

» Qusayr Amra (p236)

» Qasr Kharana (p238)

» Umm al-Jimal (p241)

When to Go

The best time to visit the remote plains of Eastern Jordan is early March to mid-April when temperate weather means getting stuck at a remote desert castle is merely inconvenient, not life-threatening.

With proper planning (including reliable transport, sufficient water supplies and a hat) May is another good time to visit. At this time, large numbers of raptors soar above the shimmering heat haze on their annual migration.

In winter, dust devils spiral on the plains as birds stop-over in the Azraq wetlands en route between Europe and sub-Saharan Africa.

History

A string of ruined pavilions, caravanserais (merchants' inns), hunting lodges and forts – known collectively (if erroneously) as the 'desert castles' – peppers the deserts of eastern Jordan, and is one of the country's most surreal attractions. Dating back to the Umayyads (AD 661–750) in the earliest years of Islam, the desert castles were once richly decorated with mosaics, frescoes, marble, plaster and painted stucco, providing oases of pleasure in the harsh and inhospitable

Eastern Highlights

❶ Chase the ghost of Lawrence through **Qasr al-Azraq** (p233), the former headquarters of this enigmatic British officer

❷ Hunker down in the bird-hide at **Azraq Wetland Reserve** (p234) and watch the drama of a waterhole unfold

❸ Meet one of Jordan's ethnic minorities, the Chechens, at **Azraq**

Lodge (p232) and enjoy a sumptuous dinner

❹ Admire the risqué frescoes in the bathhouse of **Qusayr Amra** (p236), a Unesco World Heritage site

❺ Wander the maze-like corridors of **Qasr Kharana** (p243), a mighty fortress in a lonesome desert

❻ Spot the endangered Arabian oryx on night safari

at **Shaumari Wildlife Reserve** (p235), a vital ecotourism venture

❼ Clamber through the brooding basalt ruins of **Umm al-Jimal** (p241), an ancient town of shimmering black stone

❽ Use your off-road driving skills to reach **Burqu** (p243), an unlikely lake in the wilderness desert. Here, the elite could pursue their pastimes of hawking, hunting and horse-racing during the day, while evenings were spent in wild festivities with wine, poetry and song.

The early Arab rulers were still Bedouin at heart, and their love of the desert may have led them to build these pleasure palaces, which once teemed with orchards and wild game. Or they may have come to avoid epidemics in the big cities, or to maintain links with, and power over, the Bedouin – the bedrock of their support in the conquered lands. The desert castles also served as staging posts for pilgrimages to Mecca, and along trade routes to Damascus and Baghdad – never underestimate the luxury of a hot bath in the desert!

Nature Reserves

Unlikely as it may seem on the road into the Eastern Desert from Amman, this region is home to three protected areas. The most developed is **Azraq Wetland Reserve**

UMAYYADS? WHO WERE THEY?

If you had to guess the seventh-largest empire (and fifth-largest contiguous empire) the world has ever known, chances are you wouldn't think of the Umayyads. So why is it that this critically important dynasty, central to the modern shape of Islam and responsible for building some of the best loved expressions of Arab culture, are so unfamiliar to those outside the region? It could well be because they belong to a Middle Eastern history, so often at odds with the crusading history of Western nations. It could be because the 8th century AD is generally associated, correctly or incorrectly, with the unenlightened 'Dark Ages' which tends to cast a long shadow over neighbouring cultures. Or it could be because the name 'Umayyad' just doesn't roll off the tongue.

Whatever the reason for their appalling lack of press in Western consciousness, the Umayyads deserve the odds to be evened up a little. So, in the interests of fair play, here's a few fast facts to help understand who the Umayyads were and why they were important.

» **When were the Umayyads around?** AD 661–750, in the early days of Islam

» **This huge empire of theirs, where was it?** From Portugal and Morocco in the west to Arabia and Persia in the east – about 9% of the world's land area

» **So how big is that?** 13 million sq km

» **How many people were governed by this empire?** At the time, around 30% of the world's population

» **Where was the capital?** Damascus

» **What was their impact on Islam?** Both positive and negative: they implemented a campaign of mass conversions to Islam but their dynasty was largely responsible for the damaging Sunni-Shiite split

» **How were they regarded in their day?** The minority Shiite resented the schism they caused by failing to uphold Prophet Mohammed's bloodline

» **But the Sunnis supported them, presumably?** Not exactly. Public Sunni opinion was that the Umayyad rulers were dim-witted sinners, preoccupied with earthly delights

» **Is this what caused their demise?** Partly; in 747 a rebellion of dissatisfied subjects on the fringe of the empire, combined with a huge earthquake in the region, led to a takeover of the empire by Shiite forces (known as the Abbasids) from Persia in 750

» **Are they remembered today?** Yes! The Umayyads established Arabic as the administrative language of the Middle East, their pan-Arab approach is used by nationalists to evoke an Arab Golden Age, and their association with the colour white is reflected in most modern flags of Arab countries

» **Any other cultural legacies?** They built the Dome of the Rock in Jerusalem, and the Umayyad Mosque in Damascus, two of the great icons of Islamic art

» **What was their significance in the area we now call Jordan?** The string of hunting lodges, bathhouses and pleasure palaces known collectively as the 'desert castles' were built by the Umayyads – festive expressions of their creative and exuberant reign (p234), which attracts many bird species around the gravely diminished oasis. **Shaumari Wildlife Reserve** (p235) protects endangered species such as the Arabian oryx but is currently closed to visitors (though you may be able to arrange a night safari through the RSCN), while **Burqu Reserve** (p243) is as yet an undeveloped site in the middle of remote wilderness.

Dangers & Annoyances

The desert doesn't take prisoners. At any time of year, but particularly in the middle of summer, dehydration and the threat of heat exhaustion and heat stroke – a serious condition that requires immediate medical attention – are hazards of visiting remote desert locations. Minimise the risk by carrying and drinking plenty of water, wearing a hat, avoiding exertion in the middle of the day and planning an exit route if travelling by public transport. If driving off-road, be aware that you will have to be totally self-sufficient in the event of a puncture or mechanical failure.

During the spring, flies and mosquitos are an annoyance. Bring repellent if visiting the oases.

ⓘ Getting There & Away

The easiest point of entry to the region is Amman and the towns of Zarqa and Mafraj. Desolate Hwy 5 from the south also leads into the area via Azraq. The Eastern Desert encompasses the only border crossing with Iraq. Trucks and some buses use the border crossing at Al Umau with Saudi Arabia (see p318 for restrictions).

ⓘ Getting Around

Although minimal and intermittent minibuses ply the route to Azraq from Amman, some en route to the Iraqi border, it is very difficult (and potentially dangerous in summer) to travel around this region by unreliable public transport. A much better option is to take a tour from the capital, all of which cover the main desert castles in a day trip. An even better bet is to hire a car for two days, which will allow for a stopover in Azraq and a night safari in Shaumari. To make a comprehensive tour of the region, including Umm Jimal and Burqu along the remote Eastern Desert Highway, a 4WD with camping gear is highly recommended.

AZRAQ & AROUND

Azraq is the only town of any significance in the Eastern Desert and acts as a magnet for

---

ⓘ TOURING THE DESERT CASTLES

Jumping on an organised tour of the desert castles from Amman makes a lot of sense, especially if you're short of time or on a tight budget. Tours can be arranged at the Palace, Farah and Cliff hotels in Amman (see p58), which charge about JD15 to JD20 per person for a full-day trip. You're unlikely to get a better deal by negotiating directly with the driver of a service taxi or private taxi in Amman, and regular taxi drivers are rarely keen on leaving the city. Tours can also be arranged from the Black Iris and Mariam hotels in Madaba.

trans-continental traffic looking for refreshment and company after long desert drives. The name 'Azraq' is often loosely applied to all settlements directly east of Amman and the castles that are scattered across the desert plains here. Some of the best attractions of the region lie close to the town itself, including a fort and a wetland reserve. Beyond the fringes of the town, on the two main roads into Amman, there are several desert castles, including two of the most striking, Qasr Amra and Qasr Karana.

Azraq is the only place in the whole Eastern Desert where accommodation is available. To get a real sense of the desert, it is best to plan a trip around an overnight stop that allows at least for a picnic in the wilderness and a walk off-trail between castle-spotting.

The sights here are listed in a logical, clockwise sequence, leaving Amman via Zarqa and following Hwy 30 to Azraq. The return to Amman is via Hwy 40. This is the best route on which to visit the castles if you are travelling by public transport (which nonetheless involves some backtracking and taxi rides) and it is the usual route followed by tour companies on their day excursions. Don't use up all your energy on the outbound leg as two of the best castles, Qasr Amra and Qasr Kharana, lie along the inbound Hwy 40.

Zarqa الزرقاء

◢09 / POP 910,800 / ELEV 620M

The third-largest city in Jordan after Amman and Irbid, Zarqa is now virtually part of the continuous urban sprawl of northern Amman. There's not much to this gritty working-class city that merits anything more than a passing glance, but you may have to change buses here if you're trying to visit the Eastern Desert on public transport.

In Zarqa, there are two terminals for buses, minibuses and service taxis. Transport to/from the north bus station (Tabarbour) in Amman (600 fils, 30 minutes) use the New (Amman) station. From the Old station in Zarqa, there is public transport to smaller villages in the region, such as Hallabat (for Qasr al-Hallabat and Hammam as-Sarah) and Mafraq. Minibuses also leave intermittently for Azraq (JD1.200, 1½ hours). Minibuses shuttle between the two terminals in Zarqa every few minutes.

Qasr al-Hallabat
قصر الحلابات

With a fair proportion of masonry still standing, some beautifully restored archways and a desolate perch on the edge of the Eastern Desert, this **fort** (admission free; ☉daylight hr) is an excellent introduction to the fabled desert castles of the region. Hallabat once boasted elaborate baths, intricate frescoes and mosaics, a mosque and several reservoirs, and served as a focus for a thriving farming community. Restoration of the site under Spanish direction is helping to restore an inkling of the castle's former stature although the project is likely to take many years to complete.

As with all the castles in Jordan, it takes a bit of sleuthing to peel back the layers of history. In the case of Hallabat, you need only focus on three main eras – Roman, Byzantine and Umayyad.

Look first for a fine mosaic. This sits above a large central cistern and the ruins of the **original fort**. Built by the Romans during the reign of Emperor Caracalla (AD 198–217), the fort, like many in the region, was originally built as a defence against raiding desert tribes. As you survey the land from the castle hill, you can see why they picked this location, as it would have been easy to spot men on horseback darting across the rocky plain.

Now look for additions in basaltic rock, easily distinguished by its black colour. If you venture further into the Eastern Desert you'll find this volcanic rock scattered across vast plains providing a ready supply of building materials. In the 6th century the

fort was converted by the Byzantines into a **monastery** for a short period, using the basalt blocks to expand the Roman structure.

Lastly, admire the decorated finesse of limestone walls (distinguished by their white colour), carved niches, reassembled arches and an elaborate porch with pillars. This is the work of the Umayyads (AD 661–750) who revisited the structure under the reign of the hedonistic caliph Walid II and transformed the modest fort into an imposing three-storey complex with four large towers. Look for the remains of a **large mosque** with cusped arches, an agricultural enclosure fed by an elaborate irrigation system and the ruins of a village for palace servants that were included in the Umayyad's ambitious expansion project. Wondering where the baths are? You'll have to travel 3km east to see the remains of these, at Hammam as-Sarah.

ⓘ Information

A museum is taking shape in the grounds of Qasr al-Hallabat, expected to open by 2013. In the meantime, the courtyard of the adjacent but not yet functioning visitors centre is adorned with reconstructed pillars and archways that give an idea of the decorative details bestowed on Qasr al-Hallabat by the Umayyads. Toilets are available here.

ⓘ Getting There & Away

Close enough to Amman to be visited on a half-day excursion, Qasr al-Hallabat is located near the village of Hallabat and is one of the few castles that can be easily reached by public transport. From Amman's north bus station, take a minibus to the New (Amman) station in Zarqa, another minibus to the Old station in Zarqa, and another to Hallabat village. If you're driving, the castle takes a bit of liberal navigating off Hwy 30 (it is at least signposted) and makes an excellent first stop on the desert castle circuit. To get from here to Azraq, your best bet is to return to Zarqa.

Hammam as-Sarah
حمام الصرح

There might have been considerably more to see at this hammam (bathhouse) and hunting lodge complex, once linked to Qasr al-Hallabat, if locals hadn't taken a liking to the high-quality limestone blocks in the 1950s. It's hard to complain, though, as this kind of recycling has been traditional in the region since well before the Romans. The hammam is still worth a visit, as the compact site has been extensively restored, and today you can still see the underfloor piping system that was used to heat the hot, cold and tepid bathing rooms. Outside the main building is a **well**, nearly 20m deep, an elevated tank and the remains of a nearby **mosque**.

The hammam is located along the main road to Hallabat village, about 3km east of Qasr al-Hallabat and 5km from the main road. The minibus to Hallabat village drives past Hammam as-Sarah and can drop you off on request. The site is unlocked – just push open the gate. You may well see archaeologists at work, reconstructing the dome. It's a good hour's drive from here to Azraq, the main destination on the desert castle circuit.

Azraq

الأزرق

☑ 05 / POP 8000 / ELEV 510M

Meaning 'blue' in Arabic, Azraq once lived up to its name with a shimmering lake and extensive wetlands famed throughout the entire region. This magical oasis was both a refuge for wildlife in the middle of the arid Eastern Desert and a beacon for pilgrims and caravans plying the trade routes between Baghdad to Jerusalem. And then catastrophe struck: the wetlands were all but drained to supply the ever-increasing demands of the capital for water and the fortunes of the town and surrounding farming settlements withered into the bargain.

That's not to say there is now no reason to visit. The town has reinvented itself as a pit

---

DON'T MISS

WHICH CASTLES TO VISIT?

You can't come to the Eastern Desert and miss the desert castles. There are dozens of ruins belonging to the Umayyad dynasty scattered across the gravel plains of the Eastern Desert, so how do you choose which ones to visit?

Below is a list of the main castles and a guide to their accessibility. The castles fall into two convenient sets. The most famous ones lie on the so-called 'desert castle loop'. These are accessible on a day trip from Amman via Azraq, by tour or by car. Individual castles can be reached with more difficulty by a combination of minibus and taxi.

The other set lies on the so-called 'Eastern Desert Highway', or Hwy 10, which leads from the town of Mafraq to the Iraqi border. These are much more time-consuming to visit.

Each of the two sets takes a long, full day to cover. You can combine the two sets by staying the night in Azraq and using Hwy 5 to cut between the two. See also the boxed text (p240) for a third set, all of which are thoroughly off the beaten track.

Set 1: Desert Castle Loop

CASTLE NAME	PUBLIC TRANSPORT	4WD	BY TOUR	WORTHWHILE
Qasr al-Hallabat (p230)	Yes	No	Sometimes	✓✓
Qasr al-Azraq (p233)	Yes	No	Yes	✓✓✓
Qasr 'Uweinid (p235)	No	Yes	No	✓
Qusayr Amra (p236)	Taxi from Azraq	No	Yes	✓✓✓
Qasr Kharana (p238)	Taxi from Azraq	No	Yes	✓✓✓
Qasr Al-Mushatta (p239)	Taxi from Amman	No	No	✓

Set 2: Castles of the Eastern Desert Highway

CASTLE NAME	PUBLIC TRANSPORT	4WD	BY TOUR	WORTHWHILE
Umm al-Jimal (p241)	Yes	No	Sometimes	✓✓
Qasr Deir al-Kahf (p243)	No	No	No	✓
Qasr Aseikhin (p243)	No	No	No	✓
Qasr Burqu (p243)	No	Yes	No	✓✓

stop for trucks pounding the Eastern Desert Highway between Amman and Baghdad, and for overland convoys from Saudi Arabia, and as such it has a frontier town atmosphere. The drivers who veer into this crossroads are all long haul survivors who, in many cases, contend with the hazards not just of interminably tedious roads but also of ambush and the threat of violence. Have a cup of tea with any of these warriors of the long-distance road in the restaurants or mechanic workshops that line the roads of Azraq and suddenly your journey from Amman won't seem so far.

The modern reality of Azraq apart, the town neighbours one of the best of the desert castles, **Qasr al-Azraq**, and has the region's only accommodation. In the vicinity are also **Azraq Wetland Reserve** and **Shaumari Wildlife Reserve**, making the most of what little remains of Azraq's once glorious natural inheritance.

History

As the region's most important permanent body of water and as a source for malachite, Azraq has been settled since Neolithic times. The Romans, Mamluks and Ottomans each had turns in controlling the area and in 1917–18 the town served as a staging post for the soldiers of Faisal's Arab Revolt. Lawrence of Arabia overwintered in the fort, using it as a temporary headquarter.

The town is home to two distinct communities. After WWI Druze refugees fleeing Syria settled in North Azraq, earning a living from salt production. South Azraq, meanwhile, was founded by Chechens fleeing Russian persecution, who eked out a living by farming and fishing on the shores of the oasis. Azraq Lodge is run by people from this community and the restaurant produces robust Chechen meals.

The recent settlement of Palestinian and Syrian immigrants has diluted ethnic distinctions and the virtual death of the oasis in the 1990s caused much of the local population to seek a living elsewhere. A brighter future is on the horizon, however, with the increase in tourism to the Eastern Desert injecting extra life into the local economy.

🛏 Sleeping & Eating

In a day trip it's almost impossible to cover anything more than the main desert castles that lie close to the highway. With an overnight stop in Azraq you can also add a visit to Shaumari Wildlife Reserve, which is currently only possible on a pre-arranged night

safari. Best of all, you can sample a Chechen dinner at Azraq Lodge.

TOP CHOICE **Azraq Lodge** HOTEL **$$**
(📞3835017; s/d incl breakfast from JD62/73; 🌐🖥) This former British 1940s military hospital in south Azraq has been atmospherically renovated by the Royal Society for the Conservation of Nature (RSCN) as a base from which to explore the Eastern Desert. There's an old field ambulance parked under a canvas porch and some period photographs (worth a visit in their own right) hung alongside paraffin lamps and gas masks. The RSCN has done an exemplary job of preserving the historic building while incorporating modern facilities, so thankfully there's no need to rough it on bare stretchers. As for supper, anyone raving about hospital food could normally expect to be admitted – or committed – but at Azraq Lodge the traditional Chechen dishes served from the modernised hospital canteen are likely to be some of the best you sample in Jordan. Ring ahead to request lunch or dinner (JD13) and come with a healthy appetite: the pomegranate salads and thyme-scented meat dishes arrive in generous portions on shared platters. The lodge also houses a small **handicraft workshop** (📞3835017; ⏰9am-5pm) where women from the local community produce and sell silk screen prints, ostrich-egg paintings and recycled paper products.

Al-Azraq Resthouse HOTEL **$$**
(📞3834006; s/d/tr incl breakfast from JD40/52/65; 🌐🖥) This poorly maintained hotel features unkempt rooms in need of maintenance. Given Azraq's water crisis, the swimming pool is an insensitive addition to say the least. Nonetheless, the hotel draws the crowds at weekends and with little other accommodation to choose from, the hotel is an option if Azraq Lodge is full. There is a restaurant serving standard international fare. It's about 2km north of the Azraq T-junction and 1.5km along a local track.

Zoubi Hotel HOTEL **$**
(📞3835012; r from JD10) This utterly no-frills, family-run budget option has seen better days but in the absence of other accommodation it at least provides a convenient place to kip for a night. It's located behind the Refa'i Restaurant, just off the main road, within easy strolling distance of shwarma and grilled chicken restaurants, groceries selling basic foodstuffs and toyshops selling plastic rubber rings – don't ask!

Azraq Palace Restaurant   JORDANIAN BUFFET **$**
(☑079 5030356; buffet with/without salad JD10/7, plates JD2-5; ⏱11am-4pm & 6-11pm) Apart from Azraq Lodge, this is the best place to eat in town, which is why it attracts tour groups on desert-castle excursions. The standard Jordanian fare of rice, grills, salads and dips is tasty and filling and the management helpful.

❶ Getting There & Away

Minibuses run up and down the road along northern and southern Azraq in search of passengers before joining the highway to Zarqa (JD1.200, 1½ hours). If you are driving, you have the choice here of joining Hwy 5, which leads south after at least three or four hours of utter desolation to southern Jordan. The drive to Amman along either Hwy 30 or Hwy 40 takes around two hours. Make sure you obey the rules of desert driving and fill up with petrol when you see a station, as pumps are few and far between.

Qasr al-Azraq   قصر الأزرق

> It was to be Ali's first view of Azraq, and we hurried up the stony ridge in high excitement, talking of the wars and songs and passions of the early shepherd kings, with names like music, who had loved this place; and of the Roman legionaries who languished here as garrison in yet earlier times.
>
> *TE Lawrence, Seven Pillars of Wisdom*

On the edge of the dusty town of Azraq, this imposing **fort** (admission JD1, ticket also valid for Qusayr Amra & Qasr Kharana; ⏱8am-6pm, to 4pm Oct-Mar) is where TE Lawrence and Sharif Hussein bin Ali based themselves in the winter of 1917–18 during the Arab Revolt against the Turks. Lawrence set up his quarters in the room above the southern entrance, while his loyal followers braved the elements. They were holed up here for several months in crowded conditions with little shelter from the intense cold – gaping holes in the roof were patched up with palm branches and clay.

Despite the hardships, TE Lawrence writes fondly about the time spent here with his men at arms. In the evenings they would assemble before a great fire in the open courtyard and break bread while swapping stories of war, peace and love.

The fort, built on Roman foundations, was almost destroyed in 1927 following a violent earthquake. Today busy Hwy 5 unceremoniously grinds past the front door but there is still magic in the air, particularly in the late afternoon when the castle interior is lit up by the setting sun and one can picture Lawrence, eccentric in his Arab robes, descending the stairs for supper around the fire.

History

Comparatively little is known about the history of Qsar al-Azraq, and there's been little excavation and renovation. Greek and Latin inscriptions date earlier constructions on the site to around AD 300, coinciding with Roman occupation.

The fort was renovated by the Umayyad caliph Walid II, who used it for hunting and as a military base. Its present form dates to 1237 when it was fortified by the Ayyubids as a defence against the Crusaders. The Turks subsequently stationed a garrison here in the 16th century. In a turn of the tide in 1918, it was from this building that the Arab Revolt launched an attack on Damascus that proved successful in ousting the Turks from the region.

◉ Sights

Constructed out of black basalt stone, the fort was originally three storeys high. Some **paving stones** in the main entrance have small indentations, carved by former gatekeepers who played a board game using pebbles to pass the time. By the courtyard entrance, look for the carvings of animals and various inscriptions.

Above the entrance is **Lawrence's Room**, strategically overlooking the entry and offset with arrow slits for defence. Opposite the entrance, and just to the left, are the remains of an **altar**, built in the 3rd century AD by the Romans. In the middle of the **courtyard** is a small **mosque**, angled as usual to face Mecca – it dates from the Ayyubid period (early 13th century), but was built on the ruins of a Byzantine church. In the northeast corner of the courtyard, a hole with stairs leads down to a **well**, full of water until about 20 years ago. In the northwest corner are the ruins of the **prison**.

The northern sections are residential areas with barely discernible ruins of a **kitchen** and **dining room**, and nearby **storerooms** and **stables**. The **tower** in the western wall is the most spectacular, and features a huge **door** made of a single massive slab of basalt. Lawrence describes in his book *Seven Pillars of Wisdom* how it 'went shut with a clang and crash that made tremble the west wall of the castle'.

ⓘ Getting There & Away

The fort is situated on the edge of Azraq ash-Shomali (North Azraq), about 5km north of the Azraq T-junction. From the town centre, a taxi to the fort costs around JD1 (JD5 with a 30-minute wait) – if you can persuade a taxi to bother with such a small commission.

Azraq Wetland Reserve
محمية واحة الأزرق

For several millennia, the Qa'al Azraq (Azraq Basin) comprised a huge area of mudflats, pools and marshlands, which led to the establishment of Azraq as one of the most important oasis towns in the Levant.

Although the basin was declared an 'internationally important wetland' by the Jordanian government in 1977, this largely token gesture failed to stop an environmental catastrophe. To provide fresh drinking water for the burgeoning cities of Amman and Irbid, the wetlands were all but drained by 1991.

In recent years, the RSCN has seized control of the wetlands, and established a small **nature reserve** (☑3835017; admission JD8.120; ☺9am-6pm) to help facilitate the recovery of the wetlands. Bird populations have returned but the wetlands remain a meagre reflection of their past glory. An environmental recovery project of this magnitude is certainly worth support, and the on-site visitor centre has well-documented

DIARY OF AN ECOLOGICAL DISASTER

The **Azraq Oasis** and surrounding wetlands originally fanned out over 12,710 sq km (an area larger than Lebanon), and was once regarded as the most important source of water in the region. Today it is considered one of the region's largest ecological disasters. The diary of this catastrophe makes for tragic reading.

» **200,000 BC** Human settlement and herds of elephants, cheetahs, lions and hippos are evident around the Azraq Oasis

» **8000 BC** Age of the 'fossil water' collected in Azraq

» **1950** Around 3000 cu metres of water fills the wetlands per year

» **1960s** Extraction of fossil water from the wetlands to the expanding cities of Amman and Irbid begins

» **1967** On 2 February, 347,000 birds are recorded in the wetlands

» **1975** Twice as much water is pumped from Azraq than the oasis can replenish in order to supply one quarter of Amman's water demands

» **1977** The Jordanian government signed an international wetlands-protection treaty that led to the establishment of the Azraq Wetland Reserve

» **1980** Only 10 cu metres per year of water (compared with 3000 cu metres in 1950) fills the wetlands, exacerbated by the sinking of private, illegal wells for farming

» **1991** The water table drops to over 10m below the ground, and the wetlands dry up completely

» **1994** Funding and commitment from the UN Development Program (UNDP), Jordanian government and RSCN tries to halt the pumping of water from the wetlands to urban centres

» **Mid-1990s** Over-pumping destroys the natural balance between the freshwater aquifer and the underground brine, resulting in brackish water unpalatable for wildlife, and hopeless for drinking and irrigation

» **1998** Species of killifish (Aphanius sirhani), a small fish of only 4cm to 5cm in length and unique to Azraq, is brought to the edge of extinction

» **2000** On 2 February, only 1200 birds are recorded in the wetlands

» **2011** Around 1.5 million cu metres of fresh water is now being pumped back into the wetlands every year by the Jordanian Ministry of Water

» **2015** Projected restoration of about 10% of the wetlands – providing the estimated 500 illegal deep wells operating in the area can be brought under control (if tragic) exhibits detailing the history of the basin's demise.

Sights & Activities

The RSCN estimates that about 300 species of resident and migratory birds currently use the wetlands during their winter migration from Europe to Africa. They include raptors, larks, warblers, finches, harriers, eagles, plovers and ducks. A few buffaloes also wallow in the marshy environs, and jackals and gerbils are occasionally spotted in the late evening. The best time to see birdlife is in winter (December to February) and early spring (March and April). Large flocks of raptors steadily arrive in May. Ultimately, however, bird populations are dependent on the water levels in the reserve and as the water continues to be pumped out quicker than it is pumped in, the future of the oasis remains in jeopardy.

Marsh Trail   HIKING
The 1.5km pathway through the reserve gives an idea of the former beauty of the wetlands. Take a pair of binoculars and stop at the bird hide to spot ducks squabbling between the seasonal reed beds. Bring a bird book during migration as all sorts of unusual species turn up for a drink before heading across the surrounding desert plains. A viewing platform overlooking the Shishan springs is worth noting: these springs once watered the entire wetlands. It takes a hard heart not to be moved by the scale of the ecological devastation visited on this former regional wonder.

Information

A visitor centre run by the RSCN marks the entrance to the reserve. It contains an informative interpretation room and it's hoped the gift shop selling local crafts and artwork will reopen soon.

Getting There & Away

The Azraq Wetland Reserve is located 500m east of Azraq and is signposted off the main road.

Shaumari Wildlife Reserve   محمية الشومري

Established in 1975 by the RSCN, this 22 sq km **reserve** (Mahmiyyat ash-Shaumari; www. rscn.org.jo; ⊙8am-4pm) was established with the aim of reintroducing wildlife that has disappeared from the region, most notably

the highly endangered Arabian oryx. Despite intense funding hurdles, natural predators and the continuous threat of poaching, oryx, Persian onagers (wild ass), goitered and Dorcas gazelles and blue-necked ostriches have flourished here – a testament to RSCN efforts.

At the time of research, Shaumari Wildlife Reserve remained closed to visitors while it undergoes a radical overhaul. According to RSCN staff, the new face of Shaumari will be significantly more attractive to visitors. A night safari may be possible to arrange with advanced booking from the RSCN. Alternatively, ask at Azraq Lodge for the latest status of the reserve. The project espouses such a worthy cause that it deserves all the support it can get.

Getting There & Away

The turning for Shaumari is well signposted, 7km from the Azraq T-junction, along the road to the Saudi border. A small potholed road leads a further 6km to the reserve. The last kilometre is gravel, but is easily manageable in a 2WD.

Qasr 'Uweinid   قصر عويند

If you can find this little scrap of history in the middle of the Eastern Desert, you deserve a medal! Once a robust and practical structure, built by the Romans in the 3rd century AD to protect the source of Wadi as-Sirhan (now in Saudi Arabia), this fort was abandoned less than 100 years later. All that remains to be seen now are the outline of the fort in broken walls and a couple of ruined wells and cisterns.

But you don't come to a fort like this to look at the pile of old stones, strewn across the wadi bottom – even though some of those stones have evocative inscriptions and even though you may well be one of only a handful of people to have stepped over the threshold in centuries. No, you come to a castle like this to enjoy the excuse it provides to encounter the desert. It's probably fair to say that you'll never find it without help (in researching this chapter, a Bedouin sheikh and a police escort helped us locate the pile of greyish ruins on a small tell about 8km southwest of Shaumari). A 4WD isn't strictly necessary as the gravel plain is firm and when it stops being firm, you can get out and walk the last 500m.

A shallow wadi runs alongside the fort, home to stunted tamarisk trees and shrubs of stick-tight (a type of herb). From the top

UNICORNS OF THE DESERT

The last time the Arabian oryx was seen in the wild in Jordan was in 1920 when hunting drove this magnificent, straight-horned antelope to local extinction. In 1972, the last Arabian oryx was killed by hunters in Oman, which led officials to declare the oryx extinct in the wild. However, in a remarkable conservation effort, the nine oryxes left in captivity (known now as the 'World Oryx Herd') were pooled together and taken to the Arizona Zoo for a captive breeding programme.

In 1978, four male and four female oryxes bred in Arizona were transported to Jordan in an effort to help re-establish the country's wild population. Under the auspices of the **Royal Society for the Conservation of Nature (RSCN)**, the first calf, Dusha, was born at Shaumari Wildlife Reserve the following year. Five years later, there were 31 oryxes at Shaumari. Since then, some have been released into the wild at Wadi Rum – a not altogether successful enterprise. The next step is to introduce oryx in other protected areas throughout the country. This has prompted the RSCN to overhaul their facilities at Shaumari significantly in the hopes of attracting greater interest and funding from tourists in their vital conservation project.

The return of the oryx to Jordan was the occasion of great national pride which prompts the question: what is it about this antelope that provokes such emotion? Perhaps it's the uncanny resemblance of a mature bull, with rapier-like antlers, to the mythical unicorn. This is not as far-fetched as it seems. The ancient Egyptians used to bind the antlers of young oryx so they would fuse into one. Seeing a white, summer-coated herd-bull level up to a rival in profile, it's easy to confuse fact with fiction.

---

of the ruins, a vast sky opens up across the almost entirely flat horizon. The silence is almost audible as the nothingness pulses in your ears. This is why you attempt a visit to a castle like Qasr 'Uweinid, to experience the absence of all the usual clutter and noise. If you don't find it, it doesn't matter, but you will have gained a greater understanding of why for centuries visitors have been beguiled by the desert, sand or no sand!

Qusayr Amra   قصر عمرا

One of the best-preserved desert buildings of the Umayyads, the Unesco World Heritage site of Qusayr Amra is the highlight of a trip into the Eastern Desert. Part of a much greater complex that served as a caravanserai, bathhouse and hunting lodge, the *qusayr* (little castle) is famous for its rather risqué 8th-century frescoes of wine, women and wild times.

Today Qusayr Amra appears randomly rooted on the parched desert plain, but in ancient times the site was carefully chosen for its proximity to a lush wadi famed for its wild pistachio trees. The bathhouse was supplied with underground water, tapped from the water table, which lay closer to the surface in former centuries. This potable water was accessed by deep, masonry-clad

wells – one of which can still be seen at the site a few metres north of the main building. Adjacent to this 36m-deep well a restored *saqiyah* (a contraption activated by the circular pacing of a donkey), shows how the water would have been pumped to a cistern diverted either to the baths or to be siphoned off and traded to passing caravans.

The main three-vaulted structure is well-restored but what would otherwise be a fairly modest site is made remarkable by the high state of preservation of the floor-to-ceiling frescoes decorating the interior of Qusayr Amra. An impressive restoration effort has returned much of the vividness of colour to the bacchanalian scenes of hunting, nude bathing and revelry.

History

The Umayyads built Qusayr Amra around AD 711 during the reign of Walid I (AD 705–15). Walid is most famous for launching a building campaign across the Umayyad empire that was crowned by the Umayyad Mosque in Damascus and the Dome of the Rock in Jerusalem.

In contrast to the religious solemnity of these grand projects, the bathhouse at Amra is devoted to more carnal subjects. Mind you, this is no Pompeii – a bared breast is about as daring as it gets. Walid's disapproving successor ordered the destruction of all such imagery. Fortunately for Amra, the far-reaching hand of Damascus spared this remote outpost of the Eastern Desert, allowing the modern visitor to appreciate a humour not normally associated with the early expressions of Islamic society.

Excavation at the site began in the mid-1970s under a team of Spanish archaeologists, and the frescoes were restored with funding from Austria, France and Spain. In 1985, the frescoes were formally recognised as a 'masterpiece of human creative genius' and Qusayr Amra became a World Heritage site.

◉ Sights

Walking downhill from the visitors centre towards the modest little structure, it's hard not to wonder what all the fuss is about. Even entering the main building into the **audience hall**, where meetings, parties, exhibitions and meals were once held, is decidedly underwhelming as the searing light of the surrounding desert all but obliterates the frescoes within.

But then your eyes grow accustomed to the light and you are greeted by two bare-breasted women painted on the arches, holding bowls of food (or money) against a blue background, draped in richly detailed cloth. Five centuries before the Early Renaissance in Europe, these frescoes depict a touchingly human quality – wrestlers warm up before the contest, a woman dressed in a mere strip of cloth bathes without coyness in a hinted patch of sunlight, the ear of a gazelle twitches as the herd surges ahead of the hunt, dogs pant as they race across the **west wall**, driving wild onagers into a trap

of nets. Even the mundane construction of the baths is immortalised in the frescoes – in the compartmentalised images on the ceiling, depicting quarrying, moving the stones by camel, carpentry and plastering of the walls.

These are not the normal stylised images of the day, belonging to a religious canon of signs and symbols. Instead they appear to be a unique attempt to capture daily reality – quite unlike the geometric imagery that has come to be associated with early Islamic art.

That's not to say the frescoes fail to pay homage to more weighty subject matter. Look for the defaced image of the Umayyad caliph and you'll see he is surrounded by **six great rulers**, four of whom have been identified – Caesar, a Byzantine emperor; the Visigoth king, Roderick; the Persian emperor, Chosroes; and the Negus of Abyssinia. The fresco either implies that the Umayyad ruler was their equal or better, or it is simply a pictorial list of Islam's enemies.

And if the frescoes pay lip service to concerning matters of the day, they also encompass their own mostly forgotten symbolism too. A small doorway leads to the left through the three small rooms that made up the baths. The **apodyterium** (changing room) has three blackened faces on the ceiling, said to depict the three stages of man's life. Local Christians believe the central figure to be a depiction of Christ. The left wall has a hallucinogenic painting of an exuberant bear playing the banjo, egged on by an applauding monkey which no doubt would have suggested some political vanity of the day.

THE FRESCOES OF QUSAYR AMRA

The information boards in the visitor centre at Qusayr Amra assure the visitor that: 'None of the paintings of Qusayr Amra portray scenes of unbridled loose-living or carryings-on'. Given the context of early Islam's prohibition of any illustrations of living beings, it's difficult to agree.

Just how far these boundaries were pushed is evident on the western wall of the audience hall, where there is a depiction of a nude woman bathing. Some historians speculate that she may have been modelled on the favourite concubine of the ruler of Amra. The more your eyes roam the walls, past images of musicians, naked dancers, cherubs, baskets of fruit (and even a bear playing a banjo!) the more the heresy of the frescoes becomes apparent.

And the purpose of all these paintings? Some Islamic scholars blame the Ghassanids, a pagan Arab tribe that ruled the region at the time of Rome, others mumble about rogue rulers who were not true to Islam. But most admit privately that it seems as though the rulers were simply enjoying themselves on a boys' night out, away from the confines of the court.

In the **tepidarium** (where warm water was offered and warm air circulated beneath the floor) naked women bathe a child while in the neighbouring hot-water **calidarium**, which is closest to the furnace outside, a whole Dome of Heaven spirals around the ceiling. This map of the northern hemisphere sky, accompanied by the signs of the zodiac, is among the earliest known attempts to represent the universe on anything other than a flat surface. Centaur-like Sagittarius, the Great Bear and several other zodiac signs (see the map in the visitor centre for details) would have been a fitting ultimate subject of contemplation for contemporary bathers.

❶ Information

Tickets to the site can be bought from the **visitor centre** (admission JD1, ticket also valid for Qsar al-Azraq & Qasr Kharana; ⊙8am-6pm May-Sep, to 4pm Oct-Apr). Be sure to take a look at the relief map of the site, descriptions of the site's history and the plan of the frescoes which will help in identifying some of the key highlights (such as the Dome of Heaven) that are quite hard to discern without an idea of what to expect. Public toilets are available in the visitor centre, and a Bedouin tent erected by enterprising locals sells mint tea, minimal refreshments and a few souvenirs.

Photography of the interior of Qusayr Amra doesn't appear to be regulated (perhaps because of the downturn in tourism at the time of writing there was no guard present either), but bear in mind that flash photography, and indeed touching the walls, will harm the frescoes.

❶ Getting There & Away

Qusayr Amra is on the north side of Hwy 40, 26km from Azraq. It is only signposted coming from Amman, so keep an eye out if you are approaching in the other direction as the small, dune-coloured buildings are easy to miss. No minibuses travel this route and buses will not stop at Amra making it impossible to visit by public transport. Without a car, the only option is to hire a taxi from Azraq (from JD15 return if you can persuade one to take you!).

Qasr Kharana قصر خرانه

Located in the middle of a vast, treeless plain, this imposing thick-walled structure was the most likely inspiration for the 'desert castle' moniker. There is no evidence, however, that the intimidating two-storey building, with what appear to be round, defensive towers and narrow arrow slits, was ever intended as a fort. In fact, the towers are completely solid,

which means that they couldn't be manned by armed soldiers and it would be impossible to fire bows from the bizarrely shaped 'arrow slits,' meaning that they most likely served as air and light ducts.

Although it clearly isn't a castle, Kharana was a vital building for the Umayyads as evidenced by its dramatic size and shape. Despite the fact that it has the appearance of a khan (caravanserai), Kharana wasn't located on any major trade route, and there appears to be a total absence of structures for water storage. That just leaves the supposition that the building served as a meeting space for Damascus elite and local Bedouin.

Regardless of its origins, Kharana has been impeccably restored, and is arguably the most photogenic of all the desert castles. Named after the *harra* (surrounding gravel plains), Kharana lords imposingly over a harsh and barren moonscape that appears inhospitable for human habitation. Inside, however, the internal courtyard provides a calm, protected space that even the wind fails to penetrate.

History

Very little is known about the origins of Qsar Kharana, although a painted inscription above one of the doors on the upper floor mentions the date AD 710, making it one of the earliest forts of the Islamic era. The presence of stones with Greek inscriptions in the main entrance also suggests it was built on the site of a Roman or Byzantine building, possibly as a private residence.

◉ Sights

About 60 **rooms** surround the **courtyard** inside the castle, and most likely served as meeting spaces for visiting delegations. The long rooms either side of the arched **entrance** were used as **stables**, and in the centre of the courtyard was a **basin** for collecting rainwater. Remarkably, the interior is much smaller than you'd imagine as the walls are deceptively thick.

Climb the elegant **stairways** and you'll find rooms on the upper storeys with vaulted ceilings. Some **carved plaster medallions**, set around the top of the walls, are said to indicate Mesopotamian influence.

Also in one of the rooms on the second floor are a few lines of Arabic **graffiti**, which were crucial in helping to establish the age of the fortress. Above the door in simple black script is the inscription 'Abd al-Malik the son of Ubayd wrote it on Monday three days from Muharram of the year 92'. Stairs in the southeast and southwest corners lead to the 2nd floor and the roof (closed to visitors).

ℹ️ Information

Entrance to the Kharana is through the **visitor centre** (admission JD1, ticket also valid for Qusayr Amra & Qasr al-Azraq; ⊙8am-6pm May-Sep, to 4pm Oct-Apr), which has some displays on local history. Public toilets are available. The hospitable owner of the adjacent Bedouin tent, which doubles as the site coffeehousep and souvenir stall, will brew you fresh mint tea and take time to discuss the issues of the day. Your patronage will be much appreciated if the current absence of tourism continues.

ℹ️ Getting There & Away

Kharana is 16km further west along Hwy 40 from Qusayr Amra. There's no viable public transport along the highway (although it could be included in a roundtrip by taxi from Azraq, from JD20) and the castle is only signposted coming from Amman. It's easier to spot than neighbouring Amra, especially as it's disappointingly close to a power station.

Qasr al-Mushatta قصر المشتى

Of the five major desert castles, the 'winter palace' of **Qasr al-Mushatta** (admission free; ⊙daylight hr) is the most difficult and time consuming to reach, and thus usually not part of most organised tours. This is not to say that Mushatta is located in the middle of nowhere – on the contrary, it's actually the closest of the desert castles to Amman. In fact, if you're travelling around Jordan in a rental car, the ruins may be the last thing you see in the country as they're located right next to Queen Alia International Airport!

The construction of Qasr al-Mushatta is believed to have started in about AD 743, under Caliph Walid II, who intended to establish a large city in the area. Although the fort was planned as the biggest and most lavish of all the desert castles, it was never finished. In 744, Walid II was assassinated by angry labourers, many of whose colleagues had died during construction due to a lack of water in the area. If you ignore the occasional sound of jumbo jets soaring overhead, the extensive ruins hint at the caliph's grand vision.

Many pieces have disappeared over the years, ending up in museums around the world. The elaborate carving on the facade was shipped off to Berlin (it's now in the Pergamon Museum) after the palace was 'given' to Kaiser Wilhelm in 1903 by Sultan Abd al-Hamid of Turkey. Mushatta was also partially destroyed by earthquakes, and most of the columns and watchtowers have long since collapsed. Despite the castle's slow demise, the huge exterior wall and carved facades still hint at the original grandeur of the site.

To the right of the entrance are the ruins of a mosque, with a rebuilt *mihrab* (niche in mosque, indicating direction of Mecca). The northern sections encompass the remains of a vaulted **audience hall** and **residences**. Segmented pillars lie scattered around like broken vertebrae. One unusual feature of the site is that the vaults were made from burnt bricks (an uncommon material in buildings of this style) rather than black basalt. And of course, don't miss the **ancient toilets** (complete with drains), located at the back of the hall.

ℹ️ Getting There & Away

Qasr al-Mushatta is impossible to reach by public transport. As the castle is located near sensitive areas – primarily the airport – make sure you have your passport ready to show the guards at the military checkpoints along the route.

If you're driving from Amman, head towards the Queen Alia International Airport, turn left off the Desert Highway to the airport, then turn right at the roundabout just past the Golden Tulip Airport Hotel. Leave your passport at the first security check and then follow the road for 12km around the perimeter of the airport, turning right by the second and third check posts.

An alternative is to charter a taxi from the airport (JD15) – a great idea if you have a long wait for a flight – or combine a taxi to the airport with a visit to the ruins. A visit can be made from the airport in an hour.

EASTERN DESERT HIGHWAY

To the east of the town of Mafraq in northern Jordan, the scattered fields and settlements of Druze communities gradually peter out, replaced by a stony, black basalt desert that stretches intermittently to Syria in the north and Iraq in the East. The desolate region has long been criss-crossed by pilgrimage and trade routes to Mecca and Baghdad and its position as a 'strategic corridor' continues today as the location of the Trans-Arabia Pipeline.

The region is best defined, however, by Hwy 10, otherwise known as the Eastern Desert Highway, which rolls in an interminable straight line all the way to the frontier with Iraq. Traversing the corridor between

WORTH A TRIP

FOR THE COMMITTED QASR-SPOTTER...

If the castles of the Zarqa-Azraq-Amman loop have whetted your appetite for Umayyad architecture, then you could earn your *qasr*-spotting badge by searching out one or two of the lesser *qasr* sites. Even though the ruins are not exactly spectacular, they each offer an opportunity to get off the beaten track into remote desert territory. You could visit the following three sites, all accessed via Hwy 40 between Azraq and Amman, on a day trip but it would be hard to fit any of them into the castle loop described in this chapter unless you stop overnight in Azraq.

Qasr al-Tuba   قصر التوبة

Easily the most impressive of the lesser-known castles, Tuba lies approximately 75km southeast of Amman and captures the sense of a staging post on long-forgotten incense routes. Tuba was erected by Caliph Walid II in about AD 743 and abandoned following his sudden assassination. The structure is unique for its sun-baked mud bricks and you can see an imposing doorway from the site at Amman's National Archaeological Museum. Tuba is only accessible by 4WD along dirt tracks 50km south of Hwy 40, or 35km west of the Desert Highway. A knowledgeable guide is recommended, though most local villagers can point out the castle to you. The sole nesting place in Jordan of the rare **Houbara bustard** is at nearby Thalathwat.

Qasr Mushash   قصر موشاش

Once a grand Umayyad settlement, today Mushash lies in ruin. However, it's still possible to get a sense of the original layout, and there are a number of impressive buildings left standing including the remains of a **palace**, a large courtyard surrounded by a dozen rooms, baths, cisterns and walls built to protect against possible flooding. Only accessible by 4WD, Mushash can be reached via an access road along Hwy 40.

Qasr al-Muwaqqar   قصر الموقر

Not much is known about this former Umayyad caravanserai but you can just about make out the shapes of some ancient reservoirs and a column or two. A 10m **stone tower** with Kufic inscriptions, which now stands in the National Archaeological Museum in Amman, was found by archaeologists at the site. The ruins are located about 2km north of Hwy 40.

---

eccentric borders – known as 'Winston's Hiccup' – it thunders day and night with high-sided trucks, many of which travel in convoy for safety's sake. The highway is only occasionally punctuated by a town, developed to service the passing traffic. These sparse and gritty settlements are pretty much the only manmade features of a desert otherwise left to the Bedouin and their goats.

Jordan's harsh deserts make up 80% of the country's land, yet support only 5% of its population. The day trip along the formidable Eastern Desert Highway is almost worth the tedium of the journey to be reminded of that fact. Throw in a couple of atmospheric desert castles, and a fascinating detour through the borderlands with Syria, and the excursion to this little-visited corner of Jordan may well prove to be a highlight of your trip.

There is no accommodation along Hwy 10 and a 4WD is needed if you intend to reach

Burqu, in the middle of the desert at the eastern reach of the highway. The journey from Mafraq to the Iraqi border takes a good four hours as the single-carriage road is not able to support high speeds. With your own vehicle, a two-day round trip from Amman or Irbid can be made via the town of Sefawi at the junction with Hwy 5, with a night's stopover at Azraq. With public transport, you can just about reach Umm Jimmal as a day trip from the nearest place to stay, but forget trying to get from here to anywhere else along the Hwy 10 corridor. Buses to the Iraqi border are best boarded in Amman or Irbid.

Mafraq   المفرق

✓ 04 / POP 152,900 / ELEV 700M

There really is nothing to see in this dusty and congested frontier town. However, like Zarqa, you may have to change buses here if you're heading east, or indeed northwest, on public transport.

Mafraq has two terminals for buses, minibuses and service taxis. The larger Bedouin station has minibuses and service taxis to the north bus station (Tabarbour) in Amman (JD1.300, one hour) as well as to Zarqa and Umm al-Jimal. Although occasional minibuses roam along the back roads to Deir al-Kahf (for Qasr Deir al Kahf), bear in mind that as no accommodation is available in the area, you stand a high chance of being stranded. Equally, the minibus to Ar-Ruwayshid (nearest town to Qasr Burqu) won't help you as the castle site is utterly inaccessible without a 4WD from there.

From the Fellahin station, buses, minibuses and service taxis go to places in northern Jordan, such as Jerash, Irbid and the Syrian border.

Umm al-Jimal   أم الجمال

Comparatively little is known about the ruined city of **Umm al-Jimal** (Mother of Camels; admission free; ⊙daylight hr), which has been referred to by archaeologists as the 'Black Gem of the Desert'. An extensive rural settlement in the lava lands east of Mafraq, Umm al-Jimal is located on the edge of a series of volcanic basalt flows that slope down from Jebel Druze, providing high-quality building materials.

Umm al-Jimal lacks the elaborate temples, colonnaded streets and grand amphitheatres found at Jerash, and much of what remains is unpretentious urban architecture. However, over 150 buildings standing one to three stories above ground remain, including 128 houses and 15 churches. Together, these buildings provide a fascinating insight into rural life during the Roman, Byzantine and early Islamic periods. Compared to other archaeological sites in the region, Umm al-Jimal was rarely looted or vandalised, which has left much of the original layout intact.

The famed American archaeologist HC Butler once wrote: 'Far out in the desert, in the midst of the rolling plain, there is a deserted city all of basalt, rising black and forbidding from the grey of the plain.' Indeed, Umm al-Jimal is one of the region's most captivating sites, and the opportunity to scramble across huge basalt blocks warmed by the heat of the desert sun is not to be missed.

History

Supposedly founded in 1 BC by the Nabataeans, Umm al-Jimal is notable for the inverted V-shaped roofs, constructed from black basalt. The town was taken over by the Romans who used it as part of their defensive cordon against the desert tribes and it prospered as an important trading station for Bedouin and passing caravans. From Umm al-Jimal, roads led north to Bosra (in present-day Syria) and southwest to Philadelphia (modern Amman), which firmly established the town on most of the region's major trade routes.

The city grew during the Byzantine period when churches were constructed and Roman buildings demilitarised. At the peak of growth, this thriving agricultural city boasted some 3000 inhabitants. The key to Umm al-Jimal's prosperity lay in its sophisticated method of storing water, which was a necessity for surviving the long periods

WINSTON'S HICCUP

When Winston Churchill was serving as British Colonial Secretary in the early 1920s, he once boasted that he had 'created Trans-Jordan with the stroke of a pen on a Sunday afternoon in Cairo'. As Churchill had something of a reputation for enjoying 'liquid lunches', a rumour started to fly that he had hiccuped while attempting to draw the border, and stubbornly refused to allow it to be redefined. The resulting zigzag in Jordan's eastern border subsequently became known as **Winston's Hiccup**.

Of course, Churchill was anything but drunk and foolish. The zigzag was precisely plotted to excise Wadi Sirhan, an age-old Incense Route and vital communication highway between French-controlled Syria and Arabia, from Jordan. The masterful pen stroke also created a panhandle between Azraq and Iraq, which meant that the British now controlled an unbroken corridor between the Mediterranean Sea and Persian Gulf.

Today Jordan's erratic boundaries with Syria, Iraq and Saudi Arabia are of little political consequence, at least in comparison to the heightened emotions surrounding the border with Israel. However, Winston's Hiccup does stand as testament to a time when little to no lip service was given to the colonial division of occupied foreign lands.

Umm al-Jimal

Umm al-Jimal

⊙ **Sights**

between rainfall, and for irrigating staple crops. Even today, many of the ancient town's reservoirs are still virtually intact.

Umm al-Jimal declined in the early 7th century AD, coinciding with an outbreak of the bubonic plague and an earthquake in 747 which forced the remaining inhabitants to flee the city.

The ruins of Umm al-Jimal were briefly occupied by Druze refugees fleeing persecution in Syria in the early 20th century. Today, a small modern village has sprung up around the impressive ghost town which is home now only to a few stray dogs and children trotting through the ruins on a short cut to school with their note books tucked under their arms.

⊙ Sights

The large structure just past the southern entrance is the **barracks**, built by the Romans. The towers were added later and, like the

castle at Azraq, it has a swinging basalt door that still functions. The **barracks chapel** was added to the east of the barracks during the Byzantine period (around the 5th century), and is inscribed with the names of the archangels Gabriel, Raphael, Michael and Uriel.

About 150m to the left (west) of the barracks is what some archaeologists believe is a **Nabataean temple** because of the altar in the middle. About 100m north of the barracks is the **Numerianos church**, one of several ruined Byzantine churches. Another 100m to the northeast is the **double church**, recognisable by its two semicircular naves, a wonderful structure that was renovated and extended several times over the centuries. About 80m to the right (east) is **house XVII**, whose double-door entrance, interior courtyard, fine corbelled ceilings, decorated doorways and carved pillars indicate that it was built by a wealthy family.

A few metres to the south is the **sheikh's house**, notable for its expansive courtyard, stables and stairways. Look for the gravity-defying stairs to the north and the precarious corner tower. You can just make out a double stairway to the east of the courtyard. After exiting the building you get a good view of the lovely arched window and vaulted semicircular basement in the exterior eastern wall.

About 150m north of the double church, steps lead down to the **main reservoir**, one of several around the city. Less than 100m to the left (southwest) is **house XIII**, originally a stable for domestic goats and sheep, and later renovated and used as a residence by Druze settlers. Here, take notice of the stone ventilation screen, which was used to separate the manger from the living space.

To the west (about 100m) is the **cathedral**, built in about AD 556, but now mostly in ruins – look for the lintel stone detailing the Roman emperors that ruled over the region. The **praetorium** (military headquarters) is less than 100m to the southwest. Built in the late 2nd century AD by the Romans, it was extended by the Byzantines and features a triple doorway. About 200m to the north through one of the old city gates is the **west church**, easily identifiable by its four arches and ornate Byzantine crosses.

ⓘ Information

Allow at least an hour or two to explore Umm al-Jimal, though its enormous size (800m by 500m) does invite lengthier exploration. One of the highlights of a visit to the ruins is scrambling across the shimmering black rocks, which radiate a surprising amount of warmth. It's best to visit early in the morning, or late in the afternoon, when the black basalt isn't too hot.

For more details about the site, look for the hard-to-find booklet *Umm el-Jimal* (JD3), published by Al-Kutba and available sporadically at bookshops in Amman.

ⓘ Getting There & Away

Umm al-Jimal is about 20km east of Mafraq and only 10km from the Syrian border. With an early start, it is possible to do a day trip from Amman by public transport. From the Abdali or Raghadan bus stations in Amman, catch a bus or minibus to Bedouin station in Mafraq (possibly with a connection in Zarqa), and from Mafraq catch another minibus to Umm al-Jimal.

If you're driving, head 16km east of Mafraq along Hwy 10 towards Safawi, then take the signed turn-off north for 3km to Umm al-Jimal. If you have chartered a taxi from Amman for a day trip around the desert castles, it is possible to include Umm al-Jimal on the itinerary for a little extra (about JD10) – but start early to fit it all in.

Qasr Deir al-Kahf
قصر دير الكهف

Built in the 4th century, the 'Monastery of Caves' is a purpose-built Roman fort that primarily served as a sentry post. Like its famous neighbour Umm al-Jimal, Deir al-Kahf is also constructed of black basalt, though the scattered ruins here are not nearly as extensive.

One of the highlights of Qasr Deir is approaching it along the back roads that lead for 30km or so from Umm al-Jimal. Several Druze settlements dot the way with traditional basalt buildings still in use and small farms with active dovecotes staving off the northern reaches of the Eastern Desert

There's no public transport to be relied upon to deliver you there and back in a day from Amman or Irbid via Mafraq. By car, the easiest way to be sure you are on the right road is to return to Hwy 10 and turn north at Salibayyah. After around 5km, veer right at the intersection with the road from Umm al-Jimal. There are intermittent signposts to Deir al-Kahf or just follow your nose east for a further 25km, running parallel to the Syrian border. The fort is behind a modern police station. An access road leads for 10km south of the ruins to Al-Bishriyya on the Eastern Desert Highway.

The change in scenery is quite dramatic from here as the last of the irrigated farms are left behind on the rolling high ground, replaced by occasional Bedouin tents and herds of livestock. By the time you reach Hwy 10, the dust devils take over the plains and the land extends as far as the eye can see in an uninterrupted flat disc of nothingness.

Safawi
الطفاوي

✓ 05 / POP 8000 / ELEV 700M

A welcome sight along the Eastern Desert Highway is the small town of Safawi. In itself, the ramshackle collection of mechanic shops is unprepossessing to say the least but it does offer the chance to fill up with petrol, buy water and a snack and decide on whether you have enough energy to mount the assault on Qasr Burqu. Ar-Ruwayshid, the junction for Burqu, lies at least another hour and half to the east (a round trip of four and a half hours if you factor in the off-road visit to the lake).

Qasr Aseikhin
قصر الشيخين

This small Roman fort, built from basalt in the 3rd century over the ruins of a 1st-century Nabataean building, is an hour's detour from Safawi. The small structure is worth a visit for the fantastic, commanding view of the plains, framed by a basaltic Roman arch. The vista gives you an idea of the struggle for survival endured by the Bedouin of the Badia – the local name for the Eastern Desert that stretches into Saudi Arabia; even camels are reluctant to pick their way across this rocky, basaltic plain.

The recently-sealed access road to the ruins lies about 10km southwest of Safawi along Hwy 5. For some reason the 10km access road stops about 1km short of the hilltop fort. The graded track thereafter is just about navigable in a 2WD vehicle but the walk is more rewarding if you want to get a sense of the utter remoteness of this former military outpost. From the junction with the main road, it is just 22km to Azraq.

Qasr Burqu
قصر بورقو

You have to be pretty dedicated to visit this brooding black basalt fort, which stands guard over the silent shores of Ghadir (Lake) Burqu. Of course, the apparent incongruity of the lake in the harsh desert is what makes this place so special. With a tent, some basic survival gear and a reliable 4WD, you can

ℹ VISITING THE DESERT CASTLES BY PUBLIC TRANSPORT

Although this is one region that really repays extra expenditure on a tour or on car hire, that doesn't mean the Eastern Desert is off limits to independent travellers on public transport. What it does mean is that you have to be selective about the castles you want to visit and be realistic about the time it takes to get there. There's no accommodation in the region except at Azraq so early morning trips are best, giving you enough time to return to base. If you leave Amman (or Irbid) in the afternoon for the Eastern Desert, you run a real risk of getting stranded.

You can visit the castles at **Umm Jimal**, **Hallabat** and **Azraq** by public transport, although it's almost impossible to travel between these sites without returning to Amman – or at least Zarqa. You shouldn't rely on hitching as there's little traffic.

Probably the most rewarding itinerary is to take the bus to Azraq (via Zarqa) and stay two nights. On the day of arrival you can walk from the town to **Qasr Azraq** and the following morning you can visit the **Azraq Wetland Reserve**. Take a taxi in the afternoon of the second day to **Qusayr Amra** and **Qasr Karana** and return to Azraq in the evening. On the third day, you can head back to Amman.

enjoy a serious desert adventure out here. It is precisely for this reason that the RSCN has been fighting to establish Burqu as a protected reserve, which would fit nicely into its plans to develop tourism in the Eastern Desert. At the time of writing, however, it was only possible to organise trips to Qasr Burqu from the RSCN base in Azraq by prior arrangement, though this may change in future.

The reason for the lake's existence is an ancient dam that was constructed by the Romans in the 3rd century as a means of securing water for caravans heading between Syria and Arabia. In order to secure this vital water source, the Romans also built a small fort here, though it became a monastery during the Byzantine period, and was later restored by the Umayyads in about AD 700. Remarkably, an inscription on one of the walls of the fort suggests that it may have been occupied as late as 1409.

The lake itself is home to a number of bird species (including finches, storks, sandpipers, larks, cranes, buzzards, eagles and vultures) that come to roost because the water level rarely changes, even in summer. The harshness of the surrounding landscape, as well as the lack of properly graded roads, has acted as a strong deterrent against poaching, although the Bedouin occasionally fly their birds of prey in the area. Home to gazelles, desert hares, foxes, hyenas and even caracals this remarkable little oasis has all the makings of a national reserve.

The good news for the flora and fauna – and the bad news for would-be visitors – is that Burqu is only accessible by 4WD. The lake and castle lie 22km northwest of

Ar-Ruwayshid, a forty-five minute drive across the desert on unmarked and unclear tracks from Hwy 10. The turn-off is about 3km west of Ar-Ruwayshid at a sign for Burqu spelt as 'Boarg'a'.

Although the driving is fairly straight forward, with a hard surface to within a few metres of the lake, you should not attempt to find the site without a guide unless you are confident of navigating off-road. If you have experience of desert driving, and provided you stick to the most obvious track, which is often routed between piles of white stone, the lake is fairly easy to find, although it takes quite a bit of nerve to stay your course across the barren land. More difficult is finding your way back to the highway from the lake – almost impossible if you haven't taken any reverse landmarks on the outbound journey (the pylons are helpful and so is the hint of a low, one metre-high embankment of a modern reservoir which you should keep on your left heading towards Burqu). The sense of satisfaction in finding this remarkable little oasis is worth all the anxiety and effort of getting there.

Wild camping is possible out here (don't pitch too close to the lake for the sake of the wildlife – the winged, six-legged varieties bite viciously at dusk) but don't expect that your presence will go unnoticed. The local Bedouin are bound to find you and wonder what you are doing here, on the fringes of civilisation. The good news is they are likely to insist you share tea with them.

To see if it's possible to pre-arrange a guided tour to Qasr Burqu from Azraq, contact the RSCN at the Wild Jordan Centre in Amman (see p74).

Understand Jordan

population per sq km

JORDAN · UK · SYRIA

= 73 people

Jordan Today

Home to a Seventh Wonder

When Petra was voted by popular ballot as one of the seven 'new' wonders of the world, it was a large accolade for a small country. But Jordan – straddling the ancient Holy Land of the world's three great monotheistic religions, and once an important trading centre of the Roman Empire – is no stranger to punching above its weight. Stand on Mt Nebo, consecrated by Pope John II, and survey the land promised to Moses; unfurl a veil at Mukawir, where Salome cast a spell over men in perpetuity; float in the Dead Sea beside a pillar of salt reputed to be Lot's disobedient wife – go just about anywhere in Jordan and you'll find every stone bares a tale.

Jordan circa 2011

With so much history wrapped up in this tiny desert kingdom, it's easy to overlook the modern face of Jordan – something the government is trying to address by improving productivity, making Jordan a more attractive country for foreign investment, promoting Jordan as a hi-tech service centre, and by building ambitious tourist developments, including a Star Wars theme park near Aqaba.

And 'ambitious' is an appropriate word. In a country of minimal resources – where water is in critically short supply, arable land accounts for less than 5% of the landmass, and unemployment is hovering around 13% – the disproportionate investment in Jordan's coastal pleasure domes may appear somewhat reckless, especially given the precarious nature of tourism in the Middle East. That said, with world class attractions and greater stability than some neighbouring countries, Jordan has good reason to be optimistic about its tourist potential.

» **Population:** 6.5 million

» **Population growth rate:** 1%

» **Inflation:** 5%

» **GDP:** US$34.5 billion

» **Main exports:** Clothing, fertilisers, potash, phosphates, vegetables

» **Unemployment:** 13.4%

» **Average annual income:** US$5000

A Few Facts

» Education and healthcare are highly developed in Jordan

» Average male life expectancy is 79 years

» Average female life expectancy is 81 years

» Male literacy rate is 95%

» Female literacy rate is 85%

Travellers' Tales

Travels in Syria and the Holy Land (J L Burckhardt) Account of Petra's rediscovery.

The Desert and the Sown (Gertrude Bell, 1907) The 'brains behind Lawrence's brawn'.

Seven Pillars of Wisdom (T E Lawrence, 1926) The classic.

Top Reads

Married to a Bedouin (M van Geldermalsen, 2006) Bringing a family up in Petra.

Heroine of the Desert (Donya al-Nahi, 2006) Reuniting children with their mothers.

Walking the Bible (Bruce Feiler, 2005) Biblical locations.

belief systems
(% of population)

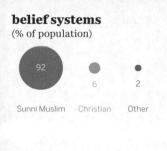

92 — Sunni Muslim

6 — Christian

2 — Other

if Jordan were 100 people

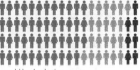

64 would be Jordanian
28 would be Palestinian
7 would be Iraqi
1 would be other

The Arab Spring & Benign Dictatorship

In the spring of 2011, Jordanians joined fellow protesters in Egypt, Tunisia, Libya and Syria in demonstrations popularly dubbed as the 'Arab Spring'. Comprised largely of young students, and peaceful in their approach, Jordanian protesters argued on the streets of Amman for higher wages and a fuller embracing of democracy. At the time of writing, the demonstrations had whittled down to a weekly gathering of die-hards after Friday prayers. Most Jordanians, in contrast, had returned to the important task of making a living in difficult economic times.

Democratic reforms have long been in place in Jordan. In November 1989 the first full parliamentary elections since 1967 were held, and women were allowed the vote. Four years later most political parties were legalised and able to participate in parliamentary and municipal elections.

Despite these concessions, democracy in Jordan is still something of an alien concept. Perceived as promoting the interests of the individual over those of the community, it runs against the grain of tribal traditions where respect for elders is paramount. In common with other parts of the Middle East, Jordan traditionally favours strong, centralised government under an autocratic leader – what might be called 'benign dictatorship'.

Of course, benign dictatorship is only as good as the leader. King Abdullah is widely regarded both at home and abroad as both wise and diplomatic in his role – a modernising monarch in touch with the sensibilities of a globalised world, supportive of social and economic reform and committed to stamping out corruption.

> Jordan is ranked 95th of 169 countries in the Human Development Index (Egypt 113th, Palestinian Territories 114th, Israel 17th). Tourism is worth 11% of GDP and US$900 million annually. In Jordan, 80% of people use mobile phones, compared with 25% in Egypt.

Troublesome Neighbours

Like his father, Abdullah has proved adept at handling foreign affairs – imperative, considering the neighbourhood Jordan shares. Wedged

---

Top Films

Lawrence of Arabia (1962) David Lean's classic.
A Dangerous Man: Lawrence after Arabia (1991) Starring a young Ralph Fiennes.
Indiana Jones and the Last Crusade (1989) Harrison Ford in Petra caper.

Unesco Sites

Petra (1985) Needs no introduction!
Qusayr Amra (1985) Best of the Eastern castles.
Umm ar-Rasas (2004) Unique 1000-year-old mosaics.
Wadi Rum Protected Area (2011) Breathtaking desert.

Religious Freedom

Although the population is overwhelmingly Islamic, Jordan is officially secular, and freedom of religion is a statutory right of the Jordanian constitution.

between Iraq, Syria and Israel and the Palestinian Territories, the country has had to shelter millions of refugees in recent decades. This has strained healthcare and education systems and driven house prices beyond the reach of many Jordanians (who often earn a minimum wage of less than $155 per month). Many Iraqi refugees have brought considerable wealth with them, allowing them to enter the Jordanian property market, inevitably bumping up prices.

More significantly, it has changed the demography of the country forever. While those of Palestinian origin belong to a prospering majority and refugees from the ongoing conflict in Iraq find permanent sanctuary in Jordan, the country is bracing for a fourth influx of refugees (following the Arab Spring) within half a century (see p277). As such, immigration is a major challenge of the coming decade.

A Bright Future

Despite the mixed origins of its people, the current political and economic difficulties and the insecurity of life in a volatile region, Jordanians are united in their pride for their country. And there's a lot to be proud of. The monarchy under King Abdullah continues the acclaimed role of peacemaker between Arab and Western interests, Jordan is a regional leader in protecting the environment and promoting sustainable tourism, and its capital city is enjoying a modern renaissance.

In common with many Arab countries, Jordan is at a crossroads as it faces integration within the modern, democratic, global community. Unlike many of its neighbours, however, Jordan has recognised that the past is part of its future, and while the politicians plan a way to maximise on the country's unique legacy, the Bedouin still herd their sheep across an unchanged landscape in effortless continuity with the ancient past.

Profiling King Abdullah

Studied in USA; attended Sandhurst in UK; succeeded father, King Hussein, in 1999; keen pilot, scuba diver and rally driver; enjoys Western food; speaks better English than Arabic; married to Queen Rania; has four children

---

Speak Easy?

» Jordan media is fairly free, tempered by local sensibilities.

» Jordan Media City transmits 120 channels.

» Criticising the king is against the law.

» Speak easy but don't talk about sex or politics.

Greeting People

» Men should shake hands with men.

» Shake hands with women only if a hand is proffered.

» Give things only with the right hand.

» Baklava or dates make a good gift.

Best to Avoid

» Using the left hand when eating.

» Pointing soles of the feet at someone.

» Exposing shoulders or knees except at beach resorts.

» Entering a mosque or home wearing shoes.

History

Blending of Past & Present

Climbing off his donkey, a shepherd in a terraced field near Madaba tethers the animal to a giant thistle and seeks refuge from the noon heat under a dolmen. Stretched full length under the cold stone roof of this ancient burial chamber, he almost blends into the landscape – until his mobile phone erupts in a rendition of 'We wish you a merry Christmas'.

In Jordan history is not something that happened 'before'. It's a living, breathing part of everyday life, witnessed not just in the pragmatic treatment of ancient artefacts but also in the way people live. Jordanians value their heritage and are in no hurry to eschew ways of life that have proved successful for centuries. The familiar lineal approach to history, therefore, where one event succeeds another in an expectation of so-called 'progress', is almost irrelevant in a country where past and present merge together so seamlessly.

The very entity of Jordan is a case in point. The political state within its current borders is a modern creation, but it encompasses territory (east of the River Jordan) that has hosted the world's oldest civilisations. Egyptians, Assyrians, Babylonians, Greeks, Nabataeans, Romans, Crusaders and Turks all traded, built cities and fought wars here, leaving behind rich cultural influences – leaning posts upon which modern Jordanians have built a proud identity.

Main Periods of History

So are there any distinct historical periods? Not exactly. With some creativity, the abundant historical clues scattered across Jordan can be shuffled into several distinct blocks of time (seven for the purpose of this chapter). Each period of history features in the experiences of a visitor to the country, not only through a pile of fallen columns by the side of the road, but in the taking of tea with old custodians of the

TIMELINE	c 250,000 BC	c 100,000 BC	c 20,000 BC
	With the aid of hand axes made of flint, early humans hunt elephants across the plains in the mild, wet climate of the Jordan Valley.	The Red Sea, lying in a branch of the great Rift Valley, retreats from Wadi Araba, leaving the Dead Sea and Lake Galilee as two separate lakes.	Hunters and gatherers live in seasonal camps and rear their own livestock, with goats forming a substantial part of the diet in the early communities at Wadi Madamagh, near Petra.

desert or the bargaining for a kilim with designs inherited from the Byzantine era.

In fact, just step foot in Jordan and you begin your encounter with history. Visit the dolmens near Madaba, for example, and you enter the cradle of civilisation; dating from 4000 BC, the dolmens embody the sophistication of the world's first villages. The era of trading in copper and bronze helped bring wealth to the region (1200 BC); you can find forgings from Jordan's ancient copper mines near Feynan Ecolodge in the Dana Biosphere Reserve. Travel the King's Highway and you'll not only be stepping in the path of royalty, but you'll see how this route helped unify city-states into a recognisable Jordan between 1200 BC and 333 BC.

The Greeks, Nabataeans and Romans dominated Jordan's most illustrious historical period (333 BC–AD 333), leaving the magnificent legacies of Petra and Jerash. The arrival of Islamic dynasties is evident from the 7th century onwards – in fact, the evidence is literally strewn over the deserts of Eastern Jordan in the intriguing Umayyad structures that dot the stark landscape. The conflict between Islam and Christianity, evident at Jordan's crusader castles in Ajloun, Karak and Shobak, is a defining feature of the next thousand years.

British imperialism dominates Jordan's history prior to the Arab Revolt of 1914. Ride a camel through Wadi Rum and cries of 'To Aqaba' hang in the wind – and so does the name of Lawrence, the British officer whose desert adventures have captured the imagination of visitors to such an extent that whole mountains are named after him! Thereafter, Jordan's history is about independence, modernisation and cohabitation with difficult neighbours.

The remainder of this chapter charts each of these periods in more detail.

Life in the 'Fertile Crescent' (10,000–4000 BC)

Early Settlements

Stand on top of the knoll at Shkarat Msaiad, on the seldom-used road from Siq Al-Barid (Little Petra) to Wadi Araba (see the boxed text, p114), and survey the minimal mounds of stone and you could be forgiven for wondering what all the fuss is about. Despite the isolated beauty of the place, there isn't much to see but some stone walling. Yet this is the kind of place that archaeologists rave about because what you are looking at, they will solemnly tell you, is a 'PPN'.

A PPN, for the uninitiated, stands for Pre-Pottery Neolithic and is significant because such sites indicate a high degree of organisation among early communities. In fact, at this sheltered spot in the hills,

c 8000 BC	c 6000 BC	c 5000 BC
Some of the world's earliest settlements are established at Ain Ghazal and Al-Beidha and neighbouring Jericho. Inhabitants tame, breed and cook domestic animals.	The Ain Ghazal fertility sculptures (among the world's oldest sculptures) and wall paintings at Teleilat Ghassul in the Jordan Valley show that early inhabitants of the region value cultural activity.	Monumental stone dolmen near Ar-Rawdah indicate that burials are now linked to concepts of afterlife. The ingenious engineering is a wonder – and a mystery.

» Statue, Ain Ghazal

WERNER FORMAN/CORBIS ©

you are looking at the very dawn of civilisation. If nothing else, the traces of shelter, water collection and farming demonstrate the basic immutability of life.

Jordan has a remarkable number of early settlements, largely thanks to its location within the 'fertile crescent' – the rich arc of lands that included Mesopotamia, Syria and Palestine. The fecundity of the soil in this region allowed early humans to move from a hunter-gatherer existence to settlement in the world's earliest villages, dating between 10,000 and 8500 BC. One such village in Jordan is Al-Beidha, near Petra. It's tempting to think of our ancient forebears as simple people living simple lives, but the inhabitants of villages such as Al-Beidha built houses of stone and wood; they tamed, bred and cooked domestic animals; they planted wild seeds, grew crops, crushed grains and kept food in mud vessels hardened under the sun; and they began wearing and forming decorative items – such as the astonishing fertility sculptures from Ain Ghazal dated around 6000 BC. These early settlers even left a record of their existence through wall paintings, such as those at Teleilat Ghassul in the Jordan Valley.

Complexity of Early Society in Jordan

If you have lingering doubts about the sophistication of the ancients, ponder the fields of dolmens that are scattered throughout the country, and were constructed between 5000 and 3000 BC. Come across the local shepherds and they may well ask you: 'Why are you here? Is anything good here?' That would be a great question to pose to the ancients who carefully aligned their last resting places along the shoulders rather than the ridges of the semi-arid hills. As for us moderns, these highly charged sites force a reconsideration of these early people: how did they lever the monumental bridging stones into place and what power of belief prompted such laborious, collaborative effort? Many of Jordan's archaeological treasures provoke more questions than they answer in our human quest to understand more about our origins.

From Metals to Massacres (4000–1200 BC)

Invest enough importance in an object and someone else will inevitably want one as well. There's evidence that Jordan's first farmers swapped desirable items among themselves well before 4000 BC, perhaps triggering the rivalry to make and trade more accurate tools and more beautiful adornments. One commodity useful for both tools and adornments was copper – of which Jordan has plenty. Visit Khirbet Feynan in present-day Dana Nature Reserve and the vast areas of black copper slag illustrate the importance of copper mining for the ancient people of the region.

From the earliest settlements, some people devoted themselves to animal husbandry, sustained by the meat, milk and wool of their livestock, while others planted olives, wheat and barley and farmed the land. This distinction between the 'desert and the sown' is apparent to this day.

c 4000 BC	c 2900 BC	c 2300 BC	c 1500 BC
Permanent settlements are established in modern-day Amman and in the south, while copper is mined at Khirbet Feynan. Arts, such as pottery, illustrate the influence of powerful neighbours in Egypt.	City-states emerge across the Middle East. Towns at Amman, Pella, Deir Alla and Tell Irbid are fortified and trade develops with neighbouring powers in Syria, Palestine and Egypt.	Sodom and Gomorrah, among the five so-called Cities of the Plain, are destroyed in a cataclysmic disaster on the southeast corner of the Dead Sea.	The Middle East enters a period of turmoil as Egypt's influence declines. The Philistines arrive west of the River Jordan, giving the land its current name of Palestine.

RIFT VALLEY & THE BIOGRAPHY OF A SEA

You can't think about history in Jordan without factoring in its position on the edge of the ancient Rift Valley. Standing beside the apologetic trickle of water that runs through Bethany-Beyond-the-Jordan today, it's hard to imagine that some 100,000 years ago the entire Jordan Valley was under the fertile waters of the Red Sea. When the sea retreated it left two landlocked stretches of water – the Sea of Galilee (known in Jordan as Lake Tiberius) and the Dead Sea.

Despite its name – given by the Greek geographer and historian Pausanias, who noticed its life-defying salinity – the Dead Sea has long been associated with health-giving properties. Book into a Dead Sea spa and you will be part of a tradition begun in biblical times. Herod visited the spa at Callirhöe near Herodus Spring to treat itching skin, and Byzantine Christians followed suit along pilgrim roads to Bethany-Beyond-the-Jordan, Mt Nebo and Lot's Cave.

Useful in extending life, the Dead Sea has been useful in death, too. Study the haunting eyes of the Ain Ghazal statues in the National Archaeological Museum in Amman (dated from around 6000 BC, they're reputedly the oldest sculptures in the world) and you'll see that they are blackened with bitumen. The Greeks and Romans named the Dead Sea the 'Sea of Pitch' on account of the bitumen that used to float to the surface. This substance was harvested by the Nabataeans who sold it to the Egyptians, who in turn used it for waterproofing funeral boats and for mummification. Ships laden with bitumen regularly crossed the sea in ancient times, as illustrated in the 6th-century Madaba mosaic map. The last piece of bitumen surfaced in 1936.

Today the area continues to contribute to health and wealth with important revenues from tourism and potash. Part of the western shore belonged to Jordan when the famous Dead Sea scrolls were discovered by a Bedouin shepherd at Qumran in 1947. Israel took control of the entire western shore in 1967 after the Six Day War, giving the term 'Rift Valley' a particularly modern resonance.

Within a thousand years, experimentation with metalwork led to the mixing of copper and tin to create bronze, a hardier material that allowed for the rapid development of tools and, of course, weapons.

During the Bronze Age (3200–1200 BC) the region's settlements showed greater signs of accumulated luxury items, growing rich on indigo, sulphur and sugar (which was introduced into Europe from the Dead Sea area). It is not by chance that the greater wealth coincided with a preoccupation with security, with defensive walls built around towns such as Pella. Early invaders included the Amorites, whose arrival in the area is often associated with the violent destruction of the five Cities of the Plain (near the southern end of the Dead Sea), including the settlements of Sodom and Gomorrah (see the boxed text, p124).

c 1200 BC	850 BC	582 BC	c 500 BC
Ammon (Amman), Moab (Dhiban) and Edom (Buseira) emerge as the dominant kingdoms to the east of the Jordan River. Moses and the Israelites are refused entry to Edom.	The divided Israelite empire is defeated by Mesha, king of Moab, who recorded his victories on the famous Mesha Stele in the Moabite capital of Dhiban.	Ammon, Moab and Edom enjoy brief unity after near annihilation by the Israelites under King David and King Solomon. The union is short-lived; they become Babylonian provinces under King Nebuchadnezzar II.	The innovation of the camel saddle transforms the lives of Arab nomads and eventually brings new caravans to Jordan's southern deserts en route to Damascus.

Invasion was not confined to the boundaries of modern-day Jordan. By the late Bronze Age (1500–1200 BC) the whole of the Middle East appeared to be at war. Wealthy city states in Syria collapsed, Egyptians retreated within their own borders from outposts in the Jordan Valley, and marauding foreigners ('Peoples of the Sea') reshaped the political landscape of the Eastern Mediterranean. The latter also brought the Philistines, who settled on the west bank of the Jordan and gave the land its current name of Palestine.

Unity in Adversity (1200–333 BC)

Emergence of a Recognisable 'Jordan'

It is difficult to talk about Jordan as a single entity for most of the country's history. That's because, at least until the latter part of the 20th century AD, its borders expanded and retreated and its peoples came and went, largely driven by the political ambitions and expediencies of more powerful regional neighbours.

Around 1200 BC, however, something akin to a recognisable 'Jordan' emerged from the regional mayhem in the form of three important kingdoms: Edom in the south, with its capital in Bozrah (modern Buseira, near Dana); Moab near Wadi Mujib; and Ammon on the edge of the Arabian Desert, with a capital at Rabbath Ammon (present-day Amman). It is unlikely that any of the three kingdoms had much to do with each other until the foundation of the new neighbouring city-state of Israel.

Succumbing to Powerful Neighbours

Israel quickly became a military power to be reckoned with, dominating the area of Syria and Palestine and coming into inevitable conflict with the neighbours. Under King David the Israelites wrought a terrible revenge on Edom, massacring almost the entire male population; Moab also succumbed to Israelite control and the people of Ammon were subject to forced labour under the new Jewish masters. However, Israelite might proved short-lived and, after King Solomon's brief but illustrious reign, the kingdom split into Israel and Judah.

By the middle of the first millennium BC – perhaps in response to Israelite aggression – Ammon, Moab and Edom became a unified entity, linked by a trade route known today as the King's Highway. The fledgling amalgam of lands, however, was not strong enough to withstand the might of bullying neighbours, and it was soon overwhelmed by a series of new masters: the Assyrians, Babylonians and Persians. It would be centuries before Jordan achieved a similar distinct identity within its current borders.

According to a German survey, 15,000 to 20,000 tonnes of copper were produced from Feynan's copper-smelting sites – some of the oldest such sites in the region. This has left 150,000 to 200,000 tonnes of slag dotting the arid landscape.

Books on Jordan's History

» *The Middle East: A Brief History of the Last 2000 Years* (Bernard Lewis, 1996)

» *History of the Arabs* (Philip Hitti, 1937)

333 BC	c 323 BC	c 100 BC	30 BC
Alexander the Great wins the Battle of Issus, defeating Persian King Darius III. He moves on Syria and Palestine, which comes under the expansive empire of Greece.	Alexander dies in Babylon. The Greek inheritance gives access to the treasures of classical learning, and the cities of Philadelphia (Amman), Gadara, Pella and Jerash blossom under Hellenistic rule.	Greek generals squabble over who rules which parts of the Trans-Jordan while a tribe of nomadic Arabs quietly makes money from passing caravans. They establish their capital at Petra.	Herod the Great expands the castle at Mukawir, which will in a few years' time set the stage for Salome's dance and the beheading of John the Baptist.

The Middle Men of the Middle East (333 BC–AD 324)

War and invasion were not the utter disaster that they might have been for the people of the region. Located at the centre of the land bridge between Africa and Asia, the cities surrounding the King's Highway were particularly well placed to service the needs of passing foreign armies. They also profited from the caravan routes that crossed the deserts from Arabia to the Euphrates, bringing shipments of African gold and South Arabian frankincense via the Red Sea ports in present-day Aqaba and Eilat. The Greeks, the Nabataeans and the Romans each capitalised on this passing bounty, leaving a legacy of imported culture and learning in return.

The Greeks

By the 4th century BC the growing wealth of Arab lands attracted the attention of a young military genius from the West known as Alexander of Macedon. Better known today as Alexander the Great, the precocious 21 year old stormed through the region in 334 BC, winning territories from Turkey to Palestine.

At his death in 323 BC in Babylon, Alexander ruled a vast empire from the Nile to the Indus, with similarly vast dimensions of commerce. Over the coming centuries, Greek was the lingua franca of Jordan (at least of the written word), giving access to the great intellectual treasures of the classical era. The cities of Philadelphia (Amman), Gadara, Pella and Jerash blossomed under Hellenistic rule, and prospered through growing trade, particularly with Egypt, which fell under the same Greek governance.

THE CITY-STATE OF ISRAEL

The kingdoms of Edom, Moab and Ammon are mentioned in the Bible, especially in connection with the wandering Jews of the Exodus. According to the Old Testament, Moses and his brother, Aaron, led their people through Sinai in Egypt looking for a permanent territory to inhabit. They were forbidden entry to southern Jordan by the Edomites but managed to wind their way north, roughly along the route of the modern King's Highway, towards the Jordan River. Moses died on Mt Nebo, in sight of the Promised Land, and it was left to his successor Joshua to lead the Israelites across the river to the West Bank where they conquered the city of Canaan, which led to the establishment of the city-state of Israel in around 1436 BC.

9 BC–AD 40	AD 26	106	111–14
Aretas IV, greatest of the Nabataean kings, presides over a city of wealth and beauty. The hidden cluster of tombs, temples and houses is adapted from Greek and Roman architecture.	Jesus Christ is baptised in Bethany-Beyond-the-Jordan by John the Baptist. The first church is built soon after at Rihab, 40km from Amman, protecting Jesus' disciples from persecution in Jerusalem.	Roman Emperor Trajan absorbs the Nabataean empire into the province of Arabia Petraea, signalling the end of Petra's heyday.	The Romans build the Nova Via Taiana, following the path of the ancient King's Highway between Bosra and the Red Sea, bringing new life to an ancient thoroughfare.

The Nabataeans

Trade was the key to Jordan's most vibrant period of history, thanks to the growing importance of a nomadic Arab tribe from the south, known as the Nabataeans. The Nabataeans produced only copper and bitumen (for waterproofing boat hulls) but they knew how to trade in the commodities of neighbouring nations. Consummate middlemen, they used their exclusive knowledge of desert strongholds and water supplies to amass wealth from the caravan trade, first by plundering and then by levying tolls on the merchandise that traversed the areas under their control.

The most lucrative trade involved the transportation, by camel, of frankincense and myrrh along the Incense Route from southern Arabia to outposts further north. The Nabataeans were also sole handlers of spices shipped to Arabia by boat from Somalia, Ethiopia and India. Suburbs at the four corners of their capital, Petra, received the caravans and handled the logistics, processing products and offering banking services and fresh animals before moving the goods west across the Sinai to the ports of Gaza and Alexandria for shipment to Greece and Rome.

The Nabataeans never possessed an 'empire' in the common military and administrative senses of the word; instead, from about 200 BC, they established a 'zone of influence' that stretched from Syria to Rome. As the Nabataean territory expanded under King Aretas III (84–62 BC), they controlled and taxed trade throughout the Hejaz (northern Arabia), the Negev, the Sinai, and the Hauran of southern Syria. Nabataean communities were influential as far away as Rome, and Nabataean tombs still stand at the impressive site of Madain Salah in Saudi Arabia.

Key Nabataean Sites
» Petra, Jordan
» Siq Al-Barid, near Petra, Jordan
» Madain Saleh, Saudi Arabia

The Romans

You only have to visit Jerash for five minutes, trip over a fallen column and notice the legions of other columns beside, to gain an immediate understanding of the importance of the Romans in Jordan – and the importance of Jordan to the Romans. This magnificent set of ruins is grand on a scale that is seldom seen in modern building enterprises and indicates the amount of wealth the Romans invested in this outpost of their empire. Jerash was clearly worth its salt and, indeed, it was the lucrative trade associated with the Nabataeans that attracted the Romans in the first place. It's perhaps a fitting legacy of their rule that the Jordanian currency, the dinar, derives its name from the Latin *denarius* (ancient Roman silver coin).

The Romans brought many benefits to the region, constructing two new roads through Jordan – the Nova Via Traiana (AD 111–114) linking Bosra with the Red Sea, and the Strata Diocletian (AD 284–305) linking

Jordan's Roman Spectacles
» Citadel, Amman
» Roman Theatre, Downtown Amman
» Oval Plaza, Jerash
» Decumanus maximus, Umm Qais
» Hint of former glories at Pella

HISTORY THE MIDDLE MEN OF THE MIDDLE EAST (333 BC–AD 324)

c 200–300
The golden age for Roman Arabia is marked by grand monuments in the cities of the Decapolis. Emperor Hadrian honours Jerash with a visit en route to Palestine.

» Columns at Jerash (p83)

c 284–305
The Romans build the Strata Diocletian linking Azraq with Damascus and the Euphrates. A string of forts in the Eastern Desert shores up the rim of the empire.

NICO TONDINI/CORBIS ©

GATEWAY TO THE AFTERLIFE: THE NABATAEAN RELIGION

A young family, arriving early for the Petra Night Tour, were waved on alone through the candlelit Siq (gorge). Haunted by the sound of their own footsteps, they soon began to feel there was something amiss. By halfway, the young daughter, overwhelmed by the towering shadows of this sacred way, begged her parents to turn back. A few moments later, all three were hastily beating a retreat. Only those who have ever been in Petra's Siq alone will understand the power this extraordinary passage has on the soul. It was chosen surely for exactly this reason, for it was no ordinary passage: it was a gateway to the afterlife.

Surprisingly little is known about Nabataean religion, considering that their preoccupation with the afterlife dominates much of their capital at Petra. It is known, however, that the early desert polytheistic religion of the original Arabian tribe absorbed Egyptian, Greek and Roman, and even Edomite and Assyrian beliefs, to create a unique faith.

The main Nabataean god was Dushara, the mountain god, who governed the natural world. Over the years he came to be associated with the Egyptian god Osiris, Greek god Dionysus and the Roman god Zeus.

For fertility, the Nabataeans prayed to the goddess Al-'Uzza (the Very Strong), who became associated with Aphrodite and Isis. Al-Kutba was the god of divination and writing, linked to Hermes and Mercury. Allat (literally 'Goddess') was associated with Athene.

Early representations of the Nabataean gods were non-figurative. Divine stones known as *baetyls* marked important wadis, junctions, canyons and mountaintops, representing the presence of the divine. Religious processions to Petra's spiritual 'High Places' were an important part of the community's religious life, culminating in a sacrifice (perhaps human) and ritual purification.

Though the secrets of Nabataean religious ceremonies are hidden in history, there is a strong sense of what one might call 'spiritual presence' enveloping Petra's high places of sacrifice: the god blocks, carved niches, altars and sacrificial basins all indicate that the hilltops were holy ground, used by the priests for mediating between heaven and earth.

Azraq with Damascus and the Euphrates. A string of forts in the Eastern Desert at Qasr al-Hallabat, Azraq and Umm al-Jimal was also built to shore up the eastern rim of the empire.

The 2nd and 3rd centuries were marked by a feverish expansion of trade as the Via Traiana became the main thoroughfare for Arabian caravans, armies and supplies. The wealth benefited the cities of Jerash, Umm Qais and Pella, members of the Decapolis (see p82), a league of provincial cities that accepted Roman cultural influence but retained their independence.

With the eventual demise of the Roman Empire, and the fracturing of trade routes over the subsequent centuries, Jordan's entrepreneurial leadership of the region never quite regained the same status.

324	614	629	c 700
Emperor Constantine converts to Christianity. Christianity becomes the dominant religion of the Byzantine Empire and many churches are built. Madaba becomes the focus of pilgrim trails to Jerusalem.	Emperor Heraclius forces invading Persians to make peace; despite this victory Byzantine Christian rule in the Trans-Jordan soon ends. A storm is brewing in Arabia, bringing Islam in its wake.	Muslim forces lose the Battle of Mu'tah against Christians. After Prophet Mohammed's death (632), they win the decisive Battle of Yarmouk (636) and Islam becomes the region's dominant religion.	The Umayyads from Syria overtake the region and build some extraordinary bathhouses, hunting lodges and fortified meeting places (known today as 'Desert Castles') in the arid desert east of Amman.

Spirit of the Age (AD 324–1516)

For 1500 years after the birth of Jesus, the history of Jordan was characterised by the expression of organised faith in one form or another. Under the influence of Rome, Christianity replaced the local gods of the Nabataeans, and several hundred years later Islam took its place – but not before a struggle that left a long-term legacy and a string of Crusader forts.

Conversion to Christianity

Think of the history of the Christian religion and most people understandably focus on the 'Holy Land' to the west of the River Jordan. And yet, if recent evidence is to be believed, the Christian church may never have evolved (at least not in the way we know it today) if it hadn't been for the shelter afforded to the early proponents of the faith on the *east* bank of the Jordan.

In 2008, 40km northeast of Amman, archaeologists uncovered what they believe to be the first church in the world. Dating from AD 33 to AD 70, the church, which was buried under St Georgeous Church in Rihab, appears to have sheltered the 70 disciples of Jesus Christ. Described in the mosaic inscriptions on the floor of the old church as the '70 beloved by God and Divine', these first Christians fled persecution in Jerusalem and lived in secrecy, practising their rituals in the underground church. Pottery dating from the 3rd to the 7th century shows that these disciples and their families lived in the area until late Roman rule.

The conversion by Emperor Constantine to Christianity in AD 324 eventually legitimised the practice of Christianity across the region. East of the Jordan River, churches were constructed (often from the building blocks of former Greek and Roman temples) and embellished with the elaborate mosaics that are still visible today at Madaba, Umm ar-Rasas and Petra. Christian pilgrims began to search for relics of the Holy Land, building churches en route at biblical sites such as Bethany, Mt Nebo and Lot's Cave. It was the archaeological rediscovery of these churches 1400 years later that confirmed the lost location of these biblical sites to a forgetful modern world (see p269).

The Rise of Islam

Reminders of Christianity are scattered across Jordan today, for instance in the observance of the faith in towns such as Madaba. But listen to the bells peal on a weekend and moments later they will be replaced by the Muezzin's call to prayer from the neighbouring mosque. Islam is present not just in Jordan's mosques but in the law, in social etiquette and at the very heart of the way people live their lives – in Bedouin camps as well as in modern city centres. So how did Islam reach here and how did it replace Christianity as the dominant religion?

The discovery in 2008 of the world's oldest church was described by senior Orthodox clerics as an 'important milestone for Christians all around the world'. Jordanian authorities are now hoping to develop the site as a tourist attraction.

Prophet Mohammed's son-in-law, the caliph Ali, was assassinated in 660. He was succeeded by Mu'awiyah, who established the Umayyad dynasty (661–750). The bitter dispute over this succession split Islam into two factions, the Sunnis and the Shiites.

747	1095	1115	1142
An earthquake shatters northern Jordan and Syria, weakening the Umayyads' hold on power. They're replaced by the Abbasids, signalling a period of Persian cultural dominance and less tolerance towards Christianity.	Pope Urban II sparks a 'holy war' in revenge for church destruction by Seljuks and to protect pilgrim routes to the Holy Land. Crusaders soon capture Jerusalem, slaughtering countless inhabitants.	Crusader King Baldwin I builds Montreal (Mount Real or the Royal Mountain) – the picture-perfect castle in Shobak. It withstood numerous attacks from the armies of Saladin.	The imposing Karak Castle is built to withstand Saladin's armies; in 1148 it is inherited by the sadistic Renauld de Chartillon of France who delights in torturing prisoners.

From 622 (10 years before the death of the Prophet Mohammed) the armies of Islam travelled northwards, quickly and easily spreading the message of submission (Islam) well beyond the Arabian Peninsula. Although they lost their first battle against the Christian Byzantines at Mu'tah (near Karak) in 629, they returned seven years later to win the Battle of Yarmouk. Jerusalem fell in 638 and Syria was taken in 640. Islam, under the Sunni dynasty of the Umayyads, became the dominant religion of the region, headquartered in the city of Damascus, and Arabic replaced Greek as the lingua franca. Within 100 years Muslim armies controlled a vast empire that spread from Spain to India.

The Umayyads' rich architectural legacy included the Umayyad Mosque in Damascus and the Dome of the Rock in Jerusalem. In eastern Jordan, the Umayyads' close attachment to the desert led to the construction of a string of opulent 'desert castles' (p231), including the brooding Qasr Kharana (built in 710) and Qusayr Amra (711).

Despite the blossoming of Islamic scholarship in medicine, biology, philosophy, architecture and agriculture over the next three centuries, the area wedged between Jerusalem and Baghdad remained isolated from the sophisticated Arab mainstream. This is one reason why Jordan possesses relatively few demonstrations of Islamic cultural exuberance.

> Maalouf's lively *The Crusades Through Arab Eyes* recasts the West's image of knights in shining armour as ruthless barbarians who pillaged the Middle East, the horrors of which still reside in the collective Arab consciousness.

The Crusades & Holy War

The armies of Islam and Christianity have clashed many times throughout history and the consequences (and language of religious conflict) resonate to this day both within the Middle East and across the world at large.

The Crusades of the 12th and 13th centuries are among the most famous of the early conflicts between Muslims and Christians. Survey the mighty walls of the great Crusader castles at Karak and Shobak and it's easy to see that both sides meant business: these were holy wars (albeit attracting mercenary elements) in which people willingly sacrificed their comfort and even lives for their faith in the hope of gaining glory in the hereafter – ironically, according to Islam at least, a hereafter shared by Muslims and the 'People of the Book' (Jews, Christians and so-called Sabians).

> Nureddin (literally 'Light of the Faith') was the son of a Turkish tribal ruler. He united the Arab world and defeated the Crusaders in Egypt. His campaign against the Crusaders was completed by Saladin (Restorer of the Faith), a Kurdish scholar and military leader.

Built by King Baldwin I in the 12th century, the castles were part of a string of fortifications designed to control the roads from Damascus to Cairo. They seemed inviolable, and they may have remained so but for Nureddin and Saladin, who between them occupied most of the Crusader strongholds in the region, including those of Oultrejordain (meaning 'across the Jordan'). The Damascus-based Ayyubids, members of Saladin's family, squabbled over his empire on his death in 1193, enabling the Crusaders to recapture much of their former territory along the coast.

1187	1193	1258
Despite superb defences at Shobak and Karak, Karak is overrun after an epic siege in 1183; Saladin goes on to beat the Crusader armies in the decisive Battle of Hittin.	Saladin dies and the ensuing family in-fighting enables the Crusaders to recapture much of their former territory.	Mongols storm Baghdad and the armies of Genghis Khan's son reach Ajloun and Salt. They are repelled by Mamluks who rebuild the castles at Karak, Shobak and Ajloun.

» Karak Castle (p145)

HISTORY OF A HIGHWAY

When pondering the King's Highway, a fair question is to ask: 'which king?' In fact, the highway was never the personal project of royalty: it gained its name through the sense of major thoroughfare, often referred to in the Arabian Orient as 'royal road'.

The highway runs for 297km between Madaba and Petra; for a thousand years before Christ it linked the kingdoms of Ammon, Moab and Edom. One of the earliest mentions of the highway is in the biblical episode in which Moses was refused passage along the highway by the King of Edom. The Nabataeans used the route to transport frankincense, originating in southern Arabia, and other exotic commodities to the important trading posts of Syria. In later times, the highway received a suitably Roman makeover under Emperor Trajan, who widened and rerouted part of the highway to facilitate the passage of troops.

The highway has great religious significance for both Christians and Muslims. Attracted by the holy sites of Mt Nebo and protected by the Crusader forces, Christians used the route for pilgrimage, building and embellishing many shrines along the way, such as the Church of St Stephen at Umm Ar-Rasas. Muslims used the route on pilgrimage to Mecca until the Ottomans developed the Tariq al-Bint in the 16th century – the approximate path of the Hejaz Railway, built in 1900, and the modern Desert Highway.

Inevitably, the importance of the King's Highway declined and it was only in the 1950s and 1960s that it was upgraded to a tarmac road. Today it's a rural, often pot-holed route, which despite ambling through some of the loveliest and most striking landscape in Jordan betrays little of its former status as a road fit for kings. For more information on the highway see www.ancientroute.com.

The Ayyubids were replaced by the Mamluks, who seized control of the area east of the Jordan River and rebuilt the castles at Karak, Shobak and Ajloun. They used these strongholds as lookouts and as a series of staging posts for message-carrying pigeons. Indeed, thanks to the superior communications that this unique strategy afforded, you could argue that the Crusaders were defeated not by the military might of Islam but on the wings of their peace-loving doves.

Western Love Affair with the Middle East (1516–1914)

The Ottoman Turks took Constantinople in 1453 and created one of the world's largest empires. They defeated the Mamluks in present-day Jordan in 1516, but concentrated their efforts on the lucrative cities of the region, such as the holy city of Jerusalem and the commercial centre of Damascus. The area east of the Jordan River once again became a forgotten backwater. Forgotten, that is, by the Ottoman Empire, but not

1453	c 1516–1916	1798	1812
Ottoman rule is established in Constantinople (modern-day İstanbul), creating one of the world's largest empires that extends throughout the Middle East.	The Ottomans lavish their attentions on Jerusalem and Damascus while the area east of the Jordan River becomes a cultural and political backwater.	Napoleon Bonaparte invades Egypt, bringing the Middle East within the sphere of Western political rivalry – a rivalry which influences the political landscape of Trans-Jordan over the next 150 years.	Burckhardt rediscovers Petra for the Western world, sparking off an enduring fascination with the fabled Pink City, and the region in general, among Western travellers, archaeologists, writers and artists.

entirely ignored by Western interests. Indeed, the period of gradually weakening Ottoman occupation over the next few centuries also marked an increasingly intense scrutiny by the Europeans – the British and the French in particular.

In the preface to *Les Orientales* (1829) Victor Hugo wrote that the whole of the European continent appeared to be 'leaning towards the East'. This was not a new phenomenon. Trade between the West and the East was long established and stories of the 'barbaric pearl and gold' of Arabia soon aroused the interests of a wider public. By the late 18th century Europeans were making pleasure trips to the Syrian desert, adopting articles of Albanian and Turkish dress, carrying pocket editions of Persian tales and penning their own travelogues.

Swiss explorer Johann Ludwig Burckhardt's monumental rediscovery of Petra in 1812 led to a further explosion of interest in the region. Societies were founded for the purpose of promoting Middle East exploration and scholars began translating Persian, Arabic and Sanskrit texts. Many aspects of the Orient were explored in Western fiction, much of which attracted a wide and enthusiastic readership. Indeed, by the end of the 19th century the fascination with the Arabian East was, to use Edward Said's phrase, no 'airy European fantasy' but a highly complex relationship defined by scientists, scholars, travellers and fiction writers.

This is the cultural backdrop upon which the political manoeuvrings of the 20th century were played out.

Fighting for an Arab Land (1914–46)

Writing of the Arab Revolt that passed through the heart of Jordan in the early 20th century, TE Lawrence described the phenomenon as 'an Arab war waged and led by Arabs for an Arab aim in Arabia'. This is a significant statement as it identifies a growing sense of political identity among Arab people throughout the last half of the 19th century and beginning of the 20th century. This pan-Arab consciousness grew almost in proportion (or at least coincidentally) to the territorial interest of Western powers in Arab lands. Slowly, in place of loose tribal interests Arabs came to define themselves as a single, unified entity – an Islamic 'other' perhaps to the Christian European threat pulsing around the Suez.

Arabs were prepared to fight for this new Arab nationalism, as Lawrence describes in the *Seven Pillars of Wisdom,* his account of the Arab Revolt:

As time went by our need to fight for the ideal increased to an unquestioning possession, riding with spur and rein over our doubts. Willy-nilly it became a faith.

The Qala'at ar-Rabad at Ajloun was built by the Ayyubids. In 1250 they were ousted by the Mamluks, a group of foreign, adolescent warriors serving as a soldier-slave caste for the Ayyubids, and the Mamluks ruled for the next 300 years.

Between 1775 and 1825, 87 volumes on aspects of the Near East were published in Britain alone and 46 reviews of the same books appeared in leading journals between 1805 and 1825.

1908	1914–18	1916	1917
The Ottoman Empire, now 'the sick man of Europe', builds the Hejaz Railway linking Damascus with the holy city of Medina, via Amman, in an effort to reassert regional influence.	During WWI Jordan sees fierce fighting between Ottoman Turks (allied with the Germans) and the British, based in Egypt. By 1917 British troops occupy Jerusalem, and Syria thereafter.	The Arab Revolt, led by Faisal and backed by the British with the famous assistance of TE Lawrence, storms Aqaba, disrupts the Hejaz Railway and marches on Damascus.	The Balfour Declaration giving Jews a home in Palestine is not the reward the Arabs are promised. In a reluctant compromise, Faisal's brother, Abdullah, becomes ruler of Trans-Jordan.

THE HEJAZ RAILWAY

The Hejaz Railway was built between 1900 and 1908 to transport pilgrims from Damascus to the holy city of Medina, reducing the two-month journey by camel and on foot to as little as three days. For Jordan, and Amman in particular, this meant a boom in trade. The 1462km line was completely funded by donations from Muslims – but functioned for less than 10 years. The trains and railway line were partially destroyed in the Arab Revolt of 1917 during WWI. The line was rebuilt as far south as Ma'an, but is now only used for cargo. There is occasional talk of introducing a tourist passenger service between Aqaba and Wadi Rum.

History shows that it was to take more than just 'spur and rein' to create viable Arab states; indeed complex diplomacy, both within Arab countries and in their relationship with the West, characterised the pursuit of nationalism throughout the 20th century.

The Arab Revolt

Ironically, the new Arab nationalist movement cut its teeth not on a Western Christian enemy but on the Ottomans, the apathetic Muslim rulers who dominated most of the Middle East, including the area either side of the Jordan River. The revolt was fought by Arab warriors on horseback, loosely formed into armies under Emir Faisal, the ruler of Mecca and guardian of the Muslim holy places, who had taken up the reins of the Arab nationalist movement in 1914. He was joined by his brother Abdullah and the enigmatic British colonel TE Lawrence, known as Lawrence of Arabia (see the boxed text, p211). Lawrence helped with coordination and securing supplies from the Allies, as well as attacking the Turkish-controlled Hejaz Railway, in a campaign that swept across the desert from Arabia, wrested Aqaba from the Ottomans and eventually ousted them from Damascus. By 1918 the Arabs controlled modern Saudi Arabia, Jordan and parts of southern Syria. Faisal set up government in Damascus and dreamed of an independent Arab realm.

Glad of the help in weakening the Ottoman Empire (allies of Germany during WW1), the British promised to help Faisal. The promise was severely undermined, however, by the 1917 Balfour Declaration:

His Majesty's Government view with favour the establishment in Palestine of a National Home for the Jewish people, and will use their best endeavours to facilitate the achievement of this object.

1923	1930s	1946	1947
Britain recognises Jordan as an independent emirate under its protection. A small defence force, the Arab Legion, is set up under British officers and the nominal control of Emir Abdullah.	The Nazi persecution of Jews accelerates Jewish immigration to Palestine, fuelling more violence between Jews and Arabs. A 1939 proposal to create a bi-national state is rejected by both sides.	Jordan gains full independence from the British; Emir Abdullah, who took a leading role in the Arab Revolt, is crowned the king of Jordan.	The UN votes for the partition of Palestine but the proposal is rejected by the Arab League on the grounds that the whole territory should remain Arab.

This contradictory acceptance of both a Jewish homeland in Palestine and the preservation of the rights of the original Palestinian community lies at the heart of the seemingly irreconcilable Arab-Israeli conflict.

The Creation of Jordan

The Arab Revolt may not have immediately achieved its goal during peace negotiations, but it did lead directly (albeit after over two decades of wrangling with the British) to the birth of the modern state of Jordan.

At the 1919 Paris Peace Conference the British came to an agreement with Faisal, who was given Iraq, while his elder brother Abdullah was proclaimed ruler of Trans-Jordan, the land lying between Iraq and the east bank. A young Winston Churchill drew up the borders in 1921 (see the boxed text, p241). Abdullah made Amman his capital. Britain recognised the territory as an independent state under its protection in 1923, and a small defence force, the Arab Legion, was set up under British officers. A series of treaties after 1928 led to full independence in 1946, when Abdullah was proclaimed king.

The betrayal of the Arab cause by Western allies was underlined by the secret Sykes-Picot Agreement of 1916 in which 'Syria' (modern-day Syria and Lebanon) came under French control, and 'Palestine' (an area including modern Israel, the Palestinian Territories and Jordan) came under British control.

Troubles with Palestine (1946–94)

If there is one element that defines the modern history of Jordan, it's the relationship with the peoples on the other side of the river – not just the Jews but also (and perhaps more especially) the Palestinians, who today make up the majority of the population of Jordan.

Much of the conflict stems from the creation of a Jewish national homeland in Palestine, where Arab Muslims accounted for about 90% of the population. Their resentment was understood by Arabs across the region and informed the dialogue of Arab-Israeli relations for the rest of the 20th century.

Modern History of Jordan

» *A History of Jordan* (Philip Robbins, 2004) Covers the 1920s to the present day.

» *The Modern History of Jordan* (Kamal Salibi, 1998) Gives an Arab perspective.

New Hashemite Kingdom of Jordan

In 1948 resentment escalated into conflict between Arab and Israeli forces, with the result that Jordan won control of East Jerusalem and the West Bank. King Abdullah, reneging on assurances regarding Palestinian independence, annexed the territory and proclaimed the new Hashemite Kingdom of Jordan (HKJ). The new state won immediate recognition from Britain and the USA, but regional powers disapproved of the annexation, added to which the unprecedented immigration of Palestinian refugees placed a strain on limited domestic resources.

In July 1951 King Abdullah was assassinated outside Al-Aqsa Mosque in Jerusalem. The throne eventually passed to his beloved 17-year-old grandson, Hussein, in May 1953. Hussein offered a form of citizenship to all Palestinian Arab refugees in 1960, but refused to relinquish

1948	1950	1951	1953
The State of Israel is proclaimed, the British withdraw immediately and renewed hostilities break out between Arabs and Jews. Half a million Palestinians flood into the 'West Bank'.	King Abdullah annexes the West Bank and east Jerusalem, despite paying lip service to Arab declarations backing Palestinian independence and expressly ruling out territorial annexations.	King Abdullah is assassinated at Al-Aqsa Mosque (Jerusalem), ending his dream of a single Arab state encompassing Syria, Lebanon, Jordan, Israel and Palestine – a dream that antagonised Arab neighbours.	Hussein becomes king of Jordan after his father is diagnosed with schizophrenia. Despite his English education, Hussein makes his mark by ousting remaining British troops.

Palestinian territory. Partly in response, the Palestine Liberation Organisation (PLO) was formed in 1964.

The Six Day War

After a period of relative peace and prosperity, conflict between Arab and Israeli forces broke out again in the 1960s, culminating in the Six Day War, provoked by Palestinian guerrilla raids into Israel from Syria. When the Syrians announced that Israel was amassing troops in preparation for an assault, Egypt responded by asking the UN to withdraw its Emergency Force from the Egypt Israel border. Nasser then closed the Straits of Tiran (the entrance to the Red Sea), effectively sealing the port of Eilat. Five days later Jordan and Egypt signed a mutual defence pact, dragging Jordan into the oncoming hostilities.

KING HUSSEIN

Since his death, King Hussein has become a legend. On succeeding to the throne on 2 May 1953 at the age of 17, the youthful, British-educated Hussein was known more for his love of pretty women and fast cars. Forty-five years later he was fêted as one of the Middle East's great political survivors, king against the odds and the de facto creator of the modern state of Jordan.

King Hussein's loyalty to his people was notable. In a role emulated by his son decades later, Hussein would disguise himself as a taxi driver and ask passengers what they thought of the king.

Hussein's lasting legacy, however, extends beyond his successful domestic policy. Throughout his reign he maintained close and friendly ties with Britain and courted trade with the West. From his sustained efforts at diplomacy to avert the 1991 Gulf War to his peace agreement with Israel in 1994, the urbane and articulate king of a country in one of the world's toughest neighbourhoods came to be seen as a beacon of moderateness and stability in a region known for neither attribute. This reputation was secured in 1997 when a Jordanian soldier shot and killed seven Israeli schoolgirls in northern Jordan. King Hussein personally attended the funeral in a public display of grief and solidarity with the Israeli families.

Hussein married four times and fathered 11 children. He was a highly popular man with many interests and was an accomplished pilot. After a long battle with cancer, during which time he continued his role as peace negotiator between Israel and Palestine, he died in Jordan in February 1999. He was greatly mourned not just by those who knew him but by Jordan and the region at large.

He is now regarded as a man who firmly steered the nascent country of Jordan through potentially devastating crises, balancing the demands of Arab nationalism against the political expedience of cooperation with Western interests. In so doing, he helped pave the way for Jordan's modern role in the world as a bridge between two ideologies.

1958

King Hussein's gesture of independence didn't last long as British troops are invited to return after Hussein's failed attempt at union with Iraq.

1960

Jordan offers partial citizenship to Palestinian Arab refugees but refuses to relinquish Palestinian territory. In response, the Palestine Liberation Organisation (PLO) is formed in 1964, backed by the Arab League.

» Men at mosque, Amman (p46)

On 5 June 1967 the Israelis dispatched a predawn raid that wiped out the Egyptian Air Force on the ground. In the following days they decimated Egyptian troops in Sinai and Jordanian troops on the West Bank, and overran the Golan Heights in Syria.

The outcome for Jordan was disastrous: it lost the whole of the West Bank and its part of Jerusalem, which together had supplied Jordan with its two principal sources of income – agriculture and tourism. It also resulted in yet another huge wave of Palestinian refugees.

Black September

After the 1967 defeat, the frustrated Palestinians within Jordan became increasingly militant, and by 1968 Palestinian *fedayeen* (guerrilla) fighters were effectively acting as a state within a state, openly defying Jordanian soldiers.

In 1970 Palestinian militants fired on King Hussein's motorcade and held 68 foreigners hostage in an Amman hotel, while the rogue Popular Front for the Liberation of Palestine hijacked and destroyed three Western planes in front of horrified TV crews. Martial law and bloody fighting (which claimed 3000 lives) followed. Yasser Arafat was spirited out of Amman disguised as a Kuwaiti sheikh in order to attend an Arab League summit in Cairo. A fragile ceasefire was signed, but it was not until midway through 1971 that the final resistance (around Ajloun) was defeated. The guerrillas were forced to recognise Hussein's authority and the Palestinians had to choose between exile and submission. Most chose exile in Lebanon.

Relinquishing Claims to Palestinian Leadership

In 1974 King Hussein reluctantly relinquished Jordan's claims to the West Bank by recognising the PLO as the sole representative of Palestinians with the right to set up a government in any liberated territory. By 1988 the King had severed all Jordan's administrative and legal ties with the West Bank.

In the meantime profound demographic changes, including a sharp rise in population, particularly of young people, had reshaped Jordan. Economic migration, both from the countryside to the city and from Jordan to the increasingly wealthy Gulf States, together with improved education changed social and family structures. Most significantly, Palestinians no longer formed an edgy minority of refugees but instead took their place as the majority of Jordan's population.

The complete integration of Palestinian refugees into all aspects of mainstream Jordanian life is due in no small part to the skilful diplomacy of King Hussein. The numerous assassination attempts (there were

PLO

When it was founded, the PLO had the blessing of the Arab League to represent the Palestinian people and train guerrilla fighters. The Palestine National Council (PNC) became the executive body of the PLO, with a remit to govern Palestine.

1967	1970	1988	1990
Israel wins Jerusalem and the West Bank in the Six Day War resulting in another influx of Palestinians. Al-Fatah dominates the PLO under Yasser Arafat, training guerrillas for Israeli raids.	Black September results in thousands being injured in clashes between the Jordanian government and Palestinian guerrillas. Three hijacked aircraft are blown up by the PLO.	King Hussein relinquishes remaining ties with the West Bank. The focus turns to home where women are now allowed to vote (from 1989) and political parties are legalised thereafter.	Saddam Hussein's invasion of Kuwait, supported by the Palestinians, requires careful diplomacy by King Hussein, who publicly supports Baghdad while suing for peace. Palestinian Gulf workers flood into Jordan.

at least 12) that dogged the early years of his reign were replaced with a growing respect for his genuine, deep-rooted concern for the Palestinians' plight – which is significant in a region where few other countries were willing to shoulder the burden.

Peace with Israel

On 26 October 1994 Jordan and Israel and the Palestinian Territories signed a momentous peace treaty that provided for the removal of all economic barriers between the two countries and closer cooperation on security, water and other issues.

But there is a twist to the final chapter of relations between Jordan and Palestine in the 20th century. There was a clause in the treaty recognising the 'special role of the Hashemite Kingdom of Jordan in the Muslim holy shrines in Jerusalem'. This inclusion aroused the suspicions of some Palestinians regarding the intentions of King Hussein, who at the outset of his long career had enjoyed more than just a 'special role' on the west bank of the Jordan. The treaty made Jordan unpopular within the region at the time, but in the longer term barely cast a shadow over the illustrious reign of one of the Middle East's most beloved rulers.

Relations with Israel & the Palestinian Territories Today

It has been a long time since the historic 1994 peace treaty and the long-term effect of peace with Israel is still being assessed. While the treaty was branded by some Palestinians as a betrayal, the world at large regarded it as a highly significant step towards vital East–West ties. Flash points between the two nations continue to occur, not just over the fate of the Palestinian people but also over issues such as water supply (see p294), which many predict will replace oil as the issue of conflict of the next few decades.

The Iraqi Dilemma (1990–2008)

Arab Federation

For the past two decades Jordan has been preoccupied with its neighbours to the East rather the West – a shift in focus necessitated firstly by the Gulf War and subsequently by the US-led invasion of Iraq.

Given that the founding fathers of the modern states of Iraq and Jordan were brothers, it is not surprising that the two countries have enjoyed periods of close collaboration over the years. In 1958 King Hussein tried to capitalise on this dynastic dimension by establishing the Arab Federation, a short-lived alliance between Jordan and Iraq that was

A PLO-Israeli declaration of principles in September 1993 set in motion the process of establishing an autonomous Palestinian authority in the Occupied Territories. With this declaration, the territorial question was virtually removed as an obstacle to peace between Jordan and Israel.

UN assessments put the total cost to Jordan of the Gulf War (mid-1990 to mid-1991) at more than US$8 billion. The UN naval blockade of Aqaba alone, aimed at enforcing UN sanctions against Iraq, cost Jordan US$300 million a year in lost revenue between 1991 and 1994.

1994	1999	2000	2001
A historic peace treaty between Israel and Jordan ends 46 years of war and gives Jordan a 'special role' over Muslim holy shrines in Jerusalem – straining relations with Arab neighbours.	King Hussein dies (7 February). His funeral is attended by former and current presidents of Israel and major powers, honouring his role as peace mediator. His son, Abdullah, becomes king.	Jordan accedes to the World Trade Organisation, and the European Free Trade Association (2001). Trade significantly increases under the free-trade accord with the USA and Jordanian Qualifying Industrial Zones (QIZ).	The US invasion of Iraq is strenuously protested by Arab countries. King Abdullah sides publicly with Baghdad while complying, officially at least, with the UN embargo on trade with Iraq.

intended to counterbalance the formation of the United Arab Republic between Egypt and Syria. Although the alliance did not last long, the connection between the neighbours remained strong, especially in terms of trade.

The Gulf War

When Saddam Hussein invaded Kuwait in 1990, Jordan found itself in a no-win situation. On the one hand, the Palestinian majority in Jordan backed Saddam's invasion, having been given assurances by Saddam that the showdown would result in a solution to the Palestinian question on the West Bank. On the other hand, King Hussein recognised that siding with Iraq would antagonise Western allies and risk Jordan's US trade and aid. As a solution, he sided publicly with Baghdad while complying, officially at least, with the UN embargo on trade with Iraq. As a result, although US and Saudi aid were temporarily suspended, loans and help were forthcoming from other quarters, particularly Japan and Europe.

Despite these new streams of income, the Gulf War exacted a heavy financial penalty on the small and relatively poor, oil-less state of Jordan. Ironically, however, Jordan's third wave of refugees in 45 years brought some relief as 500,000 Jordanians and Palestinians returned from the Gulf States. They brought with them a US$500 million windfall that stimulated the economy throughout the 1990s and helped turn Amman, in particular, into a cosmopolitan, modern city.

2005	2007	2008	2011
Three hotels in Amman are blown up in coordinated suicide attacks in Amman, masterminded by Al-Qaeda. Tourism, booming since the 1994 peace treaty, takes an immediate hit.	As one of many steps in the modernisation of the country's political, economic and social structure, 20% of seats in municipal councils are reserved for women.	Iraq contributes to the maintenance of the 500,000 Iraqi refugees in Jordan. The Iraqi arrival is the fourth influx of refugees in the modern history of this geographically small country.	Protests in Amman mark the 'Arab Spring', a period of uprising against dictatorship across the region. Jordan braces for a fifth wave of immigration – after severe disturbances in Syria.

Amateur Archaeology

Digging Up the Past

Take any path off the beaten track in central Jordan and you will be sure to stumble on something ancient – a fallen column with poppies dancing on the capital, coloured tesserae from a broken mosaic, a coin of indiscriminate currency. Look more carefully, and you'll probably see the remains of a fence enclosing a patch of land fast returning to wilderness – evidence, if any were needed, that Jordan has been the site of intense archaeological scrutiny for decades.

You don't have to be Indiana Jones to take an interest in these sites: anyone with a curiosity for the past can gain pleasure in rummaging around the hilltop at Hesban or Khirbet Tannour, or indeed at any of a hundred sites across Jordan. If just looking isn't enough, and you can't resist getting physical with the past, then you'll need to join a group of experts who will guide you in the subtle arts of archaeology. This chapter gives you a few ideas on how to get involved in amateur digs and suggests some of the sites of archaeological interest to focus on.

Two Centuries of Archaeology in Jordan

In many respects, the modern study of Western archaeology was founded in what we now call Jordan, arising out of a fascination with tracing the traditions of the Bible to the unearthed ruins of the Holy Land – on both sides of the River Jordan. For decades, this was an occupation that attracted largely foreign interest as the people of the region were more focused on the demands of the present than on digging up remnants of the past.

Today this is no longer the case, as Jordanians have the time and the means to take a greater interest in their heritage and education helps new generations to come to a better appreciation of the country's position within the cradle of civilisation. Each year more funding is put aside for archaeological exploration, with the result that some of the greatest finds, involving teams from universities in Jordan and abroad, have been made within the last 30 years, culminating in 2008 with the world's oldest church – a befitting discovery for a discipline that arose largely out of Christian curiosity.

Volunteering on a Dig

Archaeological fieldwork is a painstaking process but the rewards are great, particularly if you uncover something special like a coral bead worn by an ancient, a piece of copper cast six thousand years ago or a shard of pottery with the design intact. It's not so much the finding of an object as the sense of connection with a bygone age that makes

Digs on the Web

» **Madaba Plains Project** (www.madabaplains.org/hisban) Excavation at Tell Hesban

» **Great Temple Excavation** (www.brown.edu/Departments/Joukowsky_Institute/Petra) Brown University's Petra excavations

» **Virtual Karak** (www.vkrp.org) Castle archaeology

archaeology so compelling. In Jordan, there are numerous sites across the country, from ancient pre-pottery Neolithic (PPN) sites to more contemporary excavations in and around the crusader castles. Archaeologists, not known for consensus on many things, are at least agreed that there remains huge potential for major finds despite the intensive work in the field for the past three decades.

If you fancy being part of an archaeological team, and you have the patience and discipline to spend long hours in a dusty hole tickling dirt off a lump of masonry, then it's not too difficult to become a volunteer on one of these digs. Here are some guidelines:

» There are usually only a limited number of volunteer positions available on each site so find out who is conducting which digs and apply early.

» Make contact with the project leader and be sure to emphasise any special skills (like photography or drafting) you may have.

» Mention any travels in the region or Arabic-speaking skills.

» Emphasis your experience on group projects (archaeology is all about teamwork, despite the way it's presented in films).

» Ask how much your volunteer placement will cost. This fee helps cover the costs of adding your name to the team.

» Allow plenty of time. In order to gain access to sites, project leaders must obtain permits and security clearance, which can take up to six months to complete.

» Don't be put off if you don't succeed with your first application; it takes persistence to find a placement – a quality you'll need when you're on your first field trip!

Museums

» **National Archaeology Museum** Citadel – copy of Meshe Stele and examples of the Dead Sea Scrolls

» **Museum of Archaeology** University of Jordan – artefacts from all eras

» **Salt Archaeological Museum** Salt – good coverage of domestic history

» **Museum of Archaeology & Anthropology** Irbid – includes numismatic displays

Field Work Opportunities in Jordan

American Center for Oriental Research (ACOR; www.bu.edu/acor) Prepares an extensive annual listing of field-work opportunities in Jordan and the Middle East.

American Schools of Oriental Research (www.asor.org) This organisation supports the study of the culture and history of the Near East.

Archaeological Institute of America (AIA; www.archaeological.org) The largest and oldest archaeology organisation in the USA is a valuable resource for information.

Biblical Archaeology Society (www.bib-arch.org) Produces the magazine *Biblical Archaeological Review*, runs archaeological tours and lists volunteer openings.

Council for British Research in the Levant (CBRL; www.cbrl.org.uk) British Academy–sponsored institute with research centres in Amman and Jerusalem.

University of Jordan (☏06-5355000; www.ju.edu.jo) The archaeology department at this Amman-based university is a good contact point.

University of Sydney (www.sydney.edu.au/arts/archaeology) This prestigious Australian university runs a highly reputable field project at Pella.

Digs on the Web (Biblical)

» **American Schools of Oriental Research** (www.asor.org) Covers the sites of the Hebrew scriptures.

» **Franciscan Archaeological Institute** (http://198.62.75.1/www1/ofm/fai/FAImain.html) Excavations around Madaba and Mt Nebo.

THE CITY-STATE OF ISRAEL

The kingdoms of Edom, Moab and Ammon are mentioned in the Bible, especially in connection with the wandering Jews of the Exodus. According to the Old Testament, Moses and his brother Aaron led their people through Sinai in Egypt looking for a permanent territory to inhabit. They were forbidden entry to southern Jordan by the Edomites, but managed to wind their way north, roughly along the route of the modern King's Highway, towards the Jordan River. Moses died on Mt Nebo, in sight of the Promised Land, and it was left to his son Joshua to lead the Israelites across the river to the West Bank, where they conquered the city of Canaan and established the city-state of Israel.

Biblical Sites of Jordan

Drawing on a 200-year-old tradition, many excavations continue to be located in and around the biblical sites of Jordan. The eastern banks of the Jordan River are home to no fewer than 100 sites of biblical importance and regardless of whether or not you take 'The Word' for fact, there is strong evidence that many of the places cited in the Good Book once existed. In fact, the roots of modern archaeology in the Middle East stem from the desire to place the canon of scripture within a historical context.

Locating Bible References

Even if you're not religious, visiting sites of biblical significance can still be a moving experience, if only because this is 'hallowed, holy ground' for millions of people around the world. From Abraham and Moses to John the Baptist and Jesus Christ, the founding fathers of the three Western monotheistic traditions are all intimately tied to the Jordanian landscape and it's little wonder then that Jordan has been a destination of religious pilgrimage for centuries. The list below cites the biblical reference for each of Jordan's most famous biblical places.

'Ain Musa or Ayoun ('Ain) Musa

Biblical reference *I hen Moses raised his arm and struck the rock twice with his staff. Water gushed out, and the community and their livestock drank* (Numbers 20:11)
Historical record The exact location of where Moses struck the rock is open to debate – it's either 'Ain Musa, which is north of Wadi Musa near Petra or Ayoun ('Ain) Musa, near Mt Nebo (see p140).

Dead Sea

Biblical reference *...while the water flowing down to the Sea of Arabah was completely cut off...* (Joshua 3:16)
Historical record The Sea of Arabah (Dead Sea), also known as the Salt Sea, is mentioned several times in the Bible (see p113).

Jebel Haroun

Biblical reference *Remove Aaron's garments and put them on his son Eleazar, for Aaron will be gathered to his people: he will die there. Moses did as the Lord commanded: they went up to Mount Hor in the sight of the whole community* (Numbers 10:26-27)
Historical record Mt Hor is believed to be Jebel Haroun in Petra, which is also revered by Muslims as a holy place (see p178).

Jebel Umm al-Biyara

Biblical reference *He* [the Judean King, Amaziah] *was the one who defeated ten thousand Edomites in the Valley of the Salt and captured Sela in battle...* (2 Kings 14:7)

1812

Swiss explorer Jean Louis Burckhardt, aged 27, 'rediscovers' Petra for the West, stimulating a fascination with ancient history in the region that endures for the next two centuries.

1868

The precious Mesha Stele, one of the earliest examples of Hebrew script, is discovered by a missionary at Dhiban – and promptly shattered by bickering locals.

1900s

Jordan and the Levant are explored by British, American, French and German surveyors, including a young archaeology student from Oxford by the name of TE Lawrence (of Arabia).

1920s

Following the British mandate of Jordan, modest excavation projects aimed at consolidating the main standing monuments begin throughout Jordan.

1930s

Remarkable mosaics, regarded today as some of the finest in the Levant, are unearthed in Madaba.

1940s

The Dead Sea Scrolls are discovered by a Bedouin shepherd in Qumran at a time when parts of the western shore of the Dead Sea belong to Jordan.

1950s–60s

The Arab-Israeli wars and the aftermath of WWII leads to a lean period in archaeological study in Jordan.

Biblical Sites of Jordan

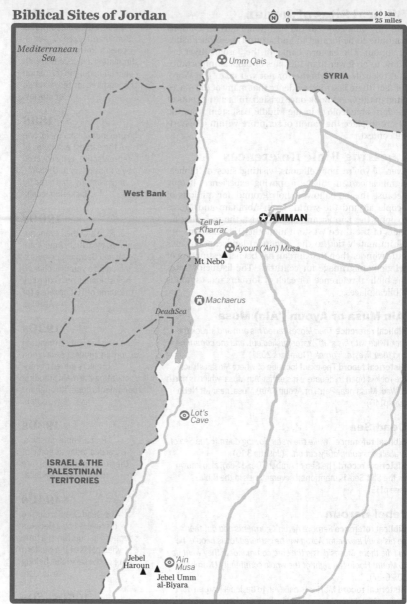

Historical record The village on top of Umm al-Biyara mountain in Petra is believed to be the ancient settlement of Sela (see p177).

Lot's Cave

Biblical reference *Now Lot went up out of Zo'ar, and dwelt in the hills with his two daughters, for he was afraid to dwell in Zo'ar; so he dwelt in a cave with his two daughters* (Genesis 19:30)

Historical record The cave where Lot and his daughters lived for years after Lot's wife turned into a pillar of salt is thought to be just off the Dead Sea Highway, not far from Safi (see p125).

Machaerus

Biblical reference *The King was sad, but because of his oaths and his dinner guests, he gave orders that her request be granted, and had John beheaded in the prison* (Matthew 14:9-12)
Historical record John the Baptist had claimed that Herod Antipas' marriage to his brother's wife, Herodias, was unlawful. So, at the request of Salome, Herodias' daughter, John was killed (see p141).

Mt Nebo

Biblical reference *Go up into...Mount Nebo in Moab, across from Jericho, and view Canaan, the land I am giving the Israelites as their own possession. There on the mountain that you have climbed you will die* (Deuteronomy 32:49-50)
Historical record Mt Nebo is revered as a holy place because it is where Moses is reported to have died, although his tomb has never been found (see p138).

Tell al-Kharrar

Biblical reference *Then Jesus came from the Galilee to the Jordan to be baptised by John* (Matthew 3:13)
Historical record Tell al-Kharrar is regarded as Bethany-Beyond-the-Jordan where Jesus was baptised by John the Baptist (see p109).

Umm Qais

Biblical reference *When he [Jesus] arrived at the other side in the region of Gadarenes, two demon-possessed men coming from the tombs met him* (Matthew 8:28-34)
Historical record Umm Qais is known as Gadara in the Bible, as well as in other ancient scriptures (see p101).

1970s
Excavations near Amman unearth the oldest statues in the world, the 8500-year-old, life-size Ain Ghazal figures.

1980s
Projects around Jordan unearth the remains of the Temple of Hercules at the Citadel in Amman, a Greek manuscript library at Petra, and ancient temple complexes in the Jordan Valley.

1990s
Early mining sites west of Karak and the baptism site of Jesus Christ at Bethany-Beyond-the-Jordan are just two of many discoveries marking the end of the century.

2008
The world's oldest church, which once sheltered 70 disciples of Jesus Christ, is uncovered under St Georgeous Church in Rihab, near Amman.

People & Society

Jordan's Bedouin Roots

Tradition of Hospitality

Ahlan wa sahlan! It's one of the most common greetings in Arabic and one that defines the way Jordanians relate to the people around them, especially guests. The root words mean 'people' or 'family' *(ahl)* and 'ease' *(sahl)*, so translated loosely the expression means 'be as one of the family and at your ease'. It's a gracious thought, and one that ends up in English simply as 'welcome' or (more commonly to tourists) 'welcome to Jordan'.

Bedouin traditions of hospitality and kindness are deeply ingrained in the Jordanian psyche. Rooted in the harsh realities of life in the desert, these traditions have been virtually codified into all social behaviour. Century-old notions of hospitality combine with a wonderful sense of humour to make Jordanians easy to connect with.

Love of the Desert

Over 98% of Jordanians are Arab, descended from various tribes that migrated to the area from all directions of the Middle East over the centuries. Most tribes trace their lineage to the Bedouin, the original desert dwellers of Arabia, perceived by many as the representatives and guardians of the very essence of 'Arabness'. Bedouins form the majority of the indigenous population, although today not more than 40,000 Bedouin can be considered truly nomadic. Living a traditional life of livestock rearing, the nomadic Bedouin who travel from oasis to oasis in quest of water are concentrated mainly in the Badia – the great desert plains of Eastern Jordan.

Despite the settlement of some Bedouin (recent examples include the Bdoul who once roamed the hillsides of Petra but who now live for the most part in the modern settlement of Umm Sayhoun), many Jordanians retain a deep sentimental attachment to the desert. This isn't always obvious given the littering and general despoliation of public access areas such as at Wadi Rum, but it is evident in the way Jordanians claim kinship with the principle tenets of desert-dwelling – hospitality, loyalty, dignity, pride and courtesy.

The checked *keffiyah* headdress is an important national symbol – red and white for Bedouin; black and white for Palestinians. It's held in place by the black rope-like *agal*. There are no official dress restrictions for women and few wear a veil. Almost none wear full-body chador.

Modern Caretakers of the Desert

Whether Zawaedha, Zalabia or Bdoul, whether from Wadi Rum, Wadi Musa or the great Badia beyond, the Bedouin are universally proud of 'their Jordan' and welcome guests who visit them in their ancient tribal lands. It's not surprising, then, that many of the country's Bedouin now make a living from tourism and many feel it is their modern mission to reveal the wonders of their country to new generations of visitors. In some senses, the Bedouin have been doing the same, albeit for slightly different purposes, for centuries, offering bread and salt to those in need on the understanding that the same courtesy will be offered to them in return. The currency today is usually money, but the principle of easing the passage of strangers through traditional tribal territories remains unchanged. Unchanged, too, is the principle of 'word of mouth' in advertising friendly encampments, though today the internet has replaced the camel caravan as the *modus operandi*.

Not everything about the modern life of the Bedouin has stayed the same, however. It is easy to romanticise the traditional way of life of the Bedouin – managing goats and sheep and looking for water – as simple and free but the reality of life in the desert is uncompromisingly hard, entailing goat-hair beds and scorpions, insufferable heat and freezing nights, not enough to eat and being forever thirsty. Add to that the modern complexities of life (compulsory education, impinging urbanisation, and the tough and fickle demands of working with tourists) and it's easy to see that there's nothing simple or free in a modern Bedouin life.

It's little surprise then that while many regret the passing of the golden age of nomadic life, the majority of Jordan's indigenous population look towards settlement and the convenience that it brings. Today, therefore, as a visitor to Jordan, you are just as likely to run into the Bedouin on a mobile phone at the bus station or in public-assisted housing at the edge of Petra. They are wistful for the stories of their grandparents but they are not nostalgic about the hardships. Television, internet and 4WD transport have changed their lives forever but as they are not regretful of this, then neither should a visitor be!

HUMOUR

The Bedouin are known for their sense of humour, which they list – alongside courage, alertness and religious faith – as one of the four secrets of life, encouraging tolerance and humility.

PEOPLE & SOCIETY JORDAN'S BEDOUIN ROOTS

SOCIAL GRACES

Standing wedged between the door and a table and with no room to back out politely, my Jordanian companion looked in horror as a foreign man proffered a large, hairy hand in her direction and gushed a greeting. 'Can you believe it,' Maryam said, 'and in Ramadan too!' I asked why she didn't simply refuse to shake hands: 'I didn't want to embarrass him', she said. This common scenario highlights both the desirability of learning a few courtesies as a traveller and also of the Jordanian good-natured tolerance of social faux pas.

Here are a few social graces that will help break the ice without breaking a friendship. If all else fails, there's not much harm that can't be undone with a smile, a box of baklava and a compliment about the lovable children.

» **Handshaking** This is an important part of the ritual of greeting in Jordan but usually only between members of the same sex. If you witness an accident, for example, the first few moments will probably be taken up with copious handshaking, greeting and asking after each man's family...before a slanging match erupts about who is to blame.

» **Public Displays of Affection** Don't think that seeing two men kissing gives you the right to do the same. All signs of affection, except between members of the same sex (and of the strictly platonic kind), is frowned upon in public. Not that you'd guess that these days from the relaxed attitudes of trendsetters in the city who openly walk arm in arm with a loved one.

» **Hands and Arms** Blundering with these limbs includes using your left hand to give something, forgetting to touch your heart when refusing something – or, for that matter, forgetting to refuse something you intend eventually to accept.

» **Feet** These appendages are both a host's and a guest's worst nightmare. For anyone contemplating a visit to a home or a mosque, the advice for feet is to wash them, unsock them and tuck them under you when sitting on the floor.

The Bedouin Inheritance
Good Manners

There are many ways in which Jordan's Bedouin roots have influenced the national psyche. For the visitor, perhaps the most easily identifiable aspects of this inheritance is the value placed on good manners. Etiquette in Jordan has been refined over centuries of tribal interaction and is an important expression of national identity. Social mores cover all aspects of life from the length and depth of an introductory 'hello' to how many cups of coffee to be offered and accepted, and who offers what to whom at supper.

For a visitor, learning the subtleties of 'custom and manner' is challenging, but making the effort to fit in is invariably appreciated, particularly if visiting Jordanians at home.

Respect for the Royals

Another noticeable trait of the Bedouin inheritance is an ingrained tribal respect for local elders, or sheikhs. This character trait is extended to the ultimate leaders of the country. Claiming unbroken descent from Prophet Mohammed, Jordan's Hashemite royal family is a nationally beloved and regionally respected institution. All monarchies have their critics from time to time, not least for seeming arcane in their function, but Jordan's modern royal family has helped to redefine the royal image through benign and diplomatic governance (especially with regard to Middle East peace issues), as well as through a history of charitable works. It was evident during the Arab Spring of 2011 (see p246) that despite protests against the government, there was no popular demand for a republic. Jordanians look to their royalty for leadership and an example of how to live a modern life in the context of their largely Islamic and Arab heritage.

In a region where men are more commonly the public face of royal initiatives, Jordan has been unusual for the high profile of its royal women. Visit many of the small women's cooperatives like Bani Hamida in Mukawir, and you are likely to find some mention of either Queen Noor or Queen Rania in the patronage or even funding of the project.

Daily Life
Importance of Family

Family ties are all-important to both modern and traditional Jordanians and paying respect to parents is where the sense of obeisance to elders is engendered. Socialising generally entails some kind of get-together with the extended family, with lines drawn loosely between the genders. This is reflected in terms of physical divisions within the house, where separate seating areas are reserved for men and women.

Meals are generally eaten on the floor, with everyone gathered around several trays of food shared by all. More traditional families are often quite hierarchical at meal times. The grandparents and male head of the house may eat in one circle, the latter's wife and the older children and other women in the family in another, and the small children in yet another.

In the evenings locals in the cities may window shop, stroll around the streets, enjoy a leisurely meal, go to the cinema or watch TV. Men may pass the time in a local coffeehouse, playing cards, smoking a nargileh (water pipe) or perhaps watching European football on the TV, while the kids play the real thing on the streets outside or diligently attend to homework.

Marriage

Marriages reflect the sense of family allegiance and are often arranged for the benefit of the families involved, with matches commonly made between cousins. It is fair to say, however, that parents do not often enforce a wedding against their daughter's wish. In 2001 the legal age of marriage was lifted from 15 years old for women and 16 for men to 18 for both, although Islamic judges are still permitted to sanction underage marriages.

The marriage ceremony takes place either at the mosque, church or home of the bride or groom. After the marriage the men of the family drive around the streets in a long convoy, sounding their horns, blasting out music and partying until sunrise.

Polygamy (by men) is rare although legal. Men who marry more than once (Islam allows four wives if each wife is assured equal treatment) are obliged to inform both their first and their new wives. Amendments to the law in 2002 made it possible for women to file for divorce if they repay the dowry given by their husband, though the social stigma regarding divorce remains strong.

The Concept of Honour

In Jordan, a woman's 'honour' is still valued in traditional society, and sex before marriage or adultery is often dealt with harshly by other members of the woman's family. In rare cases it can lead to fatalities. On average (according to government statistics) 15 women are murdered each year for bringing shame on their families by having sex out of wedlock, refusing an arranged marriage, leaving their husbands, or simply being

Jordan has two recognised ethnic minorities, though most have integrated through marriage. Around 40,000 Circassians (Muslims from the Caucasus who fled Russian persecution in the late 19th century) live near Amman. A community of around 4000 Chechens, related to the Circassians historically and ethnically, live near Azraq.

PEOPLE & SOCIETY DAILY LIFE

A DISHONOURABLE HOAX

In 2004 a book entitled *Forbidden Love*, written by Norma Khouri, arrived on the bookshelves. Within weeks the author (to the delight of her publisher, Random House) found she had a bestseller on her hands. Better and bigger than that, she had overnight become the convenient voice the West wanted to hear: an Arab woman speaking out against the supposed 'tyranny of Islam'. Soon she was feted on chat shows and courted by newspaper journalists, and her tale assumed the quality of moral crusade taken up with indignation by worthy people around the world.

Her story was a harrowing one that described the death in Jordan of her childhood friend, the legendary Dalia: a killing carried out by the girl's Islamic knife-wielding father for a harmless flirtation with a Christian soldier. This event, together with the author's description of it, apparently led to Khouri's flight to the USA from the benighted country of her birth and a *fatwa* being placed on her head. Comparisons with author Salman Rushdie begin to form...except that Rushdie never claimed his works of fiction were fact.

A 2008 documentary, *Forbidden Lies*, charts Khouri's exposure as a con artist and her book as a pack of lies. The very existence of Dalia is called into question and with it a pall of uncertainty covers the issue of 'honour killings', which is the book's central theme.

And this, of course, is the real tragedy behind one of the biggest literary hoaxes of the 21st century. Honour killings – where a woman is killed by members of the family to protect familial honour – do occur in Jordan, albeit in ever-reducing numbers. Sensationalist accounts that capitalise on the practice, however, undermine the work of various interest groups who try to work quietly and discreetly to change attitudes without compromising the sense of national pride.

A few years on and the dust is settling, and the painstaking case-by-case documentation of each crime has resumed, but it will take more than the global humiliation of the biggest con artist of the decade for Jordanians to talk about this subject openly again.

The documentary *Crimes of Honour* by Shelley Saywell, filmed in Jordan and the West Bank, gives more information on this sensitive subject.

THE ROYAL WOMEN OF JORDAN

Two influential women have helped shaped the modern face of Jordan. Both have used their marriage into royalty to make positive social changes and have set up nationally respected charities.

Queen Noor

Royal Connection Fourth wife of former king, King Hussein (now deceased); married in 1978.
Former Name Lisa Hàlaby; adopted the name Queen Noor upon conversion to Islam.
Former Occupation Architect and urban planner.
From Washington DC; studied at Princeton.
Background Born into a distinguished Arab-American family (her father served under the administration of John F Kennedy and was head of Pan-Am for a while).
Community Service Set up her own charity, the influential Noor Foundation.
Public Relations Important role in explaining Jordan's stand against the 1990 Gulf War to American audiences and active campaigner for women's rights, children's welfare and community improvement.
Further Information See Queen Noor's website (www.nooralhusseinfoundation.org).

Queen Rania

Royal Connection Wife of the present king, King Abdullah; married in 1993.
Former Name Rania Al-Yassin
Former Occupation Business administration
From Kuwait; studied at the American University of Cairo.
Background Born into a notable Jordanian family of Palestinian origin.
Community Service Set up her own charity, the influential Jordan River Foundation.
Public Relations Not afraid of a public profile; can be seen in activities as diverse as campaigning for the rights of women to running the Dead Sea Marathon.
Further Information See Queen Rania's website (www.queenrania.jo).

Women Writers on Jordan

» **Nine Parts of Desire** (Geraldine Brooks, 1995) By a former foreign correspondent.

» **West of the Jordan** (Laila Halaby, 2003) Fictionalised exploration of modernity versus tradition.

the victim of rape or sexual assault. Women in the family are often complicit in the murder.

Jordan's legal code exempts a husband or close male relative for killing a wife caught in an act of adultery and offers leniency for murders committed in a 'fit of rage'. Most perpetrators are given short prison sentences, sending the message that the state in part condones these actions.

Internationally renowned journalist Rana Husseini is one among several high-profile Jordanians who are committed not just to bringing so-called 'honour killings' to the Jordanian public's attention but also to spreading intolerance towards the practice. Even King Abdullah has tried to impose tougher sanctions against honour killings, but little progress has thus far been made. Effecting radical change of deep-rooted cultural values is not something that can be accomplished overnight and only a change of attitude, rather than a change of law, is likely to be effective in driving the practice out.

Confronting Modernity

A New Role for Women

Traditional concepts of honour *(ird)* run deep but sit uneasily with the freedoms many affluent Jordanian women have come to expect, largely thanks to universal access to one of the region's best education systems. Women are entitled to vote (Jordanian women got the vote in 1967 but didn't have a chance to use it for the first time until 1989) and a minimum of six women MPs is guaranteed by royal decree.

In 1991 only 14% of the labour force was made up of women; by 2010, according to UN data, this had risen to 25.5%, mainly in health and education. Many women now work in male-dominated industries and businesses, fewer in media or the law profession where less than 1% of judges are women.

Women in more traditional societies are also starting to gain some financial independence and a greater say in society. This is partially through the success of a number of Jordanian organisations that encourage small-scale craft production (see p284) and local tourism projects.

Urbanisation

There is an increasing polarisation in Jordanian society between town and country. In Amman, modern Western-leaning middle- and upper-class youths enjoy the fruits of a good education, shop in malls, drink lattes in mixed-sex Starbucks and obsess over the latest fashions or dreams of democracy. In rural areas, meanwhile, unemployment is high and many populations struggle with making ends meet.

For this reason, economic migration is common in Jordan and many working-class families have at least one male who is temporarily working away from home, whether in Amman, the Gulf States or further abroad. The remittances sent home by these absent workers are increasingly important to family budgets, with each economically active person supporting, on average, four other people. The absence of a senior male role model, however, is changing the pattern of Jordanian family lives and tensions inevitably rise between the expectations of those who are nostalgic for the traditions of home and those of the families left behind who are forced to steer their own course into a rapidly modernising environment.

The Ongoing Refugee Issue

The biggest catalyst of social change in Jordan is the ongoing influx of refugees. Occupying the calm eye of the storm in the Middle East, the country has a long tradition of absorbing the displaced peoples of its troubled neighbours – so much so, in fact, that the majority of its population is now comprised of people who are not Jordanian in origin.

Jordan's Female Firsts

» **1995** Mayor (in Ajloun)

» **1996** Judge

» **1997** Taxi driver

» **2010** First attorney general

» **2011** Ambassador to Washington

Official estimates put the total number of Palestinian refugees in Jordan at 1.5 million; unofficial figures, according to the UN Office for the Coordination of Humanitarian Affairs, are closer to 3.5 million. In addition, there are 500,000 Iraqi refugees (UNHCR estimate) and an unofficial estimate of 2000 Syrian 'guests'.

PEOPLE & SOCIETY CONFRONTING MODERNITY

PALESTINIAN REFUGEES

About one half of Jordan's population, according to **Minorities at Risk** (www.cidcn.umd. edu/mar), is made up of Palestinians who fled, mostly from the West Bank, during the wars of 1948 and 1967 and after the Gulf War in 1990-91.

Many Palestinians have exercised the right to Jordanian citizenship and they now play an integral part in the political, cultural and economic life of Jordan. Others, however, continue to dream of a return to an independent Palestine. Some commentators suggest that this is partly why so many have resisted integration and continue to live in difficult conditions in refugee camps that dot the landscape.

Around 350,900 refugees (17.5% of the total refugee population in Jordan) are housed in 10 official camps administered by the UN Relief & Works Agency (UNRWA), which is responsible for health, education and relief programs. As at December 2010, the largest camps were those at Baqa'a (with 104,000 inhabitants), the Amman New Camp (51,500), Marqa (53,000) and Jebel al-Hussein (23,000), with large camps also at Zarqa, Jerash and Irbid. The original tent shelters have long since been replaced with more permanent structures and often resemble suburbs more than refugee camps.

For more information, contact the Jordanian **Department of Palestinian Affairs** (06-5666172; www.un.org/unrwa/refugees/jordan.html). See www.unhcr.org for more on the Iraqi refugee situation.

By far the largest proportion of this non-Jordanian contingent is Palestinian, and no country has absorbed more Palestinian refugees than Jordan.

In contrast to the periodic assimilation of Palestinians, whose arrival is usually accompanied by much sympathy, the influx of Iraqi refugees over the past decade has provoked local resentment. This is partly due to the superior spending power of Iraqis (they brought with them an estimated US$500 million), which spiked property prices in and around Amman, fuelling a decade of high inflation.

Jordan has repeatedly appealed for international aid to cope. In 2008 Iraq gave $8 million to the UN refugee agency intended to help its smaller and poorer neighbour provide education and health services for its nationals, but this doesn't scratch the surface of the estimated economic burden on the Jordanian economy of over $2 billion.

Unlike most Palestinians, almost all (95%) Iraqi refugees have registered their intent to return home when the security situation improves.

Refugee Influxes

» 1948 Palestinians (founding of Israel)

» 1967 Palestinians (Six Day War)

» 1991 Palestinians (Gulf War)

» 2003 Iraqis (Iraq War)

» 2011 Syrian 'guests' (Arab Spring)

Islam

Faith & Society in Jordan

Islam is the predominant religion in Jordan but it is not the only religion – around 6% of the population are Christian. This mixed inheritance, together with a long tradition of hosting visitors, has led Jordanians to be tolerant towards those of other beliefs and customs.

It's probably fair to say that there is not the same overt dedication to faith as one sees in neighbouring countries such as Saudi Arabia, nor the exuberant outpouring of Islamic culture seen in the mosques and fine arts of Syria. However, this doesn't mean that Islam is any less central to Jordanian life. Islam governs what people wear, how they plan their lives, how they settle their disputes and spend their money. It gives a purpose for being and gives shape to the future. In other words, faith and culture seamlessly combine in Jordan, giving people a shared ethic upon which society is founded.

For a visitor to Jordan, understanding the country's predominantly Muslim roots will help make sense of certain customs and manners. In turn, it guides in appropriate conduct and minimises the chance of giving offence.

The words *al-hamdu lillah* (thanks be to god) frequently lace sentences in which good things are related and the words *in sha' Allah* (god willing) mark all sentences that anticipate the future. These expressions are not just linguistic decoration, they demonstrate a deep connection between society and faith.

People of the Book

Founded seven centuries after the birth of Christ, Islam shares a common heritage with the two other great monotheistic faiths, Judaism and Christianity. For Muslims, Islam is the apogee of the monotheistic faiths but they traditionally attribute a place of great respect to Christians and Jews, whom they consider Ahl al-kitab (the People of the Book).

Founding of Islam

Born into a trading family in Mecca (in present-day Saudi Arabia) in AD 570, Mohammed began receiving revelations in AD 610, and after a time began imparting the content of Allah's message to the inhabitants of Mecca. Mohammed's call to submit to God's will was not universally well

THE HOLY QURAN

Muslims believe that the Quran, the holy book of Islam, is the literal word of God, unlike the Bible or Torah which they believe were inspired by God but were recorded subject to human interpretation. Communicated to the Prophet Mohammed directly in a series of revelations in the early 7th century, the Quran means 'recitation' and is not just the principal source of doctrine in Islam, but also a source of spiritual rapture in its own right. It is recited often with emotional elation, as a blessing to the reciter and the hearer. The use of the 'sacred' language of Arabic, with its unique rhythms, gives the recitation a sacramental quality that eludes translation, and many Muslims around the world still learn large portions of the Quran in its original form to feel closer to God's words.

MECCA

Mecca is Islam's holiest city. It's the home of the sacred Kaaba – a cube-shaped building allegedly built by Ibrahim (Abraham) and his son Ismail and housing a black stone of ancient spiritual focus. Muslims are enjoined to this day to face Mecca when praying. Medina is Islam's second holiest city.

received, making more of an impact among the poor than among the wealthy families of the city, who feared his interference in the status quo.

By AD 622 Mohammed was forced to flee with his followers to Medina, an oasis town to the north, where he continued to preach. This migration (the Hejira) marks the beginning of the Islamic calendar: year 1 AH. By AD 630 his followers returned to take Mecca, winning over many of the local tribes who swore allegiance to the new faith.

After Mohammed's death in 632, Arab tribes conquered the Middle East, Egypt and North Africa, Spain and eventually France, taking Islam with them. The Arabic language and Islamic faith remained long after the military conquests faded into history, uniting large parts of Europe, Africa and Asia in a shared cultural and religious ideology. To read how Islam spread across Jordan, see p257.

Sunnis & Shiites

Islam split into different sects soon after its foundation. When the Prophet died in 632, he left no instructions as to who should be his successor, nor the manner in which the future Islamic leaders (known as caliphs) should be chosen.

In the ensuing power struggle, *shi'a* (partisans) supported the claim of Mohammed's cousin and son-in-law, while others supported the claim of the Umayyads. From that point the Muslim community split into two competing factions: the Shiites, who are loyal to the descendants of Mohammed, and the Sunnis, the orthodox bedrock of Islam.

Within Jordan most Muslims are Sunnis, belonging to the Hanafi school of thought. A minority of around 15,000 Druze in Northeast Jordan (including the town of Azraq) follow a form of Shiite Islam.

THE FIVE PILLARS OF ISLAM

A good Muslim is expected to carry out the Five Pillars of Islam.

» **Haj** The pinnacle of a devout Muslim's life is the pilgrimage to the holy sites in and around Mecca. Haj takes place in the last month of the Islamic calendar and Muslims from all over the world travel to Saudi Arabia for the pilgrimage and subsequent feast of Eid al-Adha. Returning pilgrims earn the right to be addressed as Haji.

» **Salat** This is the obligation of prayer, expressed five times a day when the muezzins call upon the faithful to pray before sunrise, noon, mid-afternoon, sunset and before midnight. Communal prayers are only obligatory on Friday, although the strong sense of community makes joining together in a *masjid* ('place of prostration', ie mosque) preferable at other times.

» **Shahada** This is the profession of the faith and the basic tenet of Islam: 'There is no God but Allah and Mohammed is his prophet' (*La il-laha illa Allah Mohammed rasul Allah*). This is part of the call to prayer, and is uttered at other events such as births and deaths. People can often be heard muttering the first half of the sentence to themselves for moral support.

» **Sawm** Ramadan, the ninth month of the Islamic calendar, commemorates the revelation of the Quran to Mohammed. As a renewal of faith, Muslims are required to abstain from sex and from letting anything (including cigarettes) pass their lips from dawn to dusk throughout the month.

» **Zakat** Giving alms to the poor is an essential part of Islamic social teaching and, in some parts of the Muslim world, has been developed into various forms of tax as a way of redistributing funds to the needy. The moral obligation towards poorer neighbours continues to be emphasised at a personal and community level, and many Islamic groups run large charitable institutions, including Amman's Islamic Hospital.

Teachings

Despite modern connotations with fundamentalism and the violent beginnings of the faith, Islam is an inherently peaceful creed. The word 'Islam' means 'submission' or 'self-surrender'. It also means 'peace'. Taken as a whole, Islam is the attainment of peace – with self, society and the environment – through conscious submission to the will of God. To submit to the will of God does not just entail paying lip service to God through ceremony, but through all daily thoughts and deeds.

The principal teaching of Islam is that there is only one true God, creator of the universe. Muslims believe that the God of Islam is the same God of Christians and Jews, but that he has no son or partner and he needs no intermediary (such as priests). Muslims believe that the prophets – starting with Adam, including Abraham and Jesus, and ending with Mohammed – were sent to reveal God's word but that none of them were divine.

Historically, this creed obviously had great appeal to the nomadic peoples of the land we now call Jordan as they were given access to a rich spiritual life without having to submit to incomprehensible rituals administered by hierarchical intermediaries. Believers needed only to observe the transportable Five Pillars of Islam in order to fulfil their religious duty. This is true to this day and is perhaps one of the reasons why Islam is one of the world's fastest growing religions.

Islamic Customs

Muslims should pray five times a day and follow certain rituals, washing their hands, mouth, ears, arms, feet, head and neck in running water. If no mosque is nearby and there is no water available, scouring with sand suffices; where there is no sand, the motions of washing must still be enacted.

Muslims must face Mecca (all mosques are oriented so that the mihrab, or prayer niche, faces the correct way – south-southeast in Jordan) and follow a set pattern of gestures and genuflections. Muslims do not require a mosque to pray and you'll often see Jordanians praying by the side of the road or at the back of their shop; many keep a small prayer rug handy for such times.

In Jordan, which has a history of welcoming tourists to its world-class sites of largely pagan origin, people may be surprised if you take an interest in Islam but they will also be delighted. Any sympathetic discussion of faith is treated as an olive branch in a region where religion has all too often led to conflict – as the great crusader castles at Karak and Shobak, and the heavily militarised border with Israel illustrates.

Islam, Judaism and Christianity share many of the same prophets: Abraham (Ibrahim), Jesus (Isa), John the Baptist (Yahya), Job (Ayyub), Joshua (Yosha), Lot (Lut), Moses (Musa), and Noah (Nuh). Mohammed is not considered divine, but rather the last of these prophets.

ISLAM

Recommended Reading

» **Islam: A Short History** (Karen Armstrong) Tackles modern dilemmas facing Islam.

» **Infidels** (Andrew Wheatcroft) Islam and Christianity's troubled relationship.

» **Concise Encyclopedia of Islam** (Cyril Glasse) Definitive A to Z.

Traditional Crafts

Walk the streets of Madaba, with bright coloured kilims flapping in the wind, hike to the soap-making villages of Ajloun, or watch elderly Bedouin women threading beads at Petra, and the country's strong handicraft tradition is immediately apparent. The authorities have been quick to support this aspect of Jordan's heritage and now craft cooperatives are widespread, resulting in benefits for local communities and ensuring that Jordan's rich legacy of craft endures for future generations.

Traditional handicrafts in Jordan are not designed to be viewed in a museum, but to be bought and bartered over. Jordan's position at the crossroads of numerous caravan routes throughout the ages has made craft, the most practical and portable of all the arts, into a currency of mutual, practical benefit.

For the visitor who chooses the right outlets, there is a special pleasure in buying something handmade, practical and aesthetically pleasing from Jordan as the craftsperson earns money that directly benefits his or her community. Taking an interest in the crafts of Jordan, then, is not a remote aesthetic exercise. It represents sustainable tourism at its best.

Fine examples of Bedouin jewellery, Jordanian crafts and traditional costumes are on display at the Folklore Museum and Museum of Popular Traditions at the Roman Theatre in Amman.

Made in Jordan
Weaving

Jordan has a long-established rug-making industry dating back to the country's pre-Islamic, Christian communities. *Mafrash* (rugs) are usually of the flat, woven kind, compared with carpets that have a pile. To this day, especially in Madaba and Mukawir, it's possible to watch kilims being made that are based on early Byzantine designs. Even if you hadn't intended to buy one of these woollen rugs, you'll find it impossible not to get carried away by the enthusiasm of the carpet vendors, who will good-naturedly unfurl all their rugs for you without much prospect of a sale.

The cost of a kilim (anywhere between JD50 and JD500) depends on whether natural vegetable dyes are used, the length, thickness of thread, intricacy of pattern and age of the rug – the older the better.

Embroidery

Embroidery is an important skill among Jordanian women and most learn the craft at a young age. Teenagers traditionally embroider the clothes they will need as married women. Embroidery provides an occasion for women to socialise, often with a pot of tea spiced up with a pinch of local gossip. Palestinian embroidery is famed throughout the region and you'll see the characteristic red embroidery cross-stitch on traditional dresses, known as *roza,* in shops across Jordan. Purses featuring intricate flower designs in silk thread make portable mementos.

Mosaics

The craft of mosaic-making has a noble and distinguished lineage in Jordan. Mosaics are made from tiny squares of naturally coloured rock called tesserae. The first part of the process is preparing the stone, which is hewn in blocks from the rock face and then cut into thin cuboid rods. These are then snipped by pincers into the tesserae. The smallest tesserae make the most intricate designs but they are much harder to work with and the mosaics take longer to assemble. It's rather like the knots on a carpet – the more tesserae per centimetre, the finer and more valuable the mosaic. Many workshops in the Madaba area will ship items home.

Copperware

Some of the oldest copper mines in the world are traceable in Jordan (especially near Feinan, now in the Dana Biosphere Reserve). Copper is used in everyday utensils, as well as for heirlooms such as the family serving dish, copper tray or coffee pot. These pieces are mostly replicated for the tourist industry, but you can still find the genuine articles – with a bit of spit-and-polish they'll light up the corner of a room back home. Quality pieces can be found in the antique stores in Amman, many of which are attached to top-end hotels. You won't find an antique older than about 50 years (and it's illegal to import anything older than 100 years), but the items are likely to have been much loved by the families who once used them.

Jewellery

A bride traditionally receives a gift of jewellery on her wedding day as her dowry, and this remains her personal property. The most common designs are protective silver amulets, such as the 'hand of Fatima'

MAKING MOSAICS

Push the door open on a mosaic workshop and it's like entering the Hall of the Mountain King. Clouds of dust plume from the masonry saws and the workspace echoes with the screech of metal against rock and the persistent snapping of the workers' pincers as they cut stone rods into tiny, coloured squares. During our visit, all the workers engaged in this dedicated craft (from the stone-cutters to the assembly teams) were women. One of the ladies dusted her hands against her overcoat and, parking her mobile phone in among the tweezers, the paste brush and the glue pot, gave us an ad hoc tour.

Artists, Mayzoon explained, sketch a design freehand or trace the image from books, in the same way as their ancient predecessors would have copied scenes from pattern books. Designs usually feature everyday life, with depictions of plants and animals (look for the chicken – almost every mosaic seems to feature one). Hunting and viniculture, personification of the seasons, and religious or mythological scenes are typical subjects. But it's the detail that captivates – the bell on a gazelle's neck, palm trees at an oasis, a wry human smile.

Once the design is in place, the tesserae are then painstakingly arranged – traditionally on a thick coating of wet lime and ash to form permanent flooring. Today they are more likely to be attached to wet plaster and affixed to wooden boards for use as table tops or wall decorations.

The tour concluded and Mayzoon returned to the assembly table. 'You took our photograph, no?' one of the ladies said. I was about to apologise when she added 'Please, take it again. This time with all of us!' A shaft of brilliant sunshine cut through the dusty air, lighting up the eight faces gathered in intense concentration around the half-built mosaic. The team worked rhythmically together, tapping and snapping, inching and coaxing the stones into a tree of life. With a little definition in malachite and sandstone, the women could have found their own immortalisation in stone.

(daughter-in-law of the Prophet Mohammed). These are used as protection from evil spirits known as *djinn* (from which we get the word 'genie'). Antique items such as silver headdresses decorated with Ottoman coins and ornately decorated Bedouin daggers (straight, rather than the famously curved Yemeni and Omani versions) are becoming harder to find. Many of the most beautiful antique pieces were crafted by Circassian, Armenian and Yemeni silversmiths in the early 20th century.

See the boxed text (p205) for an idea of the cultural significance of jewellery in Jordan.

Heather Colyer Ross looks into popular art forms in *The Art of Bedouin Jewellery*, a useful asset for those contemplating purchasing some pieces.

Added-Value Craft

Several NGOs such as the **Noor Al-Hussein Foundation** (www.nooral husseinfoundation.org) and **Jordan River Foundation** (www.jordanriver.jo) have spurred a revival of locally produced crafts as part of a national campaign to raise rural living standards, improve the status of rural women, provide income generation for marginalised families, nurture young artists and protect the local environment. For a good example of how these projects help in social regeneration, see the boxed text (p142).

If you want to spend your money where it counts, then you may like to buy from the outlets of the following community-based income-generating programs:

Beit al-Bawadi (☎5930070; www.beitalbawadi.com; Fawzi al-Qawoaji St, Jebel Amman; ☺9am-6pm Sat-Thu) Jordanian Hashemite Fund for Human Development in Abdoun runs this ceramics showroom, a weekly **farmers market** (Souq al-Ard; ☺10am-2pm Sat Oct-Jul) and community-development initiatives tackling recycling, poverty reduction and hunger alleviation.

GETTING A GOOD DEAL

Jordanians are committed shoppers and they make an art form out it, promenading the main street and popping into a shop to vex the owner without any intention of buying. Buying, meanwhile, is a whole separate entertainment, focused on the business of bartering.

Bartering implies that items do not have a value per se: their value is governed by what you are willing to pay balanced against the sum the vendor is happy to sell for. This subtle exchange, often viewed with suspicion by those from a fixed-price culture, is dependent on many factors, such as how many other sales the vendor has made that day, whether the buyer looks like a person who can afford an extra dinar or two, and even whether the vendor is in a good mood or not.

As with all social interaction, there's an unwritten code of conduct that keeps negotiations sweet. Here are a few tips for making it an enjoyable experience.

» View bartering as your chance to decide what you are willing to pay for an item and then use your interpersonal skills to see if you can persuade the vendor to match it.

» Understand that haggling is a sociable activity, often conducted over piping-hot mint tea, so avoid causing offense by refusing hospitality too brusquely.

» Don't pay the first price quoted: this is often considered arrogant.

» Start below the price you wish to buy at so you have room to compromise – but don't quote too low or the vendor may be insulted.

» Never lose your temper: if negotiations aren't going to plan, simply smile and say goodbye – you'll be surprised how often the words *ma'a salaama* bring the price down.

» Resist comparing prices with other travellers; if they were happy with what they paid, they certainly won't be if you tell them you bought the same thing for less.

» Above all, remember that a 'good deal' in Jordan generally means a good deal more than just the exchange of money. It's a highlight of travelling in the country.

JARA (Jebel Amman Residents Association; www.jara-jordan.com) A village initiative within a city, it spearheaded the now-famous **Souk Jara street market** (Fawiz al-Malouf St; ☺10am-10pm Fri May-Aug).

Jordan Handicraft Producers Association (Map p50; ☑4626295; 34 Khirfan St; ☺8am-4pm Sat-Thu) Encompassing 500 members working from home or from small workshops, it showcases the output in a 120-year-old stone building.

Jordan River Foundation (Map p50; ☑4613081; www.jordanriver.jo; Bani Hamida House, Fawzi al-Malouf St, Jebel Amman; ☺8.30am-7pm Sat-Thu, 10am-5pm Fri) The showroom in Jebel Amman displays works from three major projects – Bani Hamida Women's Weaving Project, Al-Karma Centre Jordan River Designs Project (embroidery) and Wadi Al-Rayan Handicraft Project (woven cattail-reed and banana-leaf products).

Madaba Tourism Development Association (www.visitmadaba.org) A voluntary community-based organisation, it develops tourism products that use local skills and resources.

Made in Jordan (☑2155700; www.madeinjordan.com) In Wadi Musa, it sells crafts from various local enterprises. Products include olive oil, soap, paper, ceramics, table runners, embroidery, camel-hair shawls and bags.

Nature shops These figure prominently at the **Wild Jordan Centre** (Map p50; ☑4616523; www.rscn.org.jo; Othman Bin Affan St, downtown) in Amman and RSCN visitor centres in Ajloun, Azraq, Mujib, Dana and Wadi Rum.

Noor Al-Hussein Foundation (www.nooralhusseinfoundation.org) Maintains a showroom in Aqaba as well as links to now-independent projects selling NHF-labelled products in Iraq Al-Amir, Salt and Wadi Musa (Nabataean Women's Cooperative).

Good Buys

» Silver jewellery (Wadi Musa)
» Handmade paper (Iraq al-Amir, Aqaba and Jerash)
» Ceramics (Salt)
» Painted ostrich eggs (Shaumari)
» Weavings (Mukawir)
» Traditional clothing (Madaba)
» Dead Sea soap (nature reserve shops, Amman)

TRADITIONAL CRAFTS

Shopping for Crafts

Regardless of the 'added value' element, if you are after goods of a high quality it pays to visit specialised craft centres as opposed to one-stop shopping in souvenir shops. Unfortunately, some shop owners have jumped on the cooperative bandwagon and claim to be part of charitable foundations when they are not. Check that a shop's sign exactly matches the outlet you are looking for!

Bargaining

Bargaining, especially when craft buying, is essential, although the original asking price will be not be far wide of the mark. Some cooperatives charge fixed prices.

Duty Free

Most upmarket shops offer tax rebates. If you spend over JD350, keep your receipts, fill out a tax rebate form and leave the country within 90 days, you can get the 16% tax refunded to your credit card at a booth at the airport, just before check-in.

Export Restrictions

Exporting anything more than 100 years old is illegal, so don't buy any craft or artefact (including 'ancient' coins or oil lamps) described as 'antique' – if only because it probably isn't. If you're unsure about an item's provenance, contact the **Customs Department** (☑06-4623186; www.customs.gov.jo) in Amman.

Flavours of Jordan

Our host stood by the circle, encouraging the appetite with pious ejaculations. At top speed we twisted, tore, cut and stuffed: never speaking, since conversation would insult a meal's quality, though it was proper to smile thanks when an intimate guest passed a select fragment.

TE Lawrence, *Seven Pillars of Wisdom*

Eating in Jordan is primarily a social experience, whether conducted over a chat in Amman's cafes or sitting in cross-legged silence in a Bedouin tent. Many travellers leave Jordan thinking that apart from the multicultural options in Amman and Aqaba, Jordanian food is a tedious affair of felafel sandwiches. Anyone venturing beyond the bus station kebab stands, however, will quickly find that not only is the food deliciously varied, but so is the company they will inevitably share it with.

Food

The word 'mezze' is derived from the Arabic *t'mazza*, meaning 'to savour in little bites'. Meat mezze usually comprise mutton, goat, chicken or lamb, but never pork – which is *haram* (forbidden) for Muslims. However, Jordan's Christian community is free to buy it – if they can find it.

On the crossroads of Arab caravans, bringing spices from India and rice from Egypt, Jordan's hybrid cuisine has absorbed many traditions from its neighbours, particularly from Turkey and Lebanon. Jordan's homegrown fresh fruit and vegetables are a highlight. There are two distinct cuisines in Jordan, which for argument's sake we'll call Pan-Arab and Bedouin.

Pan-Arab

The day starts for most Jordanians with a breakfast of eggs and locally produced olives, cheese, sour cream and *foul madamas* (fava-bean dish with olive oil) and, of course, bread. Arabic unleavened bread, *khobz*, is so ubiquitous at mealtimes it is sometimes called *a'aish* (life). A favourite breakfast staple is bread liberally sprinkled with *zaatar* (thyme blend) or sesame-encrusted rings of bread, which often come with a boiled egg.

Lunch is usually the main meal of the day, which could explain the habit of nap-taking in the afternoons. Invariably, lunch involves rice or potatoes and includes some form of seasonal vegetable, prepared as a slow-cooking stew with a meat bone or chicken. In a restaurant, or for a special occasion, *maqlubbeh* may be on the menu: a pyramid of steaming rice garnished with cardamom and sultanas, and topped with slivers of onion, meat, cauliflower and fresh herbs such as thyme or parsley.

The evening meal is a ragged affair of competing interests – children snacking over schoolwork, mothers preparing dishes for surprise visitors and fathers sneaking out for a kebab with friends. At the weekend, Jordanians go out as a family. In cities that could mean a Thai curry, while in small towns it will be the chef's special. In an Arab-style restaurant, the evening is whiled away over mezze – a variety of exquisite little delicacies such as peppery rucola (rocket) leaves, aromatic chopped livers, spicy eggplant (aubergine) dips or a dish of freshly peeled almonds.

Bedouin

Bedouin food consists of whatever is available at a particular time. Camel's milk and goat's cheese are staple parts of the diet, as are dried dates and water. Water takes on a particularly precious quality when it is rationed, and the Bedouin are renowned for consuming very little, particularly during the day when only small sips are taken, mostly to rinse the mouth.

The Bedouin speciality *mensaf* – consisting of lamb, rice and pine nuts, combined with yoghurt and the liquid fat from the cooked meat – was once reserved for special occasions. Now visitors can try such dishes in Wadi Rum and Wadi Musa. The dish is cooked in a *zerb* (oven), which consists of a hole in the sand and enough firewood to make glowing coals. The oven is sealed and the meat cooked for hours until succulent.

Seasonal Specialities

Spring Lamb cooked in a *zerb* (ground oven) will ruin your palate for mutton. Fresh, frothy camel's milk is abundant and giant watermelons ripen in fields alongside the Desert Highway.

Summer The fruit harvest brings pomegranates, pistachios, peaches and limes. During Ramadan, fast with the locals (dawn to dusk) and see how hunger enhances the flavours of traditional evening sweetmeats.

CHEESE

Jordan is locally famous for its dairy products, especially salty white cheese. A popular soft white cheese is *kashkawan* (or *kishkeh*) while *haloumi* and Lebanese-style *shinklish* have a firmer texture.

FLAVOURS OF JORDAN FOOD

EATING ETIQUETTE

Travel in Jordan for any length of time and inevitably you'll be invited home for a meal, especially if you are travelling alone, and most especially if you are a woman. Customs vary depending on who you are having supper with: the Bedouin, for example, share their meals from great aluminium dishes on the floor, whereas Christian communities in the hills may sit around a table. Whatever their own customs, however, Jordanians are very accommodating of other people's habits, though you will certainly impress your hosts if you manage a few of the following courtesies.

Eating in Someone's House

» Bring a small gift of baklava or, better still, a memento from home.
» It's polite to be seen to wash your hands before a meal.
» Use only the right hand for eating or accepting food. The left is reserved for ablutions.
» Don't put food back on a communal plate: discard in a napkin.
» Your host will often pass the tastiest morsels to you; it's polite to accept them.
» The best part – such as the meat – is usually saved until last, so don't take it until offered.
» If you're sitting on the ground, don't stretch your legs out until after the meal.

Eating in a Restaurant

» Picking your teeth after a meal is acceptable and toothpicks are often provided.
» It's traditional to lavish food upon a guest. If you're full, try one more mouthful!
» Leave a little food on your plate. Traditionally, a clean plate is thought to invite famine.
» It's polite to accept a cup of coffee after a meal and impolite to leave before it's served.
» Avoid eating and drinking in public during daylight hours in Ramadan. Many rural restaurants close at this time.

RAMADAN

Autumn Pluck dangling figs or grapes from the vine and sample corn drizzled with newly pressed olive oil from local groves. In the Jordan Valley bananas and mangoes ripen in subtropical warmth.

Winter Copper-coloured persimmons ripen for Christmas – a good time to try Bethany's 'Baptism Fish'. It's not carnage on the roads – it's tomatoes. Crates of them fill the fields near Safi.

Quick Eats

Local 'fast food' is safe, tasty and available in every town, usually from stands. The most popular dishes are as follows.

Shwarma Lamb or chicken sliced with great flourish from a revolving spit, mixed with onions and tomato and packed into flat bread

Felafel Deep-fried balls of chickpea paste with spices, served in a piece of rolled-up *khobz* (bread) with varying combinations of pickled vegetables, tomato, salad and yogurt

Farooj Chicken roasted on spits in large grills in front of the restaurant, served with bread, raw onion and pickles

Shish tawooq Spicy minced chicken kebabs, grilled over charcoal

Vegetarian Options

Jordan, like many countries in the region, has a strongly carnivorous bias in the national diet – at least, that is, in restaurants. At home, people enjoy their vegetables and dairy products (such as home-made cheese, yoghurt and *labneh*) and often consider meat as something to be enjoyed during *eids* (religious holidays) and special occasions.

Delicious vegetable and dairy dishes can be found in many restaurants in Jordan, especially mezze, but the concept of 'vegetarian' is still an alien one. As such, there may well be meat stock within a soup or animal fats used to prepare pastries. The following 'Vegidex' of restaurants is recommended for the variety of vegetarian options, but not for a nonmeat pedigree. Most of the nature-reserve restaurants have excellent vegetarian choices on the menu and Feynan Ecolodge gets the prize as the outstanding vegetarian choice.

Ajloun Ajloun Forest Reserve restaurant (p96)

Amman Wild Jordan Café (p66); Hashem Restaurant (p65)

During Ramadan (see p313 for upcoming dates) Muslims fast during daylight hours. They savour a large pre-dawn breakfast called *suhur* and eagerly await *iftar* (breaking the fast) at dusk. Always something of a celebration, this dish-of-the-day is a fun meal to share with hungry patrons at a busy restaurant.

COOK YOUR OWN AT PETRA KITCHEN

It was an inauspicious start one cold day in winter: the knives were seriously large, the onions eye-smartingly malevolent and the eggplants (aubergines) too big for their own good. But just as I was thinking this wasn't the activity for me, I caught sight of my fellow apprentice. With a smile of collusion across the basins of parsley, I took heart and placed myself in the hands of Mr Tariq, professional Petra chef and our teacher for the evening. Within moments, he had us shaving garlic with prodigious speed and chopping industrial quantities of tomatoes without them collapsing into sauce.

Petra Kitchen (☎ 2155700; www.petramoon.com/cuisinetours.htm) in downtown Wadi Musa is a novel idea. Instead of going out for supper, you pay a little extra to cook your own mezze, soup and a main course. The local experts who teach you how to cook Jordanian food give you valuable tips throughout the evening. If you get hooked on the flavours you learn to create, the dishes on the menu change each night so within a week you could be returning home with a whole cookbook.

The whole experience of cooking in the company of strangers makes you realise that cooking in Jordan, just like dining, isn't about the locally grown ingredients or the handed-down recipe: it's about being sociable. As Sharon Stark, my fellow apprentice from New Zealand, said: 'If we'd tasted that meal at a restaurant, without all the fun of creating it, the four of us meeting/talking to each other and our hosts, it would still have been delicious but not as nice as it tasted that night.'

COFFEEHOUSES

For men, Jordan's coffeehouses are great places to watch the world go by, write a letter, meet the locals and play a hand of cards, accompanied by the incessant clacking of slammed domino and backgammon pieces and the gurgling of fruity nargileh (water pipes). Foreign women, with a bit of courage and modest attire, are usually tolerated (see p303). Traditional coffeehouses don't generally serve food.

Aqaba Ali Baba Restaurant (p203); Blue Bay (p204); Formosa Restaurant (p204); Royal Yacht Club Restaurant (p203)
Azraq Azraq Lodge (p232)
Dana Biosphere Reserve Feynan Ecolodge (p122); Dana Guest House (p153); Rummana Campground (p153)
Jerash Lebanese House (p90)
Karak Kir Heres (p148)
Madaba Ayola Coffeeshop & Bar (p136); Haret Jdoudna (p136)
Mt Nebo Asa Moses Restaurant (Siyagha Restaurant; p139)
Petra Basin Restaurant (p184)
Umm Qais Umm Qais Resthouse (p103)
Wadi Musa Petra Kitchen (p183)
Wadi Rum Bait Ali (p221); Rum Gate Restaurant (p221)

Desserts

Jordanians have an incorrigibly sweet tooth, and there are pastry shops in every town dedicated to the sublime cuisine of baklava. The giant circular trays of filo pastry, tickled with honey, syrup and/or rose water and cut into lozenges, are almost works of art.

The sweetest highlight of travel in Jordan is *kunafa*, a highly addictive dessert of shredded dough and cream cheese, smothered in syrup. Customers generally order desserts by weight: 250g is generally the smallest portion so have some friends (or a toothbrush) at the ready.

Tea & Coffee

Tea and coffee are the major social lubricants in Jordan.

Tea *(shai)* is probably the more popular drink, taken without milk and in various degrees of sweetness: with sugar *(sukkar ziyada)*, a little sugar *(sukkar qaleel)* or no sugar *(bidoon sukkar)*. In most cafes you can ask for refreshing mint tea *(shai ma n'aana)*. Za'atar (thyme) and *marrameeya* (sage) herbal teas are especially delicious in Dana.

Coffee *(qahwa)* is served strong, sweet and flavoured with cardamom, and usually contains thick sediment. You can specify a small espresso-sized cup *(finjan)* or large cup *(kassa kabira)*. In traditional Bedouin areas coffee is served in small porcelain bowls and the host will always refill a guest's coffee cup. A good guest will accept a minimum of three cups; gently 'dancing' the cup from side to side indicates you've had enough.

Beans are traditionally roasted and then ground in a decorated mortar and pestle called a *mihbash*.

Sahlab is a delicious traditional winter drink, served hot with milk, nuts and cinnamon. Look for it at hot-drink vendors (recognisable by their silver samovars), who also offer takeaway shots of coffee or Lipton tea in white plastic cups.

Best Books for Jordanian Recipes

» **Jordanian Cooking Step by Step** (Lina Baydoun and Nada Halawani)
» **The New Book of Middle Eastern Food** (Claudia Roden)

Water is safe to drink in hotels and restaurants and is available in earthenware ewers along rural roads; bottled water, however, will minimise stomach upsets. Fresh mixed pomegranate and rockmelon juices *(aseer)* are a highlight. Discreet imbibing of alcohol, such as local wine and arak, is acceptable for non-Muslims.

The Natural Environment

The true servants of the most gracious are those who tread gently on the earth.

Quran (sura 25, verse 63)

With some application, you can have breakfast in the desert, lunch under a hilltop pine and dinner eating fresh bananas from the subtropical Jordan Valley. There are not many places in the world where the land exhibits such extraordinary diversity within such a compact area. For the naturalist, this is what makes Jordan a dream. Thankfully Jordanian authorities have been quick to recognise the country's appeal in this regard and have put in place several ecotourism projects aimed at encouraging nature-loving visitors. Whether you're a raptor enthusiast or a casual fan of flowers, there is sure to be something to please you in Jordan's modest acreage.

The Land

Jebel is the Arabic word for (usually arid) mountain. Jebel Umm Adaani (1832m), the highest peak in Jordan, lives up to that description. 'Wadi' is the word for (usually dry) watercourse or flood channel. Wadi Mujib belies that description with its permanently flowing water.

At 91,860 sq km, Jordan is slightly smaller than Portugal or the US state of Virginia. Distances are short – it's only 430km from Ramtha, on the Syrian border in the north, to Aqaba in the south. TE Lawrence was pleased that he could cover Azraq to Amman in a hard, three-day camel ride. Today you can travel by car from tip to toe in around six hours. If you want to see anything, though, there's a lot to be said for the camel.

Jordan can be divided into three major regions: the Jordan Valley, the East Bank plateau and the desert.

Jordan Valley Ecosystem

Jordan edges the Great Rift Valley, stretching from East Africa's lakes to southern Syria. The rift was created as the Arabian plate pulled away from the African plate, a geological event that gave rise to the Red Sea. Jordan's Wadi Araba, the Dead Sea and the Jordan Valley lie on this fault line. Sit under the effervescent springs at Hammamat Ma'in and it's obvious that this process of tectonic separation isn't yet complete.

Trickling through the northern part of the valley is the lowest-lying river on earth, the River Jordan, fed from the Sea of Galilee (Lake Tiberias), the Yarmouk River and hillside streams. The permanent fresh water has given rise to a humid, subtropical valley, highly fertile and intensively farmed.

Walking under the valley's flame and tamarisk trees you may see sunbirds and kingfishers or an endangered otter heading for the reeds. What you won't see is the lion, bear, elephant, rhino and herds of wild ass that Palaeolithic remains prove were once resident here.

Not everything in the region has changed, however. The fish in Madaba's famous mosaic, twisting back from certain death at the mouth of the River Jordan, show that the Dead Sea was as insupportable of life in Byzantine times as it is today.

East Bank Plateau Ecosystem

High above the Jordan Valley – cut by a series of epic gorges carved out in slow motion by the wadis of Zarqa, Mujib and Hasa – is the hilly and temperate East Bank Plateau. It comprises the forested hills of northern Jordan (less than 1% of Jordan is wooded), rich in Aleppo pines, oak and red-barked strawberry trees and home to ill-tempered wild boar, polecats, stone martens and porcupines.

In spring wildflowers, including pink hollyhocks, poppies and yellow daisies, bloom in magnificent abundance. This is the time to spot the black iris (actually a deep purple), the national flower of Jordan.

The East Bank plateau contains the main centres of population (Amman, Irbid, Zarqa and Karak) and has been crossed by caravans for centuries. The plateau landscape of fig and olive groves, occasional vineyards and closely cropped pasturelands reflects this human interaction. Hike near Madaba in the summer and you'll see Bedouin grazing their stock on the hillside; they descend to lower ground in winter to escape the bitter winds. Since the time of Moses, their husbandry has shaped the land, etching ancient paths around the closely cropped contours.

Pockets of pristine plateau wilderness remain towards the southern end of the plateau around Dana. This rocky wilderness of outstanding biodiversity is the habitat of elusive caracals (Persian lynx), felines with outrageous tufts of hair on the tips of their outsized ears. It is also home to ibex, endangered goats with enormous horns that cling to the craggy folds of limestone.

From a height of 600m to 900m above sea level, the plateau ends near the Red Sea port of Aqaba.

Desert Ecosystem

On its eastern flank, the East Bank plateau glides gradually into the desert. More than 90% of Jordan is desert, but it's home to only 5% of the population. The forbidding volcanic basalt rock of the northeast gives way to soft-whittled sandstone and granite in the south and the famous escarpments of Wadi Rum. In between, the stony wasteland known as the Badia slides into 1000km of nothingness, interrupted only by the occasional succulent, a wandering camel or camouflaged lizard.

The Dead Sea might be virtually barren, but the surrounding cliffs are not: small oases of date palm and hanging gardens of fern hide noisy Tristram's grackle (a native starling), and the sandstone bluffs shelter the elusive and endangered Nubian ibex.

JORDAN'S BIODIVERSITY

» **Birds** Jordan's location on the edge of the Great Rift Valley makes it an important migration route for birds. More than half a million birds transit between Russia, Central Europe and Africa.

» **Animals** A successful breeding program of the Nubian ibex by the Royal Society for the Conservation of Nature (RSCN) began in Wadi Mujib Nature Reserve in 1989. Some have been reintroduced into the wild and the herds are increasing.

» **Fish** The Gulf of Aqaba, part of the Red Sea, sustains 230 species of coral and 1000 types of fish.

» **Plants** Jordan boasts more than 2500 species of wild plants, including 20 species of orchid. *Wildflowers of Jordan & Neighbouring Countries* by Dawud MH Al-Eisawi has useful photographs helpful in identification.

Jordan's Nature Reserves

Jordan's Nature Reserves

Nature Reserves

1	Ajloun Forest Reserve	A2
2	Azraq Wetland Reserve	B2
3	Dana Biosphere Reserve	A4
4	Dibeen Forest Reserve	A2
5	Mujib Biosphere Reserve	A3
6	Shaumari Wildlife Reserve	B3
7	Wadi Rum Protected Area	A5
8	Yarmouk Nature Reserve	A2

Proposed Nature Reserves

9	Abu Rukbeh Reserve	B3
10	Aqaba Reserve	A5
11	Bayer Reserve	B3
12	Burqu Reserve	C2
13	Fifa Reserve	A3
14	Jebel Masuda Reserve	A4
15	Qatar Reserve	A4
16	Rajel Reserve	C2

When you travel along empty Route 10, it's impossible to imagine that anything could survive such desolation. But then, miraculously, you reach Azraq Wetland Reserve, a desert oasis attracting epic numbers of migrating birds. Herons and egrets fish patiently among the croaking toads, and predators such as the desert fox, wolf and jackal lurk beyond the fringes of oases waiting for a careless desert hare to run out of luck.

Some desert species ran out of luck a long time ago, hunted to extinction before conservation became part of the modern sensibility. In Shaumari Wildlife Reserve there's a chance to see the animals that once roamed these plains before they are reintroduced to the wild.

Protected Areas

Established in 1966, the **Royal Society for the Conservation of Nature** (RSCN; www.rscn.org.jo) is an unusual NGO in that it has a national mandate to run biodiversity projects on behalf of the nation. Indeed, it is Jordan's main environmental agency.

The RSCN has been successful in its founding remit: to help save animal and plant species from extinction and to reintroduce several locally extinct species, such as the Arabian oryx (p236). Over the past two decades, however, the RSCN has developed a much wider focus, recognising that tourism has an important role to play (see the boxed text, p297). The result has been a modern and highly successful program of ecotourism projects, centred on RSCN reserves.

Jordan's Nature Reserves

The RSCN maintains seven reserves (not the Wadi Rum protected area) and is hopeful of establishing three more (Burqu, Fifa, Rajel) soon. These should not be confused with Jordan's 'national parks', which are unstructured, recreational areas, such as Zay National Park, near Salt.

Ajloun Forest Reserve (13 sq km, established 1988) This pretty reserve has easy trails, pistachio and oak forest, spring flowers and cottage industries. See p93.

Azraq Wetland Reserve (12 sq km, 1977) In spring and autumn, hundreds of migratory birds can be seen from a bird hide and boardwalk through this damaged marshland. See p234.

Burqu Reserve (400 sq km) Remote desert lake, needing urgent protection.

Dana Biosphere Reserve (320 sq km, 1989) A spectacular wilderness area with various trails, Dana encompasses rugged mountains and desert with 600 species of plants, 200 species of bird and over 40 species of mammal. See p151.

Dibeen Forest Reserve (8 sq km, 2005) One of the last Aleppo pine forests left in Jordan, Dibeen protects endangered species such as the Persian squirrel. See p91.

Fifa Reserve (27 sq km) Rare subtropical vegetation, home to migratory water birds.

Mujib Biosphere Reserve (212 sq km, 1988) Used for the captive breeding of Nubian ibexes, Mujib has an impressive ecotourism program, with canyon walks and waterfall rappelling. See p123.

Rajel Reserve (908 sq km) Only source of water in an otherwise desolate region, with threatened desert species.

Shaumari Wildlife Reserve (22 sq km, 1975) This small reserve was established to reintroduce the locally extinct Arabian oryx, ostrich, gazelle and onager. See p235.

Yarmouk Nature Reserve (30 sq km, 2011) Undeveloped home to water birds, endangered gazelles and otters.

Wadi Rum Protected Area (540 sq km, 1998) This beautiful desert – a Unesco site since 2011 and controlled by the Aqaba government – is the Bedouin heartland, offering camping, camel treks and 4WD excursions. See p210.

THE NATURAL ENVIRONMENT PROTECTED AREAS

The RSCN conducts public awareness programs among Jordanians, especially children; sponsors environmental clubs throughout the country; trains guides; combats poaching and hunting; and lobbies against mining, helping the uphill struggle to preserve the country's natural treasures for future generations.

Nature Guides

» **Field Guide to Jordan** (Jarir Maani) A must for wildlife watchers.

» **The Birds of the Hashemite Kingdom of Jordan** (Ian J Andrews) The definitive birding guide.

Green Jordan & Ecotourism

'Green' is not a concept that has had long to mature in the Middle East, so it may come as a surprise to find that Jordan has shown both ingenuity and commitment for more than a decade in embracing a green approach. This approach extends both to an assortment of environmental challenges and to tourism, which is perhaps the biggest challenge of all. Read on to find out how you can minimise the impact of your visit in a country that at times is too popular for its own good.

Environmental Issues

Water

Swim across one of the infinity pools in Aqaba surrounded by lush gardens and you may not realise that Jordan has a chronic shortage of water. The facts are alarming. Relying mainly on rainwater and subterranean aquifers that are already in many cases overexploited (see the boxed text, p234), Jordan is the 10th most water-impoverished country in the world. With 90% of Jordan's rivers already being diverted, a population increasing by almost 3.5% annually and persistent droughts, this situation is likely to worsen rather than improve. Currently, about 60% more water is used than is replenished from natural sources and, by some estimates, the country is due to run out of water within 20 years.

Jordan is not alone in this problem. Water is a hot political issue across the region, contributing to several skirmishes over the years and continuing to spike relations between Jordan and its neighbours. Since the 1960s, for example, Israel and the Palestinian Territories has drawn around one-third of its water from the Jordan River; this river has now been reduced to a trickle, half of which is 50% raw sewage and effluent from fish farms. After the 1994 peace treaty, Israel and the Palestinian Territories permitted Jordan to extract 50 million cu metres per year from Lake Tiberias, but disputes rumble on over whether Jordan is getting its fair share.

Jordan has just 140 cu metres of renewable water per capita per year, compared to the UK's 1500, Israel's 340 and the Palestine Territories' 70. Jordan's figure is expected to fall to 90 cu metres by 2025. Anything under 500 cu metres is considered to be a scarcity of water.

Hunting

Visit a nature reserve in Jordan and you'll see lots of information about elusive animals that reside there, but the fact remains that a staggering 20 species of mammal have become extinct in Jordan in the past 100 years. Some were hunted and poached (especially after WWII, when weapons flooded the region), spelling the end for Jordan's lion, cheetah, bear, gazelle and wild ass. The last leopard was killed near Dana in 1986, although there have been unsubstantiated sightings since.

The continuing threats to bird and animal species (24 out of Jordan's remaining 77 species of mammals are globally threatened) include poor land management, such as deforestation; the pumping of water from vital areas such as the Jordan River, Dead Sea and the Azraq Wetlands with the associated consequences; urban sprawl; unremitting use of pesticides, especially near water sources in the Jordan Valley; and air and water pollution.

Overgrazing & Desertification

Survey Moses' promised land from Mt Nebo and you'll find little left of promise in the semi-arid landscape – that's if you can see it through the haze of dust kicked up by livestock. This once fertile land has been devastated by centuries of overgrazing and this, together with erosion and drought, has led to widespread desertification (the seemingly unstoppable spread of the desert to previously fertile, inhabited and environmentally sensitive areas). According to the Royal Society for the Conservation of Nature (RSCN), millions of hectares of fertile land have become infertile and uninhabitable. This means there are now fewer pastures for livestock and crops, and reduced land for native animals and plants. Jordan is home to about three million sheep and goats, but there is no longer enough pasture to feed them, resulting in their encroachment on nature reserves and urban fringes.

Overcoming the Challenges

Recognising the threat environmental problems posed to the country, the Jordanian Parliament passed the Protection of the Environment Law in 1995 as part of an impressive commitment to environmental protection. This included measures banning hunting and restricting grazing. At Dana Nature Reserve, for example, grazing within the protected area is permitted only at certain times of year.

The chief part of the environmental strategy, however, has focused on addressing the water issue. Jordan's farmers (comprising around 5% of the population) use 75% of the water (quite often inefficiently), so modernising farming practices and plugging leaks in city pipelines has been the priority of the decade. More radical approaches have included the extraction of non-renewable fossil water from aquifers near Wadi Rum and controversial plans to construct a series of desalination plants, hydroelectric power stations and canals linking the Red Sea with the Dead Sea (see the boxed text, p117), thereby raising the level of the Dead Sea and creating a fresh water supply. If the looming

Green Info on Jordan

» **Friends of the Earth Middle East** (www.foeme. org) Covers main environmental challenges.

» **Ministry of Environment** (www.environ ment.gov.jo) Environmental overviews, organisations and regional reports.

TEN TOP ECO-EXPERIENCES

» Hike to see Ajloun's soapmakers at work (p93)
» Savour a wild-berry smoothie in Amman's Wild Jordan Centre (p74)
» Learn about Azraq's Chechens over a home-cooked feast at Azraq Lodge (p232)
» Buy a hand-loomed rug from the Bani Hamida workshop (p142)
» Wake up to birdsong at beautiful Rummana campground (p153)
» Enjoy a vegetarian supper in candlelit Feynan Ecolodge (p153)
» Give your sunglasses an embroidered treat from Dana craft shop (p155)
» Splash through the permanent pools of Wadi Mujib (p123)
» Take a camel trip in the company of a Bedouin guide (p217)
» Stay overnight with the Bedouin at a camp in Wadi Rum (p220)

water crisis is not resolved swiftly, many commentators predict that 'water wars' will replace oil crises as the major source of conflict in the near future.

Ecotourism

Effects of Tourism

By 2013 Jordan expects to extract 100 million cu metres of water a year from the 30,000-year-old aquifer in Diseh near Wadi Rum. The near-billion-dollar project will have taken four years to complete, involving the drilling of 55 wells and building of a 325km pipeline from Diseh to Amman.

The impact on the environment of mass tourism is an issue that is under constant review. Tourism has caused a rapid increase in pollution from cars and industries, and has exacerbated the demand for precious water. In addition, vandalism and unwitting damage to sites such as Jerash and Petra (see the boxed text, p169), the effects of flash photography on fragile rock art, and rubbish left at hot springs and baths have made some people wonder whether tourism is worth the trouble.

But it is not all doom and gloom. In a region only recently concerned with conservation, it's refreshing to discover that Jordan is ahead of the game. Not only are the authorities keen to promote sustainable tourism with regard to Jordan's natural heritage, they are also keen to maintain the country's cultural heritage by preserving Islamic values, supporting arts and craft initiatives, and supporting traditional lifestyles (as with the employment of Bedouin drivers in Wadi Rum) within the constrains of tourism.

The RSCN has been at the forefront of attempts to promote a more sustainable form of tourism through its various ecotourism projects (for more information, see p293). Such projects provide a major means of funding environmental programs.

Of course it's not easy balancing the need for increased tourism against the environmental cost of more visitors. For example, tourism revenue at Wadi Rum is needed for the upkeep of the protected area, but it's hard to minimise the impact of more feet and wheels upon a fragile desert ecosystem. A balance can be achieved, however, with the cooperation of visitors.

Impact Neutral Checklist

Jordan's nature reserves represent about 1% of Jordan's total land area – a small percentage compared with land allocated in Saudi Arabia (9%) and the USA (11%). When measured as a ratio of habitable land versus size of population, however, the figure is considerably more generous.

If you'd like to know how to minimise the negative impact of your visit, then you may like to use the following checklist to inform the choices you make on the road.

Save water Jordan has a critical water shortage.

Use local guides and services This is an opportunity to learn about a unique way of life and help preserve local traditions.

Buy wisely Profits are returned to local communities from specialist craft centres.

Dress and behave respectfully The liberalisation of customs and manners is seen by many Jordanians as a bad habit caught from the West and an erosion of their cultural and Islamic heritage.

Pay your dues Entrance fees are the lifeline that helps to maintain Jordan's reserves.

Spend money... This will help make your visit count more positively than surviving on muesli you brought from home.

...but don't give it away Tips should only be given for services rendered (such as buying a souvenir from kids at Petra) to discourage the counterproductive activity of begging.

Leave as found For as long as outsiders have been searching for, and stumbling over, the ancient monuments of Jordan, they have also been chipping bits off, hauling items home or leaving their contributions engraved on the stones. Please don't be one of their number.

Bag it and bin it This is the one time when you shouldn't follow local example; set an example instead and take your litter home.

Follow the rules As tempting as it may be to reach out for a starfish in the Red Sea, light a fire for an ad hoc campground, take a photo without someone's permission, or skinny dip in a waterhole, these are acts that erode the natural and cultural heritage of the country.

Making Your Stay Count

There are lots of ways in which you can turn your visit from a potential burden into a blessing. By supporting any of the following enterprises, you will be contributing positively to local communities. Also don't forget that you can add value to your purchases by shopping at community-friendly outlets – see p284 for a list of craft shops.

Things to Do

Abraham Path Initiative (www.abrahampath.org) Aims to weave a path from Ajloun in Jordan through Israel and the Palestinian Territories and Syria, connecting local communities who stand to benefit from the passing trade of hikers. This ambitious international project is currently on hold due to political difficulties but is one to watch for the future.

Jordan Living History Association (JLHA; www.jerashchariots.com) Promotes accurate historical re-enactments at Jerash (where it supports 65 people, including army veterans) and other parts of the country.

Neighbours Paths (www.foeme.org) Four community-based tours along the Jordan River, focusing on cross-border issues such as water and peace-building.

Zikra Initiative (www.zikrajordan.org) Connects 'urbanites' (Jordanians and internationals) to 'ruralists' – a modest participation fee helps fund microloans for village 'entrepreneurs'.

RSCN: A BYWORD FOR SUSTAINABLE TOURISM

Teamwork is a good way of describing the Royal Society for the Conservation of Nature (RSCN) policy of environmental management. The RSCN employs 330 Jordanian people. Its role includes getting corporate business involved to back eco-ventures (such as the chic Wild Jordan Café within the RSCN headquarters building in Amman). Crucially it also involves local communities, such as those of Ajloun or Dana, through income-generating projects that complement rather than threaten traditional lifestyles. Thanks to the combined interests of all these 'stakeholders', the RSCN's work is surprisingly high-profile in Jordan, with Jordanian nationals comprising a high proportion of the annual 60,000 visitors to the country's nature reserves.

Despite being clearly passionate about what he describes as the 'golden triangle of ecotourism' (Dana, Petra and the Rift-edge landscape of Jebel Masuda), the president of RSCN, Chris Johnson, is no tree-hugging eco-warrior: 'You can't protect wildlife without thinking of economic development,' he explains. 'Tourism is the main tool being used to sustain our reserves; by visiting us, tourists make a direct contribution to preserving Jordan's natural heritage.'

With fantastic accommodation serving wonderful food in beautiful places; walking, hiking and scrambling trails to suit all legs; and a series of shops that make you wish you'd packed a bigger suitcase, the RSCN's flagship reserves are a highlight of a 'sustainable visit' to Jordan.

A successful breeding program of the Nubian ibex by the RSCN began in the Mujib Biosphere Reserve in 1989. Some have now been reintroduced into the wild and the herds are increasing well. The killifish, unique to the Azraq Wetlands, has recently been saved from extinction, and numbers are increasing slowly.

Places to Stay

RSCN (www.rscn.org.jo) Provides excellent ethical and sustainable accommodation within Jordan's reserves – reservations are necessary and can be made online.

Ammarin Bedouin Camp (p192; www.bedouincamp.net) Near Little Petra, this camp is run for the benefit of the tribe.

Bedouin cooperative campgrounds Camps at Wadi Rum (p220) and Diseh (p225) help preserve the Bedouin way of life.

Finding Fair Services

Jordan Inbound Tour Operators Association (www.jitoa.org) A voluntary umbrella organisation is a good place o research 'green' tour operators.

Fair Trade Jordan (www.fairtradejordan.org) Has an online database that reviews tourism-related products and services according to responsible criteria.

Survival Guide

Safe Travel

Democratic Uprising

Jordan is very safe to visit and, despite local dissatisfaction with issues such as Iraqi immigration, unemployment and high inflation, you are unlikely to feel any hint of the turmoil of neighbouring countries. The democratic uprising during the Arab Spring of 2011 was only fleetingly experienced in Jordan. At the time of writing, other than a few mild protests in regional towns after Friday prayers, there was no sign of trouble. King Abdullah is a respected leader and has wide public support for his efforts in introducing democratic reforms and curbing public corruption.

Terrorism

Jordan is considered locally as the 'Switzerland of the Middle East' and remains reassuringly calm. That said, there are occasional demonstrations in support of the Palestinians in Karak, Tafila and Ma'an, and in the university areas of Irbid, Mu'tah and northern Amman. A few other incidences have also

challenged Jordan's reputation as a safe haven:

2010 On 22 April and 2 August rocket attacks in Aqaba resulted in one Jordanian fatality.

2010 On 14 January a roadside explosion between Amman and the Dead Sea reportedly targeted an Israeli diplomatic convoy; there were no casualties.

2006 On 4 September 2006 a lone gunman, Nabil Ahmad Jaoura, who had no apparent ties to any terrorist organisation, randomly opened fire on tourists at the Roman Theatre, killing one Briton and injuring six others. He was found guilty in December 2006 and sentenced to death by hanging.

2005 On 9 November 2005, suicide bombers killed 60 people and injured 115 others in attacks at three hotels in Amman. The Iraqi wing of Al-Qaeda claimed responsibility.

Commitment to Safety

While they make stark reading, the terrorist incidents listed are no more numerous than in most Western

countries. If anything, these incidents have helped make Jordan a safer place. Over the past decade, the Jordanian government has invested significantly in tourism and, now, with so much at stake in terms of revenue, there is a collective desire among Jordanians to maintain Jordan's reputation as a safe destination. Some of the measures taken by the government for this purpose (see the boxed text, p70) include the following:

» A high security presence in many tourist hotels throughout Jordan.

» Metal detectors at hotels and some public buildings.

» Tourist police are present at all major sites.

» Checkpoints monitor all border zones.

Keeping Safe & Avoiding Trouble

Some Dos...

» Be vigilant in the cities, keeping clear of large public gatherings.

» Cooperate politely with security checks in hotel foyers and at road checkpoints.

» Keep abreast of the news in English-language newspapers published in Amman.

» Check the latest travel warnings online through your country's state department or ministry.

» Consult your embassy/consulate in Jordan for specific concerns.

» Register with your embassy/consulate on arrival if there has been recent public order issues.

» Trust the police, military and security services. They are overwhelmingly friendly, honest and hospitable, in common with their compatriots.

Some Don'ts

» Don't be paranoid – the chances of running into trouble are no greater than at home.

» Don't get involved if you witness political protests or civil unrest.

» Don't strike up conversations of a stridently political nature with casual acquaintances.

Government Travel Advice

The following government websites offer travel advisories and information on current hot spots.

Australian Department of Foreign Affairs & Trade (☎1300 555 135; www.smart traveller.gov.au)

British Foreign & Commonwealth Office (☎0845-850-2829; www.fco.gov.uk)

Canadian Department of Foreign Affairs & International Trade (☎800-267 6788; www.dfait-maeci.gc.ca)

US State Department (☎888-407 4747; http://travel. state.gov)

Other Dangers

Minefields

In 1999, Jordan signed the UN mine-ban convention and has been working to eradicate mines on Jordanian soil ever since. A minefield comprising 86,756 mines along the Jordan–Syria border is well off the tourist trail, but if you're in the area take heed of warnings not to enter. There are unsubstantiated reports that more mines have been laid on the Syrian side recently, but the Jordanian government has put plans in place to rid the country of mines by the end of 2012.

Theft & Crime

Crime in Jordan is much less prevalent than in many Western countries. Leaving your bag under the watchful eye of a member of staff at a bus station or hotel is generally safe so avoid jumping to conclusions if something goes missing – locals have a lot to lose by stealing in a country where thieving from guests

---

Taxi driver wouldn't use the meter? Paid more than a friend for the same item? These may sound like routine scams but there's invariably a legitimate reason. Jordanians take pride in their moral compass and tourists on the whole are treated with respect and fairness. Here are some different perspectives given by service providers that may cast so-called 'scams' in a different light.

» **Taxi fares?** The fare is set by the government and hasn't been adjusted for inflation; taxi drivers usually agree on fair fares with locals but it's harder to negotiate with tourists who don't speak Arabic.

» **Room rates?** Small hotels have to respond to fluctuations in tourist numbers or they go bust. For some this means offering unrealistic rates in low season; for others, it means raising prices to cover investments made in anticipation of a good season.

» **Minibus overcharging?** Foreigners don't like waiting until the bus is full – drivers are happy to leave early but it means making up the cost of a full load. As for luggage, that often takes up the place of a passenger.

» **Double standards?** In the bartering system, an item costs whatever a vendor is happy to sell for, balanced against whatever a buyer is happy to pay for during that one transaction. Comparison with other travellers' experiences is a pointless exercise. For more on bartering, see p284.

---

is particularly frowned upon. Punishments are harsh and, in a country where unemployment is high, there is a serious chance of losing a job without much hope of recovering a livelihood in future. Inevitably, however, there are one or two scams to look out for.

SOME COMMON SCAMS

Taken for a Ride The taxi fare quoted on the meter is in fils, not in dinars, and visitors often misunderstand this when paying. Perhaps understandably, it is rare for a taxi driver to point out this mistake.

Crafty Business Shop owners often claim something is locally crafted as part of a profit-share scheme, when in fact it is imported from abroad.

Money for Old Rope So-called 'antiques' are often merely last year's stock that's gathered an authentic-looking layer of dust.

Similarly, 'ancient' oil lamps and coins are seldom what they seem.

SOME SIMPLE SAFETY PRECAUTIONS

» Agree on a fare before you get in the taxi.

» Do some research about genuine fair-trade establishments if you want your purchase to have added value (see p284).

» Pay the sum for an item based on how much you like it and want it, not on how much you think it is worth (see p284).

» Carry wallets or purses in a front pocket and avoid carrying too much cash.

» Keep a copy of your passport buried in your luggage.

» Be careful late at night outside nightclubs in Amman: pickpockets and muggers are attracted by the patronage of intoxicated, vulnerable and comparatively wealthy foreigners.

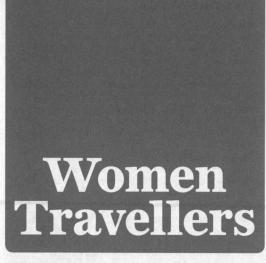

Women Travellers

Adopting the Right Mindset

Plenty of women travel through Jordan, often alone (this author included), and enjoy the experience thoroughly. That said, there are bound to be times when you'll have male company in Jordan that you'd rather do without. This may involve nothing more than irritating banter, proposals of marriage and declarations of love. On rarer occasions it will involve leering and minor physical contact – a grope in a bus for example. Where possible, it's best to ignore such behaviour or pass it off as part of the experience, or a few sad individuals will spoil your whole trip.

Attitude towards Women

Being highly gregarious as a nation, Jordanians will be surprised that you want to travel alone. Men, who have little or no contact with women, let alone sex, before marriage, may misinterpret this as an invitation to provide company. Stereotypes of foreign women based on Western films and TV convince some that all foreign women are promiscuous and will jump into bed at the drop of a hat. The fact that some women choose to do just that contributes to this impression.

Avoiding Trouble

Dressing Appropriately

Nothing gives more offense in Jordan – a country with largely conservative and Islamic sensibilities – than bearing too much flesh. To minimise harassment and to be respectful of local customs, it's imperative to dress appropriately, especially in small towns and rural areas.

In the trendy districts of Amman such as Abdoun and Shmeisani, in large hotels and resorts or even in the middle of Petra (where tour group parties generally wear whatever they feel like) you'll feel comfortable dressing as you would at home. Outside those areas, aim for knee-length dresses or loose trousers, and cover your shoulders and upper arms.

On public beaches at the Dead Sea and in Aqaba, wear a swimsuit (and preferably a T-shirt and shorts) when swimming and save the bikinis for top-end resorts and dive centres. Never go topless – especially in the wadis where skinny dipping in freshwater pools is never as unseen as you might imagine.

Some foreign women go to the extent of covering their head, but this is inappropriate for non-Muslims in Jordan and can be misconstrued – particularly by the women of Jordan's Christian communities who do not wear headscarves.

Advice from Fellow Women Travellers

The following simple dos and don'ts can make all the difference to your sanity if you are travelling alone. Here are a few tips passed on by fellow travellers.

SOME DOS...

» Sit next to a woman if possible on public transport.

» Be cautious when venturing alone to remote parts of Petra, Jerash and Wadi Rum.

» Check for peepholes in rooms and bathrooms (particularly cigarette holes in curtains).

» Place a chair against your locked hotel room door in case of 'accidental' intrusions.

» Pay for a better hotel, generally associated with less hassle.

» Be suspicious of lovelorn guides, especially the handsome ones!

» Prepare a cover story – Jordanians will be mystified you have no family or friends to travel with.

» Chat to men in the company of women – not all men are one-track minded.

» Wear a wedding ring – this will add to your respectability in Arab eyes. A photo of husband and kids will clinch it.

» Bring tampons and contraceptives – they're hard to find, and embarrassing to purchase outside Amman.

SOME DON'TS...
» Don't go to a local bar unaccompanied.
» Don't make eye contact with strangers – dark glasses can help.
» Don't sit in the front seat of a chartered private or service taxi.
» Don't go outside with wet hair – this apparently implies you've had sex recently!

Public Spaces

It's not easy finding where to eat and drink, or even just sit, in public without becoming the centre of attention. Here are some guidelines.

Coffeehouses & Local Bars Often seen as a male domain; in some places the stares will evict you even if the landlord won't.

Midrange Bars & Cafes Almost always welcoming of women in Amman and Aqaba; less 'comprehending' (of your solo status) in smaller towns.

Public Beaches Magnet for unwanted attention; best to stick to resorts.

Restaurants Most have a 'family section' where women can eat alone and in peace.

Toilets Usually only one in small restaurants and bars; avoid where possible!

Tourist Sites Counterintuitively, the best places to be 'alone' as a woman.

Responding to Persistent Harassment

Some behaviour may warrant a public scene: bystanders will quickly support you

WHAT DOES A GIRL HAVE TO DO TO GET A BEER AROUND HERE?

Author's Diary Entries of 1995, near Jerash
Thankfully times have changed since my first trip to Jordan, and solo women no longer present such an unusual spectacle. Or is it that I've grown older and no-one's interested anymore? Either way, girls be warned: eating on your own may bring more (or less) to your table than you expect. On the upside, travelling solo may well lead to home-cooked meals by locals taking pity on you.

20 April 1995 Despite the neatly laid tables there were no guests to warrant the preparation of food – except me. I braved a seat and sat shivering over the tablecloth in the corner. Eventually a waiter greeted me and brought coffee. Shocked when I drank all the hot milk, he didn't return again and there was a limit to the length of time I could sit staring at the fairy lights intermittently beaming over the concrete grotto. Another waiter came: 'Like to buy Roman coin', he said (I was thinking rather more of a kebab – with chips). 'What about guide for tomorrow?' And finally, grabbing his crotch with gusto, 'Need a man?' I said, 'No thank you, but I wouldn't mind a beer'. That was the last I saw of him, too – or of anybody for that matter.

21 April 1995 Went down to breakfast with renewed hope of food and was glad to find it arrived without further negotiation. I could have done without the services of the hotel manager who felt it necessary to put most of the breakfast things on the table in such a way that he had to brush my left breast to rearrange them. After the third 'accident', I gave him the evil eye and he went out grumbling. Gobbled a few olives, tried mixing the strawberry jam with the soured goats' milk and popped a butter pat in whole thinking it was the local cheese. Another meal to remember in Jordan!

if someone has overstepped the mark. Say out loud *imshi* (clear off): this should deter most unwanted advances. Be firm but stay calm. Swearing or losing your temper will lose you public sympathy.

What to Do in an Emergency

Assault and rape is rare in Jordan but if you do suffer a

serious problem, follow this advice:
» Go to a police station or tourist-police booth; the latter can be found at most tourist sites.
» Be clear about the facts: the tourist police in Jordan take reports seriously.
» Call the nationwide **emergency number** (911); this central coordination point has English-speaking staff.

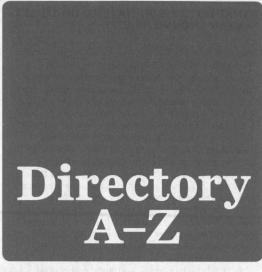

Directory A–Z

Accommodation

Jordan has accommodation to suit most budgets, although away from the main tourist centres there's limited choice. Jordan is so compact, however, that most attractions can easily be visited in day trips from the main towns.

Prices are highest during the two peak seasons, which are from September to October and from March to mid-May. Holiday weekends are also peak times in Aqaba and at the Dead Sea resorts.

High inflation and rises in taxes continue to contribute to escalating prices. Although accurate at the time of writing, expect significant increases in the cost of accommodation.

PRICE RANGES

Prices in this book indicate the cost of a double room in high season. Rooms have a private bathroom unless reviews state otherwise.

$	less than JD40
$$	JD40-90
$$$	more than JD90

Camping

For many people, spending a night under the stars – or at least under canvas – is a highlight of a trip to Jordan. One popular option is to sleep in a traditional 'house of hair' at a Bedouin camp in Wadi Rum. Facilities in these goat-wool tents are basic but it's a great experience.

Camping with your own tent is permitted in a few places in southern Jordan, especially in the desert surrounding Wadi Rum. Camping 'off piste' in the north is more problematic, not least because you'll have competition for the best spots from the Bedouin and it's surprisingly hard to find a secluded place to pitch a tent.

Bringing a tent to save money on accommodation isn't cost effective as camping is rarely possible without your own transport. Besides, cheap rooms are plentiful in areas close to the major sites of interest.

Staying in Jordan's Nature Reserves

A variety of accommodation, from camping and cabins to luxury rooms in ecofriendly lodges, is offered within several of Jordan's nature reserves. To see what is on offer in each reserve and to make an online booking, visit the website of the **Royal Society for the Conservation of Nature** (RSCN; www.rscn.org.jo). In some areas, such as the beautiful Dana Nature Reserve (open March to November), advance booking is required.

Camping in these reserves is not a cheap option. It is intended for those who are happy to pay extra to wake up in the wilds and who like to feel that they are contributing to the sustainable tourism ethic of the RSCN. Bookings can also be made through the **Wild Jordan Centre** (Map p50; ☎4616523; www.rscn.org.jo; Othman Bin Affan St, downtown) in Amman.

Hotels

From family-run guesthouses to opulent pleasure palaces on the Dead Sea, Jordan offers some interesting hotel accommodation. Reservations are recommended during peak seasons, especially at the Dead Sea Resorts, in Jerash, and for midrange and top-end hotels in Aqaba and Wadi Musa.

Accommodation prices in this book do not include breakfast, unless otherwise stated. Breakfast varies from a humble round of bread with a triangle of processed cheese in budget hotels to a delicious assortment of locally made yoghurt, hummus, *fuul* (fava bean paste) and olives in midrange hotels. The buffet-style breakfasts at top-end hotels can set a hungry hiker up for a week.

Hotels indicated as offering 'air-con' have both cooling and heating appliances available in at least some of their rooms.

BUDGET

Budget rooms are available in most towns and vary from stark and basic to simple and

BOOK YOUR STAY ONLINE

For more accommodation reviews by Lonely Planet authors, check out http://hotels.lonelyplanet.com. You'll find independent reviews, as well as recommendations on the best places to stay. Best of all, you can book online.

homey. Most are spotlessly clean.

Private rooms in less-frequented towns start from JD10/15 for singles/doubles, with less stark rooms with a private bathroom costing around JD20/35. Prices are negotiable, especially during quieter seasons. Dorm rooms are not common, but most budget places have 'triples' (rooms with three beds), which you can ask to share with other travellers, cutting the cost of accommodation considerably. In summer you can even sleep on the roof in some places for about JD5 per person. There are no youth hostels in Jordan.

Some things to consider: many budget places are located above shops and cafes that can be noisy at night; avoid windowless rooms that are stifling hot in summer; and winter in Jordan is bitterly cold so ensure the heater is working before checking in.

Payment usually needs to be made in cash in Jordanian dinars.

MIDRANGE

Midrange hotels offer the best value for money in Jordan. They are often privately owned by families who take pride in welcoming their guests. The owners are a fount of local knowledge and can provide assistance in catching transport or advising on sights of interest. Some even organise their own tours. Most family-run hotels offer some kind of home cooking for breakfast and guests may even be asked to join the family if they have ordered an evening meal.

There is at least one mid-range hotel in towns you're likely to visit, with a good selection in Amman, Madaba, Wadi Musa (near Petra) and Aqaba. Rooms in midrange hotels usually have colour TV (sometimes featuring satellite stations such as CNN), fridge, heater (essential in winter), telephone, reliable hot water and a private bathroom.

Prices are typically around JD35/50 for singles/doubles. Negotiation is usually possible, especially if you're staying for several days. Many midrange hotels accept credit cards, but it's best to ask before checking in.

PRACTICALITIES

Newspapers & Magazines available in Jordan

» *Jordan Times* (www.jordantimes.com)
» *The Times* (www.thetimes.co.uk)
» *Guardian Weekly* (www.guardian.co.uk/weekly)
» *International Herald Tribune* (www.global.nytimes.com)
» *Time* (www.time.com)
» *Newsweek* (www.thedailybeast.com/newsweek)

Radio

» Radio Jordan (96.3 FM)
» BBC World Service (1323 AM)
» Popular hits (99.6 FM)

TV

» Jordan's Channel 2 (French and English)
» Satellite channels (BBC, CNN, MTV, Al-Jazeera) available in most midrange and top-end hotels

Discount Cards

» International Student Identity Card (ISIC) for discounts at some tourist sites.
» University ID cards are not accepted.

Smoking

There are laws banning smoking in public places, but these are rarely enforced, with the following exceptions:
» Top-end hotels in Amman, the Dead Sea and Aqaba reserve a few nonsmoking rooms.
» The occasional quality restaurant enforces a non-smoking policy at selected tables.

Weights & Measures

Jordan uses the metric system. See the inside front cover for a conversion table.

WARNING – PRICE RISES

If there is one bone of contention between our readers and those involved with tourism in Jordan, it is the issue of prices. Many travellers expect to find prices exactly as quoted in this book and become suspicious of landlords and taxi drivers who charge more. By the same token, many service providers in Jordan feel frustrated when travellers insist on prices that may be unrealistic even a relatively short time after printing.

There are many reasons why prices in Jordan rise quickly. For the past five years, for example, volatile oil prices, instability among neighbouring countries and continued immigration have all contributed to high inflation. Not surprisingly, the number of people visiting Jordan also makes a difference. For some, a slump in tourism – such as that witnessed after the Arab Spring in 2011 – means there is no option but to put prices up. For others it means being forced to offer unrealistic discounts.

In summary, while every effort is made to ensure that our published prices for entrance fees, tours, accommodation, restaurants, food items and private transport is accurate at the time of writing, this book is only a *guide* to pricing, not a definitive statement of costs.

There is one piece of good news for those trying to estimate the cost of their trip to Jordan. Public bus prices, which are heavily subsidised by the government, have only minimally increased from the last edition to this edition and there is no suggestion of an imminent price hike in this sector.

TOP END

There are some excellent top-end hotels in Amman, Wadi Musa (near Petra) and Aqaba, with liveried staff, welcome drinks on arrival, marble foyers and luxurious rooms. Most have a travel agency within their shopping arcades from which you can hire a car and organise hotel bookings for the next part of your trip.

Most of the top-end hotels are owned by international chains, but they invariably reflect the local character of Jordan, with Arabian-style interior design, options for high-quality Middle Eastern dining, shops selling fine Jordanian handicrafts and bookshops with a selection of English-language titles on Jordan.

Independent travellers can often negotiate a walk-in rate. Outside peak seasons and holidays (when booking is essential), you may find a world-class room for a mid-range price.

A tax and service charge of 26% is added to the bill in top-end hotels, although it's worth checking to see if this has already been included in a discounted rate. Major credit cards are accepted in all top-end hotels.

Rental Accommodation

In Amman, the best places to check for apartments and houses to rent are the accommodation listings in the English-language newspapers, cultural centre noticeboards, and the noticeboard at Books@café in Amman. Also see www.expatriates.com/classifieds/amm/housingavailable. There is also a useful noticeboard in the office of the University of Jordan Language Center. For longer stays, wander around the suburbs of Shmeisani, or between the 1st and 5th circles: signs advertising places to rent are often displayed in residence or shop windows.

It costs about JD500 to JD1000 per month for a furnished apartment in a reasonable area of Amman; a little less if it's unfurnished. A furnished apartment or small house in a less salubrious area may cost as little as JD300 to JD500 per month, but for this price don't expect everything to work.

Resorts

If you have only one night's luxury during your visit to Jordan, plan to stay in one of the Dead Sea resorts. Not only are these state-of-the-art hotels worth a visit in their own right, but they also offer the best access to the Dead Sea – an area where there is next to no alternative accommodation. Residents of one resort can also use the facilities of the neighbouring hotels, which can take care of several nights' worth of entertainment in an area with no local nightlife.

Apart from the Dead Sea, there are also resorts in and around Aqaba – including the flagship resorts of the Mövenpick and Intercontinental chains. With access to the calm waters of the Red Sea, multiple pools, gyms and a selection of top-notch restaurants, they are bringing a touch of class to Jordan's second city.

Business Hours

Opening times vary from town to town, and from office to office across the country, but the following listings gives an idea of business hours in Jordan. Reviews only show opening times if they differ from these standards. Many sights, government departments and banks close earlier in winter.

During the month of Ramadan, working hours are greatly reduced.

BANKS
» Sunday to Thursday, 8.30am-3pm

GOVERNMENT DEPARTMENTS
» Sunday to Thursday, 8am-3pm

MONEYCHANGERS
» Daily, 9am-9pm

POST OFFICES
» Saturday to Thursday, 7am-6pm
» Some open Friday until 1pm

SHOPS & BUSINESSES
» Saturday to Thursday, 9am-8pm
» Some close 2-4pm

SOUQS (MARKETS)
» Daily, 9am-8pm

TOURIST OFFICES
» Saturday to Thursday, 8am-3pm

Visitor centres
» Daily, 8am-6pm
» See relevant destination

Customs Regulations

» 1L of alcohol
» 200 cigarettes or 25 cigars or 200g of tobacco
» A 'reasonable amount of perfume for personal use'
» Gifts up to the value of JD50 or the equivalent of US$150
» Prohibitions include drugs, weapons, and pornographic films and magazines.
» Exporting anything more than 100 years old is illegal, so don't buy any souvenir (including 'ancient' coins or oil lamps) that is deemed to be 'antique'. If you're unsure about an item's provenance, contact the **Customs Department** (☎06-4623186; www.customs.gov.jo) in Amman.

Electricity

230V/50Hz

230V/50Hz

Embassies & Consulates

The following embassies and consulates are in Amman. Egypt also has a consulate in Aqaba. In general, offices are open 9am to 11am Sunday

Climate

ACTIVITIES

Jordan offers some of the best outdoor activities in the Middle East. You can hike and climb in stunning landscapes, or painstakingly piece together the past on an archaeological dig. Don't head home without trying at least a couple of these fantastic adventures. For information on scuba diving and snorkelling, see p26.

WHAT	WHERE	HOW/HOW MUCH	ALSO SEE...	NOTES
Archaeological Digs	Around Madaba, Mt Nebo, Karak and Petra	Contact an organisation involved in archaeology in Jordan before you arrive.	p268	Even if you don't have much experience, it's possible to join a dig.
Camel treks	Petra and Wadi Rum	JD30 for two hours	p181 and p217	Choose a mounted rather than a walking guide for a more authentic experience.
Cycling	Dana and King's Highway	**Cycling Association** (www.cycling-jordan.com)	p321	Bring your own bicycle and spare parts.
Hiking	Jordan's Nature Reserves	**Royal Society for the Conservation of Nature** (RSCN; ☎06-4616523; www.rscn.org.jo)	p310	Don't expect an organised network of routes, with signposts and watering holes en route: most hiking in Jordan is an ad hoc affair passing through small villages.
Horseback Riding	Petra and Wadi Rum	**Rum Horses** (☎2033508, 079-5802108; www.wadirumhorses.com)	p181 and p218	A rare chance to ride an Arabian stallion. Prior knowledge of horseback riding is necessary and don't expect a helmet.
Hot Springs	Dead Sea and King's Highway	Entrance fees vary.	p17	Hot spring water contains potassium, magnesium and calcium, among other minerals with reputed health benefits.
Rock Climbing	Wadi Rum	The following websites detail routes: www.rumguides.com and www.wadirum.net.	p219	Popular climbs all around Jordan are detailed in the excellent books written by Tony Howard and Di Taylor.
Running	Amman, Dead Sea and Wadi Rum	**Hash House Harriers** (http://hashemitehhh.googlepages.com)	p19 and p20	Dubbed 'drinkers with a running problem' on its website, the HHH organises local runs each Monday from Amman.
Turkish Baths	Amman, Madaba, Wadi Musa and Aqaba	Around JD25, including massage	p60	A great antidote for aching muscles, the hammam is otherwise known as a Turkish bath. Women should call ahead for a female assistant.

to Thursday for visa applications and 1pm to 3pm for collecting visas.

Australia (☑06-5807000; www.jordan.embassy.gov.au; 3 Youssef Abu Shahhout, Deir Ghbar)

Canada (☑06-5203300; www.canadainternational. gc.ca/jordan; Abdul Hameed Shoman St, Shmeisani)

Egypt Consulate (☑03-2016171; cnr Al-Isteglal & Al-Akhatal Sts, Aqaba; ☺8am-3pm Sun-Thu) Embassy (☑06-5605175; fax 5604082; 22 Qortubah St, Jebel Amman; ☺9am-noon Sun-Thu) Between 4th and 5th circles.

France (☑06-4604630; www. ambafrance-jo.org; Al-Mutanabbi St, Jebel Amman)

Germany (☑06-5930367; www.amman.diplo.de; 31 Bin Ghazi St, Jebel Amman) Between 4th and 5th circles.

Iraq (☑06-4623175; fax 4619172; Al-Kulliyah al-Islamiyah St, Jebel Amman) Near the 1st circle.

Ireland Honorary Consulate (☑06-625632; King Hussein St, Jebel Amman)

Israel Consulate (☑06-5503529; Maysaloon St, Shmeisani)

Lebanon (☑06-5929111; fax 5929113; Al-Neel St, Abdoun) Near the UK embassy.

Netherlands (☑06-5902200; www.netherlandsembassy.com. jo; 22 Ibrahim Ayoub St) Near the 4th circle.

New Zealand Consulate (☑06-4636720; fax 4634349; 99 Al-Malek al-Hussein St, Downtown) On the 4th floor of the Khalaf Building.

Saudi Arabia Consulate (☑06-5924154; fax 5921154; 1st Circle, Jebel Amman)

Syria (☑06-5920684; Abdoun Prince Hashem bin Al-Hussein St, Jebel Amman) Near the 4th circle.

UK (☑06-5909200; www. britain.org.jo; Dimashq St, Wadi Abdoun, Abdoun)

USA (☑06-5906000; http:// usembassy-amman.org.jo; 20 Al-Umawiyeen St, Abdoun)

Yemen (☑06-5923771; Al-Ameer Hashem bin al-Hussein St, Abdoun Circle)

Food

See p286 for an idea of Jordanian cuisine and the general eating experience.

Gay & Lesbian Travellers

Homosexuality is illegal in most Islamic countries in the Middle East, but in Jordan (according to most sources) gay sex is legal and the age of consent is 16. Public displays of affection by heterosexuals are frowned upon and the same rules apply to gays and lesbians, although same-sex hand-holding is a common sign of friendship in Jordan.

There is a subdued underground gay scene in Amman – if you're keen to explore it, keep your enquiries discreet. Gay-friendly venues that attract young, gay and straight crowds include the multipurpose Books@café and the Blue Fig Café in Amman.

Check www.gaymiddle east.com and the gay and lesbian thread of Lonely Planet's Thorn Tree bulletin board (lonelyplanet.com) for more information.

Insurance

Travel insurance that covers theft, loss and medical problems is essential. The policy should cover ambulance fees and emergency flights home.

Some policies specifically exclude 'dangerous activities', which can include motorcycling and even trekking. You must have insurance if you plan to dive in Aqaba – decompression-chamber treatment is an expensive business!

You may prefer a policy that pays doctors or hospitals directly. Alternatively, if you submit a claim after

PRICE RANGES

The following price ranges indicate the cost of a main dish unless individual reviews state otherwise. A main dish is often accompanied by salad and various pickles, dips (such as hummus) and garnishes. These are offered free of charge and invariably served with flat Arabic bread. This means that a main dish often doubles as a meal.

$	Less than JD5
$$	JD5-10
$$$	More than JD10

the event, ensure you keep all documentation. Some policies ask you to call back (reverse charges) to a centre in your home country where an immediate assessment of your problem is made. See also Insurance (p327).

Worldwide travel insurance is available at lonelyplanet.com/travel_services. You can buy, extend and claim online anytime – even if you're already on the road.

Internet Access

Jordan is part of the cyber community, and boasts numerous Internet Service Providers (ISPs), including **Cyberia** (www.cyberia.jo).

Almost every town in Jordan has at least one public internet centre. If you have a laptop it's possible to connect to the internet from top-end and a few midrange hotels that have wi-fi facilities.

The easiest way to collect mail through internet centres is to open a web-based account such as **Hotmail** (www. hotmail.com) or **Yahoo! Mail** (mail.yahoo.com). Most places are also set up for various online chat services, such as MSN Messenger.

HIKING

Hiking is an exhilarating activity in Jordan, not least because of the pristine and varied quality of the landscape and the historical allusions that underlie almost every path.

Bear in mind that Global Positioning System (GPS) units and mobile phones may not function between steep canyon walls. Always check local conditions before setting out as flash floods can occur throughout spring and may make wadis impassable.

When to Go

» **Best** Mid-March to late April when it's not too hot, the rains have finished, flowers are blooming and wells are full.

» **Good** Late September to mid-October when it's dry but not excessively hot.

» **Avoid** November to March when rains make it dangerous to hike or camp in narrow wadis and flash floods can sweep unheralded out of the hills. Paths are often washed away and so routes change frequently. It's also very cold for camping.

Where to Go

The best places for hiking in Jordan are Ajloun Nature Reserve, Dana Nature Reserve and Wadi Mujib Nature Reserve where most trails require a guide. For more DIY options, there are some exciting hikes in Petra and in Wadi Rum. Bedouin guides also offer accompanied hikes along the old caravan routes that link these two spectacular places.

Several longer routes are possible with a tent. In particular, Dana to Petra is an excellent four-day trek that takes you through Wadi Feinan, Wadi Ghuweir and Little Petra.

What to Bring

Lightweight trousers and long-sleeved shirts are culturally sensitive and best for the terrain. Other essentials include a hat, sunscreen, water bottle, torch (flashlight) and insect repellent. Lightweight walking boots are ideal, and a watertight bag for wet wadi walks.

How to Organise a Hike

The best way to organise a trek is through the Royal Society for the Conservation of Nature (RSCN), the visitor centre in Petra or Wadi Rum, or a private tour company that specialises in hiking, as listed following. If you engage a Bedouin guide independently, make sure you understand exactly what services are on offer to avoid disappointment on either side. Rates vary (and are negotiable) between JD30 to JD100, depending on the skills required for each hike or scramble.

» **Royal Society for the Conservation of Nature** (RSCN; ✆06-4616523; www.rscn.org.jo) Wide range of guided hikes in Jordan's nature reserves; can arrange long-distance treks if given prior notice. Rates vary from JD30 for a two-hour guided hike to more than JD100 for a full-day trek.

» **Terhaal Encounters** (✆06-5813061; www.terhaal.com) For individual or group adventure hikes, including abseiling and canyoning, that minimise environmental impact and bring benefits to local communities.

» **Desert Guides Company** (✆06-5527230; www.desertguidescompany.com) Specialises in adventure hikes, treks and climbs throughout Jordan.

» **Yamaan Safady** (✆077 7222101; www.adventurejordan.com) Leads weekly hiking trips to places such as Wadi Yabis and Wadi Hasa as part of the Adventure Jordan Hiking Club.

Where to Find out More

It's best to buy both maps and books abroad as their availability in Jordan is sporadic.

Trekking & Canyoning in the Jordanian Dead Sea Rift by Itai Haviv contains numerous trekking and canyoning routes in the wadis of Central Jordan; its cultural and environmental insights alone make it worth the trouble to find.

British climbers Tony Howard and Di Taylor have spent much of their lives exploring and mapping the hiking, trekking and rock-climbing possibilities in Jordan. Their books include the following:

» *Treks & Climbs in Wadi Rum*

» *Walks & Scrambles in Wadi Rum*

» *Jordan: Walks, Treks, Caves, Climbs & Canyons*

Language Courses

For those enchanted enough by the Arab world to want to learn the language, there are some opportunities in Amman:

British Council (☑06-46033420; www.britishcouncil.org/jordan.htm) Can put individuals in touch with a private tutor.

University of Jordan Language Center (☑06-5355000, ext 2370; www.ju.edu.jo; University of Amman) Offers tailormade courses with private instruction for individuals and small groups, geared to students' special interests.

Legal Matters

The Jordanian legal system has evolved from distinct traditions. Civil and commercial law is largely based on British-style common law, while religious and family matters are generally covered by Islamic Sharia courts, or ecclesiastic equivalents for non-Muslims. In a nutshell:

» The legal age for driving and drinking is 18.

» The age of consent for men and women is 16.

» You can be prosecuted under the law of your home country regarding age of consent, even when abroad.

» Travellers are expected to respect the law.

» Penalties for drug use of any kind are stiff.

» Criticising the king is illegal.

» Excessive speeding, drunk driving and seatbelt avoidance are not tolerated.

» If you break the law, your embassy can only contact your relatives and recommend local lawyers.

Maps

The Jordan Tourism Board's free *Map of Jordan* is a handy driving map. The Royal Geographic Centre of Jordan also publishes good maps, including a hiking map of Petra.

Several detailed maps are available outside Jordan: ITMB's 1:700,000 map *Jordan* is probably the easiest map to find, *Jordan* by Kümmerly and Frey is the best driving map, and the latest edition of GEO Project's *Jordan* (1:730,000) has an excellent map of Amman.

Money

Known as the 'jay-dee' among hip young locals, the currency in Jordan is the dinar (JD) and it is made up of 1000 fils. You will sometimes hear the terms *piastre* or *qirsh:* this refers to 10 fils (10 qirsh equals 100 fils). Often when a price is quoted the unit will be omitted, so if you're told that something is 25, it's a matter of working out whether it's 25 fils, 25 piastre or 25 dinars! Although it sounds confusing, most Jordanians wouldn't dream of ripping off a foreigner, with the possible exception of taxi drivers (see p301).

Coins come in denominations of 10, 25, 50, 100, 250 and 500 fils, and one dinar. Notes come in denominations of JD1, 5, 10, 20 and 50. Try to change larger notes as often as possible – when paying for petrol, for example, or for your hotel bill – as it can be hard to pay with large notes in small establishments.

ATMs

It is possible to travel in Jordan almost entirely on plastic. ATMs giving cash advances abound in all but the smaller towns – just don't forget your PIN!

There are no local charges on credit-card cash advances, but the maximum daily withdrawal amount is around JD500, depending on your particular card. All banks have large signs (in English) indicating which credit cards they accept.

Visa is the most widely accepted card at ATMs, followed by MasterCard. Other cards, such as Cirrus and Plus, are also accepted by many ATMs (eg Jordan National Bank and HSBC).

Changing Money

It's easy to change money in Jordan. Most major currencies are accepted in cash and travellers cheques. US dollars, UK pounds and Euros are easier to change than Australian or New Zealand dollars.

There are no restrictions on bringing dinars into Jordan. It's possible to change dinars back into some foreign currencies in Jordan.

Syrian, Lebanese, Egyptian, Israeli and Iraqi currency can all be changed in Amman. Egyptian and Israeli currency are also easily changed in Aqaba. Banks and moneychangers charge about the same for exchanging cash (a little more for travellers cheques) but large hotels charge more. There are small branches of major banks at the borders and airports.

Credit Cards

Most major credit cards are accepted at top-end hotels and restaurants, travel agencies, larger souvenir shops and bookshops. Commissions of up to 5% may be added to the bill, so it may be better to get a cash advance

IRAQI MONEY

If you are a collector of notes and coins, you may be interested in old Iraqi money, bearing the portrait of Saddam Hussein, for sale on street corners in downtown Amman. Even if they're fake, they're good as a conversational gambit with the Iraqi refugees who are selling them.

and pay with the paper stuff. Make a note of the emergency numbers on the back of your credit cards in case you lose them.

Duty Free

There are duty-free shops at Queen Alia International Airport and next to the Century Park Hotel in Amman, plus small outlets at the border crossings with Israel and the Palestinian Territories.

Most upmarket shops offer tax rebates. If you spend more than JD350, keep your receipts, fill out a tax rebate form and leave the country within 90 days, you can get the 16% tax refunded to your credit card at a booth at the airport, just before check-in.

International Transfers

Some major banks (such as Arab Bank and Jordan National Bank) can arrange international money transfers. Cairo-Amman Bank is part of the international service offered by **Western Union** (www.westernunion.com). **MoneyGram** (www.money gram.com) has agreements with several banks. Fees are high with both, so obtaining a cash advance with a credit card is a better bet.

Tax

Jordan has a sales tax of 16%, but this is generally only added to the bill in midrange and top-end restaurants. Midrange and top-end restaurants and hotels may also add an additional 10% service charge. The Aqaba special economic zone has a sales tax of only 5% and many Jordanians head there on shopping sprees to take advantage of the lower consumer prices.

See Duty Free for information on tax rebates for tourists.

Tipping

Tips of 10% are generally expected in better restaurants. Elsewhere, rounding up the bill to the nearest 250 fils or giving back the loose change

is appreciated, especially by petrol attendants and taxi drivers.

Travellers Cheques

Most types of travellers cheques are accepted by money changers, with the most recognised being American Express (Amex). Check the commission before changing them.

Photography

Airport Security

All airports in Jordan have X-ray machines for checking luggage. Digital images are not affected when scanned by this equipment, but if you have print film keep it in a ziplock bag ready for manual inspection. Don't keep film in your checked-in luggage.

Equipment

Digital accessories and memory cards are widely available; a 1GB memory card costs around JD20. Many camera shops can burn photos onto a CD and print digital pictures.

Photographing People

Some Jordanians, particularly women and the elderly, object to being photographed, so ask first. Persisting in taking a photograph against someone's wishes can lead to ugly scenes, so exercise courtesy and common sense. Children generally line up to be photographed.

Jordanians are very proud of their country and can be offended if you take pictures

of anything 'negative' or suggestive of poverty and squalor; this may include the activity of a marketplace.

Restrictions

Photography in military zones and 'strategic areas' like bridges and public buildings is forbidden. Take particular care in the Eastern Desert as there are several sensitive military sites not far from the desert castles. You also need to be careful along the Dead Sea Highway where there are numerous checkpoints protecting the sensitive border with Israel and the Palestinian Territories.

Post

Stamps are available from souvenir shops where postcards are sold and there are postboxes around towns. Letters posted from Jordan take up to two weeks to reach Australia and the USA, but often as little as three or four days to the UK and Europe. Every town has a post office, but parcels are best sent from Amman or Aqaba. For more detailed postal information, **Jordan Post** (www. jordanpost.com.jo) has an informative website.

Reliable courier companies include **FedEx** (www. fedex.com.jo), which has an office in Amman, and **DHL** (www.dhl.com), which has offices in Amman and Aqaba. Half a kilo costs around JD50 to most countries, although the per-kilo rate decreases dramatically the more you send.

POSTAL RATES FROM JORDAN

	MIDDLE EAST	UK/ EUROPE	USA/ CANADA	AUSTRALIA
Letter/ postcard	600	800 fils	JD1	JD1
1kg parcel	JD9	JD18.600	JD15.300	JD14.700

ISLAMIC HOLIDAYS

HEJIRA YEAR	NEW YEAR	PROPHET'S BIRTHDAY	RAMADAN BEGINS	EID AL-FITR	EID AL-ADHA
1433	26.11.11	04.02.12	20.07.12	19.08.12	26.10.12
1434	15.11.12	24.01.13	09.07.13	08.08.13	15.10.13
1435	04.11.13	13.01.14	28.06.14	28.07.14	04.10.14
1436	24.10.14	03.01.15	18.06.15	18.07.15	24.11.15

Public Holidays

During the public holidays listed following, government offices and banks close. Shops, moneychangers and restaurants generally remain open, and public transport functions normally. During Eid al-Fitr and Eid al-Adha many shops close as shop owners join their families on these important days of celebration.

Archaeological sites and nature reserves tend to be very crowded on Fridays and public holidays.

New Year's Day 1 January

Good Friday March/April

Labour Day 1 May

Independence Day 25 May

Army Day & Anniversary of the Great Arab Revolt 10 June

Christmas Day 25 December

The main Islamic holidays are listed below. See the table of Islamic Holidays for equivalent dates in the Western calendar.

Islamic New Year First Day of Muharram.

Prophet's Birthday Celebrated on 12 Rabi' al-Awal.

Eid al-Isra Wal Mi'raj Celebrates the nocturnal visit of the Prophet Mohammed to heaven.

Ramadan Ninth month of the Muslim Calendar.

Eid al-Fitr Starts at the beginning of Shawwal to mark the end of fasting in the preceding month of Ramadan.

Eid al-Adha Commemoration of Allah sparing Ibrahim (Abraham in the Bible) from sacrificing his son, Isaac. It also marks the end of the hajj.

Ramadan

During the holy month of Ramadan, Muslims refrain from eating, drinking, having sex and smoking during daylight hours in accordance with the fourth pillar of Islam. Even gum chewing is considered haram.

Although many Muslims in Jordan do not follow the injunctions to the letter, most conform to some extent. Foreigners are not expected to follow suit, but it is bad form to eat, drink or smoke in public during this period.

Business hours during Ramadan are erratic and tempers tend to flare towards the end of the month. After 6.30pm many villages turn into ghost towns as people go home to break their fast. Tourist attractions and hotel restaurants remain open and public transport generally functions normally, but the serving of alcohol may be restricted to room service or simply be unavailable.

Telephone

The telephone system in Jordan is privatised, so visitors can make a call from a private telephone agency, call from a hotel or shop, or buy a telephone card from one of the 1000 or more payphones throughout Jordan.

Local calls cost around 150 fils for three minutes. The easiest place to make a call is at your hotel, where local calls are often free. The cost of overseas calls from Jordan varies widely: check with your service provider.

Overseas calls can be made at any card payphone or from hotels, but are substantially more expensive. Reverse-charge telephone calls are not normally possible.

Mobile Phones

Mobile phones in Jordan use the GSM system. Two main service providers are **Zain** (www.zain.com) and **Orange** (www.orange.jo), both of which offer a full range of plans and prepaid SIM cards.

Phone Codes

To make a call from a landline, you must precede the six- or seven-digit number with a two-digit area code.

✆962 Jordan country code

✆00 International access code

The following area codes precede six- or seven-digit landline numbers:

✆02 Northern Jordan

✆03 Southern Jordan

✆05 Jordan Valley, central and eastern districts

✆06 Amman district

✆07 Prefix for eight-digit mobile phone numbers

✆0800 Prefix for toll-free numbers

✆1212 Local directory assistance (Amman)

☑131   Local directory assistance (elsewhere)

☑132 or ☑133 International directory assistance

Emergency Numbers

☑911   Ambulance

☑911   Fire department

☑911   Police

Time

Jordan is two hours ahead of GMT/UTC in winter and three hours ahead between 1 April and 1 October, when daylight saving time begins. Note that Jordan's daylight saving time is slightly out of sync with summer clock changes in Europe. There are no time differences within Jordan. Jordan is on the same time zone as Israel and the Palestinian Territories, Syria and Egypt.

Toilets

Most hotels and restaurants, except those in the budget category, now have Western-style toilets. In most others you'll be using squat toilets with a hose for ablutions and a water bucket provided for flushing.

Toilet paper (the use of which is considered an unsanitary practice in most Middle Eastern countries) is seldom available, except in the midrange and top-end hotels and restaurants. Local people prefer to use the hose and then deposit any toilet paper (used for drying purposes) in the basket by the side of the toilet bowl; these baskets should be used to avoid blockages as the sewerage system is not designed for paper. For those who can't do without it, toilet paper can be bought in most grocery shops throughout Jordan.

If caught short in the desert or hillsides of Jordan, it is imperative you choose a spot well away from water courses and bury the outcome in as deep a pit as possible.

Tourist Information

Jordan has a good network of tourist offices and visitor centres. The main tourist office in Amman is located on the ground floor of the **Ministry of Tourism & Antiquities** (www.tourism.jo) in Jebel Amman.

The comprehensive website of the **Jordan Tourism Board** (JTB; www.visitjordan. com) has regularly updated information. JTB also publishes some excellent brochures in several languages. These are available from its offices in Jordan and abroad. Contact the following offices for a brochure and map package:

France (☑01-55609446; hala@visitjordan.com; 122 rue Paris, 92100 Boulogne-Billancourt, Paris, France)

Germany (☑069-9231880; germany@visitjordan.com; Weser Strasse 4, 60329 Frankfurt)

UK (☑02072231878; uk@visit jordan.com; 115 Hammersmith Rd, London, W14 0QH)

USA (☑1877-7335673, 703-2437404; contactus@visit jordan.com; Suite 102, 6867 Elm St, McLean, VA 22101)

Travellers with Disabilities

In late 2000 Jordan celebrated its first-ever Olympic gold medal, won by the female athlete Maha Barghouthi in the Sydney Paralympics. It was a proud moment for Jordan and it threw a spotlight on people with disabilities – briefly. A decade on and Jordan is still not a great place for travellers with disabilities. Although Jordanians are happy to help, cities are crowded and the traffic is chaotic, and visiting tourist attractions – such as the vast archaeological sites of Petra and Jerash – involves long traverses over uneven ground.

There is some good news, however:

» The Jordanian government has legislated that wheelchair access must be added to all new public buildings.

» Horse-drawn carriages are provided at Petra for visitors with disabilities to help with access to the main sites.

» The Royal Diving Club is a member of the **Access to Marine Conservation for All** (AMCA; www.amca-international.org), an initiative to enable people with disabilities to enjoy diving.

Visas

Visas are required by all foreigners entering Jordan (JD20). Visas can be obtained on arrival either at the airport or at most of Jordan's land borders. Tourist visas are valid for three months (that is, you must enter the country within three months of the date of issue) and allow stays of up to one month from the date of entry. Your passport should be valid for at least six months after you arrive in Jordan.

At the Airport

Visas are issued on arrival at the immigration desks in the airport in Amman. There's no form-filling involved. Payment must be made in Jordanian dinars (note that credit cards are only theoretically accepted!). There are moneychangers adjacent to the counters, but as these are sometimes closed and ATMs are only available after immigration it pays to bring the correct amount of Jordanian dinars with you.

At Land Borders

Visas for Jordan are issued with a minimum of fuss at any of Jordan's land borders, with the exception of King Hussein Bridge.

See p33 for details and information regarding border crossings.

Via the Aqaba Economic Zone

If you arrive in Jordan's southern city of Aqaba by air on an international flight, by sea from Nuweiba in Egypt or by land from Eilat, you are entitled to a free visa as part of the free-trade agreement with the Aqaba Special Economic Zone Area (ASEZA). If you stay in Jordan for more than 15 days, you must register at the office of **ASEZA** (☎03-2035757; www.aqaba zone.com) in Aqaba.

Multiple Entry Visa

Multiple entry visas (JD60) must be obtained in advance from Jordanian consulates or embassies outside the country. In the Middle East, you can find Jordanian embassies in all the neighbouring states, including Israel and the Palestinian Territories. You may want to avoid getting a Jordanian multiple-entry visa from the latter, however, if you intend to travel elsewhere in the region. This is because many Arab countries refuse entry to those who have Israeli stamps or documentation in their passports (see the boxed text, p37).

Visa Extensions

In Amman and Aqaba visas can easily be extended, at no extra charge, for stays of up to three months. The process is simple but involves a little running around, although you're unlikely to spend more than 30 minutes in each office.

» Ask staff at your hotel to write a short letter confirming where you are staying.
» Ask them to fill out two copies of a small card (or photocopy) that states all the hotel details.
» Fill out the application form for an extension on the back of this card (it's in Arabic but staff at your hotel can help your read it and answers can be in English).

» Take the form, letter, photocopies of the front pages of your passport and the Jordanian visa page, and your passport to the relevant police station (see p74 for the address in Amman and p206 for the address in Aqaba).
» Plan to arrive at the police station between 10am and 3pm Saturday to Thursday (best to go early).
» Wait for the extension (usually granted on the spot).

After assembling the necessary paperwork, it takes about 30 minutes to complete the registration process at a police station. You may be required to have an HIV test, which usually takes 24 hours to process. The maximum stay allowed on an extended tourist visa is six months. Failure to register results in a fine of JD1.500 for every day you have overstayed.

For longer-term residency, or to sort out any problems with your visa, you may be asked to go to the **Directorate of Residency & Borders** (☎06-5505360; Majed al-Idwans St, Shmeisani, Amman; ⏰8am-3pm Sun-Thu, to 1pm Sat). Take service taxi 6 or 7 from downtown to Shmeisani; from there it's a 15-minute walk. The office is next to the Shmeisani central police station (*markaz mudiret ash-shurta*).

Visas for Other Middle Eastern Countries

EGYPT

Most nationalities are issued a visa (US$20, payable in dollars) either on the boat from Jordan or on arrival in Egypt.

If you only intend to visit the Sinai Peninsula, you can get a free 'Sinai Entry Stamp', valid for 15 days.

If you wish to travel further than Sharm el-Sheikh, you need to request a full visa for Egypt on arrival (not available at Egypt's Taba border).

Single/multiple entry visas (JD20/25) can be obtained in advance from the Egyptian consulate in Aqaba or the Egyptian embassy in Amman.

IRAQ

Travel to Iraq is not advised at present. It takes two to three weeks to get approval for visa applications from the Ministry of Interior in Baghdad.

ISRAEL & THE PALESTINIAN TERRITORIES

Visas are available at the three border crossings currently open to foreigners – Sheikh Hussein Bridge, King Hussein Bridge and Wadi Araba – and many nationalities do not require one.

LEBANON

Lebanese visas are readily available at Lebanese entry points, but not at the Lebanon embassy in Amman. If you are travelling to Lebanon via Syria, it's worth noting that you will need to obtain your Syrian visa *before* you arrive in Jordan.

SAUDI ARABIA

It is not possible to visit Saudi Arabia as a casual traveller. You must either have a Saudi resident's visa to enter the country or, if you are travelling from Jordan to Kuwait or to Yemen and you can prove there is no other way of getting to your destination (ie you are travelling in your own car), you may be granted a three- or seven-day transit visa. You need to apply well in advance of travel, in your country of residence, and visas are subject to many additional stipulations. Check with the Saudi Arabian embassy in your own country before attempting this process.

SYRIA

Travel to Syria is not recommended at the time of this book going to print. If conditions improve and you intend to travel to Syria, you must obtain a visa either in your home country or in Istanbul, Ankara or Cairo *before* you arrive in Jordan. Only foreign residents in Jordan (ie expatriate workers and diplomats) and residents of a country without Syrian representation can be issued a Syrian visa at the embassy in Amman. Although some travellers have obtained a visa at the border, this can't be relied upon.

It's important to remember that you cannot enter Syria from Jordan if you have a visa stamp in your passport from Israel and the Palestinian Territories – see the boxed text, p37.

Volunteering

The list following highlights one or two opportunities. For further ideas see www.volunteerabroad.com/jordan.cfm.

New Orthodox School (☎3250636; diodoros@orange.jo) For those who like Madaba well enough to stay, there's an opportunity to teach English at this boys school that makes for an excellent gap-year experience. Run by Father Innocent (Innokentios) and attached to St George's Church, the school promotes 'mutual respect and peaceful coexistence' among youngsters of different religious communities. The school is a nonprofit organisation, supporting needy students. Volunteers receive free accommodation, pocket money and private Arabic lessons.

RSCN (www.rscn.org.jo) If you are keen to learn more about Jordan's ecological projects, there are limited opportunities to work within some of the country's nature reserves on a three-month voluntary program. Board and lodging are generally offered in return for a variety of services such as working in the visitor centres. These posts are best filled by local Jordanian people, but if you have a specialist skill in management or conservation, you may strike it lucky.

UN Relief & Works Agency (UNRWA; ☎06-5609100, ext 165; jorpio@unrwa.org) Those hoping to work with Palestinian refugees should contact the public information office of the UNRWA. There is no organised volunteer program, but if you are in Jordan for a few months (prefers longer-term commitments, rather than just a few weeks) and have a particular professional skill in education, relief or health, you may be able to arrange something. Contact them at least three months in advance.

Work

There is not much in the way of casual work in Jordan as all such jobs are in hot demand from Palestinian and Iraqi refugees. If you are interested in staying longer in the country and have a specific skill or qualification, it's best to apply for work before leaving home. That way, your employer will be responsible for paying for your air ticket and will sponsor your work permit.

Diving

Qualified dive instructors or divemasters may be able to get work at one of the diving centres in Aqaba, particularly during peak season (September to March). Keep in mind, however, that positions are hotly contested by locals.

Language Teaching

English-teaching opportunities are open to those with TOEFL qualifications. The **British Council** (☎06-4603420; www.britishcouncil.org.jordan) recruits teachers from the UK with a RSA Preparatory Certificate (the Diploma is preferred) or equivalent and at least two years' work experience. For details contact the British Council **information centre** (☎020-73894385 in the UK; www.britishcouncil.org) before arriving in Jordan. Casual vacancies within Jordan occasionally arise: address your CV to the Teaching Centre Manager.

The **American Language Center** (☎06-5523901; www.alc.edu.jo) runs the other top language school. Like the British Council, teachers are mostly recruited before arrival in Jordan.

Transport

GETTING THERE & AWAY

Ever since Jean Louis Burckhardt rediscovered Petra for the Western world in the 19th century, tourists have been finding ways of visiting Jordan, resulting in well-established and efficient inbound and onward travel routes. These include Jordan's land borders with Syria, and Israel and the Palestinian Territories. Another option is to take a boat across the Red Sea to Nuweiba in Egypt. These routes were curtailed at the time of writing by disturbances following the Arab Spring of 2011 but there is every expectation that these routes will open up again eventually.

Combining a trip to Jordan with visits to neighbouring countries is also possible by flying from Amman to regional capitals; as Amman is well connected with other Arab countries, it's also possible to combine a trip with Dubai (an increasingly important world destination) in the UAE, and other destinations in the Arabian Peninsula.

Flights and tours can be booked online at lonelyplanet.com/bookings.

Entering the Country

Entering Jordan is straightforward whether by air, land or sea, with visas and money-exchange facilities available at all borders.

Always carry your passport with you when travelling around sensitive areas such as near the border of Israel and the Palestinian Territories, along the Dead Sea Highway and roads linking the Dead Sea Highway to interior towns. Checkpoints and passport checks are common in all these areas.

It is important to remember that you cannot enter Syria (and some other Middle Eastern countries) from Jordan if you have a visa stamp in your passport from Israel and the Palestinian Territories – see the boxed text (p37).

Air

Airports & Airlines

Midway through major refurbishment, **Queen Alia International Airport** (☎06-4452700), about 35km south of Amman, is the country's main gateway. There are two terminals: Terminal 1 for most Royal Jordanian flights and Terminal 2 for other airlines. The terminals are within easy walking distance, on opposite sides of the airport road. Both terminals have ATMs, foreign-exchange counters, a post office and left-luggage counter. The departure lounge has a cafe and a good range of gift items, including Arabic sweets and Dead Sea products. Car-rental agencies are in the arrivals building.

CLIMATE CHANGE & TRAVEL

Every form of transport that relies on carbon-based fuel generates CO_2, the main cause of human-induced climate change. Modern travel is dependent on aeroplanes, which might use less fuel per kilometre per person than most cars but travel much greater distances. The altitude at which aircraft emit gases (including CO_2) and particles also contributes to their climate change impact. Many websites offer 'carbon calculators' that allow people to estimate the carbon emissions generated by their journey and, for those who wish to do so, to offset the impact of the greenhouse gases emitted with contributions to portfolios of climate-friendly initiatives throughout the world. Lonely Planet offsets the carbon footprint of all staff and author travel.

Golden Tulip Airport Hotel (☎06-4451000; www.goldentulip.com; r from JD80), the only airport hotel, is 2km from the airport terminal.

The only other international airport is at Aqaba, where some international carriers stop en route to Amman. Flights to Sharm el-Sheikh in Egypt are handled from here and occasional charter flights from Europe stop here, too.

The national airline, **Royal Jordanian** (☎06-5100000; www.rj.com), is well established with a good safety record. It has direct flights to most major cities in Europe and all Middle Eastern capitals. **Royal Wings** (www.royalwings.com.jo – website under construction), a subsidiary of Royal Jordanian, has smaller planes for short flights from Amman to Aqaba (twice daily).

The following airlines fly to Jordan and have offices in Amman:

Air France (☎06-5100777; www.airfrance.com)

British Airways (☎06-5828801; www.ba.com)

Emirates (☎06-4615222; www.emirates.com)

Gulf Air (☎06-653613; www.gulfair.com)

KLM (☎06-655267; www.klm.com)

Kuwait Airways (☎06-5690144; www.kuwait-airways.com)

Lufthansa Airlines (☎06-5200180; www.lufthansa.com)

Qatar Airways (☎06-5679444; www.qatarairways.com)

Turkish Airlines (☎06-5548100; www.turkishairlines.com)

Tickets

Jordan is not a cheap destination to fly into, but special offers are often available on the internet during non-peak seasons (November to February and mid-May to end of August). Some airlines offer 'open-jaw' tickets that allow you to fly into Amman, but

out of Beirut (Lebanon) or Damascus (Syria).

A few airlines, notably Gulf Air, still require reconfirmation of onward or return international flights at least 72 hours before departure.

Buying Tickets within the Middle East

There are regular flights from Amman to other regional capitals. Flights are not particularly cheap, but special offers over the Thursday/Friday Islamic weekend are sometimes available.

To buy discount air tickets in Amman and other regional capitals, try the following locations or agencies:

Amman Along Al-Malek Al-Hussein St, near the flyover.

Tel Aviv Israel Student Travel Association (ISSTA; ☎03-7777316; www.issta.com)

İstanbul Northern side of Divan Yolu in Sultanahmet, **Orion-Tour** (☎212-2326300; www.oriontour.com) is recommended.

Cairo Around Midan Tahrir. One of the best is **Egypt Panorama Tours** (☎02-2359 0200; www.eptours.com), just outside Al-Ma'adi metro station.

Land

It's easy to reach Jordan by land from Syria or from Israel and the Palestinian Territories. Foreign residents of Saudi Arabia (and transit passengers who can show they have no other way of reaching Jordan) are also able to cross Saudi Arabia and enter Jordan by land. For more information, together with information on visas on arrival from these countries and a map of the border crossings, see p33.

Most overland travellers arrive in Jordan by bus or service taxi. It's also possible to bring your own vehicle (see p323).

Leaving Jordan by land requires a little more planning on account of certain visa

stipulations: if you're intending to visit Syria, in particular, read the information about obtaining visas for other Middle Eastern countries (p315).

Getting to/from Jordan's Borders

EGYPT

Most people travel between Jordan and Egypt by boat (see p320). It's quicker and cheaper, however, to travel overland via Israel and the Palestinian Territories via Wadi Araba (but read the boxed text, p37, regarding the Israeli border-stamp stigma before making a decision). If you choose this route:

» Take a taxi to Wadi Araba and another taxi between Yitzhak Rabin and Taba on the Egyptian border.

» Taxis also run from either border to Eilat and there are buses from Eilat to either border.

» The whole trip takes about 1½ hours.

IRAQ

Travel to Iraq is not recommended at present. Occasional service taxis run the gauntlet between Baghdad and Abdali bus station in Amman. They use the Al-Karama–Tarbil border post, 330km from Amman. This is currently an extremely dangerous journey, however, through the notorious 'Sunni triangle'.

If the situation improves, the easiest way to reach the capital is by air-conditioned **Jordan Express Tourist Transport** (JETT; ☎06-5854679; www.jett.com.jo;

Al-Malek al-Hussein St, Shmeisani) bus service to Baghdad on Saturdays and Wednesdays at 2.30pm (JD28.400).

ISRAEL & THE PALESTINIAN TERRITORIES

Several cities in Jordan have direct bus links to cities in Israel and the Palestinian Territories. Travelling by bus directly between Amman and Tel Aviv saves the hassle of getting to/from the borders on your own, but it's more expensive than crossing independently, and you'll have to wait for all passengers to clear customs and immigration.

From Amman, **Trust International Transport** (☑06-5813427) has buses from its office at 7th Circle (p74) to Tel Aviv (six hours), Haifa (seven hours) and Nazareth (seven hours), departing daily except Saturday at 8.30am. Buses cross the border at Sheikh Hussein Bridge. Bus schedules change frequently, so check departure times and book (and collect) tickets in advance from the bus station. There is one **Jordan Express Tourist Transport** (JETT; ☑06-5854679; www. jett.com.jo) bus to King Hussein Bridge (JD7.250, one hour, 7am).

To go it alone, read the following notes.

King Hussein Bridge (Allenby Bridge)

» Take a service taxi from Amman's Abdali or South bus station to King Hussein Bridge (JD8, 45 minutes) or there's a single daily JETT bus (JD7.250, one hour, 7am).

» Buses (JD2, 10 minutes to one hour – depending on waiting time) shuttle between the two borders (expect long delays). It's not possible to walk, hitch or take a private vehicle across this border.

» To get to Jerusalem from the border, take a sherut (Israeli shared taxi; around

US$50 for the car, 30 minutes) to Jerusalem's Damascus Gate.

» Travelling in the other direction, an Israeli exit tax of 167NIS (compared to around 96NIS at other borders) is payable. If you intend to return to Israel, keep the Jordanian entrance form safe – you will have to present it on exiting the border.

Sheikh Hussein Bridge (Jordan Bridge)

» Regular service taxis travel between the West bus station at Irbid and the border (JD1, 45 minutes).

» From the bridge it's a 2km walk to the Israeli side. There is no alternative transport if you make this crossing independently.

» Taxis go to the Beit She'an bus station (10 minutes) for onward connections.

» Travelling in the other direction, take a bus to Tiberias, and change at Beit She'an (6km from the border). From there, take another bus to the Israeli border (arrive early because there are few buses).

» Israeli exit tax is 96NIS at this border.

Wadi Araba (Yitzhak Rabin)

» Taxis run between Aqaba and the border (JD8, 15 minutes).

» You can walk the short distance across the border in a matter of minutes.

» Buses run to central Eilat, 2km away (five minutes).

» Travelling in the other direction, buses from Jerusalem to Eilat will stop at the turn-off for the border (five minutes), a short walk away.

» Israeli exit tax is 96NIS at this border.

SAUDI ARABIA

Getting a visa, even a transit visa, to Saudi Arabia is very difficult – see p315 for details. If you are eligible for a visa, the main land route

for public transport is at Al-Umari, south of Azraq. The other two crossing points are Ad-Durra, south of Aqaba, and further east at Al-Mudawwara. Several companies run services to and from Jeddah and Riyadh from Amman's Abdali bus station.

The air-conditioned **Jordan Express Tourist Transport** (JETT; ☑06-5854679; www.jett.com.jo; Al-Malek al-Hussein St, Shmeisani) bus travels to Jeddah, Riyadh and Dammam.

SYRIA

If you're heading to Syria from Jordan, make sure you get a Syrian visa before arriving in Jordan (see p315), either in your home country or in Istanbul, Ankara or Cairo.

Travel to Syria is not recommended at the time of this book going to print. If conditions in Syria improve, it's quicker and cheaper to take a direct bus or service taxi between Amman and Damascus rather than negotiate local transport and border crossing formalities on your own. For visa information, see p315.

The air-conditioned **Jordan Express Tourist Transport** (JETT; ☑06-5854679; www.jett.com.jo; Al-Malek al-Hussein St, Shmeisani) bus travels between Amman and Damascus (JD8, seven hours, twice daily). JETT's international terminal is close to the Abdali bus station in Amman. The bus schedule changes frequently so check times of departure and book (and preferably collect tickets) in advance from the bus station.

From Amman, service taxis for Damascus (JD10, three hours) leave regularly throughout the day from the lower end of Abdali bus station; from Damascus, they leave from Baramke Garage. They take less time to cross the border than the buses because there are fewer passengers to process, and the drivers are experienced in helping passengers with immigration and customs formalities. Service taxis also travel between Damascus and Irbid's South bus station (JD5, 2½ hours).

The Palace Hotel in Amman (p61) may resume offering a minibus tour to Damascus, with stops in Jerash, Bosra and Shaba. Ask for details if the situation in Syria improves.

To go it alone to the border, read the following information.

Jabir (Nasib)

» Most service taxis between Amman and Damascus now use this crossing.

» If you're coming from Syria and plan to visit eastern Jordan (eg Azraq), this border is useful for connections to Zarqa or Mafraq.

Ramtha (Der'a)

» There are buses to Ramtha from Amman's North bus station (JD1, two hours) and Irbid (JD1).

» From Ramtha, service taxis and minibuses run regularly to the border.

» If hitching, ask the immigration office on the Jordanian side to flag down a vehicle for a lift to the Syrian border.

» You can also find direct transport between Irbid or Amman and Damascus, without stopping in Ramtha.

Elsewhere in the Middle East

For other destinations in the Middle East, travellers need time, patience and, most importantly, the necessary visas. Most trips involve long, hot journeys with frustrating delays so most people end up flying.

JETT has through services to Cairo (JD25), four times per week departing from the international bus office in Amman. Check with the JETT office ahead of your departure as schedules and prices change frequently.

Sea

Visiting Egypt is both a popular side trip from Aqaba or feasible as part of your onward journey. As Jordan has no land borders with Egypt, the journey involves a short boat ride. At most times of the year this is a matter of turning up and buying your ticket. During hajj, however, when Aqaba is abuzz with thousands of excitable Egyptian pilgrims returning home from Mecca, you may find the journey becomes something more epic. Most nationalities can obtain Egyptian tourist visas either on the boat or on arrival at Nuweiba – see p315 for details before making your plans.

There are two main boat services to Nuweiba in Egypt, which leave from the passenger terminal just south of Aqaba. Departure times are often subject to change so call the **passenger terminal** (☎03-2013236; www.abmari time.com.jo/english) before travelling.

The fast boat (US$75, one hour) leaves daily at noon except Saturday. Fares for children under eight are US$60. The return ferry leaves Nuweiba at 3.30pm.

There is also a slower car ferry service (US$65, three hours or more) that officially leaves at midnight. Some days it doesn't leave at all. Fares for children under eight years are US$55. The service leaves Nuweiba at around 2pm but expect delays.

Departure tax (JD6) is not included in the ticket prices. You need to show your passport to buy tickets, and return fares are not available. Note that fares from Nuweiba must be paid for in US dollars, but there are currency-exchange facilities at the terminals at Aqaba and Nuweiba. The Jordanian side offers a decent exchange rate but avoid travellers cheques, which attract a huge commission.

Passports are collected on the boat in both directions and handed back on arrival at immigration. Bear in mind, if you are travelling from Egypt you will arrive in Aqaba too late for public transport to Petra or Wadi Rum, so you'll have to stay in Aqaba or pick up a taxi from the city centre.

Tours

Organised tours from abroad are generally divided into cultural/historical tours, overland adventures that combine several Middle Eastern countries, and activity-based holidays that involve some hiking and camel riding.

See the other Tours section (p325) for details of companies inside Jordan that can organise individual tours and itineraries.

Australia

Adventure World (☎02-8913 0755; www.adventure world.com.au)

Peregrine Adventures (☎03-8601 4444; www. peregrineadventures.com)

Israel & the Palestinian Territories

Desert Eco Tours (☎972-5227 65753; www.desert ecotours.com) Specialises in camel, hiking and 4WD tours; based in Eilat.

UK

Abercrombie and Kent (☎0845-6182200; www. abercrombiekent.co.uk)

Alternative Travel Group (☎01865-315678; www. atg-oxford.co.uk) Activities in Dana, Wadi Rum and Aqaba.

Cox & Kings (☎0845-5279047; www.coxandkings. co.uk)

Exodus (☎0208-6755550; www.exodus.co.uk)

Explore (☎0845-8686487; www.explore.co.uk)

High Places (☏0845-2757500; www.highplaces.co.uk) Ten-day hiking and scrambling trips in Wadi Rum.

Imaginative Traveller (☏01473-857535; www.imaginative-traveller.com)

Martin Randall Travel (☏0208-7423355; www.martinrandall.com)

Tribes (☏01728-685971; www.tribes.co.uk)

USA

Archaeological Tours (☏1866-7405130; www.archaeologicaltrs.com; 271 Madison Ave, Suite 904, NY, NY 10016) A 14-day historical tour with archaeologists.

Jordan Tourism Board North America (☏1877-7335673; www.visitjordan.com) Professionally organised assorted tours.

GETTING AROUND

Jordan is a relatively small country, making it possible to drive the 430km from the Syrian border in the north to the Saudi border in the south in just over five hours – but of course size isn't everything. Most of Jordan's attractions lie not along the main arteries (such as the Desert Highway) but along the spectacular switchbacked mountain roads of the north or the historical, ambling and rural King's Highway. As such, if you want to make the most of your trip to Jordan, you need to factor in more time for your journey than the distance on the map may indicate.

Public transport is designed primarily for the locals and as it is notoriously difficult to reach many of the sights of interest (especially the Dead Sea, desert castles and King's Highway) consider hiring a car or using tours organised by hotels in Amman and Madaba. Alternatively, hire a yellow private taxi; often the driver adds untold value to the trip by giving you local information and cultural insights.

Air

There is only one domestic air route, between Amman and Aqaba. You can buy tickets at any travel agency or Royal Jordanian office. See p206 for details.

Royal Jordanian (☏06-5100000; www.rj.com) Flights twice daily (one way JD37, one hour).

Royal Wings (www.royalwings.com.jo, website under construction) A subsidiary of Royal Jordanian, it has daily flights.

Bicycle

Cycling can be fun or sheer folly depending on the time of year. From March to May and September to November are the best times to get on your bike – you won't have to battle with the stifling summer heat or the bitter winter winds. Spare parts are not common in Jordan, so carry a spare tyre, extra chain links, spokes, two inner tubes, repair kit and tool kit with spanner set. Also bring a low-gear set for the hills and a couple of water containers; confine

ON YOUR BIKE

It ought to be said that cycling in Jordan wouldn't be a first choice for everybody, but a few intrepid souls venture along the scenic King's Highway.

The Bad News...

There are few places to stop along the highways; the traffic is unpredictable; drivers are not used to cyclists; many of the cities and main towns, such as Amman and Karak, are sprinkled over steep hills; and spare parts are hard come by because so few locals ride bikes. If that isn't enough to put you off, then the stone-throwing might be:

There is no way to cycle along the King's Highway without getting stoned. We read it in your guidebook before leaving, but thought that kids would not stone three male adults with beards and long trousers who are looking angry. We were wrong. And it's not only *some* groups of kids who try to stone you, but basically it's becoming a major hobby for all male children between three and 20... Cycle in the morning when children are at school.

Bernhard Gerber, Switzerland

The Good News...

Roads are generally smooth and tourist attractions are well signposted in English. With some preparation, and an occasional lift in a bus, cyclists can average about 40km a day. Most major sights are conveniently placed less than a day's ride apart, heading south from the Syrian border, ie Irbid–Amman–Madaba–Karak–Dana–Petra–Ma'an–Wadi Rum–Aqaba. All these places have accommodation of some kind and restaurants, so there's no need to carry tents, sleeping bags and cooking equipment. Most other attractions can be easily visited on day trips, by bike or public transport.

OVERLAND TRANSPORT IN A HURRY

Wondering if you can get from Jerusalem to Petra in one day or vice versa? Check the following transport summary to see how far you can get in a day.

Petra & Jerusalem via Amman & the West Bank

Taking this route means you may be able to avoid evidence of a visit to Israel in your passport. Beware of long delays at the border. Note that you can't take your own car through this crossing. From Petra, catch a bus to Amman's South bus station (three hours), a service taxi or bus to King Hussein Bridge (Allenby Bridge; one hour), a bus across the border (three-hour delay; border closed by noon Friday and Saturday) and a service taxi or bus to Jerusalem's Damascus Gate (30 minutes). Also see Transport (p160), Visas (p315) and Border Crossings (p319). Take the reverse route to get from Jerusalem to Petra.

Petra & Jerusalem via Aqaba & Eilat

You can travel with your own vehicle this way. If you're arriving in Jordan at Wadi Araba (Yitzhak Rabin), you may be exempt from paying for a Jordanian visa as you'll be entering via the Aqaba free-trade zone. There are less border delays involved on this route.

From Petra, catch a bus to the main bus station at Aqaba (2½ hours), then a service taxi or bus to Wadi Araba (Yitzhak Rabin) border (15 minutes). Walk across the border (30 minutes; open every day), then take a service taxi or bus to Eilat (15 minutes) and a bus to Jerusalem's Damascus Gate (five hours). Also see Transport (p160), Visas (p315) and Border Crossings (p319). Take the reverse route to get from Jerusalem to Petra.

Petra & Damascus via Amman

This trip requires an early start in either direction. Note that the Hejaz Railway no longer operates a passenger service and there are no plans for its reintroduction in the near future. Also note that at the time of writing, travel to Syria was not recommended due to escalating violence.

From Petra, catch the JETT bus to the JETT bus station in Amman, or a bus to the South bus station (three hours). Then catch a JETT bus to Damascus (four hours; the bus waits for you to cross the border as part of the service). Also see Transport (p76), Visas (p315) and Border Crossings (p319). Take the reverse route to get from Damascus to Petra.

Petra & Sharm el-Sheikh via Aqaba & Nuweiba

Note that from Sharm el-Sheikh or Nuweiba to Wadi Rum or Petra requires an overnight stop in Aqaba.

From Petra, catch a bus to the main bus station at Aqaba (2½ hours), then a service taxi or bus to the ferry terminal (30 minutes) and catch a boat at noon to Nuweiba (one hour). From here, take the bus to Sharm el-Sheikh (2½ hours). Also see Transport (p206), Visas (p315) and Border Crossings (p320).

The trip from Sharm el-Sheikh to Petra is not possible in a day by public transport as you will arrive in Aqaba too late. First up, catch a bus from Sharm el-Sheikh to Nuweiba ferry terminal (2½ hours), then catch the 3.30pm boat to the passenger terminal south of Aqaba (one hour) followed by a service taxi or bus to Aqaba (30 minutes). Catch a private taxi to Petra or stay overnight in Aqaba and catch a bus to Petra the following day (2½ hours).

Petra & St Catherine's Mount via Aqaba

At the Taba crossing you can only get a visa for the Sinai Peninsula, so if you want to travel further than Sharm el-Sheikh, this trip needs some careful planning: full visas can be obtained in advance from the Egyptian consulate in Aqaba or the Egyptian embassy in Amman.

From Petra, catch a bus to the main bus station in Aqaba (2½ hours), then a service taxi to Wadi Araba (Yitzhak Rabin) border (15 minutes) and walk across the border (30 minutes). Catch a service taxi or bus to Taba (15 minutes) and a service taxi to St Catherine's Mount (three hours). Also see Transport (p206), Visas (p315) and Border Crossings (p318). While the reverse trip is not possible in a day on public transport, you can avoid a night's stay in Aqaba by taking a private taxi.

your panniers to a maximum of 15kg. It may be an idea to contact the **Cycling Association** (www.cycling -jordan.com) for tips before departure.

Bus

Local Bus

The two largest cities, Amman and Irbid, have efficient, cheap public bus networks. There are often no timetables available at chaotic local bus stations. Locals are always willing to help though.

Minibus

Public minibuses are the most common form of public transport. They normally only leave when full, so waiting times of an hour or more are inevitable, especially in rural areas. Tickets are normally bought on the bus. Standing is not usually allowed and some seat shuffling often takes place to ensure that unaccompanied foreign men or women do not sit next to members of the opposite sex. Locals signify that they want to get off by rapping a coin on a side window.

Tourist Bus

The larger air-con buses offer a speedy and reliable service, departing according to a fixed schedule. They don't stop en route to pick up passengers. Tickets should ideally be bought a day in advance.

The national bus company **JETT** (☎06-5854679; www. jett.com.jo; Al-Malek al-Hussein St, Shmeisani, Amman) operates the most comfortable bus service from Amman to Aqaba. It also has limited services to King Hussein Bridge border crossing, Petra and the Dead Sea. Other reliable companies with regular services from Amman:

Trust International Transport (☎06-5813427) To Aqaba.

Hijazi (☎06-638110, 02-7240721) To Irbid.

Car & Motorcycle

Jordan is an easy country to drive in (with the exception of Amman) and there are some spectacular routes linking the high ground with the Jordan Valley below sea level (see the boxed text, p114). Indeed, there aren't many countries where you can claim to be driving uphill to the sea, but if you're on the Dead Sea Highway heading for the Red Sea, then Jordan is one of them!

Strictly speaking you don't need an International Driving Permit (IDP) to drive in Jordan unless you plan on crossing any borders, but it may help if you meet with an accident.

Bringing Your Own Vehicle

If you are travelling with your own vehicle, refer to the following checklist of items to bring with you (contact your local automobile association for details) and see insurance (p324):

» The vehicle's registration papers and liability insurance

» *Carnet de passage en douane* (passport for the vehicle that acts as a temporary waiver of import duty)

» Specifications of any expensive spare parts, such as a gearbox, on board (designed to prevent car-import rackets)

» Spare parts and some mechanical knowledge for motorcycles

Royal Automobile Club of Jordan (☎06-5850626, for carnets 4622467; www.racj. com) Can arrange a carnet.

Checkpoints

There are many checkpoints in Jordan, particularly when driving along the Dead Sea Highway near the sensitive border with Israel and the Palestinian Territories, or on the roads that climb out of the Jordan Valley. Always stop at checkpoints. Foreigners are generally waved

through without any fuss, though you may have to show your passport. As such, always keep your passport, driving licence, hire agreement or proof of ownership and registration papers handy.

Fuel & Spare Parts

Petrol stations can mostly be found on the outskirts of major towns, and at some junctions. Along the Desert Highway (the only fully dual carriageway) there are plenty of stations. There are fewer along the King's Highway, and *very* few along the Dead Sea Highway. Unleaded petrol (*khal min ar-rasas*) is only reliably available in Amman and even then at only a few petrol stations.

Garages with mechanics can be found in the outskirts of most towns. They can handle most repairs. Check with your car-hire company first.

4WDs

Four-wheel drives are only necessary if you're going to remote parts of the desert, such as Burqu. You are highly advised to have prior experience of off-road driving before attempting soft sand: getting stuck in 45°C heat, for example, is a recipe for disaster if you don't know what you're doing.

Four-wheel-drive vehicles can be hired from reputable agencies in Aqaba (p207) and Amman (p75); they are far more expensive than normal sedans, costing at least JD150 per day.

Hire

Hiring a car is a great way of getting the most out of Jordan, especially if travelling the King's Highway or Dead Sea area.

There are many car-hire agencies in Amman, a few in Aqaba and one or two irregularly staffed offices at Queen Alia International Airport and the King Hussein border with Israel and the Palestinian Territories. Most

WHAT TO DO IN AN ACCIDENT

» Don't move the vehicle.

» Find a policeman from the local station to attend the scene immediately.

» Get a police report (essential for insurance – Arabic is OK) and contact the car-hire company.

» If there's a serious injury, call ☑911 for emergency services; you'll be answered by English-speaking staff.

» Contact your travel insurance company at home and your embassy/consulate in Amman.

» If your own car is involved, your driving licence and passport will be held by the police until the case is finalised in a local court – which may take weeks.

» Beware: drivers are always considered guilty if they hit a pedestrian, regardless of the circumstances.

car-hire agencies outside these areas usually consist of an office with one guy, one desk, one telephone and one car for hire (usually his!). The best deals are in Amman (see p75), where competition among agencies is fierce.

The following are some of the more reliable agencies. Daily rates run at around JD40 to JD50. This usually includes unlimited mileage. You can normally drop off the rental car in another city (eg Aqaba) for an extra fee. All companies require a deposit of up to JD400 payable upon pick-up (usually by credit card) and refunded upon return of the car.

Avis (☑06-5699420, 24hr 777-397405; www.avis.com. jo; King Abdullah Gardens, Amman) Offices at King Hussein Bridge and Aqaba; branches at the airport, Le Royal Hotel and Jordan InterContinental Hotel. The biggest car-hire company in Jordan.

Budget (☑06-5698131; www. budget.com; 125 Abdul Hameed Sharaf St, Amman)

Europcar (☑06-5655581; www.europcar.middleeast.com; Isam Al-Ajlouni St, Amman) Branches at Radisson SAS, King Abdullah Gardens and in Aqaba.

Hertz (☑06-5920926; www. hertz.com; King Abdullah Gardens, Amman) Offices at the airport, Grand Hyatt Amman, Sheraton and in Aqaba.

Reliable Rent-a-Car (☑06-5929676; www.rentareliablecar. com; 19 Fawzi al-Qawegli St, Amman) Contact Mohammed Hallak.

Road maps are not provided by car-hire agencies, but child-restraining seats are generally available for an extra fee.

Most agencies only hire to drivers over 21 years old; some stipulate that drivers must be at least 26 years. It's not possible to drive a hire car from Jordan into neighbouring countries.

Insurance

Most car-hire rates come with basic insurance that involves a deductible of up to JD400 (ie in case of an accident you pay a maximum of JD400). Most agencies offer additional Collision Damage Waiver (CDW) insurance for an extra JD7 to JD10 per day, which will absolve you of all accident costs (in some cases a maximum of JD100 excess).

Insurance offered by major companies often includes Personal Accident Insurance and Theft Protection, which

may be covered by your travel insurance policy from home. Always read the conditions of the contract carefully before signing – an English translation should always be provided.

If you're driving into Jordan in a private vehicle, compulsory third-party insurance must be purchased at the border for about JD35 (valid for one month). You also pay a nominal customs fee of JD5 for 'foreign car registration' (obtainable at the borders with Jordan and the ferry terminal in Nuweiba, Egypt).

Road Conditions

The condition of roads varies; unsigned speed humps are common, usually at the entrance to a town but also across main highways. It's important to note that the term 'highway' doesn't mean dual carriageway in Jordan – simply a main thoroughfare.

If you're driving around Jordan, read the following carefully:

» Signposting is erratic – generally enough to get you on your way but not enough to get you all the way to the destination.

» Many road signs are in English, but they are sometimes badly transliterated (eg 'Om Qeis' for Umm Qais).

» Brown signs denote tourist attractions, blue signs are for road names and green signs are for anything Islamic, such as a mosque.

» Take care when it's raining: water and sand (and sometimes oil) make a lethal combination on the roads.

» The Jordanian road system makes more use of U-turns than flyovers.

» Beware herds of goats and camels crossing all roads, including highways.

» Petrol stations are not that common, so fill up when you see one.

» Straddling of two lanes and overtaking using the slow lane are common practices.

Road Hazards

Despite the small population, and relatively well-maintained roads, accidents are alarmingly frequent.

Road Rules

Visitors from any country where road rules are rigorously obeyed may be shocked by the traffic in Jordan, especially in Amman. Indicators are seldom used, the ubiquitous horn is preferred over slowing down and pedestrians must take their chances. But anyone who has driven elsewhere in the Middle East may find the traffic comparatively well behaved. Provided that you minimise driving in Amman and take reasonable care, you're unlikely to encounter too many difficulties.

Vehicles drive on the right-hand side of the road in Jordan. The general speed limit inside built-up areas is 50km/h or 70km/h on multilane highways in Amman, and 90km/h to 110km/h on the national highways.

Wearing a seatbelt is now compulsory, though many Jordanians are reluctant to use them. Traffic police are positioned at intervals along the highways.

Hitching

Getting a Ride

Hitching is never entirely safe in any country in the world. Travellers who choose to hitch should understand that they are taking a small but potentially serious risk. That said, hitching is feasible in Jordan in areas where public transport is limited or nonexistent, such as parts of the King's Highway and to the desert castles east of Amman. Police stationed at major junctions and checkpoints are often happy to wave down drivers and cajole them into giving you a lift – or even give you a ride themselves.

Some tips to bear in mind are as follows:
» Avoid 1pm to 4pm when traffic is reduced.
» To flag down a car, raise your index finger in the direction you're heading.
» Be prepared to pay, and ask up front how much the driver wants.
» If no sum is requested, offer a token amount when you get out – it will often be refused.
» Carry a hat and lots of water.
» Don't look scruffy or hitch in groups of more than two.
» Women shouldn't hitch alone.
» Avoid riding in trucks on steep and windy roads (eg between the Wadi Rum turnoff and Aqaba) as they can be painfully slow.

Picking up Hitchhikers

Although there's no obligation to give anyone a ride, if you're driving your own or a hired car, it's hard not to feel a twinge of guilt as you fly past weary-looking locals by the roadside. On remote stretches like the Wadi Mujib stretch of the King's Highway, where public transport is limited or even nonexistent, it's customary to give a ride or two. Besides, it's a great way to meet Jordanian people. You should never charge a local for these lifts. They will assume, probably fairly, that any foreigner driving a private or hired car doesn't need the extra money.

Taxis

Private Taxis

Yellow private taxis work like ordinary taxis and can be chartered for the day. In Amman most drivers use the meter – note that fares are displayed in fils not dinars. Outside Amman negotiate a reasonable fare before you set off. Women should avoid sitting next to the driver.

Service Taxis

White service taxis (servees) run along set routes within and between many towns, as well as between Jordan and neighbouring countries. They are shared by more than one passenger and usually have writing and numbers (in Arabic) indicating their route. They usually only leave when full. They cost up to twice as much as a minibus, and about 50% more than a local bus, but are quicker because they stop less often along the way to pick up passengers. To avoid waiting for passengers, or to give yourself extra room, you can always pay for an extra seat. Lone female travellers should sit next to the driver if the back is jammed with men.

Tours

An alternative to a pricey group tour organised from abroad is to arrange your own private mini-tour with a Jordanian travel agency. Many of these can arrange hiking or archaeological itineraries and provide a car and driver.

For hiking and activities in Jordan's nature reserves contact the tourism department of the **Royal Society for the Conservation of Nature** (RSCN; www.rscn.org.jo), which can arrange short activity breaks or entire itineraries (see p293). For an extended trip to Wadi Rum it's best to contact a local Bedouin agency such as **Wadi Rum Mountain Guides** (www.bedouinroads.com).

If you're travelling independently, and on a tight budget, jumping on a budget-priced organised tour from Amman to a remote place like the desert castles of eastern Jordan is far easier, and often cheaper, than doing it yourself. See p58.

The following local agencies are reliable:

Alia Tours (☏06-5826426; www.aliatours.com.jo) Standard tours.

Atlas Travel & Tourist Agency (☏06-4642034; www.atlastours.net) Also offers side trips to Israel and the Palestinian Territories, Syria and Lebanon.

Desert Guides Company (☏06-5527230; www.desert guidescompany.com) Trekking, mountain-bike and adventure trips.

Golden Crown Tours (☏06-5511200; www.golden crowntours.com) Offers archaeological, religious and adventure tours.

Jordan Beauty Tours (☏079-5581644; www.jordan beauty.com; Petra)

Jordan Direct (☏06-5938238; www.jdtours.com; Boumedien St, Amman) Located in Amin Marie Complex.

Jordan Inspiration Tours (☏03-2157317; www.jitours.com; Petra)

Jordan Select Tours (☏06-5930588; www.select.jo) High-end tours.

La Beduina (☏03-2157099; www.labeduinatours.com)

Petra Moon (☏03-02156665; www.petramoon.com; Wadi Musa) A professional agency that also offers an interesting range of treks in remote areas of Petra and Dana.

Royal Tours (☏06-5857154; www.royaltours.com.jo) Part of Royal Jordanian, and good for stopover packages.

Zaman Tours & Travel (☏03-2157723; www.zaman tours.com; Wadi Musa) Adventure tours, camping, camel treks and hiking.

Health

Prevention and common sense is the key to staying healthy when travelling in Jordan. Infectious diseases occur in Jordan, but these can be avoided with a few simple precautions. If you need vaccinations, remember to visit the doctor around eight weeks before travelling as some require multiple injections; this will also give time to ensure immunity on arrival as some vaccinations take time to come into effect. The most common reason for travellers needing medical help is as a result of traffic accidents, which can be easily avoided if you remember to look the right way when crossing the road, wear a seatbelt even though no one else in Jordan seems to bother and stick to the speed limit on Jordan's less than perfect roads. Medical facilities are generally very good, particularly in Amman where there are some excellent modern hospitals. In case of an emergency, contact your embassy or consulate where you will at least receive sound local advice. Don't forget to take out health insurance before you leave!

BEFORE YOU GO

Insurance

You are strongly advised to have insurance (see the Insurance section in the Directory A-Z for more information) before travelling to Jordan. Check it covers the following:

» direct payments to health providers (or reimbursement later) for expenditure while in Jordan

» assistance in locating the nearest source of medical help

» emergency dental treatment

» repatriation home or aeromedical transport to better medical facilities elsewhere

Packing Checklist

Items you should consider packing:

» acetaminophen/paracetamol (Tylenol) or aspirin

» antibacterial ointment (eg Bactroban) for cuts and abrasions

» antidiarrhoeal drugs (eg loperamide)

» antihistamines (for hay fever and allergic reactions)

» insect repellent containing DEET (for the body)

» insect spray containing Permethrin (for clothing, tents and bed nets)

» iodine tablets or other water-purification tablets

» oral rehydration salts

» sunblock

Vaccinations

Note that some vaccinations should not be given during pregnancy, to people with allergies and to very young children – discuss this with your doctor.

Required & Recommended Vaccinations

The following vaccinations are recommended for most travellers to Jordan:

» diphtheria & tetanus – single booster recommended if you've not had one in the previous 10 years

» hepatitis A – a single dose at least two to four weeks before departure gives protection for up to a year; a booster 12 months later gives another 10 years or more of protection

» hepatitis B – now considered routine for most travellers

» measles, mumps and rubella – two doses of MMR recommended unless you have previously had the diseases; young adults may require a booster

» polio – generally given in childhood and should be boosted every 10 years

» typhoid – recommended if you're travelling for more than a couple of weeks

» yellow fever – vaccination is required for entry into Jordan for all travellers over one year of age if coming from infected areas such as sub-Saharan Africa and parts of South America

Travelling with Medication

Bring medications in their original clearly labelled containers. A signed and dated letter from your physician describing your medical conditions and medications, including generic names, is also a good idea. If carrying syringes or needles, be sure to have a physician's letter documenting their medical necessity and keep these handy when entering or exiting any of Jordan's borders.

Websites

It's a good idea to consult your government's travel health website before departure.

Australia (www.dfat.gov.au/travel)

Canada (www.travelhealth.gc.ca)

UK (www.doh.gov.uk)

US (www.cdc.gov/travel)

In addition to government health websites, the following provide useful health information:

Centre for Disease Control (www.cdc.gov) Overview of the health issues facing travellers to Jordan and neighbouring countries.

Lonely Planet (www.lonelyplanet.com) General advice.

MD Travel Health (www.mdtravelhealth.com) Complete travel-health recommendations for every country, updated daily, also at no cost.

World Health Organization (www.who.int/ith) Publishes a free, online book, *International Travel and Health*, revised annually.

Further Reading

Healthy Travel – Asia & India (Lonely Planet) Packed with useful information including pre-trip planning, emergency first aid, immunisation and disease information and what to do if you get sick on the road.

International Travel Health Guide (Stuart R Rose, MD)

The Travellers' Good Health Guide (Ted Lankester) An especially useful health guide for volunteers and long-term expatriates working in the Middle East.

Traveller's Health (Dr Richard Dawood)

Travel with Children (Lonely Planet) Includes advice on travel health for younger children.

IN JORDAN

Availability & Cost of Health Care

Healthcare provision is of a high standard in Jordan and any emergency treatment not requiring hospitalisation is free. The availability of health care can be summarised as follows:

» Modern, well-equipped public and private hospitals in Amman, Irbid, Aqaba and Karak.

» Good regional hospitals in Madaba, Ramtha and Zarqa.

» Basic health centres (all towns).

» Fairly modern and well-equipped dental surgeries in cities.

» Well-stocked pharmacies (most towns) dispensing advice as well as medicines.

» All doctors (and most pharmacists) speak English; many have studied abroad.

» Telephone numbers for pharmacies and hospitals in all cities are listed in the English-language newspapers.

» Ambulance number in Jordan: ☑911.

Food & Water

Water

Tap water in Jordan is generally safe to drink, but for a short trip it's better to stick to bottled water. This is readily available but check the seal has not been broken. Alternatively, you can boil tap water for 10 minutes, use water purification tablets or a filter.

The tap water in southern Jordan, particularly Wadi Rum, comes from natural springs at Diseh and so is extremely pure. Avoid drinking water from wadis in the wild as pools may have been used as waterholes for livestock. In the Jordan Valley, amoebic dysentery can be a problem.

If you get stuck in the desert without water, remember that you are more likely to be seriously ill (and even die) from dehydration than you are from a stomach upset, however unpleasant it may be. In summary, if water is offered and you need it, worry about its provenance later!

Avoiding Diarrhoea

The risk of becoming sick from unhygienic food preparation in Jordan is slim, especially if you follow this advice:

IF BITTEN BY A SNAKE...

» Don't panic: half of those bitten by venomous snakes are not actually injected with poison (envenomed).

» Immobilise the bitten limb with a splint (eg a stick).

» Apply a bandage over the site, with firm pressure, similar to bandaging a sprain.

» Do not apply a tourniquet, or cut or suck the bite.

» Get the victim to medical help as soon as possible so that antivenin can be given if necessary.

» Avoid tap water unless it has been boiled, filtered or chemically disinfected (iodine tablets).

» Beware of ice cream that may have melted and then been refrozen (eg a power cut in the last day or two).

» Be careful of shellfish such as mussels, oysters and clams, particularly outside of Aqaba, as well as the raw-meat dishes available in Lebanese restaurants.

» Eat meals only at busy restaurants and be cautious of buffets that may have been standing for more than a day.

Infectious Diseases

Diphtheria & Tetanus

Diphtheria is spread through close respiratory contact. It causes a high temperature and severe sore throat. Sometimes a membrane forms across the throat requiring a tracheostomy to prevent suffocation. Vaccination is recommended for those likely to be in close contact with the local population in infected areas. The vaccine is given as an injection alone, or with tetanus (you may well have had this combined injection as a child), and lasts 10 years.

Hepatitis A

Hepatitis A is spread through contaminated food (particularly shellfish) and water. It causes jaundice and, although it is rarely fatal, can cause prolonged lethargy and delayed recovery. Symptoms include dark urine, a yellow colour to the whites of the eyes, fever and abdominal pain. Hepatitis A vaccine (Avaxim, VAQTA, Havrix) is given as an injection; hepatitis A and typhoid vaccines can also be given as a single-dose vaccine, hepatyrix or viatim.

Hepatitis B

Infected blood, contaminated needles and sexual intercourse can all transmit hepatitis B. It can cause jaundice, and affects the liver, occasionally causing liver failure. All travellers should make this a routine vaccination. Many countries now give hepatitis B vaccination as part of routine childhood vaccination. The US Center for Disease Control says the level of hepatitis B is high in Jordan. The vaccine is given singly, or at the same time as the hepatitis A vaccine (hepatyrix). A course will give protection for at least five years. It can be given over four weeks, or six months.

HIV

This is spread via infected blood and blood products, sexual intercourse with an infected partner and from an infected mother to her newborn child. It can be spread through 'blood to blood' contacts such as contaminated instruments during medical and dental procedures, acupuncture, body-piercing and sharing used intravenous needles.

Reliable figures aren't available about the number of people in Jordan with HIV or AIDS, but given the strict taboos in Jordanian society

---

TRAVEL PROBLEMS & PREVENTION

PROBLEM	SYMPTOMS	PREVENTION/TREATMENT
Deep Vein Thrombosis (DVT) – formation of blood clots in the legs during long plane flights; some may break off and travel through the blood vessels to the lungs, where they may cause life-threatening complications.	Swelling or pain of the foot, ankle or calf, usually but not always on just one side Chest pain and difficulty in breathing – immediately seek medical attention.	Walk about the cabin. Perform isometric compressions of the leg muscles (ie contract the leg muscles while sitting). Drink plenty of fluids. Avoid alcohol and tobacco.
Jet Lag – common when crossing more than five time zones.	Insomnia, fatigue, malaise, nausea.	Drink plenty of fluids (non-alcoholic). Eat light meals. Upon arrival, seek exposure to natural sunlight and readjust your schedule (for meals, sleep etc) as soon as possible.
Motion Sickness	Nausea	Antihistamines such as dimenhydrinate (Dramamine) and meclizine (Antivert, Bonine). A herbal alternative is ginger.

ENVIRONMENTAL HAZARDS

PROBLEM	SYMPTOMS	TREATMENT	PREVENTION
Diarrhoea – occurs usually after eating unhygienically prepared food.	Onset of loose stools.	Take oral-rehydration solution containing salt and sugar; sip weak black tea with sugar; drink soft drinks allowed to go flat and diluted 50% with clean water.	Drink plenty of fluids; eat in busy restaurant; wash your hands regularly.
	More than four or five loose stools.	Antibiotic (usually a quinolone drug); antidiarrhoeal agent (such as loperamide).	As above
	Bloody diarrhoea persistent for more than 72 hours; accompanied by fever, shaking chills or severe abdominal pain.	Seek medical attention; in an emergency you can make up a solution of six teaspoons of sugar and half a teaspoon of salt to 1L of boiled or bottled water.	As above
Heat exhaustion – occurs following heavy sweating and excessive fluid loss with inadequate replacement of fluids and salt.	Headache, dizziness and tiredness; dehydration; dark yellow urine.	Replace fluids with water or fruit juice or both; cool with cold water and fans; take salty fluids through soup or broth; add a little more table salt to foods than usual.	Get fit before planning a long hike; acclimatise to the heat before exercise; wear a hat and cover your neck in the sun; avoid the midday sun in summer; wear sunscreen.
Heat stroke – occurs when the body's heat-regulating mechanism breaks down.	Excessive rise in body temperature; cessation of sweating; irrational and hyperactive behaviour; eventually loss of consciousness and death.	Give rapid cooling by spraying the body with water and fanning; seek emergency fluid and electrolyte replacement by intravenous drip.	As above
Mosquito bite – can spread dengue fever but not malaria.	Irritation; infection.	Don't scratch the bites; apply antiseptic.	Use DEET-based insect repellents; sleep under mosquito netting.
Bed bugs	Very itchy, lumpy bites.	Apply lotion from pharmacy.	Spray mattress or move hotel!
Scabies	Itchy rash, often between fingers.	Apply lotion from pharmacy; treat those you are in contact with.	As above
Snake bite	Pain; swelling.	Seek medical attention; see the boxed text (p328).	Wear boots, socks and long trousers when hiking; avoid holes and crevices; careful handling wood piles.
Scorpion bite	Intense pain.	Seek medical attention.	Check your shoes in the morning, particularly if you are camping near Little Petra.

about drugs, homosexuality and promiscuity, the disease is relatively rare. Contracting HIV through a blood transfusion is about as unlikely as in most Western countries, and anyone needing serious surgery will probably be sent home anyway.

You may need to supply a negative HIV test in order to get a second visa extension for a stay of longer than three months.

Polio

Generally spread through either contaminated food or water, polio is one of the vaccines given in childhood and should be boosted every 10 years, either orally (a drop on the tongue), or as an injection. Polio may be carried asymptomatically, although it can cause a transient fever and, in rare cases, potentially permanent muscle weakness or paralysis. Polio is not currently present in Jordan but is prevalent in neighbouring countries.

Rabies

Spread through bites or licks on broken skin from an infected animal, rabies is fatal. Animal handlers should be vaccinated, as should those travelling to remote areas where a reliable source of post-bite vaccine is not available within 24 hours. Three injections are needed over a month. If you've come into physical contact with an infected animal and haven't been vaccinated you'll need a course of five injections starting within 24 hours or as soon as possible after the injury. Vaccination does not provide you with immunity, it merely buys you more time to seek appropriate medical help.

Tuberculosis

Tuberculosis (TB) is spread through close respiratory contact and occasionally through infected milk or milk products. BCG vaccine is recommended for those likely to be mixing closely with the local population. It is more important for those visiting family or planning on a long stay, and those employed as teachers and health-care workers. TB can be asymptomatic, although symptoms can include cough, weight loss or fever, months or even years after exposure. An X-ray is the best way to confirm if you have TB. BCG gives a moderate degree of protection against TB. It causes a small permanent scar at the site of injection, and is usually only given in specialised chest clinics. As it's a live vaccine it should not be given to pregnant women or immunocompromised individuals. The BCG vaccine is not available in all countries.

Typhoid

This is spread through food or water that has been contaminated by infected human faeces. The first symptom is usually fever or a pink rash on the abdomen. Septicaemia (blood poisoning) may also occur. Typhoid vaccine (typhim Vi, typherix) will give protection for three years. In some countries, the oral vaccine Vivotif is also available.

Yellow Fever

Yellow-fever vaccination is not required for Jordan but you *do* need a yellow-fever certificate, from a designated clinic, if arriving from an infected area, or if you've been in an infected area in the two weeks prior to arrival in Jordan.

Environmental Hazards

Jordan is not a dangerous place to visit but it does have a few hazards unique to desert environments and some visitors get themselves into trouble hiking through the desert in the heat of the day, especially around Wadi Rum. While heat-related problems are the most common, don't forget that the desert can be bitterly cold in winter: there is a real risk of hypothermia if camping between December and February without adequate bedding. For hazards connected with swimming, diving or snorkelling, see p29.

Language

Arabic is the official language of Jordan. Note that there are significant differences between MSA (Modern Standard Arabic) – the official lingua franca of the Arab world, used in schools, administration and the media – and the colloquial language, ie the everyday spoken version. The Arabic variety spoken in Jordan (and provided in this chapter) is known as Levantine Arabic.

Read our coloured pronunciation guides as if they were English and you'll be understood. Note that a is pronounced as in 'act', aa as the 'a' in 'father', ae as the 'ai' in 'air', aw as in 'law', ay as in 'say', e as in 'bet', ee as in 'see', i as in 'hit', oo as in 'zoo', u as in 'put', gh is a guttural sound (like the French 'r'), r is rolled, dh is pronounced as the 'th' in 'that', th as in 'thin' and kh as the 'ch' in the Scottish *loch*. The apostrophe (') indicates the glottal stop (like the pause in the middle of 'uh-oh'). The stressed syllables are indicated with italics.

WANT MORE?
For in-depth language information and handy phrases, check out Lonely Planet's *Middle East Phrasebook*. You'll find it at **shop.lonelyplanet.com**, or you can buy Lonely Planet's iPhone phrasebooks at the Apple App Store.

BASICS

Hello.	مرحبا.	mer·ha·ba
Goodbye.	خاطرَك.	khae·trak (m)
	خاطرِك.	khae·trik (f)
Yes.	ايه.	'eeh
No.	لا.	laa
Please.	اذا بتريد.	'i·za bit·reed (m)
	اذا بتريدي.	'i·za bit·ree·dee (f)
Thank you.	شكراً.	shuk·ran
Excuse me.	عفواً.	'af·wan
Sorry.	آسف./آسفة.	'aa·sif/'aas·fe (m/f)

How are you?
كيفَك؟/كيفِك؟ — kay·fak/kay·fik (m/f)

Fine, thanks. And you?
منيح/منيحة. — mneeh/mnee·ha (m/f)
وأنتَ/أنتي؟ — oo 'ent/'en·tee (m/f)

What's your name?
شو اسمَك؟ — shoo 'es·mak (m)
شو اسمِك؟ — shoo 'es·mik (f)

My name is ...
اسمي ... — 'es·mee ...

Do you speak English?
بتحكي إنكليزي؟ — btah·kee 'inj·lee·zee

I don't understand.
ما فهمتْ. — maa fa·he·met

Can I take a photo?
يتسمحني اخذ صورة؟ — btsa·mah·nee 'aa·khud soo·re

ACCOMMODATION

Where's a ...?	وين ...؟	wayn ...
campsite	مخيّم	mu·khay·yam
guesthouse	بيت الضيوف	bayt id·du·yoof
hotel	فندق	fun·du'
youth hostel	فندق شباب	fun·du' sha·baeb

Do you have a ... room?	في عندكن غرفة ...؟	fee 'ind·kun ghur·fe ...
single	بتخت منفرد	bi·takht mun·fa·rid
double	بتخت مزدوّج	bi·takht muz·daw·wej
twin	بتختين	bi·takh·tayn

Signs	
Entrance	مدخل
Exit	مخرج
Open	مفتوح
Closed	مغلق
Information	معلومات
Prohibited	ممنوع
Toilets	دورات المياه
Men	الرجال
Women	النساء

How much is it per ...? قديش لـ...؟ 'ad·deesh li·...?

| night | ليلة | lay·le |
| person | شخص | shakhs |

Can I get another (blanket)?
أعطني/أعطيني 'a'·ti·nee/'a'·tee·nee
(بطانية) تاني. (ba·taa·nee·ye) tae·nee (m/f)

The (air conditioning) doesn't work.
(المكيف) مانه (il·mu·kay·yef) mae·nu
شغال. sha·ghael

DIRECTIONS

Where's the ...? وين الـ...؟ wayn il·...

bank	بنك	bank
market	سوق	soo'
post office	مكتب البريد	mak·tab il·ba·reed

Can you show me (on the map)?
بتورجني (عالخريطة)؟ btwar·ji·nee ('al·kha·ree·te)

What's the address?
شو العنوان؟ shoo il·'un·waen

Could you please write it down?
اذا بتريد/بتريدي 'i·za bit·reed/bit·ree·dee
اكتب/اكتبيه؟ 'ik·tu·bu/'ik·tu·beeh (m/f)

How far is it?
قديش هو بعيد 'ad·deesh hu·wa ba·'eed
من هون؟ min hoon

How do I get there?
كيف بوصل لهناك؟ kayf boo·sal la·hu·naek

It's ... هو/هي ... hu·we/hi·ye ... (m/f)

behind ...	خلف ...	khalf ...
in front of ...	قدام ...	'ad·daem ...
near to ...	قريب من ...	'a·reeb min ...
next to ...	جنب ...	jinb ...
on the corner	عند الزاوية	'ind az·zae·wi·ye
opposite ...	مواجه ...	mu·wae·jeh ...
straight ahead	للقدام	lil·'ad·daem

Turn left/right.
اتجه 'it·ta·jih
ليسار/لشمال. li·ya·saer/li·shi·mael (m)
اتجهي 'it·taj·hee
ليسار/لشمال. li·ya·saer/li·shi·mael (f)

EATING & DRINKING

Can you recommend a ...? بتوصي بـ...؟ btoo·see bi·...?

bar	بار	baar
cafe	مقهى	ma'·ha
restaurant	مطعم	mat·'em

I'd like a/the ..., please. بدي ... لو سمحت. bid·dee ... law sa·maht

| nonsmoking section | قسم غير المدخنين | 'ism ghayr il·mu·dakh·khi·neen |
| table for (four) | طاولة لـ(أربع أشخاص) | tae·wi·le li·('ar·ba·'at 'esh·khaes) |

What would you recommend?
بشو بتوصي؟ bi·shoo btoo·see

What's the local speciality?
شو الوجبة الخاصة؟ shoo il·waj·be il khae·se

Do you have vegetarian food?
في عندكن fee 'ind·kun
طعام نباتي؟ ta·'aem na·bae·tee

I'd like (the) ..., please. بدي ... لو سمحت. bid·dee ... law sa·maht

bill	الحساب	il·hi·saeb
drink list	قائمة المشروبات	'ae·'i·met il·mash·roo·baet
menu	قائمة الطعام	'ae·'i·met it·ta·'aem
that dish	ذلك الوجبة	zae·lik il·waj·be

Could you prepare a meal without ...? بتقدروا تحضروا وجبة بدون ...؟ bta'·de·roo tu·had·de·roo waj·be bi·doon ...

butter	زبدة	zeb·de
eggs	بيض	bayd
meat stock	مرق لحم	mir' lahm

I'm allergic to ... أنا عندي حساسية من ... 'a·na 'in·dee ha·sae·see·ye min ...

dairy produce	الألبان	il·'al·baen
gluten	الغلوتين	il·ghloo·teen
nuts	المكسرات	il·mu·kas·si·raet
seafood	الطعام البحري	it·ta·'aem bah·ree

beer	بيرا	bee·ra
coffee	قهوى	'ah·way
orange juice	عصير برتقال	'a·seer bur·te·'ael
mineral water	مياه	mee·yaah
	معدنية	ma·da·nee·ye
red wine	نبيذ احمر	nbeez 'ah·mer
tea	شاي	shaay
white wine	نبيذ ابيض	nbeez 'ib·yad

EMERGENCIES

Help!	ساعد!	sae·'id (m)
	ساعدي!	sae·'i·dee (f)
Go away!	روح!/روحي!	rooh/roo·hee (m/f)
Call ...!	اتصل بـ...!	'it·ta·sil bi·...
a doctor	دكتور	duk·toor
the police	الشرطة	ish·shur·ta

I'm lost.
أنا ضائع.   'a·na dae·'i (m)
أنا ضائعة.   'a·na dae·'i·e (f)

Where are the toilets?
وين الحمامات؟   wayn il·ham·mae·maet

I'm sick.
أنا مريض.   'a·na ma·reed (m)
أنا مريضة.   'a·na ma·ree·de (f)

I'm allergic to (antibiotics).
أنا حساسي/   'a·na ha·sae·see/
حساسية من   ha·sae·see·ye min
(مضاد حيوي).   (mu·daed ha·ya·wee) (m/f)

SHOPPING & SERVICES

Where's a ...?	وين ...؟	wayn ...
department store	محل المنوعات	ma·hal il·mu·naw·wa·'aet
grocery store	بقالة	ba·'ae·le
newsagency	وكالة الأنباء	wi·kae·let il·'en·baa'
souvenir shop	محل التذكارات	ma·hal it·tiz·kae·raet
supermarket	سبر مركت	su·ber·markt

I'm looking for ...
بدور عن ...   bi·daw·wer 'an ...

Can I look at it?
ورجني ياه؟   war·ji·nee yaah (m)
ورجيني ياه؟   war·jee·nee yaah (f)

Do you have any others?
في عندكن غيره؟   fee 'ind·kun ghay·ru

It's faulty.
هو خربان.   hu·we khar·baen

How much is it?
قديش هقه؟   'ad·deesh ha·'·u

Can you write down the price?
اكتب الهق.   'ik·tub il·ha' (m)
اكتبي الهق.   'ik·tu·bee il·ha' (f)

That's too expensive.
هيدا غالي اكتير   hay·dae ghae·lee 'ik·teer

What's your lowest price?
شو احسن سعر   shoo 'ih·sen si'r
طبعكن؟   ta·ba·'kun

There's a mistake in the bill.
في خطأ بالحساب.   fee kha·ta' bil·hi·saeb

Where's an ATM?
وين جهاز الصرافة؟   wayn je·haez is·sa·rae·fe

Where's a foreign exchange office?
وين مكتب صرافة؟   wayn mak·teb sa·rae·fe

What's the exchange rate?
شو سعر التحويل؟   shoo si'r it·tah·weel

Where's the local internet cafe?
وين أقرب مقهى   wayn 'a·'reb ma'·ha
الأنترنت؟   il·'in·ter·net

How much is it per hour?
قديش بتكلف   'ad·deesh bit·kal·lef
لساعة وحدة؟   la·sae·'a wah·de

Where's the nearest public phone?
وين أقرب تلفون   wayn 'a·'reb te·li·foon
عمومي؟   'u·moo·mee

I'd like to buy a phonecard.
بدي اشتري   bid·dee 'ish·ta·ree
بطاقة تلفون.   bi·tae·'e te·li·foon

TIME & DATES

What time is it?
كم الساعة؟   kam 'is·sae·'e

It's one o'clock.
الساعة وحدة.   'is·sae·'e wah·de

It's (two) o'clock.
هي (تنتين).   hi·ye (tin·tayn)

Half past (two).
(تنتين) ونص.   (tin·tayn) oo nus

At what time ...?
امتى ...؟   'em·ta ...

At ...?
في ...   fee ...

yesterday ...	مبارح ...	mbae·reh ...
tomorrow ...	بكرة ...	buk·ra ...
morning	صبح	su·beh
afternoon	بعد ظهر	ba'd zuhr
evening	مسا	ma·sae

Question Words		
When?	امتى؟	'em·ta
Where?	وين؟	wayn
Who?	مين؟	meen
Why?	ليش؟	leesh

Numbers			
1	١	واحد	waa·hed
2	٢	اثنين	'it·nayn
3	٣	ثلاثة	ta·laa·te
4	٤	اربع	'ar·ba'
5	٥	خمسة	kham·se
6	٦	ستة	sit·te
7	٧	سبعة	sab·'a
8	٨	ثمانية	ta·maa·ne
9	٩	تسعة	tis·'a
10	١٠	عشرة	'ash·re
20	٢٠	عشرين	'ish·reen
30	٣٠	ثلاثين	ta·laa·teen
40	٤٠	اربعين	'ar·be·'een
50	٥٠	خمسين	kham·seen
60	٦٠	ستين	sit·teen
70	٧٠	سبعين	sab·'een
80	٨٠	ثمانين	ta·ma·neen
90	٩٠	تسعين	tis·'een
100	١٠٠	مية	mi·'a
1000	١٠٠٠	الف	'elf

Note that Arabic numerals, unlike letters, are read from left to right.

Monday	يوم الأثنين	yawm il·'it·nayn
Tuesday	يوم التلات	yawm il·ta·laat
Wednesday	يوم الاربعة	yawm il·'ar·ba·a
Thursday	يوم الخميس	yawm il·kha·mees
Friday	يوم الجمع	yawm il·jum·'a
Saturday	يوم السبت	yawm is·sabt
Sunday	يوم الاحد	yawm il·'a·had

TRANSPORT

Is this the ... to (Petra)?	هيدا الـ ... لـ(بيترا)؟	hay·dae il· ... la·(bee·tra)
boat	سفينة	sfee·ne
bus	باص	baas
plane	طائرة	tae·'i·re
train	قطار	'i·taar

What time's the ... bus?	أمتى الباص...؟	'em·ta il·baas il·...
first	اول	'aw·wel
last	اخر	'ae·khir
next	قادم	'ae·dim

One ... ticket (to Beirut), please. تذكرة ... (لبيروت) اذا بتريد taz·ki·re ... (la·bay·root) 'i·za bit·reed

one-way	ذهاب	za·haeb
return	ذهاب واياب	za·haeb oo 'ee·yaeb

How long does the trip take? الرحلة، كم ساعة بتاخذ؟ ar·rih·le kam sae·'a bi·tae·khud

Is it a direct route? الطريق مباشر؟ it·ta·ree' mu·bae·shir

What station/stop is this? شو هيدا المحطة/الموقف؟ shoo hay·dae il·mhat·te/il·maw·if

Please tell me when we get to ... اولي/اوليلي لما منوصل عند ... 'oo·lee/'oo·lee·lee lam·ma mnoo·sal 'ind ... (m/f)

How much is it to ...? قديش الاجرة لـ ...؟ 'ad·deesh il·'uj·re la ...

Please take me to (this address). اوصلني عند (هيدا العنوان). 'oo·sal·nee 'ind (hay·dae il·'un·waen)

Please ... اذا بتريد ... 'i·za bit·reed ...

stop here	قف هون	'if hoon
wait here	استنّا هون	stan·naa hoon

I'd like to hire a ... بدي استأجر ... bid·dee 'is·ta'·jir ...

4WD	سيارة ذات الدفع الرباعي	say·yae·re zaat id·daf'er·ru·bae·'ee
car	سيارة	say·yae·re

with a driver ومعها سائق oo ma·'aa sae·'i

with air conditioning بالمكيف bil·mu·kay·yef

How much for ... hire? قديش الاجرة لـ...؟ 'ad·deesh il·'uj·re la·...

daily	يوم	yawm
weekly	أسبوع	'us·boo'

Is this the road to (Tyre)? هيدا الطريق لـ(صور)؟ hay·dae it·ta·ree' la·(soor)

I need a mechanic. لازمني ميكانيكي. lae·zim·nee mee·kaa·nee·kee

I've run out of petrol. خلص البنزين بسيارتي. kha·las il·bi·trool bi·say·yae·re·tee

I have a flat tyre. اطار السيارة ما فيه هواء. 'i·taer is·say·yae·re ma fee·hu ha·wae

ARABIC ALPHABET

Arabic is written from right to left. The form of each letter changes depending on whether it's at the start, in the middle or at the end of a word or whether it stands alone.

Word-Final	Word-Medial	Word-Initial	Alone	Letter
ـا	ـاـ	اـ	ا	alef'
ـب	ـبـ	بـ	ب	'ba
ـت	ـتـ	تـ	ت	'ta
ـث	ـثـ	ثـ	ث	'tha
ـج	ـجـ	جـ	ج	jeem
ـح	ـحـ	حـ	ح	'ha
ـخ	ـخـ	خـ	خ	'kha
ـد	ـدـ	دـ	د	daal
ـذ	ـذـ	ذـ	ذ	dhaal
ـر	ـرـ	رـ	ر	'ra
ـز	ـزـ	زـ	ز	'za
ـس	ـسـ	سـ	س	seen
ـش	ـشـ	شـ	ش	sheen
ـص	ـصـ	صـ	ص	saad
ـض	ـضـ	ضـ	ض	daad
ـط	ـطـ	طـ	ط	'ta
ـظ	ـظـ	ظـ	ظ	'dha
ـع	ـعـ	عـ	ع	ain'
ـغ	ـغـ	غـ	غ	ghain
ـف	ـفـ	فـ	ف	'fa
ـق	ـقـ	قـ	ق	kuf
ـك	ـكـ	كـ	ك	kaf
ـل	ـلـ	لـ	ل	lam
ـم	ـمـ	مـ	م	mim
ـن	ـنـ	نـ	ن	nun
ـه	ـهـ	هـ	ه	'ha
ـو	ـوـ	وـ	و	waw
ـي	ـيـ	يـ	ي	'ya
	ء			hamza
ـأ	ـَـوَـ	أ	أ	a
ـأ	ـُـوُـ	أ	أ	u
ـإ	ـِـوِـ	إ	إ	i
ـأ	ـَـوَـ	أ	أ	' (glottal stop)
ـا	ـاـ	آ	آ	aa
ـو	ـوـ	أو	أو	oo
ـيْ	ـيْـ	إيْ	إيْ	ee
ـوْ	ـوْـ	أوْ	أوْ	aw
ـي	ـيْـ	أيْ	أيْ	ay

Glossary

GENERAL GLOSSARY

This glossary lists terms used in this book that may be unfamiliar to those living outside Jordan. Most are Arabic words commonly used in Jordan but some abbreviations are also included. See the boxed text (p338) for architectural terminology, which may come in handy when visiting ancient sights such as Petra and Jerash.

abeyya – women's floor-length, black over-garment

abu – father of...

agal – black headrope used to hold a keffiyeh in place

ain (ayoun) – spring or well

amir – see *emir*

arak – alcoholic spirit

ASEZA – Aqaba Special Economic Zone Authority

Ayyubid dynasty – the dynasty founded by Saladin (Salah ad-Din) in Egypt in 1169

bab (abwab) – gate

Badia – stony desert

Bedouin (pl Bedu) – nomadic desert dweller

beit – house

beit ash-sha'ar – goat-hair Bedouin tent

bin – son of...; also *ibn*

caliph – Islamic ruler

caravanserai – large inn enclosing a courtyard, providing accommodation and a marketplace for caravans

Circassians – Muslims from the Caucasus who emigrated to Jordan in the 19th century

Decapolis (Latin) – literally '10 cities'; this term refers to a number of ancient cities in the Roman Empire, including Amman and Jerash

deir – monastery

eid – Islamic feast

Eid al-Adha – Feast of Sacrifice marking the pilgrimage to Mecca

Eid al-Fitr – Festival of Breaking the Fast, celebrated throughout the Islamic world at the end of Ramadan

emir – Islamic ruler, leader, military commander or governor; literally 'prince'

haj – the pilgrimage to Mecca

hammam(at) – natural hot springs; also a Turkish steam bath

haram – forbidden area

hejab – woman's headscarf

ibn – son of...; also *bin*

il-balad – downtown; the centre of town

imam – religious leader

jebel – hill or mountain

JETT – Jordan Express Travel & Tourism; the major private bus company in Jordan

JTB – Jordan Tourism Board

keffiyeh – checked scarf worn by Arab men

kilim – flat, woven mat

Koran – see *Quran*

Kufic – a type of highly stylised old Arabic script

mafrash – rugs

maidan – town or city square

malek – king

malekah – queen

Mamluk dynasty – Muslim dynasty named for a former slave and soldier class; mamluk is literally 'slaves'

medina – old walled centre of any Islamic city

mezze – starters, appetisers

mihrab – niche in the wall of a mosque that indicates the direction of Mecca

minaret – tower on top of a mosque

muezzin – mosque official who calls the faithful to prayer, often from the minaret

Nabataean – ancient trading civilisation based around Petra

nargileh – water pipe used to smoke tobacco (used mainly by men)

oud – Arabic lute

PLO – Palestine Liberation Organisation

qala'at – castle or fort

qasr – castle or palace

qibla – direction of Mecca

Quran – holy book of Islam

qusayr – small castle or palace

Ramadan – Muslim month of fasting

RSCN – Royal Society for the Conservation of Nature

Saladin – (Salah ad-Din in Arabic) Kurdish warlord who re-took Jerusalem from the Crusaders; founder of the Ayyubid dynasty

servees – service taxi

sheesha – see *nargileh*

sheikh – venerated religious scholar, dignitary or venerable old man

siq – gorge or canyon (usually created by tectonic forces rather than by wind or water)

souq – market

tell – ancient mound created by centuries of urban rebuilding

Trans-Jordan – Jordan's original name

Umayyad dynasty – first great dynasty of Arab Muslim rulers

umm – mother of...

UNRWA – UN Relief & Works Agency

wadi – valley or river bed formed by watercourse, dry except after heavy rainfall (plural: *widyan*)

zerb – Bedouin oven, buried in the sand

DINING & DRINKING GLOSSARY

Note that, because of the imprecise nature of transliterating Arabic into English, spellings will vary. For example, what we give as *kibbeh* may appear variously as *kubbeh*, *kibba*, *kibby* or even *gibeh*.

MEZZE

baba ghanouj – (literally 'father's favourite'), dip of mashed eggplant (aubergine) and tahini

balilah – snack of boiled salty legumes

basterma – pastrami, popular from Armenia to Lebanon

buraik – meat or cheese pie

fatayer – triangles of pastry filled with white cheese or spinach; also known as *buraik*

fatteh – garlicky yoghurt and hummus, sometimes with chicken

fattoosh – salad with sumach (a red spice mix), tomatoes and shreds of crouton-like deep-fried bread

fuul medames – squashed fava beans with chillies, onions and olive oil

gallai – sautéed tomato, garlic, onion and peppers topped with cheese and pine nuts on Arabic bread

hummus – cooked chickpeas ground into a paste and mixed with tahini (a sesame-seed paste), garlic and lemon

kibbeh – Lebanese-style kofta made with minced lamb, bulgur/cracked wheat

and onion; served raw or deep fried

labneh – cream-cheese dip

makdous – pickled eggplant, walnut and olive-oil dip

manaqeesh – Arabic bread with herbs

manoucha/manaqish – baked breads or pies with thyme (*zaatar*) and cheese

mosabaha – hummus with whole chickpeas in it

mouhamara – walnut, olive oil and cumin dip

AND A TRICLINIUM IS...?

Reading a guidebook to some of Jordan's most famous sights can seem like an exercise in linguistics encompassing Latin, Nabataean, Greek, Arabic and the languages of geography and classical architecture. Listen to any tour guide, especially at Petra and at Jerash, and you'll assume they're expert in all of them. But you don't have to be a polyglot to make the most of Jordan's wonders. Have a quick *shoofti* – Arabic word meaning 'you (female) looked' – at the glossary of architectural terms following and you'll soon know your pediments from your porticos.

agora – open meeting space for commerce

baetyls – divine stones

capitals – carved tops of columns

cardo maximus – Roman main street, running north–south

colonnade – row of columns

Corinthian – look for fluted columns with leafy capitals

decumanus – Roman main street, from east to west

Doric – look for unfluted columns with plain 'book-shaped' capitals

forum – open public space for meetings

high place – sacred site on mountaintop

hippodrome – stadium, usually for horseracing and chariot racing

Ionic – look for fluted columns with ram-horn (two curls in opposite directions) capitals

loculi – grave

macellum – indoor market building

necropolis – cemetery

nymphaeum – literally 'temple of the Nymphs'; public baths, fountains and pools

pediment – triangular crowning feature on front of building

portico – structure supported by columns

propylaeum – gateway or grand entrance

stele – commemorative stone or column with inscriptions

temenos – sacred courtyard

tetrapylon – an archway with four entrances

triclinium – Roman dining room

muttabal – eggplant dip similar to *baba ghanouj* but creamier

sambousek – meat and pine-nut pastry

shanklish – tangy and salty dried white cheese, sometimes grilled, sometimes in a salad

tabbouleh – salad of cracked (bulgur) wheat, parsley and tomato

treedah – egg, yoghurt and meat

yalenjeh – stuffed vine leaves

MAIN DISHES

fareekeh – similar to *maqlubbeh* but with cracked wheat

fasoolyeh – bean stew

gallayah – traditional Bedouin meal of chicken with tomatoes, other vegetables, garlic and Arabic spices

kofta – meatballs, often in a stew

maqlubbeh – steamed rice topped with grilled slices of eggplant or meat, grilled tomato, cauliflower and pine nuts

mulukiyyeh – spinach stew with chicken or meat pieces

musakhan – baked chicken served on bread with onions, olive oil and pine nuts

sawani – meat or vegetables cooked on trays in a wood-burning oven

sawda dajaj – chicken livers with grenadine syrup and lemon

shish tawouq – grilled boneless chicken served with bread and onions

shwarma – chicken or lamb sliced off a spit and stuffed in a pocket of pita-type bread with chopped tomatoes and garnish

DESSERT

ftir jibneh – large pastries

haliwat al-jibneh – a soft doughy pastry filled with cream cheese

halva – soft sesame paste, like nougat

kunafa – shredded dough on top of cream cheese smothered in syrup

ma'amoul – biscuits stuffed with dates and pistachio nuts and dipped in rose water

m'shekel – a form of baklava

muhalabiyya – rice pudding, made with rose water

wharbat – triangular pastries with custard inside

STAPLES

beid – egg

ejja – omelette

jibna – cheese

khobz – bread

labneh – yoghurt

makarone – all varieties of pasta

ruz – rice

shurba – soup

sukkar – sugar

MEAT & FISH

farooj – chicken

hamour – a grouper-like fish from the Red Sea

kibda – liver

samak – fish

VEGETABLES

adas – lentils

banadura – tomato

batata – potato

khadrawat – vegetables

khiyar – cucumber

FRUIT

battikh – watermelon

burtuqal – orange

inab – grape

mish-mish – apricot

moz – banana

rumman – pomegranate

tamr – date

tin – fig

tufah – apple

OTHER DISHES & CONDIMENTS

fil fil – chillies

sumach – red-spice mix

tahini – sesame-seed paste

torshi – pink pickled vegetables

tum – garlic

zaatar – thyme blend

zayt – olive oil

zaytun – olives

DRINKS

asir – juice

karkade – sweetened hibiscus tea

maya at-ta'abiyya – mineral water

qahwa – coffee

sefeeha – lemon and mint drink

shai – tea

behind the scenes

SEND US YOUR FEEDBACK

We love to hear from travellers – your comments keep us on our toes and help make our books better. Our well-travelled team reads every word on what you loved or loathed about this book. Although we cannot reply individually to postal submissions, we always guarantee that your feedback goes straight to the appropriate authors, in time for the next edition. Each person who sends us information is thanked in the next edition – the most useful submissions are rewarded with a selection of digital PDF chapters.

Visit **lonelyplanet.com/contact** to submit your updates and suggestions or to ask for help. Our award-winning website also features inspirational travel stories, news and discussions.

Note: We may edit, reproduce and incorporate your comments in Lonely Planet products such as guidebooks, websites and digital products, so let us know if you don't want your comments reproduced or your name acknowledged. For a copy of our privacy policy visit lonelyplanet.com/privacy.

OUR READERS

Many thanks to the travellers who used the last edition and wrote to us with helpful hints, useful advice and interesting anecdotes:

Obada Almaitah, Marc Almodovar, Mahed Al-nazer, Goli Amin, Karin Amnå, Tracey Anderson, Sabine Bauer, Linda Bauman, Les Bell, Rein Berkers, Lotte Bokkers, Daniel Bourne, Tim Brookes, Yuliono Budianto, Chloe Burnens, Ian Cameron, Nelly Camporeale, Julian Caruana, Ines Chabbi, Charline, James Cheng, Wouter Coppens, Fernanda Da Cruz Moscarelli, Brenda Dejager, Richard Demeester, Sandra Dietze, Sandra Eigenmann, Fabrizio Eva, Tom Gelade, Lia Genovese, Ada Gillissen & Koen Van Deudekom, Andrea Grajcar, Maud Guillet, Joshua Haber, Ofer Hadad & Hanna Lomeland, Thomas Halliday, Helen Haworth, Jimmy Hideaki, Theresa Hoelzel, Lisa Hofmann, Paul Hopkins, Luisa Houck, Montse Icart, Ahlam Idrees, Chabbi Ines, Klaus Jensen, H. Detlef Kammeier, Fadila Kettaf, Katherine Knight, Magnus Köhler, Steve Kraus, Stasja Krzeminski & Guglielmo Ravalli, David Leith, Chengxuan Liu, Bill Mania, James Merriman, Kathryn Mills, Karmen Modrijancic, Ana Moya, Serhat Narsap, Kars Neven, Thao Nguyen, Anne Og, Dek Pean, Chrissie Pegg, Cynthia Petersen, Katharina Piechocki, Gemma Pirnie, Larisa Plotnikova, Maarten Pullen, Torben Retboll, Lizzie, Richard, William & Lucy Iron, George Roach, P. Michael Rhodes, Paul Rulkens, Frieda Rusheidat-harrison, James Ryan, Yamaan Safady, Ulrike Schneider, Jeni Smith, Neil Spofforth & Emma Wilkinson, Ruth Steiner, Padraig Sweeney, Adem Terry, Denise Turcinov, Alberto Ugartemendia, Annemarike Van Egmond, Petra Van Grieken, Rob Van Elburg, Albert Verleg, Harriet Waldegrave, Jeffrey Walker, David White, Sjoerd Wiemer Sjoerdsma, Robert Wilkinsonfujii, Brent Woods and Kai Xue.

AUTHOR THANKS

Jenny Walker

It has been a huge pleasure re-encountering the people of Jordan for this project. I'd like to extend gratitude to His Excellency, Nayef Hmeidi Al-Fayez, Minister of Tourism & Antiquities, for sharing his valuable time, and to Xavier Hay for facilitating this meeting. Special thanks to Chris Johnson (Director, RSCN) and others involved in this inspirational NGO.

Guidebooks are a team effort: big thanks to LP HQ staff in Melbourne for ever-friendly support, especially Kate Morgan who assumed the duties of Commissioning Editor during this project and to Brigitte Ellemor, Managing Editor – both offered much kind assistance.

For my beloved husband, Sam Owen, I reserve the biggest thanks. Going beyond the call of duty in contributing to the research of this project, he showed unlimited patience during the many months of write-up. I couldn't have completed this edition without him. Each of our trips to Jordan felt like a treasured homecoming: heartfelt thanks to all those who helped us.

ACKNOWLEDGMENTS
Climate map data adapted from Peel MC, Finlayson BL & McMahon TA (2007) 'Updated World Map of the Köppen-Geiger Climate Classification', *Hydrology and Earth System Sciences*, 11, 1633–44.
Illustrations p162–163 by Michael Weldon

Cover photograph:
Petra Treasury by candlelight, Sean Caffrey/ Lonely Planet Images
Many of the images in this guide are available for licensing from Lonely Planet Images: www.lonelyplanetimages.com.

BEHIND THE SCENES

THIS BOOK
This 8th edition of Lonely Planet's Jordan guidebook was researched and written by Jenny Walker. The previous edition was also written by Jenny Walker and Matthew D Firestone.

This guidebook was commissioned in Lonely Planet's Melbourne office, and produced by the following:

Commissioning Editors Kate Morgan, Suzannah Shwer, Glenn van der Knijff

Coordinating Editors Susie Ashworth, Jeanette Wall

Coordinating Cartographer Ildiko Bogdanovits
Coordinating Layout Designer Lauren Egan
Managing Editors Brigitte Ellemor, Annelies Mertens
Senior Editor Martine Power
Managing Cartographers Shahara Ahmed, Adrian Persoglia, Amanda Sierp
Managing Layout Designer Chris Girdler
Assisting Editors Andrew Bain, Kate Daly, Paul Harding, Lucy Monie, Kristin Odijk

Assisting Cartographers Anita Bahn, Andras Bogdanovits
Assisting Layout Designers Kerrianne Southway, Jessica Rose
Cover Research Naomi Parker
Internal Image Research Aude Vauconsant
Language Content Branislava Vladisavljevic
Thanks to Sasha Baskett, Lucy Birchley, Laura Crawford, Brendan Dempsey, Ryan Evans, Larissa Frost, Yvonne Kirk, Alison Lyall, Trent Paton, Kirsten Rawlings, Gerard Walker

NOTES

index

how to use this book

These symbols will help you find the listings you want:

◉	Sights	☞	Tours	●	Drinking
🏄	Beaches	✸	Festivals & Events	☆	Entertainment
🏃	Activities	🛏	Sleeping	🛍	Shopping
🤿	Courses	✕	Eating	❶	Information/Transport

Look out for these icons:

TOP CHOICE	Our author's recommendation
FREE	No payment required
🌱	A green or sustainable option

Our authors have nominated these places as demonstrating a strong commitment to sustainability – for example by supporting local communities and producers, operating in an environmentally friendly way, or supporting conservation projects.

These symbols give you the vital information for each listing:

☏	Telephone Numbers	🛜	Wi-Fi Access	🚌	Bus
⊙	Opening Hours	🏊	Swimming Pool	⛴	Ferry
P	Parking	🥗	Vegetarian Selection	Ⓜ	Metro
⊖	Nonsmoking	📖	English-Language Menu	Ⓢ	Subway
✳	Air-Conditioning	👪	Family-Friendly	⊖	London Tube
@	Internet Access	🐾	Pet-Friendly	🚋	Tram
				🚆	Train

Reviews are organised by author preference.

Map Legend

Sights
- 🏖 Beach
- 🛕 Buddhist
- 🏰 Castle
- ✝ Christian
- 🕉 Hindu
- ☪ Islamic
- ✡ Jewish
- ❶ Monument
- 🏛 Museum/Gallery
- 🏚 Ruin
- 🍇 Winery/Vineyard
- 🐘 Zoo
- ◉ Other Sight

Activities, Courses & Tours
- 🤿 Diving/Snorkelling
- 🛶 Canoeing/Kayaking
- ⛷ Skiing
- 🏄 Surfing
- 🏊 Swimming/Pool
- 🚶 Walking
- 🏄 Windsurfing
- ➕ Other Activity/Course/Tour

Sleeping
- 🛏 Sleeping
- ⛺ Camping

Eating
- ✕ Eating

Drinking
- ☕ Drinking
- ☕ Cafe

Entertainment
- 🎭 Entertainment

Shopping
- 🛍 Shopping

Information
- 💲 Bank
- 🏛 Embassy/Consulate
- ✚ Hospital/Medical
- @ Internet
- 👮 Police
- ✉ Post Office
- ☎ Telephone
- 🚻 Toilet
- ❶ Tourist Information
- • Other Information

Transport
- ✈ Airport
- ⊗ Border Crossing
- 🚌 Bus
- ＋◉＋ Cable Car/Funicular
- 🚲 Cycling
- ⛴ Ferry
- Ⓜ Metro
- 🚝 Monorail
- P Parking
- 🛢 Petrol Station
- 🚕 Taxi
- 🚆 Train/Railway
- 🚋 Tram
- • Other Transport

Routes
- Tollway
- Freeway
- Primary
- Secondary
- Tertiary
- Lane
- Unsealed Road
- Plaza/Mall
- Steps
- Tunnel
- Pedestrian Overpass
- Walking Tour
- Walking Tour Detour
- Path

Geographic
- 🛖 Hut/Shelter
- 🗼 Lighthouse
- 👁 Lookout
- ▲ Mountain/Volcano
- 🌴 Oasis
- 🌳 Park
-)(Pass
- ⛱ Picnic Area
- 💧 Waterfall

Population
- ★ Capital (National)
- ◎ Capital (State/Province)
- ● City/Large Town
- ○ Town/Village

Boundaries
- – – – International
- ------ State/Province
- — — Disputed
- – – Regional/Suburb
- 🌊 Marine Park
- Cliff
- ▪▪▪ Wall

Hydrography
- River, Creek
- Intermittent River
- Swamp/Mangrove
- Reef
- Canal
- Water
- Dry/Salt/Intermittent Lake
- Glacier

Areas
- Beach/Desert
- ＋＋＋ Cemetery (Christian)
- ××× Cemetery (Other)
- Park/Forest
- Sportsground
- Sight (Building)
- Top Sight (Building)

OUR STORY

A beat-up old car, a few dollars in the pocket and a sense of adventure. In 1972 that's all Tony and Maureen Wheeler needed for the trip of a lifetime – across Europe and Asia overland to Australia. It took several months, and at the end – broke but inspired – they sat at their kitchen table writing and stapling together their first travel guide, *Across Asia on the Cheap*. Within a week they'd sold 1500 copies. Lonely Planet was born.

Today, Lonely Planet has offices in Melbourne, London and Oakland, with more than 600 staff and writers. We share Tony's belief that 'a great guidebook should do three things: inform, educate and amuse'.

OUR WRITERS

Jenny Walker

Jenny Walker's first involvement with Arabia was as a student, collecting butterflies for her father's book on entomology in Saudi Arabia. Convinced that, with her desert-savvy mum, they were the first Western women to brew tea and eat sardine sandwiches in the desolate interior, she returned to university to see if that was true.

Her studies resulted in a dissertation on Doughty and Lawrence (BA Hons, University of Stirling) and a thesis entitled *Perception of the Arabic Orient in British Literature 1780–1820* (MPhil, University of Oxford). She is currently undertaking a PhD on the role of the desert in modern literature during the period 1950–2000, through the Centre for Travel Writing Studies, University of Nottingham Trent in the UK.

A member of the British Guild of Travel Writers and the Outdoor Writers and Photographers Guild, she has written extensively on the Middle East for Lonely Planet and other publishers. With her husband, Wing Commander (retired) Sam Owen, she authored *Off-Road in the Sultanate of Oman*, about the country that has been their home for the past 14 years. This work, which is now in its third reprint, covers all parts of Oman and focuses on the geology, botany, zoology and entomology (among other 'ologies') of the country's wild and diverse desert landscapes.

Although deeply attached to Arabia, Jenny has travelled in more than 100 countries from Panama to Mongolia, on various assignments. After eight years of writing study skill courses for the Ministry of Health in Oman, Jenny has served as the Associate Dean for Professional Development at the Caledonian University College of Engineering in Muscat for the past three years.

Contributing Writer

Dr Alon Tal wrote the 'The Dead Sea is Dying' boxed text (p117). He founded the Israel Union for Environmental Defense and the Arava Institute for Environmental Studies, and has served as chair of Life and Environment, Israel's umbrella group for green organisations. Professor of the Desert Ecology Department at Ben-Gurion University, he heads the Jewish National Fund's sustainable development committee and still finds time to hike and bike around Israel with his wife and daughters.

Published by Lonely Planet Publications Pty Ltd
ABN 36 005 607 983
8th edition – July 2012
ISBN 978 1 74179 671 1
© Lonely Planet 2012   Photographs © as indicated 2012
10 9 8 7 6 5 4 3 2 1
Printed in China

Bestselling guide to Jordan – source: Nielsen BookScan, Australia, UK and USA, March 2011 to February 2012